W9-BEQ-070

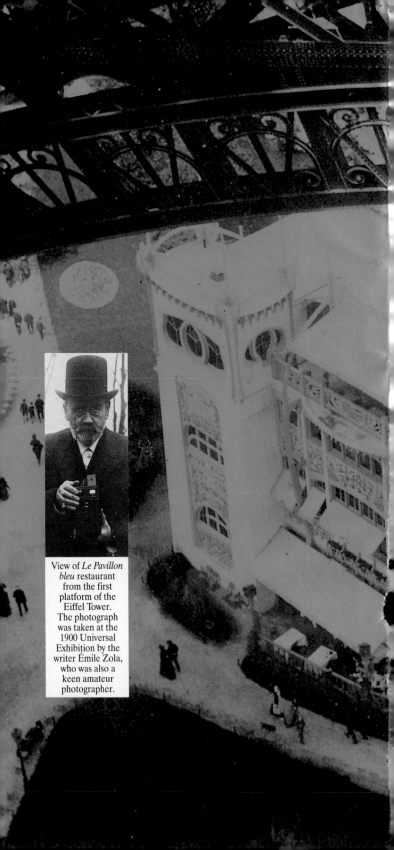

View of *Le Pavillon bleu* restaurant from the first platform of the Eiffel Tower. The photograph was taken at the 1900 Universal Exhibition by the writer Émile Zola, who was also a keen amateur photographer.

In the 1930's the *Ritz* was so popular that tables had to be set up in the gallery! In 1935 Marcel and Marthe Allard bought the *Halte de l'Éperon* in the rue Saint-André-des-Arts and established the *Maison Allard*.

Bougnats, originally coal and charcoal merchants, often doubled as local café-restaurants. Photographer Robert Doisneau came across the *Café Charbons* during his travels.

*Originally published in France by Nouveaux-Loisirs, a subsidiary of
Gallimard, Paris, 1994. Copyright © 1994 by Editions Nouveaux-Loisirs*

Restaurants of Paris. English
Restaurants of Paris/ [Gallimard editions].
p. cm.— (Knopf guides)
Includes bibliographical references and index.
ISBN 0-679-75578-0 : $25.00
1. Restaurants -- France -- Paris -- Guidebooks.
2. Paris (France) -- Guidebooks.
I. Gallimard (Firm) . II. Title.
III. Series
TX907.5.F72P376   1994
647.95443'6 -- dc20
CIP 94-8363

First American Edition

NUMEROUS SPECIALISTS AND ACADEMICS HAVE CONTRIBUTED TO THIS GUIDE:

AUTHORS: Françoise Avril, Olivier Bonnet, Alain Bradfer, Delphine Cazenave,
François Cazenave, Robert Courtine, Sylvie Desormière, Dominique Fernandes, Roger Gain,
Bruno Girveau, Patrick Jusseaux, Bernard Lehembre, Virginie Maubourguet,
Pierre-Yves Mercier, Pascale Mosnier, François Moureau, Anne Nercessian, Christophe Péry,
Jean-Luc Petitrenaud, Bernard Planche, Gilles Plazy, Anthony Rowley, Catherine Séguier,
Odile Simon, Thomas Vié, Edith Zeitlin

ILLUSTRATORS: Philippe Biard, Anne Bodin, Emmanuel Calamy, Jean-Philippe Chabot,
Jean Chevallier, Gismonde Curiace, François Desbordes, Sandra Doyle, Régis Haghebaert,
Kevin Hart, John Kent, Catherine Lachaux, Patrick Mérienne, Maurice Pommier,
Polly Raynes, Pascal Robin, James Robins

PHOTOGRAPHERS: Roger Gain, Gilbert Nencioli

WE WOULD ALSO LIKE TO THANK:
Frédéric Bellanger (CERQUA), CIDIL, Alain Garel, Christophe Péry (ATE), Pixel Impact,
RATP, Alain Raveneau, M.-C., Scotta-Loisel (C.I.V.), SEMMARIS (Rungis), SNCF,
SOPEXA, Rustica

TRANSLATED BY WENDY ALLATSON, MICHAEL CUNNINGHAM, JUDY MARCHANT;
EDITED AND TYPESET BY BOOK CREATION SERVICES, LONDON.
PRINTED IN ITALY BY EDITORIALE LIBRARIA.

RESTAURANTS
OF PARIS

KNOPF GUIDES

CONTENTS

SAINT-GERMAIN, MINISTÈRES

QUARTIER LATIN, MONTPARNASSE, PARC MONTSOURIS

TROCADÉRO, BOIS DE BOULOGNE, PÉREIRE

CHAMPS-ÉLYSÉES, ALMA, GEORGE-V

PALAIS-ROYAL, BOURSE, CONCORDE

LES HALLES, MARAIS, BASTILLE, GARE DE LYON

OPÉRA, GRANDS BOULEVARDS, RÉPUBLIQUE

▲ PARIS

I. NOTRE-DAME **II.** LOUVRE **III.** PALAIS-ROYAL **IV.** LES HALLES **V.** BEAUBOURG **VI.** HÔTEL DE VILLE **VII.** JARDIN DES PLANTES **VIII.** JARDIN DU LUXEMBOURG **IX.** MONTPARNASSE TOWER **X.** INVALIDES **XI.** EIFFEL TOWER **XII.** TROCADÉRO

This guide consists of seven itineraries, each of which covers several *arrondissements*, or districts of the city. They offer the visitor a hundred unforgettable establishments that, with their décor, their staging, and their atmosphere, are not so much restaurants as theaters.

1 SAINT-GERMAIN,
MINISTÈRES

2 LATIN QUARTER,
MONTPARNASSE ,
PARC MONTSOURIS, PLACE D'ITALIE

3 TROCADÉRO, BOIS DE BOULOGNE, PÉREIRE

4 CHAMPS-ÉLYSÉES, ALMA, GEORGE-V

5 PALAIS-ROYAL, BOURSE, CONCORDE

6 LES HALLES, BEAUBOURG, MARAIS, BASTILLE

7 OPÉRA, GRANDS BOULEVARDS, PORTE SAINT-MARTIN
RÉPUBLIQUE, PLACE CLICHY, MONTMARTRE

HOW TO USE THIS GUIDE

The mini-map locates the area of Paris corresponding to the itinerary.

The itinerary map shows the selected restaurants along the way and is intended to help you find your bearings.

The symbols at the top of each page refer to t different parts of the guide.

■ NATURAL
  ENVIRONMENT

● UNDERSTANDIN
  PARIS

▲ ITINERARIES

◆ PRACTICAL
  INFORMATION

★ The star symbol signifies that a particular restaurant has been singled out by the publishers for its special history, decorative beauty, atmosphere or cuisine.

◆ For each restaurant mentioned in the itineraries section, there is a cross-reference to the useful addresses section

●▲■◆ The symbols alongside a title or within the text itself provide cross-references to a theme or place dealt with elsewhere in the guide.

PRACTICAL INFORMATION ◆ 313
From page 313 onward, there are over 100 pages of practical information: how to get into Paris from the airports, transport, wine, restaurants on the Seine, a glossary of culinary terms and useful addresses.

THE RAW MATERIALS

RAY
Liver and cheeks are considered a delicacy by connoisseurs. Fine-textured and delicately flavored meat. No bones.

From the noble salmon to the humble herring, there are over 20,000 species of fish worldwide. Of the 160 species found in the Mediterranean and the Atlantic, only a dozen or so appear in France. Although top chefs give pride of place to the "noble" species, they do not neglect the common varieties. Quality is their sole criterion.

PIKE
Found in lakes and rivers (the best kind). Cooked in white butter sauce and white wine, roasted, used in dumplings and mousses.

CHAR
A cousin of the trout, found in the deep lakes of Savoie and the Pyrenees. Finely textured meat.

TROUT
Mostly farmed. The rainbow trout, from the United States, is the variety usually served in restaurants.

PIKE PERCH
Found in lakes. Best eaten *à la meunière, en matelote* or stuffed. Its firm, white meat is full of flavor. No bones.

GLASS-EEL OR ELVER
Eel hatchling between 2 and 3 inches long. Rare. Delicious deep fried.

EEL
Hatches in the sea, matures in rivers. Rich meat, full of flavor. Often smoked.

SALMON
Sea and freshwater. The best recipes use salmon under three years old. Uncooked, they must be fresh. The best smoked salmon comes from Scotland.

BASS
Known as *loup* (sea perch) on the Mediterranean coast and *loubine* along the Atlantic coast. Poached, grilled, braised, fried or stuffed. Finely textured and delicately flavored meat.

POLLACK
This lean Atlantic fish is eaten fried, grilled, coated in breadcrumbs or flour, poached in wine, stuffed or *en paupiettes*. Its meat is lightly flavored.

LOPHIUS OR ANGLER
Cooked in sauces, on skewers, sautéed or roasted like white meat. Cheeks and liver are used in the best recipes. Its lean meat is finely textured and firm. No bones.

JOHN DORY
Found among coastal rocks. Sautéed, *en papillote*, grilled or in soups. Its firm, white meat makes excellent fillets.

BRILL OR PLAICE
Found in the Atlantic and North Sea. At its best between November and April. A fleshy, delicately flavored fish which is grilled, served *à la normande* (with cream) or baked.

TURBOT
Found in the Atlantic and Mediterranean in summer. A choice dish. Poached in milk to preserve the whiteness of the meat, grilled or pan-fried.

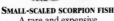

GILTHEAD BREAM
English Channel and the Atlantic. Grilled, roasted, used in soups and sashimi. Lean, tender meat.

SMALL-SCALED SCORPION FISH
A rare and expensive Mediterranean fish used in *bouillabaisse*. Smaller than the large-scaled scorpion fish.

SOLE
Found in the Atlantic. Its firm meat is easily digested. Eaten pan-fried, grilled, baked or braised.

RED GURNET OR GURNARD
A very bony fish used mainly in *bouillabaisse* and soups. Occasionally poached, grilled or baked.

RED MULLET OR SURMULLET
The Mediterranean red mullet is the choicest member of the mullet family. Fine bones, meat full of flavor. Cooked with its liver.

MACKEREL
Choose good-quality mackerel. The small mackerel caught in the English Channel are particularly good.

SARDINE
Atlantic and Mediterranean. Pilchards are the variety with the most meat.

HERRING
Best caught between October and January. Served plain, pan-fried, dried, smoked or salted.

WHITING
Atlantic. Lean, flaky meat which is easily digested. Gives body to soups. Fried, grilled, coated with breadcrumbs or flour, or poached in wine.

COD
Prefers cold waters. *Cabillaud* is fresh cod as distinct from dried or salt cod, which is de-salinated and poached.

HADDOCK
A cousin of the cod. Generally eaten smoked. Its pink-tinged meat is lean and firm.

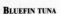

BLUEFIN TUNA
Mediterranean. Marinated and braised or cooked *en daube*. Its rich red meat is densely textured, rather like cooked veal. The choicest tuna meat comes from the much rarer albercore or germon.

SWORDFISH
Prefers warmer waters. Delicious meat.

17

Shellfish is both deliciously tasty and extremely versatile. An important meal would be unthinkable without it, and it also brings a breath of sea air to the dinner table. An added bonus is that modern methods of refrigerated transport mean that it is no longer a seasonal food. In the past oysters could be eaten only when there was an "r" in the month, which automatically excluded May, June, July and August. Those who like the rich, milky meat of oysters can now enjoy them throughout the summer.

EDIBLE CRAB
May to December. The largest species. Meat full of flavor. Females (narrow pincers, broad tail) are a better choice because of their roe.

SPIDER-CRAB
April to July. Considered more delicately flavored than the edible crab.

Prawn

Shrimp

PRAWNS AND SHRIMPS
Atlantic. Shrimps are smaller than prawns, which have a very delicate flavor.

DUBLIN BAY PRAWN OR NORWEGIAN LOBSTER
Atlantic. All the year round but more common in winter. Small yellowish-pink crustacean that turns pink when cooked. The meat is finely textured and delicately flavored. Cooked in aromatic stock or pan-fried.

VELVET SWIMMING CRAB
Difficult to shell. Its meat is used to flavor *coulis* (liquid purées) and *bisques*.

JUMBO SHRIMP
A large reddish prawn about 6 inches long, caught in the Mediterranean and along the African coast. Meat firm and full of flavor. Usually grilled.

CRAWFISH
Summer, autumn. Freshwater crustacean. Farmed or imported. The red-clawed variety is the best.

SPINY OR ROCK LOBSTER
Brittany, Corsica, America and Africa. The most expensive of the crustaceans. Delicate flavor. The Brittany lobster has more flavor.

Burgundy vineyard snail

Small snails from the south of France

SNAILS
A healthy, nourishing food although fairly bland without butter and garlic sauce. Better in summer and winter. The less choice Achatinas or Agate snails are imported.

LOBSTER
There are two types. The Breton variety has a blue shell with yellow markings. It is more fragrantly flavored than the more common, orangy-brown Canadian lobster.

ROCK SAMPHIRE OR SEA FENNEL
Clings to rocks pounded by the waves. Its fleshy stems are eaten.

WINKLE
Small marine snails, delicious cooked in a well-seasoned stock.

WHELK OR BUCCIN
Cooked. Pleasant if rather firm meat.

ABALONE
English Channel and Mediterranean. Its firm white meat is full of flavor. Pan-fried or stewed in a casserole.

CARPET-SHELL CLAM
Also known as the littleneck or cherry-stone clam. Eaten raw or cooked. Very delicately flavored.

CLAM
Also known as the American clam. Eaten raw or cooked, like oysters.

MUSSEL
Cultivated mussels are cooked while Spanish mussels are eaten raw or stuffed.

MARENNES-OLÉRON OYSTER
Cultivated, elongated, hollow-shaped *claire.* Characteristic green color.

BELON OYSTER
Flat Brittany oyster. Nutty flavor. The best and most expensive oysters.

"PORTUGUESE" OYSTER
A Creuse oyster, cultivated along the Atlantic coast.

SEA URCHIN
October to April. Eaten raw or cooked in *coulis.* Tastes strongly of iodine.

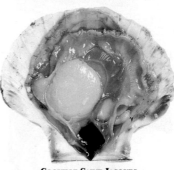

DOG COCKLE SHELLFISH
Eaten raw or stuffed. Delicious meat.

WART VENUS SHELL
Cousin of dog cockle and very similar.

COCKLE
Raw or cooked. Best species is the bucarde or sourdon.

SCALLOP
Cooked like the coquille Saint-Jacques.

COQUILLE SAINT-JACQUES
Harvesting, between October and April, is strictly regulated. Choose the simplest recipes to appreciate fully its delicious, aromatic meat.

■ Beef and veal

The *label rouge* (red label)
is the consumer's
guarantee of quality.

The labels given to certain types of meat guarantee that it has
been bred and raised according to strict specifications. The
agricultural label combines the *label rouge* and the regional label
and certifies that the meat is "a quality collective brand with a
specific set of characteristics that make it a superior-quality
product." The varied stock of French cattle includes breeds
whose meat is in great demand for its flavor.

LIMOUSIN
Bred for its meat, which is exported
worldwide. Renowned for its large yield of
"noble" grilling cuts.

SALERS
From the Cantal region. A hardy cross-breed
whose delicious meat has become extremely
popular.

MAINE-ANJOU
Bred for its milk and meat. The finely
textured, marbled meat is renowned for its
flavor well beyond its native regions.

CHAROLAIS
Accounts for 40 percent of French beef cattle.
Its excellent, marbled meat is tender, with no
outer fat.

PARTHENAIS
Formerly kept for its milk and used as a draft
animal. Has gradually been bred and made
suitable for meat again.

BLEU DU NORD
The Blanc Bleu branch of the breed provides
fine cuts of lean and tender meat for rapid
cooking.

BAZADAIS
Bred in the Gironde region and sold as
veau de Bazas (Bazas veal). Excellent for
ribsteak *à la bordelaise*.

BLOND D'AQUITAINE
Given the label *boeuf blond de l'Aquitaine* on
account of its richly flavored and finely
textured lean meat.

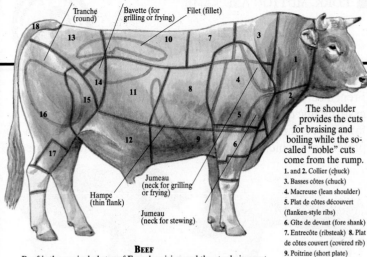

Tranche (round)
Bavette (for grilling or frying)
Filet (fillet)
Jumeau (neck for grilling or frying)
Jumeau (neck for stewing)
Hampe (thin flank)

The shoulder provides the cuts for braising and boiling while the so-called "noble" cuts come from the rump.

1. and **2.** Collier (chuck)
3. Basses côtes (chuck)
4. Macreuse (lean shoulder)
5. Plat de côtes découvert (flanken-style ribs)
6. Gîte de devant (fore shank)
7. Entrecôte (ribsteak) **8.** Plat de côtes couvert (covered rib)
9. Poitrine (short plate)
10. Faux-filet (sirloin)
11. Bavette (top or skirt for stewing)
12. Flanchet (flank)
13. Rumsteck (rump steak)
14. Aiguillette barònne (top rump of beef)
15. Tranche grasse (sirloin tip)
16. Gîte à la noix (leg muscle)
17. Gîte de derrière (hind shank)
18. Queue (tail)

BEEF

Beef is the unrivaled star of French cuisine and the staple in most French restaurants. The modern trend is for social eating. Grills are extremely popular in summer, while winter menus are characterized by a certain nostalgia for times past and the reappearance of dishes such as *boeuf en daube*, *miroton* and *gros-sel* that went out of favor for health reasons.

VEAL

Veal is tender and has a high water content, but by marinading and serving different cuts together, chefs create dishes that are rich both in texture and flavor. Veal is best eaten lightly done. The top-quality meat comes from the Limousin, where calves are raised *sous la mère* (left to suckle their mothers).

RED AND WHITE VARIETY MEATS

So-called because of the process the internal organs undergo after they have been removed rather than because of their color. Red variety meats are those that are roughly trimmed and dispatched for processing. The three types of white variety meats (tripe, feet and heads) are scalded (plunged into boiling water) to clean or cook them.

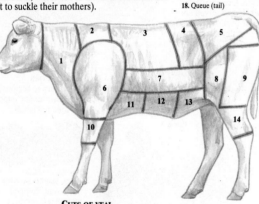

CUTS OF VEAL

1. Collier or collet (blade) **2.** Côtelettes découvertes (shoulder chops) **3.** Côtelettes premières et secondes (rib) **4.** Filet (loin) **5.** Quasi (round) **6.** Épaule (shoulder) **7.** Haut de côtelettes **8.** Noix pâtissière (boneless rump roast) **9.** Sous-noix (round steak) **10.** and **14.** Jarret (fore and hind shank) **11.** Poitrine (breast) **12.** Tendron (tendron or rib roast) **13.** Flanchet (flank)

LIVER
Rich in iron and vitamins A, D and B1 and extremely lean. Sliced and sautéed or grilled.

SWEETBREADS
Sautéed, fried or braised rapidly. Used in the preparation of sauces.

KIDNEYS
Also sautéed, grilled or braised. Sometimes browned whole in hot oil in their coating of fatty tissue.

FEET
Contain gelatin that is used to make stocks and jellies.

L'agneau des bergers de France, the new seal of quality for French lamb.

Pork, the most inexpensive white meat and the mainstay of the French culinary tradition, has regained its nutritional and gastronomic qualities since producers decided to revive pig farming. As far as mutton is concerned, modern taste tends to prefer lamb, which is more tender and more delicately flavored.

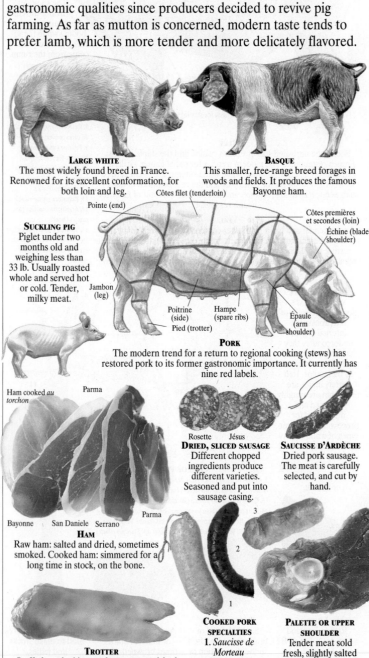

LARGE WHITE
The most widely found breed in France. Renowned for its excellent conformation, for both loin and leg.

BASQUE
This smaller, free-range breed forages in woods and fields. It produces the famous Bayonne ham.

SUCKLING PIG
Piglet under two months old and weighing less than 33 lb. Usually roasted whole and served hot or cold. Tender, milky meat.

Côtes filet (tenderloin)
Pointe (end)
Côtes premières et secondes (loin)
Échine (blade shoulder)
Jambon (leg)
Poitrine (side)
Pied (trotter)
Hampe (spare ribs)
Épaule (arm shoulder)

PORK
The modern trend for a return to regional cooking (stews) has restored pork to its former gastronomic importance. It currently has nine red labels.

Ham cooked *au torchon*
Parma

Rosette   Jésus
DRIED, SLICED SAUSAGE
Different chopped ingredients produce different varieties. Seasoned and put into sausage casing.

SAUCISSE D'ARDÈCHE
Dried pork sausage. The meat is carefully selected, and cut by hand.

Bayonne   San Daniele   Serrano
Parma
HAM
Raw ham: salted and dried, sometimes smoked. Cooked ham: simmered for a long time in stock, on the bone.

TROTTER
Stuffed, cooked in membrane or garnished or stuffed with truffles. Delicious grilled.

COOKED PORK SPECIALTIES
1. *Saucisse de Morteau*
2. Black pudding
3. *Andouillette*

PALETTE OR UPPER SHOULDER
Tender meat sold fresh, slightly salted or smoked. Can be used in sauerkraut.

MOUTON PRÉ-SALÉ
The salt-meadow sheep raised on coastal pastures graze on marsh samphire and red behen. Their delicately flavored meat is eaten mainly in spring.

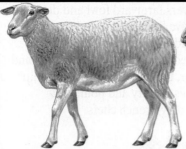

AGNEAU BLANC (MASSIF CENTRAL)
Lamb from the southern Massif Central, slaughtered at the age of fifty days. Sold under the label *agneau de Nîmes*.

BERRICHON DU CHER
A hardy breed renowned for its leg of lamb and mutton.

SOLOGNE
Lamb weighing 37 lb–44 lb. The meat is renowned for its flavor and often classified as "extra special" quality.

ROUGE DE L'OUEST (WESTERN FRANCE)
Lamb at the end of fattening. Heavy bodyweight with no excess fat.

CABRI
Male kid. The best variety is the *cabri de Poitou*.

AGNELET
Milk lamb, fed entirely on its mother's milk. Very pale meat.

BLEU DU MAINE
Crossed with a breed that has been improved for the quality of its meat. Produces excellent, lean meat.

Grilling (G); braising (B); stewing (S)
1. Gigot (leg) (G)
2. Selle anglaise (loin) (G)
3. Carré or côtes premières et secondes (rib) (G)
4. Côtes découvertes (rib) (G)
5. Collier or collet (neck) (G, B, S)
6. Poitrine (breast) (G, B, S)
7. Épaule (shoulder) (G, B)

Cuts of lamb

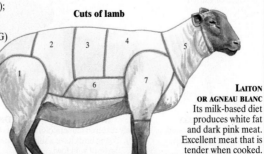

LAITON OR AGNEAU BLANC
Its milk-based diet produces white fat and dark pink meat. Excellent meat that is tender when cooked.

23

Bresse poultry has a ring on its left foot and a tricolor seal on its neck that certifies its origin and assures its authenticity.

COMITÉ INTERPROFESSIONNEL DE LA VOLAILLE DE **BRESSE**

In France the term "poultry" covers farmyard fowl and domestic rabbits. Labels of certification have been introduced to control quality and ensure that farmers adhere to a strict set of specifications with regard to breed, origin, farming methods and the age of their poultry. However, there are certain "blue chip" varieties (Bresse and Bourdonnais poultry and poultry *au torchon*) that are especially prized by French chefs.

GÉLINE DE TOURAINE
This small, rare chicken is used only by top chefs. Very finely textured white meat.

GÉLINE DU PAYS DE RACAN
An equally rare and highly prized variety of the *géline de Touraine*.

POULE DE CHALLANS
A rare chicken bred in the Vendée region. Finely textured meat.

POULET DE LOUÉ (SARTHE)
Free-range bird bred for its superior-quality meat. A recent success.

CAPON
Young cockerel that has been castrated and fattened. Its densely textured, marbled meat is extremely tender. Eaten roasted, poached or stuffed.

COQ DE BRESSE BLANC
A free-range white cockerel, bred for its delicious meat. It is never roasted but cooked in a sauce.

POULET DE BRESSE
An exclusively free-range chicken. Finely textured meat, full of flavor, with a crisp skin. Truly delicious.

HOUDAN
Now extremely rare. There has been a revival of interest among small farmers. Excellent meat. Used by top chefs.

YOUNG TURKEY
Usually eaten roasted, stuffed or in a stew. Tender meat.

GUINEA FOWL
Finely textured amber-colored meat. Young birds have a slight flavor of wild fowl.

DINDE NOIRE DE TOURAINE
This black turkey, now rare, has finely textured and delicately flavored white meat.

> "THE TURKEY IS THE FINEST THING
> THAT THE NEW WORLD EVER
> GAVE TO THE OLD."
>
> A. BRILLAT-SAVARIN

FOIE GRAS
France produces 8,250 tons of *foie gras* per year. It comes in various forms: "raw" (cooked like calf's liver or *en terrine*), "fresh," "semi-cooked" (very fashionable) or canned. The best *foie gras* has one or several lobes and no other additional stuffing.

CANARD DE CHALLANS
Crossed with the mallard. Renowned for the flavor of its finely textured and fairly fatty red meat. Best eaten rare.

OIE BLANCHE DE TOURAINE
White goose. Its meat is often served in the form of sliced breast, *confit* or *rillette* (a kind of paste).

Pigeon

White king

JAPANESE QUAIL
Imported from Asia and raised like poultry. The finely textured, fairly bland meat is eaten roasted, grilled, stuffed or *en terrine*.

PIGEON
Its meat was once believed to be an aphrodisiac. The meat of the domestic pigeon is pale and less strongly flavored than that of its wild cousin. Only young pigeons are eaten.

NEW ZEALAND WHITE
This plump, hardy rabbit is bred intensively.

FAUVE DE BOURGOGNE
Plenty of firm, densely textured meat.

CALIFORNIAN
Recently included on the French standards list. Particularly meaty shoulders, back and haunches.

BLANC DU BOUSCAT
A meaty animal from the Gironde. One of the major French breeds at the turn of the century. Bred widely throughout France for the quality of its meat.

EGGS
Eggs laid by brown hens are the most common. White eggs are laid only by Leghorns. Eggs are a food in themselves but are also used in a wide variety of dishes, for binding and in stuffings, for example. Quail's eggs, eaten hard-boiled or in jelly, and the more exotic ostrich egg!

GIZZARD
Pan-fried or roasted. Duck or goose gizzard is the best.

LIVER
Duck's liver is the most delicately flavored. The pale liver of the Bresse poularde is also extremely tasty.

Fresh game appears on the menu in French restaurants according to the official opening and close of the hunting season, the dates of which vary in each *département*. On average, connoisseurs of game have three months in which to indulge themselves. The season generally runs from mid-September to December for small game and to the end of February for large game and wildfowl. It should be noted that it is forbidden to serve woodcock in restaurants.

PHEASANT. Generally a forest-dweller. The meat of the modestly plumed hen pheasant is extremely tender. That of the cock is comparable only in birds up to fifteen months old. The meat of a young pheasant, identifiable by its gray, shiny, spurless feet, is particularly tender. Wild pheasant is rarer and much more strongly flavored than pheasant reared in captivity.

RED-LEGGED PARTRIDGE Found in the south and southwest of France. White, very lightly flavored meat.

GARENNE RABBIT
Meat more delicately flavored than that of its domestic cousin. Usually cooked *en terrine* or *en civet*.

DEER
Does and fawns under three years old have delicious meat. The choicest cuts are the loin or saddle, haunch and cutlets.

ROE-DEER
Very flavorful, dark red meat. The haunch and loin are roasted. The meat is also cooked *en civet* and accompanied by chestnuts, *poivrade* (pepper), cherry, gooseberry or cranberry sauce.

WILD BOAR
Young boars are hunted from the age of one year. The haunch, fillet and loin are cooked *en civet*. Pig's and boar's head-cheese is considered a delicacy. The meat of boars under six months old (recognizable by their striped coat) is tender and has a milder flavor.

HARE
Year-old hares and leverets (two to four months old) are roasted, and animals older than one year are eaten *en civet*. Hare meat is known as "black" meat (by comparison to rabbit meat).

SADDLE OF HARE
This excellent cut, from the lower part of the back, is roasted, marinated or cooked *en civet*.

YOUNG PARTRIDGE
Male or female partridge under one year is deliciously tender. The meat of the *pouillard*, young partridge shot at the opening of the hunting season, is much sought after.

GRAY PARTRIDGE
One of the most highly prized game birds, found throughout France.

WOOD PIGEON
Known as the ring dove in southwestern France. Densely textured, aromatic meat.

MALLARD
France's most common wild duck, with delicious meat. It is not hung. Legs and breast only are roasted, used in spiced sausage or fricasséed.

In recent years fresh vegetables have tended to replace those three old favorites, potatoes, rice and pasta, on French menus. Using shorter cooking times and following the modern trend toward lighter dishes, restaurateurs have been able to cater for weight- and health-conscious customers as well as for gourmets, who revel in rediscovering a whole range of forgotten delights.

BF 15

Bintje

Roseval

Ratte

POTATO
The wide variety of potatoes includes the Bintje, the BF 15, the small, delicate Rattes, the Charlotte and the Roseval. They are eaten cooked, in salads, puréed or chipped.

TURNIP
Spring and autumn. The purple Nantais and the long white Croissy are delicately flavored. Eaten cooked or raw.

LEEK
May to winter. The "white" variety is the most highly prized. Strong aroma. Cooked and served hot or cold.

CARDOON
Winter. A flavor reminiscent of artichokes. A Lyonnais specialty served *en gratin*.

SWISS CHARD
A fibrous, crunchy vegetable. The midribs or chards are eaten. Cooked *en gratin* and in sauces.

RADISH
Served as an aperitif or used to add piquancy. Eaten raw, dipped in salt.

SPINACH
Spring. Young shoots delicious in salads. Steamed, cooked in cream, soufflés and quiches. The green juice is used to color pasta.

FENNEL
Autumn, winter. A crisp bulb tasting of anise. Eaten raw, braised or steamed.

RED BEETROOT
Summer, autumn. Fleshy, sweet, dark-red root vegetable. Grated raw or cooked and served in salads.

BROCCOLI
October to April. Eaten raw in salads. Fragile when cooked.

BRUSSELS SPROUTS
September to March. Nutty flavor when eaten raw.

CAULIFLOWER
Autumn, winter. Cooked plain, in sauces or gratin dishes.

RED CABBAGE
Autumn, winter. Leaf vegetable. White-, green- and red-headed cabbage. Mild flavor. Red cabbage turns purplish blue on cooking. Eaten raw or cooked, braised or boiled.

WHITE CABBAGE

SAVOY CABBAGE
Autumn, winter. Eaten raw or cooked, stuffed and *en potée*.

> "IN THE BEGINNING, MAN HAD TO LIVE ON THE SAME FOOD AS ANIMALS. IN OTHER WORDS THE SIMPLE FRUITS OF THE EARTH: LEAVES, FRUIT, HERBS AND HAY."
>
> HIPPOCRATES

Sicilienne   Perline

TOMATO
Summer vegetable. Varieties include round, plum or cherry tomatoes. Eaten cooked or raw.

PEPPER
Summer. Fruit of the sweet pepper. Green, red or yellow (the mildest). Eaten raw or cooked, stuffed or grilled.

CUCUMBER
Summer, autumn. A sprinkling of salt removes excess water. Eaten raw in salads.

SALSIFY
Winter. Thin black or white root. Peeled and washed in water with added lemon juice. Eaten boiled and in gratin dishes.

Camus

Poivrade

ASPARAGUS
May to June. Found in the Rhône, South of France, Loire and Alsace. Cooked as a vegetable or in soups.

AUBERGINE (EGGPLANT)
Summer. Long or round, black, purple or white. Eaten braised, fried and in ratatouille.

ARTICHOKE
Summer, autumn. The Camus (Brittany) is cooked, braised or fried, while the Poivrade (Provence) is eaten raw.

COURGETTE (ZUCCHINI)
Spring, summer. Boiled or fried. The dwarf variety is eaten raw in salads.

French (green) bean

Soissons haricot bean

Pea

Spanish (white) bean

CARROT
Early spring vegetable. Eaten raw or cooked, boiled, *à l'étouffée* (slowly cooked in tightly covered casserole) or baked.

HARICOT
Green-podded variety (spring, summer), mange-tout and the fleshy, yellow butter bean (spring, autumn). Cooked and served hot or in salads. Dried beans are used in cassoulet, other regional dishes and in soups and salads.

GARDEN PEAS
Summer. Delicious, sweet. Fresh or dried (split peas). Used in slow-cooked dishes and soups.

PLEUROTE
Autumn, winter. Found beneath deciduous trees. Tender, varying in flavor. Cooked.

TROMPETTE DE LA MORT
Summer, autumn. Supple, aromatic. Cooked or dried as a seasoning.

GIROLLE
From July onwards. Firm, full-flavored, spicy. Cooked.

CULTIVATED MUSHROOM
Specialty of Saumur. Firm. Eaten in salads or cooked.

White truffle

Black truffle

SHITAKE
Grown in the Périgord on oak. Tastes similar to the edible Boletus. Cooked.

MOREL
Spring. Rare mushroom. Earthy flavor. Cooked or dried.

TRUFFLE
Winter. The black Périgord truffle is a great delicacy. Cooked.

BOLETUS (CÈPE)
Summer, autumn. The Bordeaux variety is a great delicacy. Cooked, dried.

The word "salad" originally referred to savory dishes based on herbs seasoned with oil, vinegar and salt. Today the term conjures up an image of health, freshness, natural ingredients and an easily prepared dish. Yet the art of preparing salads, apparently so simple, is extremely subtle. Chefs vie with each other in the use of color and texture and, above all, in producing the dressings that are to a salad what scent is to flowers. Indeed, flowers can be added to salads to enrich their flavor and color.

BATAVIAN LETTUCE
Autumn to spring. Curled, crunchy leaves.

CHICORY OR ESCAROLE LETTUCE
Autumn to spring. This curly lettuce has fresh, crunchy, flavorsome leaves.

MESCLUN
Mesclumo in Provençal means "mixture." A mixture of young lettuce shoots and herbs.

LOLLA ROSSA
Summer, autumn. This hardy lettuce has fine, curled, crunchy leaves that are graduated from green to red.

FRISÉE
Summer, autumn. Curly-leafed chicory with a spicy flavor ideally suited to well-seasoned dressings and croûtons.

CABBAGE LETTUCE
Delicately flavored and easily digested, with a round, pale heart. Also eaten braised and in soups.

LOOSE-LEAF LETTUCE
No heart. Reddish purple, with floppy, very curly leaves. Delicate flavor.

DANDELION
Tender shoots in spring. Spicy flavor. Aids digestion. Ideal with well-seasoned dressings.

LAMB'S LETTUCE
Autumn, winter. Mild and nutritious, slightly sharp-tasting. Ideal with beetroot.

BELGIAN ENDIVE
Autumn, winter. Tender and crunchy with a hint of bitterness. Eaten raw, braised, or baked.

CRESS
Autumn to spring. Sharp, slightly piquant flavor. Used in salads and soups.

ROCKET
Spring. Thick leaves. Spicy, piquant flavor. Mixed with other salad greens.

TREVISO CHICORY
Autumn, winter. Bitter-tasting spear-shaped leaves. Eaten raw or grilled.

RED CHICORY
Bitter-tasting rosette-shaped leaves. Used with other salad greens.

NASTURTIUM
Summer. Delicately flavored and aromatic. Served as fritters or in salads.

COURGETTE FLOWERS
Summer. Mild, tender flowers used in salads, cooked, or in fritters.

> "WHATEVER THE VARIETY OF HERB, THEY ARE ALL COVERED BY THE TERM SALAD."
>
> MONTAIGNE

BAY
Fresh or dried leaves. Strong aroma. Bouquet garni used in terrines, pâtés, stuffing, stocks, marinades, and as a flavoring.

BASIL
Spring to autumn. Delicate, spicy flavor. Used in salads, pâtés, with tomatoes and fish.

ROSEMARY
Pungent aroma. Used to flavor meat, grills and Mediterranean dishes.

CHIVES
Onion-like taste. Chopped in salads, soups, omelettes and cottage cheese.

COMMON (FLAT-LEAFED) PARSLEY
Stronger flavor than the curly-leafed variety. Used in many different dishes.

SORREL
Sour-tasting. Fresh sorrel is chopped in salads, cheeses and sauces. Cooked in soups.

CURLY-LEAFED PARSLEY
Mild flavor, frizzy leaves. Widely used to season salads, sauces and soups.

CORIANDER
"Arab" or "Chinese" parsley. Citrus, spicy flavor. Used fresh or as a powder in salads, sauces and soups.

TARRAGON
Distinctive flavor. Used in grills, omelettes, sauces and vinaigrettes, and to flavor pickles in vinegar.

THYME
Aromatic herb used in bouquets garnis for meat, grills and sauces. Wild thyme has a more subtle flavor.

MINT
Dark or light green with a spicy flavor (pennyroyal). Fresh mint is used in stuffings, drinks, salads and ice cream.

DILL
Fresh, aniseedy flavor. Dill is used freshly chopped (marinated fish, salads and sauces) and dried (oils and cakes).

WHITE ONIONS
April to September. Crisp and full flavor. Eaten chopped, sliced or whole, raw or cooked.

YELLOW ONIONS
Available all year. Slow cooking preserves sweet flavor. Eaten raw, cooked, or stuffed.

RED ONIONS
June to March. Milder flavor. Used in various ways, in sauces and tarts.

BILLOM PINK GARLIC
Spring garlic with a mild and slightly sweet flavor. Dried garlic has a more pungent flavor.

WHITE GARLIC
Strong flavor made milder with cooking. Raw garlic is chopped or made into a paste.

BUTTON ONION
Picked when small. Fresh button onions are braised, sautéed, glazed, or pickled.

SHALLOT
Gray shallots have a stronger flavor than red shallots. Used as flavorings.

PEAR SHALLOT
Delicately flavored shallot used raw (chopped) and in sauces.

France boasts more than 400 varieties of cheese, with 6 families of fully matured cheeses and 32 AOC (*appellation d'origine contrôlée*) labels. The vast range of regional specialties includes fully matured and fresh cheeses, cheeses made from cow's, goat's and sheep's milk, salted cheeses and cheeses with added cream. Each cheese has its own trade secret.

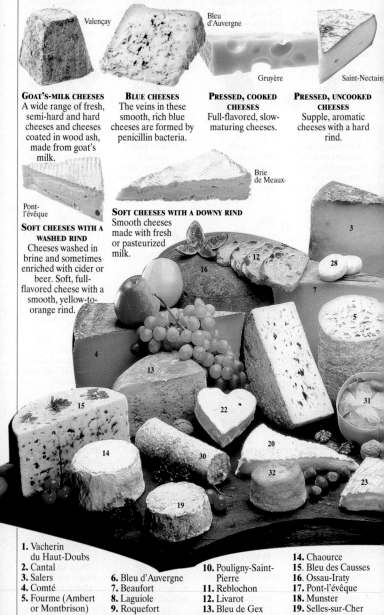

Valençay

Bleu d'Auvergne

Gruyère

Saint-Nectaire

GOAT'S-MILK CHEESES
A wide range of fresh, semi-hard and hard cheeses and cheeses coated in wood ash, made from goat's milk.

BLUE CHEESES
The veins in these smooth, rich blue cheeses are formed by penicillin bacteria.

PRESSED, COOKED CHEESES
Full-flavored, slow-maturing cheeses.

PRESSED, UNCOOKED CHEESES
Supple, aromatic cheeses with a hard rind.

Brie de Meaux

Pont-l'évêque

SOFT CHEESES WITH A WASHED RIND
Cheeses washed in brine and sometimes enriched with cider or beer. Soft, full-flavored cheese with a smooth, yellow-to-orange rind.

SOFT CHEESES WITH A DOWNY RIND
Smooth cheeses made with fresh or pasteurized milk.

1. Vacherin du Haut-Doubs
2. Cantal
3. Salers
4. Comté
5. Fourme (Ambert or Montbrison)
6. Bleu d'Auvergne
7. Beaufort
8. Laguiole
9. Roquefort
10. Pouligny-Saint-Pierre
11. Reblochon
12. Livarot
13. Bleu de Gex
14. Chaource
15. Bleu des Causses
16. Ossau-Iraty
17. Pont-l'évêque
18. Munster
19. Selles-sur-Cher

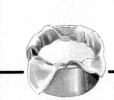

CURDLING
Fermentation, and adding rennet to the milk, causes the casein (milk protein) to coagulate.

DRAINING
The curdled milk is cut, stirred and separated from the whey to obtain a mass of curds to be made into cheese.

MOLDING
The curds are molded in containers of varying shapes and materials, such as wood or cloth, which give the cheese its final shape.

SALTING
Salt is rubbed into the surface of soft cheeses. It acts as an antiseptic and also determines the taste and appearance of the cheese.

RIPENING
Cheeses are ripened for anything from a few days to several months, under conditions where humidity and temperature are carefully controlled.

PACKAGING
A wooden or cardboard box or simply a label, preserves the product and provides information for the consumer.

"APPELLATIONS D'ORIGINE CONTRÔLÉES"
The AOC label (currently awarded to thirty-two French cheeses) indicates that they are "recognized, original products from a specific region, produced by traditional methods". There are, however, many superior-quality cheeses that do not have an AOC label.

20. Brie de Meaux
21. Crottin de Chavignol
22. Neufchâtel
23. Brie de Melun
24. Maroilles
25. Saint-Nectaire
26. Camembert de Normandie
27. Abondance
28. Picodon (Ardèche and Drome)
29. Chabichou du Poitou
30. Sainte-Maure de Touraine
31. Époisses
32. Langres

Sunflower oil

Various ingredients are used to season and accompany meat and vegetables considered bland and lacking in taste. The quest for highly prized spices prompted many voyages of discovery.

UNSALTED BUTTER
Isigny (Normandy) and Charentes butter (Échiré, Saint-Varent, Surgères) are AOC.

SALTED BUTTER
Guérande, Marennes and Noirmoutier butter. Salt helps to preserve butter.

THICK CREAM
Used in Normandy to sweeten vegetables, soups, sauces and patisserie.

LIGHT CREAM
Thin, semi-liquid, low-fat cream. Served with cakes, fruit and coffee.

SEA SALT
Ré and Guérande (AOC). Sharp-tasting, obtained by evaporation.

PURE SALT
Crust formed on the surface of salt pans. Rich in iodine.

GOOSE FAT
Used in gastronomy of Béarn, Gascony, the Landes and Languedoc.

COOKING LARD
Made from clarified pork fat. Used for frying in eastern France.

BLACK AND WHITE PEPPER
Black is piquant, green is full flavored, white is mild, and gray is a blend.

PAPRIKA
Powder from sweet peppers. Used in stews, stuffings, dishes with sauces and cheese.

RED PEPPERCORNS
Red or Cayenne pepper. The kernel is slightly piquant. Used in salads.

CORIANDER
Dried seeds of a parsley-like plant. Used in marinades and cooked meats.

CINNAMON
Bark of several tropical trees. Used in desserts and mulled wine.

NUTMEG
Grated nutmeg has a spicy aroma. Used to flavor potatoes, eggs and cakes.

CARDAMOM
From Malabar (India). Used in Indian cuisine, gingerbread, coffee.

OREGANO
Also known as marjoram. Used in Mediterranean dishes.

CUMIN
Seeds with a hot, slightly bitter taste. Used in bread, meats, soups and cheeses.

CARAWAY
Plant tasting like aniseed. Used in stews, sauerkraut, bread and patisserie.

CURRY
A mix of spices, in paste or powder, from India. Used in more exotic dishes.

GINGER
Root from India and Malaysia. Used to season exotic dishes and in patisserie.

| Olive oil | Grapeseed oil | Corn oil | Walnut oil |

OLIVE, GRAPESEED, CORN AND WALNUT OIL

Extracted from seeds or fruit. Full of flavor or tasteless, depending on how far the oil has been refined. Consisting of 100 percent lipids, with 135 calories per tablespoon (½oz), and with varying proportions of essential fatty acids. Groundnut and olive oil are used hot for cooking; virgin olive oil and grapeseed oil are used as a seasoning or to make mayonnaise.

SAFFRON
Stigmas of a species of crocus. The most expensive spice in the world.

CLOVE
Piquant flavor. Used in medicine and in stocks, marinades, pickles, patisserie.

JUNIPER
Spicy berries. Used in northern dishes such as marinades, game, and sauerkraut.

CITRONELLA
The lemon-scented citronella is used in Asian cuisine.

VANILLA
Pod from species of orchid. Used in patisserie and chocolate-making.

SESAME
Oily plant from which a very mild oil and a flour are extracted.

BUCKWHEAT AND WHEAT FLOUR
Wheat flour is the most widely used. Buckwheat flour is used for traditional patisserie. Whole-meal flour consists of wheat ground with bran and wheat germ.

EGG PASTA
Made with eggs and served as a side or main dish. Spaetzle is the most popular type.

ITALIAN PASTA
Used in soups, on its own, in gratin dishes, for stuffing, and as an entrée.

WILD RICE
A grass that grows in the marshes of North America. Rare and expensive.

BASMATI RICE
Long, thin-grained Indian rice. Full of flavor. Served as an accompaniment.

COCOA
From Venezuela, Brazil, Africa and Sri Lanka. Used as a paste or butter.

SUGAR
Extracted from beet (temperate regions) and sugarcane (tropical regions).

VERGEOISE
A low-grade, light- or dark-brown sugar. Solid residue from sugar refining.

CASSONADE
Raw crystallized cane sugar. Light brown and often used in patisserie.

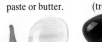
Tarragon

Balsamic   Cider

Sherry   Marsh samphire

VINEGAR
Obtained by fermenting alcoholic liquids such as wine, cider or sherry. It can be flavored with herbs, seasoning and spices.

DIJON MUSTARD
"Strong" or "white" Dijon mustard. Made with verjuice and white wine.

MEAUX MUSTARD
Piquant mustard made from vinegar and crushed mustard seeds.

Whether sweet or sharp-tasting, fleshy or watery, fruit appears on the menu in many guises. It may take center stage (desserts are its *pièce de résistance*) or play a minor part. Restaurateurs use it liberally: in entrées, with poultry and meat (*magret* with fresh figs) and in sweet-and-sour dishes.

Canada   Reine des Reinettes   Cox's Orange   Williams   Beurré-Hardy   Passe-Crassane

APPLE
All year round. The most widely eaten fruit in France. Crisp, juicy flesh. Kept in fruit stores or cold storage rooms. Eaten raw or cooked.

PEAR
Summer, autumn, winter. Tender, juicy, aromatic flesh, sometimes granular. Delicate flavor. Eaten raw or cooked. Desserts, side dishes, confectionery, liqueurs, sorbets.

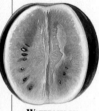   

WATERMELON
Summer. Refreshing, sweet, crunchy flesh with large black seeds.

CAVAILLON MELON
Summer. Its orange flesh is sweet and very flavorsome. Served chilled for hors d'oeuvre, sometimes with spices, or as a dessert.

MUSKMELON
The Sucrin is the best-known variety. June to October. Eaten *à l'italienne* with ham.

BANANA
All year round. Soft, nourishing flesh. Eaten raw or cooked, in compotes, flambéed, grilled, or dried.

Mandarin   Clementine

MANDARIN, CLEMENTINE
Winter. Sharp and sweet-tasting. Eaten raw or as candied fruit.

NAVEL ORANGE
Winter. The navel is sharp and sweet-tasting. Eaten raw or as candied fruit.

MALTESE BLOOD ORANGE
Winter. Sweet and very juicy. Eaten raw, in desserts, or squeezed for juice. Cooked in marmalade. Its peel is used in confectionery.

AVOCADO
All year round. Rich, fleshy tropical fruit with a nutty flavor. Served for hors d'oeuvre and in salads.

YELLOW GRAPEFRUIT
All year round. Sharp-tasting. Used for its juice, for hors d'oeuvre, or in salads. Cooked in patisserie and ice cream.

PINK GRAPEFRUIT
Winter. Pink (Sunrise and Thompson) and red (Ruby). Sweet and juicy.

LIME
From Tahiti. Fine-skinned, seedless flesh. Extremely juicy and flavorsome. Used in cocktails and sauces.

LEMON
All year round. Sharp-tasting and juicy. Used in main dishes, sauces, drinks, confectionery and patisserie.

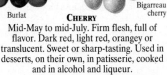

Victoria
(Réunion) Ivory Coast
PINEAPPLE
Winter. Tropical fruit. Sweet, juicy, fibrous
flesh. Sliced lengthwise and eaten raw. The
base is sweeter. Used for its juice, canned, in
syrup, in kirsch, or as an accompaniment to
rich meats.

Black
Hamburg

Muscat
(Italy) Chasselas
GRAPES
Summer, autumn. Sweet and refreshing. Firm,
fresh fruit, covered with a fine bloom. Used
raw (for juices, desserts and side dishes),
cooked (for main dishes and confectionery),
and dried (for patisserie and sauces).

FIG
June to November.
From the Orient.
White figs are
juicier; purple figs
have more flavor.

BLACKBERRY
Summer. Black,
fleshy, sharp-tasting
fruit. Eaten on their
own or used in jams,
tarts and liqueur.

CRANBERRY
All year round. Sharp-
tasting. Used as an
accompaniment to
northern dishes, in
sauces, as a condiment,
in compotes.

BLUEBERRY
Also huckleberry.
Summer. Blue-black
berry. Delicately
flavored. Eaten on
their own, in tarts,
jellies and jams.

Gooseberry

Redcurrant

**CURRANTS AND
GOOSEBERRIES**
Summer. Red, pink
and white. Sweet and
sharp. Eaten on their
own, in purées and
jellies.

BLACKCURRANT
Summer. Black berry
with a distinctive
taste. Used in juices,
syrups, ice cream,
sorbets, jams and
liqueur (Dijon).

Montmorency

Burlat

English Cherry

Bigarreau
cherry

CHERRY
Mid-May to mid-July. Firm flesh, full of
flavor. Dark red, light red, orangey or
translucent. Sweet or sharp-tasting. Used in
desserts, on their own, in patisserie, cooked
and in alcohol and liqueur.

White
Pêche de vigne
(late, red)

Yellow **PEACHES**
May to September. The white peach has
delicate flesh and is full of flavor. Used as a
dessert fruit and in sorbets. The firmer, less
juicy yellow peach is used in patisserie, brandy
and liqueur. The small, red *pêche de vigne* is
full of flavor but much less common.

Gariguette Solognote

RASPBERRY
Summer. Delicate,
fleshy, highly flavored
berry. Eaten on their
own, in purées and
sorbets.

STRAWBERRY
Spring, summer.
Delicate fruit,
aromatic and highly
flavored. Eaten on
their own, with
cream, or used in
patisserie, sorbets and
liqueur.

NECTARINES
Summer. Close cousins
of the peach. Smooth,
mottled skin. Sweet
flesh, similar to plum.
Eaten on their own.

APRICOT
Mid-June to August.
Tender, highly flavored
flesh. Eaten fresh,
canned or bottled, and
in patisserie.

**PLUMS: QUETSCHE, MIRABELLE,
REINE-CLAUDE**
July to September. Juicy, highly flavored.
Eaten on their own, in patisserie and
confectionery. Used in brandies and as an
accompaniment to pork and game.

■ WINES

WINE LIST
A good wine list should not only include a wide selection of wines from the five wine-growing regions of France but also take account of different vineyards and vintages.

The most comprehensive wine lists indicate the *cru* (vineyard where the wine was produced), the *millésime* or year (there are usually between three and five very good years every decade), and the *appellation d'origine* (quality grading for regional products whose characteristics meet certain geographical criteria). There are three main gradings: the AOC (*appellation d'origine contrôlée*) label, a quality guarantee reserved for wines of superior quality; the VDQS (*vins délimités de qualité supérieure*), excellent regional wines; and the *vins de pays*. Except in top establishments, restaurateurs often stock average years of the more prestigious wines ◆ 322.

| Dry White | Sweet White | 1947 | 1985 | 1992 |

BORDEAUX

A very young Bordeaux is deep red in color with purplish-blue highlights. As it matures it turns a rich ruby red that becomes brick red in very old vintages. Sweet white wines are initially a pale gold color and acquire a brownish tinge as they mature.

Côtes de Blaye
Côtes de Bourg
Graves
Pessac-Léognan
St-Emilion
Puisseguin-St-Emilion

Lalande de Pomerol
Pomerol
Fronsac
Barsac
Sauternes
Ste-Croix-du-Mont

Côtes de Castillon
Entre-Deux-Mers
Premières Côtes de Bordeaux

CHÂTEAU MARGAUX

Château Margaux is the jewel in the crown of the Margaux *appellation d'origine*, the most extensive and productive in the Médoc.

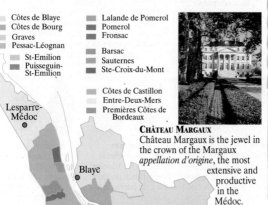

Lesparre-Médoc

Blaye

Libourne   St-Emilion   Ste-Foy-la-Grande

BORDEAUX

Médoc
Haut-Médoc
St-Estèphe
Pauillac
St-Julien
Listrac
Moulis

Langon

SOIL AND SUBSOIL

The left bank of the Gironde produces pleasantly smooth, finely balanced wines (Médoc and Graves), while the right bank produces full-bodied wines (Saint-Émilion and Pomerol). The dominant variety of vine for Médoc and Graves is the *Cabernet Sauvignon*.

Champagne
Loire
Als[...]
Burgundy
Bordelais
Côtes-du-Rhône

DOM PÉRIGNON
The wines of the Champagne region owe their sparkling quality to Dom Pérignon, *cellérier* at the Abbaye de Hautvillers in the 18th century.

REIMS

Mailly-Champagne

Château-Thierry

Ay Louvois

Bouzy

Epernay

Cramant

Avize

TYPOLOGY
The character of a champagne – *brut* (extra dry), *sec* (dry), or *demi-sec* (medium dry) – is determined by the addition of a champagne liqueur, a sugar-based syrup.

Bar-sur-Aube

Bar-sur-Seine

CHAMPAGNE
Wine made predominantly from the Pinot (black) grape combined with the Chardonnay (white) grape. If only Chardonnay grapes are used, it becomes a *Blanc de Blancs*. A rosé is generally obtained by adding a few drops of red wine.

Steinklotz

Altenberg de Bergbieten

Engelberg

Bruderthal

STRASBOURG

Altenberg de Wolxheim

Kirchberg de Barr

Wiebelsberg

Kastelberg

Wisenberg

Muenchberg

Frankstein

Kanzlerberg

"Late-picked"   Riesling   Pinot noir

ALSACE
Depending on the variety of grapes used, Alsace wines range from the very dry Sylvaner to the fruity Gewürztraminer. The "late-picked" vintages are made from selected overripe grapes that produce sweet wines.

Gloeckelberg

Altenberg de Bergheim

Kirchberg de Ribeauvillé

Schoenenbourg

Rosacker

Sporen

Sonnenglanz

Schlossberg

Marckrain

Brand

Mambourg

COLMAR

Hengst

Pfersigberg

Eichberg

Goldert

Hatschbourg

Zinnkoepfle

Saering

Pfingstberg

Ollwiller

ALSACE VINEYARDS
Each of the 110 official *communes* produces a wine named after the main variety: Chasselas, Sylvaner, Pinot Noir (ordinary varieties); Riesling, Tokay, Gewürztraminer (noble varieties).

Rangen

| Rosé de Marsannay 1991 | Côte de Beaune 1985 | Puligny-Montrachet 1987 | Romanée Saint-Vivant 1978 |

BURGUNDY WINES

Red Burgundy is ruby-colored when young, maturing to the color of red onion skins. White Burgundies are a golden-yellow, with a greenish tinge for Chablis. Burgundy wines are produced mainly from two *cépages* (varieties): Pinot Noir (red) and Chardonnay (white).

BURGUNDY VINEYARDS

The Burgundy vineyards are divided between the Côte de Nuits (Gevrey-Chambertin, Clos de Vougeot) and the Côte de Beaune (Corton, Montrachet), with the Chablis vineyards lying farther west. To the south the Côte Chalonnaise is now recognized as an *appellation contrôlée*.

Auxerre

Dijon

Chablis	
Côtes de Beaune	
Corton	
Montrachet	Beaujolais
Mâcon Villages	Beaujolais Villages
Côtes de Nuits	St-Véran
Chambertin	Pouilly
Morey-St-Denis	Rully
Chambolle-Musigny	Mercurey
Vougeot	Givry
Vosne-Romanée	

Nuits-St-Georges

Beaune

Chalon-sur-Saône

CLIMATES

The landscape of the wine-growing region of Burgundy is a mosaic of vineyards. The "climates" define the different vineyards, their specific type of soil, hours of sunshine and level of humidity.

Mâcon

Villefranche-sur-Saône

BEAUJOLAIS

Gamay is the only grape used to produce the predominantly red Beaujolais wines. The young Beaujolais Nouveau is ruby red and characterized by a distinctive fruity bouquet. The very pale white Beaujolais has a honeylike bouquet. The superior-quality wines are Juliénas, Chénas, Chiroubles, Saint-Amour, Morgon, Brouilly, Côte de Brouilly, Fleurie, Moulin-à-Vent and Régnié.

"APPELLATIONS" AND CLASSIFICATIONS

Beaujolais (9°), the richer Beaujolais Supérieur (10°), the superior-quality Beaujolais-Village with ten crus. Beaujolais Nouveau appears in mid-November.

The vines of Condrieu are planted on narrow terraces.

Vienne

Côtes du Rhône-Villages
Châteauneuf-du-Pape
Côte-Rotie
Vacqueyras
Muscat de Beaumes de Venise
Cornas
Lirac
Tavel
Clairette de Die
Gigondas
Hermitage

COTE-ROTIE

DOMAINE du CAYRON
GIGONDAS

Le Gréal
Hermitage

Valence

Montélimar

CÔTES DU RHÔNE
Northern Côtes du Rhône wines (Condrieu, Côte Rôtie) are made from a single variety of grape. The southern Côtes du Rhône (Châteauneuf-du-Pape, Gigondas) are produced from a blend of several grapes.

Rosé 1991   Châteauneuf blanc 1991   Gigondas 1988

HERMITAGE

Carpentras

Avignon

CÔTES DU RHÔNE VINEYARDS
Often steep hillsides in the north and vast plains in the south. Wines produced on the right bank (Châteauneuf-du-Pape) said to be heavier than left-bank wines (Gigondas, Vacqueyras, Villages), and naturally sweet wines (Beaumes-de-Venise, Rasteau).

Bourgueil

DOMAINE BOURILLON D'ORLEANS
VOUVRAY

CHINON

TOURAINE
For Touraine wines, the vintage and vineyard are important.

Sancerre 1990   Muscadet 1990   Vouvray Moelleux 1989

SANCERRE

LOIRE WINES
An extensive region producing a wide variety of wines: dry white wines from the Nantes region, the velvety Côteaux du Layon, red wines suitable for laying down, and the fruity Gamays, which are drunk young.

LOIRE REGION
Four wine-growing regions: Pays Nantais, Anjou-Saumur (fruity rosés and sparkling wines), Touraine (eleven AOCs), Pouilly and Sancerre (dry white wines).

Muscadet
Gros Plant
Coteaux du Loir
Jasnières
Savennières
Saumur
Saumur-Champigny

St Nicolas-de-Bourgueil
Bourgueil
Chinon
Vouvray
Menetou-Salon
Sancerre
Pouilly
Quincy

Orléans

Angers   Tours

Nantes

Poitiers

BRANDY AND CIGARS

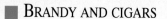

CIGAR BANDS
Cigar bands bear the brand name
of the cigar.

An unwritten but entirely logical
rule requires a meal to end with a brandy from
the region that produced the wine served with the various
courses. According to Zino Davidoff, Europe's expert on
Havana cigars, the choice of cigars should also be determined by
the wines served. For example, the Montecristo is
ideally suited to Bordeaux and the Romeo y
Julieta to Burgundy wines. The
caliber of the cigar depends
on the individual taste of
the smoker and the time
available to enjoy it.

Should cognac or armagnac be drunk after
Bordeaux wines, marc after Burgundies and a
fruit brandy after wines from Alsace and
Champagne? Is there a marc that goes with
Champagne? Cognac, armagnac, vintage rum
and marc are served at room temperature,
while fruit brandies should be chilled so that
they frost the glass.

Chicos

Small Corona

Lonsdale No. 1

Panetelas

Demi-Corona

Small Bouquet

Corona

COGNAC
After distilling,
cognac is left in a cask
where the alcohol
diminishes as it
evaporates. This is
"la part des anges,"
the angels' share.

SIZE AND COLOR
Calibers range from
the Demi-Corona (2½
to 3 inches long and
about ½ inch in
diameter) to the large
Corona (9½ inches
long and from ½ inch
to 1 inch in
diameter). The most
widely smoked cigars
in France range from
the Chicos (4 to 4½
inches long) to the
Corona (5½ inches
long). The mildest
cigars have the
lightest (green) outer
leaves and the
strongest cigars have
the darkest (black)
leaves.

CIGAR-CUTTER
The opening, which
must be neither too
big nor too small, can
also be made with a
fingernail or a knife.

HISTORY

1765–82: THE BIRTH OF THE RESTAURANT

1765
Boulanger opens the first "restaurant" in Paris, in the Rue des Poulies.

"BOUILLON RESTAURANT." Until the 18th century the term restaurant referred to a *bouillon restaurant* (nourishing meat broth) and the establishments that served it soon became known by the same name. The first of these to accept diners opened only in 1765 in the Rue des Poulies, the present-day Rue du Louvre. It was owned by a certain Boulanger, nicknamed "Champ d'Oiseau," who served restaurants and other dishes by the portion. His sign read: *Venite ad me omnes qui stomacho laboratis et ego restaurabavos* (Come to me all of you who are suffering with your stomach and I will restore you). His reputation (and his prices) increased rapidly. His establishment offered a wide choice of dishes served, at individual tables, and in this respect it differed from taverns (*Ramponneau* was the archetype), which offered only a few simple dishes to accompany the drinks served, from inns, which offered a table d'hôte (a communal table where a fixed meal was served), and from *traiteurs* (caterers), who did not retail their specialties. The *traiteurs* took legal action against Boulanger based on the regulations of their guild, according to which the right to serve cooked meats was reserved for its members. They were unsuccessful and the event marked the official birth of the restaurant.

Ramponneau

1774
Death of Louis XV and accession of Louis XVI.

Beauvilliers

1783
Beaumarchais presents "The Marriage of Figaro".

1786
Restaurateurs are permitted to remain open until 11pm in winter and midnight in summer.

1789
Fall of the Bastille. Paris has about one hundred restaurants.

ANTOINE BEAUVILLIERS. The first "luxury" restaurant was opened in Paris in 1782 by Antoine Beauvilliers ▲ *272* ◆ *410* at No. 26, rue de Richelieu. The sign of the *Grande Taverne de Londres* indicated the British origins of the culinary traditions that the former steward to Monsieur, Count of Provence, the future Louis XVIII, tried to introduce in Paris. The practice of eating a good meal outside the home was unthinkable to the French aristocracy of the Ancien Régime, who maintained a large kitchen staff. However, the habit was widespread in England, where taverns had long served a sophisticated clientele.

18TH–19TH CENTURIES: FROM THE PALAIS-ROYAL TO THE BOULEVARDS

THE PALAIS-ROYAL. In 1791 Beauvilliers opened a restaurant in the Galerie de Valois of the Palais-Royal. Shortly afterward Robert, former chef to the Prince de Condé, opened an establishment in the Rue de Richelieu. In the Galerie du Beaujolais, the Frères Provençaux offered *bouillabaisse* and *brandade de morue* (salt cod and garlic purée). As its name suggests, the *Boeuf à la mode* served a dish

Madame Véry

based on the aristocratic *boeuf à la royale*. The *Café de Chartres* became the *Véfour* ▲ *213*. The reputation of the Palais-Royal soon spread beyond France. In *Paris à table* (1846), Eugène Briffaut tells how, when France was attacked by her European neighbors in 1814, the commanders of the various armies were united in their battle cry: Paris! Once in Paris they asked for the Palais-Royal, and once inside the Palais-Royal they asked for a meal to be served. In 1789 there were less than one hundred restaurants in Paris. By the turn of the century there were over five hundred. The abolition of the guilds, the availability of chefs following the demise of the aristocracy and the rising popularity of public life (in which restaurants played an important role) were the main reasons for this increase.

THE BOULEVARDS. The golden age of the Palais-Royal came to an end in 1836, when Louis-Philippe closed down the gaming houses and drove out the prostitutes. Both had in fact contributed as much as the restaurants to the success of the Palais. The boundaries of Paris "restauration" had rapidly expanded and now included the district near Les Halles, which had the advantage of fresh supplies on the doorstep, although it had been a merchants' district long before the central market was built. However, the top restaurants were located in the vicinity of the Boulevards, in the Rues Montorgueil and Vivienne. Since the early 19th century Alexis Baleine had served shellfish to an appreciative clientele at the *Rocher de Cancale* at No. 61 Rue Montorgueil, where the Paris oyster market was located. The *Rocher* was a favorite venue for the high society of Louis-Philippe's reign. At about the same time *Champeaux* opened at the corner of the Rue Vivienne and the Rue des Filles-Saint-Thomas and, when the Palais Brongniart was completed in 1827, it became the first "business restaurant" in Paris, and was renowned for its winter garden. In 1795 the *Café Hardy* opened on the Boulevards, which had replaced the Palais-Royal as a center for social outings, theaters and entertainment, reaching its peak under the Restoration and the Second Empire.

Rocher de Cancale

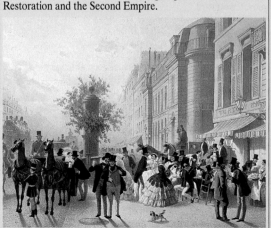

The Café de Paris *and* Tortoni

Private room at the Maison Dorée

1815
Fall of the Empire and restoration of the monarchy.

1825
About one thousand restaurants are now open in Paris.

1830
The July Revolution. Louis-Philippe becomes King of France.

19TH CENTURY: THE RESTAURANT'S GOLDEN AGE

1841
The architect Hittorff builds a leisure complex on the Champs-Élysées.

BOULEVARD DES ITALIENS. The boulevard *par excellence* was the Boulevard des Italiens. It was known as the "Petit Koblenz" during the Directoire, and during the Restoration was renamed the "Boulevard de Gand" after the city where Louis XVIII had sought refuge during the Hundred Days. It was the meeting place for returning exiles and, therefore, a place of celebration. It was here in the theater district, during the first quarter of the 19th century, that such restaurants as *Tortoni*, the *Café Riche*, the *Café Anglais*, the *Café de Paris*, and the *Maison d'Or* (formerly the *Café Hardy* and later the *Maison Dorée*) opened and served well and expensively everyone who was (or aspired to be) anyone in Parisian high society. Food was abundant and of the finest quality. Princes and actresses, courtiers and dandies, bourgeois and divas all frequented their luxurious private rooms, the most famous of which was the *Grand Seize* at the *Café Anglais*. Until the end of the 19th century it was in fact considered bad taste to take one's wife to a restaurant. Although certain individual establishments survived beyond the 19th century and into the 20th, the fashion for the Boulevards did not, and the epicenter of Parisian gastronomy moved westward.

1846
Daumier publishes "Nos Bons Bourgeois", a collection of his drawings.

1848
The monarchy is overthrown and the Second Republic is founded.

1850
About two thousand restaurants are now open in Paris.

1850
Labiche presents his play "Un garçon de chez Véry".

"BRASSERIES" AND "BOUILLONS." During the Second Empire two types of establishment grew up alongside the top restaurants. Brasseries, where since the 16th century customers had been able to drink beer and enjoy Alsatian cuisine in Paris, became more numerous after the end of the Franco-Prussian war in 1871 and the arrival of large numbers of refugees from Alsace-Lorraine. This led to the opening of such Alsatian restaurants as *Bofinger* ● *76* ▲ *240*, near the Place de la Bastille, and *Floderer* (better known as *Flo* ▲ *259*) in the Passage des Petites-Écuries. During the same period *Lipp* ▲ *129*, on the Boulevard Saint-Germain, also served sauerkraut, the national dish of Alsace, while the *Brasserie Universelle* in the Place de l'Opéra could seat eight hundred diners. The

Gambrinus

The *Boulant* "bouillons."

appearance of the *bouillons* was a result of the economic success of the French capital during the second half of the 19th century. To provide inexpensive and nourishing fare for the workers in Les Halles, a butcher by the name of Pierre-Louis Duval decided to open an inexpensive restaurant in the Rue de la Monnaie serving cheap cuts of boiled beef. Duval opened a number of *bouillons* across Paris. His son, Alexandre Duval (known as "*Godefroi des Bouillons*"), inherited a large fortune and became one of the "kings" of the Boulevards. The idea was taken up by Chartier ▲ 262, Boulant and Rougeot, who also established *bouillon* chains.

19TH CENTURY: THE RISE OF THE RIVE GAUCHE

FAUBOURG SAINT-GERMAIN. The oldest of the famous establishments in the Faubourg Saint-Germain is the *Café Desmares*, on the corner of the Rue de l'Université and the Rue du Bac. After 1830 it was renowned as the meeting place of the Legitimists, and was patronized mostly by ministry officials and directors. The *Café d'Orsay* opposite the Pont Royal served high-class food to the last officers of the First Empire and the first men of letters of the Second. Such a clientele is not in the least surprising. Members of the military, writers, politicians and students formed the bulk of customers at the restaurants on the Rive Gauche (left bank). In the 1840's the *Magny* opened in what is now the Rue Mazet, but the students who frequented it were soon replaced by a wealthier clientele, and from 1862 the writer Sainte-Beuve would preside over famous literary dinners there. In 1848 a certain Foyot, a former cook to Louis-Philippe, took over an establishment on the corner of the Rue de Tournon and Rue de Vaugirard, to which he gave his name. Throughout the 19th century and during the first third of the 20th century it remained the mecca of Parisian gastronomy, patronized in particular by members of the Sénat (upper chamber). By the end of the 19th century, the *Café Voltaire* (founded in 1750) in the Place de l'Odéon had become a political and literary venue. It maintained its gastronomic reputation until the 1950's.

Lapérouse

THE TWO "BIG NAMES" OF THE QUAIS. The last of the top restaurants on the Rive Droite (right bank) was located on the Quai de la Tournelle. Although the *Tour d'Argent* ▲ 147 was already a very popular inn with the courtiers of King Henry III in the 16th century, it was not until the late 1880's that Frédéric Delair established its reputation. All the crowned heads who had previously dined at the *Café Anglais* feasted on his numbered pressed duck. In 1913 Frédéric Delair was succeeded by André Terrail, the last manager of the great Boulevard restaurant. In 1878 Jules Lapérouse

1852
Louis Napoleon is proclaimed Emperor.

1853
Baron Haussmann becomes Prefect of the Seine département.

1854
Baltard begins the construction of Les Halles.

1854
Bois de Boulogne designed by Alphand.

1861
Garnier begins to build the Opéra.

1866
Offenbach presents "La Vie Parisienne".

1867
Louis Bignon of the "Café Riche" is awarded the "Légion d'honneur".

1870
End of the Second Empire.

1871 *The Paris Commune.* **1873** *Zola's "Le Ventre de Paris" is published.*	opened a restaurant on the corner of the Rue and the Quai des Grands-Augustins and gave it his own name. The small restaurants that made his reputation date from the turn of the century. His golden age, sustained by a fine menu and intimate settings, lasted until World War One ▲ *135*.

20TH CENTURY: PLACE DE LA CONCORDE TO THE BOIS DE BOULOGNE

1875 *Founding of the Third Republic.* **1889** *Eiffel Tower completed.* **1899** *Feydeau writes his play "La Dame de Chez 'Maxim's.' "* **1900** *Exposition Universelle held in Paris. The Belle Époque reaches its apogee.*	**PLACE DE LA MADELEINE AND RUE ROYALE.** The Universal Exhibition of 1900 led to the appearance of dozens of new restaurants and the renovation of many others. Its location on the Place de la Concorde, marked by a monumental entrance, guaranteed the fortunes of the establishments in the Rue Royale and the Place de la Madeleine. *Maxim's* ▲ *217* (opened in 1893) became the torchbearer of the *Belle Époque*, assisted by its famous coterie of cocottes. *Weber*, an English restaurant that opened in 1865, put up strong competition, while *Lucas*, an 18th-century tavern that was renamed *Lucas-Carton* ▲ *216* in 1925, was not far behind. Two more top restaurants in the district were *Larue* and *Chez Durant*.

Maxim's

1900 *First edition of the "Guide Michelin" is published.* **1913** *Proust publishes the first volume of "A la Recherche du Temps Perdu".* **1914** *Jean Jaurès, philosopher and socialist, is assassinated at the "Croissant".* **1914–18** *World War One.*	**THE CHAMPS-ÉLYSÉES AND THE BOIS DE BOULOGNE.** The lower end of the Avenue des Champs-Élysées and its restaurants, which had been popular for social outings since the mid-19th century, now also became extremely fashionable. During the Revolution the *Ledoyen* ▲ *197* was considered an unacceptable establishment. In 1848 it was renovated by Hittorff, who was also the architect of *Laurent* ▲ *196*, which opened in 1842. The *Pavillon de l'Élysée* ▲ *192*, dating from 1898, offered the bucolic charm of a shady terrace. On public holidays the citizens of Paris walked up the "most beautiful avenue in the world," stopping en route at *Fouquet's* ▲ *180*, a former coaching inn, before reaching the Bois de Boulogne for the *Grande Cascade* ▲ *171* and the *Pré Catelan* ▲ *173*.

20TH CENTURY: BOHEMIAN RESTAURANTS

1920's *The Roaring Twenties.* **1925** *Exhibition of the Decorative Arts in Paris.*	**STUDENTS AND ARTISTS.** Since students have always formed an impoverished and hungry clientele, it follows that there are no top restaurants near the Paris universities. The success enjoyed by *Flicoteaux* in the 19th century was due largely to the fact that bread was served in almost unlimited

quantities. In 1931 university lecturers started to patronize *Balzar* ▲ *150*, a brasserie bought by Marcellin Cazes in the Rue des Écoles, and their equivalent of *Lipp* ▲ *129*. During the golden age of the Boulevard Saint-Michel (1870 to 1940) students on the many café terraces, from the *Café Vachette* to the *Capoulade*, drank more than they ate. The reputation of the Faubourg Saint-Germain was made by its clientele of artists and writers. In 1930 the *Méditerranée* ▲ *152* in the Place de l'Odéon enjoyed a brief period of glory when Picasso and Jean Cocteau were among its customers. However, *Lipp* continued to be the left bank restaurant *par excellence*. The *Brasserie des Bords du Rhin* (opened in 1880) was given this name and its present character in 1926. Its reputation, already well established before 1939, reached its peak after World War Two, when the Faubourg Saint-Germain became fashionable. The *Procope* ▲ *132*, which doubled as a literary salon virtually from the time it opened in 1686, was first and foremost a café. When it became a restaurant it attracted more tourists than writers.

1939–45
World War Two.

1946
Founding of the
Fourth Republic.

THE GOLDEN AGE OF MONTPARNASSE. According to Paul Léautaud the *Closerie des Lilas* ▲ *159*, situated opposite the *Bullier* ballroom at the intersection of the Boulevard Montparnasse and

La Coupole

the Avenue de l'Observatoire, became the mecca of literary café society at the beginning of the 20th century. It stood here until the Roaring Twenties, when it was knocked down to make way for a new intersection on the boulevard. The *Dôme* ▲ *308*, the *Rotonde* and later the *Coupole* ▲ *156* and the *Sélect* on the Carrefour Vavin attracted the bohemians from Montmartre, who were to be followed by rich American tourists. From the late 19th century to the 1930's, the *Lavenue*, a restaurant with gastronomic pretentions, stood on the former Place de Rennes.

1950's
The great days of
Saint-Germain-des-
Prés, Paris.

1958
Founding of the Fifth
Republic.

TODAY: REMEMBRANCE OF THINGS PAST

MIDDLE-CLASS AND BUSINESS DISTRICTS. The present-day location of restaurants echoes their historical development. With one or two noteworthy exceptions, few top restaurants in the east and north of Paris have survived. Today the speed with which districts come into and go out of fashion makes it difficult to predict whether restaurants in such districts as Les Halles and the Bastille will continue to thrive. The establishment of new top restaurants on the Rive Droite within the middle-class and business districts is nothing new, and intellectuals and politicians still dine on the Rive Gauche, in restaurants redolent of times gone by. On Saturday evenings diners crowd into the modern equivalents of the *bouillon* chains.

1993
Paris has 5,500
restaurants.

● CHEFS AND GOURMETS

The French writer Honoré de Balzac once explained to a diner who was gulping down a good wine: "That wine, my friend, should be caressed with the eyes. – And then what? – And then inhaled. – And then what? – And then put back on the table, devoutly, without being tasted. – And then what? – And then it should be discussed." This dialogue goes on.

ALEXANDRE GRIMOD DE LA REYNIÈRE (1758–1837)

Rejected by his aristocratic family, Grimod hated the rich but dined at their tables. Between 1803 and 1812 this gourmet and dilettante published *L'Almanach gourmand* and set up teams of tasters who assessed the dishes. He was the father of restaurant critics.

ANTONIN CARÊME (1783–1833)

Carême was born of modest parents and placed with an innkeeper who raised him as his son. He later served an apprenticeship under the famous pâtissier Bailly but had ambitions of becoming an architect. He became chef to members of the European nobility and wrote several works in which he devised and set out the rules of modern, decorative cuisine.

JEAN-ANTHELME BRILLAT-SAVARIN (1755–1826)

An educated and cultivated man who was a député at the Estates General but first and foremost a gourmet. He brought the recipe for Welsh rarebit back from the United States and wrote *La Physiologie du goût*, which earned him posthumous renown ● 90.

CURNONSKY (1872–1956)

Maurice Edmond Sailland wrote under the pseudonym *cur non?* (why not?), adding a Slavic flavor by making it Curnonsky. This "prince of gourmets" wrote the 28-volume *La France gastronomique*, which heralded the middle-class family cooking of Auguste Escoffier.

PLEASURE AND UTILITY

You should eat to live and not live to eat. This famous maxim, immortalized by Molière in his play *The Miser*, encapsulates the distinction between *gourmet* (connoisseur) and *gourmand* (greedy eater).

NOUVELLE CUISINE

"New" but just one of a succession of novelties, this type of nouvelle cuisine, promoted by Gault and Millau, emerged in 1968 as a result of the desire for healthy eating and attractive presentation.

BIBENDUM

The first *Michelin*, the forerunner of modern gastronomic guides, appeared in 1900. From 1926 it included a selection of the very best French restaurants. The *macarons* (the Michelin equivalent of stars) appeared in 1930. Over one million copies of the guide are published every year.

RAYMOND OLIVER (1909–90)

Oliver was born into a family of innkeepers. He became the chef at the *Grand Véfour* ▲ *213–14* and was responsible for popularizing haute cuisine on television.

TALLEYRAND (1754–1838)

Napoleon liked eating as little as he did sleeping and entrusted the task of receiving his dinner guests to Talleyrand and Cambacérès. So enthusiastically did these hosts carry out their duty that they earned the Empire the reputation for being the most "gastronomic" reign until that of Louis XVIII, who was himself an extremely fine cook. Government dinners no longer have this reputation.

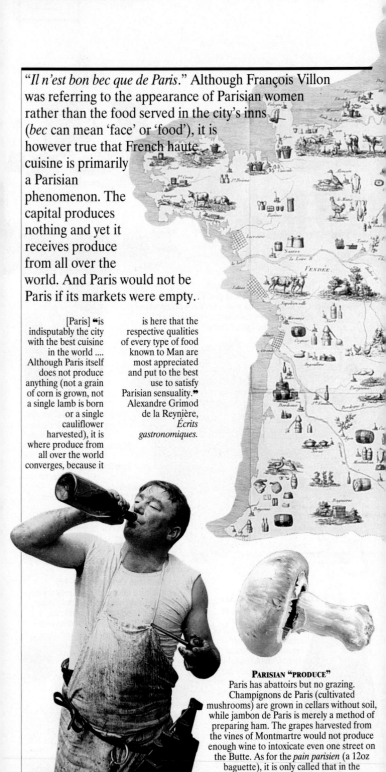

"Il n'est bon bec que de Paris." Although François Villon was referring to the appearance of Parisian women rather than the food served in the city's inns (*bec* can mean 'face' or 'food'), it is however true that French haute cuisine is primarily a Parisian phenomenon. The capital produces nothing and yet it receives produce from all over the world. And Paris would not be Paris if its markets were empty.

[Paris] **"is indisputably the city with the best cuisine in the world .... Although Paris itself does not produce anything (not a grain of corn is grown, not a single lamb is born or a single cauliflower harvested), it is where produce from all over the world converges, because it is here that the respective qualities of every type of food known to Man are most appreciated and put to the best use to satisfy Parisian sensuality."** Alexandre Grimod de la Reynière, *Écrits gastronomiques.*

PARISIAN "PRODUCE"

Paris has abattoirs but no grazing. Champignons de Paris (cultivated mushrooms) are grown in cellars without soil, while jambon de Paris is merely a method of preparing ham. The grapes harvested from the vines of Montmartre would not produce enough wine to intoxicate even one street on the Butte. As for the *pain parisien* (a 12oz baguette), it is only called that in the provinces.

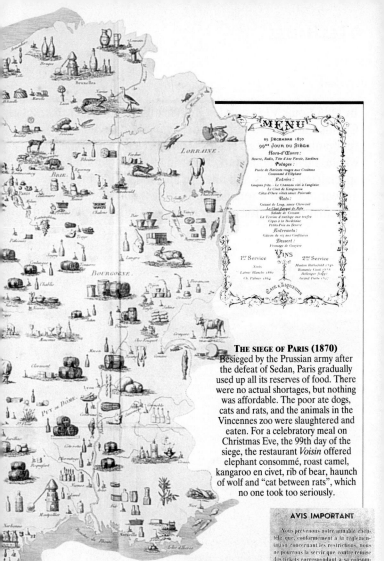

MENU

25 Décembre 1870
99ᵐᵉ Jour du Siège

Hors-d'Œuvre :
Beurre, Radis, Tête d'Ane Farcie, Sardines

Potages :
Purée de Haricots rouges aux Croûtons
Consommé d'Éléphant

Entrées :
Goujons frits. - Le Chameau rôti à l'anglaise
Le Civet de Kangourou
Côtes d'Ours rôties sauce Poivrade

Rôts :
Cuissot de Loup, sauce Chevreuil
Le Chat flanqué de Rats
Salade de Cresson
La Terrine d'Antilope aux truffes
Cèpes à la Bordelaise
Petits-Pois au Beurre

Entremets :
Gâteau de riz aux Confitures

Dessert :
Fromage de Gruyère

1ᵉʳ Service **VINS** 2ᵐᵉ Service
Xérès *Mouton Rothschild 1846*
Latour Blanche 1861 *Romanée Conti 1858*
Ch. Palmer 1864 *Bellenger frappé*
Grand Porto 1827

Café & Liqueurs

THE SIEGE OF PARIS (1870)

Besieged by the Prussian army after the defeat of Sedan, Paris gradually used up all its reserves of food. There were no actual shortages, but nothing was affordable. The poor ate dogs, cats and rats, and the animals in the Vincennes zoo were slaughtered and eaten. For a celebratory meal on Christmas Eve, the 99th day of the siege, the restaurant *Voisin* offered elephant consommé, roast camel, kangaroo en civet, rib of bear, haunch of wolf and "cat between rats", which no one took too seriously.

AVIS IMPORTANT

Nous prévenons notre aimable clientèle que, conformément à la réglementation concernant les restrictions, nous ne pourrons la servir que contre remise des tickets correspondant à sa consommation de PAIN, VIANDE, FROMAGE et MATIÈRES GRASSES.

WICHTIGE MITTEILUNG

Wir teilen unserer werten Kundschaft mit, dass wir sie nur – gemäss den Einschränkungs-verordnungen - gegen Abgabe von Lebensmittelmarken bedienen können, welche ihrem Verbrauch von BROT, FLEISCH, KÄSE und FETTEN entsprechen.

THE GREAT WAR

"Provided the rear holds out!" was the ironic caption to certain caricatures showing Parisians indulging in good food. *La Baïonnette* preferred propaganda: "No meat...Out of potatoes... What's the meaning of this?!?!?! - To make our customers feel better, sir, we feature the menu of the day in Berlin before the French menu."

WORLD WAR TWO

The war years were marked by rationing and the black market. The writer Pierre Benoit was at *Ledoyen* when he heard the news of the Allied landings in Normandy. "The butter route has been cut!" was his immediate response.

In 1136 Louis VI (Louis le Gros) instituted the public market of Champeaux. In the 16th century Francis I ordered the reorganization of Les Halles, which became a national wholesale and retail market. During the Revolution Les Halles specialized in food, and under Napoleon III it took on the appearance that it retained until its demolition. It became the principal supplier for restaurateurs who did not obtain their produce directly from farmers in the provinces.

VICTOR BALTARD
Winner of the Grand Prix de Rome, director of works in Paris and a schoolfriend of Baron Haussmann, Prefect of the Seine département. In 1851 he completed a huge stone pavilion to house Les Halles Centrales. Ironically the pavilion, nicknamed the "Fort de la Halle," was soon destroyed. Baltard later designed the iron structure that was begun in 1854. He also designed the Church of Saint-Augustin.

CONSTRUCTION OF LES HALLES CENTRALES
The first six pavilions were completed in 1857, the next four in 1868, and the last two in 1936. The thirteenth and fourteenth pavilions that Baltard designed were never built.

"ONLY ONE ORIGINAL MONUMENT, WHICH GREW NATURALLY IN THE SOIL OF THE PERIOD, HAS BEEN BUILT SINCE THE BEGINNING OF THE CENTURY ... LES HALLES CENTRALES."

ÉMILE ZOLA

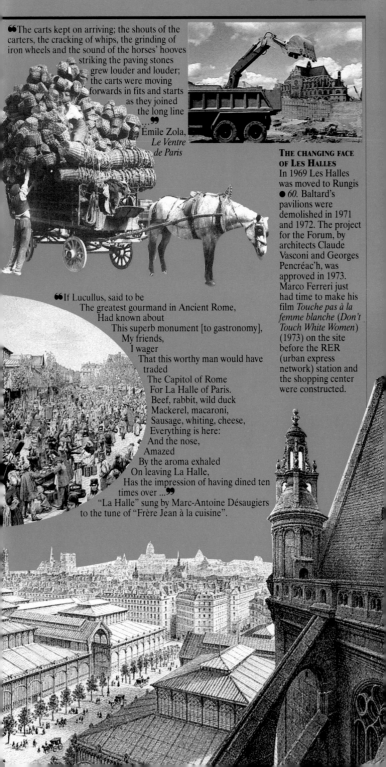

❝The carts kept on arriving; the shouts of the carters, the cracking of whips, the grinding of iron wheels and the sound of the horses' hooves striking the paving stones grew louder and louder; the carts were moving forwards in fits and starts as they joined the long line ...❞
Émile Zola,
Le Ventre de Paris

THE CHANGING FACE OF LES HALLES

In 1969 Les Halles was moved to Rungis ● 60. Baltard's pavilions were demolished in 1971 and 1972. The project for the Forum, by architects Claude Vasconi and Georges Pencréac'h, was approved in 1973. Marco Ferreri just had time to make his film *Touche pas à la femme blanche* (*Don't Touch White Women*) (1973) on the site before the RER (urban express network) station and the shopping center were constructed.

❝If Lucullus, said to be
The greatest gourmand in Ancient Rome,
Had known about
This superb monument [to gastronomy],
My friends,
I wager
That this worthy man would have traded
The Capitol of Rome
For La Halle of Paris.
Beef, rabbit, wild duck
Mackerel, macaroni,
Sausage, whiting, cheese,
Everything is here:
And the nose,
Amazed
By the aroma exhaled
On leaving La Halle,
Has the impression of having dined ten times over ...❞
"La Halle" sung by Marc-Antoine Désaugiers to the tune of "Frère Jean à la cuisine".

CHURCH OF SAINT-EUSTACHE
Built between 1532 and 1640.
The façade dates from 1754.

"MARCHANDS D'ARLEQUINS"
Leftovers from the tables of the rich were sold to the poor. The sellers set out their offerings haphazardly, like the pieces in a harlequin's costume, which is how they got their name.

❝As he came out on to the great central street, it brought to mind a strange city, with its clearly defined districts, its suburbs, its villages, its avenues and its roads, its squares and its intersections, which had been gathered together in one vast shed, on a rainy day, on some gargantuan whim.❞
Émile Zola, *Le Ventre de Paris*

❝On the ground, the piles of unloaded goods spilled over into the roadway. Between the piles, the truck farmers cleared a narrow path so that people could get through. The broad

pavement stretched away into the darkness, covered from end to end with dark mounds of vegetables. All that was visible in the intermittent light cast by swinging lanterns were the fleshy flowers of a bunch of artichokes, the delicate greens of the salads, the pink coral of the carrots ...❞
Émile Zola,
Le Ventre de Paris

"RESTAURANT DES PIEDS HUMIDES"
This open-air restaurant, at the foot of the Fontaine des Innocents, served thin vegetable broth to the workers of Les Halles and the local poor.

> **"AGILE, BURLY MEN SEEMED, WITH THEIR BARE, MUSCULAR ARMS, TO BE MILKING THE HUGE UDDER OF A BOUNTIFUL NIGHT."**
>
> LOUIS ARAGON

❝Pell-mell, on the chance casting of a net, the seaweed which harbors the mysterious marine life of the ocean's watery depths had surrendered its secret: cod, haddock, brill, plaice, dab, ordinary, dirty gray creatures with white markings; congers, those huge, mud-blue snakes with narrow black eyes, still alive and so viscous with slime that they seemed

to crawl; broad, flat rays with their pale under-bellies bordered with soft red and the protruding line of their backbone extending along their superb backs, marbled to the stiffened bones of their fins with patches of vermilion crossed by stripes of Florentine bronze ...**❞**
Émile Zola, *Le Ventre de Paris*

FORTS DES HALLES
The Forts des Halles (market porters), whose guild was established during the reign of Louis IX (Saint Louis), gradually became responsible for enforcing regulations in Les Halles. However, even up until the time that the market was moved to Rungis, would-be forts still had to show that they could carry a 440-lb load over 65 yards.

● LES HALLES

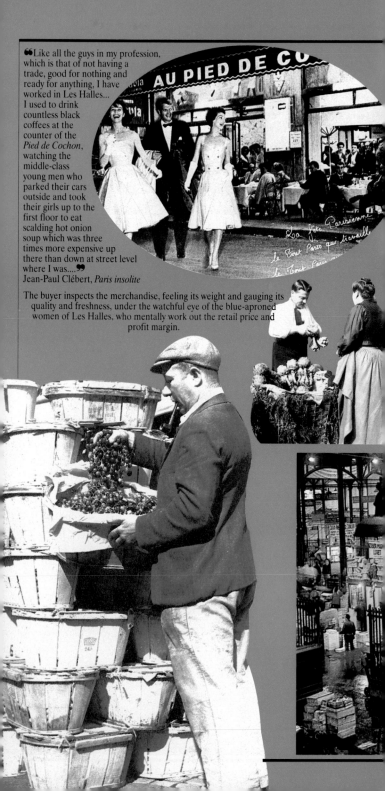

66Like all the guys in my profession, which is that of not having a trade, good for nothing and ready for anything, I have worked in Les Halles...
I used to drink countless black coffees at the counter of the *Pied de Cochon*, watching the middle-class young men who parked their cars outside and took their girls up to the first floor to eat scalding hot onion soup which was three times more expensive up there than down at street level where I was.....99
Jean-Paul Clébert, *Paris insolite*

The buyer inspects the merchandise, feeling its weight and gauging its quality and freshness, under the watchful eye of the blue-aproned women of Les Halles, who mentally work out the retail price and profit margin.

❝I found myself before the vast pantry which would provide the food for the day's orgy. In the pale light, I caught a glimpse of piles of red meat, baskets of gleaming silver fish, mountains of vegetables piercing the shadows with splashes of green and white.**❞**
Émile Zola, *La Tribune*
October 17, 1869

❝Morpheus has certainly never scattered his poppy seeds in La Halle. No silence, no rest, no let-up there... The constant hubbub contrasts sharply with the sleep that envelops the rest of the city: at four o'clock in the morning, only thieves and poets are awake.**❞**
Louis-Sébastien Mercier,
Tableau de Paris

RUE DES HALLES
The Rue des Halles was laid out in 1854 on the site of a cul-de-sac and three streets. Like the other streets in the district it was lined with shops and businesses connected with the activity of Les Halles, and by bistros.

PAVILLON DE NOGENT-SUR-MARNE
Napoleon III to Prefect Haussmann: "All I want are huge, iron umbrellas!" The only surviving "iron umbrellas" can be seen at Nogent-sur-Marne (Val-de-Marne) a few miles east of Paris. The only one of Baltard's pavilions to have been preserved has been rebuilt as a cultural center. The town's museum also has displays relating to Les Halles.

● RUNGIS

Tastes are changing. The market for tropical fruits, African fish, baby vegetables and edible flowers continues to grow ◆ *328*.

On March 1, 1969, after seven years' work, Rungis, France's new purpose-built central market located 9 miles south of Paris, opened its doors to market traders formerly based at Les Halles. Within 48 hours a string of trucks had filled the market with merchandise and trading was soon under way, seemingly unaffected by the relocation of the "stomach of Paris".

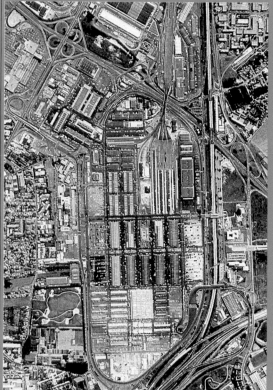

RUNGIS: A WORLD APART

Spread over 545 acres (including 598,000 square yards of covered buildings), the market is larger than the Principality of Monaco. It is the leading international market for fresh produce, handling 2,425,000 tons of food per year. Around 17,000 people are employed by 800 wholesale companies. Rungis feeds 18 million people. In the Paris region alone it provides 60 percent of the fresh- and saltwater fish and seafood, 50 percent of fruit and vegetables, 45 percent of fresh and cooked meats, and 60 percent of cut flowers and pot plants. On the other hand Rungis also generates 127,000 tons of waste per year, the equivalent of a town of 350,000 inhabitants.

La Marée is the most famous of Rungis's twenty-five restaurants. Like the *Pied de Cochon* in the days of Les Halles Centrales, *La Marée* is a two-tier restaurant. On the ground floor market workers snatch a quick snack washed down with a glass of wine, while the basement houses a specialist seafood restaurant.

The mere sight of food in such vast quantities is enough to kill anyone's appetite!

Produce is sold by the tray, trolley or container load. The basic unit is the crateful.

TRADITIONS

In the catering business, everything depends on there being food of the very highest quality available in the first place. Every chef knows what he wants and, for the most part, has the names and addresses of the best shops and markets; these are essential if his customers are not to be disappointed. Claude Peyrot, chef at the *Vivarois* restaurant in the 16th *arrondissement*, tours the markets regularly. Although food is often delivered direct to his restaurant, he likes to keep in touch with his suppliers; this is vital if he is to get hold of the best raw materials. Here is a chef's guide to intelligent shopping.

FISH
The criteria to follow when buying fish are that it should be whole, and that its flesh must not be delicate or flaky. Freshness can be judged from the firmness of the meat, a sharp, distinct smell that does not suggest rottenness, bright eyes that are not sunk in their sockets, shiny scales, and bright red gills.

QUALITY AND FRESHNESS
A windswept market in rue Gerbillon in the 6th arrondissement, towards the end of the 1900's.

Freshness is essential if food is to be of good quality; frozen food is not acceptable. To ensure that the food he buys is good quality and fresh, Claude Peyrot offers his clients a seasonal cuisine. As often as possible, he also selects local French produce from areas that are always utterly reliable.

CHEESE
Like so many restaurateurs, Claude Peyrot prefers dairy cheese made from milk straight from the cow. He orders his butter and cream from Échire, a name that guarantees the highest quality.

POULTRY AND GAME
Only poultry with an official seal of quality can be guaranteed to be any good; Claude Peyrot has a preference for chicken, capon and fatted chicken from Bresse. Game is, of course, seasonal and is normally supplied by professional hunters.

FRUIT
Like vegetables, ordinary fruits are best chosen according to what is in season; the same goes for exotic fruit. In this way, the quality is always likely to be best. The appearance of the fruit is also important, but it should not look "too perfect".

VEGETABLES
Many great chefs like to cook vegetables that come from a particular region or are seasonal; they also love humble, rustic vegetables such as potatoes, pumpkins, aubergines, courgettes and sweet peppers. How vegetables look is important, and it is sometimes advisable to be suspicious of vegetables that are too big, too beautiful, or too shiny. They will quite possibly turn out to be tasteless!

MEAT
The favorite meat at the *Vivarois* is beef. Points to bear in mind when buying beef are that the meat should be bright red and have a pleasant appearance, it should feel firm yet "elastic", and should smell fresh and light. The fat distributed among the lean meat should be in white or slightly yellowish threads – this may vary from breed to breed – and must weave in and out of the lean tissue to form a marbled effect.

OYSTERS
"An oyster the size of a small pebble has a rougher appearance and is not one single color, and is yet brilliantly off-white."
Francis Ponge,
Le parti pris des choses

63

SERVICE COVER
This dome-shaped dish cover
keeps food warm when it leaves
the kitchens.

To prevent last-minute preparations from turning
into disasters, restaurant kitchens must be highly
organized. This is how the basement kitchens of
Les Ambassadeurs, the restaurant of the Hôtel
de Crillon, operate, under the iron rule of chef
Christian Constant. This carefully planned
layout, completed in 1993, brings the benefits of
modern expertise to the culinary tradition.

BAHUT
Deep, cylindrical
container (with no
lid) into which solids
or liquids are
transferred, during
preparation, from
another saucepan.

SHALLOW FRYING PAN
A shallow pan for poached
eggs and sauces.

RUSSE
Saucepan for cooking
food in stock.

PATISSERIE
Marble-topped work
surface (1) in the
center of the room.
Cold-storage room
(2) and freezer (3).

**THE KITCHENS AT
"LES
AMBASSADEURS"**

**POTS, PANS AND
KITCHEN UTENSILS**
Saucepans and heavy
equipment (4) are
near the dishwasher.

MEAT AND FISH
Work surfaces (5),
stoves ("piano" in
kitchen jargon) (6), and
the warm pantry (7).

A: delivery of fresh food;
B: preparation; **C:** cleaning;
D: distribution to chefs;
E: to the dining room.

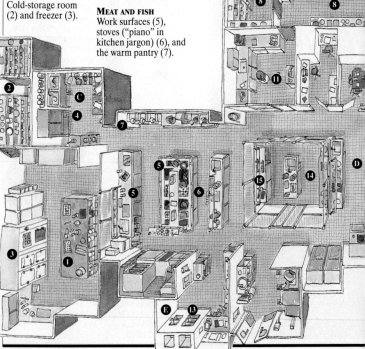

Fork for meat and poultry, either as a roast or cut in pieces.

KNIVES
1. Bacon knife: for cutting even slices of meat.
2. "Surgical" knife: for taking meat off the bone.
3. Peeler: for peeling fruit and vegetables.

COLD-STORAGE ROOM
All the fresh food is stored in one of these huge refrigerators.

SKIMMER
For draining.

WHISK
For mixing and beating.

SKIMMING LADLE
For straining.

FOOD PROCESSOR WHISK
For large quantities.

RUSSE
Saucepan used for reducing.

SAUTÉ PAN
For food cut into small pieces.

COLANDER
For straining and draining.

STOVES
Each chef is responsible for his own particular section (sauces, fish, meat, etc.) and has his own stoves.

CONICAL SIEVE
For straining thick sauces.

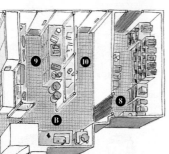

PREPARATION OF FOOD
Cold-storage rooms (8) with sections for fish (9), vegetables (10), and meat (11).

CHEF'S ROOM
Serves both as an office and dining room (12).

DUMBWAITER
The kitchens are in the basement. Plates and dishes therefore have to be carried up to the restaurant (13).

"BANQUETS FROIDS" (COLD BANQUETS)
This aseptic, air-conditioned room is used for preparing receptions with a cold menu (14). Cold pantry (15).

MESH CONICAL SIEVE
With fine mesh for straining thin sauces and broths.

PATISSERIE
The top restaurants have a patisserie chef.

DISHWASHER
An integral part of every kitchen and in constant use.

BANQUETS CHAUDS (WARM BANQUETS)
These ovens are located in the staff dining-room (room service) (16) and used for large receptions.

PLACE SETTING
Forks, knives and spoons.

Standards of service depend largely on the class of restaurant. If the quality of the cuisine is the primary reason for eating in a restaurant, so a large, uniformed staff, working efficiently and courteously, also contributes to the reputation of such prestigious establishments as the Hôtel de Crillon's *Les Ambassadeurs*. Each member of staff has a clear-cut function that they diligently fulfill. In the dining-rooms of *La Tour d'Argent*, *Le Louis-XIV*, *Lucas-Carton* and *Sébillon-Élysées* and many others, proceedings unfold with the magic of a theatrical performance. Enjoy!

THE STAFF OF "LES AMBASSADEURS"

CAR PARKING ATTENDANT
Brings customers' cars to the door as they leave.

BELLBOY
Operates the revolving door and carries messages.

DOORMAN
Welcomes the customers.

MAÎTRE D'HÔTEL
Seats the customers and oversees service.

THE PRESTIGE OF A UNIFORM

The organization at the top Paris restaurants exemplifies the art of living through gastronomy. Collectively the staff possesses a wide range of skills. They can be recognized individually by their uniform. Staff at *Les Ambassadeurs* must be soberly dressed, and the uniforms of the reception staff are decorated with gilt buttons and braid.

CRUMB TRAY
A small scoop or roller, usually in silver plate or sometimes solid silver.

CLOAKROOM ATTENDANT
When customers leave the attendant is waiting by the door with their coats.

SOMMELIER
An expert on wines who manages the wine cellar and advises customers.

CHEF
Supervises the cooks and checks the various dishes at the stoves.

WAITER
Uncovers the dishes at the customer's table.

67

A meal should delight the senses. It cannot be enjoyed to the full unless it is both pleasing to the eye and thrilling to the palate. The desire to meld the toothsome and the visually attractive has given rise to an entire ritual covering not only the way the table is laid and the napkins folded but also the presence of beautiful serving accessories made of wood, silver, ivory, or other sensual materials. These still play a part in a first-class restaurant.

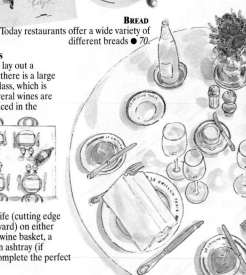

❝Against the snowy whiteness of the cloth, heavy silverware

Adds its brilliance to that of glass and crystal, Through which tapered light shines clear and bright Next to coldly reflecting cutlery.❞
Albert Couvreur

BREAD
Today restaurants offer a wide variety of different breads ● 70.

TABLE SETTINGS
In the past restaurants used to lay out a complete set of glasses. Today there is a large glass for water and one wine glass, which is changed during the meal if several wines are served. The table napkin is placed in the

center of the plate with the knife (cutting edge inward) and fork (tines downward) on either side. A bottle of red wine in a wine basket, a butter dish, salt and pepper, an ashtray (if required), and fresh flowers complete the perfect table setting.

> **"I should like death to take me
> During a grand repast;
> ...And that this inscription
> Be writ upon my tomb:
> 'Here lies the first poet
> To die of indigestion."**
> Antoine Désaugiers

HOTEL DE CRILLON

BRANDY AND LIQUEURS TROLLEY

Customers can select armagnacs, cognacs and calvados – even their producer and vintage.

ROAST OR CARVING TROLLEY

Under the silver cover is a heated carving table on which poultry and roast meats are carved.

THE ART OF FOLDING TABLE NAPKINS

For reasons of hygiene napkins are not folded at the Hôtel de Crillon. But this is an art that continues in some establishments.

CHEESE TROLLEY

The cheeses are laid out under a domed cover. The lower shelves carry plates, knives, and a selection of breads.

White brandies are served in chilled glasses.

DUCK PRESS

This silver duck press is used to compress a duck carcass, from which the breast and legs have been removed. The juice is collected and used to thicken the sauce in the preparation of pressed duck ▲ *147*.

DESSERT TROLLEY

Ice creams and sorbets set out below the patisserie and desserts on the upper trays. The lower trays are for plates and cutlery.

● BREAD

Traditionally a good restaurant is also judged by the quality of its bread, that unassuming but essential accompaniment to every meal and the indispensable complement to all haute cuisine. For a long time bread, a symbol of France, was a staple food. Today it takes very varied forms and can even be a luxury food. Parisian bakers belong to traditional guilds and their reputation is closely allied to that of the restaurants they supply. Some chefs, like Joël Robuchon of *Jamin*, are not only master cooks but have also become bakers so as to supply their restaurant.

BREAD IN ANCIENT TIMES
Bread first appeared in Egypt in 2500 BC. It has been part of the staple diet of various civilizations throughout the ages and was also a means of payment. In Ancient Greece alone there were seventy-two varieties of bread, which was cooked in the first wood-burning ovens. In Rome, where bread was a key to power, daily deliveries were organized by the Emperor.

THE MEDICINAL PROPERTIES OF BREAD
In the Middle Ages bread, when combined with certain substances, was believed to have medicinal properties that cured illness and even impotence.

MAIN TYPES OF BREAD
1. Organic bread made with whole meal flour and unrefined salt
2. Rye bread with raisins
3. Fancy corn bread
4. *Poilâne* corn bread
5. Rye bread
6. *Gana flûte*
7. Baguette
8. Leavened *boule de campagne* (brown bread), with added wheat germ
9. Walnut bread

8

9

BREAD AND THE FRENCH REVOLUTION
In 1793, following the law on equality for all citizens, the Convention decreed that only one type of bread could be sold.

FROM THE MIDDLE AGES TO THE REVOLUTION
Cereals remained the staple European food crop. Bread was made at home, baked once a week to save on fuel. Good wheaten bread was a rare luxury enjoyed by the wealthy classes. The price of bread (88 percent of the average family budget in 1789) was one of the causes of the French Revolution.

A GOOD BAGUETTE
A good baguette has a crisp, brown crust. The tender undercrust, the baker's signature, should be deep. When cut, the soft crum should not be too white but a creamy, almost grayish color with irregular air pockets. If the crust comes away in large sections and if the bread crumbles when touched, it is a sign that it has been defrosted.

70

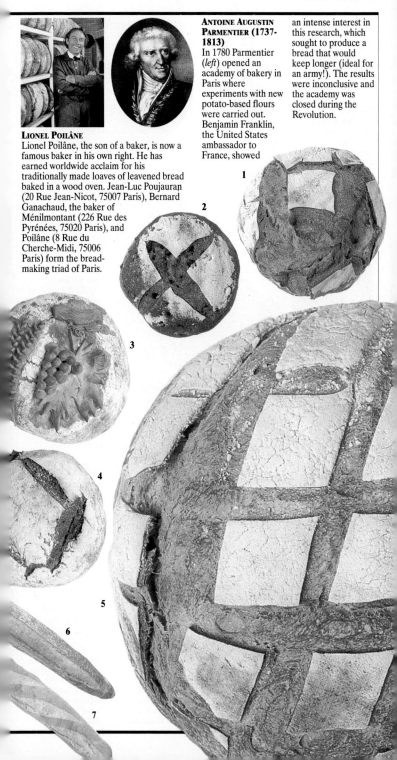

> **"BREAD IS GENEROUS AND CONFINING IT WITHIN A RIGID SET OF RULES SMACKS, IN MY OPINION, OF OPPORTUNISM... I RESERVE THE RIGHT [FOR BREAD TO BE] SUBJECTIVE, IMAGINATIVE AND FREELY CREATED."**
>
> LIONEL POILÂNE

LIONEL POILÂNE

Lionel Poilâne, the son of a baker, is now a famous baker in his own right. He has earned worldwide acclaim for his traditionally made loaves of leavened bread baked in a wood oven. Jean-Luc Poujauran (20 Rue Jean-Nicot, 75007 Paris), Bernard Ganachaud, the baker of Ménilmontant (226 Rue des Pyrénées, 75020 Paris), and Poilâne (8 Rue du Cherche-Midi, 75006 Paris) form the bread-making triad of Paris.

ANTOINE AUGUSTIN PARMENTIER (1737-1813)

In 1780 Parmentier (*left*) opened an academy of bakery in Paris where experiments with new potato-based flours were carried out. Benjamin Franklin, the United States ambassador to France, showed an intense interest in this research, which sought to produce a bread that would keep longer (ideal for an army!). The results were inconclusive and the academy was closed during the Revolution.

1

2

3

4

5

6

7

● BREAD

SAINT HONORÉ
In the 14th century bakers made Saint Honoré their patron. According to legend Honoré was still an impetuous young man when he announced to his old housekeeper that he intended to become a priest. The housekeeper, who was putting her bread in the oven, replied: "The day my oven peel sprouts leaves, then you'll be a bishop." Immediately the peel began to flower!

BREAD AND RELIGION
Bread has a strong symbolic significance for Christians. In the sacrament of the Holy Eucharist it becomes the body of Christ. It is also greatly respected in the Jewish religion and is blessed before being shared during a meal. Although it does not enter into the rituals of Islam, Muslims consider it a gift from God.

FROM OVEN TO TABLE
Bakers control the acidity of their bread. It should be subtle so that it doesn't spoil the taste of the dish that it accompanies. Bread should be served at the table in a basket, preferably wicker, and not (as is all too often the case) on a table napkin.

TO EACH DISH ITS OWN BREAD
Top chefs recommend rye bread rather than whole meal bread with oysters. Lemon bread is ideal with entrées and fish, and seaweed bread with fish that is fairly bland. Special breads, such as vegetable loaf, with layers of celery, spinach and carrot, make an excellent accompaniment for meat dishes.

Walnut, hazelnut and currant breads go well with cheese, but avoid strongly flavored ones such as cumin, poppy seed and onion breads.

To express their appreciation of a particular dish, the French often say: "You could eat it on bread!" The phrase harks back to the days when bread was often used instead of plates.

"LA FEMME DU BOULANGER"
In Marcel Pagnol's *La Femme du boulanger* (*The Baker's Wife*) (1939), the baker welcomes his errant wife back to the fold with a heart-shaped bread roll.

FOIE GRAS
Pâté de foie gras is best served with slices of toasted baguette or leavened bread rather than white bread.

DECORATION
AND FURNISHINGS

"Julien"
A restaurant opened in a former baker's shop in which the original décor has been kept.

Although they have fulfilled an increasingly social function, restaurants have never been thought of in exclusively architectural terms. Since they were usually opened in an existing building, décor was the only way their identity could be established and their image defined. Décor was initially sober and governed by regulations, but from 1845 onward it became bolder and much richer, particularly on the façades. Sculptures and moldings juxtaposed with patterned frosted glass produced an endless repertoire of embellishments which ultimately took on the generously undulating forms of Art Nouveau.

"Drouant" ▲ 204
Drouant opened in 1880 in an 1830's building. The first floor has a casing consisting of a row of elegant wooden arcades sympathetic with the style of the rest of the façade, with its curious wrought-iron balconies supported by consoles.

"L'Escargot-Montorgueil" ▲ 233
The façade is decorated with green and orange lozenged woodwork dating from 1875 and decorative elements from the 1900's known as *fixés sous verre* (inscriptions in gold leaf and polychrome scenes placed against a black background and covered with a sheet of glass), medallions in relief and acid-etched glass.

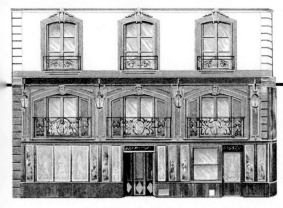

"LAPÉROUSE" ▲ 135
A casing of wooden panels on the façade of this 18th-century private residence, large wrought-iron balconies (also 18th-century) and beautiful hanging lanterns create a classic effect.

"LAURENT" ▲ 196
This is one of the few buildings constructed with the intention of housing a restaurant. It was designed by architect Jacques Ignace Hittorff (1792-1867), who directed the laying out of the Champs-Élysées gardens and the Place de la Concorde.

"LAURENT" AND THE NEO-CLASSICAL STYLE
The meticulously ordered arrangement of pillars, pediments, capitals and palmettes on the façade of *Laurent*, built in 1841, is usually reserved for interiors. The façade reflects the elegance of the dining-rooms. The building's neo-classical, almost Pompeian, image was originally highlighted by polychrome decoration.

"BISTRO DE LA GARE" ▲ 154
Despite alterations in 1977, the façade of this former *bouillon*, opened in 1906, gives a foretaste of the undulating plant-like forms that curve luxuriantly round the interior of the building. The ironwork (detail above left) and mirrors create an interplay of reflections that accentuates the rhythm of the décor. By contrast, the design of the broad, flat canopy at the front of the bistro is much more restrained.

"AU PETIT RICHE" ▲ 261
The dark woodwork of the façade dates from the 1880's. The trompe-l'oeil effect of curtains engraved on the windows preserves the privacy of the diners within.

75

Between 1880 and 1890 furniture was the vehicle of new decorative trends, starting with Art Nouveau and, from 1914, the Art Deco style of the inter-war years. New and fashionable restaurants and some *bouillons* adopted these fascinating modern styles of furniture and interior décor to keep up with the tastes of their bright and somewhat flashy clientele.

PILLAR AT "LA COUPOLE" ▲ *156*
The upper sections of the pillars in the brasserie (built in 1927) are decorated with paintings by Montparnasse artists. Below these a molded quirk serves as a bracket-lamp. From the base of the bracket-lamp the pillar is covered with "lap," a sort of green, lapidary enamel that was extremely fashionable during the Art Deco years.

THONET CHAIR FROM "JULIEN" AND "PHARAMOND"
Curved wooden Art Nouveau chairs like these, easy to stack, were widely adopted.

ART NOUVEAU CHAIR FROM "MAXIM'S"
Its simplicity is in contrast with the décor.

ART NOUVEAU COUNTERS
The dark wood counter at *Julien* ▲ *264* was installed in 1902. The pilasters alternate with panels that open out into broad, plant-like curves. The soft lines complement the more energetic exuberance of the restaurant's Art Nouveau décor, designed by Fournier. The pay-desk (opposite) at *Lucas-Carton* ▲ *216* (c. 1904–5) was the joint creation of cabinetmakers from the firm of Lucas and the sculptor Paul Planel. The use of marquetry represents a more figurative aspect of Art Nouveau.

BANISTER AT "BOFINGER"
● *46, 76* ▲ *240*
This wrought-iron banister is part of the décor designed for the brasserie (c. 1920) by Mitgen.

FROM ART NOUVEAU TO ART DECO
In this pleasing composition the curves of Art Nouveau, still present in the floral elements, are being discreetly replaced by the stronger geometrical forms of the Art Deco style, which already permeates the decorative scheme.

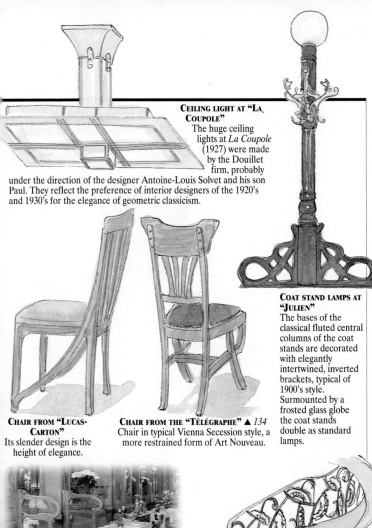

CEILING LIGHT AT "LA COUPOLE"

The huge ceiling lights at *La Coupole* (1927) were made by the Douillet firm, probably under the direction of the designer Antoine-Louis Solvet and his son Paul. They reflect the preference of interior designers of the 1920's and 1930's for the elegance of geometric classicism.

COAT STAND LAMPS AT "JULIEN"

The bases of the classical fluted central columns of the coat stands are decorated with elegantly intertwined, inverted brackets, typical of 1900's style. Surmounted by a frosted glass globe the coat stands double as standard lamps.

CHAIR FROM "LUCAS-CARTON"

Its slender design is the height of elegance.

CHAIR FROM THE "TÉLÉGRAPHE" ▲ 134

Chair in typical Vienna Secession style, a more restrained form of Art Nouveau.

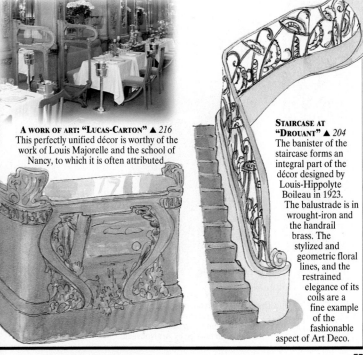

A WORK OF ART: "LUCAS-CARTON" ▲ 216

This perfectly unified décor is worthy of the work of Louis Majorelle and the school of Nancy, to which it is often attributed

STAIRCASE AT "DROUANT" ▲ 204

The banister of the staircase forms an integral part of the décor designed by Louis-Hippolyte Boileau in 1923. The balustrade is in wrought-iron and the handrail brass. The stylized and geometric floral lines, and the restrained elegance of its coils are a fine example of the fashionable aspect of Art Deco.

Fixé sous verre at the *Grand Véfour*

Toward the end of the 19th century there was a revival of interest in the decorative arts. Rejecting conventional artistic values, Art Nouveau appealed to the poetic imagination, incorporating plant forms and other natural motifs and systematically using certain materials (notably glass and *pâte de verre*, terracotta and faience). After World War One the movement was superseded by Art Deco, which in its turn reacted against the exuberance of Art Nouveau, fulfilling the need to adapt to industrial production by taking a functional and rational approach to design. Many Parisian restaurants followed these fashions but the designers, materials and the decorative themes that they chose deferred to the taste of the owner.

THE DÉCOR OF THE "GRAND VÉFOUR"
▲ *213–14*
Here the assurance of the Second Empire is combined with the classicism of the Directoire.

"JULIEN" ▲ *264*
Pâte de verre panel by Louis Trezel in the style of Mucha.

Apple tree on *pâte de verre* panel at *Pharamond* ▲ *234*.

PAINTING ON "PATE DE VERRE"
The décor of *Pharamond* makes good use of the effects of relief and the scope and variety of painting on *pâte de verre*, a material much favored by Art Nouveau.

ART DECO AT THE "CLOSERIE DES LILAS" ▲ 159
The dining-rooms are separated by acid-etched or enameled glass panels (above).

ART NOUVEAU AT "MOLLARD" ▲ 258-9
Marble is combined with figurative mosaics and Sarreguemines ceramics. The mosaic wall panels (right), the cornice friezes (above), the ceilings and floors are covered with *pâte de verre* plants, fish and cabochons, creating the effect of semi-precious stones against a gold background.

ENAMELED GLASS
The décor of *La Fermette Marbeuf* ▲ 193, executed under the direction of Émile Hurtré in 1898, includes several enameled glass panels. The decoration of bees buzzing around sunflowers creates an interplay of light and transparency. This is a fine example of the stylized plant forms that characterize Art Nouveau.

A MODERN BRASSERIE
Mollard, whose bright and colorful decorative scheme was designed by Édouard Niermans between 1894 and 1895, was a classic brasserie and a symbol of modernity. It won the acclaim of a number of decorative arts reviews and, above all, of the general public and the press.

WINTER GARDEN OF "LA FERMETTE MARBEUF 1900"
For the small dining room Hurtré designed a cast-iron framework on pillars in the form of stylized plants. It is surmounted by a glass roof decorated with stained glass panels, echoing the theme of the winter gardens, fashionable since the early 19th century.

EXOTIC ART NOUVEAU
In 1900 the ceramist Léon Fargues designed eight faience panels for the brasserie *Lipp* ▲ 129. The panels were inspired by plates from botanical collections and depicted luxuriant, exotic plants such as banana trees, palm trees and bamboo. They alternated with large mirrors which, as in many restaurants of the same period, created the effect of infinitely reflected space and décor.

● FLOOR MOSAICS

Frieze at the *Prince de Galles*
▲ *185*, inspired by the designs of
classical antiquity.

Although diners rarely give them a second glance, floor mosaics with their widely differing patterns closely reflect the various decorative movements and to a large extent dictate the restaurant's atmosphere. The designs at *Bofinger* and *Au Petit Riche* are both simple and traditional, while customers at the *Drouant*, *La Coupole* and *La Closerie des Lilas* have all the imaginative geometry of 1930's and 1940's Art Deco at their feet.

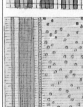

SIMPLE BANDS
The criss-crossed bands of the floor of *Au Petit Riche* ▲ *261* (top) are a variation on the theme of simple borders that are often a feature of restaurants opened between the 1870's and 1890's. As in the case of *Bofinger* ▲ *240* (above) they often stand out against a background of speckled mosaics of varying density.

ART DECO SHAPES AND COLORS
The bright, contrasted colors of these Art Deco mosaics reinforce the geometric effect and dynamic design of the floors.

SCATTERED MOSAICS
The muted colors of the traditional scattered mosaic pattern of the floor of the *Télégraphe* ▲ *134* (1905) are repeated in the border of parallel bands.

SEMICIRCLES
At the *Prince de Galles* ▲ *185* (1928) semicircular motifs create an energetic pattern in which repetition is hard to spot. The red and gold of the design and the broken border bring a touch of Classical antiquity to this Art Deco scheme.

CURVES
The pattern of intersecting circles on the floor of *La Closerie des Lilas* ▲ *159* (1925) gives the surface a sense of movement.

TOWARD CUBISM
One of the most interesting floor patterns is that at *La Coupole* ▲ *156* (1927). It reflects the influence of Delaunay's geometric abstraction and the Cubist movement rather than a pure Art Deco style. The same openness of approach inspired the contemporary paintings that decorate the pillars of the restaurant.

RESTAURANTS
AS SEEN BY PAINTERS

"MODERNISM IS TRANSITORY, FLEETING, CONTINGENT.
IT IS ONLY HALF AN ART. THE OTHER HALF
IS ETERNAL AND IMMUTABLE."

CHARLES BAUDELAIRE

The modern art movement, which originated in the 1860's and '70's with such artists as Manet, Degas, Daumier and the Impressionists and the lesser-known Lépine, Jongkind and Guillaumin, not only developed new techniques but also introduced new themes. The urban environment, and more specifically Paris and its suburbs, was one of the central themes of the movement, much more so than for artists such as Corot or Bonington who several decades earlier had painted the city in luminous watercolors.

Paris was, in fact, a city of social gatherings and social pursuits. Not surprisingly, its cafés and, to a lesser extent, its restaurants featured prominently. JEAN-LOUIS FORAIN (1852-1931) (above) was an artist of the Verist school who, like Degas, was fascinated by life behind the scenes at the theater and ballet. His paintings of social mores were usually inspired by a fierce hatred of politics, money and pleasure, and his palette creates harsh, violent contrasts as illustrated in *Entrée au restaurant* (*Entering the restaurant*) (1879).

> ## "I HAVE A HORROR OF ANYTHING SUPERFLUOUS. WE HAVE BEEN PERVERTED BY THE CONTRIVANCE OF ART. HOW DO WE RID OURSELVES OF IT? WHO WILL DELIVER US FROM ALL THIS SUPERFICIAL ORNAMENTATION?"
>
> ÉDOUARD MANET

ÉDOUARD MANET (1832-83) (4) was born into an educated and conservative upper middle-class family. His extreme freedom of style played an important part in the development of modern art: original distortions, a lack of regard for certain details and his sense of color earned him the admiration of new artists such as Monet and Renoir, whose influence caused Manet to lighten his palette and paint in the open air.

Chez le père Lathuille (*At Father Lathuille's*) (1879) (1) is a fine example of the naturalism that Zola and Maupassant embodied in their writing. A young dandy is trying to seduce an older woman seated stiffly at his side. The modesty of the scene, the woman's hands and averted gaze, and the half-hesitant, half-pressing attitude of the young man combine to make this painting a masterpiece of delicacy. Confronted by the rigidity of academic art, Manet remarked, "There is only one truth: to reproduce what you see spontaneously." Manet was an elegant, bourgeois socialite and a regular visitor to fashionable cafés.

Early on in his career HENRI DE TOULOUSE-LAUTREC (1864–1901) (5) was attracted by the clarity and light in the paintings of Manet and the Impressionists and became the friend of Van Gogh. In the early 1890's he became fascinated by the work of Degas, and began to concentrate on composition and the power of painting, through which he captured the mood of the period, particularly in the world of brothels and cabarets. One such painting is *Cabinet Particulier au Rat mort* (*Private room at at the Rat Mort*) (1899) (2). Japanese

artist TSUJUHARU FOUJITA (1886–1968) (6) was a fashionable artist among the intellectuals of Montparnasse at the turn of the century. But his work lacks force, as illustrated by *Souper dans un Cabinet Particulier chez Maxim's* (*Supper in a Private Dining Room at Maxim's*) (3).

			5
	1		4
2	3		6

"COME NOW! MODERN ART HAS SOME GOOD POINTS. YOU MUST ADMIT ... THAT GERVEX IS A GIFTED ARTIST WHOSE WORK COMBINES GREAT VISUAL AWARENESS WITH A UNIQUE TONAL QUALITY." ROGER-BALLU, *L'ILLUSTRATION*, 1887

HENRI GERVEX (1852–1929) was originally a pupil of the dull academic artist Cabanel, but after meeting Manet and Degas in 1876 he adopted the Verist style of painting. Scenes depicting the social mores of the period and the

uncompromising portraits that followed constitute the best part of the artist's work. Unfortunately from the 1880's Gervex (above) limited himself to society portraits and works glorifying the Third Republic. His scenes of fashionable restaurants fall within this category: *Armenonville, le soir du Grand Prix* (*Armenonville, on the Evening of the Grand Prix*) (1905) (1), *Une soirée au Pré Catelan* (*An Evening at the Pré Catelan*) (1909) (2) and *Aux Ambassadeurs* (1895) (3). These themes found a loyal following among the contemporary middle classes, who were fascinated by the pomp and mystery of a high society that only admitted commoners to its ranks if they were influential financiers. The restaurant was a magical window.

Maurice Utrillo (1883-1955) was a self-taught artist, renowned for his evocative depiction of life in Montmartre with its peeling façades and provincial calm (*La Savoyarde* and *Aux Vignobles de France*).

RESTAURANTS
AS SEEN BY WRITERS

ORIGINS OF THE RESTAURANT

Before it came to mean an establishment, the word "restaurant" meant a "bouillon qui restaure" (a nourishing broth). It was not until the mid-18th century that the word was synonymous with the places that served the restoring bouillon. The first restaurant worthy of the name was the Grande Taverne de Londres, *opened in 1782 by Antoine Beauvilliers in the Rue de Richelieu ● 44 ▲ 272. According to the "Larousse gastronomique", it was different because it served meals at set hours, at small, individual tables, and provided a bill of fare. The idea caught on during the Revolution when former cooks to the aristocracy found themselves without employment and set up restaurants on their own account.*

BEAUVILLIERS, THE FOUNDING FATHER

Jean-Anthelme Brillat-Savarin (1755–1826), magistrate and mayor of the town of Belley (in the département of Ain) and "député" at the Estates General, was first and foremost a gourmet ● 50. In 1825 he published an excellent treatise on the art of living entitled "La Physiologie du goût, ou Méditations de gastronomie transcendante", which he described as a "theoretical and historical work and, in line with the fashion of the day, dedicated to Parisian gourmets by a teacher and member of several literary and academic societies." It consists of alternate recipes and anecdotes.

❝In about 1770 ... [foreign visitors] were forced to partake of the fare provided by inn-keepers, which was generally speaking of poor quality. Several hotels offered a table d'hôte but, with few exceptions, they served only a very basic menu and at fixed hours. There were, of course, the *traiteurs* but they delivered only whole joints of meat and anyone wanting to entertain a few friends had to order in advance. This meant that visitors who were not fortunate enough to be invited into a wealthy home left the city without experiencing the resourcefulness and delights of Parisian cuisine... One intelligent man finally realized that all active causes must have their effect and that, if the same need manifested itself at about the same times every day, customers would flock to a place where they could be certain that this need would be agreeably satisfied. He also realized that, if the first customer were served with a poultry wing, then there would certainly be a second who would be happy with a leg; that the cutting of the first slice in the privacy of the kitchen would in no way dishonor the rest of the joint; that people would not mind paying more if they had been well, promptly and efficiently served; that the situation would be untenable if, in this necessarily extensive retail trade, customers were able to dispute the price and quality of the dishes they had ordered and, finally, that the combination of a variety of dishes at set prices would have the advantage of suiting every type of pocket.
... Beauvilliers opened his restaurant in 1782 and, for fifteen years, remained the most famous restaurateur in Paris.
First of all he had an elegant establishment, well-dressed waiters, a carefully chosen wine cellar and top quality cuisine. ...
Beauvilliers had a prodigious

memory. After twenty years he recognized and greeted customers who had dined at his restaurant only once or twice. In certain cases he also adopted his own particular "method." When he knew that a group of rich customers was eating in his restaurant, he would approach them in a most obliging manner, kiss the ladies' hands and appear to give his guests an entirely individual attention.

He would advise against certain dishes, thoroughly recommend others, order a third that no one had even considered and send for wine from a cellar to which he alone had the key. In fact his manner was so agreeable and engaging that all these 'little extras' appeared to be just so many kindnesses on his part. But the role of host did not last long; it was no sooner fulfilled than forgotten and not long afterward the size of the bill and the bitterness of the 'hour of reckoning' were enough to make customers realize that their charming host was also a restaurateur. **99**

JEAN-ANTHELME BRILLAT-SAVARIN,
PHYSIOLOGIE DU GOÛT, 1825

"TABLES D'HÔTES," INNS AND RESTAURATEURS

Louis-Sébastien Mercier (1740–1814) was a remarkable chronicler of Parisian social life who devoted twelve volumes to the subject. His "Tableau de Paris" is an irreplaceable account of life in the capital on the eve of the French Revolution. In particular he considers the advantages and disadvantages of the various ways of eating in Paris and the etiquette required.

66Although foreign visitors find the French tables d'hôtes unbearable, they really have no alternative. Once they have managed to locate a place, they have to eat in the company of a dozen or so strangers, and the more timidly polite among them certainly do not get value for their money. The central section of the table (near the so-called *pièces de résistance*) is occupied by the 'regulars' who commandeer this strategic position and don't waste time discussing the latest gossip. Their indefatigable jaws are ready to devour at the first opportunity. Their thick, ineloquent tongues are, on the other hand, skilled at dispatching the largest and choicest morsels down to their stomachs. Like so many Milos of Crotona, these accomplished athletes strip the table of its dishes, and are cursed after only a few minutes, just as Sancho Panza cursed the treachery of his doctor. Woe betide the man who eats slowly! Seated between these avid, darting cormorants, he will fast in the midst of feast. His calls for assistance will fall upon deaf ears: the servants will ignore his plight and the table will be cleaned out before he is served. They are accustomed to reiterated requests and immune to shouts and threats. The best way is to know how to eat, as it is impossible to make yourself heard.... Would you like to hear of another way of ensuring that you are well served in an inn? Well, here it is. Errant diners find out which new inn-keepers have recently hung up a sign: for a month or so, the service is good, the table linen is clean, the servants are attentive to your needs, the host is polite and the dishes well served. ... If you want to eat in a restaurant, you will soon be put off by the prices: people of modest means cannot afford such places which, in spite of their wonderful promises, are not in the least 'restoring.' Restaurants have been compared to the refectories of Capuchin monks; there are no tablecloths, nobody speaks and you are still hungry when you leave, while the helpings are so small that you can spend up to six pounds without satisfying your hunger. You will study the menu in vain, since you will be served with samples! It would seem that simply entering a restaurant is considered to be enough, that breathing in the air, smelling the aroma of the dishes and perusing the menu should satisfy your hunger. **99**

LOUIS-SÉBASTIEN MERCIER,
TABLEAU DE PARIS, 1781–8

TOP RESTAURANTS

It is not by chance that the Académie Goncourt holds its meetings at the "Drouant" ▲ 204. An empty page and a full plate are two extremes in the life of a writer, who spends his days seated at a table. All writers are (or have been) hungry. They frequent all the top restaurants, if only to find settings for their novels, but they don't all order from the same menu.

THE CAFÉ DE FOY

Aurélien Scholl (1833-1902) was born in Bordeaux but rapidly became the most Parisian of journalists. This prolific writer, who tends to be somewhat neglected, paints a wonderful picture of life on the Grands Boulevards, especially in his "Annales", which his caustic humor invests with a lively Parisian charm. In this extract he is not afraid of upsetting Louis Bignon, the famous Second Empire host, who made his fortune at the "Café de Foy" before taking over the management of the "Café Riche" ● 46.

❝How many people must have turned the corner of the Chausée- d'Antin and the Boulevard des Italiens without so much as a glance at this modest establishment and certainly without imagining that its proprietor, who had the idea of putting sea turbot and pot-au-feu on the menu, would be able to retire after a few years with savings of 200,000 francs! Bignon rented the shop, and decorated the ceiling so lavishly that it was the height of bad taste; a gilt-covered wooden colonnade and generally Moresque decor produced something resembling a traveling Alhambra. There were around twenty tables on the first floor and half a dozen private rooms on the mezzanine. He called the whole thing the *Café Foy*. All the titled gentry and unbelievably wealthy people from England, Russia, Austria, Prussia, Italy and America came to eat at the *Café Foy*.... 'Monsieur Bignon, a salted, smoked herring for two francs fifty; that seems a little excessive!' 'But these prices are fixed in your interest, replied the restaurateur. It is the barrier that I erect between my customers and the rank and file. Why do you come to my restaurant? To be among friends, to avoid irritating or compromising encounters. If I altered my prices, the place would be overrun and you would all go somewhere else!' A dissatisfied customer: 'This sauce is terrible!' 'That would surprise me, sir.' – Taste it and see for yourself.' Bignon suddenly changed the subject: 'But you didn't dine here last night, did you?' 'No.' 'Well, that's it. You went and ruined your taste buds in another restaurant.**❞**

AURÉLIEN SCHOLL,
LES ANNALES POLITIQUES ET LITTÉRAIRES

WEBER

Léon Daudet (1867–1942), son of writer Alphonse Daudet, was introduced to Parisian literary circles at an early age. This strongly nationalist writer edited the newspaper of the "Action française" and was also one of the best memorialists of the 1900's. He was fond of well-worked formulae and in this extract describes evenings at Weber ● *48, the famous restaurant in the Rue Royale that opened in 1865 and only closed in 1961.*

❝Men of letters and artists don't gather in cafés like they used to thirty or forty years ago. However, between 1900 and 1905, a number of my contemporaries and men of the older generation used to enjoy meeting in the evenings at *Weber* in the Rue Royale ... There was much more variety, more of the unexpected and the picturesque in those meetings than in society at large. We were less formal. We could move about more freely and get rid of the bores. Opinions were expressed more good-naturedly and more directly. If I said at *Weber*: 'What a dolt that Doumic is, he is a schemer who causes trouble wherever he goes,' such a statement would not provoke surprise or indeed much of a reaction at all. The same could not be said of *La Revue des Deux Mondes* or the homes of certain people I could mention. The empty chatter and poetic and dramatic vacuity of various members of the Rostand family, which were proverbial at *Weber*, were still being disputed in certain aristocratic and middle-class literary circles. An academic election had no effect on Charles or 'Monsieur Chantepie,' while it certainly ruffled the feathers of fifty or so Parisian parakeets, parrots, blackbirds and woodcocks. ...At about seven o'clock a pale young man with soft, brown eyes arrived at *Weber*. He was wrapped up like a valuable piece of porcelain and either sucked or played with one half of his drooping brown moustache. He asked for a bunch of grapes and a glass of water, announcing that he had just left his sickbed, that he had the flu, that he was going back to bed, that the noise gave him a headache. He glanced nervously then mockingly around him and finally gave a delighted laugh and decided to stay. Before long extraordinarily original remarks and diabolically clever observations were spilling hesitantly and hurriedly from his lips. These unexpected images flew straight to the heart of the matter, like a kind of elevated music, as is said to have happened at the *Globe* tavern among the companions of the great Shakespeare. He was more like Mercurio or Puck, following several lines of thought at once, quick to excuse himself for being too pleasant, 'tormented' by scruples, naturally complex, nervously delicate. He was the author of that original, often bewildering but promising work: *Du côté de chez Swann* (*Swann's Way*). It was Marcel Proust.❞

LÉON DAUDET, SOUVENIRS LITTÉRAIRES, GRASSET, PARIS, 1968

LIPP

Restaurants played an important part in the life of Léon-Paul Fargue (1876–1947). This poet and dilettante, the 'pedestrian of Paris,' as he called himself, made his mark as one of the prominent figures of Parisian literary life, which was often led around a table. Furthermore his father and uncle managed the factory that supplied the ceramics for the decor of the brasserie Lipp ● *49* ▲ *129. Less happily Fargue was dining with Picasso at the* Catalan *in the Rue des Grands-Augustins in 1943 when he suffered a stroke. He died four years later.*

❝I first visited *Lipp* some thirty years ago when it was still relatively unknown. My uncle and father, who were specialist engineers, had just finished the ceramic and mosaic decoration for the brasserie. ... Since then, and for all these reasons, I have been in the habit of dining at *Lipp*. I'm not 'one of the crowd,' like so many others, I'm still in the tenth grade, but I go there like an Englishman to his club, sure of finding a real friend with whom I can spend the evening and (how time flies!) start a new day, that unknown quantity that weighs so heavily. ... Eating at *Lipp* involves observing a strict code of practice. Some dishes require a tablecloth, others do not. It's a mystery to me. It's impossible to enjoy something simple, something a bit greasy or strongly flavored, with a 'jar,' on the wood or marble surface of the table, like we used to at the good, old *Pousset*, so exquisitely dark and cosy, at the crossroads Le Peletier. If it's hot and you're on the terrace and you suddenly feel hungry, then you have to go inside ... However, you can't write thirty lines in a newspaper in Paris, paint a canvas or express remotely specific political opinions without spending at least one night a week at *Lipp*. Today *Lipp* is as indispensable a part of the Paris décor and the smooth running of its social scene as the Ministry of the Interior, the Foire du Trône or the cross-Paris swim. *Lipp* is undoubtedly one of those places (and possibly the only one) where, for the price of a 'half' you can obtain a faithful, daily résumé of the French political or intellectual scene. This makes it easier to understand why, at two-thirty in the morning, hints dropped by the staff are ignored as they switch off all the lights in this Agency, this Audit Office of the 'Événement parisien', refuse any form of refreshment to latecomers, and finally have to push the customers outside with the dustbins. **99**

LÉON-PAUL FARGUE, *LE PIÉTON DE PARIS*,
GALLIMARD, PARIS, 1932

FOUQUET'S

The "pedestrian of Paris" has no compunction about deserting the "paternal brasserie" to praise the café terraces of the Champs-Élysées, starting with Fouquet's ● *48* ▲ *180.*

66When you come out of any of the buildings on the Champs-Élysées you have the impression of being on the open sea. I walked for a long time, as if I was on the bridge of a ship, before going into *Fouquet's*, the unrivaled capital of the avenue. While the *Select* absorbs, as a matter of course, the most questionable and ephemeral elements of the district, *Fouquet's* only welcomes the least questionable elements. If you go to the *Select*, you look as if you go to *Fouquet's*. When the 'top people' in the world of movies, who from time to time need a change of scenery, come to *Fouquet's*, they usually come in the evening and prefer the dark corners. Their vanity keeps them on the terrace until the first cold weather drives them inside. In fact they are deeply humiliated by *Fouquet's* clientele, who are full of joie de vivre and in whom they recognize people who make movies that are actually shown. They see Tourneur; Raimu, who is difficult to miss; Murat; Pierre Benoit,who wrote screenplays; people for whom the movies are reality. For others, who mix with people from the Stock Exchange or the race track, *Fouquet's* is a delightful anteroom room with excellent cuisine. *Fouquet's* is one of those establishments that will not go out of fashion unless a bomb is dropped on it. And probably not even then! Other cafés and restaurants lose business, lose their clientele, close and go bankrupt. *Fouquet's* persists like an organ that is indispensable to the bodily health of Paris. It is a place for male tittle-tattle, for men like to gossip as much as women. In the fall, men go there to tell each other

about their successes of the summer, or to pick up tips for the Stock Exchange or the race tracks, which most of them don't need since *Fouquet's* can boast that it welcomes the well heeled. But as the saying goes: when in Rome... **99**

LÉON-PAUL FARGUE,
LE PIÉTON DE PARIS,
GALLIMARD,
PARIS, 1932

LA CLOSERIE DES LILAS

In 1921 Ernest Hemingway (1899–1961) became the Paris correspondent of the "Toronto Star". Gertrude Stein welcomed him to her salon in the Rue de Fleurus where, among others, he met Ezra Pound. "The Sun Also Rises" and "A Moveable Feast" are the romanticized accounts of his life in Paris during the Roaring Twenties. The Closerie des Lilas ● 49 ▲ 159 *was only a few yards from where he lived in the Rue Notre-Dame-des-Champs, a distance often covered by this frequenter of bars.*

❝The *Closerie des Lilas* was the nearest good café when we lived in the flat over the sawmill at 113, rue Notre-Dame-des-Champs, and it was one of the best cafés in Paris. It was warm inside in the winter, and in the spring and fall it was very fine outside with the tables under the shade of the trees on the side where the statue of Marshal Ney was, and the square, regular tables under the big awnings along the boulevard. Two of the waiters were our good friends. People from the *Dôme* and the *Rotonde* never came to the *Lilas*. There was no one there they knew, and no one would have stared at them if they came. In those days many people went to the cafés at the corner of the Boulevard Montparnasse and the Boulevard Raspail to be seen publicly and in a way such places anticipated the columnists as the daily substitute for immortality. The *Closerie des Lilas* had once been a café where poets met more or less regularly and the last principal poet had been Paul Fort whom I had never read. But the only poet I ever saw there was Blaise Cendrars, with his broken boxer's face and his pinned-up empty sleeve, rolling a cigarette with his one good hand. He was a good companion until he drank too much and, at that time, when he was lying, he was more interesting than many men telling a story truly.❞

ERNEST HEMINGWAY, *A MOVEABLE FEAST*,
FIRST PUBLISHED BY CHARLES SCRIBNER'S SONS,
NEW YORK, 1964

LE TRAIN BLEU

Her association with writers such as Antoine de Saint-Exupéry set Louise de Vilmorin (1902–69) on the path to a literary career. André Malraux encouraged her to publish her first book, "Sainte-Une fois" (1934). The "taxi" in which she wrote this famous "letter" was taking her to the Train Bleu ▲ 243.

❝The restaurant of the Gare de Lyon is the most beautiful restaurant in Paris. Imagine a vast, rectangular, richly decorated room whose vaulted ceiling, a basket-handle arch, seems to start two meters above the floor. While placid-faced mascarons watch over certain of its soaring ribs, sirens, mere caryatids of fantasy in this vast structure, serve only to support the dreams of travelers. The latter, afraid, no doubt, of missing their train if they allow themselves to be seduced by the sirens' charms, run their gaze instead along the grandiose lines of the massive moldings that frame regional scenes from the south of France, painted in oils by the 'official' artists of the 1900's. The further the eye travels upward, the more it is distracted for, on the ceiling, paintings of various forms and formats, depicting landscapes and allegories, are set in a series of caissons which, while obeying the laws of symmetry, relieve its monotony by their varying size. Opposite the entrance, toward the far end of the room, the cashier sits in a glass kiosk dominated by a full moon, called a clock because it has hands. From her vantage point, the cashier presides over the comings and goings of the maîtres d'hôtel and the waiters who move to and fro between the customers and a huge sideboard shaded by green plants.

Tables to which chairs can be added are placed in front of a double line of gaboon and brown-leather benches, attached to a thick back rest, surmounted by brass rails, which both joins and separates them. These tables, kept permanently laid, and benches, flanked by coat stands, form well-ordered, solidly established islands on a sea of parquet flooring. They bear the hallmark of a dignity conferred by weight and are sufficiently distant from each other so as not to disturb the intimacy of conversations ....The extraordinary thing is that the exuberant ostentation of this extravagant decor contains a not inconsiderable truth that challenges the refinements of beauty and taste by the spectacle of republican opulence. This amazing establishment was created not only to satisfy the pretensions of the 'grand dukes' of the bourgeoisie and the more bourgeois of the grand dukes but also to inspire wonder in little Rémi and his mother, Barberin, in *Sans Famille (The Adventures of Rémi)*. 99

LOUISE DE VILMORIN, *LA LETTRE DANS UN TAXI*,
GALLIMARD, PARIS, 1973

LA CASCADE

Louis Aragon (1897–1982) published "Les Beaux Quartiers" during the year of the Front Populaire. It was the second novel in the series "Le Monde réel", which this Communist writer had begun two years earlier. Aragon, who was a Dadaist and Surrealist before he became a Realist, uses the plot of his novel to paint a picture of Paris before World War One in which the prestigious restaurant in the Bois de Boulogne naturally has its place ● 48 ▲ 171.

66The restaurant was full of people returning from Longchamp. The dusty, slanting rays of the late afternoon sun shone through the trees and rivers of the parched and dying Bois de Boulogne, settling on this diverse crowd in which the picnicking populace, with its greasy papers, noisy games and balls that suddenly flew off into the path of oncoming cars, served to emphasize the image of La Cascade as an oasis of champagne, a place of refuge after the enclosure, with the freshness of its water and grotto, like a décor at the Châtelet theater. The shouts, the car horns, the general clamor of the crowd epitomized the general weariness of the landscape. In the distance, as if in mockery, were the mill of Longchamp, the villa of Chauchart, the Tour du Prince Impérial and the flattened carpet of already yellow stretches of grass. In the spring of 1913, April in this substitute countryside already felt like autumn. Cyclists reinforced this feeling at all levels of perspective. Factory smoke beyond the Seine acted as a reminder of the real world that began when idleness and Sunday ended. A Viennese orchestra near the ice cream pavilion dominated the garden of the restaurant, which is like a flat tray, sloping toward the confluence of the Acacias and the roads to Longchamp. The customers, packed so tightly around the tables that they could not move, had to stand up to make way for the black and white waiters, carrying their electroplated trays high above their heads. They seemed to have reconstructed another world in the aftermath of the races. A world that was perfumed, polished and well washed had crystallized here after the excitement of the turf, the uninhibited spectacle of horses, dust, sweat and dung. Shining patches of flesh were revealed as the ladies relaxed and stoles slipped lower down backs that were not designed for the open air, while the men sported a singular mixture of morning coats and jackets, light gray and beige. After the intense excitement of risk, after the game of chance that had rendered them oblivious to anything else, these gentlemen, still fingering their betting slips in their pockets, were becoming suddenly aware of their re-awakened virility, as at the end of a sleepless night. Moustaches, to which pistachio or raspberry ice cream still clung, leant toward their nervously laughing companions. 99

LOUIS ARAGON, *LES BEAUX QUARTIERS*,
DENOËL, PARIS, 1936

MAXIM'S

Henri Calet (1904–56) had a series of different jobs, from solicitor's clerk to journalist, before turning to Parisian literature, an occupation at which he excelled. In "Le Croquant indiscret", he gives an account of his exploration of the high society and demi-monde of Paris in the 1950's that led to a dinner invitation from the manageress of Maxim's ● 48 ▲ 217.

❝No one was taken in by my overly cavalier manner. The bellboy paid no more attention to me than he had on the previous occasion. What an agreeable temperature, neither too warm nor too cool. And what a distinctive aroma, possibly unique in the entire world! It was the composite and heady aroma of sauces, alcohol, meat, spices, fruit, brine, tobacco and perfume. And only the very best quality. A concentrate of wealth. It was a far cry, momentarily at least, from the *Rendez-vous des Camionneurs* where I sometimes have my meals. I advanced like a sleepwalker, caught up in the fibers of his dream. Mme V– invited me to sit beside her. And there I was, me, part of this fairyland, amid the purple plush, the polished brass and the dark, shining woodwork. The ceiling lamps gave off a finely (of course) filtered, pink-tinged light. Their shape and the very transparency of the veined glass made one think, rightly or wrongly, that their designer had been inspired by the wings of some neuropteron. A fine example, in any case, of art imitating nature. Yes, it was certainly the right setting for so many, so very fragile left-overs. What was I served? Oysters? Well. In a technical and very well-executed 'briefing,' an extremely eloquent wine waiter recommended Sancerre wine. He was perfect, apart from the mannerism of pulling nervously at his cuffs. Wasn't it here (at our very table perhaps) that a minister had been poisoned by eating oysters? I decided it was better to keep this thought to myself. The oysters were delicious...While we ate, Mme V– told me *Maxim's* long history, which at times became confused with the History of France and even of the world. Only the choicest aspects of History, of course. In front of me the smart set, referred to by a contributor to *Chic* in 1895 as the 'smart set,' gathered in the confined space known as the 'omnibus.' From where they were sitting, they could watch the great cocottes go by: Liane de Pougy, la Belle Otero, Caroline, Émilienne d'Alençon, Blanche de Marcielle, Odette de Brémonval, Irma de Montigny... All these handles to their names; you find the 'nobility' in the most unexpected places these days. And how can you possibly talk about 'noblesse de robe' when they take them off so often? Noblesse de... 'nightdress' perhaps? No, not even that.❞

HENRI CALET, *LE CROQUANT INDISCRET*, GRASSET, PARIS, 1955

POPULAR RESTAURANTS AND CHEAP EATING-HOUSES

There were other establishments where writers, or their characters, kept their napkin ring, either out of habit or necessity. Such establishments made it quite clear that they were in the business of providing food rather than gastronomy. They are, in their own way, equally memorable and equally invested with history as their more prestigious counterparts.

FLICOTEAUX

In "La Comédie humaine", which consists of no less than ninety-five volumes, Honoré de Balzac (1799–1850) is the genial observer of his century and the human nature of his contemporaries. In "Les Illusions perdues" ("Lost Illusions"), Lucien de Rubempré, recently arrived in Paris, is forced to eat at Flicoteaux ● 48. He goes on to experience his moment of glory before once again falling on hard times.

❝The name of *Flicoteaux* is engraved on many memories. Few indeed were the students who lived in the Latin Quarter during the last twelve years of the Restoration and did not frequent that temple sacred to hunger and impecuniosity. There a dinner of three courses, with a quarter bottle of wine or a bottle of beer, could be had for eighteen sous; or for twenty-two sous the quarter bottle became a bottle. *Flicoteaux*, that friend of youth, would beyond a doubt have amassed a colossal fortune but for a line on his bill of fare, a line which rival establishments are wont to print in capital letters, thus: bread at discretion, which, being interpreted, should read 'indiscretion'. *Flicoteaux* has been nursing-father to many an illustrious name. Verily, the heart of more than one great man ought to wax warm with innumerable recollections of inexpressible enjoyment at the sight of the small, square window panes that look upon the Place de la Sorbonne and the Rue Neuve-de-Richelieu. *Flicoteaux II* and *Flicoteaux III* respected the old exterior, maintaining the dingy hue and general air of a respectable, old-established house, showing thereby the depth of their contempt for the charlatanism of the shop-front ... . The potato is a permanent institution; there might be not a single tuber left in Ireland, and prevailing dearth elsewhere, but you would still find potatoes at *Flicoteaux's*. Not once in thirty years shall you miss its pale gold (the colour beloved of Titian), sprinkled with chopped verdure; the potato enjoys a privilege that women might envy; such as you see it in 1814, so shall you find it in 1840. Mutton cutlets and fillet of beef at *Flicoteaux's* represent black game and fillet of sturgeon at *Véry's*; they are not on the regular bill of fare, that is, and must be ordered beforehand. Beef of the feminine gender there prevails; the young of the bovine species appears in all kinds of ingenious disguises. When the whiting and mackerel abound on our shores, they are likewise seen in large numbers at *Flicoteaux's*.❞

HONORÉ DE BALZAC,
LOST ILLUSIONS: A DISTINGUISHED PROVINCIAL AT PARIS,
TRANSLATED BY ELLEN MARRIAGE, EVERYMAN'S LIBRARY, LONDON, 1913

LA BOHÈME

Henri Murger (1822–61) is best known for having inspired the libretto for Puccini's opera "La Bohème". "Scènes de la vie de bohème", the novel from which this extract is taken, describes the artistic and literary milieux of the 19th-century Romantics. He described a "bohème" as the phase of artistic life, the preface to the Académie Française, the Hôtel-Dieu or the Morgue. The musician Schaunard and his friends Rodolphe, Marcel and Colline are members of the Bohemian set and always in search of a good meal.

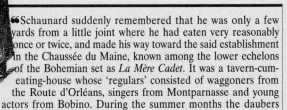

❝Schaunard suddenly remembered that he was only a few yards from a little joint where he had eaten very reasonably once or twice, and made his way toward the said establishment in the Chaussée du Maine, known among the lower echelons of the Bohemian set as *La Mère Cadet*. It was a tavern-cum-eating-house whose 'regulars' consisted of waggoners from the Route d'Orléans, singers from Montparnasse and young actors from Bobino. During the summer months the daubers from the many studios near the Luxembourg, the unpublished men of letters and the hacks from mysterious gazettes, flocked to dine at *La Mère Cadet*, famous for its rabbit stew, its genuine sauerkraut and a rather good little white wine with a bouquet reminiscent of gun flint. Schaunard went and sat under the arbour, the name given to the rather sparse foliage of two or three rickety old trees that had been trained above a sickly looking patch of grass. 'Well, that's it,' Schaunard said to himself. 'I'm going to enjoy myself and have a really good tuck-in.' And without further ado he ordered soup, a half-portion of sauerkraut and two half-portions of rabbit stew. He had discovered that by ordering half-portions, you got at least 25 percent more than if you ordered a full portion. This order attracted the attention of a young woman dressed in white, with orange blossom in her hair and wearing evening shoes. An imitation veil (or what purported to be a veil) floated on her shoulders, which would have done better to remain covered. She was a singer from the Montparnasse theater, which virtually backed on to *La Mère Cadet*. She had come to eat during an interval in *Lucia di Lamermoor* and, at that moment, was finishing a meal consisting entirely of an artichoke in vinaigrette and half a cup of coffee.

– 'Two rabbit stews, that's some dinner!, she said to the girl who acted as waiter. There's a young man who looks after himself. How much do I owe you, Adèle?'
– Four sous for artichokes, four for half a cup of coffee and one for bread. That's nine sous.'
– 'There you are,' said the singer, and she went out humming:
This love that God has given me!
– 'I say, she was a bit over-generous with the lah,' said a strange individual sitting at Schaunard's table, half-hidden behind a huge pile of books.
- 'Over?' said Schaunard; 'I thought she was rather too under-generous.'
- 'And would you credit it,' the stranger went on, pointing to the plate from which Lucia di Lamermoor had eaten her artichokes, ' marinating her falsetto in vinegar like that!❞

HENRI MAUGER, *SCÈNES DE LA VIE DE BOHÈME*, LEVY, PARIS, 1851

THE "RENDEZ-VOUS DES MARQUISES"

In the work of Henri de Montherlant (1885–1972) emotions and intellect were in continual conflict. They were finally reconciled through the medium of irony until separated forever by his suicide. "Le Fichier parisien" is a little-known collection of writings about love, women and death, written by this native of Neuilly who returned to the 7th arrondissement after a detour via the countries of the Mediterranean. His comparison of twelve-franc and seven-franc restaurants in the Faubourg Saint-Germain is a wonderful opportunity for a delightfully wicked social satire.

❝In the heart of the Faubourg Saint-Germain in Paris I know two little restaurants; or I should say two places where you can eat at mealtimes, since the term 'restaurant' is somewhat ambitious. In one, the cooking is not exactly unpleasant. You can eat à la carte but it is difficult to eat for less than twelve to fifteen francs. In the other the cooking is ... How can I best describe it? Let's say that it is in great need of attenuating circumstances. You eat a set meal that costs seven francs. And I've rarely seen anyone have an extra dish. The first of these two places, the twelve-to-fifteen franc one, is mainly frequented by taxi drivers and private chauffeurs. The second, the seven-franc one, is frequented almost exclusively by high-ranking officers, fairly important civil servants ('heads' of something or other) from the nearby ministries, and the nobility... At around midday the ladies from the War Office arrive, dressed up to the nines with their glass necklaces and 'emerald' rings, the very best of petit bourgeois luxury, and their cheap, over-powering perfume: these are the queens à la Pomaré, the marquises. When they enter the 'restaurant,' the gentlemen's backs arch almost imperceptibly; one has the impression that they feel cornered: ah! I'd rather have my cavalry squadrons any day! The marquises waste no time in firing their first round: their evening with the sub-prefect's wife; a case of the crawlers being entertained by the pen-pushers: 'How are you, commander? – Please don't get up, colonel! – Oh, yes, *médéme*! – Oh, no, *médéme*! – But of course, *médéme*!' You have the feeling that these people are all vying for a place in society, continuing their petty 'office' intrigues in this cheap eating house, cooking up something in the 'reek and steam' of the other awful concoctions... Sometimes the owner cries in a stentorian voice: 'Come on, Emma! serve Mme la Marquise's camembert a little better than that! What's got into you!' ... In the seven-franc restaurant, I met a man who had a fine apartment in the district, full of works of art, and a car, and so on, a man who had never had to worry about money in his entire life. As I expressed my surprise he explained (he was a bachelor and therefore half mad): 'I don't eat at home, partly because organizing meals is an unworthy occupation (a woman's job that I would never lower myself to doing) and partly because I don't want to have to keep regular hours at the risk of having to listen to remonstrations from my cook. I don't eat at the chauffeurs' restaurant because I would meet mine there. I don't eat regularly at X– (a fashionable restaurant a hundred yards from where we were) because the people that eat there are terrible pigs. In spite of that I go to X- when I want a good meal, but the rest of the time I come here, where at least I can eat among people from my own set.**"**

HENRI DE MONTHERLANT, *LE FICHIER PARISIEN*,
GALLIMARD, PARIS, 1974

INSIPID AND INCONSEQUENTIAL

Albert Camus said of "Le Parti pris des choses" that it was the first time a book had made him feel that inanimate objects were an incomparable source of feeling, both emotionally and intellectually. In "Le Parti pris" Francis Ponge (1899–1988) "poeticizes" familiar objects, making us see them for the first time. The Lemeunier *restaurant in the Rue de la Chaussée-d'Antin is subjected to his method of transforming real objects into archetypal abstractions.*

"There is nothing more moving than the sight of the crowds of employees and salesgirls who eat at *Lemeunier*, that huge restaurant in the Rue Chaussée-d'Antin, at lunchtime. Light and music are dispensed with a prodigality that is the stuff of

"COME ON, EMMA! SERVE MME LA MARQUISE'S
CAMEMBERT A LITTLE BETTER THAN THAT!
WHAT'S GOT INTO YOU!"

HENRI DE MONTHERLANT

dreams. There are beveled mirrors and gilt everywhere. You enter through a dark passageway lined with pot plants and extra diners who are already being packed in along the walls. This leads into a vast dining-room whose several pitchpine balconies form a single, irregularly shaped gallery, and where you are met by gusts of warm aromas, the clatter of knives and forks against crockery, the shouts of the waitresses and the noise of conversations.

... Here our insipid and inconsequential world reaches the height of perfection! Every day an entire generation unwittingly apes the ostentatious frivolity in which the middle classes indulge eight or ten times a year, when the banker father or the kleptomaniac mother has received some additional and totally unexpected bonus and wants to outdo the neighbors. Smartly attired, in what their provincial relatives would only wear on Sundays, these young employees and their female companions luxuriate in the atmosphere of *Lemeunier*, in all good faith, every day. They cling to their plates as the hermit crab clings to its shell, while the rich strains of a Viennese waltz dominate the clatter of the waltzes executed by the crockery, stirring stomachs and hearts alike.

... A little later, the cigarette lighters compete for the leading role, depending on the mechanism that activates the knurl or the way in which they are operated. The women, raising their arms in a gesture that reveals their armpits and, consequently, their personal approach to transpiration, adjust their hair or touch up their lipstick. This is the moment, in the renewed hubbub of chairs being pushed back, napkins being flicked and croutons bring crushed, of the final ritual in this singular ceremony. The waitresses, bringing a notebook out of their pocket and a little pencil from their hair, advance their stomachs, so appealingly enveloped by the strings of their apron, as they stand beside one customer after another and execute a rapid calculation, entirely from memory. **99**

FRANCIS PONGE, *LE PARTI PRIS DES CHOSES*,
GALLIMARD, PARIS, 1942

FORCE OF HABIT

The prolific writer Georges Simenon (1903–89) created Maigret in 1929. The inspector's cases sometimes force him to abandon his wife's boeuf en daube and visit the restaurants, both small and large, of the capital. But when he has time on his hands, he automatically makes his way to the brasserie Dauphine near his office on the Quai des Orfèvres.

66 At the bar he found at least ten familiar faces, men from the Criminal Investigation Department who had as little to do as himself and who had left early. This happened from time to time: a lull for a few days, flat calm, with things 'ticking over' as they say. And then suddenly there would be incidents occurring one after the other, with no time to draw breath. They acknowledged him with a gesture and moved along to make room at the bar. Pointing to the glasses full of semi-opaque, whitish liquid, he muttered:

'Same again ...'

The patron had been there thirty years ago when the inspector first came to the Quai des Orfèvres, but at the time he was still the son of the family. Now he had a son of his own who, like his father before him, wore a white chef's hat and worked in the kitchen.

'OK, chef?'

'Yes, thanks.'

The smell of the place hadn't changed. Each small Paris restaurant had its own individual smell. Here, for example, against a background of aperitifs and brandy, a connoisseur would have identified the slightly sharp bouquet of the less expensive Loire wines. The kitchen smelt of tarragon and chives.

Maigret automatically read the menu on the slate: Brittany whiting and calf's liver *en papillottes*. It was then that he caught sight of Lucas. He seemed to have taken refuge among the paper tablecloths of the dining-room, not to eat, but to talk to someone undisturbed. Lucas, in turn, saw Maigret, hesitated and then stood up and came over to him.

'Have you got a moment, patron? I think there's something here that might interest you.**"**

GEORGES SIMENON, *LA COLÈRE DE MAIGRET*,
PRESSES DE LA CITÉ, PARIS, 1990

GOURMANDS AND GASTRONOMES

Cooks delight us with their art, and so do writers. The latter sometimes surpass the former, whether they are writing about gastronomy itself or betray their own love of good food in a particular scene or description in their work. Food and meals play an important part in the works of two writers in particular: François Rabelais and Alexandre Dumas ● 108, who deserve to be brought into this discussion, even though their prose does not relate directly to restaurants.

FRANÇOIS RABELAIS, A HUMANIST AT THE DINNER TABLE

Contrary to the general belief of those who have not read Rabelais (1494–1553), his works have nothing "Rabelaisian" about them. Although his characters eat and drink their fill, his intention is not to produce a complacent description of the satisfaction of a vice, but rather to help his readers understand the world through the medium of comedy and the grotesque. For, like all good humanists of the Renaissance, Rabelais (who was also a priest and a doctor) was inspired by a thirst for knowledge. In the following extract he describes the birth of the giant Gargantua who was born through his mother's ear. It should be said that he was born in the middle of a banquet ...

"The good man *Grangousier* drinking and making merry with the rest, heard the horrible noise which his sonne had made as he entered into the light of this world, when he cried out, Some drink, some drink, some drink; whereupon he said in French, *Que grand tu as et souple le gousier,* that is to say, *How great and nimble a throat thou hast;* which the company hearing said, that verily the child ought to be called *Gargantua* because it was the first word that after his birth his father had spoke ... . in the mean while, to quiete the childe, they gave him to drink *à tirelarigot*, that is, till his throat was like to crack with it; then was he carried to the Font, and there baptized, according to the manner of good *Christians*. Immediately thereafter were appointed for him seventeen thousand, nine hundred and thirteen Cowes of the towns of *Pautille* and *Brehemond*, to furnish him with milk in ordinary, for it was impossible to find a Nurse sufficient for him in all the Countrey, considering the great quantity of milk that was requisite for his nourishment ... . **"**

FRANÇOIS RABELAIS, *GARGANTUA & PANTAGRUEL* (BOOK I),
TRANS. BY SIR THOMAS URQUHART AND PIERRE LE MOTTEUX,
EVERYMAN'S LIBRARY, LONDON, 1994

Pantagruel is the son of Gargantua. Like his father he is endowed with Herculean strength and a huge appetite from an early age. The young giant has a unique way of drinking his milk.

"One day in the morning, when they would have made him suck one of his Cows, (for he never had any other Nurse, as the History tell us), he got one of his armes loose from the swadling bands, wherewith he was kept fast in his Cradle, laid hold on the said Cow under the left fore hamme, and grasping her to him, ate up her udder and half of her paunch, with the liver and the kidneys, and had devoured all up, if she had not cried out most horribly, as if the wolves had held her by the legs,

at which noise company came in, and took away the said cow from *Pantagruel*....
which when they saw that attended him, they bound him with great cable-ropes ...
But on a certain time, a great Beare, which his father had bred, got loose, came
towards him, began to lick his face, for his Nurses had not thoroughly wiped his
chaps, at which unexpected approach being on a sudden offended, he as lightly rid
himself of those great cables ... and, by your leave, takes me up my Lord the Beare,
and tears him to you in pieces like a pullet ...**99**

FRANÇOIS RABELAIS, *GARGANTUA & PANTAGRUEL* (BOOK II),
TRANS. BY SIR THOMAS URQUHART AND PIERRE LE MOTTEUX,
EVERYMAN'S LIBRARY, LONDON, 1994

*Society condemns the most innocent of transgressions, and it takes the judgment of a
fool to show, with great humor, the ridiculousness of certain situations.*

66At Paris, in the roast-meat cookery of the *Petit-Chastelet*, before the cook-shop of
one of the roast-meat sellers of that lane, a certain hungry porter was eating his
bread, after he had by parcels kept it a while above the reek and steam of a fat
goose on the spit ... and found it so besmoked with the vapour, to be savory; which
the cook observing, took no notice, till after having ravined his penny loaf ... the
master-cook laid hold upon him by the gorget, and demanded payment for the
smoke of his roast meat ... The altercation waxed hot in words, which moved the
gaping hoydens of the sottish Parisians to run from all parts thereabouts, to see
what the issue would be of that babbling strife and contention. In the interim of
this dispute, to very good purpose Seyny John, the fool and citizen of Paris,
happened to be there, whom the cook perceiving, said to the porter, Wilt thou refer
and submit unto the noble Seyny John, the decision of the difference and
controversy which is betwixt us? Yes, by the blood of a goose, answered the porter,
I am content. Seyny John the fool, ... after that the reasons on either side ...had
been to the full displayed and laid open before him, commanded the porter to draw
out of the fob of his belt a piece of money, if he had it. Whereupon the porter
immediately ... put the tenth part of a
silver Philip into his hand. This little
Philip Seyny John took, then set it on
his left shoulder, to try by feeling if it
was of a sufficient weight. After
that, laying it on the palm of his
hand, he made it ring and tingle, to
understand by the ear if it was of a
good alloy in the metal whereof it
was composed. Thereafter he put
it to the ball or the apple of his left
eye, to explore by the sight, if it was
well stamped and marked; all of
which being done, in profound
silence of the whole doltish
people, who were the spectators of
this pageantry, to the great hope of
the cook's, and the despair of the
porter's prevalency in the suit that
was in agitation, he finally caused
the porter to make it sound

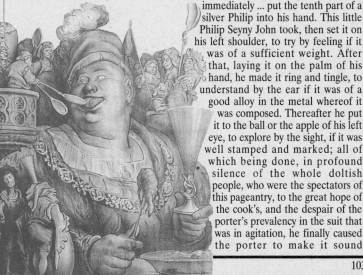

several times upon the stall of the cook's shop. Then with a presidential majesty holding his bauble, sceptre-like, in his hand, muffling his head with a hood of marten skins, each side whereof had the resemblance of an ape's face, sprucified up with ears of pasted paper, and having about his neck a bucked ruff, raised, furrowed and ridged, with pointing sticks of the shape and fashion of small organ pipes, he first with all the force of his lungs coughed two or three times, and then with an audible voice pronounced this following sentence. The Court declareth, that the porter, who ate his bread at the smoke of the roast, hath civilly paid the cook with the sound of his money. And the Court Ordaineth, that everyone return to his home, and attend his proper business, without costs and charges, and for cause. 99

FRANÇOIS RABELAIS, *TIERS LIVRE*,
LE SEUIL, PARIS, 1973

THE FIRST CRITIC

Alexandre Grimod de la Reynière (1758–1837) was the inventor of the literary genre of gastronomic criticism, and a new type of publication, the gastronomic guide ● 50. "The Almanach gourmand", which appeared for the first time in 1802, accompanied the development of restaurants in Paris. His 'team of tasters,' established a year later, was the first authority to award a seal of quality to food served in restaurants. In the following extract he praises the fish dish known as 'matelote' prepared by the widow Guichard at La Rapée. *Although not part of central Paris at the time, the district later gave its name to the Quai de la Rapée.*

66In our first year, we said a few words about the matelotes served at *La Rapée* and expressed our surprise that they were far superior to those prepared in the best middle-class establishments by the very best cooks. The mystery is explained when we consider the only way to ensure a perfect matelote: the dish requires constant attention, active surveillance; once it is on the stove, it cannot be left for a moment. In short, the person preparing the matelote must do that and nothing else. This is an impossible task for a cook who has to supervise his ovens and spit and constantly divide his attention between all the dishes that will make up his dinner.

However skilful and active he may be, he cannot be in several places at once, or stand in front of the cooking pot when he has to supervise his saucepans. He is therefore compelled to divide his time, to come and go from one to another and, as he does so, the matelote either disintegrates or burns; for it is a well-known fact that one burst of heat too many can cause it to lose most of its qualities.

But let us suppose, and this is extremely difficult to imagine, that one day the cook only has a matelote to prepare; however skilled he is, he will still not achieve the quality of the matelotes served at *La Rapée*, because not only must the cook be used

"AND SHE CALLED THE WAITER 'YOUNG MAN', STRUCK HER GLASS WITH HER KNIFE, AND THREW HER BREAD UP TO THE CEILING."

GUSTAVE FLAUBERT

to preparing this dish, but it also requires patience and a series of minute attentions that can scarcely be expected of a man and of which possibly no man is capable. Thus the matelotes that are so widely acclaimed, and rightly so, are always the work of a woman, who has been entirely occupied by that task, devoting all her talent, attentions, vigilance and patience to the preparation of that one dish. Add to this familiarity with the task, a practised eye and a skilful hand and we will see a person incapable of making the simplest entrée ... prepare a matelote which makes the artists of Paris pale into insignificance. This is proved every day at *La Rapée*, where you can eat the best matelotes in the world, especially those prepared by Madame Guichard who makes the best matelotes at *La Rapée*. ""

ALEXANDRE GRIMOD DE LA REYNIÈRE, *ALMANACH GOURMAND*,
MADARAN, PARIS, 1803

"APPELLATIONS" NOT "CONTRÔLÉES"

Gustave Flaubert inherited his Viking's physique from his Norman mother, while his scientific taste for the objective analysis of the social and spiritual anatomy was inherited from his father, who was a surgeon. "L'Éducation Sentimentale" ("Sentimental Education") is the account of his youth, and of the hopes and disillusionment experienced by the generation of the 1848 revolution. The book, which gives a faithful account of the period and its personalities, is considered to be the "bible" of the Naturalist school. The scene takes place in the Café Anglais ● 46, one of the most prestigious Boulevard restaurants that, at the time, was the center of Parisian social life.

"" Rosanette began to read through the menu, pausing at all the most extraordinary dishes. 'Supposing we were to eat a dish of rabbit *à la Richelieu*, and a pudding *à la d'Orléans*?' 'Oh! no Orléans!' exclaimed Cisy, who was a Legitimist and thought he was making a joke. 'Would you prefer a turbot *à la Chambord*?' she continued. Frederic found these civilities offensive. She decided in favour of a plain steak, some crayfish, truffles, a pineapple salad, and some vanilla ices. 'After that, we'll see. Now get on with it! Oh, I forgot! Bring me a sausage, but not with garlic!' And she called the waiter 'young man', struck her glass with her knife, and threw her bread up to the ceiling. She wanted to drink burgundy straight away. 'You don't serve burgundy at the beginning,' said Frederic. According to the viscount it was occasionally done. ""

GUSTAVE FLAUBERT, *SENTIMENTAL EDUCATION*,
TRANSLATED BY ANTHONY GOLDSMITH, EVERYMAN'S LIBRARY, LONDON, 1941

PRESSED DUCK

"Paris vécu" by gourmet Léon Daudet obviously includes references to a number of good restaurants. We have already read his description of Weber in the Rue Royale ● 93. Here he has crossed the Seine to dine at the Tour d'Argent ▲ 147 and takes the opportunity to describe Frédéric Delair, owner of the restaurant and "inventor" of the famous pressed duck.

"" Frédéric was preparing the duck in a special way. He got two servings (and two lots of profit) out of it, one pressed, the other grilled. Although they are both equally delicious, I think I still prefer the grilled version. Frédéric was really quite a sight, with his *lorgnon*, his graying side-whiskers and his imperturbably serious expression, as he cut up his plump 'quack-quack,' already trussed

105

and flambéed, threw it into the saucepan and made his sauce, salting and peppering just as Claude Monet painted, with the objectivity of a judge and the precision of a mathematician, preparing to open up new gastronomic horizons with his firm artist's hand. He recognized in dear Ali Bab, a connoisseur and taster, an artist of the same caliber as himself, in short, a master. On this particular occasion we also sampled brill soufflés, an unparalleled recipe that melted in the mouth. These were followed by Strasbourg foie gras, which must certainly have come from Gerst; for many years later, on Christmas eve 1907, I found its pendant at Dr Boucher's in the Rue de la Nuée-Bleue, in that very town that was still under the control of the dull-witted Germans. A discussion got under way at the *Tour d'Argent* as to whether the chicory salad, which was lightly sprinkled with absinthe, should or should not accompany the foie gras. It seems to me that it was a mistake and that the flavor of the oil does not go with the pâté. English cuisine, with its delicious, mouthwatering 'pies,' would appear to agree with me. **99**

LÉON DAUDET, *PARIS VÉCU*, GALLIMARD,
PARIS, 1929

THE ART OF MAKING ASPIC

Marcel Proust (1871–1922) wrote his great work "À la recherche du temps perdu" ("Remembrance of Things Past") at the turn of the century. This description of the social mores of the period could not fail to include the fashionable restaurant rendez-vous, for this was the golden age of restaurants. The scene below, taken from "À l'ombre des jeunes filles en fleurs" ("Within a Budding Grove"), provides an overview of some of the most prestigious restaurants of the Belle Époque ● 48.

66'Well then', inquired my mother, 'and how do you explain that nobody else can make an aspic as well as you (when you choose)?' 'I really couldn't say how that becomes about,' replied Françoise, who had established no very clear line of demarcation between the verb 'to come', in certain of its meanings, and the verb 'to become'. She was speaking the truth, moreover, if only in part, being scarcely more capable (or desirous) of revealing the mystery which ensured the superiority of her aspics and creams than a well-dressed woman the secrets of her toilettes or a great singer those of her voice. The explanations tell us little; it was the same with the recipes of our cook. 'They do it in too much of a hurry,' she went on, alluding to the great restaurants, 'and then it's not all done together. You want the beef to become like a sponge, then it will drink up all the juice to the last drop. Still, there was one of those cafés where I thought they did know a little bit about cooking. I don't say it was altogether my aspic, but it was very nicely done, and the soufflés had plenty of cream.' 'Do you mean *Henry's*?' asked my father (who had now joined us), for he greatly enjoyed that restaurant in the Place Gaillon where he went regularly to regimental dinners. 'Oh, dear no!' said Françoise with a mildness which cloaked a profound contempt. 'I meant a little restaurant. At that *Henry's* it's all very good, sure enough, but it's not a restaurant, it's more like a ... soup-kitchen.' '*Weber's*, then?' 'Oh, no, Monsieur, I meant a good restaurant. *Weber's*, that's in the Rue Royale, that's not a restaurant, it's a brasserie. I don't know that the food they give you there is even served. I think they don't even have any table-cloths; they just shove it down in front of you like that, with a take it or leave it.' '*Cirro's*?' Françoise smiled. 'Oh! there I should say the main dishes are ladies of the world.' (Monde meant for Françoise the demi-monde.) 'Lord! they need them to fetch the boys in.' We could see that, with all her air of simplicity, Françoise was for the celebrities of her profession a more ferocious 'colleague' than the most jealous, the most self-infatuated of actresses. We felt, all the same, that she had a proper feeling for her art and a respect for tradition, for she added: 'No, I mean a restaurant where it looked like they kept a very good little family table. It's a place

of consequence, too. Plenty of custom there. Oh, they raked in the coppers, there, all right.' (Françoise, being thrifty, reckoned in coppers, where your plongeur would reckon in gold.) 'Madame knows the place well enough, down there to the right along the main boulevards, a little way back.' The restaurant of which she spoke with this blend of pride and good-humoured tolerance was, it turned out, the *Café Anglais*.**99**

MARCEL PROUST, *WITHIN A BUDDING GROVE*,
VOL. II OF *REMEMBRANCE OF THINGS PAST*, TRANSLATED BY C.K. SCOTT
MONCREIFF AND TERENCE KILMARTIN, CHATTO & WINDUS, LONDON, 1992

"CERVELAS"

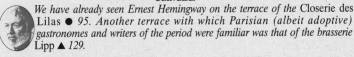

We have already seen Ernest Hemingway on the terrace of the Closerie des Lilas ● *95. Another terrace with which Parisian (albeit adoptive) gastronomes and writers of the period were familiar was that of the brasserie* Lipp ▲ *129.*

66...do you know where you are going to eat right now? *Lipp's* is where you are going to eat, and drink too. It was a quick walk to *Lipp's* and every place I passed that my stomach noticed as quickly as my eyes or my nose made the walk an added pleasure. There were few people in the *brasserie* and when I sat down on the bench against the wall with the mirror in back and a table in front and the waiter asked if I wanted beer I asked for a *distingué*, the big glass mug that held a liter, and for a potato salad. The beer was very cold and wonderful to drink. The *pommes à l'huile* were firm and marinated and the olive oil delicious. I ground black pepper over the potatoes and moistened the bread in the olive oil. After the first heavy draught of beer I drank and ate very slowly. When the *pommes à l'huile* were gone I ordered another serving and a *cervelas*. This was a sausage like a heavy, wide frankfurter split in two and covered with a special mustard sauce. I mopped up all the oil and all of the sauce with bread and drank the beer slowly until it began to lose its coldness and then I finished it and ordered a *demi* and watched it drawn. It seemed colder than the *distingué* and I drank half of it.**99**

ERNEST HEMINGWAY, *A MOVEABLE FEAST*,
FIRST PUBLISHED BY CHARLES SCRIBNER'S SONS, NEW YORK, 1964

THE ICONOCLAST

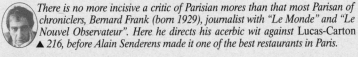

There is no more incisive a critic of Parisian mores than that most Parisan of chroniclers, Bernard Frank (born 1929), journalist with "Le Monde" and "Le Nouvel Observateur". Here he directs his acerbic wit against Lucas-Carton ▲ *216, before Alain Senderens made it one of the best restaurants in Paris.*

66Long before I ever dined there with my mother, Lucas-Carton began to try my patience. It was too expensive and not particularly good. And then there was the grotesque habit of putting out the ovens at an hour when only chickens go home to roost. I could imagine Lucas' reasoning: 'This is not a brasserie, monsieur. This is haute restauration, and haute restauration needs its beauty sleep.' Gastronomic critics greeted this piece of antiquated logic with little cries of delight, a logic which, after all, was due largely to the death of Larue. He was a marvel, Larue! ... Larue had contributed significantly to my irritation ... Rather like de Gaulle at the time of the Libération (who according to Malraux had said that the French ought to think about something other than their sardines and swedes), in 1967 I was well and truly fed up with these chroniclers who cluttered up the columns of our newspapers with their 'grub.' And so, to paraphrase Bataille, I wrote a 'Hatred of gastronomy' for my paper, which earned me a pleasant letter from La Reynière. ... I went even further. Having just eaten very well and very reasonably in a cheap eating house in the Rue de Verneuil, I said that if we no longer had any choice and that if, after 9 o'clock in the evening, certain famous restaurants were going to drift off to sleep like puppies or old men who go to bed at dusk, and become mere mockeries of great restaurants, making extravagant excuses for their inability to make a simple crêpe, then long live cheap eating houses!**

BERNARD FRANK, *UN SIÈCLE DÉBORDÉ*, FLAMMARION, PARIS, 1987

ALEXANDRE DUMAS, WRITER AND GASTRONOME

Alexandre Dumas (1802–70) handled fork and pen with equal ability. He frequented the top restaurants of his time, chose his cooks with great care and did not hesitate to take to the kitchen to prepare his own recipes. Toward the end of his life, Dumas retired to Roscoff to write his last will and testament, "Le Grand Dictionnaire de Cuisine". Raymond Oliver ● 51 said of Dumas: "I have a lot of cookery books, including several 19th-century editions. I consult them from time to time. But I read Dumas because Dumas tells a story. To my knowledge he is the only writer to have told the story of recipes."
On the subject of beef, to which he devotes a long and richly detailed article, Dumas criticizes the masters who do not know how to encourage the talent of their cooks, as illustrated by this anecdote about Cardinal Richelieu.

**It was during the war of Hanover, and the countryside around the French army was devastated for a distance of 80 kilometers. All the princes and princesses of Ostfrise (numbering twenty-five in all), plus a fairly substantial number of ladies-in-waiting and chamberlains, had been taken prisoner. Cardinal Richelieu had decided to set them free but had had the idea of offering them a supper before releasing them, which caused his stewards to despair. But when Monsieur de Richelieu had made a resolve, then the thing had to be done. He called his stewards together.
'What do you have in your kitchen, gentlemen?' he asked them. 'Sire, there is nothing.'

'What do you mean, nothing?'

'Nothing at all.'

'But only yesterday I saw a pair of horns go past the window.'

'You are right, sire, there is an ox and a few roots, but what do you expect us to do with them?'

'What I expect you to do, of course, is to make the finest supper in the world.'

'But sire, that is impossible.'

'Come now, impossible. Rudière, write down the menu I am about to dictate, and we'll break the back of the work for these gaping fellows.'

'Do you know how to write out a menu, Rudière?'

'Sire, I must confess ...'

'Give me your seat and your pen.'

And the commander-in-chief sat down in his secretary's place and improvised a classic supper ...**

ALEXANDRE DUMAS, *LE GRAND DICTIONNAIRE DE CUISINE*, 1873

In his "Dictionnaire" Dumas includes several anecdotes concerning the great figures who frequented the restaurants of the Boulevard ● 45. Romieu de Vieil-Castel is one of those to whom Dumas concedes "gastronomic tendencies". The following scene illustrates Dumas' idea of gastronomy.

**One day, in a mixed gathering consisting partly of artists and partly of members of Parisian high society, the Viscount of Vieil-Castel, brother of Count Horace de Vieil-Castel, one of the most prestigious gourmets in France, made the following observation:

'One man can eat a five hundred-franc dinner.'

'Impossible!' exclaimed the assembled company.

'It is understood', the viscount continued, that the word "drink" is included in the word "eat".'

'Good Lord, yes!' exclaimed the company.

'Well, then! I say that a man, when I say a man, I don't mean a waggoner, I mean a gourmet, a pupil of Montron or Courchamps ... Well, I say that a gourmet, a pupil of Montron or Courchamps, can eat a five hundred-franc dinner.'

'You, for example?'

'Me, or any other gourmet.'

'Could you?'

'Of course I could.'

'I've got the five hundred francs,' said one of the company. 'So, let's get establish the rules.'

'Nothing could be easier: I eat at the *Café de Paris*, I choose my menu as I think fit, and I eat a five hundred-franc dinner.'

'Without leaving anything on the dishes or on your plate?'

'Yes, I'll leave the bones.' Oh, that's cutting it a bit fine!'

'And when will this wager take place?'

'Tomorrow if you like.'

'So you won't be having lunch?' asked one of the company.

'I'll have lunch as usual.'

'So be it. Tomorrow, seven o'clock at the *Café de Paris*.'

... At the appointed time, the viscount entered the restaurant, greeted the referees and sat down at his table. The menu was a mystery to his challengers; they would have to wait and see. The viscount sat down. He was brought twelve dozen Ostend oysters and half a bottle of Johannisberg.

The viscount was hungry: he ordered another twelve dozen Ostend oysters and another bottle of the same vintage.

Then came bird's nest soup, which the viscount poured into a bowl and drank like a broth.

'My goodness, gentlemen,' he said, 'I'm on form today, and I feel like treating myself to something extravagant.'

'Be our guest, you are doing the ordering.'

'I love steak and chips.'

'No advice, gentlemen, if you please,' said a voice.

'Bah! Waiter,' said the viscount, 'steak and chips, please.'

The waiter looked at the viscount in amazement.

'Well!' said the latter, 'didn't you understand me?'

'Yes, but I thought Monsieur le Vicomte had ordered his dinner?'

'True, but I'm treating myself to a little something extra; I'll pay for it separately.'

The referees looked at each other. The steak and chips arrived and the viscount devoured it down to the very last morsel.

'Now then! Let's have the fish!'

The fish was brought.

'Gentlemen,' said the viscount, 'this is a type of salmon found only in Lake Geneva. But it can be obtained. It was shown to me earlier while I was having lunch. It was

still alive and had been brought from Geneva to Paris in water from the lake. I can thoroughly recommend it, it is a delicious fish.'

Five minutes later, only the bones remained on his plate.

'The pheasant, waiter!' said the viscount.

And he was brought a pheasant garnished with truffles.

'Another bottle of Bordeaux, the same vintage.'

The bottle arrived. In two minutes the pheasant had been dispatched. ...

'Waiter! the ortolan casserole!'

There were ten ortolans, and the viscount made short work of them.

'Gentlemen,' said the viscount, 'this is a simple menu. Now for the asparagus, peas, a pineapple and strawberries. As for the wine: a half-bottle of Constance, a half-bottle of sherry sent from India. Then coffee and liqueurs, of course.'

Each arrived in turn: the vegetables and fruit were eaten conscientiously, the wine and liqueurs drunk to the last drop. The viscount had taken one hour fourteen minutes to eat his dinner.

'Gentlemen,' he said, 'have things gone according to the rules?'

The referees nodded.

'Waiter, the menu!'

The term 'bill' was not yet being used. The viscount glanced at the total and passed the menu to the referees.

... They took it to the viscount's challenger, who was dining in a private room at the far end of the restaurant. He appeared five minutes later, greeted the viscount, took six one-thousand franc notes out of his pocket and presented them to him. It was the total amount of the wager.

'Oh, sir,' said the viscount.

'There was no hurry; perhaps you would have liked a return match.'

'Would you have agreed to one?'
'Certainly.'
'When?'
'At once.'**"**

ALEXANDRE DUMAS, *LE GRAND DICTIONNAIRE DE
CUISINE*, 1873

*In his "Dictionnaire" Dumas also describes cooking
utensils, taking the opportunity to recount anecdotes relating
to them.*

"Spoons and forks were introduced relatively
late into Europe. Before they were invented,
people ate with their fingers and used a roughly
carved wooden bowl as a serving spoon. Instead
of a fork they used two little pieces of wood to
convey pieces of solid food to their mouths. In 1610
the English dismissed the 'useless' utensils brought
back from Italy by Thomas Coryate as one of the
traveler's many foibles. However, their usefulness
was later acknowledged and they became
increasingly widely used among the wealthy
classes. The populace imitated them by using
wooden spoons and forks, but these were fragile and soon
replaced by iron and pewter.
One day, at a grand dinner, a prince wanted to embarrass one of his royal friends
and had given orders that this particular guest should not be given a spoon. As they
sat down to eat, the prince said to him: 'People who don't eat soup are silly b......!'
The doctor, seeing that they were playing a trick on him, hollowed out his bread,
stuck his fork in it and used it as a spoon to eat his soup. Having thus avoided
embarrassment in this way, he wanted in turn to embarrass the prince and his
friends who had been prepared to laugh at his expense. So he took the bread that
he had used as a spoon, ate it and said: 'People who don't eat their spoons are silly
b......!' Who won the day? The prince openly admitted his defeat and praised the
doctor's imagination.**"**

ALEXANDRE DUMAS, *LE GRAND DICTIONNAIRE DE CUISINE*, 1873

*The cook Denis-Joseph Vuillemot (1811–76) was a friend of Dumas and a pupil of
Carême. He was Dumas' principal adviser for the "Dictionnaire". On his return from a
journey to Tiflis, Dumas was invited by Vuillemot to preside at a banquet attended by
his closest friends. The dishes were named after the titles and heroes of Dumas' novels.*

"Menu for the dinner held in Alexandre Dumas' honor on his return from Russia.
September 1869.

Miscellaneous hors d'oeuvre

Soups
À la Buckingham
Aux Mohicans

Entrées
Trout à la Henri III
Lobster à la Porthos
Tenderloin of beef à la Monte-Cristo
Bouchées à la reine Margot (chicken vol-au-vent)

Roasts
Pheasant, partridge, quail, woodcock

> *Side dishes*
> Aux Mousquetaires
> Peas aux Frères corses
> Prawns à la d'Artagnan
> Bombe à la dame de Monsoreau
> Crème à la reine Christine
> Salade à la Dumas
> Vase d'Aramis
> Gâteau à la Gorenflot
> Fresh fruit Mlle de Belles-Isle
> Assorted desserts. **99**

ALEXANDRE DUMAS,
LE GRAND DICTIONNAIRE DE CUISINE, 1873

LOVE AND RESTAURANTS

The doors of private dining-rooms in restaurants of the Belle Époque did not have handles on the outside, while their benches very obviously doubled as divans. There was often very little separating the indulgence of pleasures of the palate and pleasures of the flesh. In fact the sensations to which both forms of pleasure give rise are not dissimilar. And the term "consume" is applied to both food and passion.

PROSTITUTES

Émile Zola (1840–1902) was the leading light of the Naturalist school of writers and artists, who have given us a true and accurate account of an entire era. Nana, daughter of Gervaise and the heroine of the ninth book in the "Rougon-Macquart" series, is an actress in light opera and a prostitute. The account of her life provides Zola with an ideal opportunity to denounce the hypocrisy of 19th-century Parisian society. In the following extract, Nana has been invited to dine by her friend Satin in a very particular kind of restaurant.

66They arrived early at Laure's, and not wanting to hang around outside on the pavement, they went upstairs twenty minutes before the restaurant was due to open. It consisted of three rooms, all empty. They took their seats at a table in the room where Laure Piedefer was presiding on a high bench behind the counter. Laure was 50 years old, a lady of exuberant curves tightly strapped up in belts and corsets. Women were arriving in quick succession, leaning familiarly across over the saucers and placing on her mouth tender kisses which the monster herself, misty-eyed, was trying to dole out evenly in an endeavour not to arouse any jealous feelings. The waitress serving these ladies was, on the other hand, a tall, gaunt woman with ravaged features, black eye-lids, and darkly glowing eyes. The three rooms quickly filled up; there must have been about a hundred female customers spread out at the tables, most of them verging on 40, huge women bloated with fat, with flabby, vicious, thick lips; and amidst these bulging busts and bellies, you could see a few thin, pretty girls, still innocent-looking in spite of their saucy demeanour, novices who'd been picked up in some cheap dance-hall and brought along to Laure's restaurant by a female customer, where the herd of fat women, unsettled by the smell of their young flesh, were competing with each other for their favors like anxious old bachelors by offering them tasty little titbits. There were also a few men (ten or fifteen at the most) lying very low in this invading wave of skirts, apart from four lively young sparks making themselves very much at home, who'd come to watch and were cracking jokes. 'The grub's not bad, is it? Satin remarked. Nana nodded her agreement. It was the standard solid fare of country hotels: sweetbread-and-mushroom vol-au-vent, chicken and rice, French beans, caramel cream. ...When she was finally able to look up, she was amazed to see that the chair

next to her was empty. Satin had vanished into thin air. 'Where on earth can she be?' she exclaimed. Seeing her annoyance, the stout blonde who'd been so attentive to Satin gave a little laugh, and when Nana appeared irritated and looked threateningly in her direction, she said in a soft drawl: 'No, of course it's not me, it's that other woman who's snaffled her.'"

ÉMILE ZOLA, *NANA*,
TRANSLATED BY DOUGLAS PARMÉE, OXFORD UNIVERSITY PRESS, 1992

PRIVATE ROOM

In "Bel-Ami" Guy de Maupassant (1850–93) combines the skills learned from his mentor Gustave Flaubert and his experience of the pleasures of Parisian life to criticize the political and social milieux of the capital. The nickname of his unscrupulous protagonist Georges Duroy comes from his great success as a lady's man. Here he has been invited to dine at the Café Riche ● 46, one of the great Boulevard restaurants.

"Having hired, for the second time, a dress suit (his funds not yet allowing him to buy one), he arrived first at the rendezvous, a few minutes before the time. He was ushered up to the second storey, and into a small private dining-room hung with red and white, its single window opening into the boulevard.

... The door was opened, and, followed by a waiter, the two ladies appeared, veiled, muffled, reserved, with that charmingly mysterious bearing they assume in such places, where the surroundings are suspicious.

... The Ostend oysters were brought in, tiny and plump like little ears enclosed in shells, and melting between the tongue and the palate like salt bonbons. Then, after the soup, was served a trout as rose-tinted as a young girl, and the guests began to talk. They spoke at first of a current scandal; the story of a lady of position, surprised by one of her husband's friends supping in a private room with a foreign prince. ... As the first entrée was slow in coming, they sipped from time to time a mouthful of champagne, and nibbled bits of crust. And the idea of love, entering into them, slowly intoxicated their souls, as the bright wine, rolling drop by drop down their throats, fired their blood and perturbed their minds. The waiter brought in some lamb cutlets, delicate and tender, upon a thick bed of asparagus tips.

... And the conversation, descending from the elevated theories, concerning love, strayed into the flowery garden of polished blackguardism. It was the moment of clever double meanings; veils raised by words, as petticoats are lifted by the wind; tricks of language; clever disguised audacities; sentences which reveal nude images in covered phrases; which cause the vision of all that may not be said to flit rapidly before the eye and the mind, and allow the well-bred people the enjoyment of a kind of subtle and mysterious love, a species of impure mental contact, due to the simultaneous evocation of secret, shameful, and longed-for pleasures. The roast, consisting of partridges flanked by quails, had been served; then a dish of green peas, and then a terrine of foie gras, accompanied by a curly-leaved salad, filling a salad bowl as though with green foam. They had

partaken of all these things without tasting them, without knowing, solely taken up by what they were talking of, plunged as it were into a bath of love.

... Madame de Marelle rang for the waiter, and asked for the bill. It was brought almost immediately. She tried to read it, but the figures danced before her eyes, and she passed it to Duroy, saying: 'Here, pay for me; I can't see, I am too tipsy.'

... 'Shall I see you to your door?'

'Certainly. I am incapable of finding my own way home.' **99**

GUY DE MAUPASSANT, *BEL-AMI* IN *THE WORKS OF GUY DE MAUPASSANT*, HARPER & BROTHERS PUBLISHERS, LONDON, 1909

THE RESTAURANT OF THOSE GENTLEMEN...

The diary that Paul Léautaud (1872–1956) kept for sixty-three years is a racy chronicle of the minor literary figures of the first half of the 20th century. In it this so-called misanthropist and cynic shows himself to be a man of great sensitivity who writes with all the freshness of youth. In this extract, written in December 1928, he gives an account of a discussion with Rachilde, an influential woman of letters of the period.

66Then Rachilde said: 'I must tell you a really good story. I don't know if you know *Le Boeuf sur le toit,* the restaurant of those gentlemen ...' Valette interrupted, laughing: 'Him? (me), Come on now! He doesn't know the first thing about it...' She went on: 'An unbelievable décor. Pillars with strange lighting. On one pillar, there is a portrait of Cocteau and, on another, a portrait of Z. Well, one day, Moïse, the proprietor, asked me if I wouldn't like my portrait up there with the other two. You can imagine what a start it gave me. But I didn't want to be rude, so I merely replied: That's going a bit far, isn't it? I'm not exactly Liane de Pougy.' I started to say: 'I don't know much about these places, but it does all strike me as a bit dissolute.' Rachilde laughed: 'A bit? A lot, I should say. It makes you want to throw up. All you see is the intrigues of those contemptible young men and young women. I started to say: 'Today ... We tend to take fright ... They are children of their time. They've been born into an age when such behavior is commonplace. For them, what they are doing seems normal. Perhaps they see doing something naturally as abnormal.' Rachilde said that there was a strange and extremely interesting book to be written on this reversal in matters of love, that there were unbelievably frightening things to be said.**99**

PAUL LÉAUTAUD, *JOURNAL LITTÉRAIRE*, MERCURE DE FRANCE, PARIS, 1954–66

THE CHARMS OF THE "PATRONNE"

Emmanuel Bove (1898–1945) is a reserved and unjustly neglected writer who was only twenty-three when he wrote "Mes amis". The novel is a fine example of the sinister atmosphere that pervades his work, while the following scene illustrates his 'sense of touching detail' that Samuel Beckett admired so much.

❝I prefer to eat at the little wine shop in the Rue de la Seine, where I am known. The patronne is called Lucie Dunois. Her name is written in enamel capitals on the shop window. Three letters are missing. Lucie has the plumpness of a beer drinker. On the forefinger of her left hand she wears an aluminium ring, in memory of her husband who was killed at the Front. Her ears are soft. She wears shoes without heels. She is constantly blowing away the hair that has escaped from the knot of her hair. When she bends down, the folds of her skirt crack open like a chestnut. Her pupils aren't in the middle of her eyes: they are too high, like an alcoholic's eyes.

The dining-room smells of empty wine casks, rats and cheap wine. The asbestos fan above the gas mantle never moves. At night, the gas burner throws its light into every nook and cranny, even under the tables. A poster (Law on the suppression of drunkenness) is pinned to the wall in full view. A few pages stick out of the printed edge of a Bottin. A stained mirror, scratched on the back, decorates one wall.

... Lucie is always kind to me. She serves me steaming hot soup, fresh bread that makes crumbs, a plate of vegetables and sometimes a piece of meat. When I have finished my meal, the grease congeals on my lips.

Every three months, when I receive my allowance, I give Lucie one hundred francs. She can't make much of a profit out of me. At night, I wait until all the customers have gone because I close the shop for her. I always hope that Lucie will ask me to stay. One night she did.

... We were embarrassed, because the all-too-obvious reason for my presence anticipated our intimacy.

'Let's have a drink,' she said, wiping the neck of the bottle with her apron.

We talked for an hour. I would have liked to kiss her, if I hadn't had to go round the table to do it. Better wait for a more suitable moment, especially for the first kiss. Suddenly she asked me if I had seen her room. I replied quite naturally: 'No.' **99**
EMMANUEL BOVE, *MES AMIS*, FLAMMARION, PARIS, 1977

BEHIND THE SCENES

Restaurants are like theaters. They have their stage and their backstage, and the contrast between the two is sometimes quite striking. Everything is arranged so that customers only see the tip of the iceberg... until the day when they find themselves in the unfortunate predicament of the passengers on the "Titanic".

WASHING UP

George Orwell (1903–50) is well-known as the author of "1984". His father was a colonial civil servant and Orwell served in the imperial Indian police force in Burma before returning to Europe, where he experienced several years of poverty. These years were the subject of his first book, in which he describes, among other things, his experiences as a "plongeur" in a Paris restaurant.

66 The patron had engaged me as kitchen plongeur; that is, my job was to wash up, keep the kitchen clean, prepare vegetables, make tea, coffee and sandwiches, do the simpler cooking and run errands ... .
I should add, by the way, that the Auberge was not the ordinary cheap eating-house frequented by students and workmen. We did not provide an adequate meal at less than twenty-five francs, and we were picturesque and artistic, which sent up our social standing... .
The kitchen measured fifteen feet long by eight broad, and half this space was taken up by the stoves and tables. All the pots had to be kept on shelves out of reach, and there was only room for one dustbin. This dustbin used to be crammed full by midday, and the floor was normally an inch deep in a compost of trampled food ... .
There was no hot water laid on. Water for washing up had to be heated in pans, and, as there was no room for these on the stoves when meals were cooking, most of the plates had to be washed in cold water. This, with soft soap and the hard Paris water, meant scraping the grease off with bits of newspaper. ...
Looking round that filthy room, with raw meat lying among the refuse on the floor, and cold, clotted saucepans sprawling everywhere, and the sink blocked and coated with grease, I used to wonder whether there could be a restaurant in the world as bad as ours. **99**
GEORGE ORWELL, *DOWN AND OUT IN PARIS AND LONDON*, PENGUIN BOOKS, 1940

RESTAURANT CRITICS

Restaurant critics have the unique power to make or break culinary reputations. In this extract, Hubert Monteilhet (born in 1928, below), a brilliant writer of detective novels, describes one of these censors. Himself a restaurant critic, he takes the opportunity to settle a few scores.

66 But let's take a closer look. After examining the menu, the indispensable kitchen inspection gives the full picture and the tasting becomes a mere formality.
'How many apprentices on your staff work at the stoves?'
Dumas had to admit there were nine. Only a few of the very top restaurants could afford to pay the salaries of an entire team of hand-picked, qualified staff.
Having made a mental note of this 'black mark,' Sartine paced about like a caged bear, assessing everything critically ...

'Grill for meat, salamander stove for delicate fish, are where they should be, but where is the spit? Where is the spit? Haven't you got a spit?

'You know very well, Monsieur Sartine, that proper cooks don't use them any more! The spit is out of date. It has become a piece of hardware associated with unhygienic-looking chickens in the windows of none-too-particular delicatessens.'

'You will find one, even several, rotating vertically in front of the braising wall at Dumonet, at the top end of the *Rue du Cherche-Midi*, next door to Joséphine. That's one of the reasons why they serve the tastiest legs of lamb in Paris. They are to be highly recommended for many cuts of meat, and spits over a wood fire are essential for roasting poultry and small fowl.' ...

It was the moment for me to find out more about this strange profession of 'restaurant inspector,' and I expressed my surprise that these gentlemen could, in particular, break out into such competent excesses entirely free of charge ...

'How do you become a reporter?'

'By knowing the right people and sheer cheek, my friend! There's no special college and no diploma. That's why food journalism is littered with nonentities who contrive to make allusions, but whose ignorance is staggering, and whose honesty is more than suspect. And thus we witness the sad spectacle of pretentious individuals who don't know how to boil an egg destroying the reputations of experienced restaurateurs.'❞

HUBERT MONTEILHET, *LA PART DES ANGES*,
ÉDITIONS DE FALLOIS, PARIS, 1990

THE WAITER

Jacques Faizant (born 1918) is famous for his caricatures, which are a daily thorn in the side for French politicians, as well as for the tenderness with which he describes old ladies. He is less well-known for his partly auto-biographical novels, in the first of which he remembers his days as a waiter.

66My talents were variously appreciated. Generally speaking, I was required to keep quiet and use a tray for anything more than four plates. However, one day a customer took it upon himself to congratulate me on the masterly way in which I loaded my left arm. He had scarcely finished speaking when, like a high diver, I had disappeared into the depths of the kitchen, to re-emerge soon afterward bearing fourteen plates of jam, seven on my left arm and another seven placed on my right (at my request) by the steward, who saw nothing wrong with the maneuver. With the help of a great deal of technical advice, I made my way to the table of my admirer and displayed my superbly laden arms before him and his guests. But crowds are fickle. They had resumed their conversation about contemporary art and were no longer interested in my professional acrobatics. Furthermore, they were still eating their soup and made it abundantly clear that they would not be interested in gooseberry jam for quite some time. I must admit I was disappointed. Disappointed and embarrassed. For while, generally speaking, it is possible to unload your left arm with your right hand, it is infinitely more difficult to unload both arms when you have no hands at all. Of course my worthy colleagues pretended not to notice my dilemma. It was, they thought, the moment when actions speak louder than words. My arms were becoming dangerously tired. I ended up near an ancient English gentleman who had just got to the jam stage. Making one last, supreme effort I held out my arms and asked him if he would like to help himself. I thought, of course, that he would take the top plate on the pile, and perhaps even, realizing my predicament, unload one of my arms. But the English are lacking in such subtleties. He took the plate closest to him, pulling at it absent-mindedly. A few seconds earlier, he had been wearing a pair of beige trousers. He looked around him at the debris caused by my arms (for in my alarm, I had also lowered my left arm) and then, placing his plate of jam, intact, on the table before him, he said:
- The service is poor here! I haven't got a spoon!
The least any one could have said **99**

JACQUES FAIZANT, *ALLEZ VOUS RHABILLER!*, DENOËL, PARIS, 1972

POETS' RESTAURANTS

Only a poet could invest a character with the ability to disrupt the service; only a poet could demonstrate the impossibility of adding up the bill; only a poet could invent a restaurant that doesn't serve food.

A SURREALIST DINNER

Nadja, the strange young woman that André Breton (1896–1966) met in the street in 1926, became the guardian angel of Surrealism. The writer pays homage to her in his most celebrated work. Is her fascination part of the "suspension of conscious control" so dear to the Surrealists?

6610 October. We dined on the Quai Malaquais, at Delaborde. The waiter distinguished himself by his extreme clumsiness. It would seem that he was fascinated by Nadja. He fussed about at our table, flicking away imaginary crumbs, moving her handbag for no reason, and proving himself totally incapable of remembering our order. Nadja chuckled and told me it was not over yet. Indeed, while he served the neighboring tables quite normally, he spilled the wine he was pouring into our glasses and, while taking infinite precautions when placing a plate in front of one of us, he knocked against another, which fell to the floor and smashed. From the beginning to the end of the meal (and here we re-enter the realm of the fantastic), I counted eleven broken plates. It is true that every time he came out of the kitchen he was facing us, and when he looked up at Nadja he seemed to lose his balance. It was both comical and painful to watch. In the end he didn't come near our table and we had great difficulty in finishing our meal. Nadja was not in the least surprised. She knew she had this effect on certain men and, among others, on black men who, wherever she is, seem compelled to come and speak to her.**"**

ANDRÉ BRETON, NADJA, GALLIMARD, PARIS, 1963

THE IMPOSSIBLE BILL

Jacques Prévert (1900–77), who was half Breton and half Auvergnat by birth, was essentially Parisian or, more accurately, "Parigot". His poetical works are characterized by fantasy and an irreverence for situations that always border on the fantastic. This, for example, is a totally nonsensical dialog between a waiter and a customer.

CUSTOMER
> Waiter, the bill!

WAITER
> Here you are, sir. (He takes out his pencil and writes.) You've had... two hard-boiled eggs, one portion of veal, one pea, one asparagus, one cheese with butter, a green almond, a filter coffee, a telephone call.

CUSTOMER
> And cigarettes!

WAITER
> (Beginning to add up...)
> Yes, you're right... cigarettes...
> ...So that makes....

CUSTOMER
> Stop there, my friend, you won't be able to add it up.

WAITER
> !!!

CUSTOMER
> Didn't they teach you at school that it's ma-the-ma-ti-ca-lly impossible to add up different types of items.

WAITER
> !!!

CUSTOMER (Raising his voice...)
> Really, you've got to be joking!... You must be quite mad to try and "add" veal and cigarettes, cigarettes and a filter coffee, a filter coffee and a green almond, hard-boiled eggs and peas, peas and a telephone call... Why not peas and an officer of the Légion d'Honneur, while you're at it! (He gets up.) No, my friend, believe me, you might as well give up. You'll wear yourself out, and you'll get nowhere, d'you hear, nowhere, absolutely nowhere... and you won't even get a tip! (And he goes out taking the napkin ring free of charge.)

JACQUES PRÉVERT, *HISTOIRES*, GALLIMARD, PARIS, 1963

THE "BONNE PEINTURE"

The best novels of Marcel Aymé (1902–67), "La Jument verte" (The Green Mare) and "La Vouivre" (The Serpent Swallowing a Child), were dedicated to the countryside where he was born and brought up. When he moved to Paris, he lived in Montmartre, which as everyone knows is a village. One of the short stories in "Le Vin de Paris" ("Wine of Paris"), set during the war years, describes a restaurant that is more pleasing to the eye than to the palate. It is true that, at the time, restaurants were not very well stocked.

❝They agreed immediately. A third of the takings would go to the proprietor of the restaurant, while the rest would be divided between the two owners of the painting. The next day the restaurant was closed 'for refurbishment' and, a few days later, was ready to welcome customers under its new name, the *Bonne Peinture*. The menu was displayed in huge lettering by the door: *Effet de soleil sur la rue des Saules* (*Sunlight on the Rue des Saules*), by the illustrious artist Lafleur.' In the dining room, the tables had been replaced by two hundred chairs, arranged on either side of a narrow aisle. Customers sat as if they were at the movies, looking at Lafleur's painting, which was hung on the wall in front of them and lit by a strip light, while a record player in the kitchen played swing and tango through the serving hatch. Generally speaking, the customers had had enough after twenty minutes and, since there was nothing else to do, they left their seats. A few customers had more healthy appetites and stayed for forty minutes or three quarters of an hour. A seat cost forty-five francs. Moudru and the proprietor issued entrance tickets. Balavoine, who didn't want to be seen, stayed in the kitchen, where he operated the record player. From the first day, business boomed. Several thousand brochures distributed in the district had brought the Bonne Peinture to the public's attention and the restaurant was full from ten o'clock in the morning until midnight. The average daily takings were in the region of 200,000 francs. Moudru and Balavoine wore fine suits, huge gold rings and little Hollywood moustaches, which suited them very well. The establishment of this restaurant of painting contributed to the general excitement. Parisians were undernourished, and their hopes of improved food supplies were continually dashed. But their imaginations were haunted by the inexhaustible reserves of food represented by the works of Lafleur. The artist's name was on everybody's lips. Having learnt that he had donated paintings to several schools in Montmartre, the newspapers sent reporters to find out about the results. Thus the public was informed that the pupils of these privileged schools, where they had two meals of painting per day, were in excellent health.❞

MARCEL AYMÉ, *LE VIN DE PARIS*,
GALLIMARD, PARIS, 1947

Gastronomic Itineraries
100 memorable restaurants

▲ The *Jules-Verne*, on the second platform of the Eiffel Tower.

▼ The *Benkay* and, at the Trocadéro, the *Totem* ▲

▲ The restaurant of the Institut du Monde Arabe

View of the Eiffel Tower from *Morot-Gaudry* ▲ and the *15 Montaigne*. ▼

▲ *Vagenende*, Bd Saint-Germain, and *Ledoyen*, at the Carré des Champs-Élysées. ▼

Les Jardins de Bagatelle in the Bois de Boulogne. ▼

▲ *Fouquet's* on the Champs-Élysées, and the *Méditerranée*, Place de l'Odéon. ▼

The *Grande Cascade*. ▼

The kitchens of *Les Ambassadeurs*.

"Cookery is the most ancient of arts." *Anthelme Brillat-Savarin*

1.
SAINT-GERMAIN, MINISTÈRES

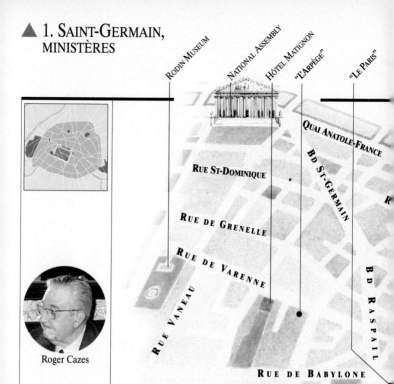

RODIN MUSEUM

NATIONAL ASSEMBLY

HÔTEL MATIGNON

"L'ARPÈGE"

"LE PARIS"

QUAI ANATOLE-FRANCE

BD ST-GERMAIN

RUE ST-DOMINIQUE

RUE DE GRENELLE

RUE DE VARENNE

RUE VANEAU

B D   R A S P A I L

RUE DE BABYLONE

Roger Cazes

THE BRASSERIE DES BORDS DU RHIN
"Brasserie on the banks of the Rhine" was *Lipp*'s original name. The reference to the Rhine disappeared during World War One, and thereafter the restaurant was simply called the *Brasserie des Bords*.

The Boulevard Saint-Germain is like a great river tapping into the activity of the streets on either side: Republicanism at the end near the National Assembly, a more military posture as it passes the Ministry of Defence, a more bourgeois manner in the area known as "noble," and then more "down-market" round Saint-Germain-des-Prés, before it pours all over the tourists and students swimming along yet another great watercourse, the Boulevard Saint-Michel. On either side stretch the picturesque hinterlands of Sèvres-Babylone and Saint-André-des-Arts with their quiet streets lined with Ministry buildings, and embracing the quays along the Seine and the Esplanade

BIÈRE HATT DE KRONENBOURG

BRASSERIE DES BORDS DU RHIN

Photo Lange

Brasserie LIPP

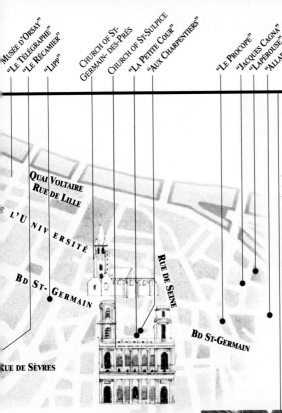

QUAI VOLTAIRE
RUE DE LILLE
E L'UNIVERSITÉ
BD ST-GERMAIN
RUE DE SEINE
BD ST-GERMAIN
RUE DE SÈVRES

> **"**Then I started to think in *Lipp*'s about when I had first been able to write a story after losing everything. It was up in Cortina d'Ampezzo when I had come back to join Hadley there after the spring skiing which I had to interrupt to go on assignment to the Rhineland and the Ruhr.**"**
> Ernest Hemingway
> *A Moveable Feast*

des Invalides. The eastern end connects with the old part of Paris and the left bank; the western extremity, long occupied by the grounds of the Abbey of Saint-Germain-des-Prés, dates only from the 17th and 18th centuries.

LIPP ● 49, 79, 93 ◆ 370

LÉONARD AND ÉLISE. In 1880, Léonard Lipp and his wife Élise pulled up outside 151 Boulevard Saint-Germain and, at the sign of the *Brasserie des Bords du Rhin*, a tiny restaurant with no more than a dozen tables, began the daunting task of trying to make a living. The portents for the area were good and the restaurant was popular with actors and poets from the outset, and the Lipps were able to retire in the early years of this century. In 1914, on the eve of World War One, *Lipp* took a big step toward being the legend it has now become when the new owner, Martin Barthélémy-Hébrard, decided to decorate the premises afresh with large, beveled mirrors set in faience tiles, and ceramic panels on the walls. They are still there. The actors now only needed someone to direct them. When Marcellin Cazes bought *Lipp* in 1920, Saint-Germain-des-Prés was already a busy district and the premises were soon too small to cope. He decided to extend them by covering over the courtyard and turning it into a room. The reopening of *Lipp* was celebrated with a huge banquet on December 26th, 1926.

A MEETING PLACE FOR SAINT-GERMAIN SOCIETY. The *Brasserie Lipp* became the meeting place for the powerful and the intelligentsia, and leading figures from the *Vieux-Colombier*, the *Nouvelle Revue Française* and the Third Republic came to

THE FAIENCE DÉCOR. It dates from 1914 and was the work of the Fargue brothers, father and uncle of the poet Léon-Paul Fargue, who wrote of *Lipp* in his *Le Piéton de Paris* ● 93–4.

129

"L'ATTENTAT"
Yves Boisset's film tells the story of the Ben Barka affair. On October 29, 1965, Ben Barka, an opponent of King Hassan II of Morocco, was abducted outside the Brasserie *Lipp* by General Oufkir's Moroccan agents, assisted by the French secret service.

❝Imagine the fuss if they announced that *Maxim's* was to be pulled down and replaced by a snack bar. *Vagenende* is no *Maxim's*, and its disappearance is unlikely to lead to rioting in the streets, but it is still a remarkable building dating from the Paris of 1900, and it is now under threat.❞
Paris-Presse, 1966
Lovers of Art Nouveau! Rest assured! *Vagenende* is still there!

relish its saveloy salads and sparkling wines. Marcellin himself showed guests to their tables: the downstairs dining-room was reserved for regulars, while newcomers were sent upstairs, and being given a table in the right-hand corner near the entrance was as good as being awarded the Prix Goncourt or the *Légion d'honneur*. Roger Cazes succeeded his father in 1976 and managed *Lipp* until his death in 1987, when his nephew Michel-Jacques Perrochon took over. *Lipp* has remained impervious to changing fashions and the restaurant has now become a legend. The brasserie's customers are astonishingly faithful, and Robert Sabatier still carves his meat with his own special knife as a mark of respect to Marcellin's memory.

VAGENENDE ◆ 373

AN OLD BOUILLON CHARTIER. Between 1878, when the premises at No. 142 were built on the new Boulevard Saint-Germain, and 1905, when Édouard and Camille Chartier bought the site, the first floor housed a cake shop. The building's culinary traditions were not to be cut short, as it was here that the Chartiers, who had founded a chain of *bouillons*, opened another of the many popular eating-places that were to make their fortune ● 46. As in other *Chartier* establishments ▲ 262, the décor was much more opulent than their innumerable customers. Beveled mirrors, interlaced rounded paneling, tiles made of colored glass decorated with pastoral scenes, copper coat-racks, and lamps with engraved bulbs vividly recall the style of the period, now known as Art Nouveau. Low partitions divide the room and give the tables an element of intimacy. The restaurant was sold a few years later to the rival *Rougeot* chain, which sold it on to the Vagenendes in 1920.

The Carpenters' Guild forms the central theme of the decoration in Pierre Bardèche's restaurant, once the eating-place of journeymen carpenters.

SAVED FROM DEMOLITION. Mme Vagenende remained faithful to the spirit of the old *bouillons*, and kept prices down while making the décor even grander than before. In 1966 Minister of Culture André Malraux saved the restaurant from being pulled down by placing it on the list of protected buildings. Like many former *bouillons*, *Vagenende* sought to match its culinary aspirations to the magnificence of its décor when it was taken ovet by Jean-Pierre Egurreguy in 1977. In a district full of fast-food outlets, that is very good news.

AUX CHARPENTIERS ◆ 364

THE CARPENTERS' EATING-PLACE. Before it became one of the most picturesque restaurants in the entire Saint-Germain quarter, 10 Rue de Mabillon was, from 1874, the eating-place of a guild of carpenters. The society's general meetings took place here, and carpentry courses were given upstairs. This masterpiece (below right), which won a bronze medal at the Universal Exhibition of 1889, was designed and executed at Rue de Mabillon by a guild member by the name of Théodore. Following restoration, the carpenters' eating-place was hugely popular in the years after both World Wars, when all the reconstruction work was taking place, and then, as guild members declined in number, it found a new role – without losing any of its atmosphere. In an official address delivered in the 1950's, a guild member said, "The restaurant where so many members took their meals, often on credit and always served by the revered 'mothers', is now owned by a restaurateur who has nothing to do with our society. He has, however, shown respect for our organization and its history by decorating the restaurant on the basis of advice given by an elderly member of ours and in the style of our guild." The anonymous retaurateur was then given the new name "Bordelais" after an introduction ceremony.

A friendly atmosphere. Pierre Bardèche has owned *Aux Charpentiers* since 1976. He wanted to preserve the spirit of the place and decorated it with mementoes of the Carpenters' Guild. There is even something indefinably fraternal about the cuisine. The recipe has worked perfectly. Today, celebrities and ordinary families sit round the table once used by the Guild and share the pot-au-feu. Mayor of Paris Jacques Chirac celebrated his sixtieth birthday there, and François Mitterrand is a regular customer. George and Barbara Bush have also been seen here, dining incognito.

Aux Charpentiers has the atmosphere of a local bistro.

THE MASTERPIECE. This work of art by a Carpenters' Guild member occupies a place of honor in the *Charpentiers* restaurant. It was executed by a member who, in order to achieve a defined standard of skill, had to abide by precise rules laid down by the Guild. His degree of skill was appraised by a jury of master carpenters.

VOLTAIRE
Voltaire was the most regular of the *Procope*'s famous customers, a list of whom appears on the façade. It was his second home. The first time Voltaire entered the *Procope*, he came disguised as a priest to eavesdrop on what people were saying about his play *Sémiramis* (1748), which had received its première the night before at the *Comédie-Française*.

CAFÉ PROCOPE
ICI
PROCOPIO DEI COLTELLI
FONDA EN 1686
LE PLUS ANCIEN CAFÉ DU MONDE
ET LE PLUS CÉLÈBRE CENTRE
DE LA VIE LITTÉRAIRE ET PHILOSOPHIQUE
AU 18e ET AU 19e SIÈCLES.
IL FUT FRÉQUENTÉ PAR
LA FONTAINE, VOLTAIRE,
LES ENCYCLOPÉDISTES
BENJAMIN FRANKLIN, DANTON, MARAT,
ROBESPIERRE, NAPOLÉON BONAPARTE,
BALZAC, VICTOR HUGO,
GAMBETTA, VERLAINE,
ET ANATOLE FRANCE.

LE PROCOPE ◆ 372

THREE CENTURIES OF HISTORY. The *Procope* is one of the few Parisian restaurants that can boast a history going back three centuries. Paris's first café-ice cream parlor opened in 1686; it was situated on Rue des Fossés-Saint-Germain, later re-named Rue de l'Ancienne-Comédie after the *Comédie-Française* left in 1770. The owner was Francesco Procopio dei Coltelli, and his establishment replaced public baths known as the *Saint-Suaire de Turin*. In those days, cafés were smoky, dilapidated and unsafe places, but Procopio, a man of taste, got rid of the partitions to give more space, covered the walls with tapestries and mirrors, hung crystal chandeliers from the ceilings, and introduced marble tables with attractively curved legs. The *Procope* soon became popular for liqueurs distilled by Procopio himself, cocktails (including *Rosée du soleil* (Sundew), which is made with crushed fennel, aniseed, coriander, dill and caraway left to macerate in brandy), crystallized fruit, and fruit ice creams – the first to be sold in Paris. Francesco Procopio dei Coltelli acquired French nationality and took the name of François Procope Couteau. Then, in 1689, the *Comédie-Française* moved opposite, and the café predictably became the theater foyer. And that is how it came about that the casts of Molière's *Le médecin malgré lui* and Racine's *Phèdre* could go for coffee together between performances.

VOLTAIRE, A TRUE REGULAR. In the 18th century, the *Procope* was in competition with exclusive clubs and private salons, but Diderot, Rousseau and Voltaire (whose play *Le Caffé, ou l'Écossaise* was set in the *Procope*) preferred the café once patronized by Molière and Racine. Some of *L'Encyclopédie* came into being beneath the *Procope*'s chandeliers, and Montesquíeu once wrote that it was a place where the coffee was so good that it quickened the pulse of all who partook of it. The restaurant continued to be successful after the *Comédie-Française* departed and, in 1784, Beaumarchais chose the *Procope* to celebrate the première of *Le Marriage de Figaro*. At the time of the French Revolution, Danton, Marat, Robespierre, Desmoulins and Guillotin all ate here, undeterred by the threat of the scaffold. Musset, Hugo and Balzac – and later Verlaine, Wilde and Huysmans – all maintained the intellectual reputation of the place.

DEATH AND RESURRECTION. There was no knowing what the 20th century would bring. In fact, the *Procope* closed its doors in 1900, and re-opened and closed again many times until 1937, when it was taken over by Jacques and Pierre Blanc, who restored it. Today, it is like a museum with its rather flashy splendor and plateaux of seafood lacking all sense of history. Students still ask for the table where Voltaire sat.

ZOPPI
Zoppi succeeded Procopio as manager. He was Italian, like his predecessor, and gave the capital's most famous revolutionaries the best ice creams in Paris.

Prior to its recent renovation by the Blanc brothers, the *Procope* was more like the literary café it once was, rather than the tourists' museum it has now become.

133

A paved courtyard, window boxes, the gurgle of a fountain and a flight of worn steps conspire to lure Parisians seeking provincial calm, but who never like provincial life so much as when it is right in the middle of the city.

THE POST OFFICE'S SOCIAL OBLIGATIONS At the beginning of the 20th century, the Post Office management took it upon itself to provide accommodation for its female employees, many of whom were single, hailed from the provinces and had modest family backgrounds. The refectory in the women's hostel in

Rue de Lille has been turned into a refined and charming restaurant.

LA PETITE COUR ◆ 372

THE PROVINCES COME TO PARIS. A keen sense of direction is needed to find this, an exceptionally peaceful restaurant in an otherwise noisy area. It is situated in Rue de Mabillon below street level and, as its name suggests, it gives on to a small courtyard adorned with flowers and a fountain. The courtyard used to be at the same level as the road, until the constant ebbing and flowing of the Seine became too much. Those looking for a quick snack are likely to be put off by the steep flight of steps, but that will not apply to more mature souls who have some time on their hands and like to enjoy their food in peace. With its aura of provincial life, the *Petite Cour* is particularly attractive in summer for simple, elegant meals outdoors. For a while, you could almost believe that you were in the countryside.

LE TÉLÉGRAPHE ● 77, 80 ◆ 373

THE POST OFFICE WOMEN. The success enjoyed by the *Télégraphe* demonstrates yet again that good cooking needs a good décor, and that the social architecture of the early 20th century can provide an excellent setting for a fashionable restaurant of the 1990's. The hostel for women once employed by the *Postes, Télégraphes et Téléphones* in Rue de Lille shows that management were genuinely concerned about their staff's housing needs. The building was constructed in 1905 to plans drawn up by the architect Bliault, and is an example of enlightened avant-garde practice. The ceilings are high, the rooms are large and well ventilated, and on the first floor bay windows give on to a courtyard filled with flowers. The furniture, some of which has survived, was the work of Belgian designer Gustave Serrurier-Bovi.

A VIENNESE ATMOSPHERE. When Bernard Marck was searching the area looking for somewhere to open a new restaurant, he must have been absolutely delighted to come across these premises, used originally as a refectory for women Post Office employees before being turned into office space. He entrusted the decoration to his friend François-Joseph Graf, who had just finished work on the *Ambroisie* restaurant in Place des Vosges. Graf restored the magnificent mosaic floor, made accurate copies of the early 20th-century furniture, installed an entirely new lighting system, renovated the huge sideboard that dominates the main room, and in an adjoining room built a bar that works well with the rest of the furnishings. He also designed plates, cutlery and chandeliers that give the whole place an entirely unforced Viennese atmosphere. The *Télégraphe* opened in 1987 and swiftly became a popular haunt for all manner of fashionable people: when the weather is fine, the tiny covered courtyard is particularly popular.

The design of the *Télégraphe* restaurant is a perfect example of early 20th-century social architecture. It was influenced by such important innovators as the Austrian Secession movement of Josef Hoffmann and Otto Wagner, and the German Jugendstil of Henry van de Velde and Joseph Maria Olbrich whose slogan "Only the functional is beautiful" paved the way for Walter Gropius and the Bauhaus.

LAPÉROUSE ● 47, 75 ◆ 369

WINE MERCHANT AND POULTRY MERCHANTS. The story of this famous restaurant on the Quai des Grands-Augustins is riddled with misconceptions. No, Lapérouse is not the celebrated French navigator, the Count of La Pérouse, although the latter's name has long been taken in vain. No, the famous rooms were not built to cater for local prostitutes but to store the merchandise of chicken farmers. And no, the décor does not date from the 18th but from the late 19th century. What we do know is that, in the 18th century, a certain Lefèvre, victualler to the King, bought the private house belonging to Forget, Count of Bruillevert, Master of the Louis XIV's Waters and Forests, as a base for his wine business. The proximity of the Marché de la Vallée, Paris' main poultry and game market, attracted numerous merchants to his establishment. In those days business was transacted in

LITERARY RENDEZ-VOUS
Marcel Proust had Swann take dinner on the Quai des Grands-Augustins because the sign above the restaurant reminded him of the name of the street where Odette de Crécy lived. Jules Romain had Haverkamp lunch here to celebrate the discovery of the mineral water spring that had made him rich. And Georges Simenon chose *Lapérouse* for a meeting between Maigret and Dr Paul, the forensic pathologist and gourmet who gave his name to the *Poulet Docteur* that is still on the menu.

135

THE SALON LA FONTAINE
The La Fontaine Room is one of the *Lapérouse*'s fourteen rooms. It is decorated with eight painted wooden panels showing rustic scenes. The celebrated writer of fables is depicted on a medallion. Other rooms include the *salon des Glaces* (mirrors) and the *salon des Singes* (monkeys).

JEAN FRANÇOIS DE GALAUP, COUNT OF LA PÉROUSE. The Count commanded an expedition comprising two frigates, the *Boussole* and the *Astrolabe*, to

reconnoiter the American and Asian shores of the North Pacific. The ships set sail in 1786 but disappeared in 1788. His name is used by the restaurant, and is almost identical to that of the man who founded it.

silver or gold, and Lefèvre had the ingenious idea of constructing on the first floor of his establishment a line of small rooms where merchants could negotiate in peace and quiet, and toast their deals away from prying eyes. By the time Jules Lapérouse bought the premises in 1870, however, the clientele had changed: the poultry market had moved into Les Halles and was about to be replaced by establishments selling books.

SOME VERY PRIVATE ROOMS. Printers, publishers and authors were among the first to patronize Jules Lapérouse's new restaurant, which he opened in 1878. It was decorated with paintings mounted in the manner of Watteau and Boucher, and with gilding, painted ceilings, ornamental moldings, mirrors and fine carpets. It is known that the establishment was largely used for a certain purpose – but was that by accident or design? In any event, the small rooms soon became popular with gentlemen seeking the company of young ladies. Surely French law had something to say about this sort of thing? One way and another, fact and fiction then became hopelessly intertwined with bawdy stories of sofas, bidets, concealed staircases – and even secret underground passages. The scratch-marks on the mirrors in

> ## "THE MOTOR CAR HAS KILLED OFF THE PRIVATE DINING-ROOMS TO THE ADVANTAGE OF SUBURBAN HOTELS."
>
> CECIL SAINT-LAURENT

some of the rooms were probably caused by ladies of the night checking that the jewels given to them in gratitude for their services were indeed genuine ... To ensure guests' peace of mind, food was neither served nor cleared away unless a bell rang down in the kitchens. One final anecdote: Victor Hugo is remembered bringing his grandchildren here to buy them sweets.

TOPOLINSKI AND ALEXANDRE. Jules Lapérouse sold out in 1885, and was followed by a string of proprietors until Roger Topolinski bought the restaurant in 1923. The *Lapérouse*'s great period of gastronomic and worldly glory then lasted until after World War Two, when it fell into oblivion. Then in 1985, Georges Alexandre, who had already saved the *Bofinger* brasserie, turned his attentions to this sleeping beauty on the Quai des Grands-Augustins. He entrusted the task of renovating the establishment to interior designer Pierre Pothier: a bar and an oyster stall were built downstairs, and a large room with trompe l'oeil décor upstairs. What is more, after a long succession of chefs, the *Lapérouse*'s reputation for good food also revived. Serious business lunches soon became the order of the day – and when the time came to light up the cigars, that was the signal for a little nostalgia for the good old days when there were no parking restrictions in the area.

INTIMACY
The *cabinet aux Raisins* (Grape Room) seats only two people, and is particularly noted for a medallion depicting a young man leaning over a young woman. It is decorated with this short poem: "Your luscious grapes, so full and fruity/ are the answer to a young man's prayers./ Indulge his whims – it is your duty! –/ and let him inspect your wares!/ And if the rascal shining bright/ should procrastinate and quibble,/ make sure, fair daughter of the night,/ to let him have a nibble!"

L'ARPÈGE ◆ 364

IN PERFECT HARMONY. *L'Arpège* is strategically situated between the National Assembly and the Hôtel Matignon, and close to the Rodin Museum. The area has been popular with gourmets for many years. Alain Senderens ▲ 216 started his career at what was then the *Archestrate* before handing the keys over to Alain Passard, one of his faithful and talented pupils. Passard re-named the establishment *L'Arpège* (Arpeggio), a reminder of his earlier dreams of becoming a conductor. Music would probably have been the winner, and cooking certainly the loser, but this Breton chef still likes nothing better than playing the saxophone between courses. Arpeggios also hint at Alain Passard's classical inventiveness and his dishes carefully prepared with the precision of a metronome. *L'Arpège* long had the reputation of having the most uncomfortable kitchens and dining-room in Paris, but in 1991 it turned over a new leaf. A wood, steel and glass-fitted interior now gives the restaurant an element of sobriety and better use of space.

LOUISE PASSARD
The gold frame surrounding the photograph of Louise Passard, Alain Passard's grandmother and his inspiration, occupies a place of honor in *L'Arpège* restaurant. It is in sharp contrast with the modern style adopted in her grandson's restaurant. The difference perfectly illustrates Alain Passard's cooking, which skilfully marries traditional cooking and bold new ideas.

137

This sideboard decorated with brightly colored ceramic tiles, and illustrated with a splendid illustration of Mucha's paintings, is representative of a "poor" Art Nouveau style.

LE PETIT ZINC

♦ 371

MAXIM'S, RUE SAINT-BENOÎT. In 1991, the news that *Le Petit Zinc* was closing down spread like wildfire. However, like *Muniche*, another of the Layrac brothers' establishments, this narrow and permanently crowded bistro in Rue de Buci was simply moving to Rue Saint-Benoît and making way for *Arbuci*, the Blanc brothers' latest success story. *Le Petit Zinc* now stands on a site previously occupied by the *Assiette au*

Beurre, a restaurant once patronized by Maurice Casanova and Raymond Oliver. It is in the shape of a theater (which is what it once was) and its somber décor, renovated in the early years of the 20th century, recalls *Maxim's* ▲ *217*; there are also some fine ceramic tiles. Identical *sole meunière* and *boeuf gros sel* are served at the nearby *Muniche*. People are turned away every night!

LE MUSÉE D'ORSAY ◆ 370

FROM PALACE TO MUSEUM. This superb room has been a palace drawing-room and a hotel foyer; it is now a museum restaurant, and customers sit beneath the gilding and frescoes of the sumptuous ceilings as the Seine flows on, past the museum of the *Légion d'honneur*. The Palais d'Orsay was built between 1810 and 1838 on plans supplied by architects Bonnard and Lacornée. At one point, it housed the *Cour des comptes*, the State auditing office. It was set on fire during the time of the Commune in 1871, and in 1898 it was turned into a railway station by architect Laloux. The façade overlooking the Seine incorporates two enormous clocks and is surmounted by three monumental statues, allegories of Bordeaux, Toulouse and Nantes, the three main destinations for trains departing from the Gare d'Orsay. The station was opened on July 14, 1900, the same year as the new Gare de Lyon, and it even incorporated a hotel for the use of travelers. The building ceased to be used as a station in 1939, but the hotel survived until 1973. It was saved from threatened demolition by Jacques Duhamel, Minister of Culture from 1971 to 1973, who had it listed as a historic monument which should therefore be protected. For a few years the hotel hosted theatrical productions by the Renaud-Barrault Company, as well as concerts, fashion shows and exhibitions.

GAE AULENTI. In 1977, the French Government decided to turn the building into a museum, and appointed the Italian interior designer Gae Aulenti to take charge of the transformation. The new museum was opened by President François Mitterrand in 1986. A restaurant was built on the second floor, and the two superb ceilings – one adorned with allegories painted by Gabriel Ferier, the other with airline routes by Benjamin Constant – were restored to their former glory. The impressive decorations of the restaurant include extravagant crystal chandeliers, gilt moldings, magnificent marble fireplaces and a light oak floor. To a critical eye, the only weak points are the green cane chairs and lacquered sidetable and wood benches that needlessly conform to the fashion of the period.

ル・レストラン・デュ・ル・ドルセー

M'O

L'restaurant du Musée d'Orsay

オルセー美術館

THE MUSÉE D'ORSAY Works of art from the second half of the 19th century and the early part of the 20th, previously dispersed in the Louvre, the Jeu de Paume and the Palais de Tokyo, are displayed here. The various collections include not only paintings (from Millet to Bonnard) and sculptures (from Carpeaux to Maillol), but also decorative arts, photography and architecture.

Before it was converted into a museum, this building was the Gare d'Orsay, a railway station.

The tall windows of the restaurant overlook the entrance to the museum, on the west side of the building.

Le Récamier

♦ 372

MADAME RÉCAMIER
Mme Récamier, née
Bernard in 1777,
brought together in
her salon all the
leading figures in arts

and letters at the
time of the
Consulate. On her
husband's first
bankruptcy in 1806,
she went to live with
Mme de Staël at
Coppet, in
Switzerland. In 1811,
when suspected by
Napoleon of
consorting with the
opposition, she was
exiled "40 leagues"
(about 120 miles)
from Paris.

Grapes and vines are
the main themes of
the sculptures by
Léon Binet and Paul
Belmondo (father of
the actor, Jean-Paul

Belmondo) that
adorn the façade of
the *Hôtel Lutétia*.
They commemorate
the famous vines that
covered the left bank
in Roman times.

JEANNE FRANÇOISE JULIE ADÉLAÏDE RÉCAMIER. For many
years, the *Théâtre Récamier* was used solely for rehearsals, but
performances now take place in the restaurant of the same
name at lunchtime and in the evening, both indoors and out
on the terrace. The theater and restaurant bear the name of
the Impasse Récamier, a cul-de-sac named to mark an
episode in the life of Mme Récamier, the famous society
beauty. In 1819, when her husband had gone bankrupt once
too often, she retired to the Abbaye-aux-Bois, which stood on
this site in Faubourg Saint-Germain, and it was here that her
relationship with the poet Chateaubriand flourished. Mme
Récamier died in 1849 and the abbey was demolished in 1906
to make way for Boulevard Raspail, then
under construction. Martin Cantegrit
discovered the *impasse* in 1969 when, after
getting the *Hôtel Montalembert* into the
Michelin Guide, he was looking to go into
business for himself.
A PUBLISHERS' EATING PLACE. *Chez Jules*
was once a so-called "clerics' restaurant,"
but Cantegrit wanted it to cater to the
worlds of publishing, movies, television
and politics, and he named it after a famous patron of the
arts. Gaston Gallimard, once a regular at the *Montalembert*,
transferred his allegiance to *Le Récamier* and became one of
its most loyal customers. The *impasse* was not yet
pedestrianized, but Georges Pompidou, who was dining there
one evening, promised to see what he could do. However,
Martin Cantegrit had to wait until 1978 before he could add
the terrace that is the *Le Récamier*'s second main attraction.
The primary attraction is unquestionably the cooking, which
combines Burgundian classicism with superb technique. The
hour at which today's customers leave the *impasse* coincides
with the time that Chateaubriand paid
Mme Récamier his daily visit to
read her his *Mémoires d'outre-
tombe* (Memoirs from Beyond the
Grave).

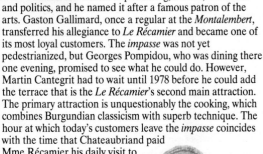

> **"WE OFTEN COMPARE STEAMSHIPS TO FLOATING HOTELS; WE MIGHT JUST AS WELL COMPARE HOTELS TO STATIONARY STEAMSHIPS."**
>
> LÉON-PAUL FARGUE

ART DECO DÉCOR
The walnut and citron wood paneling, the Art Deco chandeliers, the dark brown carpet with geometrical motifs and the mid-1920's armchairs give the room a great feeling of warmth. It is a small restaurant, seating only thirty-five people.

LE PARIS ◆ 371

THE PAQUEBOT. The Parisii were a tribe of Celtic fishermen who sailed up the Seine and became the region's first inhabitants. It was here, on the left bank, that they built a town that, under the Romans, would be known as Lutetia. The only luxury hotel now on the left bank is the *Lutétia*, and it is decorated in the style of an ocean-going liner. The hotel was built between 1907 and 1910 by architects Louis Boileau (who was also responsible for the *Drouant*, the *Prunier* and the *Bon Marché*) and Henri Tauzin, and the overall style allows the rigor of Art Deco to impose on the flowing lines of Art Nouveau. The *Lutétia*, strategically placed at the Sèvres-Babylone crossroads between Montparnasse and Saint-Germain, has played a part in the history of both districts; customers to its American bar included *Montparnos* in the Roaring Twenties and *Germano-Pratins* in the post-war years. Charles and Yvonne de Gaulle spent the first night of their honeymoon there; other famous guests have included Henri Matisse and André Gide, and more recently the sculptor César and the director of the Paris Opéra, Pierre Bergé.

THE PARIS RESTAURANT IN THE HÔTEL LUTÉTIA. The *Paris* opened in 1985. In an attempt to retain the hotel's ocean-going style, interior designer Sonia Rykiel was commissioned to recreate the form and atmosphere of the dining-room of the *Normandie,* which was destroyed by fire in New York harbor in 1942.

THE HÔTEL LUTÉTIA
According to a publicity brochure dating from the beginning of the century, "the beautiful, capacious *Hôtel Lutétia* stands in one of the safer, cleaner parts of Paris opposite the Square Boucicaut. Its tall bays and casement windows are bathed in light from all directions, the decoration is elegant and graceful ... The hotel is directly served by several omnibus routes and by the *Nord-Sud* and underground stations."

141

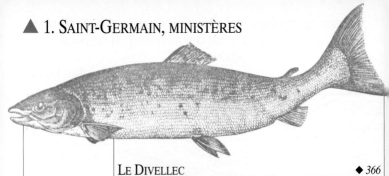

Le Divellec ◆ 366

La Rochelle comes to Paris. Jacques Le Divellec settled here in the early 1980's, on the second floor of a sumptuous building close to the Hôtel des Invalides – and a long way

from the sea. However, "grand Jacques" (Big Jacques) did not leave La Rochelle without having his fisherman friends promise to send him their fish and crustaceans in record time. He serves them in a beautiful, blue and white dining-room with yachting furnishings, and windows that open out on to the lawns of the *Esplanade*. His seafood cooking is simple and impeccable. He got the idea of a lobster press from the famous duck press at the *Tour d'Argent* ▲ *147* and, with the assistance of Christofle, the Parisian goldsmiths, designed a press to extract the juices from his superb crustaceans. No sympathy, then, for those food writers who lack the most elementary sense of poetry, and maintain that the lobster press is merely decorative rather than functional!

Ambassador of the sea. This gentle giant with the piercing eyes is in charge of the kitchen, but also takes an interest in the dining-room and even opens doors for customers on occasion. He is everywhere – in the restaurant itself, of course – but also on book covers, on television and radio, and any other place where he can expertly perform his self-appointed role of "ambassador of the sea". His chic seafood cooking has been hugely popular, drawing not only businessmen but also devotees from the diverse worlds of politics, the arts and the media to *Le Divellec*. François Mitterrand is a regular customer.

Seafood menu
The restaurant's menu reads like a simple confession of faith: *Le Divellec*, Seafood Cuisine. The philosophy is all about minimizing the stages between the product in its natural state and its presentation on the customer's plate; a light touch is the key.

The lobster press
This gadget was made famous by Jacques Le Divellec, who also designed it. It now appears in the catalogue of Christofle, the goldsmiths. There are certainly cheaper kitchen utensils!

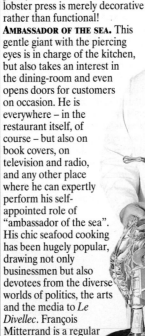

LE BISTROT DE PARIS ◆ 365

MICHEL'S BISTRO. A man is ill-advised to stay in his father's
shadow for ever. This is especially so when the father is a
celebrated chef, and the son eager to make his own way in the
world. In 1965, when Raymond Oliver was in charge at the
Grand Véfour ▲ 213, his son Michel, who
was then Manager and *maître-d'hôtel* of the
Palais-Royal restaurant, decided to go it
alone. He was drawn to the Saint-Germain
district and, with his friend André Allard,
started looking for a genuine bistro. In
Rue de Lille, he found the *Poënsin*, a
former *bouillon* that had been closed for
many years. He then contacted Slavik, at
that time the most fashionable of Parisian
interior designers, who offered his services free to the
penniless restaurateur. The molded mirrors of the old
bouillon have been preserved, more mirrors have been added
to the ceilings, and a winter garden and a bar have been built
in the covered courtyard. The restaurant has the feel of a
billiard room in a provincial café: the tables, set close
together, encourage conviviality, and the bistro food is
hugely popular.

JACQUES CAGNA ◆ 369

AN 18TH-CENTURY INN. This restaurant is hidden amid a
tangle of quiet old streets lying between the noisy Boulevard
Saint-Germain and the Seine. The 17th-century façade is a
protected monument, and the whole building was once part of
the College of the Charités-Saint-Denis, which gave the
narrow street its original name. The Convent of the Grands-
Augustins once stood opposite. So atmospheric is the locality
that one could almost slip on a doublet and arrive at this 18th-
century inn on horseback. In 1975 Jacques Cagna and his
sister Anny Logereau decided to open a business there and
they have respected the building's history without falling for
medieval pastiche. Interior designer Daniel Pasgrimeau, a
friend of Cagna's, blended the white paneling with the
massive oak beams of the upstairs dining-room, designed
furniture and a table service to match the surroundings and
devised an authentic décor using some of Jacques Cagna's
personal collection of minor 17th-
century Dutch masters. A small room
upstairs also has three 16th-century
frescoes depicting three of the twelve
apostles.

HIGH-PRECISION CUISINE. With such
elegantly made tables, it is hardly
surprising that the food served on them
is some of the best in Paris. The finest
quality ingredients are prepared with
respect and simplicity – and no fuss.
This is often the secret that helps to
explain how the Parisian chef can
prepare high-precision dishes,
which are at the same time not
too costly.

THE OPENING
Oliver did not realize
that the gas lamps he
had kept from the old
bouillon would
produce far too much
heat and make
everything look
green. On the
opening night, make-
up ran like rivers and
the guests looked
sickly, although that
had nothing to do
with the food.
Electricity was soon
installed and gas was
used solely for the
ovens in the kitchen.

MEMORIES
In 1573, the Duke of
Anjou, the King of
Poland, his brother
Charles IX and the
Duke of Navarre
invited themselves to
the home of the
Provost of Paris in
Rue des Grands-
Augustins. When
they departed, they
took with them the
silver table service to
punish the Provost
for refusing to marry
a mistress whom the
Duke of Anjou was
leaving behind.

ALLARD ◆ 364

À LA HALTE DE L'ÉPERON. The vulgarity that now disfigures the ancient district of Rue Saint-André-des-Arts conceals a few gems that pre-date the days when the drab uniformity of *crêperies* and stalls selling frippery and second-hand clothes descended on the area. *Allard* is situated on the corner of Rue de l'Éperon and Rue Saint-André-des-Arts, and the building's façade complies with an ordinance of 1720 requiring wine merchants to close their premises with grilles. The establishment's gastronomic reputation does not go back quite that far. In the early years of the 20th century, Vincent Candré opened a bistro here at the sign of the *Halte de l'Éperon*, serving wines from his native Sancerre over the zinc counter that is still in place today. The wine was accompanied by local food prepared by Joséphine, who was soon to open her own restaurant in Rue du Cherche-Midi. In 1935, when Vincent Candré handed the restaurant over to Marcel and Marthe Allard, 41 Rue Saint-André-des-Arts already enjoyed a solid reputation among *gourmets*. This reputation remains. The walls are still decorated with green lacquer, and the new owners continue to serve the traditional dishes of lamb stew, duck with olives, and partridge with cabbage, for which the restaurant has been so well-known.

"GENEROUS HELPINGS." The restaurant is always packed, seven days a week. Maurice Chevalier, Yvonne Printemps and Pierre Fresnay were already regulars, but it was Marcel's son André and his wife Fernande who really put the *Allard* on the gastronomic map of Paris after 1946. Juliette Gréco and Philippe Lemaire had their wedding banquet here, and rich foreigners temporarily forsake their luxury hotels on the right bank to enjoy "slumming it" at this left bank bistro. A measure of its authenticity is that the entrance to the dining area is through the kitchen. However, snobbery has no place in an awowedly "anti-*Lipp*" establishment where Socialist ex-Ministers like Roland Dumas and Robert Badinter can lunch in private, just as Georges Pompidou used to do. "Generous helpings" is still *Allard*'s consistent theme. André Allard died in 1983 and Fernande sold up in 1985, but wisely the new owner, Bernard Bouchard, has not touched the décor and has preserved the established custom of offering generous helpings of the restaurant's traditional specialties to the still loyal clientele.

2.
LATIN QUARTER, MONTPARNASSE, PARC MONTSOURIS, PLACE D'ITALIE

VAL-DE-GRACE HOSPITAL

"CLOSERIE DES LILAS"

SENATE

GARE MONTPARNASSE

MONTPARNASSE TOWER

MONTPARNASSE CEMETERY

"LE BISTRO DE LA GARE"

"LA COUPOLE"

"LE DUC"

RUE D'ASSAS

JARDIN DU LUXEMBOURG

RUE DE RENNES

BD DU MONTPARNASSE

BD. EDGAR QUINET

BD RASPAIL

NUMBERED DUCKS
Canard au sang had long been a famous dish at the *Tour d'Argent* and in 1890 Frédéric Delair devised a system for numbering the ducks. Some of the diners and their ducks were illustrious: the Prince of Wales, the future Edward VII: duck 328 (1890); Grand-Duke Vladimir of Russia: duck 6043 (1900);

King Alfonso XIII: duck 40,362 (1914); Franklin D. Roosevelt: duck 112,151 (1929); and Princess Elizabeth (before she became Queen Elizabeth II): duck 185,397 (1948). The 500,000th duck, named Frédéric, was released from the roof of the restaurant on March 17th, 1976, with an invitation for two to the *Tour d'Argent* attached to its feet.

It is a long time since Latin was spoken in the Latin Quarter, and since Montparnasse was the home of poets. The district came to be known as the Latin Quarter because this was the language spoken by students and teachers up to the time of the French Revolution; moreover, the Sorbonne, founded in the 13th century, remains one of the most important buildings in a district that is positively alive with history. In the early 17th century, students named the artificial hill in the south of the district *Mont Parnasse* (Mount Parnassus), but it was demolished when a boulevard, which acquired the name, was laid out in the 18th century. From the second half of the 19th century until 1930, Montparnasse was popular with artists and students and, because they had very little money, many of the restaurants in both quarters were originally inexpensive.

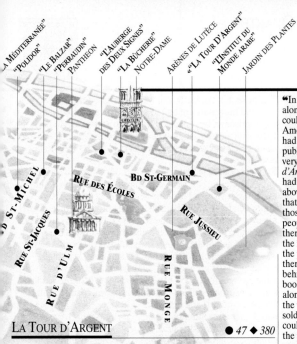

BD ST-MICHEL

RUE DES ÉCOLES

BD ST-GERMAIN

RUE ST-JACQUES

RUE D'ULM

RUE JUSSIEU

RUE MONGE

LA TOUR D'ARGENT

● 47 ◆ 380

FOUR CENTURIES OLD. At the time of Philip II of France (1165–1223) the wall that encircled Paris stopped at a stone tower on the banks of the Seine. It was speckled with mica that glittered in the sunlight, and was called the *tour d'argent* (silver tower). There is evidence of there having been an inn in these parts since the 16th century, and Henry IV was known to treat himself to heron pâté here, but it was not until 1780 that a proper restaurant was built. On July 14, 1789, revolutionaries returning from the Bastille mistook the restaurant's coat of arms for that of a prince and sacked the building.

THE GREAT FRÉDÉRIC. When the *Tour d'Argent* was bought by Frédéric Delair a century later, it rapidly acquired the reputation that it has to this day. Delair had side-whiskers that made him look like an Austrian archduke, he wore tiny iron-framed spectacles and was a notoriously difficult person. But he was an absolute genius in the kitchen ● 105. It was also his idea to number the *canard au sang*!

TERRAIL, FATHER AND SON. André Terrail took over from Delair in 1912. André was lucky enough to be married to the daughter of Claudius Burdel, proprietor of the celebrated *Café Anglais* ● 46. When that establishment closed in 1913, its wine cellar was transferred to the *Tour d'Argent* on Quai de la

"In the bookstalls along the quais you could sometimes find American books that had just been published for sale very cheap. The *Tour d'Argent* restaurant had a few rooms above the restaurant that they rented in those days, giving the people who lived there a discount in the restaurant, and if the people who lived there left any books behind there was a bookstall not far along the quai where the *valet de chambre* sold them and you could buy them from the proprietress for a very few francs."

Ernest Hemingway
A Moveable Feast

"July 4, 1942. Spent the evening at the *Tour d'Argent* ... from where there is a view of the Seine and its islands as if from the dining compartment of an aeroplane .... One has the impression that the guests eating their sole and duck can, with a certain amount of diabolical satisfaction, look down on the grey sea of roofs under which the poor eke out a living. At times like these, eating, eating well and abundantly, gives one a feeling of power."

Ernst Jünger
Journal

When the red and blue flag emblazoned with a tower flies over the restaurant, it means that Claude Terrail is in residence.

THE WINE CELLAR IN THE CAFÉ ANGLAIS
In 1912, André Terrail transferred the *Café Anglais* wine cellar to the *Tour d'Argent* (he was married to Augusta, the daughter of the owner of the *Café Anglais*). Whenever her praises were being sung, he liked to add, with a knowing smile, "And what a wine cellar!"

Tournelle, but André Terrail was conscripted the following year and his restaurant had to close. He was wounded and taken prisoner, but managed to escape and return to Paris. In 1916, with a carnation fastened in his buttonhole, he was once again graciously welcoming members of high society to his restaurant.

SIXTH FLOOR, SEVENTH HEAVEN. A rooftop terrace was added in 1937 for eating *au plein air* in fine weather. It has a quite magnificent view out over the Seine ● *81*. However, the unpredictability of the Parisian climate obliged André Terrail to cover it over, although the restaurant remained on the sixth floor, where the kitchens were also moved a year later. A concealed bell in the lift tells the staff that the boss is on his way. The entrance is now at No. 17, and there is a small museum on the ground floor. Of particular interest is the table brought from the *Café Anglais* where, on June 7, 1867, three emperors, William I of Hohenzollern, Bismarck and Tsar Alexander II and his wife, had dinner after attending the première of Offenbach's *La Grande-Duchesse de Gérolstein*. Claude Terrail's son, André, who inherited the old man's carnation, had large bay windows added by way of enhancing the dining-room's charm. There is ample visual gratification, but it is the perfection of the cooking and the service that make the *Tour d'Argent* one of the wonders of the world.

L'INSTITUT DU MONDE ARABE ◆ *378*

INSTITUT DU MONDE ARABE
This cultural center for Arab countries opened in 1987. It contains meeting rooms, a library, a documentation center, a shop, exhibition rooms and a restaurant.

A terrace facing Notre-Dame. A ninth-floor dining-room giving on to a terrace and facing the Seine and Notre-Dame clearly represented stiff competition for Claude Terrail and his *Tour d'Argent* ▲ *147–8*. However, any comparison between the restaurant on Rue de la Tournelle and the *Institut du Monde arabe* stops there. This restaurant on Quai Saint-Bernard is made of glass and steel and was designed by Jean Nouvel. Since 1992, it has been managed by Fakr el Dinh, owner of a chain of Lebanese restaurants. He removed Philippe Starck's furniture (not always safe to use, it has to be said) and refurnished the dining-room in Louis XVI style. The Seine and Notre-Dame, however, are still there.

L'AUBERGE DES DEUX SIGNES ◆ *374*

COAL AND A FLASH OF LIGHTNING. Rue Galande marks the beginning of the old Roman road that led back to Rome via Lyons, and it was this route that Georges Dhulster, a young charcoal deliveryman, took in 1930 to woo the daughter of a local innkeeper-charcoal seller. Love at first sight gave way to a flash of lightning that destroyed the inn, and the ageing proprietors sold the charred furniture to their son-in-law.

Metal moucharabieh panels cover the south façade of the *Institut du Monde arabe*. The tiny openings change shape according to the light, like the diaphragms of a camera.

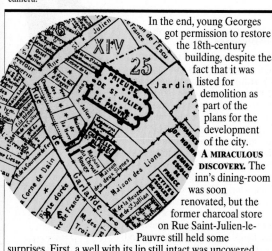

In the end, young Georges got permission to restore the 18th-century building, despite the fact that it was listed for demolition as part of the plans for the development of the city. **A MIRACULOUS DISCOVERY.** The inn's dining-room was soon renovated, but the former charcoal store on Rue Saint-Julien-le-Pauvre still held some surprises. First, a well with its lip still intact was uncovered, and water could be seen about 150 feet below. That was just the beginning. A chance blow with an axe then revealed the Gothic window of the former Chapelle Saint-Blaise, which had been destroyed around 1770. The chapel dated from the 15th century and was attached to the 12th-century church of Saint-Julien-le-Pauvre. The window has now been incorporated into the main wall of the inn, and the wine cellars, which contain the vaulted storerooms of the former priory, have been turned into a dining-room. A final curiosity is the spiral staircase leading to the owner's private apartments, which was hewn from a single block of stone. In these medieval surroundings, Georges Dhulster's cuisine is characterized by what might be termed a "classical revival," so that past and present are united in one of the most picturesque settings of any restaurant in Paris.

BERTY'S MAP OF PARIS, 1770
The map, reproduced on the menu, shows that there was once a *Maison des deux Signes* (House of Two Signs) on the spot where the restaurant now stands, although the origin of the name is unknown. Georges Dhulster chose two swans (*deux cygnes*) as the punning motif of his restaurant.

SAINT-BLAISE
The saint to whom the chapel adjoining the restaurant is dedicated was the Bishop of Samaria, in Armenia. He was martyred in 316. He is the patron saint of carders, his executioners having reputedly hacked him to death with iron doffing knives.

LE BALZAR ● *49* ◆ *375*

FROM AMÉDÉE OVER TO MARCELLIN.
On arriving in Paris from his native Picardy in the closing years of the 19th century, Amédée Balzar first worked for his brother, who ran the *Taverne des Escholiers* in Rue Soufflot. That was before he decided to recreate the formula in Rue des Écoles, running it as his own establishment. Amédée is remembered as a short, stocky character, with a jet-black beard, though he was going bald, and he always welcomed guests with a broad smile and a glass of beer in his hand. Predictably, students and teachers were enthusiastic customers. However, the post-war period was disastrous for him as it was for others, and there was a long succession of proprietors until Marcellin Cazes, the jovial owner of *Lipp* ▲ *129*, decided to restore the place to its former glory. For this he called on Madeline, the interior designer who had enlarged *Lipp*.

SIMILARITIES
This brasserie sign demonstrates the close links between *Lipp* and *Balzar*. It has the same foaming tankard of beer in a circle surrounded by the same red neon lights bearing the establishment's name.

❝There were just two waiters, Marius, whose tables were to the right of the door, and Alexandre, whose were to the left .... Either Balzar or a buxom cashier sat at the cash register, and

Madeline introduced imitation leather sofas, tables covered in white cloths, bistro chairs, and lights that were reflected in large, slightly distorting mirrors in such a way that they bent the perspective. No concessions were made to Art Deco, which was enormously popular at the time. *Balzar* reopened its doors in November 1931, with Clémence Cazes at the helm, while Marcellin took charge of *Lipp*. Clémence's son Roger was meanwhile making his debut in the *Balzar* dining-room.

A SECOND LIPP? The Cazes sold the restaurant in 1961, and in 1979 Jean-Claude Marolleau, following in his parents' footsteps, installed angled mirrors on the ceiling, which enabled him to watch discreetly what was going on in the brasserie. Since 1987 Jean-Pierre and Michèle Egurreguy, who were already managing the *Vagenende* ▲ *130* on Boulevard Saint-Germain, have maintained Amédée and Marcellin's traditions with a somber décor and traditional brasserie dishes. After Roger Cazes left, some of his loyal devotees still came to the *Balzar* in search of the special atmosphere that they thought was now fading at *Lipp*. Marcellin's wish had always been to make the *Balzar* a second *Lipp*. What he did not foresee was that one day *Lipp* would become a second *Balzar*.

to one side stood the local 'soak', a young man with biceps almost as beautiful as his boss's, who poured himself halves until two in the morning.❞
René Martal, 1931

RESTAURANT POLIDOR
SERVICE À PRIX FIXE
Cuisine très Soignée | 41, Rue Monsieur-le-Prince -- PARIS (6e)

POLIDOR ◆ 379

BUTTER, EGGS AND CHEESE. *Polidor* stands in Rue Monsieur-le-Prince but would Monsieur le Prince have chosen to dine at *Polidor*? If he liked purée of black pudding and a *blanquette* of veal or *boeuf bourguignon*, and enjoyed good company, good humor and the simple things in life, he most certainly would have. He would also have been pleased to know that Maurice Barrès, Paul Léautaud and Max Ernst would come here one day, and that the restaurant would never really grow old. The street was named after the Prince de Condé, who owned a house close to this road, which skirted Phillip II's ramparts and the ditches of Charles V's wall. The *Crèmerie Restaurant Polidor* did not open until the 19th century. The food was simple, consisting mainly of things like butter, eggs and cheese, which could be bought in the shop. They were mainly consumed in the morning by women customers.

A BOHEMIAN CLIENTELE. When in 1890 the *Polidor* ceased to be a café and became a proper restaurant, it went on to feed generations of poverty-stricken students and artists, before switching to a more snobbish bohemian clientele and tourists seeking the "authentic" Bohemian experience. *Polidor*'s many famous customers have ranged from Verlaine to Joyce, and from Valéry to Hemingway. In 1948 Alfred Jarry's "College of Pataphysics" began to hold its "scientific dinners" there, although the shepherd's pie was at several removes from the "imaginary solution" of which pataphysics claimed to be the science. Boris Vian (pictured above right) was promoted to the rank of "Transcendant Satrap" in 1953. Even today customers sit very close to one another while they eat. In an area infested with restaurants of the worst type, *Polidor* is a veritable jewel.

THE POLIDOR RESTAURANT AT THE FRENCH ACADEMY Writer Pierre Benoit referred to the *Polidor* restaurant in his speech of acceptance.

❝November 21, 1941: had lunch with Marie Dormoy in an excellent restaurant: *Polidor* in Rue Monsieur-le-Prince. I am sure we shall carry on going there.❞
Paul Léautaud,
Le Journal littéraire

A GOOD PRESS
This restaurant is the "local" used by the staff of the *Guide du Routard*, whose offices are nearby. The gentleman on the menu (monocle and big cigar, wearing top hat and frock coat, and sipping a glass of champagne while waiting for his table) has not exactly left his rucksack at the door.

PERRAUDIN ◆ 379

AN OLD COAL STORE. It may be hard to believe, but *Perraudin*, from its foundations, furniture, the restaurant front and the windows, is almost wholly constructed of extremely old wood. This, the old *Via Superior* that led to Orléans, is one of the oldest streets in Paris, and it derived its later name, Rue Saint-Jacques, from its proximity to the Jacobin convent. Perraudin himself sold coal in the street during the second half of the 19th century. The coal dust made everyone thirsty, and he went into the trade so beloved of coalmen – selling red wine by the glass. In the years leading up to World

War One, the sale of coal gradually tailed off, and the place became a simple, local restaurant. Over four generations altogether, the Perraudins have tirelessly served students and teachers from the Sorbonne, as well as tourists (it is in all the guidebooks), dishing out the same *boeuf bourguignon* and *andouillette* with the same tablecloths in the same burnished décor. And there hasn't

been a single complaint!

Toward the end of the 19th century, Paul Arène's club for Frenchmen from the south of France then Frédéric Mistral's provençal writers would meet in the *Café Voltaire*, Place de l'Odéon. Fifty years on, they would undoubtedly have chosen the *Méditerranée*.

LA MÉDITERRANÉE ◆ 378

PLACE DE L'ODÉON. The story of this famous restaurant in the Place de l'Odéon, like much of the business in this district past and present, owes much to the proximity of the *Théâtre de France*. It was built between 1779 and 1782, in what had been the gardens of the Hôtel de Condé, in the hope of attracting customers from the *Comédie-Française* which had temporarily settled in the Tuileries. After the theater was closed down during the Reign of Terror (1793) for offering

> **"THANKS TO THE LA MÉDITERRANÉE, THE SEA LAPS THE PLACE DE L'ODÉON WHERE IT SCATTERS FRUIT AND FLOWERS. BUT THEY DO NOT WITHER AWAY AS THEY DO ON THE SAND; THEY COME BACK TO LIFE AND ARE EATEN IN THE SUNSHINE."**
> JEAN COCTEAU

shelter to Monarchist actors, it was occupied in 1797 by Mlle Montansier's company, which named it the *Odéon*. It was burnt down in 1799, rebuilt in 1808, and burnt down again in 1818, and from 1819 operated as a second *Théâtre-Français*. The first restaurant to make an impact in the area was the *Café Voltaire* ● 47; it was built at the same time as the square and, from the 1880's onward, was to be a well-known political and literary meeting-place. It was frequented not only by Gambetta and Vallès but also by the likes of Gauguin and Mallarmé. The *Café Voltaire* was the first non-smoking restaurant in Paris, and its reputation continued until the 1950's.

PICASSO AND COCTEAU. Around 1930, a certain M. Pêche from the south of France opened the *Méditerranée* on the other side of Rue de l'Odéon, specializing in the sale of stuffed mussels and *bouillabaisse*. It attracted many lovers of seafood, Picasso and Cocteau ▲ *201* among them. Marcel Vertès and Christian Bérard painted the frescoes that were partly responsible for giving the restaurant the reputation it still enjoys. Works donated by artists by way of payment of their bills include a cat (appropriate in a fish restaurant!), painted by Balthus.

Americans in Paris tend to follow the artists' trail, and Charlie Chaplin and Orson Welles (who always ordered for two) are well remembered. The dining-room has been faithfully looked after by Yves Moutier, and the covered terrace gives onto one of the loveliest squares in Paris.

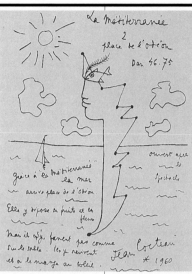

THE MÉDITERRANÉE MENU
It features a drawing and text (above) by Jean Cocteau dated 1960.

LA BÛCHERIE

◆ *375*

PORT-AUX-BUCHES. Wood for construction and heating once came to Paris by river. Until the 16th century, the *port-aux-bûches*, the port where this wood was unloaded, was on the left bank at the bottom of the 13th-century Rue de la Bûcherie, and was later moved to Louviers island. For many years, the building that now houses Bernard Bosque's restaurant, stood close to the sinister Petit Châtelet. Before it was pulled down in the 18th century, it defended access to the city at Petit-Pont and was an annexe of the Grand Châtelet prison. The restaurant now has a view overlooking Notre-Dame.

VOLTI'S STATUE
A statue by sculptor Volti of a generously endowed young lady welcomes customers to the *Bûcherie* from her place over the vast fireplace.

RUE DE LA BÛCHERIE
The façade of a restaurant can be made out in this early 20th-century photograph.

The main dining-room at the *Bûcherie*.

MODERN ART AND CLASSIC CUISINE. It is a matter of consummate pleasure to have either lunch or dinner in one of the *Bûcherie* restaurant's huge bay windows. First, while the table is being made ready, there is time for drinks by the fireplace, which is where the *Bûcherie*'s cat and dog sprawl out between sittings. Then, if one has not had the good fortune to be seated near the front of the building, there is the warmth of the wood-paneling, the rare sight of a Lurçat tapestry, and a few well-executed contemporary paintings to compensate. Either way, there is an opportunity to relish the strict classicism of Bernard Bosque cooking.

LE BISTRO DE LA GARE   ● 75 ◆ 375

ART NOUVEAU MOTIFS Plants, flowers and the female form were the principal decorative motifs used in Art Nouveau. The *bouillon Chartier*, later to be named the *Bistro de la Gare*, was no exception. The young woman in bronze (right) holds up a light that illuminates the dining-room.

Bistro de la Gare's Art Nouveau exterior.

THE MONTPARNASSE CHARTIER. In 1903, Édouard and Camille Chartier ▲ 262 bought the restaurant at 59 Boulevard Montparnasse with a view to making it part of their chain of *bouillons* ● 46. This came about three years later after major alterations and building work had been carried out. The Chartiers characteristically served popular dishes in a splendidly, and for those days boldly, decorated room. The *Bistro de la Gare* has the same lay-out as many other *bouillons*, with an entrance area leading back to a bar, and the dining-room situated behind that. After buying the *Bistro de la Gare* in 1977, the Bistro Romain group commissioned interior designer Slavik to redo the interior and exterior glasswork and the façade. The result was a faithful imitation of Art Nouveau.

ART NOUVEAU DÉCOR. The dining-room is on two levels, divided by a carved wood balustrade that also supports lights and opalescent green shades held aloft by scantily dressed peasant girls. The walls are covered with beveled mirrors in frames that are adorned with rounded moldings, set against a background of ceramic tiles with blue trelliswork motifs intertwined with convolvulus and mulberry fronds. Rustic landscapes painted on colored glass by Louis Trézel ▲ 264 decorate the dining-room. What a crime it would be

The long dining-room in the *Bistro de la Gare*.

to hide all this Art Nouveau décor behind hat and coat stands!

FROM BOUILLON TO BISTRO. In 1924, the *bouillon Chartier* became a *bouillon Rougeot*, like *Vagenende* ▲ *130* on Boulevard Saint-Germain. In 1977, after the restaurant was bought by the Bistro Romain group, which was in process of replacing the chains of old *bouillons* with newer establishments, it was listed as a historic building.

LE DUC ◆ *377*

THE MOST BEAUTIFUL YACHT IN PARIS. There is a sense that this restaurant on Boulevard Raspail, on the corner of Rue Campagne-Première must have been washed up by some freak wave. Outside, the façade is eggshell-white and the rounded window frames remind one of portholes; inside, the warmth and glow of wood and copper suggest the opulence of a *de luxe* cabin. The *Duc* is the most beautiful yacht in Paris. It has occupied its present site since the 1950's and is a favorite haunt of fish lovers. Paul Minchelli, who has run the restaurant on his own since the death of his brother Jean, concentrates on fresh ingredients, which he cooks lightly and very skilfully to bring out the natural flavors. A few dishes from the Seychelles give an exotic touch to a cuisine in which only the freshest produce is used. Dishes are therefore subject to seasonal availability.

A DEGREE OF SOBRIETY. It is important to stress that the grilled red mullet, baked bream and lobster are cooked with great simplicity and sobriety. The menu also informs customers that the sea urchin come from Brittany and the oysters are from the Ile de Ré – always a good thing to know. This strong point is sufficiently rare today to make it worth stressing.

MEMORIES OF SEA JOURNEYS
Customers are seated in what appear to be gangways and cabins, and eat to the sound of breakers. Even the floor seems to rock gently from side to side.

In his *Histoire et Géographie gourmandes de Paris* (1956), René Héron de Villefosse describes *La Coupole* as a "well-heated railway waiting-room with a good feel to it." He says it has become "a Parisian monument that is as solid as the 'Colonne de Juillet'. It is the very center of Montparnasse," he goes on, "and all around, less prestigious restaurants go about their business without any sense of rivalry or competition."

THE PAINTERS OF THE PILLARS
Their names were Chantal Queneville, Guillaume Guindet, Isaac Grünewald, Auguste Clergé, Pierre Girieud, Pierre Dubreuil, Jean Lombard ... A few, like Othon Friesz and Marie Vassilieff, have subsequently become well-known. Since 1988 work by painter and restaurateur Michel Bourdon has covered the only pillar not to have been decorated.

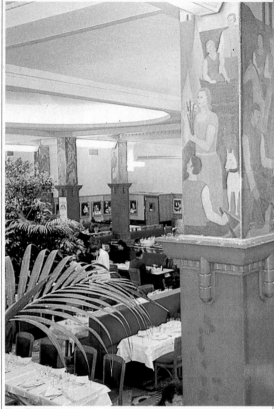

LA COUPOLE
● *49, 76, 80* ◆ *376*

THE MONTPARNOS. In 1923, the area around the crossroads formed by the boulevards Montparnasse and Raspail had a Bohemian atmosphere that drew artists who had moved down from Montmartre at the beginning of the century and never returned. First, the *Select* opened its doors, and Michel-Georges Michel published *Les Montparnos* with a reproduction of a gouache by Picasso on the cover. Then in 1923 Ernest Fraux and René Lafon, business partners related by marriage, took over as managers of the *Dôme,* with an option to buy. Three years later, the owner withdrew his offer, and Ernest and René found themselves out on the pavement but with ample compensation jingling in their pockets. Then, just across the road from the *Select*, they saw something they had somehow never noticed before: the Juglar wood and coal store with over 900 square yards of prime land. They promptly obtained a 20-year lease, an option to buy and, most important of all, permission to build.

THE LARGEST DINING-ROOM IN PARIS.
The idea of building several restaurants (those were the days of small, smoky rooms) was

replaced by a plan to construct a single, large establishment, the biggest in Paris. Architects Barillet and Le Bouc joined forces on the building work, while competitors sniggered from the sidelines. The presence of galleries in the basement meant that the foundations had to be strengthened, and twenty-four pillars projecting into the dining-room were inserted. Their dream of a vast open space had come to nothing, but what Ernest and René did not know was that the pillars would one day make the restaurant famous. Responsibility for the interior decoration was entrusted to the highly respected Alphonse-Louis Solvet and his son Paul, who had just completed work on the *Closerie des Lilas* ▲ *159*; they endowed the furniture, chandeliers, mosaics and the table service with a neo-classical stamp that had been so fashionable since the Paris Exhibition of the Decorative Arts in 1925. The pillars were clad in lap, a highly resistant, synthetic material that could be tinted; in this case it was green. The pillars were also corbeled about 12 feet above the ground so as to break the vertical

"Any obscure poet or painter hoping to succeed in Bucharest or Seville must, given what the Old Continent is like these days, first do a little military service at the *Rotonde* or the *Coupole*, both of them pavement schools which teach Bohemian life, distrust of the middle classes, humor and getting very drunk. The war did serious harm to Montparnasse, but soon taxis were driving up and down Rue Delambre, Rue Vavin and Rue Campagne-Première all night long, transporting long-haired versifiers, Chileans in sweaters painting with snail forks, black intellectuals, Abyssinian philosophers, and Russian refugees expert in the art of inventing soporifics, lotteries and fashion houses."
Léon-Paul Fargue,
Le Piéton de Paris

A DAY AT LA COUPOLE
Breakfast on the terrace as soon as it opens, cocktails in the bar from 11 o'clock onward, lunch in the brasserie near the

bar, dinner in the main dining-room, evening in the basement discotheque.

MONTPARNASSE IN THE 1920'S
The farms, stables and coach-houses of this once-rural district have now become

bars, dance halls and restaurants. And as soon as stables come on the market, they are turned into artists' studios. Van Dongen (above), author of *Montparno's blues*, was one of the first to move in.

lines. Round about this time, a Montparnasse painter friend of Ernest and René suggested that local artists would be attracted to the restaurant if the upper part of the pillars was decorated. He was there and then given the task of finding thirty-two artists to do the thirty-two paintings. And that is how the pillars that hold up the bar came to be painted ... by artists who normally held up the bar themselves.

HOW ABOUT LA COUPOLE? The restaurant was about to open. All it needed was a name. There was already a *Dôme* and a *Rotonde* nearby, so why not *La Coupole*? It was a brilliant idea, even though there was no sign of any cupola on the roof. The restaurant opened on December 20, 1927, and 1,200 bottles of Mumm champagne were not enough to satisfy the thirst of the 2,500 guests. They had to send out for more in the middle of the night. *La Coupole* became an institution overnight, and its competitors were already looking worried. The *La Pergola* restaurant opened on the terrace in the spring of 1928, and by the end of the year there was also dancing in the basement. The Parisian climate forced the *Pergola* to be covered over in 1931, and the builders took the opportunity to add a real cupola. It was made of a mosaic of stone tiles and was visible from the upstairs dining-room through an opening made in the ceiling. It was supremely successful. *Montparnos* like Kisling, Soutine, Foujita and Léger now mingled with English-speaking artists and writers such as Miller, Rhys, Hemingway and Pound. Louis Aragon even met Else Triolet in the bar of the *Coupole*. As they used to say between the two World Wars, "Governments are made at *Lipp* ▲ *129*, but they fall at *La Coupole*."

A COMEBACK. *La Coupole* suffered badly during the Occupation, and had to wait until the 1950's for intellectuals and artists, and later the liberal professions, to return. Ernest Fraux departed in 1960 and René Lafon continued to manage the establishment, but he was by now getting old and losing enthusiasm for the place. In 1985 *La Coupole* was put up for sale. It was bought by a property developer who had plans to turn it into profitable housing, but his schemes did not come off. Offices were eventually built on top, the building having been listed as a historic monument in 1981. The Flo group ▲ *259* took over responsibility for managing the concern and, in December 1988, after eight months of renovation work, *La Coupole* reopened its doors. "My *Coupole* has been stolen!" cried the writer Philippe Sollers, but others soon realized that the original decoration, which had fallen into disrepair, had been reproduced. True, the Bohemian feel had evaporated, but the restaurant was still full of nostalgia and it had at least been rescued from oblivion.

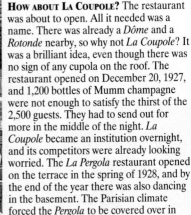

gran sala

LA CLOSERIE DES LILAS ● 49, 79, 80, 95 ◆ 376

LILAC TIME. At the beginning of the 19th century, the further extremity of Avenue de l'Observatoire was still in the country, and the area could boast only a handful of small bars frequented by students. In 1847, a gentleman by the name of Bullier, a lamp-trimmer at the *Grande-Chaumière*, an immensely fashionable establishment during the Restoration (1814-30), bought one of these bars, the *Chartreuse* dance hall. It was situated not far from where Marshal Ney had been executed in 1815, and on the site of what is now the Jean Sarrailh university center. Bullier transformed it into a palace of the One Thousand and One Nights with shrubbery, fountains and flowerbeds, and he planted rows of lilac bushes. Dancers such as Marie la Gouape, Clémentine Pomponette and even Pauline la Folle performed at *La Closerie des Lilas* (Lilac Garden), and Théophile Gauthier, Théodore de Banville, Émile Zola, Paul Cézanne and the Goncourt brothers were among those who flocked to this den of iniquity.

THE CLOSERIE CROSSES THE BOULEVARD. In the meantime, Marshal Ney had been rehabilitated and, in 1853, his statue

MICHEL NEY
Marshal of the Empire and dubbed "bravest of the brave", Ney was among those who urged Napoleon to abdicate. He was made a peer by the Bourbons but rallied

by Francis Rude, an artist better known for his *Marseillaise* at the Arc de Triomphe, was erected on the spot where he had been executed. *La Closerie des Lilas* became the *Closerie-Bullier*, and then the *Bullier* dance hall. In 1895, the extension of the Sceaux railway line meant that Ney's statue had to be moved, and it was taken to the other side of the boulevard on the

corner of Boulevard Montparnasse and placed outside a coaching inn serving the Paris-Orléans route. The *Bullier* dance hall continued to be popular (it did not close until 1932) and Jean Richepin and Raoul Ponchont persuaded the owners of the coal store to switch to a new business and revive

to Napoleon's side during the Hundred Days. On December 6, 1815 the Chamber of Peers condemned Ney to death.

THE BULLIER DANCE HALL
Thursday evenings were given over to students with long hair and flowing cravats. They mingled

with artists and writers who already had a reputation for seeking to re-live their earlier Bohemian lives. It was also a meeting-place for disreputable members of both sexes.

the name *Closerie des Lilas*. The new establishment, with its bar of Cuban mahogany and flanked by flowering arbors, was soon luring customers away from the *Bullier* dance hall, who had by this time followed Ney from the other side of the road. Life was rarely uneventful at the *Closerie*. One day, Alfred Jarry, another regular customer, interrupted a turbulent discussion by firing blanks from his revolver. When an indignant lady pointed out that there were children in the room, he replied, "Don't worry, madam! We'll get you some more of those!" Ernest Hemingway moved here from Notre-Dame-des-Champs immediately after the war.

AT THE CENTER OF THINGS. One day in 1925 the *Closerie* was the scene of a remarkable brawl. At a banquet in honor of the Symbolist poet Saint-Pol Roux, the Surrealists decided to attack Rachilde, a woman of letters who frequently courted scandal. She had published an anti-German interview in *Paris-Soir* that the others considered to be insulting to their friend Max Ernst. The temperature rose when Robert Desnos called out, "Long live Germany!" and Michel Leiris shouted, "Down with France!" This led to blows and, with confusion mounting, the police were called. Once again, the *Closerie* had proved that it was, to say the least, at the center of things. The same year, the establishment bowed to current tastes and chose to modernize, and Alphonse-Louis and Paul Solvet, the father and son who would soon be working on the *Coupole* ▲ *156*, were asked to take charge.

> **"WHAT IS EVEN MORE REAL IN THIS WORLD AT THE OBSERVATOIRE CROSSROADS, IT SEEMS TO ME, IS THE FISHPOND AT LA CLOSERIE DES LILAS – THE PEACEFUL, MAJESTIC, UNMISTAKABLE LOBSTER..."**
>
> PHILIPPE SOLLERS

PAUL FORT
This Symbolist poet, who was elected "Prince of poets" in 1912, worked on the *Mercure de France* and edited *Vers et Prose*. He is best-known for his *Ballades françaises,* based on old French popular stories. Fort organized meetings at the *La Closerie des Lilas*.

The porch roof was replaced by two covered terraces; the one on the boulevard side housed the brasserie, while the one on the avenue side accommodated the restaurant. Basically life continued where it had left off. In 1933, Paul Fort was again presiding over his Tuesday poetry evenings that would launch the famous Battle of the Two Banks, a crusade aimed at writers of the right bank. By the time of the Liberation, the Montparnasse quarter was very run down. It was not until 1953 that the *Closerie* rediscovered its former glories and charmed a new generation of artists and writers. It was by then under the management of Jaqueline Milan, who has now been succeeded by her son Jean-Pierre. The writer Jean-Edern Hallier is one of those who re-live the restaurant's history. A hundred years of Parisian history awaits anyone today pushing open the door of the *Closerie.*

"On the corner of Boulevard Montparnasse and Avenue de l'Observatoire there is a tavern, until recently flanked by flowering arbors, called *Closerie des*

Lilas ... the customers were students, local residents, and Russian revolutionaries with conspiratorial expressions and speaking in low voices at a table pushed to one side. One of them was bald and had a Kalmuck look about him; we were struck by the sparkle in his somber face. It was Lenin.**"**

Léon Daudet,
Paris vécu

161

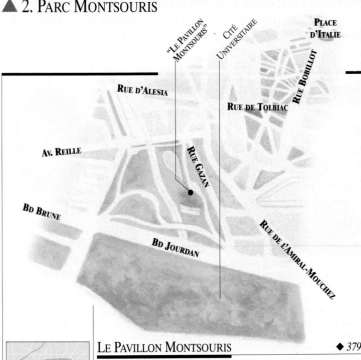

"LE PAVILLON MONTSOURIS"   CITÉ UNIVERSITAIRE   PLACE D'ITALIE

RUE D'ALESIA

RUE DE TOLBIAC

RUE BOBILLOT

AV. REILLE

RUE GAZAN

BD BRUNE

BD JOURDAN

RUE DE L'AMIRAL-MOUCHEZ

LE PAVILLON MONTSOURIS
◆ 379

A BELLE ÉPOQUE JEWEL. The Parc Montsouris and its restaurant offer the visitor an exceptional combination of park and spa in the middle of Paris – a bandstand, an artificial lake with a waterfall, and a *fin de siècle* chocolate-box pavilion. The garden, which was designed to extend between the wall of the *Fermiers généraux* and the fortified wall built (1841) beyond the *octroi d'Enfert*, was constructed by Napoleon III to designs by Jean-Charles Alphand. Together with the Bois de Boulogne, the Bois de Vincennes and the Parc des Buttes-Chaumont, which were also the work of Alphand, the Parc Montsouris was one of the "green lungs" that the Emperor wanted for Paris; the Mocque-Souris windmill is perched at the top of a small hill. The laying out of the park began in 1867, but the 40 acres were not completed until 1878. Part of the reason for this was that many buildings and a nursery of trees had to be removed, and two tracks cut, one for the Petite Ceinture, the other for the Sceaux railway lines. On the day the park was opened, the artificial lake suddenly emptied of water and it was discovered that there had been an error in its construction; the man responsible for the work was unable to live with the shame and committed suicide. The Palais du Bardo, the pavilion in the Tunisian section of the Universal Exhibition of 1867, was transferred from the Champ-de-Mars

The glass was added on to the terrace in 1930 in a manner that scrupulously respected the *Belle Époque* style of the rest of the building. The same goes for the recently constructed awning above the entrance. The turn of the century was undoubtedly the golden age of Parisian restaurants!

to the Parc Montsouris by Ferdinand de Lesseps; this Moorish building is a replica of the summer residence of the Bey of Tunis. A meteorological observatory was installed in the building in 1872. More recently it lay abandoned for many years and then was destroyed by fire in 1991. The palace had not been maintained properly, and it had also suffered from years of equivocation over what should be done with it. A sad business indeed! The Park also contains a 13-foot metal stela, built for the Paris Observatory in 1806, and one of the more agreeable garden-restaurants in Paris.

FORGETTING PARIS. The restaurant was built in 1898 and enlarged in 1912, then enlarged yet again in 1930 by the addition of a glass canopy running the length of the building. Customers in the early days included Mata Hari, Lenin and Trotsky, Braque and Foujita, Jouvet and Carné, and Sartre and de Beauvoir. In 1987, Yves Courault, former manager of the *Grand Véfour* ▲ 213, bought the restaurant, re-named it the *Jardin de la Paresse* (Garden of Idleness) and renovated it. He need not have

bothered with the name as the area was already notorious for its indolence. When the sun comes out, customers meet under the overhanging branches and, to the strains of a nearby band, enjoy the skilful cooking and the unique atmosphere – and pretend they are no longer in Paris.

"The Parc Montsouris is frequented mainly by orphan girls. They seem to have a fondness for this park, which seems to be as sad as they are ... There are also elderly people there reading old newspapers ... Most people wear black in case there is an accident. Better Safe than sorry."
Henri Calet
Le Tout sur le tout

The sculptures on the restaurant's façade show artisans at work, although Bacchus is depicted as a bishop! The craftsmen include masons, glassmakers, butchers, blacksmiths, carpenters and, of course, chefs.

LES VIEUX MÉTIERS DE FRANCE   ◆ 381

A MEDIEVAL INN. The presence of this provincial inn built in the neo-medieval style and with concrete facing – and in such a featureless road off Place d'Italie – is quite unexpected. Its name refers to the old craft trades. Michel Moisan, the proprietor, took expert advice on furnishing

the premises, and this is a key to understanding the restaurant's name and appearance.

A TEMPLE TO SKILL. The windows, which are reminiscent of those of a cathedral, and the carved wood frontage decorated with depictions of various crafts, announce that this is an extraordinary temple to knowledge. The slate floor, the false beams, the mock stone walls, the pieces of art metalwork, and the heavy tapestries that divide up the room could easily give guests the impression that they are about to share a table with a knight in armor. There is no chance of that, however. Michel Moisan's cooking is decidedly modern even if the menu is on the traditional side. The biggest problem is trying to leave the place. It feels like the Périgord, but it is in fact the 13th *arrondissement*.

LA-BUTTE-AUX-CAILLES

Boulevard Blanqui is at the northern end of a picturesque quarter of Paris marked by a maze of alleyways, courtyards and housing estates stretching as far as Rue de Tolbiac, Rue du Moulin-des-Prés and Rue Barrault. The first journey in a hot-air balloon started from here on November 21, 1783. The balloon was built by the manufacturer of Révillon wallpaper and piloted by Pilâtre de Rozier and the Marquis d'Arlandes. Although they achieved a height of almost 3,120 feet, it took them two hours to cover the 5 miles between the Château de la Muette and the Butte-aux-Cailles.

3.
TROCADÉRO,
BOIS DE BOULOGNE,
PÉREIRE

"Jean-Claude Ferrero"

"Le Vivarois"   Passy Cemetery   "Faugeron"   Palais de Chaill   "Joël R

Av. Georges-

Av. Paul-Doumer   Jardins du Trocadéro

Av. des Nations-Unies

Av. du Pt Kennedy

A private *hôtel* is to an ordinary house what a made-to-measure suit is to something hired. The *Jean-Claude Ferrero* restaurant occupies one of the many private houses in the district and provides made-to-measure cooking.

For Parisians, the very notion of "west" is not simply a compass direction. It is more a state of mind, a way of living, a kind of world of its own. The west of Paris is mainly on the right bank, not too far to the south, not too far to the north, and covers a good half of the 16th and 17th *arrondissements*. In 1800, it was still in the country, and included the villages of Auteuil, Passy and Chaillot, with their vast properties and hedge-lined roads. During the 19th century Haussmann turned it into an assortment of middle-class residential areas. They were there to stay, and it is therefore not surprising to come across restaurants catering for the kind of people who live in large private houses.

Jean-Claude Ferrero   ◆ 386

Truffles and mushrooms. A 19th-century deed states that the owner of 38 Rue Vital "must carry out graveling in Rue Vital the length of the house's façade up to the middle of the road in so far as the road is not communal property." And that indeed appears to be what he did in this tiny, quiet street in the 16th *arrondissement*, only a few steps from the humming business activity of Rue de Passy. The house at No.

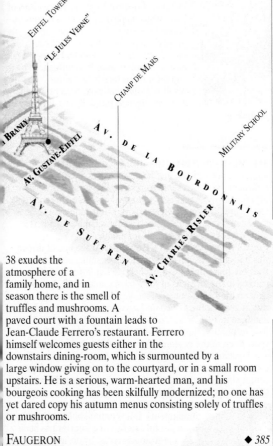

The "all truffles" meal is the surprise item on Jean-Claude Ferrero's menu.

38 exudes the atmosphere of a family home, and in season there is the smell of truffles and mushrooms. A paved court with a fountain leads to Jean-Claude Ferrero's restaurant. Ferrero himself welcomes guests either in the downstairs dining-room, which is surmounted by a large window giving on to the courtyard, or in a small room upstairs. He is a serious, warm-hearted man, and his bourgeois cooking has been skilfully modernized; no one has yet dared copy his autumn menus consisting solely of truffles or mushrooms.

FAUGERON

♦ 385

CHARM AND CIRCUMSPECTION. In the 18th century Rue de Longchamp was a cart track used mainly by farms, and by the inhabitants of Chaillot going to Longchamp Abbey. How things have changed! Today Rue de Longchamp is one of the most elegant roads in the 16th *arrondissement*, and Henri Faugeron's restaurant has no connection with farming. The décor, which is typical of the *arrondissement*, may be on the gaudy side, but the legendary charm of Faugeron's wife, who welcomes all guests in person, put the decorations completely out of one's mind. Henri Faugeron himself would win a prize for good judgment, if food guides were ever to award one.

GOOD SENSE, SKILL AND PERFECTION. Faugeron, who comes from Corrèze in southwest France, did not become a chef by chance, his grandmother, father, brother and sister all having been chefs as well. He learnt a lot with Fernande Allard ▲ 144, and still cooks in what is known as a "woman's" style. He opened his own restaurant, the *Belles Gourmandes*, in the 7th *arrondissement* and then moved to Rue de Longchamp in 1977. In 1989 he took part in preparing the great banquet served to the Heads of State of the seven leading

THE PALAIS DE CHAILLOT
Following its construction in 1937, this palace replaced much of the Palais du Trocadéro . It overlooks the gardens and the Seine and faces the Eiffel Tower. The area includes museums and a theater, and is one of the most visited parts of Paris.

ÉDOUARD NIGNON
Nignon was the author of *L'Heptaméron des gourmets ou les Délices de la table* (*Gourmets' heptameron, or Gastronomic delights*) which inspired the text that appears on the *Faugeron* menu. Born in 1865, he worked in all the great Parisian houses before taking charge of the Emperor's kitchens and then those of the Tsar. On his return to Paris in 1904, he made *Larue* the best restaurant in Place de la Madeleine.

The somewhat over-gilded décor at the *Faugeron* is typical of restaurants in the area.

industrialized countries at the Arche de la Défense. Édouard Nignon's professions of faith, which appear on his menu, sums up his own cooking: "Understand and properly appreciate the value of each ingredient" and "A chef who knows the past well understands it, is influenced by it, and must in his turn be a creator." The result is dishes that have been prepared with intelligence and skill, and are close to perfection.

JOËL ROBUCHON ◆ 386

JUDGMENT AND PERFECTION. Joël Robuchon is sound judgment personified, and he never ceases to amaze his many followers. His impeccable cooking, which he seems to carry off effortlessly, is regularly remarked upon, and his creations can be breathtaking. Often exploring untrodden paths, he is rarely imitated, and the price his admirers have to pay is a wait of weeks or even months for a table.

FROM POITIERS TO AVENUE POINCARÉ. At the age of fifteen this fine chef gave up all thought of becoming an architect to start his apprenticeship as a chef. He left Poitiers in 1963 and worked in the kitchens of the *Berkeley*, and by 1970, he was a chef on the Île-de-France. Four years later he was in charge of the kitchens at the *Concorde-Lafayette* hotel at Porte Maillot, and then in 1978 at the *Nikko* hotel. In 1981, he opened his own restaurant, the *Jamin*, in Rue de Longchamp. Thirteen years later, at the beginning of 1994, Robuchon moved just a short distance away, to 59 Avenue Raymond-Poincaré. The private hotel set up there was built in the early part of this century by the architect Charles Letrône. Its façade, with sculptures by Camille Garnier, and its wrought-iron Art Nouveau staircase, are themselves historic monuments. If it is unthinkable to alter the beautiful exterior, the interior has been meticulously recast by designers Christian Ferré and Alberto Bali, under the careful guidance of Joël Robuchon, who wants to return a sense of their former style to all the rooms, from the *salons* at street level, to the dining rooms on the floor above, and to the kitchens, modernized to perfection by the chef.

MULTIPLE STYLES
On the second floor, the dining-room merges Renaissance, Louis XV and Dutch styles. Mahogany paneling and original trompe l'œil bookcases by Alberto Bali surround a large neo-Gothic-style fireplace, also in wood, carved with motifs. There is Art Nouveau-style glass by Gallé, Daum and Legras, hanging lamps by the Muller brothers and furniture by Majorelle.

THE LAST WORD IN COOKING. With Joël Robuchon nothing is left to chance. The kitchen squad's moves are measured to the inch and timed to a fraction of a second. Every new dish (and there are plenty) is tried out again and again from concept to presentation, long before it appears on the menu. When the dish eventually arrives, even the minutest detail has been checked by the chef; his peerless stewed *tête de veau* and its no less wondrous *purée* may be the most "working class" of his creations, but it is certainly not short of sophistication. As for the clientèle, it would be easier to count the famous names who have not dined here than of those who have. However, Joël Robuchon is not the kind of "media chef" who spends more time in front of cameras than in the kitchen. He is neither seen nor heard, but his presence is felt everywhere.

LE JULES VERNE ◆ 386

CHILDLIKE PLEASURES. In all of Paris this is unquestionably the most beautiful restaurant with a view. Sit at a table at the *Jules Verne*, over 400 feet above the ground, and Paris simply seems to stretch out beneath one's feet, one of the most extraordinary experiences ever. Thank you, Gustave Eiffel, for toasting the triumphs of industrialization at the Universal Exhibition of 1889, and building a tower that serves no purpose whatsoever except to feed childlike pleasures. The Eiffel Tower is like some gigantic Meccano model made for Gargantua's son. It consists of girders weighing over 7,700 tons and has come within a hair's breadth of being knocked down. It was intended only to be a temporary edifice but in 1910, the date fixed for its demolition, it was saved by advances being made by wireless telegraphy, which needed a raised structure. In 1920, it was coveted by the construction industry for its iron, and on this occasion survived thanks to developments in radio communications. In 1957 French television installed aerials, and in 1964 the Eiffel Tower was listed as an historic monument.

VIEW AND SERVICE INCLUDED. The *Jules Verne* restaurant, which opened in 1983, is on the second tier on a 600-square-foot platform set between the pulleys and wheels that operate the lifts. Slavik, the interior designer, faced with the problem of decorating a place whose main attraction was outside, came up with a black and grey non-décor that does not draw attention away from the view over Paris. Walls of grey laminated wood, a black ceiling and a dark carpet allow the eye to wander through the glass ogives of the façade and the glass pyramids of the ceiling. Such is the restaurant's popularity with tourists and French visitors from the provinces that tables have to be reserved well in advance. The *Jules Verne*'s simple cooking does not disappoint. Try the mouthwatering menu of Arc de Triomphe, Sacré-Coeur, Saint-Louis des Invalides, Grand Palais, Notre-Dame ... coffee and bill.

JULES VERNE
Nobody embodied the spirit that imbued the building of the Eiffel Tower better than the celebrated French writer of science fiction and adventure stories. After *Around the World in Eighty Days*, he might have considered the possibility of *Around*

Paris in Twenty-six Months, the time taken to build the Tower. By 1889, the year the Eiffel Tower was completed, Verne had published most of his works. The story of his "extraordinary journeys" could have been the subject of the entire Universal Exhibition.

▲ 3. Trocadéro, bois de Boulogne, Péreire

Square Lamartine

The charming Square Lamartine is not far from the *Vivarois*, between Avenue Victor-Hugo and Avenue Henri-Martin. It was built in 1863, and is where the Passy artesian well was dug between 1855 and

1866 to supply water for the numerous lakes and streams in the Bois de Boulogne, then under construction, and to irrigate various clumps of trees. The temperature of the water, which smells strongly of hydrogen sulphide, is 60° Fahrenheit; the underground water table, over 190 feet down, is the same as the Grenelle water table in the 15th *arrondissement*.

The Ardèche

"Vivarais" or "Vivarois" is the name of the old province now in the *département* of the Ardèche, Claude Peyrot's homeland. The Ardèche forms one of the southern-most borders of the Massif Central between Velay, Cévennes and Rhône.

Le Vivarois

◆ 390

Peyrot and Lacan. The picture of a couch next to a Knoll chair just about sums up the strange relationship between restaurateur Claude Peyrot and the famous psychoanalyst Jacques Lacan, his friend and frequent guest. Claude Peyrot, chef at the *Vivarois* and a man with a reputation for total loyalty and discretion, is certainly not going to tell us. Some describe Peyrot as moody, unpredictable and a perpetual worrier. Others, and they are in the majority, claim that he is one of the best, if not the very best, of men. With his clear gaze and his resemblance to Pierrot lunaire, Claude Peyrot is both a loner and an inimitable chef, although that has not stopped competitors from trying to copy him. Indeed, since the menu at the *Vivarois* has hardly changed since the restaurant opened on Avenue Victor-Hugo in 1966, his rivals have had plenty of time to absorb his ideas. His cooking is the fruit of much research and inventiveness matched with Peyrot's ideas and unparalleled skills. The results are as surprising as they are obvious, but that is what genius is all about.

Knoll, cherrywood and marble. 1960's design has proved less enduring than good cooking, and has not really come back into fashion, although it will undoubtedly do so in time. The *Vivarois*'s décor has often been criticized for being dated, and, after a period of Knoll furniture with its clean lines marrying functionalism and aestheticism against a background of white walls, the restaurant was finally "warmed up" in 1981. Carved cherrywood and grey marble were used to decorate the large, well-lit dining-room, on the first floor of this modern block in a quiet 16th *arrondissement* avenue; then in 1992 the contemporary paintings that adorned the paneling were replaced by tapestries with brightly colored geometrical motifs. There is altogether an air of softness, tranquility and, if the cooking is to be included, serenity. As for the atmosphere, the *Vivarois* is the least typical of 16th *arrondissement* restaurants, and it is unlikely that anyone will complain about that.

170

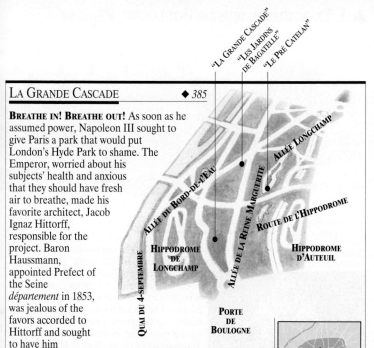

"LA GRANDE CASCADE"
"LES JARDINS DE BAGATELLE"
"LE PRÉ CATELAN"

ALLÉE LONGCOURSE

ALLÉE DU BORD-DE-L'EAU

ALLÉE DE LA REINE MARGUERITE

ROUTE DE L'HIPPODROME

QUAI DU 4-SEPTEMBRE

HIPPODROME DE LONGCHAMP

HIPPODROME D'AUTEUIL

PORTE DE BOULOGNE

BREATHE IN! BREATHE OUT! As soon as he assumed power, Napoleon III sought to give Paris a park that would put London's Hyde Park to shame. The Emperor, worried about his subjects' health and anxious that they should have fresh air to breathe, made his favorite architect, Jacob Ignaz Hittorff, responsible for the project. Baron Haussmann, appointed Prefect of the Seine *département* in 1853, was jealous of the favors accorded to Hittorff and sought to have him dismissed. However, it was Jean-Charles Alphand, appointed to administer the capital's public promenades in 1854, and Gabriel Davioud, who had designed the *Théâtre du Châtelet* and the Saint-Michel fountain, who were responsible for the Bois de Boulogne as we know it today. The whole park abounds with winding avenues, pretty pathways, kiosks and little huts, lakes with artificial islands, rockeries, grottoes and, of course, waterfalls. The biggest of these waterfalls, over 30 feet wide and some 45 feet high, was called "La Grande Cascade" so, when a restaurant opened in 1900 in Napoleon III's pavilion opposite the Universal Exhibition, it had a ready-made name. Over the years, many vendors have established themselves at the *Grande Cascade* ● 48.

BELLE ÉPOQUE ATMOSPHERE. In 1988 André Menut and his son Georges, with whom he managed the establishment, decided to restore a *Belle Époque* atmosphere to *La Grande Cascade,* as the old pavilion had undergone many changes in its lifetime. The stairwell, which had been the axis of all communications, was removed, and a bar was built where it had once stood, and a ceiling decorated with blue mirrors suggesting the nearby waterfall was added. The floor was paved in the style of a Florentine palace, but the ceiling decoration in the Napoleon III room proved impossible to restore and was replaced. Lastly, the corner stones and cornices were regilded, and the crystal chandeliers, the windows and the glass porch were all restored. *La Grande Cascade* was reborn. The cooking is less rococo than the décor, and combines seriousness and elements of serene classicism. The customers are mostly lovers and businessmen who like a touch of greenery.

TWO RACECOURSES *La Grande Cascade* lies between two racecourses, Longchamp and Auteuil, and has therefore always been popular with race-goers.

The monumental bronze gates at the main entrance to the Bagatelle garden (below).

Les Jardins de Bagatelle ◆ 386

A LOVERS' PAVILION. This building has an unusually long history. The "*bagatelle*" itself was a "little house" that the elderly Maréchal d'Estrées, Marquis of Coeuvres, had built for his young wife not far from the Château de Madrid. Soon afterward he turned it into a pavilion for amorous assignations. Louis XV was a regular visitor and, as the Marquis of Argenson wrote, "One dines at Madrid with Mademoiselle, one takes supper at the Muette, in the afternoon one goes to Bagatelle, the home of the Maréchal d'Estrée's lady, where one passes the time most pleasantly, even making love if one wishes. Everything is extremely well regulated." When the Marquis of Mauconseil succeeded the Maréchal in 1745, Louis XV continued to come, but in 1775 the building was bought by the Count of Artois, Louis XVI's brother, who razed the "little house" to the ground and bet Marie-Antoinette 100,000 *livres* that he would build a castle there in under sixty-four days. Nine hundred

THE ORIGINS OF THE BOIS DE BOULOGNE
The Bois de Boulogne is a vestige of the Forest of Rouvray, which until the modern period covered the entire area to the west of Paris. In 1308 Phillip the Fair had a chapel built there to commemorate a pilgrimage he had just made to Notre-Dame-de-Boulogne-sur-Mer. This was to become Notre-Dame-de-Boulogne-sur-Seine.

workmen toiled day and night, and the Count won his bet, but he had to spend 1,200,000 *livres* instead of the 600,000 he had budgeted for. The castle, which was constructed on plans by François-Alexandre Bélanger, is magnificent. It was also notorious for the debauchery that took place there: some of the bedrooms had erotic paintings on the walls and the floors were covered with mirrors, and it was said that the women had to "turn their dresses into trousers"! The grounds were designed by the English landscape gardener Thomas Blaikie.

A ROSE-GARDEN-CUM-ORANGERY. The Count of Artois's folly was spared during the Revolution, and from 1797 onward it was a restaurant until it reverted to its owner during the Restoration. Lord Seymour, Earl of Hertford and a close

friend of the future Napoleon III, bought the property in 1835, redesigned the gardens, and built the orangery, stables and outhouses. His adopted, and probably natural, son Richard Wallace (who gave his name to the fountains in Paris) took over in 1870, but the Municipality of Paris bought it from his heirs in 1905. The famous rose-garden was built the following year by Jean-Claude Nicolas Forestier, and is still one of the most famous in France. The castle outhouses had fallen into decay but from 1921 onward they were the site of the *Henri* restaurant, and the park and restaurant have since proved a popular destination for Parisians out walking. The Bagatelle garden is in the middle of a somewhat neglected wood. *Les Jardins de Bagatelle*, was bought by the Bouquet family in 1984 and is frequented by people visiting the numerous exhibitions that are staged at the orangery.

THE OUTHOUSES
This brick construction reminiscent of a farm building now houses the restaurant.

LE PRÉ CATELAN ● 87 ◆ 388

THE TROUBADOUR AND THE LEADER OF THE HUNT. *Le Pré Catelan* is a restaurant, but it is mainly a center for seminars and business meetings, and is a must for businessmen and nature lovers. The drawing-rooms are magnificent and the paintings of forests quite enchanting. The building itself dates only from the beginning of the 20th century, but its history goes back much further. The story goes that, in 1306, a troubadour by the name of Arnould de Catelan was murdered in the Forest of Rouvray, what is now the Bois de Boulogne, while on his way to the court of Philip the Fair, and that the King erected a cross on the site of the crime in memory of the poet. However, the cross, replaced by a stone pyramid in the 18th century, is more likely to commemorate Théophile Catelan, Captain of the Hunt in the Bois de Boulogne toward the end of Louis XIV's reign, and Governor of the royal Castles of Madrid and La Muette.

THE BOIS DE BOULOGNE AND ITS WALLS
In 1556 Henri II had the Bois de Boulogne, a bandits' hideout, encircled by a wall with eight gates. Later Louis XIV and Louis XV used to hunt there, and it was given to the people by Louis XVI on the occasion of his accession to the throne. During the French Revolution, the Bois was used by people on the run, by police suspects and by others who rebelled against the new system, and later on by bandits again. These days, it has new inhabitants. The police close some of the paths at night in their fight against prostitution.

THE BIGGEST TREE IN THE BOIS DE BOULOGNE
The *Pré Catelan* restaurant overlooks a vista of impeccably kept lawns and magnificent flowerbeds. In the center stands a two-hundred-year-old copper beech, the largest tree in the Bois de Boulogne.

A DAIRY, AN AQUARIUM AND MARIONETTES. The area began to be known as a *pré* (meadow) during the 19th century. This was when the quarries that had supplied stone to build roads through the Bois de Boulogne were finally covered over with grass. When the Bois began to be used more frequently by walkers, the "Pré Catelan" was handed over to Nestor Roqueplan, who built a café, restaurant, dairy, aquarium and some small theatrical and marionette stalls. The current building, designed by Guillaume Tronchet, marries Louis XV, Louis XVI and Empire styles, and was erected on the same site in 1905. A model farm and stables in the Normandy style, standing back from the main buildings, have also been built. *Le Pré Catelan* was henceforth noted for its florid lunches and more worldly dinners. Under the Fourth Republic Antoine Pinay, who lived nearby on Boulevard Suchet, was a regular customer and frequently chatted with "Monsieur Paul" who, as the owner of *Le Pré Catelan*, *Fouquet's*, the *Pavillon d'Armenonville* and the *Café de Paris*, knew just about everything that went on in the city.

A CEMETERY IN THE BOIS DE BOULOGNE
Henri III wrote that, "in a hundred years' time, this will be an amusing promenade; it will have at least two hundred graves in it." He was a monarch much given to black humor! Perhaps he was already thinking of building a mausoleum for himself. His plan was for a building on which six paths converged; they were to be planted with yews and cypresses, and lined with the tombs of Knights of the Order of the Holy Spirit, an order that he had just created. The plans came to nothing.

UNDER PARASOLS OR BY THE FIRE. In 1976 Colette Lenôtre, wife of Gaston ▲ *191*, took over *Le Pré Catelan* from Jean Drouant, owner of the *Drouant* ▲ *204*. She had much work carried out. This included restoration of the gardens as well as the building itself, and the construction of an orangery and a terrace. Come the winter, guests could abandon the large Italian parasols for the warmth of the marble fireplace.

APICIUS ◆ 382

MARCUS GAVIUS. Four men by the name of Apicius, each of them noted for their culinary skills, lived in Rome between the 1st century BC and the 2nd century AD. The most famous of the four was undoubtedly Marcus Gavius, who lived in the reign of the Emperor Nero and was quoted by the philosopher Seneca. He wrote one of the earliest known books on cooking, *De Re Coquinaria*, and from it we learn that he force fed sows with dried figs and wine sweetened with honey, enjoyed flamingos' tongues, liked the contrast of sweet and sour, and recommended seasoning with garum, a Roman sauce made of fermented fish entrails. He also enjoyed inviting his friends to sumptuous banquets. One day, realizing that he could no longer afford his lifestyle, he organized one final feast and poisoned himself. You can't take the responsibilities of a host any more seriously than that!

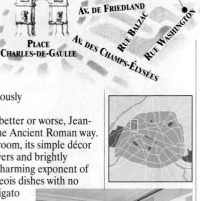

PLACE DES TERNES

AV. MAC MAHON · AV. DE WAGRAM · RUE DU FBG ST-HONORÉ · AV. HOCHE · AV. DE FRIEDLAND · RUE BALZAC · RUE WASHINGTON · PLACE CHARLES-DE-GAULLE · AV. DES CHAMPS-ÉLYSÉES

A LOVELY, UNSOPHISTICATED MAN. For better or worse, Jean-Pierre Vigato has no skill in cooking the Ancient Roman way. In his warm and beautifully lit dining-room, its simple décor lightened by splendid bouquets of flowers and brightly colored contemporary paintings, this charming exponent of Parisian cuisine boldly prepares bourgeois dishes with no ungainly sophistication. Jean-Pierre Vigato owes his vocation to his mother; in a way, he does not seem to have quite grown up, and still cooks with the spontaneity of a precocious ten-year-old. Ideally, Vigato, like Apicius, should occasionally reincarnate himself over the next few centuries!

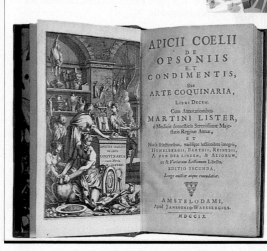

APICII COELII
DE
OPSONIIS
ET
CONDIMENTIS,
Sive
ARTE COQUINARIA,
LIBRI DECEM.
Cum Annotationibus
MARTINI LISTER,
è Medicis domesticis Serenissimæ Maje-
statis Reginæ Annæ,
ET
Notis selectioribus, variisque lectionibus Integris,
HUMELBERGII, BARTHII, REINESII,
A. VAN DER LINDEN, & ALIORUM,
ut & Variarum Lectionum Libello.
EDITIO SECUNDA,
Longe auctior atque emendatior.

AMSTELODAMI,
Apud JANSSONIO-WAESBERGIOS.
MDCCIX.

DE RE COQUINARIA
Apicius' book consists of ten chapters each written by ten imaginary cooks explaining their recipes. The main cooks are Epimeles the Diligent, Sarcoptes the Pork Butcher, Cepuros the Market Gardener, Politeles the Magnificent and Alies the Fisherman. Apicius' book has been reprinted many times, and Jean-Pierre Vigato owns a fine 18th-century edition.

175

MICHEL ROSTANG ◆ 387

A MAN WITH COOKING IN HIS BLOOD. René Sualem, also known as Rennequin, left Wallonia at the end of the 17th century to design the Marly high tower and aqueduct that supplied the Château de Versailles with water. Michel Rostang, for his part, came down the Alps and must have dreamed of building a machine for supplying Paris with Chignin-Bergeron, a dry white wine from Savoie. Chance presumably brought them together on a street in the 17th *arrondissement*. Michel had not long succeeded his father Jo in the family restaurant in Sassenage, near Grenoble, when he came to Paris in 1977; his brother, then catering for the gastronomic needs of the inhabitants of Antibes, and his cousins were also chefs. In other words, the Rostangs have cooking in their blood. They are also constantly on the move. Michel himself travels the world, but this does not prevent him from adding to his menu, even though it is still dominated by regional dishes from the Rhône, the Alps and southern France. He is a modest man, believing that there is no inventiveness in cooking, a theory that one meal at *Michel Rostang* immediately dispels!

REFINED DÉCOR. He welcomes guests in a room elegantly decorated with wood carvings and dark lacquer, and with glass cases containing culinary objects including precious porcelain statuettes by Rodj. Between two marvelous meals at *Rostang* one can always "slum it" at the *Bistro d'à Côté*, an old *épicerie* two doors away that Michel bought as a place where he could entertain his friends informally.

LE JARDIN ◆ 386

FROM MONCEAUX TO MONCEAU. This garden at the end of the avenue was named after Monceaux, a hamlet that stood there in medieval times; it now occupies only a third of the land bought by the Duke of Chartres from gastronome Grimod de la Reynière ● 50 in 1778. The future king then had a garden and a folly built to plans by Carmontelle, his favorite dramatist; the folly was later used as a theater, but all that now remains is an oval bowl of land surrounded by a Corinthian colonnade. The garden was later bought by the State, then acquired by the municipality under the Second Empire. Later some of it was divided into lots. The rest was originally laid out in the English manner by Jean-Charles Alphand, designer of the Bois de Boulogne. The Third Republic honored General Lazare Hoche, who had been responsible for putting down the Vendée uprising, by re-

> **"NO RESTAURANT IS MORE DESERVING OF ITS NAME THAN LE JARDIN AT THE ROYAL-MONCEAU, A LUMINOUS GLASS BUBBLE SET AMID GROVES AND MASSES OF FLOWERS."**

The modernity of the bubble-shaped *Royal-Monceau*, which is approached via a passageway also made of glass, contrasts with the more conventional design of the rest of the establishment.

naming after him Avenue de la Reine-Hortense which had previously been called Boulevard Monceau and Rue Sainte-Marie. The suppression of religious orders under the Third Republic freed large plots of land for property speculation. The retreat house of the Augustinian nuns of the Order of Notre-Dame became vacant on the eve of World War One.

1928. The *Royal-Monceau* opened on this site in 1928. The owner was Pierre Bermond, who had started a hotel chain that included the *Miramar* hotels in Biarritz and Cannes. The *Royal-Monceau* stayed in his family until 1978, when it was bought by the Ciga group. It has always been a key player in the events of the day: for example, the French and German delegations attending the armistice talks in June 1940, and the Allied general staffs in 1945, all stayed at the *Royal-Monceau*, and it was also here that in May 1948 David Ben Gurion signed the proclamation creating the State of Israel.

A GLASS BUBBLE. No restaurant is more deserving of its name than *Le Jardin* (The Garden) at the *Royal-Monceau*, a luminous glass bubble set amid groves and masses of flowers. Guests and local businessmen can enjoy splendid bourgeois cuisine in a truly rural setting.

GUY SAVOY ◆ 386

An Alechinsky painting adorns the dining-room of the *Guy Savoy*, whose eponymous owner is a great chef and lover of modern art.

POULTRY AND PAINTING. Constant Troyon, the 19th-century painter, filled his rustic compositions with cows, horses and poultry in the style of Albert Cuyp and Paul Potter. *Return to the Farm* is a good example of his work, and he would undoubtedly have appreciated the guinea fowl or the duckling which feature on the menu at the *Guy Savoy*. However, Savoy himself is unlikely to hang these paintings in his well-lit, simply decorated dining-room in Rue Troyon. He prefers contemporary canvases, and these are admirably set off by the wood paneling and the room's generally soft tones.

"MASTER" SAVOY. The décor reflects Guy Savoy's cooking: rigorous and simple, and mingling the bold and the traditional with a fundamental respect for the taste buds. The cellist Rostropovich once called him "Master" and, when the chef returned the compliment, the great Russian musician responded by saying that cooking was a more noble art than music. Like

The Guy Savoy
The *Guy Savoy*, in a little street behind Rue Étoile, is one of the best restaurants in Paris, and boasts a delightful décor.

Rostropovich, Guy Savoy is not a man to take himself too seriously, and he seems to be in ten places at once without getting flustered. Not only is he an outstanding chef but also a lover of art, theater, music and fashion. Although he spends every evening at Rue Troyon supervising the cooking, he is also opening up bistros all over Paris, offering humbler dishes but still "in the Guy Savoy style". He can have no better advertisement than the amazing woman who dresses like a famous diva and has had lunch there every day of the week since the restaurant opened.

Taillevent ◆ 389

Guillaume Tirel. Like Alexandre Dumas' musketeers, ambassadors of Parisian cuisine abroad number four: the *Tour d'Argent* ▲ 146, *Maxim's* ▲ 217, *Lasserre* ▲ 188 and *Taillevent*. The latter takes its name from the first great French chef, Guillaume Tirel, known as Taillevent (1310-95). He was also the first cook to write about his art. *Le Viandier* (Tirel's authorship is now disputed) describes how spicy, non-fatty sauces were considered important at the time and that swans and peacocks were hugely popular. Taillevent was also an alchemist and, like all chefs, was always searching for the quintessence of good food.

CHEF TO THE COURT
Taillevent entered the service of Jehanne d'Évreux at the age of sixteen. He subsequently served Philip VI of Valois, the Dauphin, the Duke of Normandy, and lastly Charles VI as chef and head chef.

Perfect judgment. There are no half measures at *Taillevent*, nor does the Vrinat family practise alchemy in their kitchen. André Vrinat started the *Taillevent* restaurant in Rue Saint-Georges, then, as his business prospered, moved to the former town house of the Duke of Morny in Rue Lamennais in 1946. For several years, he offered a different provincial cuisine every day. When his son Jean-Claude, an outstanding sommelier, took over, culinary know-how and a love of living contributed both to the preparation of classic dishes that avoided conformity and to excellent service. The décor has an English rigor about it, the dark paneling carved with neo-classical motifs and the blue benches producing an atmosphere of retrained luxury. There is nothing showy about this restaurant: the *Taillevent* is the least Gascon of the four musketeers.

COOKING AND ALCHEMY
The coat of arms on Taillevent's tombstone in Hennemont, southwest of Paris, depicts the alchemical symbols of three pots between two groups of three roses.

4.
CHAMPS-ÉLYSÉES, ALMA, GEORGE-V

«CHEZ EDGARD»
«LES PRINCES»
«LE PRINCE DE GALLES»
«FOUQUET'S»
«LA FERMETTE MARBEUF»
«15 MONTAIGNE»
«LE PLAZA»

AV. KLÉBER
AV. D'IENA
RUE DE PONTHIEU
RUE MARBEUF
AV. MARCEAU
AV. GEORGE V
AV. MONTAIGNE
RUE JEAN-GOUJON
PLACE DE L'ALMA
COURS ALBERT-1
PT DE L'ALMA

The magnificent promenade, the views and the golden triangle all call for the most brilliant superlatives. For is this not the most chic and expensive part of Paris? The promenade was what is now the Champs-Élysées, which was crossed by the Jardin des Tuileries when Le Nôtre extended it in 1670, and which during the 18th century was extended as far as the Rond-Point and then up to the Étoile and Pont de Neuilly. Magnificent private townhouses were built here during this period, and the Arc de Triomphe, the finishing touch, was added in 1836. The Champs-Élysées now forms part of the great vista stretching from the Louvre to the Grande Arche de La Défense. The golden triangle, bounded by the Champs-Élysées, avenue Montaigne and avenue George-V, owes its name to the luxury stores, the palaces and the sumptuous offices that grace the area. It goes without saying that local restaurants are a cut above the average.

FOUQUET'S

● 48 ● 94 ◆ 393

A COACHMEN'S RENDEZ-VOUS. There is an air of Saint-Tropez about *Fouquet's*. Even the terrace brings to mind the *Sen.nequier*, with its Mercedes and Jaguars, ocean-going yachts and cabin cruisers. The sun always seems to be shining. It was the first restaurant in the Champs-Élysées, and is now the

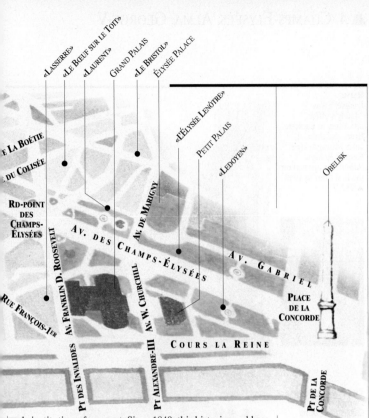

«LASSERRE» «LE BŒUF SUR LE TOIT» «LAURENT» GRAND PALAIS «LE BRISTOL» ÉLYSÉE PALACE

«L'ÉLYSÉE LENÔTRE» PETIT PALAIS «LEDOYEN» OBELISK

E LA BOÉTIE

DU COLISÉE

RD-POINT
DES
CHAMPS-
ÉLYSÉES

RUE FRANÇOIS-1ER

AV. FRANKLIN D. ROOSEVELT

AV. DES CHAMPS-ÉLYSÉES

AV. DE MARIGNY

AV. W. CHURCHILL

AV. GABRIEL

PLACE
DE LA
CONCORDE

PT DES INVALIDES

PT ALEXANDRE-III

COURS LA REINE

PT DE LA
CONCORDE

only institution of any sort. Since 1840, this historic road has been lined with superb private houses, and at the end of the 19th century, "the most beautiful avenue in the world" resembled Avenue Foch much as it is today. It used to be patrolled by nannies taking perfectly groomed children out for walks. Now there is an air of decline about the place. Only one bar, the *Critérion*, is allowed. It is level with No 99, and the coachmen just have to kick their heels!

LOUIS'S OR FOUQUET'S? In 1901, the *Critérion* was bought by Louis Fouquet, who had the good sense to marry the daughter of the owner of the *Maire*, a well-known restaurant of the time. He renovated it, put in some tables and immediately charged astronomical prices as a way of attracting the rich, and sometimes snobbish, local clientele. As for a name, anglomania ruled supreme in those days. *George's* and *Maxim's* ▲ 217 in Rue Royale were all the rage. "*Louis's*" was unpronounceable, so *Fouquet's* seemed as good as any, and anyway there was a sign that read "American Drinks, Cocktails"! Louis Fouquet died in 1905 without knowing how successful his establishment would one day be. The restaurant was then taken over by Léopold Mourier, a former chef at the *Maire* and now owner of the *Café de Paris*. *Fouquet's* soon became a meeting-place for race-goers returning from Longchamp, and in 1913 Mourier enlarged and redecorated the premises: improvements included a real "grill room" with mahogany walls, and an "American" bar of the type only found in English clubs. Moreover, in an attempt to imitate

Fouquet's

❝In 1934, as a young starving actor, he [Raymond Pellegrin] walked up to the bar in *Fouquet's*. He was so hungry-looking that Raymond [the barman] gave him some knuckle of beef and a carafe of Bordeaux wine which the young man immediately devoured. And he could not bring himself to turn down the *tarte Tatin* either. Raymond passed over a saucer but, instead of the bill, there was a banknote on it. Raymond Pellegrin looked up in amazement. 'Your change, sir,' was the impassive reply.❞

Raymond Castans,
*Parlez-moi du
Fouquet's*
(Talk to me
about *Fouquet's*)

RAIMU
Fouquet's was "daddy's office," according to Paulette Brun, daughter of Jules Muraire, alias Raimu. A *salon Raimu* was opened on the first floor in 1989 ▲ 242.

THE ESCADRILLE BAR
During World War One, some young men sporting white scarves would invade the bar at *Fouquet's*, jostling the regulars. Their names were Jean Navarre, René Fonk and Georges Guynemer. When these pioneers of the air were not flying the skies above Champagne and Picardy, they came to forget the threat of death in the hot spots

of Parisian life. The *Escadrille* bar at *Fouquet's* perpetuates their memory.

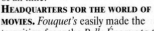

British customs even further, he banned unaccompanied women. The most superb food was served in the upstairs restaurant. It was an immediate success. For some time now, the Champs-Élysées had been the hub of Parisian life, and *Fouquet's* became the deluxe eating-place for those in show business, the arts and politics. Regular customers included Liane de Pougy, Paul Poiret, Georges Feydeau and Raymond Poincaré. On the eve of the Battle of the Marne, the *Kronprinz* booked a table there to toast his expected victory with champagne. He must have been the most disappointed customer of all time.

HEADQUARTERS FOR THE WORLD OF MOVIES. *Fouquet's* easily made the transition from the *Belle Époque* to the Roaring Twenties. Léopold Mourier died in 1923, and was succeeded by Louis Barraya and by Maurice Drouant, owner of *Drouant* in Place Gaillon. With that, *Fouquet's* virtually became the movies' international headquarters, catering for the many cinema offices in the locality. Jules Muraire, better-known by his pseudonym "Raimu," brought along such leading figures in the golden age of French cinema as the Pagnols, Sacha Guitry, Pierre Brasseur, Jules Berry and Elvire Popesco, among others. In 1958 the establishment was

> **"FOUQUET'S IS WHERE YOU DISCUSS FILMS MADE ON BUDGETS OF MILLIONS OF FRANCS, WHILE YOU SIT IN FRONT OF GLASSES OF BEER – AND DON'T KNOW HOW YOU'RE GOING TO PAY FOR THEM."**
>
> HENRI JEANSON

renovated with a splendidly decorated staircase, crystal chandeliers and heavy curtains. *Fouquet's* was going slightly downmarket, but the Champs-Élysées itself was also losing much of its pomp. Things were moving on, the magic was no longer working, and Maurice Druant decided to sell.

A NEW LIFE. Only the King of the left bank could save the jewel of the right bank. In 1976, Maurice Casanova, who had opened many restaurants in Faubourg Saint-Germain, came to *Fouquet's* accompanied by his daughter, Jenny-Paule. As part of a plan to revive the restaurant's fortunes, he added two covered terraces, one giving on to Avenue George-V, the other overlooking the Champs-Élysées, and Georges Cravenne, grand Master of Ceremonies of Parisian life, found himself landed with the task of attracting customers. Gala evenings thereupon proliferated, and featured show business events, gastronomic competitions and popular radio programs. They were duly successful and during the 1980's different rooms were named after James Joyce, Roger Nimier and Raimu.

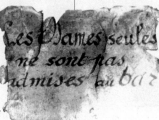

EVICTED? In 1985, the building's freeholder refused to renew the lease, and three years of legal battles ended with an order to move. However, in 1988, following an outcry by *Fouquet's* many friends, the restaurant was listed as an historic building, and Louis Fouquet could rest in peace.

> **"**Which Paul Bourget will give us a novel about the sporty, worldly, affected, cultivated, intolerable, charming airplane-man-cocktail-man of 1930-1938? If such a person exists, and he is short of local color, let him go to *Fouquet's*, the National Library of Elegant Parisianism.**"**
> Léon-Paul Fargue,
> *Le Piéton de Paris*

LES PRINCES ◆ *394*

AMERICAN AND ENGLISH. The *George-V* is both the most English and the most American of Parisian hotels: English because it is named after a former king of England and stands in a street of the same name; American because, ever since it opened in 1928, it has combined luxury and modern style. Predictably, 60 percent of the clientele in the 1930's were American, and 30 percent British. At that time, the hotel introduced an air-taxi service linking Le Bourget with various European capitals. The service still runs. In 1978, on the occasion of the *George-V*'s fiftieth anniversary, a plane was chartered to bring 150 American millionaires over to spend a dream weekend in Paris.

THE 1920'S AND 30'S. The *George-V* was the luxury hotel of the 1920's and 30's *par excellence*. As Léon-Paul Fargue put it in "Le Piéton de Paris" ("A Pedestrian in Paris"), the *George-V* is "ideally suited to a clientele that has nothing to do with

the years before the war; it is a clientele that is hooked on jazz, speed, and the fluctuations of a changing world." The hotel was launched in February 1929 with a meeting of the committee of experts charged with determining

> **SACHA GUITRY'S ANNIVERSARY**
> In 1932, Sacha Guitry celebrated thirty years in the theater and the beginning of his affair with Jacqueline Delubac. The menu included *Consommé Jacqueline, Salade de Printemps, Bombe illusioniste, Madeleine du Théâtre* and *l'Eau de la Fontaine, système Pasteur*. The names of the dishes referred to some of his previous conquests or to titles of his plays.

GRAND HOTEL

Vicky Baum's novel celebrated the high point in the history of luxury hotels. It was made into a film by Edmund Goulding in 1932. Greta Garbo, a regular at the *Hôtel George-V*, starred with Joan Crawford, John Barrymore and Wallace Beery.

war reparations; the committee was chaired by Owen D. Young and attended by American banker John P. Morgan. When Young left he took as souvenirs the chair he had occupied and the green cloth that had covered the negotiating table. Ever since, financiers and businessmen staying at the hotel have rubbed shoulders with celebrities such as Buster Keaton, Greta Garbo, Gene Kelly, Bob Dylan and Liza Minnelli. The *George-V* contains one of the finest collections of works of art of any Parisian hotel: the drawing-rooms and apartments display a wealth of 17th-century tapestries, sculptures and paintings by the great masters, as well as a number of pieces of period furniture.

RENOVATION AND RESTORATION. The *George-V* restaurant has long prided itself on being able to serve its guests with any dish they desired. This prompted a rich American in the 1950's to order for himself and friends his favorite dish, lobster coated in chocolate sauce. However, Americans do love French specialties as well. Burt Lancaster was so struck by snails, when he ate them for the first time, that he instructed his entire family to have them every day throughout their stay. The *Princes* restaurant opened in the 1970's under the management of André Sonier; it gave the hotel a new lease of life, and between 1989 and 1992 was restored along with the rest of the hotel. The designers concentrated on re-creating the 1930's décor that characterizes the architecture of the hotel, and they preserved the stucco wall decoration of papyrus motifs, which provide evidence of the new-found interest in Egyptian art that followed the discovery of Tutankhamen's tomb in 1922. In the course of the renovation work a splendid oak floor and sculpted reliefs by Raymond Delamarre depicting putti against a background of leaves were also discovered and restored. Dinner is served in four intimate rooms decorated with frescoes in the manner of Puvis de Chavanne. However, the cuisine of *Les Princes* can best be enjoyed in summertime, under red parasols out on the patio, sheltered from the world and shaded by the nine-story hotel. For a moment, while taking coffee, you can almost imagine yourself the heir to the throne.

GEORGE V

George V, second son of Edward VII, acceded to the throne on his brother's death in 1910. He remained on the throne throughout World War One, and died in 1936.

> "FINALLY, DOMINATING THE BASEMENT LIKE THE CAPTAIN'S CABIN, IS AN EVEN NARROWER GLASS CAGE OCCUPIED BY THE CLERK CHECKING OFF EVERYTHING COMING OUT OF THE KITCHENS."
>
> GEORGES SIMENON

LE PRINCE DE GALLES ● *80* ◆ *394*

"I SERVE." Like all heirs to the British throne, George V was Prince of Wales before he became king. The *Prince de Galles* hotel opened in the same year as the *George-V*, but opted to keep its princely name. The prince's coat of arms, a crown surmounted by three ostrich plumes and bearing the motto *Ich dien* (I serve), is to be seen above the red awnings over the entrance to the hotel. Winston Churchill and Neville Chamberlain were regular guests, as were Erich Maria Remarque, Nat King Cole, Gina Lollobrigida and Henry Kissinger.

ART DECO MOSAICS. André Millon, already owner of the *Meurice*, the *Grand Hôtel* and the *Café de la Paix*, staked all on a rise in the fortunes of the Champs-Élysées district. He decided to settle in Avenue George-V, a road built over the old Chaillot quarries that had supplied stone for the construction of the Arc de Triomphe. Success came immediately. It is not called the golden triangle for nothing! The high point of the décor at the *Prince de Galles* consists of the blue, ocher and gold Art Deco mosaics which adorn the

THE RED AWNINGS
Like the *George-V* and many other comparable hotels, the *Prince de Galles* boasted red awnings and blinds that shielded the windows from the rays of the sun.

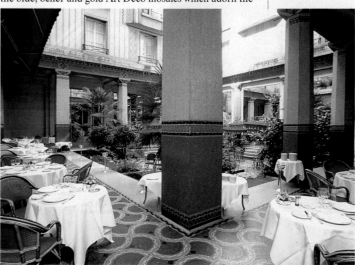

hotel's delightful patio and sumptuous bathrooms.

COOKING IN A CLASS OF ITS OWN. You do not have to stay at the hotel to enjoy what it has to offer. In summer, the restaurant's tables spill out under the veranda surrounding the patio, and on two sides the back of the veranda is covered with mirrors, which increase the impression of space. In the middle of the veranda is an octagonal fountain consisting of three superimposed basins that in the warm months of the year are smothered in vegetation. Rattan armchairs and exotic plants accentuate the colonial atmosphere created by the mosaics. The winter restaurant, which is decorated with trompe l'oeil painted paneling and a mural depicting swans swimming round a fountain, is more in keeping with the conventional

BLUE MOSAICS
The mosaics decorate both the patio and the hotel's magnificent bathrooms. In 1928, such bathroom facilities placed hotels in the luxury class.

concept of a luxury hotel restaurant. The cooking, however, avoids the limitations within which top-class hotels seem to work, and proves once again that it is possible to eat well in such establishments.

CHEZ EDGARD ◆ 391

MINISTERS AND DEPUTIES. After every election and ministerial reshuffle, the new deputies and ministers go to test their popularity at *Chez Edgard*, where they tackle media interviewers and ribs of beef with equal gusto. There are also private rooms where confidences can be exchanged, and alliances cemented or broken. The restaurant is equally popular with politicians, past and present, and radio and television journalists. *Chez Edgard* is right next to the National Assembly and is a regular *rendez-vous* for politicians and journalists. On an average day it will be patronized by leading television presenters, journalists from the national press, members of the cabinet and even the Prime Minister himself. It is the sort of place where casual, one-off remarks can easily end up being lead stories on the television news.

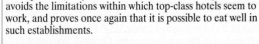

"MONSIEUR PAUL." If the Left Bank, including the National Assembly and the Palais de Matignon, ceased to exist (and it would be inconvenient if this were to happen at lunchtime) a government in exile could immediately be formed at *Chez Edgard* on the right bank. Just for information, there is no such person as Edgard; the owner's name is Paul Benmussa. "Monsieur Paul", as he is known, is better informed than the satirical magazine *Le Canard Enchaîné*, and much more discreet. He is very much a consensus man, and is ideally equipped to form the next government.

LE RÉGENCE AND LE RELAIS-PLAZA ◆ 395

Until 1852 Avenue Montaigne was known as Avenue des Veuves (Avenue of the Widows), as it had been a popular haunt of ladies of easy virtue during the 18th century. Moreover, many of the royal jewels stolen in September 1792 were hidden at the foot of one of the elm trees that line this ill-lit road. Under the Directoire, Madame Tallien gave memorable parties in her little "cottage". These were not equalled until evenings at the *Mabille*, a nearby famous pleasure garden and temple of the can-can, started up many years later. Avenue Montaigne is still known as a street for merrymaking and for women. There are shops owned by big names in the leisure and fashion industries and another of Paris's leading hotels, the *Plaza Athénée*.

FROM THE ATHÉNÉE TO THE PLAZA. The first *Grand Hôtel de l'Athénée* was opened in Rue Scribe in 1863 by a businessman, Louis

WINSTON CHURCHILL
A regular at the *Prince de Galles*.

WHO DINES WITH WHOM?
This little game attracts anonymous customers to the red room in *Chez Edgard* as much as the menu and the excellent service.

1930'S FASHIONS
Stained-glass decoration in one of the pillars dividing the two dining-rooms in the *Relais-Plaza*, the bar grill in the *Plaza-Athénée* hotel.

> "FOR FRENCHMEN ABROAD, DO YOU KNOW WHAT COMING BACK TO PARIS MEANS, OH PARISIANS? ... IT MEANS REDISCOVERING FRENCH WINES. OUTSIDE FRANCE, THEY HAVE A MYTHOLOGICAL STATUS"
>
> HONORÉ DE BALZAC

Raphaël Bischoffsheim; his son then sold it to Émile Armbruster, director of the *Plaza* chain of hotels, in the 1900's. It was renamed the *Plaza-Athénée* and moved to Avenue Montaigne, where it opened in 1911. The hotel's cosmopolitan clientele has included Mata Hari, who regularly stayed in Room 120 and was arrested outside 25 Avenue Montaigne in 1917. In 1919 the hotel was enlarged to its present dimensions. Rich Americans, royalty and film stars often took apartments there, and Josephine Baker, who was appearing at the *Music-Hall des Champs-Élysées*, frequently came in the 1920's, in the company of Maurice Chevalier.

1930'S LUNCH OR GRAND SIÈCLE DINNER. In 1936 Managing Director François Dupré built the *Relais-Plaza*, a grill room more in keeping with the atmosphere of a transatlantic voyage than with annual holidays from work. The enormous dining-room, which is in two parts and decorated by Jacques Dupuis, is something straight out of a luxury liner, and has plate-glass windows to protect guests from the curiosity of passers-by. A large mirror covering one wall increases the impression of space, and light descends from the coffered ceiling on to beige leather wall-sofas. The immensely chic clientele knows the brasserie menu by heart. Cocktails are served from a huge bar behind which rises a bas-relief by Francine Saqui depicting an allegory of Diana the Huntress; if this were a real liner, the guests would be more than happy to sip their Bloody Marys and return to their cabins later. There is a totally different ambience in the hotel's gastronomic restaurant, the *Régence*, which was built shortly after the *Relais*, and was completely renovated in 1984. Walls hung with silk or covered

> "Paris ... could not possibly be indifferent to the admirable law that allows the most obscure citizen to live like a prince for a few hours; since the war we have had a dozen or so establishments that can arrange anything."
>
> Léon-Paul Fargue, *Le Piéton de Paris*

DIANA THE HUNTRESS
The most important painting in the dining-room of the *Régence* (above, left) and the bas-relief in the dining-room and restaurant bar of the *Relais* (below) both depict Diana the Huntress. One is 18th-century, the other dates from the 1930's.

THE THÉÂTRE DE L'ATHÉNÉE
The old theater in the *Grand Hôtel de l'Athénée* in Rue Scribe survived the hotel's move to Avenue Montaigne. It became the *Théâtre de l'Athénée* in 1899, and was directed by Louis Jouvet between 1934 and 1951. His company performed the majority of the plays by Jean Giraudoux.

187

with weathered paneling, a ceiling adorned with gold wood moldings, crystal chandeliers and a marble fireplace combine to make the *Régence* the archetypal luxury hotel restaurant. The cooking is just as outstanding. In the spring, tables are put out on the patio, where the walls are covered by a carpet of young vines punctuated by the red of the awnings, which match the flowers and borders on the tablecloths. What with a liner saloon, a Regency dining-room and shaded terrace, guests at the *Plaza* are somewhat spoilt for choice.

LASSERRE ◆ 393

THE RISE OF RENÉ LASSERRE. Back in Bayonne, on high days and holidays, Irma Lasserre would serve *mesclagne*, a concoction of *foie gras* and breast of chicken, and *mesclagne Mère Irma* figures on the *Lasserre* menu to this day. René Lasserre loves to recall his childhood and how far he has come since then. By the age of twelve, he was already out earning money, but he was soon in Paris where he began to climb the ladder of his new profession. *Chef de rang* at seventeen, *maître d'hôtel* at nineteen, he had worked at the *Pavillon d'Armenonville*, the liner *Île de France*, the *Lido*, the

Irma Lasserre.

PAUL LORÉE
The bartender who once served coffee to street sweepers in René Lasserre's ramshackle bar is still at his post – or very nearly. Like most of the restaurant staff, Paul Lorée got by with on-the-job training, and became head wine waiter in 1942. He held that job until 1977.

DOVES GIVEN THEIR FREEDOM
On the numerous gala evenings at *Lasserre*, it is the custom to allow the doves to fly freely round the dining-room.

Drouant-Est (now no longer in existence) and the *Prunier* ▲ *222* before he even dreamed of working for himself.

A PLACE OF HIS OWN. In 1942 an opportunity presented itself in the form of a dilapidated bistro built for the Universal Exhibition of 1937 in the garden of a private house on Avenue Victor-Emmanuel III. The restaurant was in an isolated locality but it soon attracted custom, and its reputation spread rapidly. In 1948 René Lasserre founded the "Club de la Casserole", which brought together a wide range of personalities, most of them friends of his. In 1951 he decided to expand (building works in progress are shown below), and the following year a small neo-classical building with a white façade was ready for its first customers. The restaurant was on the first floor, and the ceiling incorporated a sliding roof decorated with scantily dressed dancers by the painter Touchagues. They proved too much for the first few customers, and Touchagues had to come back and cover them up. The retractable ceiling was a brilliant idea as the restaurant could now be ventilated or illuminated, and guests could even gaze straight up at a star-lit sky. Unfortunately, stars fall to earth occasionally. *Lasserre* won its third Michelin star in 1962, but has since lost it!

CHOCOLATE BOX. At the entrance to *Lasserre*, there are cages of doves and a glass cabinet containing a collection of small porcelain cooking pots made especially for the restaurant. The dove and the cooking pot are the establishment's motifs, and they also appear on the floor decoration. A lift resembling a sedan chair takes guests up to the chocolate-box dining-room. Balustrades and window boxes give diners a degree of intimacy without isolating them completely, but it is the profusion of Chinese porcelain vases, vases from Saxony, and solid silver trinkets that distinguish *Lasserre* from other comparable establishments. Here, each table is individually adorned, and the furniture, cutlery and table service have been exclusively designed.

TIMELESS COOKING. It would be astonishing if the cooking was not unique. Rather than describe it as classic or traditional, it would be more accurate to say that it is timeless. The *canard à l'orange*, for example, is out of this world and the flambé dishes are also hugely popular, while the wine

SOLID SILVER
Like all other objects that decorate the tables at *Lasserre*, this 18th-century knight in solid silver is unique.

CHANDELIERS AND A SLIDING ROOF
The center of the dining-room is dominated by an eighteen-bulb chandelier made by the Cristalleries de Saint-Louis. Because of the sliding roof, a chandelier cannot be suspended from the ceiling.

DALÍ, MALRAUX AND SAN ANTONIO
Salvador Dalí and André Malraux were almost daily customers at *Lasserre*. Dalí's fantasies are inscribed for ever on the memories of the staff. As for Malraux, it was at *Lasserre* that he persuaded

Chagall to paint the ceiling of the Paris Opéra. Another regular was Commissaire San Antonio, whose creator, the writer Frédéric Dard, frequently had him dine at *Lasserre*.

LASSERRE AND THE OCCUPATION
Former Prime Minister Jacques Chaban-Delmas, a noted figure in the Resistance, recalls, "There are indelible memories that attach me to your restaurant because of the courage you showed during the Occupation and the help you gave me and my comrades in the Resistance."

THE THÉÂTRE DES CHAMPS-ÉLYSÉES
The theater was built between 1911 and 1913 on plans by the brothers Auguste, Gustave and Claude Perret; it is one of the earliest examples of the use of reinforced concrete. The Perret brothers were the first to contrive a new aestheticism using this revolutionary material, but without flouting the rules of classical architecture. The marble ornamentation matches the structure of the building admirably.

cellar, with its 230 different *appellations* and 700 vintage *crus*, is almost peerless. The wine is decanted into *aiguières*, silver-lined crystal ewers, of which René Lasserre has a fine collection. Finally, service at table benefits from the fact that many of the staff have been working there for several decades. *Lasserre* celebrated its fiftieth anniversary in 1992; the youngster from Bayonne has come a long way in fifty years.

15 MONTAIGNE ♦ 395

IT ALL DEPENDS ON ONE'S POINT OF VIEW. It was a public scandal! To lay so much as a finger on a triumph of modern architecture, which also just happens to be a temple of music, is bad enough! And the fact that work started before a permit was granted was outrageous! Maybe the *Théâtre des Champs-Élysées* did not really deserve to be decked out in some post-modernist style and turned into a restaurant anyway. But it does, quite literally, rather depend on one's point of view. Guests sitting in the huge bay in *15 Montaigne*, or out on the open-air terrace overlooking the Seine, the Eiffel Tower and the Invalides, may have different ideas. In the evenings particularly, when the street lights draw a twinkling map of the city, the view is breathtaking.
FROM BOULEVARD LEFÈVRE TO AVENUE MONTAIGNE. In 1900, after months of argument and a number of law suits, José Lempréia finally took over as proprietor, and brought to the *15 Montaigne* the cherries and brandy motif he had used at his previous restaurant, the *Maison Blanche*. He had managed to attract Parisian society to one of the city's outer boulevards in the 15th *arrondissement*; he therefore had no problem persuading them up to the balcony of one of the most popular concert halls in Paris. The restaurant lift takes customers up to a huge dining-room that looks like a New York penthouse.
PARISIAN DÉCOR. The wooden ceiling and carpet-strewn floor compensate for the coldness of the grey walls, furniture and structural elements; other decoration includes contemporary works of art and superb bouquets of exotic flowers. The real décor, however, comprises one whole side of the restaurant: Paris itself, seen through glass. Being a theater, the *15 Montaigne* offers seats everywhere from the orchestra pit up to the balcony, but at the end of their meal, customers cannot get to their feet and applaud the visionary Lempréia, as that brilliant, good-looking man is of course no longer with us. His many inventive southern dishes, not least the celebrated *brandade* (salt cod), are still on the menu, though. Service is in the hands of a group of young waiters wearing a uniform midway between a dressing gown and kimono. One way and another, the *15 Montaigne* is an absolute marvel.

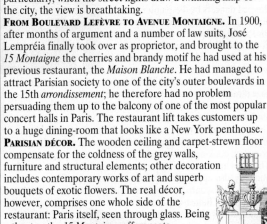

> **"THE PAVILLON PAILLARD IS AN INCOMPARABLE JEWEL-CASE OF CHAMPAGNE BUCKETS, ORCHIDS AND RED VELVET."**
> RENÉ HÉRON DE VILLEFOSSE

A breathtaking night-time view from the *15 Montaigne* restaurant, which was originally designed as a theater.

L'ELYSÉE LENÔTRE ◆ 392

THE PETIT PAILLARD. In 1878, the *Paillard* was founded in the premises of the *Bignon* in Chaussée d'Antin, and it quickly became one of the great restaurants of the period. On being invited there by actor Lucien Guitry in 1902, writer Jules Renard observed, "It gives him pleasure to ask me ... whether I prefer Chablis or Graves and to ponder my indecisiveness in front of the waiters who smile at me." The April 30, 1898 issue of the building magazine *Construction Moderne* announced that architect Albert Ballu was to start work on a "charming little building that will accommodate a branch of one of the boulevard's leading restaurants". It was to be built in the gardens of the Champs-Élysées. The restaurant in question was none other than the *Paillard*, whose owner saw that there was money to be made from being so close to the site of the impending Universal Exhibition. It was later nicknamed *Le Petit Paillard*. The *Paillard* has gone now, but it survives in a new form and with a no less prestigious name. The Louis XVI building is flanked by a Renaissance-style

BALLU, FATHER AND SON Albert Ballu, architect of the *Petit Paillard*, had plenty to live up to. His father Théodore was responsible for the Église de la Trinité, the 1st *arrondissement* Mayor's Office and Paris' new *Hôtel de Ville*. Albert himself was a diocesan architect in Algiers, and designed Oran Cathedral.

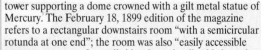

THE ÉLYSÉE LENÔTRE
The terrace and main dining-room.

PAILLARD
The *Paillard* was one of the great Parisian restaurants at the end of the 19th century.

tower supporting a dome crowned with a gilt metal statue of Mercury. The February 18, 1899 edition of the magazine refers to a rectangular downstairs room "with a semicircular rotunda at one end"; the room was also "easily accessible from all sides through tall, wide bays that allowed air and light to pour in". There is an overhanging podium for musicians halfway up the wall, while access to the private rooms is by the stairway in the tower. "One of these rooms is in the Empire style, two are Louis XV, and the remaining three are Louis XVI." The article goes on to say that "the architect cannot have been consulted" about the two frescoes of Venus on Mount Parnassus and Neptune in his chariot that appear on the ceiling, as "they are not in harmony with the interior design". In fact these frescoes are works by minor masters executed in the style of Delacroix, and they are now an integral part of the restaurant's charm. The materials used for the rest of the decoration can be summed up in two words: stucco and staff.

A VERANDA AND A TERRACE. Over the years, the *Pavillon Paillard* has welcomed royalty as well as several characters in the novels of Marcel Proust. The restaurant was known as *Chez Langer*, and then the *Pavillon Élysée* after it was bought and renovated by Gaston Lenôtre in 1984. In 1989, a metal and glass veranda was added around the rotunda to make guests feel as though they were eating out in the open, even in the midst of winter. As soon as the good weather returns, the terrace beneath the chestnut trees does a brisk trade as business people arrive to enjoy the very best service and food.

THE FRENCH LINE ◆ *393*

A RE-LAUNCH. The Compagnie générale transatlantique (CGT) was founded by the Péreire brothers in 1855. It won the transatlantic postal concession in 1861 and opened up the Le Havre-New York line in 1864. The CGT's last flagship was

the liner *France,* which was sold in 1974. Now the jewel in the crown of "the French Line" is its restaurant of the same name, although that will come as no surprise to those who love ocean cruises and appreciate fine food. This initiative by the CGT is now located in Faubourg Saint-Germain, and the splendid brasserie seeks to recreate the atmosphere of the novels of Scott Fitzgerald and Paul Morand; there are chaises longues on the promenade deck, tangos and charlestons, sables and white dinner jackets. Having climbed the gangway, guests can choose between three decks, each with an uninterrupted view over the dining-room. The mood of nostalgia is completed by a décor comprising mahogany, polished steel, chrome, black and white marble, and engraved ground glass; the dinner wagons are in the form of cabin trunks and the glass cabinets are closed with pretty little models of boats; even the lighting simulates a night sky full of stars, seen from a ship out at sea. The menu continues the maritime theme. To maintain the illusion, staff are dressed in stewards' uniforms, and "passengers" (or clients) wonder when they are going to be invited to sit at the captain's table.

LA FERMETTE MARBEUF
1900
● 79 ▲ 392

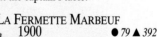

ONE BLOW OF A PICKAXE.
The large glass and wrought-iron awning over the entrance to 24 Rue Boccador is the only reminder that the *Hôtel Langham* stood on this spot at the end of the 19th century. Until recently, little was known about this institution.

In 1978 Jean Laurent bought the rundown restaurant that was located at 5 Rue Marbeuf, proposing to turn it into something a little more grand. The premises were rather stuffy, so he had to install ventilation shafts. Then a workman's pickaxe revealed a marvelous décor of metal columns, ceramic tiles and carved glass: Jean Laurent had just rediscovered the *Hôtel Langham*'s original dining-room. The restored interior is now listed .

"What can I say about the ships run by the *Compagnie générale transatlantique*? They are wonders that sum up the refinement of French art, and Americans who travel on them have a foretaste of what awaits them in France. And for those who travel on the *Île-de-France* or the *Champlain* – What cuisine! What service! What staff!"
  Alexandre Dumaine, 1935

HURTRÉ AND WIELHARSKI.
In the course of a few weeks in 1898, the architect Émile Hurtré and painter Jules Wielharski constructed a strictly Art Nouveau pavilion in the tiny courtyard of the *Hôtel Langham*. The decorative elements include women (a ceramic panel based on Botticelli's *Spring*), animals (peacocks and herons), flowers (irises, gladioli and sunflowers) and vegetables (gourds).

In 1982, Jean Laurent was fortunate enough to acquire furniture from the winter garden of a contemporary Maisons-Laffitte villa. He placed them in the dining-room overlooking the street. *La Fermette Marbeuf 1900* was deservedly listed as a protected building in 1983.

"The two artists have succeeded in producing a joyful, yet discreet, harmony. The softness of the snowy whites, the caress of the pale greens and the subdued warmth of the gold bring a gentle peace to our eyes, which are daily assaulted by lurid contrasts and by refulgence that is as useless as it is unexpected."
Art et Décoration, 1898

Nothing remains of the original carpet with its motifs of water lilies, frogs and dragonflies.

FEAST YOUR EYES. The décor alone would be enough reason to eat at *La Fermette Marbeuf 1900*, but of course the fine, wholesome cuisine is quite superb. In 1992 Jean Laurent was the first to put on a meal comprising solely *appellation d'origine contrôlée* products. Parisian society came flocking.

LAURENT ● 48, 75 ◆ 393

JACOB IGNAZ HITTORFF
Hittorff was born in Cologne in 1792 and went to the École des Beaux-Arts in Paris in 1810, where he studied under Charles Percier. In 1822 he undertook a long journey to Sicily where he discovered the polychromy of Greek temples. Louis-Philippe made him responsible for work on the Place de la Concorde and the Champs-Élysées, but the principal legacy of this precursor of cast-iron architecture was the Gare du Nord which he built between 1861 and 1865. Hittorff died in 1867.

The motif that appears on the menu (above right) is also the recurrent decorative element of the panels that adorn the walls of the *salon Élysées* (Élysées Room), one of the *Laurent's* many dining-rooms.

THE CAFÉ DU CIRQUE. Work on the *Laurent* restaurant in the late 1970's uncovered the remains of a very old building, probably a hunting lodge in the reign of Louis XIV or an open-air café at the time of the French Revolution. It was on this site that Jacob Ignaz Hittorff built the *Café du Cirque* in 1842. Two years earlier, Louis-Philippe had asked him to draw up a plan for this section of the Champs-Élysées, incorporating restaurants, a rotunda with a view and a circus. The "view" was to be the *Théâtre Marigny*; all that now remains of this summer circus (it was pulled down in 1899) is the ring, which children use as a sandpit. The original *Café du Cirque* consisted of a metal framework with brick walls, a revolutionary structure at the time; pilasters, columns and capitals bear witness to Hittorff's liking for the neo-classical. He was one of the first architects to show that Greek temples were polychrome, and painted the façades with bright colors. "Painting a building," he said, "brings out form and emphasizes the detail." The result is reminiscent of Pompeii.

LAURENT BECOMES LAURENT. The concession was given to a man named Guillemin, and the café, which was a lovers' meeting-place, became known as the *Chalet des Amoureux*. In his *La Table à Paris* of 1845, Victor Bouton wrote, "The *Café du Cirque* welcomed us ... the dinner was excellent ... we expressed our gratitude to M. Guillemin for the way he ran the restaurant and the fine service ... This is no utopia, mind ... you eat well here, but you get what you pay for." It seems that the *Café du Cirque*, soon to be re-named the *Café Guillemin*, rapidly became too expensive for local people, although the fact that Caroline Otero, an actress appearing at the nearby *Théâtre Marigny*, patronized the *Café* could only increase the number of well-heeled male customers. Nobody knows why the *Café* continues to be called *Laurent*, after its third manager from 1860 to 1879, although it was during his time that this part of the Champs-Élysées was at its most fashionable before it began to decline around the turn of the century.

TRANSFORMATIONS. The restaurant was renovated and enlarged in 1906: two glass-covered wings in the form of semi-rotundas were added to the end of Jacob Ignaz Hittorff's building, and an awning hung over the entrance. The restaurant was closed in 1939, and until 1948 it served as the

mess for officers of the 2nd Armored Division. In 1957 the new manager opened up three bays in the front of the building, turned the small upstairs rooms into a large dining-room and built terraces over the two wing extensions. Then in 1976 the decoration and organization of the restaurant were entirely overhauled, and the original façade restored. Only the décor in some of the upper rooms was preserved. There is an English-style mahogany bar at the entrance, but the *Laurent*'s great charm, apart from its superb menu and impeccable service, is its shaded terrace. A hedge prevents guests from being looked at, and in summer the restaurant is one of the city's main business and political meeting-places. The chef, Philippe Braun, was a protégé of Joël Robuchon. Enough to make the President, in the nearby Élysée Palace, quite jealous!

The recent renovation to the façade recalls Hittorff's love of polychromy.

LEDOYEN ● *48* ◆ *393*

ANTOINE NICOLAS DOYEN. "Beyond the Tuileries, and running along the river, is a magnificent walk known as the 'Cours de la Reine' as it was the Medicis Queen who had it built and planted in 1628 ... The huge, round promenade in the middle ... takes one into a plain on the right-hand side called the Champs-Élysées." So wrote Piganiol de la Force in his *Description de Paris* of 1742. It was in this rustic setting that Antoine Nicolas Doyen, who came from a family of restaurateurs, bought a tumbledown bar called the *Dauphin* and gave it his own name. He painted the shutters green, whitewashed the façade, and began serving meals accompanied by a white wine from Suresnes, west of Paris. The *Montagnards* soon made it their meeting-place, while the

❝At the far end of the Avenue des Champs-Élysées, and to the left, as you walk up between Place de la Concorde and the Rond-Point toward the Arc de Triomphe, you come to the *Ledoyen* restaurant, where lunch was compulsory on days when there were private viewings. In those far off days, one met there Benjamin Constant ... Henri Gervex ... Jean-Louis Forain ... Caran ... and, of course, Mme Madeleine Lemaire ... Mme Lemaire's flowers came from the tops of boxes of chocolates, and not as good as those you can get at Boissier's. 'D'you know how much those cauliflowers cost?' Caran used to say. 'No. Five – six thousand francs?' 'Four francs fifty dead.' And he would add, 'Good enough for a Grand-Duke.'❞
Léon Daudet, *Paris vécu*

Ledoyen

A REVOLUTIONARIES' MEETING-PLACE
The *Ledoyen* restaurant was a popular haunt of the *Montagnards* during the

French Revolution. One day in 1794, as Jean-Lambert Tallien and his friends plotted the downfall of Robespierre in an upstairs room, Robespierre himself was lunching below.

Girondins opted for Rue Saint-Honoré. The premises were frequently enlarged and redecorated, and after Doyen's departure in 1830, a new manager by the name of Drouhin gave his own name to the restaurant.

FROM LE DOYEN TO LEDOYEN. The restaurant was given the name *Le Doyen* (as two words) after Jacob Ignaz Hittorff rebuilt it in 1848 as part of the Champs-Élysées development. At the time of the Second Empire, this neo-classical building flanked by a vast terrace became a favorite haunt of young gallants and of duellists who came here to make it up with each other after firing off a few cartridges in the surrounding woods. The proprietor commented thus after one such episode: "A fine duel, gentlemen. One of the best. It got through six bottles of champagne!" In 1870, the restaurant was laid waste by the mob for not closing down during a march-past by Prussian troops along the Champs-Élysées, and its reputation slowly declined thereafter. In 1962 a new manager called Lejeune had some renovation work carried out and renamed the restaurant *Ledoyen*, in one word. The terrace was covered over, and the whole place rejuvenated by the presence of a certain Guy Legay in the kitchen, but unfortunately the restaurant failed yet again. A celebrated figure in Parisian night life by the name of Régine became the proprietor in 1988 but her reign was even briefer than Lejeune's. Finally, in 1992 the restaurant was taken over by another woman, Guislaine Arabian, who left her restaurant in Lille to try her luck in Paris. She went for a new formula, offering gourmet cooking upstairs in a Napoleonic dining-room and simpler fare downstairs. Her cuisine is influenced to an extent by her Flemish origins and, at its best, is very inventive. Her commercial logic also seems sound. After all, why should something that works so well on the other side of the Champs-Élysées – at *Laurent* ▲ *196* and also at the *Élysée Lenôtre* ▲*191* – fail to work equally well here? And of course the flowery, shaded terrace is as charming as ever!

MME DE POMPADOUR'S TOWN HOUSE. On the site of 112 and 114 Rue du Faubourg-Saint-Honoré, there once stood a private townhouse built in the second half of the 18th century, and now mainly remembered as the home of Mme de Pompadour. Count Jules de Castellane bought it in 1829 and enlarged it in 1835 to make an amateur theater to seat four hundred. But Hippolyte Jammet, son of the great chef and hotelier, acquired the building and turned it into a hotel, the *Bristol*, which opened in 1924. Frederick Hervey, Earl of Bristol and Bishop of Derby, was one of the great travelers of the 18th century and a friend of Goethe and Voltaire. He traveled on horseback, ensured that he was always preceded by his chef, who decided where his master would spend the night, and was followed by beasts of burden carrying his baggage. Dozens of hotels were named after him during the 19th century. However, by 1924 this custom was dying out, and the itinerant earl was in danger of being forgotten. Whereupon Hippolyte Jammet, taking advantage of the fact that the last *Bristol* hotel in Paris in Place Vendôme had disappeared, re-launched the name.

CHIC AND DISCREET. In those days the Faubourg Saint-Honoré stayed aloof from Parisian high life, a handicap that was eventually turned to advantage. The hotel was always sought out by aristocrats and diplomats for its chic and discretion, and so it remains to this day. It was here on the night of September 10-11, 1993 that Israeli negotiators and PLO representatives met two days before the historic signing of the Declaration of Principles. The hotel had been enlarged in 1948 when a congregation of French nuns, the Petites Soeurs de la Bonne Espérance, left their convent for Canada, and in 1978 the cloister was converted into 1450 square yards of French garden. The *Bristol* had in the meantime become one of the most admired hotels in the world for its service and magnificent decoration, just at a time when the Faubourg Saint-Honoré was turning into one of the smartest quarters of Paris. A roll call of royalty and film stars who have stayed at the *Bristol* would be like reading *Who's Who*. The rooftop covered swimming pool is one of the establishment's more recent improvements. It was conceived by the designer of Niarchos' and Onassis' yachts; the massive décor is made of teak, and there is a

IRISH CONNECTIONS
Hippolyte Jammet, who founded the *Bristol* hotel, was Irish (there is a Jammet Hotel in Dublin), as was Frederick Hervey, one of the great travelers of the 18th century.

THE BRISTOL AND THE OCCUPATION
When the main Parisian hotels were being requisitioned by the occupying forces, the *Bristol*

management had the ingenious idea of placing their hotel at the disposal of the United States, which was then still neutral. Many embassies were temporarily housed there, and twelve serving ambassadors were still there at the time of the Liberation.

CÉCILE SOREL
When Sorel moved from the *Comédie-Française* to the *Casino de Paris* in 1933, she became a permanent resident at the *Bristol*. She must have thought she had done the right thing as she swept down the superb wrought-iron staircase every day.

Marguerite Moreno in the role of the Mad Woman of Chaillot at the *Théâtre de l'Athénée* in 1945.

trompe l'oeil view of a sailing-ship coming into view at Cap d'Antibes.

A RESTAURANT-THEATER. Count Jules de Castellane's small theater, which was never pulled down, now houses the *Bristol*'s winter restaurant and is one of the hotel's more beautiful rooms. The glass roof through which daylight filters is adorned with gold leaf. The atmosphere of the Regency-style oval dining-room, with its tapestries, crystal chandeliers and walls covered with Hungarian oak wainscoting, is of the utmost refinement. The ceiling is adorned with frescoes depicting the four seasons, executed in the 1940's by Gustave-Louis Jaulmes, who also decorated the *salle Pleyel*, one of the main concert halls in Paris. In the summer, guests prefer to lunch overlooking the patio beyond the huge bay windows that open up and are framed by large doors resembling garden screens. The cuisine is classic but, winter or summer, the *Bristol* is unique.

CHEZ FRANCIS ◆ 391

THE MAD WOMAN OF CHAILLOT. On the terrace of *Chez Francis* in Place de l'Alma, a group of shady businessmen are sitting over a few glasses of port plotting how to take some gullible fools for a ride. They opt for mine prospecting, and agree to open a bank to finance work on the land underneath Paris, and Chaillot Hill in particular. Regular customers of *Chez Francis* and residents of the 16th *arrondissement* can relax! This is just a scene from the beginning of *The Mad Woman of Chaillot*, a two-act play by Jean Giraudoux, premiered at the *Athénée* on December 19, 1945. It has a happy ending. Poetry and freedom triumph, and the crooks fall over the precipice above the cave in the side of the hill where the Mad Woman lives.

THEATRICAL GOINGS-ON. There are no more two-faced prospectors or mad women on the *Chez Francis* terrace, just fashionably dressed diners who have come for a meal after the theater or a show at the *Comédie des Champs-Élysées* or the *Crazy Horse Saloon* nearby. This elegant

"CHEZ FRANCIS TERRACE, PLACE DE L'ALMA. DO BE SEATED, BARON. THE WAITER WILL POUR YOU SOME OF MY BEST PORT. WE MUST CELEBRATE WHAT IS GOING TO BE A HISTORIC DAY."

JEAN GIRAUDOUX

brasserie is ideally placed opposite Pont de l'Alma and at a confluence of the quays running along the Seine and the Montaigne, George-V and Marceau avenues. It is as if *Chez Francis* is right down by the theater footlights, with the Eiffel Tower as its backdrop; it has been thus for over a century. A hundred years ago, when the building was a bistro patronized by coach drivers, it was called *A la Vue de la tour Eiffel*. With the arrival of Francis, *Chez Francis* became a fashionable grill room of the 1950's, but twenty years later interior designer Slavik redecorated it in the characteristically flamboyant style that it has retained to the present day. The semicircular main dining-room is situated next to the bar near the entrance; it is adorned with mirrors that reflect ad infinitum the chandelier decorated with beetles, and large ceiling fans keep the room at an even temperature. As soon as the clouds blow over, guests hasten out on to the covered terrace, with awning supported on copper brackets. When the sun comes out, everybody moves to the outside terrace. At one time, Francis used to set out tables on the Pont de l'Alma itself.

"Jouvet burst out laughing ... We were at *Chez Francis*, just outside his theater and a short walk from

LE BŒUF SUR LE TOIT   ◆ *391*

A PANTOMIME BALLET. *Le Boeuf sur le toit* (*The Ox on the Roof*) is the title of a pantomime ballet first performed on February 21, 1920 at the *Comédie des Champs-Élysées* by the Fratellini company. To music by Darius Milhaud, the piece portrayed the dandified customers of an American bar called "The Ox on the Roof". The production was by Jean Cocteau and the sets by Raoul Dufy. It was one of the high spots in the Roaring Twenties. Bohemians and the upper classes were united by the frenzy and sense of urgency that so

my home ... The whole of Parisian society had paraded down the fashionable grill room, down what was once a cabmen's *bistrot* ... When our friend Francis threw us out – for it was very, very late – we went home laughing."

Blaise Cendrars, *Bourlinguer*

characterized the era, and together they applauded this homage to impertinence. After the show, everyone – Gide, Diaghilev, Picasso, Mistinguett, Chevalier, Satie, Poiret, Tzara, Radiguet, Daudet, Fargue, Léger, Poulenc and others of whom nobody had ever heard – gathered at the *Gaya*, a bar in Rue Duphot where Jean Wiener played fashionable syncopated pieces on the piano.

"The sign of the bar where our scene takes place, wrote Cocteau, is at the *Boeuf sur le toit*. Only look for any meaning in the signs that say *Chien qui fume* (Smoking dog) and *Chien borgne* (One-eyed dog)."
Maurice Sachs,
Au temps du Boeuf
sur le toit

"At one table, there is André Gide, Marc Allégret …. Beside them, Diaghilev, Kochno and Picasso. A little further on, Mistinguett, Voltera and Maurice Chevalier. Leaning against a wall, Erik Satie, René Clair, his wife and Bathori. Then I catch sight of Francis Picabia who is talking to Paul Poiret and Tzara ... Cocteau and Radiguet want to go and have a word at every table. They embrace Anna de Noailles, who is joined by Lucien Daudet who has just come in."
Jean Wiener,
Souvenirs

FROM RUE BOISSY-D'ANGLAS TO RUE DU COLISÉE. Success soon forced the company to move out of Rue Boissy-d'Anglas into a bar that came to be called *Le Boeuf sur le toit*. Doucet replaced Wiener on the piano, Cocteau stayed on percussion, but the artists gradually gave way as fashionable Parisians poured in. In July 1922, a few months before his death, Marcel Proust put in an appearance wearing a white tie, but the atmosphere was fading. In 1925, *Le Boeuf sur le toit* moved to Rue de Penthièvre and then in 1934 it moved again to Avenue Pierre-Ier-de-Serbie, before finally settling in Rue du Colisée in 1941. The magic had not been working for a long time; it closed down in 1943 on the orders of the occupying forces but re-opened in 1949. It then just about managed to keep going until it was bought by Jean-Paul Bucher, director of the Flo group, in 1985. The manager of Flo ▲ *259*, *Julien* ▲ *264*, the *Vaudeville* ▲ *208* and, before long, *La Coupole* ▲ *156* was once more remarkably successful in attracting to this restaurant close to the Champs-Élysées a lot of Parisians who would never normally dream of eating in such an area. More than 750 meals are now served every day.

AN OVERDONE DÉCOR. It has to be said that Flo did not stint with the décor. The restaurant is on several levels, and the vast area in the style of a dining-room on a luxury liner is decorated in what is almost a caricature of Art Deco. Stucco friezes with replicated motifs, huge engraved mirrors, geometrically formed chandeliers and lamp brackets, sideboards adorned with dark paneling, and sharp-angled, velvet-upholstered chairs all recall the era of *Le Boeuf sur le toit*. A reproduction of Picabia's painting *L'Oeil Cacodylate*, and a Jean Marais sculpture dedicated to Cocteau depicting an ox's head with horns made into a lyre, hang on the wall just in case there is any doubt. The place is like a beautiful but empty jewel case. However, anyone pursuing the spirit of Milhaud, Cocteau and Dufy will find the oysters excellent!

5.
PALAIS-ROYAL,
BOURSE,
CONCORDE

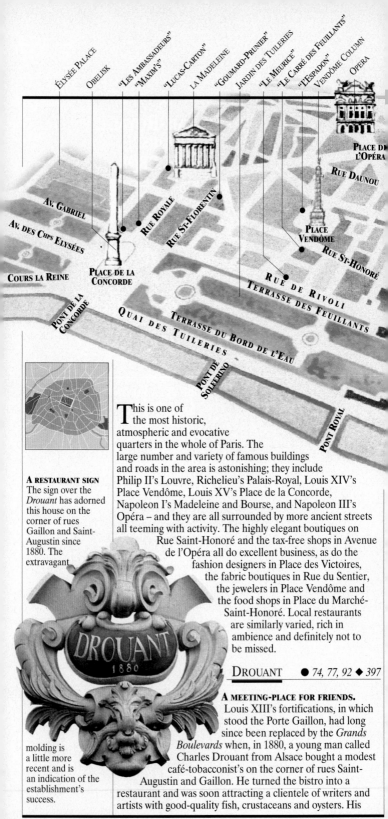

ÉLYSÉE PALACE — OBELISK — "LES AMBASSADEURS" "MAXIM'S" — "LUCAS-CARTON" — LA MADELEINE — "GOUMARD-PRUNIER" — JARDIN DES TUILERIES — "LE MEURICE" — "LE CARRÉ DES FEUILLANTS" — "L'ESPADON" VENDÔME COLUMN — OPÉRA

PLACE DE L'OPÉRA

RUE DAUNOU

AV. GABRIEL

AV. DES CHPS ELYSÉES

RUE ROYALE

RUE ST-FLORENTIN

PLACE VENDÔME

RUE ST-HONORÉ

COURS LA REINE

PLACE DE LA CONCORDE

RUE DE RIVOLI

TERRASSE DES FEUILLANTS

PONT DE LA CONCORDE

QUAI DES TUILERIES

TERRASSE DU BORD DE L'EAU

PONT DE SOLFERINO

PONT ROYAL

A RESTAURANT SIGN
The sign over the *Drouant* has adorned this house on the corner of rues Gaillon and Saint-Augustin since 1880. The extravagant

molding is a little more recent and is an indication of the establishment's success.

This is one of the most historic, atmospheric and evocative quarters in the whole of Paris. The large number and variety of famous buildings and roads in the area is astonishing; they include Philip II's Louvre, Richelieu's Palais-Royal, Louis XIV's Place Vendôme, Louis XV's Place de la Concorde, Napoleon I's Madeleine and Bourse, and Napoleon III's Opéra – and they are all surrounded by more ancient streets all teeming with activity. The highly elegant boutiques on Rue Saint-Honoré and the tax-free shops in Avenue de l'Opéra all do excellent business, as do the fashion designers in Place des Victoires, the fabric boutiques in Rue du Sentier, the jewelers in Place Vendôme and the food shops in Place du Marché-Saint-Honoré. Local restaurants are similarly varied, rich in ambience and definitely not to be missed.

DROUANT ● 74, 77, 92 ◆ 397

A MEETING-PLACE FOR FRIENDS.
Louis XIII's fortifications, in which stood the Porte Gaillon, had long since been replaced by the *Grands Boulevards* when, in 1880, a young man called Charles Drouant from Alsace bought a modest café-tobacconist's on the corner of rues Saint-Augustin and Gaillon. He turned the bistro into a restaurant and was soon attracting a clientele of writers and artists with good-quality fish, crustaceans and oysters. His

"PIERRE GAILLON"
"DROUANT"
PYRAMIDE DU LOUVRE
"L'INCROYABLE"
"LE GRAND VÉFOUR"
"LE VAUDEVILLE"
"LE GRAND COLBERT"
"GALLOPIN"
BOURSE
"LE CROISSANT"

RUE DES P'TITS CHPS

AV. DE L'OPÉRA

PLACE DES VICTOIRES

RUE DU MAIL

RUE D'ABOUKIR

RUE Ce DES P'TITS CHPS

RUE J. J. ROUSSEAU

RUE DE RIVOLI

RUE BERGER

QUAI DU LOUVRE

RUE DU LOUVRE

RUE DE L'ARBRE SEC

PONT DES ARTS

FATTED OX
When Drouant decided to enlarge his café-tobacconist's in the 1880's, he bought up the adjoining shop, a former butcher's called *Flesselles*. It had been famous in the Second Empire for supplying the famous fatted ox that was walked through the streets of the capital for three days at carnival time. He also acquired the cellars of neighboring houses.

JULES AND EDMOND DE GONCOURT
If the *Journal* he wrote with his brother Jules is correct, Edmond de Goncourt (1822–96) dined at *Drouant* for the first time on October 30, 1894. On his death Edmond left a fund to establish the *Académie Goncourt*, which was to award an annual prize for the "best work of imagination in prose." It was set up in 1902. The first jury met in 1903 at the *Grand Hôtel*, but subsequently convened at the *Champeaux* and the *Café de Paris*. Then, almost twenty years to the day after Edmond dined at *Drouant* for the first time, the Goncourt jury met there again on October 31, 1914. The restaurant seemed to come up to the jurors' expectations as they have gone there ever since.

regulars at this stage included the Daudets, father and son, Renoir, Pissaro and Rodin. With even greater success on the horizon, he decided to expand and his gamble paid off when, in 1885, a group of friends, writers, journalists and artists chose to hold their regular Friday evening dinners at the *Drouant*. The bistro's original customers were later joined by other artists, including Gustave Geoffroy, Octave Mirbeau, Jean Ajalbert, the Rosny brothers, Paul Neveu, Paul and Georges Clemenceau, Toulouse-Lautrec, Monet and Edmond de Goncourt.

THE GONCOURT BROTHERS.
The Goncourt jury met at the *Drouant* for the first time in 1914, and has continued to do so ever since. Léon Daudet, the leading gourmet among the Goncourt academicians, may no longer determine what is on the menu, but the *Blanc de Blancs* ■ 38 that he was the first to introduce still accompanies all their meals.

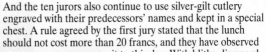

And the ten jurors also continue to use silver-gilt cutlery engraved with their predecessors' names and kept in a special chest. A rule agreed by the first jury stated that the lunch should not cost more than 20 francs, and they have observed it to this day. With blithe disregard for inflation, the academicians continue to pay just 20 centimes for their meal!

AN ART DECO SETTING. In 1923 Charles Drouant decided to rebuild his restaurant, which was now rapidly expanding, and he entrusted the task of renovation to Louis-Hippolyte Boileau, who had designed the *Bon Marché* and the *Lutétia*, and to the interior designer Jacques-Émile Ruhlmann. They installed a wide wrought-iron staircase, and restyled the old café with a ceiling of gilt staff decorated with reliefs of fish, shellfish and crustaceans, and brackets in the form of dolphins. The restaurant remained in the Drouant family until Jean, nephew of Charles' son, decided to sell all his restaurants in 1976. Robert Pascal, who had started at the *Drouant* at the age of eighteen, took over but in 1986 he too sold out to the Élitair group, which immediately carried out extensive building work. As so often happens, there is a sense that the restoration is little more than a copy of what was there before. Perhaps we need to let time take its course, and just enjoy the excellent food served in both the café and the Goncourt academicians' restaurant.

PIERRE "À LA FONTAINE GAILLON" ◆ 401

SPOILT FOR CHOICE. Those wishing to patronize Jules Hardouin-Mansart can choose between *L'Espadon* ▲ 224, the *Ritz* restaurant in Place Vendôme, and *Pierre "A la Fontaine Gaillon"* in Place Gaillon. The Duke of Lorgues' townhouse was built in 1672 for Frémont, first a footman and then

Guardian of the Royal Treasure, whose daughter married the Duke in 1676. Over the years, the house belonged to several royal families: Princess Marie-Anne of Bourbon-Conti, daughter of Louis XIV and the Duchess of La Vallière; then her grand-nephew the Duke of La Vallière, later Christian IV, Duke of Deux-Ponts-Birkenfeld; and finally the Duke of Richelieu, who bought it in 1795.

FINE RENOVATIONS, FINE CUISINE. It was in 1880 that the *Pierre* restaurant moved into the first floor near the fountain, and introduced the *bouillon* formula – providing hundreds of inexpensive meals a day. Custom flowed in and it met with immediate success. The *Pierre*'s style evolved as proprietor succeeded proprietor, and in the 1930's it acquired much of the reputation that it enjoys today, although it was not until 1984 that the décor began to match the culinary

standards. That was the year when Roger Boyer, a distant cousin of Marcellin Cazes, who founded *Lipp* ▲ *129*, decided to redecorate the *Pierre* in a manner befitting its setting. On the suggestion of Monuments de France, government heritage advisers, the criss-cross façade was restored, and new rooms were added, each one representing a particular style. The *salon Régence* has superb oak paneling and an enormous Louis XIV stone fireplace, while the bar is done out in the style of Charles X. When the weather is fine, it is possible to eat out on the covered terrace by the fountain. The *Pierre*'s fine classical cuisine comes close to outshining the "other" restaurant in Place Gaillon, which was opened in the same year by a certain Charles Drouant ▲ *204*.

GALLOPIN   ◆ *398*

"STOCK EXCHANGE LUNCHEON BAR." The short trip from the Palais Brongniart to the *Gallopin* is like going into a pub in another financial bear garden, the City of London. That is not an overstatement: it does say *Stock Exchange Luncheon Bar* on the frosted glass door, after all! Gustave Gallopin, who was married to an Englishwoman, had the interior decoration carried out in his London

establishment before moving to Rue Notre-Dame-des-Victoires in 1876. The style of the *Gallopin* is resolutely Victorian. The dark tones of the decorative scheme come from the mahogany paneling, which is broken up by mirrors framed with ribbed columns surmounted by gilt Ionic capitals, while the chandeliers with their glass shades and the coat stands along the walls give the room a warm, cosy and hospitable feel. A cream-colored ceiling with abundant moldings equally typical of the Victorian age features strongly in both dining-rooms, and a corner of one of them is lit up by a glass ceiling adorned with floral motifs. An enthusiast for

THE FONTAINE GAILLON
This fountain, made by Jean Beausire in 1707, was the only water point in the quarter. It bears a Latin inscription: *Rex loquitur, cadit e saxo fons, omen amemus, instar aquae, o cives, omnia sponte fluent*. It was originally called the Louis-le-Grand, and then the Antin, Fountain. It was restored in 1828 by Louis Tullius Joaquim Visconti, who also designed the fountain in Place Saint-Sulpice and Napoleon I's tomb in Les Invalides.

The *Gallopin* restaurant's customers include journalists from Agence France-Presse in Place de la Bourse, as well as staff from the Palais Brongniart and the Stock Exchange.

RUE NOTRE-DAME-DES-VICTOIRES
The church that gave its name to the road where *Drouant* is situated dates from 1666. It replaced a chapel built in 1629 to commemorate the taking of La Rochelle two years earlier. The present church, which was not completed until 1740, attracts many pilgrims and its walls are covered with ex-votos. The composer Lully (1632–87) is buried there.

ART DECO STYLE
The present décor of the *Vaudeville* dates from the 1920's. It is characterized by the elegance of the design, as demonstrated in this statue of a woman archer.

the genuine article and a stickler for authenticity, Gustave Gallopin also had a revolving door brought over from New York, but all it did was stop corpulent bankers from getting in and out. It has now been replaced by swing doors.

FLUTES AND BOCKS. The establishment was an immediate hit with locally based financiers, and the district's considerable affluence rapidly ensured that more champagne was consumed at the *Gallopin* than anywhere else in Paris – except for cabarets. Actresses from nearby theaters inevitably followed, and on slack days champagne flutes were replaced by *bocks* (small beer glasses). As time went by, artists such as Jules Berry, Albert Préjean, Arletty and Raimu became regulars, and the Communist Party leader, Marcel Cachin, recalls how he would strike the fear of God into the speculators' hearts by his very presence. It was certainly the only thing that put a stop to the passing of "tips," which together with the clanking of plates, formed the only background noise at the *Gallopin*. The financial honeypot has now gone, but the "golden boys" still meet there. The best value dishes in the house fluctuate even less than the Stock Exchange's top share prices.

VAUDEVILLE ▲ *202* ◆ *401*

A CAFÉ THEN A THEATER. The *Vaudeville* dates from 1827, and must initially have had a different name since the Vaudeville theater, after which it was eventually named, was at the time situated in Boulevard des Capucines. When the building in which it was housed was burned down in 1838, the theater transferred to Place de la Bourse, although it was moved again in 1868 when Rue du 4-septembre was being constructed, and returned to the

Boulevards. In 1927 it was turned into a movie theater. This café in Rue Vivienne may have called itself after the theater when *La Dame aux camélias* was put on at the Vaudeville in 1852. At all events, the success of Alexandre Dumas' play was good for business.

BETWEEN THE PALAIS-ROYAL AND THE BOULEVARDS. Rue Vivienne, which is situated between the Palais-Royal and the Boulevards, and between the Bourse and the theaters, won its gastronomic spurs when the *Champeaux* restaurant opened there around 1800. The *Champeaux* was patronized by bankers, businessmen and merchants, while the future *Vaudeville* catered for more humble Stock Exchange employees. The Palais-Royal had been at its peak at the end

RUE VIVIENNE
The name of the road where the *Vaudeville* stands is the feminine form of the name of the Vivien family, who were lords of Saint-Marc and also owned the land on which the road was constructed in 1652. A nearby street dating from the same period is called Rue Saint-Marc.

of the previous century, but was now in decline; meanwhile, Rue Vivienne attached itself to the Boulevards, which were on the way up ● *45*.

THE FLO GROUP. In their turn, the Boulevards fell away as well, and speculators and theater-lovers were the *Vaudeville*'s sole remaining customers. It then joined the Flo group ▲ *259* in 1979, and Jean-Paul Bucher turned the café into a brasserie serving hundreds of meals every day. The good-natured crush and the waiters' balletic contortions as they bring the seafood platters to the tables provide much entertainment. These days, brasserie food is a surefire winner. What more could one ask for? Perhaps a little more soul – and even *La Dame aux camélias* on the menu?

THE PRESS
In 1914 the offices of *L'Humanité* were at No. 142 Rue Montmartre. By that time, the area between the Stock Exchange and Le Sentier had become the capital's press center.

LE CROISSANT ◆ *396*

"JAURÈS HAS BEEN KILLED!" The *Humanité* journalist tells the sad story thus: "It was dinner time ... We went down to the *Croissant* restaurant and sat down at the long table on the left as you go in. Jaurès had Landrieu on his left and Renaudel on his right ... *Le Croissant* is a busy place. People were coming and going. We did not

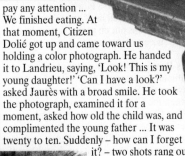

> **"**A crime always precedes the greatest crimes of all ... The abominable carnage that the military and nationalists of all countries are at this very moment planning in the darkness of their minds has begun with a shocking murder ... May the blood of this just man who has perished at his post, the victim of unforgivable hatred, so appal the world that peoples already opposed to war may find the strength – and there is still time – to stay the murderers' hands.**"**
> *L'Humanité*
> August 1, 1914

pay any attention ...
We finished eating. At that moment, Citizen Dolié got up and came toward us holding a color photograph. He handed it to Landrieu, saying, 'Look! This is my young daughter!' 'Can I have a look?' asked Jaurès with a broad smile. He took the photograph, examined it for a moment, asked how old the child was, and complimented the young father ... It was twenty to ten. Suddenly – how can I forget it? – two shots rang out, there was a flash, and I heard the blood curdling screams of a terrified woman: 'Jaurès has been killed! Jaurès has been killed!' Jaurès had just slumped on to his left side, and we were all on our feet shouting, gesticulating and running. There was a moment of complete confusion and disbelief. Some ran out into the street – the two shots had been fired point-blank from outside, and through the window that Jaurès had had his back to. The rest of us looked at Jaurès. He was struggling for breath, and had his eyes closed ... Renaudel was using napkins to mop up the blood pouring from the wound – a small hole at the back of his head with some whitish matter around it. 'Gentlemen,' announced the doctor, who had just arrived, 'I am afraid there is nothing I can do.' "

WINDS OF CHANGE. "Jaurès assassinated" was *L'Humanité*'s front page banner headline for August 1, 1914. The previous evening, the Socialist leader and chief of *L'Humanité*, who had worked so hard for peace, paid for his efforts with his life, and a few days later the country would be at war. History had chosen a fine summer's evening to visit this peaceful café-restaurant, the *Croissant*, which had stood on the corner of rues Montmartre and du Croissant since 1850. Photos taken shortly after Jaurès' murder show black marble plates on the wooden shop front announcing in gold letters: "Open all night. 'Plat du jour' 75 centimes. Sauerkraut, ham, sandwiches, fine wines,

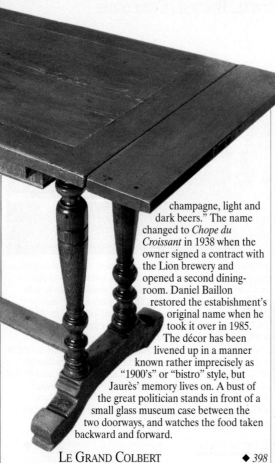

champagne, light and dark beers." The name changed to *Chope du Croissant* in 1938 when the owner signed a contract with the Lion brewery and opened a second dining-room. Daniel Baillon restored the estabishment's original name when he took it over in 1985.

The décor has been livened up in a manner known rather imprecisely as "1900's" or "bistro" style, but Jaurès' memory lives on. A bust of the great politician stands in front of a small glass museum case between the two doorways, and watches the food taken backward and forward.

LE GRAND COLBERT ◆ 398

LOUIS XIV'S GREAT BOOKKEEPER. There is no question that Jean-Baptiste Colbert deserves the sobriquet "great." As Louis XIV's principal minister for twenty-five years, he presided over the kingdom's economic expansion that financed the Sun King's successes. In 1665 he bought a townhouse built thirty years earlier by Le Vau for Guillaume Bautru de Serrant when Rue Vivienne was under construction. He therefore lived not far from the house where his former protector Cardinal Mazarin lived until he died, and which later became the National Library. In 1789, Bautru's house was given to the king, who installed in it the department of state that administered Crown property. The Vivienne and Colbert Galleries were opened on this site in 1826.

FROM BOUILLON TO BRASSERIE. The *Grand Colbert* restaurant, which gives on to Rue Vivienne and the Galerie Colbert, is not the first commercial undertaking to use the name. During the reign of Louis-Philippe (1830-48), for instance, there was a large draper's shop at this address, and it was replaced by a *bouillon* a hundred years later. Thereafter the building underwent much restoration and various alterations before closing down in 1987. The Fisher group, specialists in arts administration, then bought the site and did it up with a view to converting it into an elegant brasserie. A large bar was added, mirrors were hung on the walls, and

JEAN-BAPTISTE COLBERT (1619–83) He began his service with Cardinal Mazarin, who subsequently recommended him to Louis XIV. Colbert was appointed Intendant of Finances in 1661, but was unable to revive the finances of a state permanently at war. The application of mercantilism enabled him to develop French industry, and he also concerned himself with the arts. His influence declined as that of his great rival, Louvois, rose.

THE PASSAGE COLBERT

❝I adore the passage Colbert. I am enraptured by the elegant proportions of its ... architecture and the majesty of its appearance ... I recommend you take a look at the rotunda. The chandelier that illuminates it looks like a coconut palm in the middle of the savannah. Priestesses of lingerie and perfumes have pitched camp round about. How many generations of linen maids have I seen pass to and forth and die out round the chandelier!❞

Amédée Kermel
Le Livre des Cent et Un

Pleasing bric-a-brac makes the *Incroyable* look like a tavern from the set of an operetta.

polychrome décor found on the premises which dated back as far as the mid-19th century served as a model for mural frescoes. The room is now divided by molded glass panels, while the red velvet benches, the copper bar and the chandeliers all add to the general air of jollification. Joël Fleury, late of the Flo group, took the establishment over in 1992, and its future still rests with him. Colbert, who has always been so fond of covered galleries, is commemorated in a dish – *whiting Colbert* – that bears his name. It is thought that Audiger, the great statesman's chef, may have invented it. Audiger was the author of a work entitled *The Well-Kept House and the Art of Housekeeping for a Great Land and Others, both in Town and Country, and the Duties of all Officers and Other Domestic Servants*.

L'INCROYABLE   ◆ 398

"IT'S INCEDIBLE!" They wore enormous wigs *en oreille de chien* (dog's ear style), tucked their chins behind huge cravats, wore coats with long tails and habitually sported canes made of knotty wood. This sartorial affectation was then capped by the use of affected speech in which the pronunciation of the the letter "r" was dropped. For example, instead of saying *"C'est incroyable!"* (It's incredible!) "they used to say *"C'est incoyable!"* (It's incedible!), and so came to be called the

Incroyables (Incredibles). The meeting-place for these affluent young men was the Palais-Royal, where they met their sisters, the *Merveilleuses* (Marvelous), whose generous gowns in the ancient style left little to the imagination. There are two pictures on the wall of the *Incroyable*, which stands between rues de Richelieu and de Montpensier; one is of the *Incroyables*, the other is of the *Merveilleuses*. The pictures are sold each time the restaurant changes hands. This has happened frequently since the 1930's when the bistro became a restaurant – and where *huîtres* (oysters) presumably are never on sale as the menu does not have words with an "r" in them!

A PROVINCIAL HAVEN IN PARIS. The *Incroyable* occupies the first floor of a townhouse dating from 1643. It was owned first by Jean-Baptiste Bochard de Saron, President of the French Parliament and astronomer, who was beheaded in 1794; then by Rose Bertin, who served as dress designer to Marie-Antoinette, and whose shop was on the corner; and later, during the Restoration, by a famous *Comédie-Française* actor of the time called Potier. The latter has given his name to the flower-decked space where the restaurant puts out a few tables in fine weather. On such days, it is easy to imagine oneself many miles from Paris.

A WARDROBE AND A BUFFET. The interior looks like a tavern out of an operetta with its engravings, mirrors, plates and jugs hanging on the wall. In the smaller of the two dining-rooms, dinner is taken next to a mirror wardrobe – the sort that is left in the dining-room because it will not fit into the bedroom. However, dancing is absolutely forbidden in front of the buffet; this is a discreet establishment, even allowing for the fact that it is popular among American and Japanese tourists.

LE GRAND VÉFOUR ● 45, 78 ◆ 398

THE DUKE OF ORLÉANS' COMMERCIAL CENTER. The layout of the Palais-Royal as we know it today was occasioned by debts once amassed by the Duke of Orléans. To pay them off the future Philippe-Égalité decided to sell by lots the palace gardens that had been in his family since 1692. Richelieu's Palais-Cardinal had become the Palais-Royal in 1643 when Anne of Austria, now Regent, came and settled here with her two sons, Louis XIV and Philip of Orléans, but the size of the huge garden was substantially reduced by the Duke's building

THE INCROYABLES AND THE MERVEILLEUSES
The *chansonnier* Ange Pitou pilloried the Royalist youth of the Directoire with these words:
❝Everything is unbelievable about you, from your heads to your toes: Revolting hats, huge feet in tiny shoes ... You wear shoes as if you were St George and hats as if you were Marlborough. Double-breasted waistcoats hugging your chests and golden pins at your necks, three enormous cravats concealing your chins – and the ends of your plaits look like horns sticking out of your foreheads.❞
Then it was the turn

of the *merveilleuses*:
❝You leave your dresses gaping open for everyone to stare at you and it is no doubt a sacrifice that your stockings are turned up ... All the clothes you wear – jaunty heels, embroidered buckles and shoes, riding boots, stockings with set-in clocks – they are all ridiculously worldly. Deep down, you yearn for the trappings of queens and Roman ladies.❞

> "The *Café de Chartres* has just been reborn amid the luxurious remains of the merveilleuses and the incroyables. The *Véfour* has remained intact because it has fragile things that endure for ever and, with its Louis XVI ceiling and Directoire passe-partout mounting, could extend a terrace into the garden. In the *Florian* café, Paris has become a village with plenty of leisure time.

> It is impossible to love Paris without making a pilgrimage to this scene of desolation. There, you will dine with the shadows of Fabre d'Églantine, Saint-Just, Bonaparte, Barras, Rastignac and Delphine de Nucingen."
> Jean Cocteau
> *Plaquette du bicentenaire du Grand-Véfour*

The Fair Otero.

plans. Between 1781 and 1784 the architect Victor Louis constructed round three sides of the garden an arcaded building consisting of sixty pavilions for rent or sale. Each of them was three arcades wide and comprised a first floor to be used as a shop, a mezzanine, a floor with windows, a garret, and an attic story lined with balustrades. The garden has been open to the public since it was acquired by the Orléans family. It was now transformed into Paris' first commercial center, and also became noted for merrymaking, and not all of it reputable, as the Duke always refused to allow the forces of law and order on his property. Arcades 79-82 were let to a certain Aubertot, who opened the *Café de Chartres* (the Duke of Orléans was also Duke of Chartres). It was soon well-known, serving as a Revolutionary headquarters, then a loyalist meeting-place during the Terror, before embracing Bonapartism and the nobility. A *café-chantant* known as the *Café Montansier* was located on the same site and attracted many visitors. The *Café de Chartres* was bought by Jean Véfour in 1820, and although he ran the place for only two years, he at least bequeathed it his name. Théophile Gautier and Sainte-Beuve dined here with Victor Hugo on the evening of *Hernani*'s tempestuous première in 1830.

AGGRANDIZEMENT. When and why did the *Véfour* become the *Grand Véfour*? Was it in the 1850's when it was decorated and enlarged? Or could it have been a reaction to the opening of a *Petit Véfour* in Galerie de Valois? Perhaps the little *Véfour* acquired its name *after* the big *Véfour*! Either way the appearance of the *Véfour* certainly changed. The Tavernier brothers bought the premises in 1852, and in 1859 enlarged arcades 83–5, which had hitherto been occupied by the *Véry* restaurant, and carried out building work. Each floor was then equipped with its own kitchens, and the current decorations probably date from this period. When more recent restoration was carried out, it became clear that painted panels under glass in the downstairs dining-room dated from the mid-19th century and not from post-Revolutionary times, as the allegories and neo-Pompeian style might have suggested. In 1892 a thirteen-year-old girl from Cadiz, who was later to become *la belle Otero*, used to dance on the tables for a party of gentlemen. They forecast a brilliant future for her, but fashions change. The fashion for the *Grand Véfour* did not survive the century either. Two wars and the years in between did not blow away the dust that had settled on the venerable establishment, and all that remained were the two downstairs dining-rooms. The building was acquired by the association of court bailiffs for the Seine region, and in 1945 Louis Vaudable, former owner of *Maxim's* ▲ *217*, bought the *Grand Véfour*. Unfortunately his customers did not follow him, and he sold out to Raymond Oliver in 1948.

RAYMOND OLIVER ▲ *51*. Oliver was instantly successful. The French writer Colette became a regular and, when rheumatism eventually prevented her from walking, Raymond Oliver would actually carry her to her usual table, the one at which Josephine had waited for Bonaparte. The playwright Jean Cocteau, another regular, designed the menu. Thus, following in these famous footsteps, the whole world came to sit on the lovely black and gold Directoire chairs. The *Grand Véfour*'s star was once more in the ascendant, and Oliver was busy collecting the more earthly but practical Michelin stars. A terrorist attack on the restaurant in 1983 brought an ubrupt end to this prosperous period and, exhausted and dispirited, Oliver finally sold the restaurant over to the Taittinger group, which then carried out refurbishment work in the dining-room. A large number of chefs have been affiliated to the restaurant since this time but, at the *Grand Véfour*, simply having the opportunity to appreciate the atmosphere is half the pleasure anyway.

This wooden trompe l'oeil fireplace is in what was once the *Véfour*'s main dining-room on the second floor. It is now the meeting-place of the association of court bailiffs for the Seine region.

THE PALAIS-ROYAL
"The promenade is superb – ideal after the excellent dinners and lunches in the numerous restaurants that surround this garden, and which are known all over the world ... Strictly speaking, in spite of its two flower beds, its pond and two or three avenues of lime trees, it is not a real garden. Either that, or we no longer have the right to make fun of the *bourgeois* who call their window boxes gardens."
Alfred Delvau
Les Plaisirs de Paris,
1867

"When we dine at *La Taverne anglaise*, we whet our fading appetites with some English mustard."

The Goncourt brothers
Journal, 1860

"I shall never eat again at *La Taverne anglaise*. There is an anaemic woman in her fifties behind the counter, her face emaciated and exhausted from making up the bills, her hair clinging to her temples ... – her savagely serious head is unpleasant to look at when I am eating my food."

Edmond Goncourt
Journal, 1878

LUCAS-CARTON ● *48, 77, 107* ◆ *399*

LUCAS. Almost two centuries separate the Lucas and the Carton who gave their names to this, one of Paris' top restaurants. In 1732 Robert Lucas opened a tavern in Rue Boissy-d'Anglas, which was then called Rue de la Bonne-Morue due to its proximity to a cod restaurant. Good Englishman that he was, Lucas served cold meat and steamed pudding and not unnaturally called his establishment *La Taverne anglaise* (The English Tavern). His reputation was such that, 130 years later, the new buyer, who also owned the *Restaurant de la Madeleine*, which opened in 1851 in Place de la Madeleine, decided to call his new establishment *La Taverne Lucas* in an attempt to retain the *Taverne anglaise*'s customers.

PLANEL. A certain Monsieur Scaliet, who bought the *Lucas* restaurant in 1890, decided in 1902 to change its internal decoration to that of the modern, that is to say Art Nouveau, style. Maple wood, sycamore and bronze dominated the new somber décor, which was somewhat at odds with the more flamboyant style to be found at *Maxim's* ▲ *217* and at popular *bouillons*. The light paneling carved with plant motifs frame smaller decorative panels and, between the pillars separating the two dining-rooms and at either end of the benches, wood carved with intertwining and rounded motifs is set in small sheets of glass. The bronze wall brackets have women's heads emerging from flower stems surrounded

by three bright lampshades. It looks like the work of Louis Majorelle but it is in fact by Planel. This is his only known work, and is a fine example of Jugendstil (German Art Nouveau).

CARTON. It was not until 1925 that Francis Carton, who had learned his trade and won his spurs at the *Café Anglais* ● 46, bought the *Lucas* and added his name to make it the *Lucas-Carton*. A new era brought with it a new style. At the entrance, Carton installed a revolving door. It was set within an Art Deco grille and projecting above it was a half-moon awning that diffused indirect light; mirrors replaced the original decorative panels, although one still remains by the cash desk. There are seven small rooms on the second floor, which can be reached through a door on Passage de la Madeleine. It is popular with politicians requiring discreet meeting-places, while envious Parisian society enters by the main door. In 1945 Francis Carton passed the restaurant on to his son-in-law, who in turn left it to his daughter in 1982. Little by little, *Lucas-Carton* is beginning to rest on its laurels.

ALAIN SENDERENS. The establishment was saved from total oblivion by the Henri Martin group, which bought it in 1984. The décor, blackened over many years by cigar smoke and flambé lobsters, has been cleaned up, the staff ceiling has been remade, the benches have been upholstered in tobacco velvet, and the chairs have been redesigned in 1900's style. Also, the upstairs rooms have been renamed *Le Cercle*, an elegant area including an "uptown" New York bar and Louis XVI dining-rooms. Alain Senderens, formerly of the *Archestrate*, is in charge in the kitchen, where he continues to produce his celebrated masterpieces. Equally distinctive is the fact that restaurant was listed as a historic monument in 1987. In 1989 it was bought by Asahi, which replaced the revolving door with a functional but ugly entrance. It is unfair to cast slurs on such a fine combination of décor and cuisine. The next person to buy the *Lucas-Carton*, perhaps two hundred years hence, will do well to call it the *Taverne Senderens*, or even the *Taverne Planel*.

MAXIM'S

● 48, 76, 85, 97 ◆ 400

MAXIME AND GEORGES. At the end of the 18th century No. 3 Rue Royale was a shop called *Imoda* that was noted for its outstanding ice creams; however, on July 14, 1890 it was ransacked by a mob for displaying flags, including the German flag, on the front of the building. It was then put up for sale just at a time when Maxime Gaillard, who worked at the nearby American bar *le Reynolds*, and her friend Georges Evernaert were getting into serious debt. Somehow *Maxim's et George's* opened in 1893, but success was not immediate. Georges soon retired, and Maxime died in 1895. The establishment was bought by two *maîtres d'hôtel*, Cornuché, formerly of *Durand*, and Chauveau from the *Café Anglais*. They had the restaurant redecorated in the then fashionable Art Nouveau style.

LE CHASSEUR DE CHEZ MAXIM'S ●

WHORES AND GRAND DUKES

During the *Belle Époque*, everything that Paris knew about dukes and grand dukes with their little actresses and their courtesans could be summed up at the *Omnibus*. In the popular big room, or the little rooms

upstairs, the champagne flowed till morning to the strains of a gypsy band.

ALBERT

The most admired *maître d'hôtel* at the beginning of the century.

THE "S" IN MAXIM'S

❝What he [Cornuché] discovered was the 's' in *Maxim's*. He could have called the place *Maxime* except that he would only have been half as successful.❞

Léon Daudet, *Paris vécu*

THE IMPÉRIALE

Parisian society used to flock to the *Impériale*, the most popular basement in the capital. This photograph, taken on October 6, 1955, shows musician Georges Van Parys, singer Juliette Gréco, actress Martine Carol and explorer Paul-Émile Victor.

LOUIS MARNEZ

Louis Marnez, the man employed by Cornuché and Chauveau to redecorate *Maxim's*, was an Art Nouveau specialist. He covered over the courtyard with a glass roof adorned with plant motifs, and constructed the dining-room underneath. He decorated the walls with carved mahogany set off with decorative elements in copper that contained rounded mirrors and painted panels depicting nymphs. The benches and armchairs were upholstered in red leather. By contrast with the strict décor of the *Lucas* ▲ *216*, a restaurant that was no less Art Nouveau and dated from the same period. Marnez here introduced a more flamboyant 1900's style. *Maxim's* has been the toast of Paris for a century.

CUSTOMERS

The most eccentric were Max Lebaudy, Georges Feydeau, author of *La Dame de chez Maxim's*, and Yves Mirande, author of *Le Chasseur de chez Maxim's*. The more normal customers were Boni de Castellane, Robert de Montesquiou and Hélie de Talleyrand.

THE TERRACE

The restaurant was taken over by the Germans during World War Two, and it was expropriated at the time of the Liberation. The owner, Louis Vaudable, bought it back and attracted a wider range of clients. In 1952 the *Maxim's* façade was hidden behind a glass terrace surmounted by a red dais.

THE CUISINE

The cotton industrialist MacFadden had served to him on a silver salver a girl wearing only her dancing shoes. *Maxim's* cuisine has never been as well-known as the ghosts that live on in its peerless décor.

SPIFFING"

Maxim's only sees a ...ction of this army ...fashionable, ...iffing', roistering, ...wdy whores ... One ...them suggests a ...me of knuckle-...nes to an entire ...neration; another ...e with an alluring ...hind, proves to the regulars that the old guard never gives up ... Next to the orchestra is yet another whose diamond clasps on her garters are almost as well known as Botticelli draperies. **

Le Chic magazine, 1895

MAXIM'S AND THE MOVIES
Several films have been based on Yves Mirande's play *Le Chasseur de chez Maxim's*. Above is a still from Maurice Cammage's 1939 film with Félicien Tramel in the leading role.

FIRST COMMUNIONS
❝The restaurant slowly became a public dining-room, and where there had previously only been gentlemen with their mistresses, there were now First Communion lunches. There were also large dinner parties that had become too complicated to prepare in the apartments.❞
Maurice Sachs
Au temps du Boeuf sur le toit.

LE CHASSEUR DE CHEZ MAXIM'S
Chaim Soutine's series of Expressionist portraits is from the 1920's series remembered for the deformed facial traits and exuberant color.

THE BAR
The famous first-floor bar was closed during Louis Vaudable's building works of 1952. It was rebuilt identically on the second floor after couturier Pierre Cardin arrived in 1979 and commissioned Pierre Pothier to renovate the restaurant. It was listed as a historic monument the same year.

PLACE DE LA CONCORDE

When the square was completed in 1772, it was called Place Louis-XV; then in 1792 it was renamed Place de la Révolution and in 1795 Place de la Concorde. In 1814 it reverted to Place Louis-XV, in 1826 it was changed to Place Louis-XVI, and in 1830 it was changed yet again to Place de la Charte, before settling once and for all for Place de la Concorde in 1830.

LOUIS XV REPLACED BY AN OBELISK

Bouchardon's statue of Louis XV initially graced the square before it was pulled down in 1792. A statue of liberty replaced it a few months later. As Madame Roland remarked as she walked to the guillotine, "Ah, Liberty! How many crimes are committed in your name!" Napoleon had it removed in 1800, and in 1831 Louis-Philippe installed the obelisk presented by Mehmet Ali.

LES AMBASSADEURS ● 64 ◆ 396

WHERE HISTORY WAS MADE. The "ambassadors" in question gave their name to a 19th-century theater that was later turned into the restaurant of the *Crillon* hotel. They were also the ambassadors whom the king wanted to lodge in a house built by architect Louis-François Trouard behind the colonnaded façade in Place Louis-XV and completed by his colleague Jacques-Ange Gabriel in 1772. It was finally leased to the Duke of Aumont, and then passed on to the Duke of Crillon in 1788. After providing less aristocratic accommodation during the Revolution, it was revived and refurbished by the Crillon family under the Restoration and remained their property until 1904. In 1907, it was bought by the *Société des grands magasins et hôtel du Louvre* with a view to converting it into a deluxe hotel, and the *Crillon* hotel, one of the smartest in Paris, opened in 1909. It occupies a small place in history; the British and American general staffs using the premises during World War One, but the *Ambassadeurs'* location told against it when the building was requisitioned by the occupying forces during World War Two, and it was damaged by fire in 1944. The hotel was completely redecorated after the war, when its cosmopolitan guests returned.

SUPERB FOOD. The dining-room at *Les Ambassadeurs*, which looks rather like a little hall of mirrors, boasts an unusual display of marquetry consisting of six different kinds of marble, and below the cornice there are extraordinarily detailed frescoes depicting the construction of the hotel by chubby-cheeked little angels. The room is lit by crystal chandeliers and adorned with dark-blue drapes, and the overall atmosphere is one of restrained elegance. Sonia Rykiel designed the table service and has produced seasonal illustrations for chef Christian Constant's menu. The greatest compliment one can pay this talented chef is that the *Crillon* is one of the few deluxe hotels in Paris that are noted for both their traditional and their modern cuisines.

GOUMARD-PRUNIER ◆ 398

THE BEST OYSTERS IN PARIS. Rue Duphot was built in the early 1800's through the grounds of the Convent of the Conception between Boulevard des Capucines and Rue du Faubourg-Saint-Honoré. By 1872 it was a red light district, but that did not discourage Alfred and Catherine Prunier from opening a modest restaurant at No. 9 comprising a counter and ten tables, and specializing in oysters. Grills, snails and lamb's trotters were also on the menu. Its reputation spread

"APRIL 29, 1941. WENT TO PRUNIER IN RUE DUPHOT. THE SMALL ROOM ON THE SECOND FLOOR – COOL, SPICK AND SPAN, WITH A HINT OF AQUAMARINE – IS A POSITIVE INVITATION TO TRY THE SEAFOOD."

ERNST JÜNGER

rapidly, and in 1878 an appreciative American passing through Paris left the Pruniers recipes for oyster soup and fried oysters. These became the first of a series of many dishes imported from the United States that were to be glory of the *Prunier* menu. The establishment was enlarged in 1897. Although it was now Paris' leading oyster restaurant and, as its publicity claimed, it had "frequently appeared in stage representations," it nonetheless remained "a simple, hospitable place." Moreover, it is worth adding that "a woman may lunch or dine here without being harassed ... Almost eighty deliverymen are continually criss-crossing Paris bringing their oysters at specified hours." The restaurant's current motif depicts one of these porters delivering oysters.

"EVERYTHING THAT COMES OUT OF THE SEA." On taking over from his parents in 1904, Émile Prunier asked Louis Majorelle (1859–1926) to redecorate the restaurant in the then fashionable Art Nouveau style. The following year was marked by an epidemic of typhoid fever, which was wrongly blamed on oysters, but Émile turned the disaster to advantage by introducing fish, crustaceans and shellfish on to his menu. This was such a successful maneuver that he decided to buy breeding grounds and oyster beds on the Atlantic coast and chartered small boats for his exclusive use. He also tried to have live fish delivered, but the city tollhouse either emptied the water out of the containers to weigh the fish or included the weight of the water in the cost. Prunier was forced to abandon the idea. Instead he began importing products and specialties from across the Atlantic, and his customers came to know oysters from Blue Point, East River and Lynn Haven, clams from Long Island, and Newburg lobster. After World War One *Prunier* was the only restaurant to import caviar from the former Soviet Union, and later went in for sturgeon fishing and processing sturgeon's eggs in the Gironde. Both Soviet and French caviar were triumphs for Prunier.

A NEW BRANCH AND A NEW NAME. Émile's daughter Simone and Jean Barnagaud opened a branch of *Prunier* in Avenue Victor-Hugo in 1924. The *Prunier Traktir*, as it was called, was furnished and decorated by Louis Hippolite Boileau and remained one of the capital's finest Art Deco restaurants until it closed in 1989. It is scheduled to reopen in 1994. Claude Barnagaud-Prunier of the fourth generation of Pruniers managed the group from 1949 to

CELEBRATED CUSTOMERS

So as not to overload the plane, the only food that the French aviators Charles Nungesser and François Coli took on their unsuccessful flight across the Atlantic was caviar from *Prunier*. The restaurant is also quoted in Marcel Proust's *La Prisonnière*: "Before I had time to tell her that they [the oysters] were better at *Prunier*, she was already asking for everything that the fishwife was calling out." Other regulars, including Georges Clemenceau and his friend Claude Monet, often met over a plate of mussel soup.

THE DON JUAN
The *Goumard-Prunier* restaurant entertains its guests on a superb 100-foot motor yacht built in 1937; it is moored in the port of Javel. The mahogany décor of the dining-room is an ideal setting for seafood meals on the Seine, or even further afield ♦ *326*.

THE BAR AT THE RITZ
"Many years later at the Ritz bar, long after the end of the World War II, Georges, who is the bar chief now and who was the *chasseur* when Scott lived in Paris, asked me, 'Papa, who was this Monsieur Fitzgerald that everyone asks me about?'...

'He was an American writer of the early 'twenties and later who lived some time in Paris and abroad.'...

'It is strange that I have no memory of him,' Georges said... 'You must tell me something about him for my memoirs.'"
Ernest Hemingway
A Moveable Feast

1980 but in 1992 Jean-Claude Goumard stepped in to save *Prunier*, whose director had abruptly walked out. He knew the restaurant well, having worked there for a spell immediately after leaving catering school, and he opened the *Goumard* restaurant in 1980 with his father, Jean, at No. 17 Rue Duphot. Like Émile Prunier, Goumard had a number of excellent seafood suppliers and it was only logical that he should subsequently open the new *Goumard-Prunier* at No. 9 Rue Duphot. Claude Lafond's restoration work preserved everything that could possibly be salvaged in a building that was over a hundred years old: he redesigned some of the rooms as well as the splendid first-floor kitchen, which is separated from the entrance by a mirror, and he also redecorated the façade. The largely fish and seafood cuisine carries on the fine traditions of the two earlier restaurants from which this establishment developed.

L'ESPADON ♦ *397*

CÉSAR RITZ. César Ritz was born in Niederwald, Switzerland, in 1850. After working as a shepherd, assistant sommelier and sacristan, he came to Paris, where he was employed by a third-rate establishment, the *Fidélité* hotel, performing a wide range of tasks. Ritz then began to move in loftier circles at the *Voisin*, a fashionable Second Empire restaurant in Rue Saint-Honoré where, according to his wife, "authentic dishes were served to authentic guests". Following the *Voisin*'s decline, Ritz worked in deluxe hotels in France and abroad where he rapidly climbed the managerial ladder. In 1889, he was appointed manager of the *Savoy*, which with the help of Auguste Escoffier as chef he turned into the best hotel in London.

A MAGNIFICENT TOWNHOUSE. César Ritz finally realized his dream in 1898 when he opened the luxury hotel of all luxury hotels, offering "all the refinements that a prince could ask for in his own home." The prestigious location for such an enterprise was the town house of the Dukes of Gramont built in 1705 by Jules-Hardouin Mansart and Germain Boffrand in Place Vendôme. Architect Charles Mewes redecorated the building in a manner that preserved its outward appearance as a townhouse, but he also installed the latest hotel furnishings such as electricity on every

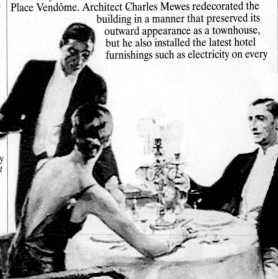

> **"I'M GOING TO DISMISS MY CHEF. I WOULD BE FOOLISH TO TRY AND COMPETE WITH RITZ AND ESCOFFIER."**
>
> BONI DE CASTELLANE

floor and a bathroom in every suite. The chef was Auguste Escoffier and the opening evening was attended by such notables as the Duke and Duchess of Mornay, the Duke and Duchess of Uzès, the Prince of Furstenberg, the Aga Khan, and a pale, shy, nervous, dark haired young man by the name of Marcel Proust. The *Ritz* was now the touchstone for luxury hotels. During World War One, the Rue Cambon wing, which had been built in 1910, and the second floor of the Vendôme wing were turned into a hospital.

AUTHENTICALLY "RITZY." César Ritz died in 1918, and did not live to see the Roaring Twenties, which turned the *Ritz* into a Parisian pied-à-terre for wealthy young Americans like Louis Bromfield, Scott Fitzgerald, Cole Porter and last but not least Ernest Hemingway. In 1944 General Leclerc took command of the *Ritz* bar and declared it "liberated" after four years' occupation by Goering's men; the event was celebrated over numerous bottles of champagne. In 1953 Marie-Louise Ritz, César's widow, passed the hotel over to her son Charles. He was a fish fanatic, and it was he who opened the *Espadon* restaurant in 1956. The dining-room is behind the bar in Rue Cambon, and its authentically "ritzy" décor, as rich American guests like to call it, somehow marry the materials and the timeless neo-Louis XVI baroque style. All in all, *L'Espadon* avoided the coldness often associated with such design and offered its clients a much more inviting and hospitable atmosphere.

GUY LEGAY. In the circumstances there was a temptation to continue with the cuisine of a bygone age, but Guy Legay would have none of it. Since 1980 Legay (an Auvergnat and one of France's greatest chefs, who had already learned his trade at *Maxim's*, the *Bristol* and *Ledoyen*) has offered the hotel's sophisticated clientele a subtle, country cuisine, one that is chic without being pretentious and satisfies the "Ritziest" of palates. The sommelier, Jean-Michel Deluc, supervises the magnificent cellars, and the smartly dressed waiters provide impeccable service. The seventy-strong kitchen staff can provide hotel guests with any dish on the menu twenty-four hours a day. Since 1979 the *Ritz* has belonged to Egyptian businessman Mohammed Al Fayed, who has breathed new life into the enterprise by combining one of the best restaurants in Paris and one of the world's greatest hotels.

MONSIEUR RITZ
"It is not widely known that the founder of the *Ritz Hotel* is an ordinary man like you and me, and that his real name is Monsieur Ritz, just as Flaubert called himself Monsieur Flaubert. Far from Paris, where

the *Ritz* finds most of its glittering clients, people think that "Ritz" must be a word like "Obelisk," "Eiffel Tower," the "Vatican" or "Westminster" – even "Jerusalem" or "Himalayas." The legend dies hard.**"**
Léon-Paul Fargue
Le Piéton de Paris

Le Carré des Feuillants ◆ 397

"The king of maîtres d'hôtel"
Olivier Dabescat, who was immortalized in the character of Antoine in Édouard Bourdet's *Le sexe faible*, worked at the *Ritz* for forty years and was known as the "king of *maîtres d'hôtel*."

What do well off young women dream of?
- Living in a hotel.
- Which are their favorite hotels?
- They all go for the same one – the *Ritz*.
- What is the *Ritz*?
- Paris.
- And what is Paris?
- The *Ritz*.
- "'There is no higher praise,' murmured Proust" to whom Léon-Paul Fargue was relating a conversation which he had had, he claimed, "with the most beautiful eyes in Chile".

The Couvent des Feuillants
The convent stood between Rue Saint-Honoré and the Tuileries, and its main door opened on to the middle of Place Vendôme.

❝As a child brought up amid the mountain torrents of the River Adour, I learned from my ... childhood to respect and appreciate fresh produce. The Pyrénées ... and the forests gave me a vocation to be a chef and the will to be someone who 'captured the real taste.' Tradition may be my first source of inspiration, but simply the thought of giving you pleasure is certainly the second.❞
Alain Dutournier

An abbot, some kings ... The Cistercian monks who occupied the convent founded in Rue Saint-Honoré in 1587 by Henry III came from Feuillants, near Toulouse. Alain Dutournier, too, comes from the southwest of France, but that is where the comparison ends between the excellent chef at the *Carré des Feuillants* and the austere abbot Jean de la Barrière, who made his monks eat bread that the dogs turned down and drink out of hollowed human skulls. Marie de' Medici came to the convent (Couvent des Feuillants) to pray to St Bernard for a son, who later became Louis XIII, and Anne of Austria also came with the same request to St Joseph one year before the birth of future Louis XIV. And it was in the convent gardens that a small riding school was built in 1721 for the young Louis XV to learn horseriding. During the Revolution, the dining-room resounded to the heated debates of the Constituent and Legislative Assemblies and the National Convention; the last king to come here was condemned to death. The moderate Jacobins under La Fayette met in the nearby convent whose name they adopted, but it was here that the painter David executed his celebrated *Tennis Court Oath*.

... and a chef. The convent was pulled down in 1804 and rues de Castiglione and de Rivoli were constructed over the site. This work was begun in 1811 and finally completed in 1815. At No. 14 Rue de la Castiglione, under the arcades where nestle the district's most antiquated shops, is a light modern courtyard leading to Alain Dutournier's restaurant,

which opened in 1987. The simple light-colored décor, including pictures with vegetable themes is an ideal setting in which to savor his delicious southwestern French cuisine. Dutournier is a master at cooking with a mixture of boldness and respect.

LE MEURICE
◆ 400

ENGLISH CLIENTELE. As postmaster in Calais, Augustin Meurice was well placed to acquaint himself with the particular tastes of the English travelers who flocked to Paris after the fall of Napoleon; his coach line then took them from the Channel port to Rue Saint-Honoré in thirty-six hours. Meurice decided to open a hotel on the site of the convent of Feuillants, which had been demolished a few years earlier. This was the first *Meurice* hotel and it succeeded in attracting much custom from Britain in the early 19th century partly on the basis of his claim that the "linen is washed with soap, and not beaten or brushed as is usually the case in France." After Rue de Rivoli was laid out and completed, the establishment transferred there in 1835 and took up ten arcades, and this second *Meurice* became one of Paris' top luxury hotels. In 1907 the hotel's new owner appointed Frédéric Schwenter, a highly skilled hotelier, as manager. The *Meurice* was completely refurbished. During the renovation, workmen found a greyhound that they kept as a mascot; that was how the greyhound became the hotel's motif.

A HOTEL FIT FOR KINGS AND QUEENS. A third *Meurice* emerged from the renovation work. It was in the luxury class, and was one of the city's leading hotels from 1920 to 1940. The decoration of the dining-rooms and bedrooms is largely in a Louis XVI style, and the restaurant in the *Salon des Tuileries* resembles a miniature Versailles. The elevator, in many ways ultra modern, is a replica of Marie-Antoinette's sedan chair. It takes guests to the *Roof-Garden* restaurant, where tables are separated by a trelliswork of greenery; sadly, it will soon disappear, a victim of Paris' pollution problems. As Léon-Paul Fargue has said, "Kings and queens around the world were waiting for the *Meurice* to reopen so that they could claim Rue de Rivoli as one of their addresses." That was true as long as there were still kingdoms, and kings and queens in exile. During World War Two, the Germans, frustrated at their failure to invade England, set up their headquarters at the *Meurice*.

THE SALON DES TUILERIES. Decorations have continued apace at the *Meurice* since the end of the war, and in 1990 the restaurant was restored to its original home in the superb *Salon des Tuileries*. This is an outstandingly beautiful room, truly a feast for the eyes. In this sumptuously regal setting the chef, Marc Marchand, serves dishes that are at once simple and sophisticated to a discerning clientele.

REGULARS
The postwar period was notable for two regulars. Salvador Dalí used to stay at the *Meurice* one month every year. On discovering one day that the polished wooden toilet seat had been replaced since his last stay, he called out in a loud voice for "the seat of Alfonso XIII," the exiled Spanish king currently staying at the hotel. It was found and hung on a wall in his villa at Cadaqués! For thirty years Florence Gould held weekly literary lunches that were attended by writers of the period from Marcel Jouhandeau to Jean d'Ormesson, and including Paul Morand and Paul Léautaud.

ANGÉLINA ◆ 396

◆ 396

RUMPELMEYER
The son of the founder of the *Angélina* was an aviation enthusiast, but he inherited a love of tearooms from his father. He

opened two more establishments, one in Rue Saint-Honoré and the other in London. He died at the controls of his fighter plane in 1916 somewhere in the sky above Champagne.

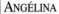

THOROUGHLY MODERN CLIENTELE
When the *Angélina*'s standards began to improve, society ladies could stop off there between fittings at nearby couturiers. And knowing grandmothers brought their grandchildren to take their first steps in the world. *Angélina* was also the favorite meeting-place for fashionable young men and women to come and talk about the latest motor rally. Well-known faces came more and more often, unable to resist the temptation of what was thought to be best chocolate in the world.

FROM VIENNA TO PARIS VIA NICE. Rumpelmeyer, a word brimming over with Strudel and Sachertorte, sounds an ideal name for a tearoom boasting the elegant comfort of a Viennese café. Angèle did not think so, and renamed the place *Angélina*. It was the right decision. Her Austrian forebear Antoine Rumpelmeyer had opened his first deluxe patisserie in Nice just after the war of 1870 and, flushed with success, opened more in Menton, Aix-les-Bains and finally in Paris, at No. 226 Rue de Rivoli, in 1903. Responsibility for decorating and furnishing the establishment was entrusted to Édouard Niermans, architect of numerous hotels and restaurants of the *Belle Époque*. Niermans designed an anteroom for the cash desk and display units, and behind it a dining-room, which he illuminated by a glass roof. Stucco moldings highlight the cornices and carved pillars, and paintings by Lorans Meilbronn, the biggest of which depicts the Baie des Anges in Marseilles, adorn the walls. Calashes and the first motor cars brought Faubourg Saint-Honoré high society to Rumpelmeyer's as well a few crowned heads, including George V when he was staying in Paris. Marcel Proust and Coco Chanel were also known to while away the time over cups of frothy chocolate.

RUMPELMEYER BECOMES ANGÉLINA. Angèle renamed the restaurant *Angélina* in 1950. It was then that the name of the tearoom was set in mosaic in the pavement of the Rue de Rivoli. But it was already beginning to go downhill. The only customers in those days were old ladies in hats, and in 1974 *Angélina* was bought by Jacques and Pierre Gauthier, proprietors of the brasserie *Mollard* ▲ *258* in Rue Saint-Lazare and enormous fans of the work of Édouard Niermans. The move was an overnight success, and *Angélina* was suddenly brought up-to-date. Not everyone can afford to spend the afternoon over a coffee and a cake, so the establishment now offers customers a menu of simple, well-cooked dishes that they can enjoy, along with the décor, at lunchtime as well.

6.
LES HALLES, BEAUBOURG, MARAIS, BASTILLE, GARE DE LYON, CHARONNE

"VÉRO-DODAT"
"CHEZ LA VIEILLE"
"AU PIED DE COCHON"
ST-EUSTACHE CHURCH
"L'ESCARGOT MONTORGUEIL"
"PHARAMOND"
"BENOÎT"
G. POMPIDOU CENTER
NOTRE-DAME
"L'AMBASSADE D'AUVERGNE"
HÔTEL DE VILLE
"DÔMARAIS"

RUE RAMBUTEAU

RUE DU LOUVRE
RUE ST-HONORÉ
RUE DE RIVOLI
QUAI DE LA MÉGISSERIE
RUE BEAUBOURG
RUE DES ARCHIVES

PONT NEUF
ÎLE DE LA CITÉ
BD DU PALAIS
BD DE SÉBASTOPOL
RUE DE LA CITÉ

ÎLE ST LOUIS

É mile Zola called Les
Halles "the stomach of Paris"
● 54, but an area that runs from the
Louvre (the kings' palace) to Place de la
Bastille (whose fall led to the fall of the monarchy)
could just as validly be dubbed "the heart of Paris."
To the west, Les Halles had been a market since the 12th
century before it was taken over by the Pompidou
Center and the Forum des Halles. To the east, the Marais,
formerly marshland standing on a dried-up branch of
the Seine and increasingly built on during the reigns
of Henry IV and Louis XII, now contains rows of superbly
restored townhouses. The restaurants are mostly very
picturesque.

"NIGHT OWL"
The iron-grille gate in
Passage Véro-Dodat
closes at 10pm;
thereafter, customers
have to be
accompanied to the
exit. This does much
for the restaurant's
"night owl"
reputation.

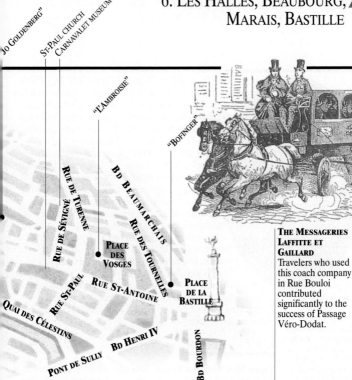

JO GOLDENBERG"

ST-PAUL CHURCH

CARNAVALET MUSEUM

"L'AMBROISIE"

"BOFINGER"

RUE DE TURENNE

RUE DE SÉVIGNÉ

BD BEAUMARCHAIS

RUE DES TOURNELLES

PLACE DES VOSGES

RUE ST-PAUL

RUE ST-ANTOINE

PLACE DE LA BASTILLE

QUAI DES CÉLESTINS

BD HENRI IV

BD BOURDON

PONT DE SULLY

THE MESSAGERIES LAFFITTE ET GAILLARD
Travelers who used this coach company in Rue Bouloi contributed significantly to the success of Passage Véro-Dodat.

LE VÉRO-DODAT ◆ 409

FOUNDED BY PORK BUTCHERS. The Galerie Véro-Dodat was built in 1826 on land bought by two rich pork butchers, M. Véro, based in Rue Montesquieu, and M. Dodat, who had a shop in Rue du Faubourg-Saint-Denis. It was a clever move of theirs, as the passageway linked Rue du Bouloi and Rue de Jean-Jacques-Rousseau, thus facilitating communication between the Palais-Royal and Les Halles districts. What is more, the proximity of the *Messageries Laffitte et Gaillard*, whose yellow coaches covered the length and breadth of Europe from Rue du Bouloi, ensured regular business. From the day it opened the Galerie Véro-Dodat has always been praised for the high quality of its décor: in addition to the black and white marble paving stones, the shops' wooden façades, their windows encircled with yellowish-golden copper beading, are divided by double pilasters framing a mirror whose capitals support globes containing gas lamps. The glass that filters the daylight is cut by four ceilings decorated with allegorical paintings.
DAUMIER AND RACHEL. The various businesses that settled in Galerie Véro-Dodat included the bookseller and engraver Aubert, who published *Le Charivari*, a newspaper that carried caricatures by Daumier and Gavarni. And the tragic actress, Rachel, who was making her debut at the *Théâtre-Français*, lived on

> "Of the many passageways and galleries built for business purposes in the last few years, Passage Véro-Dodat excels for the richness and integration of its decoration."
> Quoted from an 1837 anthology on woodwork and interior decoration

> "While crossing Paris by night, one finds oneself transported into a fairyland lit up by illuminations repeated by mirrors reflecting the lights."
> F. M. Merchant
> *Le nouveau Conducteur de l'étranger à Paris*, 1830

the second floor of No. 38 from 1838 to 1842. In 1854 the construction of Rue du Louvre disrupted links with Les Halles. Then competition from the railways forced the coaches of *Messageries Lafittte et Gaillard* to go out of business in 1880, after which the Galerie Véro-Dodat sank into oblivion.

ONLY THE VERY CHIC. The gallery has made a comeback in recent times. It now plays host to art publisher Franco Mario Ricci, antique doll and puppet specialist Robert Capia, film producer Yannick Bellon, a designer and producer of fabrics, an Italian leatherworker, a gemologist, an anarchist bookseller, a modern glassmaker – and a restaurant. Once upon a time this ancient establishment sold eggs and dairy produce. It was turned into a proper restaurant in 1973 and was called the *Clémentine*. On being renamed the *Véro-Dodat* in 1982, it adopted a sophisticated menu befitting the select clientele that frequents the gallery. Catherine Deneuve, one of Robert Capia's best customers, is sometimes seen there.

1839. The actress Rachel and the poet Alfred de Musset reading *Phèdre* by candlelight: Hippolytus: "Madam, forgive me: with shame I admit it,/I misinterpreted an innocent speech./I cannot stay here, having so disgraced myself/And I am going..." Phaedra: "Do not be so cruel!/ You understand too well ..."

GOLDEN BOOK
The painter Moretti signed the precious Golden Book at *Chez la Vieille* "for Adrienne."

CHEZ LA VIEILLE

◆ 404

FROM NEW YORK TO TOKYO. Rue de l'Arbre-Sec is home to a Parisian institution. Not, however, the gallows that stood for many years at the northern end of the road and gave their name to this street in the 13th century! The institution in question is Adrienne, and she dispenses a somewhat gentler discipline at *Chez la Vieille*. She moves secretly from New York to Tokyo, but politicians and media types come here in their droves, for nothing is more Parisian these days than to be lectured by the manageress of a restaurant that looks more like a provincial inn – and that just happens to serve the best stuffed tomatoes on earth.

MORE SNOBBISH THAN LIPP. The entrance to *Chez la Vieille* is through a hall with a staircase at the far end. It does not feel like a restaurant at all, and that can be disconcerting, but suddenly Adrienne emerges from what looks like the concierge's cubby hole, and from which tantalizing smells are already wafting. Whether "one of the gang" or not, each guest is then led to the other side of the hall into a room like a truckdrivers' café, before being taken up to another room straight out of "White Horse Inn". It is just like *Lipp* ▲ *129*, but much more snobbish, and nobody dares complain about that! President Mitterrand and former Prime Ministers Raymond Barre and Jacques Chirac certainly don't! They get what she cares to serve them – pickled pork with lentils, calf's liver or *sole meunière* – and have their lips wiped clean before being returned to their chauffeurs.

Only one establishment rivals Adrienne in this quarter, and that is a large store called "La Samaritaine."

L'ESCARGOT MONTORGUEIL   ● 74 ◆ 405

OYSTERS AND SNAILS. The hill on Rue Montorgueil (Mount Pride Street) is a former rubbish tip, and present-day Boulevard Bonne-Nouvelle slices straight through it. The street's real pride is that it was once the route used to transport seafood and fish products into Paris from the northern ports, and for a long time was also the site of the capital's oyster market. In the early 19th century the street became fashionable and acquired an interest in food (the two often go hand in hand). The *Rocher de Cancale* was one of the leading restaurants during the Restoration, and until 1874 No. 38 was occupied by a wine merchant by the name of Bourreau when he and a restaurateur called Mignard joined forces to open the *Escargot d'Or*. The board announced "Wines, snails and restaurant". *Gastropods* did not seem out of place in a street focused on molluscs. Shellfish and snails, also in a shell, are not after all so different, although at the time snails were what poor people ate. The restaurant eventually moved upmarket and in 1890 a M. Lecomte, whose name still appears on the front of the building, bought the establishment and added oysters to the menu. The *Escargot Montorgueil* thereupon became the most popular restaurant in Les Halles, and it was there that Allied representatives celebrated the Armistice of 1918. The restaurant was a favorite haunt for *Belle Époque* Parisian society, soon to be replaced by the flappers of the Roaring Twenties.

> **"For as long as there are gourmets left in Paris, France and Europe, Rue Montorgueil will be remembered. Rue Montorgueil – bounteous heaven! A veritable Cockaigne where one can lunch at the *Philippe*, dine at the *Rocher de Cancale*, and have supper of Lesage pâtés – and as many oysters as one can eat."**
> Louis Lurine
> *Les Rues de Paris en 1843*

▲ 6. LES HALLES, BEAUBOURG, MARAIS, BASTILLE

"Snails have the good fortune to be both male and female ... They give and receive at the same time. Their pleasure is not just twice ours

it also lasts much longer ... They are in rapture for three or four hours: not long compared with eternity, but a long time for you and me."

Voltaire
Correspondence

SARAH BERNHARDT'S DINING-ROOM. André Terrail, already the owner of the *Tour d'Argent* ▲ *147*, bought the *Escargot Montorgueil* in 1919, and the second floor, which was reached by a spiral staircase, became a famed meeting-place for post-World War One politicians. In 1923, at the dispersal of Sarah Bernhardt's estate, he purchased the painting that had decorated her dining-room ceiling; the great actress had demanded that chef François Lespinas bring her lunch at home when she was doing matinees. This work featuring culinary angels (right) is mounted on the ceiling at the restaurant entrance. In 1974 Kouikette Terrail, André's daughter and Claude's sister, bought the restaurant. They renovated it but preserved the 1875 décor with its dark wood carving, red upholstered benches with backs, gold moldings, and lighting provided by lamps with bronze shades. Standing proudly above the shop sign is a golden snail with its clutch of children that must be the proudest animal in the street!

PHARAMOND
● 76, 78 ◆ 406

HOW TRIPE CAME TO PARIS. The *Pharamond* has led a charmed life, having survived several brushes with demolition. In a quarter that has undergone many changes, it somehow escaped the destructive instincts of Rambuteau and Haussman, prefects of the Seine *département*, in the mid-19th century. It was on the right side of the road when the houses between rues de la Grande- and de la Petite-Truanderie were pulled down in 1919, and it survived the upheaval of Les Halles' move from the center of Paris to Rungis ● *60*, on the outskirts, in 1969. According to an alternative version of the restaurant's origins, the *Pharamond* was founded in 1832, and was situated in one of the innumerable streets that have long disappeared in the district, and did not move to its current location until 1879. The building, beside the old central Halles, is now listed as a historic monument.

RUE DE LA TRUANDERIE
The *Pharamond* restaurant gives onto a square where there were once some houses separating Rue de la Grande-Truanderie from Rue de la Petite-Truanderie. They were knocked down in 1919. That is why the former street has only odd numbers, and the latter only even numbers. These 13th-century streets are named after the *truands* (vagrants) who used to live in a nearby courtyard.

> "ABOUT TEN O'CLOCK IN THE EVENING, A MAN LEFT THE RESTAURANT WHERE THE RICH WERE ABOUT TO EAT TRIPE."
>
> GEORGES SIMENON

A LA PETITE NORMANDE

☎ (1) 42.33.06.72

Restaurant PHARAMOND

24, Rue de la Grande-Truanderie, Les Halles

Tripes à la mode de caen

PÂTE DE VERRE FROM 1900. The original name of *Pharamond*'s, *A la petite Normande*, has now been replaced by the original owner's name, and it still serves tripe *à la mode de Caen*; this is the kind that simmers for over fifteen hours and is placed over a hotplate on the table to keep it warm. Like many other restaurants, the *Pharamond* was transformed in 1900 during the period leading up to the Universal Exhibition. The friezes on the façade were decorated with plant motifs covering four stories, and the building was subsequently restored in the style of a half-timbered Normandy cottage. The interior décor remains intact. In the downstairs dining-room the friezes and the *pâte de verre* (colored glass) panels with floral and plant motifs frame large mirrors beneath which the upholstered benches; other recurring decorative elements include apple trees (suppliers of cider and calvados), a special pot for cooking tripe, and an assortment of different vegetables. The *Pharamond* has not belonged to the Normandy family since 1946, but the traditions have not died out. Couturier Claude Montana eats there regularly, and Les Halles society comes to feast their eyes on Victor Baltard's fantasies. Tripe will always be in fashion – Caen-style, of course!

TRIPE UP FOR AUCTION
The success of the *Pharamond* restaurant encouraged the first owner to organize sales of tripe by auction. Horse-driven

carriages in the restaurant's colors toured Paris to cries of "Tripe for sale!", and left behind them the smell and the reputation of *Pharamond*'s famous dish.

OUT IN THE GARDEN
In the summertime the *Benoit*'s façade is invisible behind bushes where garden tables are shaded by parasols.

BENOIT

◆ 403

THE NUMBER ONE BISTRO. When the *Benoit* was first opened in 1912, the menu stated, "At *Benoit*, food and drink just like home"; today a different notice is posted: "At *Benoit*, you can drink like a king". Does this perhaps mean that *Benoit* has now forgone home cooking for a more regal choice of cuisine and moved upmarket? Maybe, but bistro food is highly regarded these days, particularly in the hands of chefs such as Benoit Matray, Benoit I, a former butcher. The throne at No. 20 Rue Saint-Martin is now occupied by Benoit III; he is the founder's grandson, and his name is

"At that time, [of all] the bistros that my friends and journalists, writers and painters went to ... Benoit Matray in Rue Saint-Martin ... was famous for its scallops, its hot sausage and fried potatoes, and the best Beaujolais in Paris.**"**

Jean-Galtier Boissière
Mémoires d'un Parisien

Michel Petit. Virtually nothing has changed since before World War One. *Benoit* is a little like *Allard* ▲ *144* in Les Halles, and the timeless carved wood, weathered paint, copper bars, engraved glass and tiling make it an unusually typical Parisian bistro. Its cuisine, particularly the *boeuf mode* and the calf's kidneys, makes it a leader among bistros. The day will eventually come when the Pompidou Center, the neighboring streets and the fast food outlets will remind us of an era we never knew. That will be the day to visit *Benoit*.

It is like returning home, even it you have never been there before. Customers simply sit themselves down and spread their napkins over their laps as if they had never left!

THE GRAND-COMPTOIR
Recalling the early days of this restaurant, which predates the *Pied de Cochon*, writer Paul Mahalin observed: "The rooms, divans and tables were crowded with disparate and contrasting people: there were local market gardeners in long blue overalls, hats with earflaps, sheepskin gloves, and clubs hanging from their wrists by a leather cord; then there were gentlemen in fur-lined overcoats, black coats, white ties and waistcoat ... And in the midst of all that, swooping hither and thither between the overflowing glasses of beer ... plates of steaming sauerkraut, saveloy dripping with fat, and onion soup replete with cheese ... Meanwhile, foraging around the plates, and guzzling out of the glasses ... were women, women, and more women."

AU PIED DE COCHON ● *58* ◆ *403*

ROUND THE CLOCK SERVICE. The ovens of the *Pied de Cochon* have never been turned off since December 6, 1946. The front door or the restaurant does not even have a key, because the seafood and pork are served round the clock, 365 days a year. This tradition dates from the days when Les Halles was still in the center of town, and the restaurant's success has enabled it to carry on even after the market moved to Rungis in 1969. The atmosphere is not quite the same, though. In former times, early risers (the market porters) would easily rub shoulders with late owls (show-business folk moving downmarket to slum it in Les Halles). One memorable evening Lady Hervey, wife of the British Ambassador to France, gave her dancing shoes to a 400lb

porter called Coco who had boldly admired her "beautiful dancing pumps" and asked how she could possibly dance in them. Moreover, tramps were sometimes employed by the establishments to provide local color and mix with the inebriated revelers. The sight of bloodstained overalls on the butchers as they downed large glasses of red wine at the bar were guaranteed to unnerve elegant women in evening dress having a night out on the town.

85,000 PIGS' TROTTERS A YEAR. The early mornings are quieter these days. The afternoons, however, are reserved for tourists and visitors partaking of oysters, and later on the early evening diners eventually give way to the post-theater crowds. A ton of shellfish and crustaceans a day, and 85,000 pigs' trotters a year are consumed at the tables on various floors of the establishment. The interior has been recently decorated by the Blanc brothers in a rather gaudy, *Grand Véfour ▲ 213* style. Fashions may change and eras come and go, but at least pigs' trotters still have twenty-eight bones in them!

JO GOLDENBERG ◆ 406

THE "SOUP KITCHEN." *Jo Goldenberg* is Central Europe come to Paris, the ambassador of the Ashkenazi Jewish community in France ▲ 284, and one of the most exotic and typically Parisian of restaurants in the capital.

In 1950, Jo Goldenberg moved his father's shop at No. 15 Rue des Rosiers to No. 7 and opened up a kind of "soup kitchen," the *Fourneau alimentaire*, an eating-place with long tables that was just the thing for cold and hungry immigrants. He stripped it of any charitable connotations, and developed it into exactly the sort of place people would return to even after an absence of many years, where they embrace as if they will never meet again, or promise to meet up again there the next day.

GEMÜTLICHKEIT. The entrance is through the grocer's; just like at other places where you enter through the kitchen. Hungarian sausages are hung out in the front, jars of gherkins stand on the counter, and bottles of Bordeaux line the shelves. The first dining-room serves bortsch washed down with beer, as customers lean up against the bar, but stuffed carp or Wienerschnitzel are only available in the second room, where you sit on red leather-covered benches beneath mirrors and a host of pictures hung on the walls. Anyone unfamiliar with Prague, Cracow or Thessaloniki should be adventurous and sample the zakuski, the krupnik, the *pickelfleisch* and the cholent like a tourist getting to know a town by its side streets. After terrorist violence struck the establishment in August 1982 and six people were killed, it was only the *Goldenberg's Gemütlichkeit* that enabled happy memories and a whole cultural tradition to survive.

On the stairs leading to the upper floors, there is a glass case containing various objects connected with pigs.

AUGUST 9, 1982
Two men armed with automatic pistols entered the *Goldenberg*, threw a grenade, opened fire and fled. Six people were killed. Members of the Palestinian Abu Nidal group were suspected.

RUE DES ROSIERS
This street has been documented since 1230. Its name comes from the *rosiers* (rose bushes) in the gardens adjoining.

▲ 6. LES HALLES, BEAUBOURG, MARAIS, BASTILLE

The tower over the *Dômarais* restaurant cannot be seen from the outside. Access is by a corridor overlooking the street and giving on to a small courtyard with plants.

NATURAL LIGHTING
The *Bourse du Commerce* and the *Dômarais* tower, built to plans by Charles-François Viel de Saint-Maux, are the finest examples of circular buildings with central, natural lighting in the 18th-century neo-classical Parisian tradition. In the mid-19th century, the stone dome was replaced by a cupola in engraved glass.

LE DÔMARAIS ◆ 405

HOME COOKING. The nearest that Paris comes to old-style, provincial home cooking is the *Dômarais*. In 1777 Louis XVI introduced into France a system of *Monte di Pieta* (pawnshops) that had for over a century been trying to combat usury in Italy, and the institution was given premises in two townhouses in Rue des Blancs-Manteaux. Business commenced a year later. It was an immediate success, and those who ran the pawnshops sought to expand their activities by purchasing extra property. Two houses were acquired in Rue de Paradis, today Rue des Francs-Bourgeois. Charles-François Viel de Saint-Maux, the architect charged with the task of decorating the new buildings, drew up plans for a tower surmounted by a balustraded dome in the middle to let in natural light, and a mezzanine circular gallery. It was here that the *Mont-de-Piété* sold unredeemed goods. However, around 1930 the *Crédit municipal*, which had replaced the *Mont-de-Piété* in 1918, moved out of the saleroom, which was now far too small, and the tower was no longer used.

PERFECT ACCORD. In 1981 Julien Rispal obtained a lease from the *Crédit municipal* allowing him to open a restaurant on the premises. The saleroom's platform and circular benches were removed, and interior designer Roger Bénévant was asked to take charge of decorations. The base of the dome and the moldings were painted the same deep red as the carpet, and the skirting of the gallery was highlighted in gold, as were the surrounds of the niches up as far as the ogee molding. The addition of numerous plants gives the impression of a glasshouse in an Italian *palazzo*. In 1987 the *Dômarais* (the word comes from *dôme* [dome] and the quarter of Paris known as the "Marais") was bought by Dominique Ratni, who organizes dinners accompanied by singing. Then, the eyes, the ears and the palate are gratified in equal proportion and in perfect accord. The only cloud on the horizon is that the *Crédit municipal* is threatening to terminate the lease and replace the restaurant with a high-class auction room.

L'AMBROISIE ◆ 403

PLACE ROYALE. Place des Vosges, then known as Place Royale, was formally declared open on April 5, 6 and 7, 1612 on the occasion of the forthcoming marriages of Louis XIII to Anne of Austria, and of Elizabeth of France to the future Philip IV. Henry IV, who had decided to have the square built in 1605, did not attend the opening; two years later he was assassinated by Ravaillac. In 1985 Bernard Pacaud opened the *Ambroisie* restaurant of the first floor of No. 9 Place des Vosges in what was once a silversmith's shop.

ITALIAN CHARM, VIENNESE DASH. Pacaud's friend, interior designer François-Joseph Graf, has provided a restrained, refined setting, not unlike the restaurant's cuisine. He has one large room with a ceiling over 16 feet high and a smaller room, and he has introduced a distinctive note of elegance, mixing Italian charm, monastic rigor and Viennese dash. The large marble flagstones which are decorated with black, four-leaved clover date from the 18th century and come from a religious institution in Paris, the walls have been treated with a paint rendering and watercolor highlights, and the doors are framed in imitation marble moldings. Some of the windows in the smaller room, with their internal wooden shutters, are decorated with trompe l'œil paintings, while the larger room is adorned with a huge tapestry and an enormous bouquet of flowers. The chairs come from a Viennese theater, and the small sideboards are reproductions whose design is based on a model found in a market: both are typical of the Austrian Secession Movement, and were designed by Viennese artists at the beginning of the 20th century. Customers at this quiet restaurant enthuse over the technical

RUE DES FRANCS-BOURGEOIS
In the early 16th century an almshouse was opened here to care for the needs of the *francs*, or those "freed" of all obligation to pay taxes. This refuge for the *"francs-bourgeois"* later became a red light district.

NO. 9 PLACE DES VOSGES
It was the evening of the opening of Place Royale. After watching dancing by 1,300 knights, after listening to 150 trumpeters, and after applauding the 4,000 fireworks hurled from the top of the Bastille, the future Louis XIII, then aged eleven, went to sleep at the home of Counselor Pierre Fougeu-Descures at No. 9 Place Royale. The Counselor's house subsequently belonged to the Chaulnes, Luynes, Nicolaï and Moreau families, and in 1857 was inhabited by Rachel, the

celebrated tragic actress who died in it the following year. Bernard Pacaud opened the *Ambroisie* restaurant there in 1985.

ESTOFINADO
The Auvergne offers curiosity-hunters a delight called *estofinado*, the only fish dish in a landlocked province. It has a way of inspiring pleasant dreams of the Auvergne as a region dotted with charming fishing ports!

In the 1925 issue of *La France gastronomique*, food writer and critic Curnonsky ● *50* wrote this about *Bofinger*: "One of the best brasseries in Paris. Excellent beer.

Succulent sauerkraut ... Do not be afraid to try and inveigle the landlord – a delightful man and a Great War hero – into letting you have his strawberry and mirabelle plum brandy."

skills and artistry displayed by Bernard Pacaud, one of Paris' best chefs and a one-time pupil of Claude Peyrot ▲ *170*. *L'Ambroisie*, in what was once Place Royale, offers divine food at a princely address.

L'AMBASSADE D'AUVERGNE ◆ 402

AUTHENTIC FOOD AND DÉCOR. At the beginning of the 20th century the area was much frequented by people working in Les Halles market. Today no restaurant is more deserving of its name than the *Ambassade d'Auvergne* (Embassy of the Auvergne). This splendid eating-place at No. 22 Rue du Grenier-Saint-Lazare is like any typical café down in the Auvergne and is just like a provincial inn. The joke runs that, after tasting the regional specialties, many a customer has been tempted to seek political asylum with the Petrucci family, the restaurant's owners since 1967. Make no mistake about it, the rustic décor at the *Ambassade* is absolutely authentic, as is the food; the Auvergne has been sending the Embassy its best produce for over a quarter of a century. Week in week out, the dishes on the menu consistently disregard fashion, and yet demonstrate that Auvergnat cuisine, with its reputation for richness, can be as light as so-called nouvelle cuisine. The wines of Chanturgue, Châteaugay and Saint-Pourçain are, of course, perfect partners. Former Minister Robert Sabatier, himself from the Auvergne and a regular customer, has written thus of the cuisine: "The names of the recipes are more beautiful than poems. Who will sing of salmon from the River Allier, stuffed freshwater trout and local coq au vin...?" The *Ambassade*, of course. Who else?

BOFINGER ● 46, 76 ◆ 403

DRAUGHT BEER. "An excellent soup, a succulent slice of beef, a boiled leg of capon running with grease and tender as butter, one small plate of fried marinaded artichokes and another of spinach, a beautiful *crassane* pear, some fresh grapes, a bottle of mature Burgundy and the best Moka coffee." That was the delicious meal served to writer Jean-François Marmontel in 1761, though not at *Bofinger* in Rue de la Bastille (the restaurant did not open for another hundred years) but in the prison that stood in the neighboring square and was fated to achieve notoriety on July 14, 1789 ... In fact, the Bastille was noted for its food, although it was usually

served to some rather grand people who had brought their furniture and servants with them! In 1864 Frédéric Bofinger from Alsace opened a small restaurant at No. 5 Rue de la Bastille. It was not the first brasserie in Paris as the publicity suggested (the *Hofbraühaus* dates from 1589) but it was at least the first place to sell draught beer. The froth that poured all over the counter was *Bofinger*'s best publicity. The establishment's reputation grew, and was becoming even more successful when in 1906 Frédéric handed the restaurant over to his son-in-law Albert Bruneau, a business associate of Louis Barraud.

ARCHETYPAL BRASSERIE. After World War One, it may have been the reconquest of Alsace and Lorraine that gave the restaurant's owners their energy. At all events, they bought Nos. 3 and 7 Rue de la Bastille in 1919, and enlarged the premises, and the architect Legay and interior designer Mitdgen produced a setting of extraordinary coherence. The bar and entrance area at the front are separated by a sweeping curved staircase from the dining-room, which is lit

by a cupola adorned with floral motifs. There are further rooms upstairs. Here, carved wood, large mirrors, bronze wall brackets and lampshades, copper coat and hatstands, black leather benches with backs, ceramic vases by Clément Massier (1844–1917) decorated with plant motifs, marquetry on decorative panels by Panzani, and ceramics in the toilets combine to produce a restaurant that is halfway between a gentlemen's club

and a country inn. It is situated close to the Austerlitz and Lyon railway stations and to the Bastille (now closed) and is open for the sustenance of travelers 24 hours a day.

Politicians from southern France who pass through these stations on their way to and from the Chamber of Deputies are regular callers. It was also here, in room 9, that Édouard Herriot and his *Cartel des gauches* plotted their bid for power.

eggs laid by his own hens to make an omelette, and Maurice Chevalier, who would partake of some sauerkraut when he was appearing in the *Pacra*, a nearby *café-concert*.

"HANSI." In 1930 interior designer Jean-Jacques Waltz, better known as "Hansi," decorated the second-floor room and designed the restaurant's board, depicting two youngsters from Alsace in folk costume. However, the postwar period of the 1940's proved less energizing and, when Louis Barraud sold out in the 1950's, he was followed by a number of new owners. Then, in 1982, *Bofinger* was taken over by Georges and Marie-Louise Alexandre, Jean-Claude Vigier and Michel Vidalenc, who breathed new life into it; the area's new fashionable status and the opening of the Opéra Bastille did the rest. With a little help from sauerkraut, oysters and Alsatian wine, *Bofinger* has once again become one of Paris' most popular brasseries.

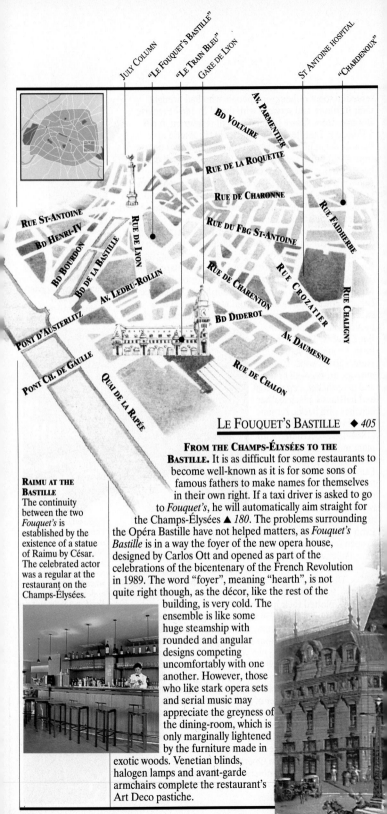

JULY COLUMN
"LE FOUQUET'S BASTILLE"
"LE TRAIN BLEU"
GARE DE LYON
ST ANTOINE HOSPITAL
"CHARDENOUX"

Av. PARMENTIER

Bd VOLTAIRE

RUE DE LA ROQUETTE

RUE DE CHARONNE

RUE DU FBG ST-ANTOINE

RUE FAIDHERBE

RUE ST-ANTOINE

Bd HENRI-IV

Bd BOURDON

Bd DE LA BASTILLE

RUE DE LYON

Av. LEDRU-ROLLIN

RUE DE CHARENTON

RUE CROZATIER

RUE CHALIGNY

Bd DIDEROT

Av. DAUMESNIL

PONT D'AUSTERLITZ

PONT CH. DE GAULLE

QUAI DE LA RAPÉE

RUE DE CHALON

FROM THE CHAMPS-ÉLYSÉES TO THE BASTILLE. It is as difficult for some restaurants to become well-known as it is for some sons of famous fathers to make names for themselves in their own right. If a taxi driver is asked to go to *Fouquet's*, he will automatically aim straight for the Champs-Élysées ▲ *180*. The problems surrounding the Opéra Bastille have not helped matters, as *Fouquet's Bastille* is in a way the foyer of the new opera house, designed by Carlos Ott and opened as part of the celebrations of the bicentenary of the French Revolution in 1989. The word "foyer", meaning "hearth", is not quite right though, as the décor, like the rest of the building, is very cold. The ensemble is like some huge steamship with rounded and angular designs competing uncomfortably with one another. However, those who like stark opera sets and serial music may appreciate the greyness of the dining-room, which is only marginally lightened by the furniture made in exotic woods. Venetian blinds, halogen lamps and avant-garde armchairs complete the restaurant's Art Deco pastiche.

RAIMU AT THE BASTILLE
The continuity between the two *Fouquet's* is established by the existence of a statue of Raimu by César. The celebrated actor was a regular at the restaurant on the Champs-Élysées.

242

REAL SURPRISES IN THE KITCHEN. *Fouquet's* in Avenue Champs-Élysées is patronized as much for the setting as it is for the food. At *Fouquet's* in Place de la Bastille, however, the setting has little to offer but the cuisine has plenty of surprises in store. This applies both in the "gastronomic" restaurant upstairs and in the downstairs bistro, two eateries under one prestigious roof.

LE TRAIN BLEU

● 95 ◆ 409

THE APOTHEOSIS OF RAILWAY ARCHITECTURE. In the years leading up to the 1900 Exposition Universelle, the *Compagnie du Paris-Lyon-Méditerranée* railway company (PLM) decided to build a new Gare de Lyon to cater for the thousands of visitors that were expected to flock to the capital. With a façade 328 feet long, decorated with allegorical sculptures and surmounted by a tower over 200 feet high bearing clocks on each of its four sides, the Gare de Lyon was indeed the very apotheosis of railway architecture. The restaurant, like the station itself, is monumental.

BASTILLE, CHARONNE AND THE GARE DE LYON
The Faubourg Saint-Antoine stretches away to the east of the Bastille. The district has been inhabited by craft workers since Louis XI granted franchises to all trades placed under the patronage of the Abbey of Saint-Antoine-des-Champs. The *faubourg* (area), which also took its name from the Abbey, has retained its popular atmosphere.

CINEMA LOCATION
The *Train Bleu* is often used as a film location. Luc Besson's *Nikita*, some of which was shot in the restaurant, came out in 1990. There is a fine scene set in the *Grande Salle* (Main dining-room), starring Tcheky Karyo and Anne Parillaud.

MARIUS TOUDOIRE
Architect Marius Toudoire not only designed the new Gare de Lyon but also the Gare Saint-Jean in Bordeaux.

The fame of the restaurant in the Gare de Lyon rests mainly on the sublime décor, which is characteristic of the turn of the century. Numerous artists were asked to illustrate the French towns and regions to be served by the PLM Company. In addition to these paintings, the restaurant boasts fine ornaments, statues, moldings and furniture.

THE NEW RESTAURANT
This is an engraving of the *Salle Dorée* (Golden Room) in the new Gare de Lyon restaurant. It shows the cash desk already in place.

THIRTY PAINTERS
The architect commissioned thirty painters to produce forty-one paintings to cover the walls and ceiling. They had five months to complete the task, and their fee was 2,500 francs.

THE BATTLE OF FLOWERS
The ceiling of the *Salle Dorée* is decorated with this painting by Henri Gervex ● 87. It represents Nice and its folklore, and features the Battle of Flowers and orange-picking. An early sketch depicted tourists at the scene of the carnival; in the end, this was seen to symbolize the town's life very well. The woman standing up in the calash is probably Mme Gervex, and the orange-picking scene is an allegory of Summer Abundance.

"P" FOR PARIS
Beside the woman representing Paris is an angel holding a scroll that reads "Intelligence." The painting also includes a church, the tower of Gare de Lyon, and allegories of Fine Arts, Science and Fortune.

"L" FOR LYONS
Lyons is a woman lying back against the city's coat of arms. An old man and a naked woman represent the Rhône and the Saône, which are separated by the Church of Notre-Dame de Fourvière. A bishop is blessing the town.

"M" FOR MARSEILLES
The port is facing the Mediterranean. Marseilles is holding a tiller, and is being offered various local produce while Mercury has placed one foot on chests marked "PLM."

Writer Jean Giraudoux once remarked: "This place is a museum, but nobody knows about it. In time, people will appreciate it for what it is ... I myself love the "Old France" dining-room which throws down a challenge of adventure and is not ashamed of its smells of stuffed animal, encaustic and large canvases." The restaurant of the Gare de Lyon was listed as a historic monument in 1972 following interventions by a number of prominent individuals including film director René Clair and the former President of the SNCF Louis Armand.

THE SALLE DORÉE
The "Golden Room" (above left), measuring 61 by 30 feet, takes its name from the golden stuccowork adorning its walls. Like the *Grande Salle*, it is 36 feet high. The paintings on the ceiling represent landscapes from the southeastern quarter of France and the Mediterranean. They include *Alger* (Algiers) by R. Allègre, *Le Mont Blanc* by Eugène Burnand, *Sousse* by P. Buffet, *Le Lac d'Aiguebelette* (Lake of Aiguebelette) by M. Carl-Rosa, *Battle of Flowers* by Henri Gervex ▲ *244*, *Antibes* by Gaston de Latouche, *La Meije* by Maurice Leenhardt, *Vendanges en Bourgogne* (Harvest time in Burgundy) by A. Maignan, *Le Vieux Port de Marseille* (The Old Port of Marseilles) and *Saint-Honorat* by J.-B. Olive, *Le Puy* by E. Petit-Jean, *Beaulieu* by A.-G. Rigolot, *Le Lac du Bourget* (Bourget Lake) by P.-E. Rosset-Granger, and *Hyères* by P. Vayson.

7.
Opéra,
Grands Boulevards,
Porte Saint-Martin
République,
Place Clichy,
Montmartre

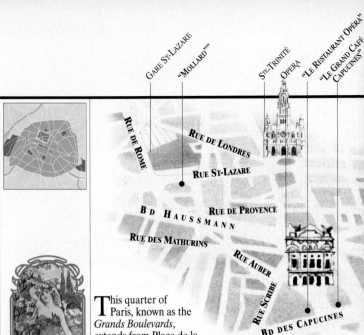

GARE ST-LAZARE · "MOLLARD" · STE-TRINITÉ · OPÉRA · "LE RESTAURANT OPÉRA" · "LE GRAND CAFÉ CAPUCINES"

RUE DE ROME

RUE DE LONDRES

RUE ST-LAZARE

RUE DE PROVENCE

B D   H A U S S M A N N

RUE DES MATHURINS

RUE AUBER

RUE SCRIBE

BD DES CAPUCINES

THE LUMIÈRE BROTHERS
With the help of his brother Auguste (1862–1954), Louis Lumière (1864–1948) worked in their father's photographic laboratory in Lyons from an early age. In 1878 he discovered a process for instantaneous photographs, and in 1895 he invented the movies.

This quarter of Paris, known as the *Grands Boulevards*, extends from Place de la République to Place de la Madeleine. These days it is but a pale shadow of what it was between the Restoration and the *Belle Époque*. It is here, and more particularly in *the* boulevard – the Boulevard des Italiens – that we find the heart (and stomach) of 19th-century Paris. The *Nouveau Cours* (New Walk), constructed over the site of the ancient fortifications put up by Charles V, Charles IX and Louis XIII, became more and more built up as the 18th century progressed. It then turned into an area noted for walks and entertainment, and theaters and cafés sprang up everywhere. These show business and gastronomic traditions have survived to the present day.

LE GRAND CAFÉ CAPUCINES   ◆ 412

THE FIRST CINEMA. The Blanc brothers, who own the *Grand Café Capucines*, took full advantage of the fame that the Lumière brothers brought to the *Grand Café*. The *Grand Café* itself no longer exists, but the *Grand Café Capucines* is in the same boulevard, just ten numbers away and beyond Place de l'Opéra. On December 28, 1895 a man stood on the corner of Boulevard des Capucines and Rue Scribe handing out leaflets; for the price of one franc they invited passers-by to the Lumière brothers' first public cinematographic representation. It was cold, pedestrians hurried on past, and the man had little success. And so it came about that the discovery that was to revolutionize the entertainment business for decades attracted no more than thirty-three curious individuals to the *salon Indien* in the basement of the *Grand Café*. A magic lantern perched on a wooden stool then projected on to a tiny screen two films that are still famous. The first, a short comedy entitled *L'Arroseur arrosé*, was about a man watering

CINÉMATOGRAPHE LUMIÈRE

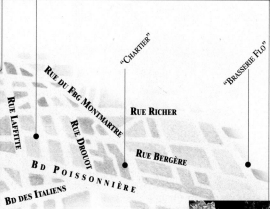

RUE DU FBG MONTMARTRE

RUE LAFFITTE

RUE DROUOT

RUE RICHER

RUE BERGÈRE

BD POISSONNIÈRE

BD DES ITALIENS

The covered terrace and dining-room of the *Grand Café Capucines*, with their extravagant Art Nouveau décor.

his garden who gets water splashed in his face; the second, *L'Entrée d'un train en gare de La Ciotat,* had the audience leaning back in their seats as the train loomed up, and then caused nervous coughs when smoke seemed to fill the screen. It was a brilliant success. The movies had triumphed, even though the press did not turn up as the showing had clashed with a concert by singer Yvonne Guilbert. The film show brought the inventors three francs, and the owner of the *Grand Café* preferred a daily rental of thirty francs, rather than the 20 percent return on receipts that the Lumière brothers had suggested. That evening, he was happy enough. But a few days later, when the cinema was already catching on, he must have been having second thoughts!

THE CASHIER AT THE GRAND CAFÉ. Like its neighbor the *Café de la Paix,* the *Grand Café* had been built to coincide with the opening of the Opéra in 1875, and it rapidly became one of the most popular establishments on the Boulevards during the Second Empire and the *Belle Époque.* The whole quarter seemed to host permanent festivities. Even the horses of the "Madeleine-Bastille" omnibus seemed to trot in time to an Offenbach air, and in the evening the Opéra disgorged its smartly dressed patrons into neighboring restaurants. And at all hours of the day and night, customers would come in singing Izoird's famous love song to the cashier of the *Grand Café*: "She is fair, she is beautiful. She's just the girl for me." Today, the bright lights and the rousing choruses are no more. The Opéra itself has moved on ▲ *242.* The boulevards may not be as fashionable as they once were, but they remain lively and popular with tourists.

ART NOUVEAU CARICATURE. Beware of imitations! The décor at the *Grand Café Capucines* is an amazing caricature of Art Nouveau. The glass roof overflows with flowers and fruit, and the wall tiles are decorated by the Czech painter Alfons Mucha's pastiches. This style calls for little ornamentation. Bourgeois and brasserie cuisine is served to latter-day film-goers as they emerge from the area's many movie theaters.

JACQUES OFFENBACH Offenbach, born in Germany and a naturalized

Frenchman, was the Second Empire composer *par excellence.* Before his compositions became well known, he conducted at the *Théâtre-Français* and founded the *Bouffes-Parisiens* theater.

THE MAIN HALL
In 1906 the Main Hall was covered over by a glass roof, and a popular tearoom was installed. The glass roof was destroyed in 1960 and was temporarily replaced by an ordinary roof; after extensive renovation, rebuilding began in 1985.

ALI THE COFFEE MAKER
Ali was one of the best-known characters at the *Café de la Paix* during the 1960's.

LE RESTAURANT OPÉRA ◆ 414

THE GONCOURT BROTHERS ▲ 205
The first *Académie Goncourt* luncheon took place at the *Grand Hôtel* in 1903, on the advice of Léon Daudet, who admired Auguste Escoffier's cooking. However, Octave Mirbeau found the hotel too solemn, and they subsequently went to *Champeaux*, the *Café de Paris* and, finally, *Drouant*.

9,600 SQUARE YARDS. Charles Garnier's Opéra was still at the foundations stage when Alfred Armand's *Grand Hôtel* was opened in 1862, and it needed fully thirteen years to build the Opéra, whereas only fifteen months were necessary to complete this huge hotel. In a typically Haussman style, it occupies a triangle covering an area of 9,600 square yards between the Boulevard des Capucines and rues Auber and Scribe. The Empress Eugénie attended the opening night, which included extracts from *La Traviata* conducted by Jacques Offenbach in person, a one-act piece by Eugène Labiche, and a grand society ball. With eight hundred rooms, a façade 550 yards long and two thousand windows looking on to the street, the *Grand Hôtel* certainly lives up to its name.

A "TABLE D'HÔTE" FOR SIX HUNDRED. The establishment was ultramodern for its day. There were fifteen bathrooms in the basement, Turkish baths, hydrotherapy and massage rooms, and a hairdressing and manicure salon. It also boasted the first hydraulic lift in the capital; it was the size of a small room and, as the hotel's brochure put it, was also capable of taking guests downstairs! Until 1914 the "table d'hôte" dining-room, now known as the *salon Opéra*, catered for up to six hundred people at a single sitting.

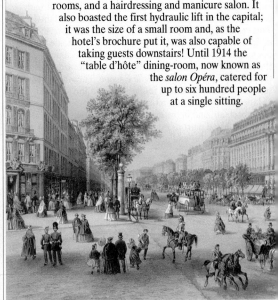

It was a semicircular space on three levels covering an area of 540 square yards; it was unequaled anywhere in Paris. The twenty-seven mirrors magnified the light that the crystal chandeliers poured over the flamboyant décor of marble, gilt molding, stucco and staff, caryatids and table centerpieces: the very essence of Second Empire style. Charles Garnier took his inspiration from the decoration in the foyer of the nearby Opéra. In addition to the "table d'hôte," there is a gastronomic restaurant on the right of the central hall. Its refined and distinguished clientele was making writers, artists and their mistresses feel uncomfortable, and they preferred to patronize other establishments on the Boulevard des Capucines.

UNPARALLELED POMP. The *Café de la Paix*, which had opened back in 1863, was entirely refurbished and renovated in 1974, and *Le Restaurant Opéra* was opened in the part facing Place de l'Opéra. As a result of this refurbishment, the fluted columns with Corinthian capitals supporting the carved beams are once again visible, and the ceilings themselves are decorated with Italian skyscapes framed in medallions with angel motifs. The center of each section of the dining-room is occupied by a dark wood dinner wagon surmounted by a candelabrum that also contains large bunches of flowers. The ceiling was listed as a historic monument immediately after it was renovated. In 1991 chef Jacky Fréon left the *Lutétia* ▲ *141* for the *Grand Hôtel*. He is a former pupil of Joël Robuchon ▲ *168*, and his strictly classical cuisine is entirely in keeping with the superb décor of this deluxe restaurant. The staff are impeccably turned out, the table service is luxurious, and the silver is suitably heavy. This is the *Grand Hôtel*, a throwback to a forgotten age of unparalleled pomp.

THE HORSE BANQUET
On February 6, 1865, naturalist Isidore Geoffroy Saint Hilaire invited two hundred people to a dinner at the *Grand Hôtel* consisting of horse products, with the aim of promoting their popularity. The guests numbered 132, and included Alexandre Dumas *père*, the chef Charles Monselet, Gustave Flaubert, and the celebrated gastronome, Dr Véron. It was the first time horse had been on a restaurant menu. There was meat served with noodles in a horse stock, cold (horse) meats, boiled horse, horse *à la mode*, horse ragoût, fillet of horse with mushrooms, sauté potatoes in horse fat, and horse marrow cake; the meal was accompanied by Bordeaux wines from Château du Cheval Blanc. The practice of eating horse never caught on in France. It was not until the siege of 1870 that starving Parisians once again turned to the meat of horses – and several other animals, too.

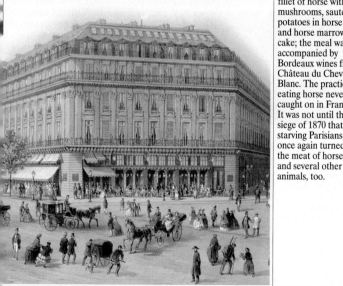

Rich décor

The interior is similar to the terrace. The décor consists of marble columns, Saargemünd faience with decorative panels, teak beams and tiles, Baccarat crystal adorned with flowers in colorful mosaic, ceilings depicting game, fish, fruit and vegetables against a golden background, tiled floors, a roof in colored glass, and

numerous ornaments in wrought-iron and bronze. The cool- and warm-air grilles are magnificent pieces of goldsmith's art, and the teak chest adorned with marble and faience is a work of art in its own right.

MOLLARD ● 79 ◆ 413

A LIVELY PART OF TOWN. Whatever is a Savoyard doing running a coal store? Cafés that sold wood and coal were usually run by Auvergnats who had moved to Paris, so why did Louis Mollard not open an Alsatian brasserie while he was about it? In 1867 the Saint-Lazare quarter was undergoing enormous changes and everything was in a great state of upheaval: construction work on the Gare de l'Ouest, as it was then known, was almost completed, and it was to become the most important suburban station in Paris; the *Grands Magasins* were opening their doors; and, so it was said, as many as five thousand horses pulled omnibuses, cabs for hire and private carriages every day! Louis Mollard was making a fortune. In 1895 Mollard decided to enlarge his premises and turn it into a brasserie. A special edition of the *Gil Blas* revue reported the opening of the *Brasserie Mollard* as follows: "At first, *brasseries* were nothing more nor less than old-style cafés – large, dark, airless, gloomy rooms. But Paris, already humiliated by not being able to compete with public eating-places in the provinces, is committed to change. For this reason, Renaissance taverns have been built, some of them interesting copies of what we have seen in Germany for many years. These German-looking brasseries are springing up so fast that people are asking for something new – and now! Architects are working on devising new, original and, above all, Parisian formulas. One of them, Édouard Niermans, has seen his efforts crowned with great success." **ÉDOUARD NIERMANS.** The plans for the "scintillating trinket" that came to be known as *Mollard* were the work of the man who had also designed the *Casino de Paris*, the *Brasserie universelle* and *Angélina* ▲ 228. "How fresh! How charming!" exclaimed the local newspapers. Passers-by were immediately struck by the elegant porch, its metal framework decorated with stained-glass windows, and the alabaster stucco façade

adorned with blocks of granite highlighted in gold letters. The whole thing was completed by metalwork that included a frieze of acanthus leaves decorated with shaded lamps that provided the lighting. And then there were the bronze ornaments and the plaques in Saargemünd faience. The effect was nothing if not overpowering. As the *Gil Blas* article put it, "One's eye is drawn to every detail: there is not a single empty space, not one unoccupied surface." The façade is no longer standing.

"FRESH AND CHARMING." *Mollard* was considered "fresh and charming," and it proved very popular, the brasserie's opening having been as grand as that of the Gare Saint-Lazare six years earlier. It also owned five floors of the *Hôtel Franco-Américain*, whose fifty rooms provided the highest class of accommodation. It was successful until the eve of World War One, when Louis Mollard died. After the war was over, Louis' children decided to refurbish the restaurant in a fashionable style. The glass roof was replaced, the tiles were painted, the faience was hidden behind mirrors, and the ornaments removed, but it did not lead to commercial success.

REDISCOVERED. In 1930 the brasserie was sold to Georges Gauthier, who was succeeded by his sons Pierre in 1941 and Jacques in 1945. Then in 1960 an employee who had started in the restaurant in 1907, and who was on the point of retiring, told Jacques, "When I was younger, I used to see some amazing things at *Mollard's*. You should go and look for them." After ten years of research and hard work, *Mollard*'s past was eventually rediscovered and its original décor restored. As a reward, the Ministry of Culture listed it as a historic monument in 1988 and, a hundred years after it opened, *Mollard* was once again a place where "customers come in ever greater numbers, attracted as much by the splendor of the décor as by the excellent cuisine."

FLO ● 46 ◆ 412

HANS. Every day at this authentic Alsatian brasserie, the jewel in Jean-Paul Bucher's crown and center of his empire, customers must queue before taking their seats for their seafood platter and plate of sauerkraut. The restaurant's success is as much to do with its atmosphere as with Jean-Paul's managerial talents. *Flo*'s history goes back to 1886, when Jean Voitenleitner opened an alehouse in Cours des Petites-Écuries. He linked up with the *Brasserie Hans* in 1901 and used the new name before selling out in 1909 to a man named Floderer, another exile from Alsace whose homeland had been annexed by the Germans in 1870.

COUR DES PETITES-ÉCURIES
The street and *cour* (courtyard) of the *Petites-Écuries* (small stables) stand on the site of the royal stables in the 18th

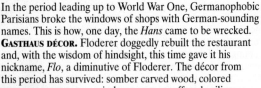

century. They are not far from the brasserie *Flo* at No. 14 rue des Petites-Écuries; it was also here that Joseph Santerre, a celebrated brewer and Revolutionary warrior who led Louis XVI to the scaffold, died in 1809.

In the period leading up to World War One, Germanophobic Parisians broke the windows of shops with German-sounding names. This is how, one day, the *Hans* came to be wrecked.

GASTHAUS DÉCOR. Floderer doggedly rebuilt the restaurant and, with the wisdom of hindsight, this time gave it his nickname, *Flo*, a diminutive of Floderer. The décor from this period has survived: somber carved wood, colored window panes, a coffered ceiling, painted panels depicting Alsace landscapes and the heavy tavern furniture combined to produce a *gasthaus* atmosphere that was at once austere and welcoming, without being at all folkloric. At the time, *Flo* was very popular with exiles from Alsace in Paris rather than with tourists. The establishment remained in the Floderer family until 1964.

PAUL MEURISSE AND JULIEN CLERC. When the political upheavals and student revolution of May 1968 were in full flow, the restaurant was sold to a young twenty-seven-year-old from Alsace, Jean-Paul Bucher. Two shows were about to bring the Parisian public to *Flo*'s doorstep. One was Françoise Dorin's *Un Sale Égoïste,* which was playing at the nearby *Théâtre Antoine*; during this time the leading actor, Paul Meurisse, regularly ate there and brought his admirers along in tow. Shortly afterward, the musical *Hair* came to the *Théâtre Porte Saint-Martin* and the star, Julien Clerc, attracted a completely different clientele. Success was now assured. Eventually, Jean-Paul Bucher got tired of refusing bookings every day, and decided to spread his wings. He expanded his operation and acquired *Terminus Nord, Julien* ▲ *264, Le Boeuf sur le toit* ▲ *201* and *La Coupole* ▲ *156*. It was an inspired move and a highly successful piece of empire-building for the Flo group.

TY COZ ◆ *415*

This splendid sketch is one of the most delightful pieces of decoration in the *Ty Coz*.

HORSES LEAD THE WAY. The horse-drawn carriages linking the Palais-Royal and Montmartre used to stop here and rest the horses. The large openings in the restaurant façade are the last traces of the carriage gateways in this staging post dating back to the days of Henry IV. When it became a coal store, people walking up Rue Saint-Georges would drop in for a drink, but it was not until M. and Mme. Libois bought

ON MANGE BIEN ICI...
VIVE LA BRETAGNE LIBRE...

1969

> "THE PLEASURE OF EATING IS OF ALL AGES, ALL CONDITIONS, ALL COUNTRIES AND ALL DAYS. IT CAN BE COMBINED WITH ALL OTHER PLEASURES, AND REMAINS THE LAST PLEASURE TO CONSOLE US WHEN ALL OTHERS HAVE GONE." J-A BRILLAT-SAVARIN

the establishment in the 1960's that it was enlarged and turned into a proper restaurant. It was then that is acquired the name the *Ty Coz*.

BRETON CUISINE. The *Ty Coz*, which is now run by the Libois' daughter, attracts all lovers of Breton cuisine, with its salty and sweet *crêpes*, fish and seafood. The upmarket clientele are certainly assiduous in telling

their friends about it, if the "golden book" is to be believed. The décor, that of a simple inn, includes flagstones and bare stone walls, enormous beams, antique furniture and lovely objects connected with the sea. They emphatically contribute to the restaurant's reputation just as much as does the cuisine in the pleasant eatery.

AU PETIT RICHE ● 75, 80 ◆ 410

IMITATION. The *Café Riche* was opened on Boulevard des Italiens in 1804, not far from the celebrated *Café Hardy* ● 45. The poor quality of the food prompted the anti-Royalist arch-councilor Cambacérès, a noted statesman and great gourmet, to say, "You have to be rich to eat at *Hardy*, and hardy to eat at *Riche*." However, it became one of the best-known restaurants in the boulevard, and even in France, after Louis Bignon bought it in 1847. In 1854, a certain M. Chansart is said to have commented, "Only borrow from the rich," slightly modifying a saying well-known in a part of Paris that had become the city's financial center. Then, on the corner of rues Le Peletier and Rossini, he opened a restaurant called *Au Petit Riche*. He was not to know that it would survive the *Café Hardy*, which closed in 1916, and would also become one of the most attractive and popular eating-places in the area. Meanwhile, Chansart fed and watered the coachmen and workers at the Le Peletier building which housed the Opéra at the time. Act I closed on *Au Petit Riche* when, in 1873, a fire that lasted an entire day destroyed the Opéra and the rest of the buildings in Rue Le Peletier.

ACT II. In 1880, the restaurant was bought by a certain M. Besnard from the wine-producing region Vouvray, who turned it into an establishment specializing in produce from the Val de Loire, even buying his own cellars in Vouvray and Bourgeuil, The dark woodwork, the molded ceilings, the engraved glass, the mirrors and copper railings, and the row of small rooms of this crowded bistro have scarcely changed since they were installed a few years after the place was first opened. In 1920 it was enlarged by the addition of the adjoining *Hôtel de Rothschild* stables, which Besnard had purchased. With bankers and politicians coming in for lunch at noon, and

THE CAFÉ RICHE SAUCE
In his *Les Plaisirs de Paris* (*The Pleasures of Paris*), Alfred Delvau recalls Louis Bignon's cooking, saying that the sauce in particular contained no especially flavored concentrate, no white wine, no mysterious ingredient. "It was," he wrote, "quite simply the *Café Riche* sauce, and the recipe was the chef's secret." In fact, the sauce came from Normandy and contained butter, lobster, cognac and cayenne pepper. It accompanied sole with shrimps, one of Bignon's specialties.

actors and theater-goers preferring to dine in the evening, the *Petit Riche*'s clientele became more select, and there were many more who came for the Vouvray, Bourgeuil, Gamay and other Saumur wines. One of them was a director of the Rothschild Bank, Georges Pompidou. In 1980 there was a major break with a French catering tradition according to which the chef could go home at 9pm; now, it is possible to be served up till midnight. The resulting increase in business has meant that almost twice as many staff have had to be taken on. The *Petit Riche*'s adventure has gone on for longer than its predecessor's, and it shows no sign of running out of steam.

CHARTIER   ● 46 ▲ 130, 154 ◆ 411

GOOD VALUE FOR MONEY. Good quality does not necessarily have to cost a lot of money. Camille and Édouard Chartier opened their first restaurant in Rue du Temple in 1895. They may not have invented the *bouillon* formula, which they borrowed from a former butcher, Pierre Duval, but they certainly improved upon it greatly. Duval, it is true, was most

"On Sunday, we ate at *Chartier* among the green plants. I ordered *vol-au-vent financière,* perhaps because of the name -

and a *timbale milanaise* for dessert, perhaps because of the little almonds. We were becoming bourgeois."

Henri Calet
Le Tout sur le tout

certainly the first to have a chain of popular restaurants serving up cheap pot-au-feu and a bowl of bouillon (a kind of soup), but it was the Chartiers who opened *bouillons* in smart surroundings. The *Vagenende* ▲ 130 in Boulevard Saint-Germain and the *Bistro de la Gare* ▲ 154 in Boulevard du Montparnasse are two excellent examples that have survived. Just the same, the big *bouillon Chartier* in Rue du Faubourg-Montmartre, which opened in 1896, is the only one to

RESTAURANT CHARTIER

continue the inexpensive *bouillon* formula and keep Chartier's name. Since 1945 *Chartier* has been run by René Lemaire (the restaurant has had only three owners) with the assistance of his son Daniel.

A STATION CONCOURSE. The entrance to *Chartier*, which has all the trappings of a truly "great" restaurant, is at the back of a dark courtyard and through a revolving door. Customers are sometimes surprised to be welcomed by a waiter in a long white apron, black waistcoat and bow tie. Their amazement is all the greater when they see the enormous dining-room. With its huge clock and the glass roof covering the entire ceiling, the room bears a striking resemblance to a station concourse. The walls, whose marble sub-foundations are half-covered with woodwork, are broken up by false bays adorned with mirrors, and are otherwise decorated with stucco moldings incorporating Camille Chartier's initials in the manner of a prince's monogram. The ceiling lamps with their large, bright bulbs and the coat stands on the low, wooden partitions are made of copper.

PIAF AND FRÉHEL. The place seems to be in utter turmoil as the waiters waltz frantically about, and one is quite likely to be given a seat between a little old lady finishing off her sardines fried in oil and a couple of students waiting for eggs mayonnaise. Over in another corner of the dining-room some American tourists tuck into their beef stew. Meanwhile, well-dressed gentlemen order *hachis parmentier*, a kind of shepherd's pie, and muse dreamily of their long-departed youth. Mistinguett and Maurice Chevalier, Édith Piaf and Marcel Cerdan, all came here as lovers, as did journalists on the newspaper *L'Équipe* before it moved. At one point, Fréhel decided to turn the restaurant into a movie theater, but fortunately that idea never got beyond the stage of a drawing on the back of an envelope. A good thing, too, bearing in mind what has become of most movie theaters in the area. The *Chartier* was listed as a historic monument in 1989, and faces the future with confidence.

A FINE JOB
The *bouillon Chartier* has just one painting – but it is enormous. It is signed "Germont" and dated 1929, and depicts a garden with unexpected perspectives, with a fragile airship flying overhead. The artist painted this picture in exchange for food, and must have eaten free for many weeks as he completed his vast picture ....

F. PLACE

263

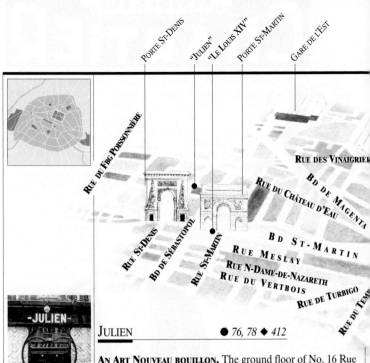

PORTE ST-DENIS "JULIEN" "LE LOUIS XIV" PORTE ST-MARTIN GARE DE L'EST

RUE DU FBG POISSONNIÈRE

RUE DES VINAIGRIERS

BD DE MAGENTA

RUE DU CHÂTEAU D'EAU

RUE ST-DENIS

BD DE SÉBASTOPOL

RUE ST-MARTIN

BD ST-MARTIN

RUE MESLAY

RUE N-DAME-DE-NAZARETH

RUE DU VERTBOIS

RUE DE TURBIGO

RUE DU TEMPLE

JULIEN

● 76, 78 ◆ 412

A BOY CALLED JULIEN
Another version of the origin of the *Julien* involves a bar owner from Montmartre called Barbarin who is alleged to have left La Butte and settled in the Saint-Denis quarter because of his love for a "dancer." The dancer is said to have had a child whom she called "Julien," and Barbarin named his establishment after him.

AN ART NOUVEAU BOUILLON. The ground floor of No. 16 Rue du Faubourg-Saint-Denis has been a restaurant since the mid-19th century. In 1902 the owner of the building, one M. Fournier, decided to rebuild it and align the front with the road; he renovated the establishment at the same time. Fournier employed the best designers, and he made it clear that he wished the décor to be exceptional. Art Nouveau was by now all the rage, and the result undoubtedly surpassed his wildest dreams. The *Gandon-Fournier* restaurant was no longer just a *bouillon*, no matter how popular *bouillons* may have been at the time; the décor must have made many a smart establishment on the nearby Boulevards green with envy!

LOUIS TRÉZEL
Trézel was expert in the fashioning of *pâte de verre* (colored glass), a basic decorative element in Art Nouveau at the turn of the century.

LA RÉPUBLIQUE
"CHEZ JENNY"

C\ ST-MARTIN
RUE DU FBG DU TEMPLE
QUAI DE JEMMAPES
QUAI DE VALMY
AV. DE LA RÉPUBLIQUE
BD VOLTAIRE
BD DU TEMPLE
RUE BÉRANGER

LOUIS MAJORELLE AND LOUIS TRÉZEL.
Behind the entrance area near the door is a bar made of Cuban mahogany. It is the work of Louis Majorelle, the celebrated interior designer and member of the school of Nancy. The furniture, with its rounded forms, is decorated with motifs and elements of worked metal, but it is dominated by a mirror that is also rounded and framed by stucco moldings. It is a magnificent example of Art Nouveau. The poor architectural qualities of the long, simple dining-room are amply compensated by quite breathtaking décor. Three glass sections in the ceiling provide filtered lighting, and three large mirrors, alternating with panels of colored glass, hang on each wall. These extremely interesting mirrors by Louis Trézel, influenced by Alfons Mucha, represent four young women personifying the Four Seasons, and the flower-women's dresses are set off by cabochon inlay and colored pearls. Here Trézel, a prominent French glass painter, used a technique of applying colored metals on colored glass at high temperature. A mirror at the far end of the room is framed by two more panels depicting two peacocks against a background of the moon, stars and flowers; they are signed "A. Segaud".

STAFF MOLDINGS. The glass and wood panels

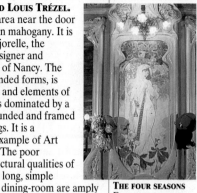

THE FOUR SEASONS
Four young women personifying the Four Seasons are shown against a background of flowers for spring, green leaves for summer, dead leaves for autumn, and bare branches for winter.

and the mirrors are clad with staff moldings which also cover the beams, cornices and structures with motifs based on flowers, animals and the female form. The central partition separating the rows of tables support coatstands surmounted by light bulbs, and on the walls above each panel there are gilt and bronze wall brackets supporting five lamp shades. The tiled floor is decorated with plant motifs. The *Julien* is a relic from a departed era that Jean-Paul Bucher, director of the Flo group and lover of "places of historic interest" ▲ 259, bought in 1975 in an attempt to revive the tradition of Parisian brasseries. It has certainly gone down well with theater-goers. At the *Julien*, part of what you pay for is visual gratification.

❝Each piece of meat is a kind of factory, mill and blood press. Tubes, ovens and vats stand next to sledge-hammers and bolsters. Boiling steam shoots out. Dull and bright fires glow...❞

Francis Ponge
"Le morceau de viande"
in *Le Parti pris des choses*

The Boulevard Saint-Denis between Porte Saint-Martin and Porte Saint-Denis, shown here in a late 18th-century picture.

THE MAIRE
RESTAURANT
One of the *Louis XIV*'s predecessors in this locality was called the *Maire*. It stood on the corner of boulevards Saint-Denis and Strasbourg. The Goncourt brothers referred to it in their 1857 *Journal*: "Ah! The Maire restaurant! Around 1850, when he was just a wine merchant, behind the zinc counter he had a little room that fitted six people if they squeezed up. There, on real old silver, and to people whose culinary tastes he respected, old Maire himself served haricot mutton with morel, wonderful macaroni with truffles, and several bottles of

LE LOUIS XIV ◆ 412

TRIUMPHAL ARCHES AND BILLIARDS. The construction of the Boulevard Saint-Denis in the 1670's (it was formerly known as the Nouveau-Cours) caused the old fortified gates of Charles V's wall to be pulled down and replaced by two monumental triumphal arches glorifying and commemorating Louis XIV's military victories. They were the Porte Saint-Denis and the Porte Saint-Martin, both which opened onto the streets of the same name. These were the new north-south arteries of Paris. New taverns and bars must soon have sprung up, and an early 19th-century engraving of the boulevard shows a billiard hall at No. 16. A century later, the game of billiards had become very popular in the district, which had itself become a kind of billiard player's paradise, and the hall itself was turned into a café-restaurant with a few felt-covered tables.

GRAND SIÈCLE STYLE MAKES A COMEBACK. Jean Descombes bought the establishment in 1939, and after the war entrusted the architect Larrivière with the task of renovating it and turning it into a proper brasserie. Larrivière came up with a design for a sober décor consisting mainly of mahogany carved with rounded niches. In the niches Larrivière placed mirrors, and decorative wooden panels painted in a marquetry style and representing the Sun King either in

delightful Burgundy from Louis-Philippe's cellars which he had bought up almost completely." On becoming a proper restaurant, the *Maire* acquired an excellent reputation.

a coach or on horseback. However, the most prominent features of the decorative ensemble were pieces of art metalwork dispersed around the room. The tables, armchairs and bar stools were all made of wrought-iron, and the wallbrackets, ornaments in niches and partitions were in bronze. Recurring elements included the fleur-de-lis, scallops and intersecting "L"s in honor of the illustrious monarch after whom the restaurant is named. The result was an astonishing 1950's pastiche of *Grand Siècle* style. One reason why it was so surprising was that it was virtually unique in Paris, the style no longer finding favor with contemporary arbiters of taste.

AN OLD-FASHIONED ATMOSPHERE. In the 1960's, when modern style was developing and alone distinguished the postwar

XIV

period, Jean Descombes found himself beset by doubt. Could the *Louis XIV*'s décor possibly be already out of date? First to fall victims to his uncertainty were the sun-shaped, wrought-iron ceiling lights set in stained glass, and the wooden panels covered with canvases by the Parisian painter Le Beuze, a specialist in the Parisian school of "miserabilism" and street urchins. The pillaging would doubtless have gone on but for Jean Descombes' death in 1965: his successor,

Gérard Flottes-Descombes, was a stout defender of the restaurant's extraordinary décor, and found a willing listener and powerful ally in Michel Guy, Minister of Culture between 1974 and 1976. How many restaurants have been saved, thanks to this man, officially listed as "places of historic interest"? Anyone in any doubt should simply go into the *Louis XIV* and find a table next to the second-floor spit-roaster. The old-fashioned atmosphere is totally enchanting, and many customers have not hesitated to add their names to the Golden Book next to such lovers of aesthetic incongruity as the artists Salvador Dalí and Andy Warhol.

The Porte Saint-Denis commemorates the taking of Maastricht, the defeat of Holland and the conquering of the Rhine; the Porte Saint-Martin recalls the taking of Besançon and Limburg and the break-up of the Triple Alliance.

PARIS — LA PORTE St-MARTIN

267

LE TEMPLE

The name of this quarter derives from the commandery of the Knights Templar that once stood there. It was like a town surrounded by ramparts, the dungeon lying between the Mayor's office in the 3rd *arrondissement* and Square du Temple. The Order was banned in 1313 by Philip the Fair, who handed their land over to the Hospitallers of St John of Jerusalem.

This lifesize wooden figure is of an Alsatian woman in traditional costume holding a bunch of grapes portending a good harvest. It stands in the restaurant at the foot of the staircase.

CHEZ JENNY

◆ *411*

FROM EXHIBITION STALL TO DANCE HALL. Robert Jenny had a stall at the 1930 Colonial Exhibition at which he sold produce from his native Alsace such as sauerkraut, sausages and beer. They went down very well and, attracted by the Parisian way of life, he looked for a place to settle. He eventually chose premises near Place de la République, the former *Victor* dance hall at No. 39 Boulevard du Temple. Did he know, when he bought it, that it had been a Russian restaurant in 1906, and then a Belgian restaurant in 1914? This is a lively area, although it is no longer a "boulevard of crime"; it acquired this reputation in the 18th century when plays put on in neighboring theaters were based on dubious local events.

GASTRONOMIC REPUTATION. The Boulevard du Temple's gastronomic reputation dates from this period. Prior to the Revolution, this road was a favorite Parisian promenade and offered idlers an endless choice of bars and some excellent restaurants. The *Cadran Bleu* opened in 1773 on the corner of the Boulevard and Rue Charlot and, in the years leading up to the Revolution, was highly successful under one M. Henneveu, formerly a chef to the nobility. The private rooms soon became much better-known than the food; however, the *Nouvel Almanach des gourmets* (*New Gourmets' Almanach*) of 1825 spoke highly of the canapés, and the following year, "*Batteur de Pavé*" (the novelist Honoré de Balzac) wrote in his *Dictionnaire des enseignes de Paris* (*Dictionary of Parisian Restaurant Signs*) that the clock in the *Cadran Bleu* shows 4 o'clock "announcing wedding meals, Beaune and champagne". The *Café Turc*, owned by Bonvalet from 1811 onward, competed with the *Cadran Bleu* next door for the reputation of best restaurant in the street, and Balzac and his heroes soon abandoned the Boulevard du Temple for the Boulevard des Italiens ● 46.

SPINDLER AND ERNY. The atmosphere of the *Chez Jenny* restaurant, which opened in 1932, was that of an Alsatian bar especially recreated by Robert Jenny's designers. The marquetry expert Charles Spindler decorated the rooms on the brasserie's top two floors with typical regional scenes, and

> "THE ONLY PROMENADE OF ANY NOTE,/THE ONLY ONE I REALLY
> LOVE,/THE ONLY ONE THAT GIVES ME ANY PLEASURE/IS THE
> BOULEVARD DU TEMPLE IN PARIS."
>
> DÉSAUGIERS

THE "FORK MURDERER"

The "fork murderer" died in Boulevard du Temple, and not at *Chez Jenny* (which had not yet been built) but at the *Cadran Bleu*. It all came to pass in the early 19th century. A rich landowner by the name of Old Gourier had a peculiar yearning to make his dinner companions die of indigestion. He would have designs on some unfortunate acquaintance whom he invited out and fed till he expired. The best eaters lasted a few months at the most. The ninth victim, called Ameline, an assistant executioner, held out for one year, then two years ... and then it was Gourier's turn to feel the pace. One evening, at the *Cadran Bleu*, he collapsed over his fourteenth slice of sirloin and died, killed by his latest victim.

an ensemble of Moroccan citron-wood, Indonesian Amboyna, Canadian maplewood and Finnish birch, providing a remarkable, contrasting harmony of colors. In 1934 Robert Jenny was succeeded first by Jean-Baptiste Fleck, who enlarged the restaurant, and then in 1939 by Charles Bayer. In the late 1950's Bayer asked Jean-Jacques and Albert Erny to add some carved woodwork to the restaurant's interior,

PLACE DE LA RÉPUBLIQUE

Until the mid-19th century, Boulevard du Temple crossed Rue du Faubourg du Temple at the tiny

and a splendid wooden statue of a sturdy Alsatian woman holding an enormous bunch of grapes in her left hand and a basket over her right arm; today she still stands in the same position, at the bottom of the stairs. Waitresses wearing folk dress – looking like living versions of the statue – serve marvelous sauerkraut and wine, as they have since the day *Chez Jenny* first opened in 1932. This authentic restaurant has lost none of its appeal and remains an extremely popular meeting-place.

Place du Château-d'Eau, named after the fountain in the middle. The present square was built between 1856 and 1865; the Statue de la République was unveiled on July 14, 1884.

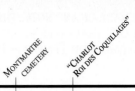

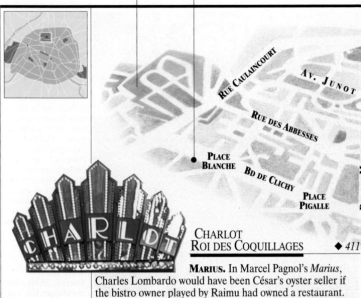

RUE CAULAINCOURT

AV. JUNOT

RUE DES ABBESSES

PLACE BLANCHE

BD DE CLICHY

PLACE PIGALLE

RUE DES MARTYRS

CHARLOT ROI DES COQUILLAGES ◆ 411

MARIUS. In Marcel Pagnol's *Marius*, Charles Lombardo would have been César's oyster seller if the bistro owner played by Raimu had owned a restaurant. And he would have played *belote* (a card game) with Panisse, Escartefigue and Monsieur Brun if he had not been employed while still young to open shellfish for some fish restaurant in Marseilles' *Vieux Port* or the Cannebière. So, did he acquire the nickname of "Charlot" in Marseilles or when he went up to Paris in 1935? It is well-known that fashionable Parisian society had a weakness for signs of worldly familiarity, like calling servants by their first rather than their second names. At all events, Charlot was soon attracting that high society to *Marius* in Rue du Faubourg-Saint-Martin with a mixture of southern charm and culinary skills.

"CHARLOT I." In 1948 he opened his first restaurant called *Charlot I*,

PLACE CLICHY
Place Clichy was the scene of a historic episode in the history of Paris. On March 28, 1814, a large number of peasants fleeing before the Cossack invasion entered Paris to find shelter. They set up camp near the Porte de Clichy just where Rue de Clichy meets the wall of the *Fermiers généraux*. On the night of March 29 and 30, men under Moncey, a major-general in the National Guard, which had made its headquarters in the *Père Lathuile* bar in Avenue de Clichy, were defending this route into Paris with assistance from students from the *École polytechnique*. They resisted the Cossack attacks of the Count of Langeron until Marshal Marmont resolved to sign the armistice.

270

"BEAUVILLIERS"
SACRÉ-CŒUR
RUE RAMEY
RUE DE CLIGNANCOURT
BD DE ROCHECHOUART
AV. TRUDAINE

in Boulevard de Clichy. *Marius* lost ground while Charlot successfully concentrated on the shellfish, leaving the catering side to his brother-in-law. Unfortunately the two men soon fell out, and it even reached the point where Charlot was thrown out of his own restaurant one day while lunch was being served. Regulars who had witnessed the scene had no hesitation in following Charlot out, taking the tables, chairs and crockery with them. They later deposited their booty at the *Astor*, a restaurant in Place de Clichy that Charlot soon purchased. He had to leave the name *Charlot I* with his brother-in-law, and this time called himself *Charlot, Roi des Coquillages* (Charlot, King of Shellfish) with a subtitle saying, "This is the real Charlot." He need not have bothered: everybody knew!

SACHA GUITRY AND HIS SHRIMPS. After complaining that Sacha Guitry was the only major theatrical personality not to have come to his restaurant, Charlot decided to telephone the great man. Guitry explained that his doctor had forbidden him to leave his room and asked for some shrimps to be delivered. And he carried on having them sent round until he was completely recovered! That was how *Charlot* treated customers. Later, Charlot the man retired to Marseilles, leaving the restaurant to others and, during this time, Jean-Pierre Rémon executed his famous mural frescoes inspired by Breton landscapes. The brothers Jacques and Pierre Blanc bought the new *Charlot* in 1984 and commissioned the designer Pierre Pothier to carry out renovations on the establishment. He devised a scheme of tiles and tortoise shells on the walls, mirrors on the ceiling, 1925-style wall brackets and furniture, partitions in engraved glass, and a multiplicity of objects relating to the sea. The grand result is a Marseilles version of Art Deco to accompany the outstanding seafood cuisine.

THE BLANC brothers take over THE ASTOR
At first, *Charlot* kept the *Astor*'s anonymous façade, and even the name remained on the awning next to *Au Roi des Coquillages*. The Blanc brothers then turned it into an enormous mirror reflecting the bustle of Place Clichy, and the name *Charlot* appeared on a fan of peacock feathers that advertised the restaurant's caricatured Art Deco style.

A CAUTIOUS WINNER
On being offered champagne by Charlot after winning a race, champion cyclist Fausto Coppi declined, saying that the cork might make too much noise when it popped out!

THE 1798 MENU

The only surviving copy of the *Beauvilliers* menu is the one made by an English traveler passing through Paris in 1798. There were 178 dishes in all, including *fricandeau* with spinach, herring in mustard, sauerkraut with sausages, veal chops grilled in buttered paper, partridge with cabbage, and duck with turnips. Pies, too, figured prominently on the menu: fillings included soft roe of carp, fillet of cod and eel stew.

SMARTLY DRESSED

Leading Revolutionary figures did not object to Beauvilliers strutting about the restaurant, smartly dressed and carrying a sword at his side. His bearing and haughtiness simply reminded the sarcastic emigrés that it was he that would be catering for *them* after 9 Termidor. He was, after all, no more than an ex-servant.

BEAUVILLIERS ◆ *410*

A GENTLEMAN SERVANT. The name of this restaurant is a throwback to late 18th-century aristocratic cuisine; the setting recalls late 19th-century boudoirs. Antoine Beauvilliers was a gentleman servant of the Count of Provence, but in 1782 he was obliged to open his own restaurant in Rue de Richelieu ● *44* when his master emigrated. He opened the first "grand restaurant" in Paris and it was

popular with fashionable society ● *90*; indeed, such was his reputation that the name did not disappear until 1925. Édouard Carlier was responsible for renovating this splendid restaurant when he opened his own restaurant in Rue Lamarck – "on the slopes of 'Mont-Martre'," as he was fond of saying.

OLD-FASHIONED REFINEMENT. Carlier proved to be the equal of Beauvilliers in terms of both gastronomy and etiquette. The classical food is of the very highest quality, and the same may also be said for both the welcome and the advice with the menu accorded to the select clientele. Carlier himself supervised the interior renovation of the dining-rooms: lovers of high tech and rooms reduced to the bare essentials are advised to stay away as the décor here will not be to their taste. *Beauvilliers* is truly a world of old-fashioned refinement where a mistress's whims vie with aesthetic caprice. The Empire Bar adjoins three dining-rooms: the first of these is decorated with wedding bouquets, the second with portraits of children, and the third with etched engravings and charcoal sketches of the mills of Montmartre. However, everything is overshadowed by enormous bouquets of flowers that are reflected in the mirrors and lacquered ceilings. This restaurant is a favorite haunt of gourmets who do not believe that best is opposed to good. The stairway on the side of the restaurant leads to three small covered terraces that command a fine view over the old streets of Montmartre.

FOREIGN CUISINE

Where would Italian cooking be without olive oil?

Pizzerias flourished in Paris throughout the 1960's and 1970's, and businessmen, opportunists and enterprising hipsters simply spread out their dough and covered it with tinned tomato sauce. But pizza is to Italy what "steak frites" are to France: good quality is hard to find. Other distinctive Italian dishes include seafood risotto, spaghetti with anchovies and Venetian ratatouille. Such specialties are among the best of this most convivial of all cuisines.

LE GRAND VENISE ◆ 369
A truly great Italian restaurant run by the whole family, including the *mamma* who presides over the kitchen and the daughter who organizes the service. Dishes are accompanied by anecdotes of life in Italy.

ITALIAN WINES
Chianti comes from Tuscany, from 150,000 acres of vineyard between Florence and Siena. "Original" Chianti is called Chianti Classico, and on the neck-label there is a black rooster, the sign of authenticity; it also guarantees a tannic, heady, powerful wine with a slight bouquet of violets and liquorice. *Villa Antinori* (opposite), a Chianti Classico, should be drunk with meat and well-flavored pasta dishes. Also shown here is an Orvieto Classico, a white wine recommended for fish and seafood lasagne.

PASTA
There are thousands of different kinds of pasta: apart from spaghetti and tagliatelle, the best-known types in France are fettucine (narrower than tagliatelle), gnocchi (made with potato), penne (short and flat), tortellini, macaroni, farfalle (butterflies) and cannelloni (filled with a meat stuffing).

ESPRESSO
Coffee can be *ristretto* (small and strong) or *lungo* ("long").

WATER
There are many kinds of Italian water; most of it is carbonated.

"ANTICA PIZZERIA"
This engraving of 1881 shows another popular Italian dish, pizza. It is hugely popular in Paris, though less so in "real" Italian restaurants.

HAM
Thinly sliced Parma ham and salami make excellent starters. Alternatively, they may be used as ingredients in a main dish.

CARPACCIO AND THE AMERICANS

At the end of World War Two, the American army left a stock of corned beef in the south of Italy. The starving Italians sliced the meat and dressed it with olive oil – and so carpaccio was born.

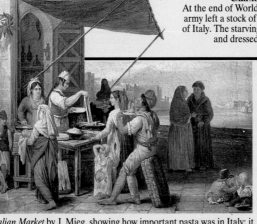

Italian Market by J. Mieg, showing how important pasta was in Italy; it is a dish that can be eaten anywhere at any time.

SOME TERMS

BOLLITO MISTO: various meats boiled in the same pot.
CARPACCIO: raw beef dressed with olive oil.
FEGATO ALLA VENEZIANA: calf's liver sautéed with onions.
MINESTRONE: vegetable soup.
POLENTA: cornmeal porridge; at one time, it accompanied meals in the way that bread does today.
RISOTTO: a rice dish.
TIRAMISÙ: a pudding made with *mascarpone* and coffee.
VITELLO ALLA PIZZAIOLA: veal with tomato and garlic sauce.

Fettucine genovese (pasta with fresh basil, pine nuts and garlic).

Pasta is excellent when cooked *al dente*, that is, still a bit firm, and served with a knob of butter, fresh tomato sauce, basil and a sprinkling of Parmesan.

Tortellini alla ricotta (a gratin of pasta with cream and cheese).

Spaghetti Napoli (with tomato sauce).

THE ORIGIN OF SPAGHETTI

It is said that spaghetti originated in China and was introduced to Venice, and then Europe, by Marco Polo.

"GRISSINI"

It is common to munch *grissini* while waiting for the food to arrive. These are thin sticks of dry bread that are placed in a glass or simply straight on the table.

When Marco Polo was in the Far East, he is said to have seen Chinese women make a paste of flour, eggs and water, and then press it through a plate pierced with many holes. The long filaments that were produced were then cooked in boiling water. The dish is now known throughout the world.

CHEESES

Finely grated Parmesan (opposite) is sprinkled on pasta. Pecorino, ewe's milk cheese, is delicious, although not as well-known as Ricotta or Mozzarella.

Spain is a land of contrasts and has no single cuisine. Instead, there are several. Garlic, bread and olive oil are very common everywhere, but the cuisines of Andalusia, Catalonia and the Basque country are quite different, if only because they use local products. A good Spaniard lunches at three and dines at ten, and the food is sophisticated and sensual. There are also charming tapas bars all over the country; the word comes from *tapar* (to cover). These bars serve small snacks with glasses of wine; an evening in Spain is almost unimaginable without them.

SAN VALLERO ◆ 390
The cuisine is authentically Spanish, and each dish is prepared with refinement and imagination. The young chef was trained in the great French restaurants, and this gives him a fresh approach to classical Spanish cuisine. The *San Vallero* is a far cry from from tasty, but less sophisticated, tapas and empañadas.

PAELLA
Paella is widely thought to be the Spanish culinary specialty *par excellence*, but in fact it is typical only of the Valencia region. Fish and meat are never mixed: there is fisherman's paella, and one made by peasants with rabbit and chicken. *Paella* takes its name from the dish it is cooked in, a two-handled frying-pan.

BRANDY AND FORTIFIED WINES
The fine wines of Jeréz in Andalusia are known as "sherry" in English. There are different kinds, all derived from the basic *fino* and *oloroso*: *fino* (below left) is a dry white wine (15-16°), while *oloroso* is fuller-flavored, has a strong bouquet and is a popular aperitif on account of its high alcohol content. There are two popular after-dinner drinks in addition to *anís escarchado* (above): they are Andalusian brandy (opposite), which is very different from Cognac, and *Pacharán* from Navarre, made from sloes macerated in *anís*.

COCIDO
Each region has its own dish of boiled meat; the ingredients vary with what is available locally. *Cocido gallego* (above) is from Galicia.

GAZPACHO. A cold soup from Andalusia, with a tomato base.

SAFFRON
This famous spice is found in Aragon, southern Catalonia and Andalusia. The women who gather saffron are called *roseras*. It is pounded in a mortar with a little stock before being added to the paella, which it colors and flavors without dominating the dish.

In Spain, houses used to be built around the kitchen. It was the main room, and was full of life, heat and wonderful smells.

DESSERT
Oranges and pomegranates are found everywhere; they even appear on the Spanish coat of arms. The nuns of Andalusia are famous for their pastry-making skills. Other desserts include *flan con nata* (baked custard) and almond tarts.

SOME TERMS
BODEGA: a cellar where wine is stored and sold.
CALLOS A LA MADRILEÑA: tripe with chickpeas, potato and *chorizo*.
FABADA ASTURIANA: dried haricot beans with salt pork and sausages.
SERRANO: country ham.
TORTILLA: a potato omelette often eaten as tapas.

OLIVE OIL
Like other Mediterranean cuisines, Spanish cooking relies heavily on olive oil. If the oil is green, it means the olives have been picked young, and the oil is then very fruity.

RIOJA
Rioja now stands comparison with the best Bordeaux wines, and nowadays has a high reputation. The vineyards in northern Spain cover about 100,000 acres, and the main grape variety, the *tempranillo*, resembles the Pinot Noir of Burgundy. Rioja is aged in oak barrels, and this makes it a very classy, elegant wine. Catalan wines like *cava* are lighter.

CHARCUTERIE
Spanish sausages such as chorizo, *butifarra* and *botillo* have an excellent reputation.

AÏOLI
This variant of mayonnaise is made with garlic and olive oil, but without egg. The *aïoli* is perfect when the mortar can be turned upside down, and neither the pestle nor the *aïoli* falls out.

▲ PORTUGUESE CUISINE

It is said that an English nobleman by the name of Forester, an enthusiast for the wines of the Upper Douro Valley, decided to add brandy to his favorite wine because it did not travel well, and that he thereby stumbled upon the invention of port.

Portuguese cuisine is not well-known in Paris, although there are a few excellent restaurants. Back home, the Portuguese need no encouragement to gather around the table and sip a little port while waiting for their cabbage soup, grilled sardines or salt cod. It is said that the Portuguese have 365 recipes for salt cod, "one for every day of the year." Portuguese cuisine includes some very good desserts but, like the people who produce them, they are not ostentatious.

SAUDADE ◆ 408
This is the best Portuguese restaurant in Paris. It is splendidly decorated with blue and white tiles called *azulejos*, which are often found on the façades and in the interiors of Portuguese houses. The wine list is impressive, and the salt cod dishes are perfectly executed. The restaurant is run by a proprietor who talks of his country as if singing a *fado*.

PORT
Port is blended from nine great grape varieties, and is the product of lengthy fermentation. It is still common for the grapes to be pressed to the sound of traditional songs. At the end of the fermentation period, about 20 percent grape spirit is added. Strict selection determines whether the port is "vintage" (a wine of a single exceptional year, bottled early), "crusted" (more than one year, bottled early), "late bottled vintage" (bottled later, once developed) and so on. Red ports can be dry or sweet, the whites dry or very dry, and a good vintage port is drunk at 20–30 years old. Apart from being drunk as an aperitif, port goes well with certain cheeses and desserts.

OLIVES AND MEAT
Portuguese cuisine uses a great deal of fish in the main course. Red meat is rare; the Portuguese prefer poultry and rabbit, and these are frequently accompanied by olives (*azeitonas*).

Olives are also served at the beginning of a meal, and are eaten with bread, salted butter and cheese as a tit-bit before the main course.

The Lisbon fish market in the early 20th century.

VINHO VERDE

"Green wine" (below right) is, like port (below left), produced in the north of Portugal. It is a young, fresh, fruity wine with a hint of sparkle. *Vinho verde* is a wonderful accompaniment for fish.

"BACALHAU A ESCONDIDINHO"

Salt cod is covered by a sauce of tomatoes, onions and olive oil, and is gratinéed in the oven. This dish is usually accompanied by boiled potatoes (see center page illustration for ingredients).

WINE REGIONS

750,000 acres are planted with vines. Port was officially defined in 1765, and 280,000 hectolitres are produced each year. Madeira, with 80,000 hectolitres a year, is also excellent, as are the lively *vinhos verdes*.

SOME TERMS

ARROZ DOCE: a rice pudding.
CAMARÃOES A BRASA: grilled shrimps.
CARNE A ALENTEJANA: meat with shellfish.
COZIDO A PORTUGUESA: boiled beef and pork with sausages.
LINGUIÇA: traditional dry sausage.
MARISCOS: seafood.
PUDIM-FLAN: crème caramel.
SARDINHAS ASSADAS: grilled sardines.

MADEIRA

Madeira wine is produced on the island of that name and comes from vines planted in the ashes of burnt down forests.

Madeira is known as "the wine that never dies" as it never stops improving; it is decanted before being served. The sweetest is Malmsey; Bual is lighter and less sweet.

BACALHAU (SALT COD)

Cod, whether fresh or salted, is the national dish. It combines perfectly with olive oil, another famous Portuguese product, and with onions, another common ingredient in Portuguese cookery. Salt cod is also served in slices.

OLIVE OIL

Many Portuguese dishes contain liberal quantities of olive oil. Once upon a time, the quality of a first pressing of olive oil was judged by cooking salt cod in it: the flavors had to reinforce each other, rather than cancel each other out. Popular Portuguese sayings include: "Truth is like oil, it always comes to the surface" and "To pick oneself up as easily as olive oil."

After the Bolshevik Revolution, Rue Daru in the 8th *arrondissement* became the center of Russian life in Paris, and in the 1920's and 1930's, the Russian community was some 300,000 strong. News of flats and jobs traveled by word of mouth, much of it on the pavements opposite the Cathedral of St Alexander Nevsky, and in little bistros, now sadly closed. Some Russians opened restaurants and bars that served Russian specialties and vodka while Russian songs were sung in the background.

DOMINIQUE ◆ 376

The *Dominique* is considered to be the best Russian restaurant in Paris. Both up at the bar (the zakuski is strongly recommended) and in the dining-room at the back, the surroundings are elegant, and the cooking refined. This is a meeting-place for famous Russians. Alexander Solzhenitsyn, the cellist Mstislav Rostropovich, the Russian-French writer Gabriel Matzneff and the beautiful pianist Brigitte Engerer are often seen here.

LE BORTSCH

BORTSCH
The Russian national soup is based on cabbage, beetroot and other vegetables (ingredients shown above) and meat, and it is eaten boiling hot as a way of keeping out the cold. Sometimes a spoonful of sour cream is added as it is served. Simone de Beauvoir was very fond of

bortsch, and often had it for lunch at the *Dominique*.

VODKA

Russians use barley, wheat or rye to make their national drink; the Poles use potatoes. Sometimes pepper, orange or lemon peel or even bison grass are added. Besides the pleasure that it gives them, Russians drink vodka for its alcoholic strength, which not only warms them up in the long winters, but helps the digestion of often fatty, smoked fish. But beware! Some brands of vodka are neither Russian nor Polish, despite their names. *Smirnoff*, for example, is American!

A START TO THE EVENING

Place a bottle of vodka in the freezer, in the middle of a small bucket of water containing flowers and leaves. When it is frozen, peel the ice off the bottle, and serve the vodka in the resulting block of ice.

A TRADITIONAL RUSSIAN BANQUET

The existence of a range of traditional dishes means that there is a certain unity in the cuisine of this vast country. All dishes are put on the table together, and people help themselves in an expression of Russia's famous hospitality.

Russians drink a great deal of tea served in glasses (opposite: a glass decorated with silver-gilt).

RUSSIAN PASTRIES

This woman is selling *baranki*, dry biscuits eaten with tea, or perhaps *bubliki*, made with sour cream.

DRINKING RUSSIAN STYLE.

There is a story that, once when a Grand Duke dropped his glass of vodka at a reception, it broke and his guests immediately copied him. It is said that this was the origin of the custom of throwing away empty glasses. It is traditional at weddings to break a vodka glass while bride and groom embrace, so as to ward off bad luck.

BLINIS

These thick buckwheat pancakes are eaten with melted butter and sour cream. They go

A large selection of zakuski, or starters.

Pirozhki, tiny pasties of meat, cabbage or fish.

wonderfully with caviar and with smoked fish such as salmon.

RUSSIAN CRAFTSMANSHIP

This box of compressed papier mâché comes from a workshop that used to produce icons. It diversified into new products after the Bolshevik Revolution.

A doll in traditional 19th-century rural costume.

The famous nesting dolls, or *matriochka*.

CAVIAR

Connoisseurs prefer Iranian to Russian caviar, but wherever it comes from, it is always eaten chilled by the teaspoonful - or the ladle! It does not necessarily go best with vodka; white Burgundy and Champagne are also very popular.

SOME TERMS

CUTLETS POJARSKI: veal meatballs.

LAMB GOULASH TOLSTOY: with paprika and sweet pepper sauce.

SALMON COULIBIAC: a salmon pie with rice and mushrooms.

MOLOSSOL: lightly salted cucumber.

NA ZDAROVYE: Good health!

VATRUSHKI: curd cheese buns.

ZAKUSKI: Russian hors d'oeuvres (herrings, marinated fish, aubergine caviar, cabbage salad).

A good Scandinavian dinner always begins with the *skal* ritual. The word originally meant "bowl," but is nowadays best translated as "Good health!" During the Middle Ages, it was the custom for a bowl of mead or beer to be passed from guest to guest and for each to drink from it. It was also customary for a basket to be hung beneath the roof of each farm facing the road; this told passing travelers that they could ask for bread, butter, meat and smoked sausages. These rituals are an illustration of Nordic conviviality and hospitality. Scandinavian cuisine typically evokes thoughts of smoked salmon or herring, washed down with plenty of aquavit.

LA MAISON DU DANEMARK ◆ 387
This has a café-bar and a restaurant, both of which serve delicious meals.
OLSEN ◆ 394
Both restaurant and traiteur sell very good quality salmon. Like the herring, it is caught off the Danish island of Bornholm in the Baltic.

SMOKED FISH
Danish people still smoke fish traditionally by rubbing filleted fresh salmon and herring with coarse salt, and then hanging them in the smoke of different kinds of wood, preferably alder. Top: a salmon with its smoky exterior; above: with the exterior removed.

AQUAVIT
Like vodka ▲ 280, aquavit is drunk iced, and may be flavored with cumin, orange, spices or herbs. In Denmark, a yellow flower, the Pericum, is often placed in the bottle to color the aquavit. Aquavit is capable of matching the strong flavors of smoked fish and piquant sauces.

SMOKED SALMON AND GRAVADLAX
Salmon ■ 16 are born in fresh water, and then migrate at the age of approximately two years to the Baltic, where they fatten up, mainly feeding on mackerel. This is what gives them their pale color. Salmon goes well with various sauces using cream and dill.

SCANDINAVIAN BEER
The Scandinavians were the first people in the world to brew beer. A glass of aquavit sharpens the taste buds, and is typically followed by a beer.

Rodgrod med flode, a thickened purée of red fruits with cream.

JAM MADE WITH ARCTIC BERRIES

Arctic berries only grow north of the Arctic Circle and are slightly sour. They are therefore mostly

eaten in the form of jam, which is added to puddings like pancakes or cream cheese.

Ready-made *smorrebrod* are sold in all Scandinavian countries.

SMORREBROD

Danish *smorrebrod*, literally "buttered bread," is a national institution. It consists of a slice of bread with one of a range of toppings - herring, salmon, cream, cheese, egg yolk, radish or herbs. This "open sandwich" is eaten as a dish in itself, with a knife and fork.

CRISPBREAD

This is made with whole rye, and frequently accompanies meals. *Smorrebrod* is made with either crispbread or black bread (rye, buckwheat and wheat flours).

SOME TERMS

JEG ER SULTEN (Danish): I'm hungry.
KIITOS (Finnish): thank you.
LAX (Swedish): salmon.
LOHI (Finnish): salmon.
ROGET LAKS (Danish): smoked salmon.
SILD (Danish): herring.
SILL (Swedish): herring.
SILLI (Finnish): herring.
SKAL (Danish): Good health!
VELBEKOMME (Danish): Bon appétit!

WIENERBROD

Wienerbrod are Viennese-inspired Danish pastries. They are light, and particularly delicious at teatime.

FISHING IN THE BALTIC

The fishing season lasts from August to April. Fishermen go out at nightfall to spread their nets, and the herring and salmon are separated when they return to port in the early morning. Below is a Danish engraving of a fisherman's wife selling her wares in Copenhagen.

HERRING

This is the main Scandinavian specialty. The very best herring are fished off the Danish island of Bornholm. It can be eaten as part of a *smorrebrod*, or fresh with different sauces and garnished with herbs that bring out the flavors.

▲ CENTRAL EUROPEAN CUISINE

At one time, Central European restaurateurs flavored their own vodka with cumin, pepper or lemon. Vodka is always drunk iced.

Central Europe has been influenced gastronomically by the cuisines of surrounding countries, including Russia (bortsch, piroshki and zakuski), Austria (strudel), Italy (pasta and polenta), Greece (stuffed vine leaves and cabbage leaves) and Turkey (mezze); in Paris, this cuisine is mostly to be found in Ashkenazi Jewish restaurants. While drawing on Hungarian and Slav cuisines, they have retained traditional recipes (e.g. stuffed carp or glazed onions with a meat stuffing) that are often linked to the religious calendar. The use of kosher food lends a great freshness to the cooking.

GOLDENBERG ◆ 385
Patrick Goldenberg is the nephew of the celebrated Jo who has a restaurant in Rue des Rosiers ▲ 237. The *Goldenberg* offers some of the best Central European cooking, including pastrami sandwiches served at the counter. There is both a restaurant and a take-away section. The proprietor is a mine of information about the customs and traditions linked to the food.

WINES
Kosher wines (made in accordance with the prescriptions of Jewish ritual law) give great pleasure to many. Many of them come from Israel: red Gamla goes with meat, and Yarden, a dry white, is ideal with fish. Red, white and rosé Carmel wines are also well known.

ECONOMY
This is a cuisine of the poor, and everything is used, including the roe of the pike (*icra* in Romanian), offal, feet and necks. Opposite: the ingredients for stuffed goose's neck. This is served with horseradish (the roots grated and marinated in vinegar), and beetroot provides the sweetness; it is sometimes accompanied by *molossol* (pickled cucumber) ▲ 281.

PASTRAMI
Pastrami, a salted, smoked and highly seasoned brisket of beef eaten between two slices of bread, is of Romanian origin. Veal, goose or chicken pastrami is now available, and the main ingredient is prepared in the same marinade.

A VARIETY OF BREAD
There is a wide range of bread: this includes caraway bread, bagels, *wassel* (a bagel cooked in water), *matzeler* (a salted biscuit with poppy seed), and unleavened bread that is eaten during the eight days of Passover.

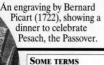

An engraving by Bernard Picart (1722), showing a dinner to celebrate Pesach, the Passover.

FARFEL
This is a kind of toasted pasta, an ideal garnish for various dishes.

PEARL BARLEY
This is the basis for two traditional dishes: *krupnik* and *cholent*.

KASHA
These buckwheat grains have a honeyed taste. They are cooked like rice.

CARMEL CHÂTEAU-RICHON
This sweet red wine is drunk on all festive occasions, particularly

FISH
Freshwater fish like salmon (opposite, on a bagel) is enormously popular. In Hungary, carp is served with gingerbread and paprika, and in Poland in the Kracow style.

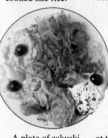

A plate of zakuski.

A TRADITIONAL ASHKENAZI MEAL
There are three well-known zakuski ▲ *281*, or starters. They are chopped chicken liver, salt herring, and Romanian aubergine caviar. Zakuski are typically followed by the most famous Central European dish of stuffed carp served jellied with horseradish and pickled cucumbers. This may in turn be followed by boiled beef, and the meal ends with stewed apple.

at the New Year meal, in the hope that the next year will be a happy one.

PASTRIES
Pastries include *vatruschka*, a Russian cake made with cream cheese, apple and cherry strudel, and poppy-seed cake.

285

▲ FRENCH WEST INDIAN CUISINE

COLOMBO
Each family jealously guards its own recipe for colombo.
This subtle combination of curry powder, thyme flowers
and saffron goes well with pork, poultry, fish and crab.
Sometimes garlic, cumin, cloves and ginger are added.
Delicious!

The cuisine of the Antilles, the French West
Indies, is extraordinarily colorful and
varied, and is typically accompanied by a
glass of punch. There are also as many
recipes as there are families, and as many secret little ·
tricks as there are spices. Accra and black pudding, fish and land
crabs, sucking pig and kid – the list is as mouthwatering as it is
endless! Every dish is a taste of paradise, and delicately
combines European, African and Indian cuisines.

LA PLANTATION ◆ 407
Lisette Gagelin, originally from an Indian
family in Guadeloupe, has cooking at her
fingertips. Her husband Réginald has also
reworked the recipes and thereby lent them
an exceptional delicacy. Their restaurant is a
great success, and boasts the best Creole
cuisine in Paris.

CHATROU IN RED SAUCE
Chatrou, the Creole
name for a small
squid or octopus, is
cooked with lemon,
chili, and spring
onions, a plant much
used in the West
Indies. It is frequently
accompanied by
kidney beans.

SALT-COD ACCRA
This fritter is crunchy
on the outside and
succulent inside, and
was named after the
Ghanaian capital by
African slaves. The
fritters are sometimes
made with salt cod
and peppers,
cabbage, carrots and
herbs. Drinks before
dinner are
inconceivable without
accras and punch!

BLAFF
This typical Creole
dish is based on fish
cooked in a highly
spiced court-bouillon.
Sea-urchin blaff is
very popular; blaff of
John Dory (above) is
well-known, too.

A CREOLE SAYING
"*Kote ki pa ni wonm, pa ni plesi.*": "Where there is no rum, there is no pleasure."

Daube de lambi Shellfish stew.

Dombré Kidney beans and meat.

Creole black pudding, a spicy dish, is eaten with the fingers.

TI-PUNCH
The recipe for punch used to be the words of a song: "*One of sour*" (lime juice), "*Two of sweet*" (cane syrup), "*Three of strong*" (the rum), "*Four of light*" (water and ice).

RUM
For many years, rum was looked down on and was drunk by slaves; it acquired respectability at the end of the 19th century. In France today, there is industrial rum, which is obtained from molasses and is artificially colored, and *rhum agricole*, distilled from the fermented juice of the sugar cane; the latter is better. When rum is young, it is white and is used as a base for cocktails. After aging in oak casks, it becomes brown rum.

COCKTAILS
Tantalizing drinks like punch and planter's punch (in which the lime is replaced by fruit juice) vary from island to island and family to family, with different combinations of spices, fruit and rum.

SOME TERMS
CASSAVE: cassava bread.
COUI: half a gourd, used as a dish.
CHADRON: sea-urchin.
DIDICO: a snack.
FÉROCE: a dish made of cassava, avocado and salt cod or herring.
OUASSOUS OR Z'HABITANTS: bluish-grey crayfish.
SAUCE-CHIEN: sauce of onion, spring onion, lemon and peppers.

THE WEST INDIAN ORCHARD
Each fruit is believed to have particular medicinal qualities.

1. Pineapple
2. Cinnamon
3. Vanilla
4. Passion fruit
5. Red pepper
6. Yam
7. Sweet potato
8. Papaya
9. Physalis
10. Garlic
11. Mango
12. Avocado
13. Coconut
14. Lime
15. Melon
16. Plantain
17. Banana

▲ SOUTH AMERICAN CUISINE

No discussion of South America is complete without mention of tequila. This famous Mexican spirit is typically swallowed in one with a pinch of salt.

In Paris, it is Brazilian restaurants that most successfully evoke the sun, dancing and sense of fiesta associated with South American cuisine. The cooking is very colorful, not unlike Brazilians themselves, whose ancestors came from every corner of the world, bringing their favorite ingredients with them. Brazilians have succeeded in combining them in new dishes with locally grown black and brown beans and corn. Like all truly fascinating cuisines, the cuisine of this vast country consists of specialties from different regions. Making *Churrasco*, charcoal grilled beef, is an excuse for enormous parties that bring the whole family together, and recall the gauchos, the cowboys of central South America.

GUY ◆ *369*

Erica Limouza now runs Guy Leroux and Cléa de Oliveira's restaurant but the atmosphere is the same and it is still a favorite meeting-place for those who miss Brazil. In the evening, customers enjoy their *feijoada* (the national dish), and few resist the rhythms when Brazilian music plays.

ALCOHOL

The Brazilians are great beer-drinkers, and three brands dominate the market: Brahma, Skol and Antartica. *Vinho verde* ▲ *279* from Portugal (Brazil was once part of the Portuguese empire) also goes well with Brazilian food.

LATIN AMERICAN WINE

Chilean wines are of high quality; they are robust and well made, and go very well with highly seasoned dishes.

Argentina also produces large quantites of popular wine. Brazilian Merlot is similar to Médoc.

COCKTAILS AND APERITIFS

Preprandial drinks are an essential ritual in South American life. Cocktails are usually based on *cachaça* (cane spirit). A *batida* is made with *cachaça* and fruit juice - passion fruit for *batida de maracuja*, coconut milk for *batida de coco*, and lime juice for *batida de limão*. *Capirinha* is made with *cachaça*, lime juice and cane sugar. Drinks are accompanied by *tiragosto*, appetizing tit-bits including quails' eggs, cod cakes, *empañadas de camarão* (shrimp), and *pasteizinhos de carne* (small fried meat turnovers).

POPULAR ACCOMPANIMENTS

Cassava meal, ground fine, is cooked in a frying pan with oil or butter, and slivers of bacon, olives or banana may be added. Shredded Portuguese green cabbage (*couve*) is also delicious. The many ways of cooking rice include the addition of onion and coconut. In Brazil, black beans are more common than bread.

288

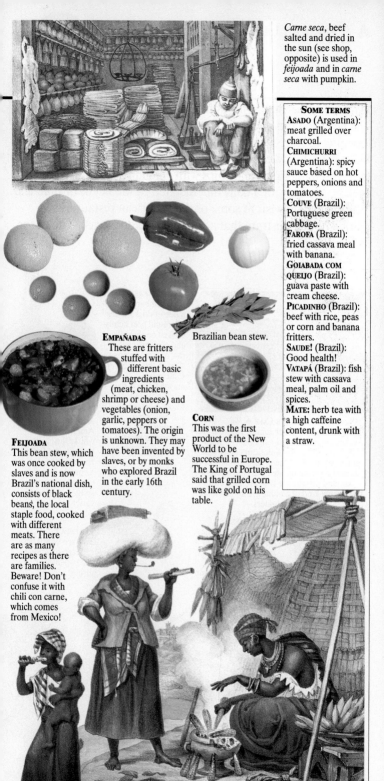

Carne seca, beef salted and dried in the sun (see shop, opposite) is used in *feijoada* and in *carne seca* with pumpkin.

EMPAÑADAS
These are fritters stuffed with different basic ingredients (meat, chicken, shrimp or cheese) and vegetables (onion, garlic, peppers or tomatoes). The origin is unknown. They may have been invented by slaves, or by monks who explored Brazil in the early 16th century.

Brazilian bean stew.

CORN
This was the first product of the New World to be successful in Europe. The King of Portugal said that grilled corn was like gold on his table.

FEIJOADA
This bean stew, which was once cooked by slaves and is now Brazil's national dish, consists of black beans, the local staple food, cooked with different meats. There are as many recipes as there are families. Beware! Don't confuse it with chili con carne, which comes from Mexico!

289

▲ AMERICAN CUISINE

American cuisine has never been so much in the news in France as it has been since the opening of EuroDisney. It has perhaps been a chance for the French to discover that North American food does not consist solely of hamburger and chips with ketchup and cola. That may well be the basis of a daily diet dictated by the needs of time and economy, but a visit to some of the American restaurants in Paris will demonstrate that a wider choice does exist. The décor is good, too.

JOHNNY ROCK CAFÉ ◆ 393
The French rock singer Johnny Hallyday has taken over what used to be the *City Rock Café*, a well-known American eatery that appears to strive for the maximum number of decibels. This immense bistro has a central bar, and the kitchen staff produce every imaginable kind of hamburger in full view of the customers.

HAMBURGERS
Real hamburgers are made of thick patties of ground beef lightly cooked on the grill and accompanied by raw or fried onions, a slice of cheese, bacon, sometimes mayonnaise on the side, and salad. The whole is served on a soft round bun. Hamburgers are sometimes served with an egg on top.

AMERICAN WHISKY
Americans make whisky, just as their Scottish and Irish ancestors did. Kentucky Bourbon (51 percent grain spirit) is one such variety.

SOFT DRINKS
Americans often have a soft drink, usually a cola, with their hamburgers. Colas are also sold in sugar-free and "*diet*" versions.

COLESLAW
This is a sweetened cabbage salad that accompanies many dishes.

FRENCH FRIES
Despite the name, these thick-cut fries are only distantly related to what Parisians would recognize as *frites*. Ketchup is optional but very common.

BUNS
These special rolls for American hamburgers are often very different from the type imported by French fast-food chains.

TEX-MEX
This is a popular marriage of Mexican (*nachos*, *tacos* and *guacamole*) and Texan (chili con carne) cuisines.

THE FOOD
Meat is served with a choice of sauce, perhaps ketchup, accompanied by potatoes: French fries, mashed, or baked in their skins. The more popular dishes include barbecued ribs, grilled chops and salads often served in generous quantities. Family cooking rarely appears on restaurant menus; it is delicious and often rustic in presentation.

CALIFORNIAN WINES
Their history goes back to the conquest of Mexico in the 16th century, and they are now big business. Wines from the Napa Valley are well structured, with an admirable combination of fruit and oak.

American food available to the homesick traveler in Paris includes: Caesar salad (based on romaine lettuce, anchovies, Parmesan, croutons and a raw egg), cheesecake, cookies, pecan pie, pancakes, pumpkin pie and T-bone steak.

BEER
American restaurants in Paris generally sell two light American beers, Budweiser and Michelob. Mexican beers, such as the lighter Corona and the reddish Dos Equis, are also available.

The brownie is a sort of chocolate cake, often served with ice cream.

TEA
Tea, whether in leaf or powder form, is an essential element of Japanese culture.

The highly decorative cuisine of Japan is organized around fish and vegetables. It is truly a feast for both eyes and palate, and the food is always wonderfully fresh and flavorsome. All the dishes are placed together on the serving table, and people come and go, tasting one thing and then another. The traditional Japanese menu is made up of five dishes: *gohan* (rice), *shirumono* (soup), *sake no sakana* (vegetable or salad dish), *nimono* (boiled dish), and *yakimono* (grilled dish). Japanese cooking is frugal yet elaborate, and is an art that makes the best of a limited number of ingredients through the changing seasons.

LE BENKAY ◆ 365
This is part of the *Nikko* hotel, and is one of the best Japanese restaurants in Paris. The view over the Seine is splendid, the décor is extremely refined, and the food itself superb. By way of ensuring that customers have only authentic cuisine, *Le Benkay* employs only genuine Japanese chefs.

RICE
In Japan rice plays the same role as bread does in France. The word *gohan*, which means boiled rice, also means "meal". Japanese rice can be combined with various sweet and savory ingredients, and is absolutely superb.

A UTENSIL FOR EACH DISH
Chopsticks for every meal, skewers for the grill, wooden moulds for sushi, a *nabe* (earthenware pan) for sukiyaki, and long thin bladed knives for sashimi.

SOYA
The soya bean is a basic foodstuff. It is consumed in many forms: in salads, as tofu, in puddings, as flour and of course as the ever-popular soy sauce.

ALCOHOLIC DRINKS
Sake is one of Japan's oldest drinks. It is fermented from rice, and reaches 16° or 17°. Depending on the season and the outside temperature, it may be drunk hot, at room temperature or iced. The Japanese also drink the stronger *syochu*, distilled rice spirit, and beer. There is a sweetened sake, *mirin*, which is used only in cooking.

BOWLS
Soup is drunk from a lacquered wooden bowl (1); porcelain bowls (2,3) are used for the remaining courses.

1 2 3

NABE DISHES
These recall ancient rites according to which guests cooked their food by dipping it into a pan boiling over a fire.

MAKISU
Rolled *sushi* is made with a *makisu*, a small bamboo mat that helps keep the other ingredients in the middle of the rice as it is rolled up in the seaweed.

WASABI (JAPANESE MUSTARD)
Fresh grated horseradish mixed with soy sauce is used to season *sashami* and *sushi*.

Noodles, like the *soba* (above), are made with wheat, rice or buckwheat.

SUSHI
Delicately prepared *sushi* is food for high days and holidays. They are little cakes of vinegared rice topped with a fine slice of fish or piece of omelette, or else they are stuffed with different ingredients according to taste. Sometimes they are wrapped in seaweed.

SASHIMI
This popular dish consists of finely sliced fish and other seafood, all eaten raw. The Japanese are among the world's greatest consumers of fish and seafood.

THREE WAYS OF COOKING
Charcoal grill for *yakimono*, steam for *mushimono* and deep fat for *agemono*.

EATING AS AN ART
Japanese food is enjoyed for its own flavors and particular qualities, and it is not thought that sauces and drinks improve the taste in any way.

▲ CHINESE CUISINE

Eating is a serious matter in China. Even the question *"Chi guo le ma?"* ("Have you eaten?") used to be the equivalent of "Good morning" or "Good afternoon." The Chinese eat food for its flavor and nutritional value, but also for its therapeutic qualities. A well thought-out meal should both afford pleasure and contribute to long life. In this vast country there are four main styles of cooking: Cantonese, light, inventive, and slightly sweet; Szechuan, highly spiced; Shanghai, noted for its fish dishes; and Peking and north Chinese cuisine, based on wheat, sorghum and millet.

RESTAURANT A ◆ 380
From the front this looks like an apothecary's shop, but Huynh Kien is more like a walking encyclopedia on all the traditions of Chinese cuisine. He was trained by the greatest chefs, and is particularly expert at rice-paste sculptures, which he makes at the table.

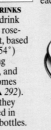

1   2

SPRING ROLLS
Spring rolls are made with rice pancakes that are steamed and stuffed, and then fried crisp and golden-brown in oil. The filling is succulent and full of flavors. Before each mouthful, the roll is dipped in a sauce made with soy, sesame oil and ginger.

ALCOHOLIC DRINKS
The Chinese drink *mei kuei lu* (a rose-flavored spirit, based on sorghum, 54°) ▲ *297*, ginseng liqueur (35°), and sake which comes from Japan ▲ *292*). At one time, they were all served in earthenware bottles.

3

1. The processed monkfish is placed on the seaweed.
2. The seaweed is rolled up.
3. Seafood rolls and their accompaniments.

SCULPTURE
Traditionally, every chef is an artist who carves figures from fresh vegetables and models rice-paste.

Rice growing.

Dishes are often very beautifully decorated, as the Chinese believe that food should please the eye as well as the nose and palate.

DRINKS
For a banquet, the opening courses are traditionally accompanied by rice- or sorghum-based spirits, although beer and soft drinks are more common these days. The Chinese never drink tea with their meals – quite unlike Chinese restaurants in Paris.

THE WOK
Chinese cooking only needs a small number of cooking utensils. The wok is a large round-bottomed frying pan whose

CHOPSTICKS
For most Asians, chopsticks are simply extensions of the fingers. Carved ivory chopsticks trimmed with silver are used at banquets and official meals, while bamboo chopsticks are for everyday use. Bamboo is very practical; plastic is thought to be a little slippery.

design helps save on time, fuel and cooking fat.

STEAMING
Noodles, dumplings and other cereal-based foods are often cooked in water or steamed in small baskets.

SEASONING
Dishes can be seasoned with sesame oil or soy sauce, which are dispensed from bottles on the table.

SOME TERMS
PICKLED CABBAGE: Chinese cabbage marinated with vinegar, salt, hot peppers and sugar, with a sweet-and-sour taste.
FENSZU: transparent bean noodles.
HOA-CHEO: a reddish-colored wild pepper.
JIAOZI: meat or vegetable ravioli, fried, boiled or steamed.
1000-YEAR-OLD EGGS: duck's eggs coated in lime, mud and ashes and matured for two to three months.
TO BAN CHIEN: a sauce based on soya beans, chili and sesame oil.
YU: fish, but also "abundance"; the fish is thus a symbol of wealth.

A COMPLETE MEAL
Cold starter dishes, such as marinated meats or vegetables, are followed by hot fish or meat dishes accompanied by rice or noodles and a variety of sauces. There are no desserts.

▲ SOUTHEAST ASIAN CUISINE

TEA
A lot of tea is drunk in Asia, especially between meals.

Each country of southeast Asia has its own gastronomic tradition, but they all share the same ingredients: fresh and dried fish, shrimp paste, rice, lemon grass, coconut, onion, garlic and chili. In Paris, such food is mainly to be found in Vietnamese, Thai and Cambodian restaurants, and these can be sampled in the "Chinese" areas in Belleville (11th and 20th *arrondissements* and at Porte de Choisy (13th *arrondissement*). The Oriental atmosphere is extremely exciting, and there are plenty of eating-places ranging from cheap cafés to miniature palaces with beautiful carved wooden screens.

NIOULAVILLE ♦ 413
This is a vast restaurant such as you would find in Hong Kong. In the glassed-in kitchens, Cambodian, Chinese, Thai and Vietnamese chefs compete to impress the customers greedily looking over the *dim-sum* trolleys.

THAILAND
Thai desserts, which include fruits and sweetmeats, are among the most delicious in southeast Asia (below: a salad of papaya with glutinous rice). Thai gastronomy is very much like those of its neighbors, except for one thing: Thais use knives and forks!

SERVING PEKING DUCK
The duck is eaten in three stages: first, the crisp, roasted skin, rolled up in a little pancake, with spring onion and a few mint leaves; second, the meat served as a stew with mushrooms or noodles; and third, the carcase made into a soup. Divine!

PEKING DUCK
This special roast duck requires long preparation. It is coated several times with a mixture of sugar and soy sauce, and the skin caramelizes as the duck cooks. It is one of the great delights of Chinese cuisine.

Preparation of noodles in Indo-China, 1874.

A CAMBODIAN PROVERB
❝No one can live without rice, because it is rice that gives us strength, as it gives strength to the king. Rice is not to be looked down on.❞

Mei kuei lu is a rose-flavored spirit distilled from sorghum.

RICE
Rice is eaten fried, boiled (bottom of page) or, in Vietnam (above), as a type of pastry wrapper.

Tsingtao Chinese beer and rice wine. They are both used in cooking or drunk warm.

FISH AND SEAFOOD
Fish and seafood are prepared in all kinds of ways in Asia (above: Cambodian shrimp pancakes; below: the ingredients).

POUDRE DE CURCUMA

FARINE DE RIZ

FÉCULE DE POMME DE TERRE

NEM
These small Vietnamese spring rolls are rolled in a lettuce leaf with a little mint, and are then dipped in *nuoc-mam*, a sauce made from fermented fish.

SOME TERMS
CHE DAU (Vietnam): grated coconut.
CHIEN (Vietnam): fish.
HO MOK (Thailand): steamed fish with spices.
KAI (Thailand): chicken.
KOUAYTIO (Laos, Thailand): rice noodle sheet.
MI KHO (Vietnam): hot and spicy soup with noodles.
MI KROB (Thailand): spicy fried noodles.
NAM PLA (Thailand): fermented fish sauce.
NEM (Vietnam): spring roll.
NUOM PRA CNOCK (Cambodia): traditional soup.

THE DIM-SUM TROLLEY
In the big, popular restaurants of Hong Kong, waitresses walk from table to table pushing trolleys, each carrying a selection of steamed dishes. Customers choose what they want, and pay per item.

297

▲ INDIAN CUISINE

Indian cuisine cultivates difference and subtlety, and across India there are very many different cultures and eating habits. In an Indian meal, the dishes are placed in the middle of the table and changed periodically. The art of presentation is very important: dishes are sometimes decorated with edible gold or silver leaf. Recipes are approximate, because nothing can replace the cook's palate and intuition. Paris only discovered Indian cooking in the mid-1970's, and by then it was already adapted to European tastes, particularly with regard to spicing.

KAMAL ◆ 369
This restaurant serves outstanding Punjabi (north Indian) food. The dishes have an uncommon finesse, and the flavors are subtle and carefully balanced.
YUGARAJ ◆ 373
The Sri Lankan owner is married to a Frenchwoman. The result is perfect cuisine, and a good selection of French wines.

Aperitifs include beer and fruit juices with rose water.

SUPARI
At the end of a good Indian meal, it is common to chew a mixture of aromatic seeds called *supari* to freshen the breath.

SPICY DISHES
Apart from providing subtle flavors, spices are useful for preserving food. They also disguise the effects of heat on perishable ingredients.

DRINKS
Indians drink spiced teas (with mint, ginger and cardamom), and yoghurts with fruit (below left: a rose-

flavored *lassi*) or with fruit juices (above right). These drinks match the colorful, highly flavored cuisine very well. Indian restaurants in Paris often serve Provençal rosé, far too insipid a wine for most Indian food.

TANDOORI FOOD
Tandoori dishes are cooked in a tandoor, a clay oven shaped like a big tall jar. A charcoal fire burns in the bottom, and the fat is thereby roasted off; this is considered a very healthy way of cooking. Meat, poultry and prawns can be prepared in this way. The orange color comes from the use of saffron.

The façade of an Indian restaurant is often restrained and decorated with carved wood. It is what happens inside that counts. Opposite: part of the interior decoration of the *Kamal*.

BREAD

Each dish is accompanied by bread. Nan (above) is made with white flour and is cooked in the tandoor; it is sometimes filled with cheese. *Roti* is a kind of bread made with wholemeal flour.

1   2   3   4

CHUTNEY

Chutneys give a distinctive accent. They can be hot (raw mango with chili – 1), sweet (with mango in syrup – 2) or fresh-flavored (with mint – 3, or coriander – 4).

FOOD AND RELIGION

Eating habits in India are strongly influenced by religion: for instance, Hindus are forbidden beef, and Muslims are forbidden pork. However, most Indians exclude both fish and meat from their meals anyway as they believe that a vegetarian diet encourages purity of mind and spirit. Rice is the staple, especially in the south, although more bread is eaten in the north.

SOME TERMS

CHAPATI: flat bread.
DALCHINI: cinnamon.
ELAICHI: cardamom.
GHEE: clarified butter.
LASSI: a yoghurt drink.
SAMOSA: a small deep-fried triangular pie.
SEEKH KEBAB: minced lamb cooked on skewers.
THALI: a big round tray on which the food and accompaniments are served together.
WARAK: edible, handmade, gold or silver leaf placed on food.

SOME SPICES

From left to right starting at the top: green cardamom, ground green cardamom, garam masala (a spice mixture), zaifal, cloves, cinnamon, cumin, ground cumin, aniseed, black cardamom, chili, turmeric and grated coconut. Above: a special spicy rice from Kashmir. Left: a fish dish from Calcutta.

▲ Middle Eastern Cuisine

Middle Eastern cuisine is well-known, not for its traditional dishes, which are still hardly known in France, but for *mezze*. This consists of a large number of small and sophisticated starters and, if it is to be enjoyed properly, plenty of time is needed to taste and compare the flavors. Otherwise, it makes more sense to settle for a *chawarma* sandwich, which is just as tasty. Lebanese restaurants are the standard bearers of Middle Eastern cuisine in Paris, and over the last few years they have been springing up at an astonishing rate. Syrian and Jordanian restaurants offer similar food.

MEZZE
This bewildering assortment of small starters is typically consumed with a glass of arack. *Mezze* is usually served in small round or oval dishes (opposite), and is ample for a single meal. Hot dishes are followed by cold dishes, and bread takes the place of cutlery.

LOUBNANE ◆ *378*
The *Loubnane* is authentically Lebanese: the whole family, including cousins and nephews, is involved, while the piano is played by an ex-chef from a private household. The owner's uncle had the first restaurant in Paris that served Middle Eastern cooking. Their *mezze* is superb. A vaulted cellar has been set aside for those who wish to discover Lebanese music and dance in the course of their meal.

MOUTABBAL
Purée of aubergines with sesame oil, also known as *batenjane moutabbal*. It is sometimes called aubergine caviar. With hummus (chickpea purée), it is one of the mainstays of *mezze*.

CHANKLICH
This is a cheese flavored with thyme, and is served with tomato, onion and olive oil.

WARAK ENAB
Warak enab comprises vine leaves stuffed with a mixture of rice, onion, tomato, parsley mint and olive oil.

BREAD
The bread (*khobz*) is a round, thin, flat cake and has no crumbs.

ARACK
Arack is an aniseed-flavored spirit that can be diluted with water and taken as an aperitif. It is usually drunk, very cold, with *mezze*.

OLIVE OIL
Olive oil is extremely common, and is used to dress salads, stuffed vegetables and mezze.

SAMBOUSEK
These small rissoles can be stuffed with minced meat and onions, or with cheese and parsley.

MANAKICH
This is a kind of *mezze* similar to a miniature pizza with thyme.

TABOULEH
Real Lebanese tabouleh is mainly green. It is made with chopped parsley and large amounts of mint, to which burghul (cracked wheat) and chopped tomato and onion are added. It is then dressed with olive oil and lemon juice, and served with leaves of cabbage or lettuce.

This delightful dish has a wonderfully fresh taste. This is

authentic tabouleh, but the word can be used to describe any concoction using *burghul* and a few vegetables.

JAWANEH
Chicken wings with garlic and lemon juice.

AHWE
Ahwe is finely ground coffee, sometimes flavored with cardamom (*haal*) and boiled with water in a kind of small long-handled saucepan called a *rakwé*. "White coffee" (*ahwe bayda*), which is made with orange-flower water rather than coffee, is very pleasant too.

A Damascus café on the banks of the River Barada, in the 19th century.

SOME TERMS
CHAWARMA: lamb grilled on a vertical spit.
FALAFEL: spicy balls made with chick-peas.
FATAYER: spinach fritters.
HUMMUS BI TAHINA: puree of chick peas with sesame paste.
KIBBÉ: meatballs made with cracked wheat.
KIBBÉ NAYÉ: raw meat with cracked wheat.
LABAN: yoghurt.
LABNA: drained and salted yoghurt (the most common cheese in Lebanon).
LAHM BI AJEEN: a kind of meat pizza.
MA ZAHR: orange-flower water.
MAKANEK: little spicy sausages.
SAMKÉ HARRA: fish with chili.
TAHINA: sesame-seed paste.
ZAATAR: thyme.

WINE
Lebanon has about 40,000 acres of vines in the Bekaa Valley, northeast of Beirut, and produces a good quantity of red wine aged in oak barrels. The most common grape varieties are Cinsault, Syrah and Cabernet. There are also white and rosé wines. The oldest vineyard belongs to a religious house founded by the Jesuits at Ksara in 1857. More recent wines come from Kefraya and Château Musar.

North African restaurants sprang up all over Paris quite suddenly in the 1960's. The food continues to be popular, and is available from run-down cafés run by a blue-jacketed Tunisian, where you go to enjoy a sugary pastry, to more upmarket establishments often run by French ex-colonials, where more refined fare is on the menu. To appreciate to the full this sweet and subtle cuisine, with its perfumed harmonies of spice and sun, it is advisable to have a robust, complex wine with it, or perhaps just a mint tea!

LE CAROUBIER ◆ 375

This excellent establishment is run by a French ex-colonial couple. The wife is in the kitchen, and cooks some of the best couscous in Paris, while her husband runs the dining-room diligently and without fuss. The décor is restrained and includes just a few photos from pre-Independence days to add a touch of nostalgia. Remarkable wines.

SPICES

The most common spices are hot peppers, sweet peppers, saffron, black pepper, cinnamon and cumin.

Once ground, they are added to tajines and couscous with the dried beans and chick peas, fruit (raisins) and almonds.

WINES

There are about 420,000 acres of vines, producing 4.5 million hectolitres of wine. The rosés, which should be drunk young, are popular, and the *Vin Gris de Boulaouane* (2) from south of Casablanca is very pleasant. The best Moroccan reds are found near Rabat; Guerrouane (1), a fairly heavy wine, is one of them. In Tunisia, wine was grown by the Phoenicians at Carthage; today's wines, like Tebourba (4), are reliable and good. The best Algerian wines, like Medea (3), are still those whose vineyards were planted before the 1960's.

COUSCOUS

"Rolling" the couscous is an art, and perfection is achieved when all the grains are separate, small and the same size. Whether spicy, hot or mild, proper couscous is a subtle dish, made with couscous grain, vegetables, meat (shoulder of mutton, shin of veal and merguez), raisins (opposite) and spices.

1 2 3 4

MINT TEA

Green tea flavored with mint, drunk boiling hot and perhaps with sugar, is part of North African culture. It is a lot more popular than coffee.

TAJINE

This is a stew usually prepared with mutton or veal, though sometimes with fish or poultry. It gets its name from the round earthenware dish with a pointed cover in which it is cooked. Different vegetables and fresh and dried fruits, such as dates and prunes, are used to produce interesting combinations of sweet and savory flavors.

PASTRIES AND SWEETS

Pastries are typically rich and honeyed, and made with semolina or many-layered pastry, together with sugar, honey, almonds, dates and other dried fruits; they can also be flavored with orange-flower water. Turkish delight (above) is one of the region's better-known sweets.

Other specialties include Moroccan pancakes called "judge's ears."

SOME TERMS

BRIK: a small deep-fried pie made with *malsouqua* pastry (similar to filo), with a filling of chicken, egg or tuna.

CHAKCHOUKA: a stew of meat with vegetables (carrots or potatoes).

KEFTA: ground meat grilled on skewers.

MÉCHOUI: a sheep roasted on a spit.

MEHRAZ: a brass mortar and its pestle.

PASTILLA: a pie made with *ouarka* pastry (similar to filo) with a filling of pigeons and almonds.

TAJINE: a meat and vegetable stew.

THE ART OF COOKERY

North African cooking has always been done by women, and in years gone by it was the duty of mothers and grandmothers to teach young girls how to cook. They say that couscous can only be "rolled" with the patience and finesse of a woman's hand, and that this skill cannot be learned, but must be passed on as part of the cultural heritage.

BREAD

Bread is traditionally baked at home, and is usually made of hard wheat flour, although sometimes of fine sieved flour. It has the advantage of staying fresh for 24 hours.

GINGER
Ginger is best-known for its flavoring properties; however, if it is pounded and a juice extracted from the roots, a delightful drink is produced.

There is little African cuisine in Paris as the ingredients are rarely available outside Africa. Furthermore, its somewhat rustic quality lies uneasily with French tastes and cooking habits. An African meal is traditionally organized around a single dish, prepared as a stew or cooked without water in an earthenware jar. The colorful and highly flavored cuisine of Senegal is similar to that of the French West Indies.

PARIS-DAKAR ◆ 413
The owner, M. Mamadou, is famous for his warm welcome and ritual question: "What brings you here?" *Yassa*, the national dish, is served here in a pleasant and simply decorated environment and, between courses, against a background of traditional Senegalese songs, the owner will tell you all about his country. It is a sure sign of quality that Senegalese traveling through Paris always drop in for a meal.

FRUIT
Africans are not very fond of cakes and pastries, but they love fruit and fruit juices

such as papaya, coconut, *bouye*, the fruit of the baobab (above, left), red sorrel (above, right) in cocktails (above).

SOME TERMS
CAÏDOU: fish soup with rice.
CASSAVA: a starchy vegetable.
DIBITERIE: grilled food.
DJIDIERE: ginger juice.
GOMBO: okra, an edible pod.
KINKELIBA: a Senegalese herb tea.
MAFFÉ: a stew of various meats (beef, pork, chicken or mutton) with vegetables and peanut butter.
PASTEL: a small fritter.
TARO: a vegetable, also called tannia or eddo, which is as tender as an apple.

ACCOMPANIMENTS
An African dish is always accompanied by a cereal like millet or brown rice (above), or by a starchy vegetable such as cassava, yam or sweet potato.

SPECIALTIES
Each country specializes in its local resources, such as seafood, monkeys and reptiles.

TRADITIONAL SENEGALESE DISHES
The Senegalese have several specialties, which they prepare with style. *Tiep bou dienn* (above) combines fish (often grouper), rice and vegetables. Chicken, mutton or fish may be served in a *yassa* – that is, marinated in lime juice and then fried. Beef, sautéed with a peanut sauce, is called *maffé*. Soups such as *caïdou* are very common.

FRENCH
SPECIALTIES

◆ CASSOULET

There is a long-running battle between the cassoulets of Castelnaudary and Toulouse, because each town claims to be where the dish originated. The matter is still unresolved. It was the Arabs who first introduced white beans to the southwest, where they were used for mutton stew. However, there is a legend that during the Hundred Years War, when Castelnaudary was besieged by the English, its inhabitants created the first *estofat* with beans. Directed by the town's provost, the inhabitants emptied out their storehouses and cellars and each made a contribution to the experimental dish. This first cassoulet, which was accompanied by plenty of wine, put new fire into the fighters' bellies and, it is said, they pushed the English all the way back to the Channel!

AU TROU GASCON ◆ 403
Alain Dutournier, who now runs the *Carré des Feuillants* ▲ 226, opened this restaurant twenty years ago. It is now run by the very talented Nicole Dutournier. Here south-western cuisine flourishes and the cassoulet is excellent. Anyone who needs convincing should catch chef Jacques Faussat in the early hours of the morning, as he makes his sausages and cooks the haricot beans. Here, cassoulet is nothing short of a devout ritual.

THE DISH
The word cassoulet comes from *cassole*, the earthenware dish used for simmering the ingredients. The *cassoles* made by the potters of the small village of Issel (Aude) are particularly famous. Making a cassoulet requires patience: the longer and slower it cooks, the better it tastes. It is always served in the dish in which it is cooked.

BOUQUET GARNI
The different herbs are tied together to prevent them spreading through the dish. They are removed before serving.

ARMAGNAC
This grape brandy has three *appellations*: Bas-Armagnac (often the best), Haut-Armagnac and Ténarèze. For Armagnac to be at its best, the bottom of the glass should be warmed in the palm of the hand.

AROMATICS
Aromatics are vital to French cooking. The most commonly used are onions, carrots, de-seeded tomatoes, garlic, cloves and nutmeg.

Sausages being made by hand.

A *toupin* is used to keep duck *confit*.

An appetizing description

In 1911, the poet Fourès wrote: "Fragrant cassoulet under your crusty coat, Cassoulet blessed and praised by one and all, Especially when, deep within, we find a choice piece of goose, A fine loin of pork and some delicate rind."

Wines

The red wines of the southwest are a perfect accompaniment to cassoulet. Particularly good are smooth and full-bodied Madiran and a young Cahors. Dry white wines also go well.

Beans

Beans are essential for a successful cassoulet, as they give it its taste and slightly greasy texture. The best are the delicious flat beans from Tarbes.

1

2

3

4

5

The choice of meat

There must always be pork (sausage, 3; spare ribs, 5; pork rind for flavor, 2) and a piece of goose or duck *confit* (4). Then there is lamb (1), and at Carcassonne they use partridge when in season. The Toulouse recipe includes bacon and Toulouse sausage.

A hymn to cassoulet

Prosper Montagné, from Carcassonne, was a great early 20th-century chef. He composed a homage to cassoulet that attempted to reconcile the different factions: "Cassoulet is the God of Occitan cuisine, one God and three persons: the Father is the cassoulet of Castelnaudary; the Son, the cassoulet of Carcassonne; and the Holy Spirit, the cassoulet of Toulouse."

Cheese

Some cheeses from the southwest, like goat's cheese from Rocamadour and ewe's milk cheese from the Pyrénées, go very well after cassoulet.

The name of this southwestern recipe comes from the Provençal *bouiabaisso*, a contraction of two verbs meaning "to boil" and "to lower": "When the saucepan boils, lower the heat." This fish stew used to be eaten by the poor, and was made after market from what was left in the fishermen's baskets. It was then eaten when they returned from fishing, sometimes on the beach itself. Its ingredients vary from day to day according to the season and the catch. Many people think that bouillabaisse is only the fish, but this is a mistake because the liquid, with its inimitable taste, is an integral part of the dish. As Georges Simenon said, "More rubbish has been written about bouillabaisse than about any other dish!"

LE DOME ♦ 376
This is one of the best fish restaurants in Paris. The modern décor is a little disappointing but the bouillabaisse is of the highest quality, and is particularly attractive when the price of seafood is so high. The *Dôme* also has a retail shop in Rue Delambre behind the restaurant.

KINDS OF BOUILLABAISSE
At Martigues, bouillabaisse is usually made with red mullet, and sometimes small cuttlefish called *daubes de muscadins* are added, together with their ink-sacs, to make "black bouillabaisse." At Toulon they like "sardine bouillabaisse," and "pot-luck bouillabaisse" made with sea water. *Bourride*, a fish soup from Sète, is lightly thickened with *aïoli* ▲ 276.

Herbs give the true taste of Provence.

ROUILLE
Rouille is a garlic mayonnaise spiced with a couple of pinches of hot red pepper and a fresh red pepper peeled and seeded. Léon Daudet once said that *rouille* "raised the liquor and the lips to the power of two." There are two ways of using the sauce: diluted with a little of the liquid before being added to the bouillabaisse, or spread on garlic croutons. *Rouille* also goes well with cuttlefish and octopus.

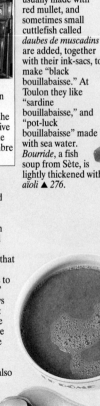

Fishermen at
Martigues.

> "But to be true and good, without
> a fault,
> A real wonder,
> More than fish, oil, garlic and
> fennel,
> You need Marseilles air!"
>
> Jacques Normand
> "La Bouillabaisse"

INGREDIENTS FOR A GOOD STOCK

A successful stock
needs olive oil,
onions, de-seeded
tomatoes, fennel,
garlic, bay leaf,
saffron, orange peel,
star anise, white wine
and water.

DEPENDING ON THE MOOD

There are as many
bouillabaisses as
there are fishermen,
housewives and chefs.

In Martigues, they
cook the potatoes
separately and add
them later.

THE REAL BOUILLABAISSE

According to Marcel
Pagnol, rock lobsters,
langoustines and
other "noble"
shellfish have no
place in a proper
bouillabaisse. It is not
unknown, however,
for certain chefs to
disregard this
tradition.

WINES

Well chilled rosés
from the Côtes de
Provence, Bandol
and Cassis go very
well with
bouillabaisse; they
are very effective at
evoking the dreamy
atmosphere of
Provence. White
wine is also very
suitable.

THE FISH

The fish must be very
fresh, and best
straight from the sea.
Ordinary fish like
small rockfish,
rascasse, weever and
moray eel are usually
only eaten in
bouillabaisse or fish
soup, and they
disintegrate in the
stock. Pieces of sea
bass, John Dory and
monkfish are actually
eaten - depending on
inclination and
availability.

BOUILLABAISSE ON THE TABLE

Diners should sit
waiting for their
bouillabaisse, not the
other way round.
Here, it is attractively
decorated with
parsley, and
surrounded by the
bouillon, the *rouille*
and the croutons.

Pot-au-feu remains one of France's most popular dishes. Alexandre Dumas was one of its most outspoken admirers: "You will not find this word in any dictionary, but if ever I am one of the Forty [members], I will make sure it gets into the Dictionary of the Académie Française." Pot-au-feu originated in Lyons, but it has since become the French national dish, even if each individual region insists on its own particular ingredients. It is an ideal winter dish, and is much loved for its mouthwatering smell.

LIFE AS FINE ART
Pot-au-feu is cooked slowly over a low heat, and for more than two days if the bouillon is to be fat-free. The top of the liquid has to be skimmed frequently, and the smell changes and develops as vegetables are added.

THE POT
It should be wide and deep, as big as the pot-au-feu itself - perhaps even a little bigger.

LE VIN DES RUES ◆ 381
This restaurant takes its name from a popular novel, but the pot-au-feu prepared by Jean Chanrion, its ruddy-cheeked owner, is little short of a miracle. The bistro looks a little like an old-fashioned café, with its bar and wine sold by the carafe. Ah! Those were the days!

THE BOUILLON
Before pot-au-feu is served, the liquid is cleared of fat and poured into bowls. This is eaten as a first course before the meat, and when the bowl is almost empty, a drop of red wine is sometimes added; this custom is called *faire chabrot*. A starter is sometimes made by pouring the bouillon over thick slices of country bread then heating these in the oven.

Certain accompaniments are very important. They include coarse salt, pepper, gherkins, mustard and shallots.

A DISH THAT GOES ON FOREVER
The bouillon from the pot-au-feu can be reheated in the evening, and cold meat is popular at suppertime with a bit of mustard - if it has not already gone into the cottage pie! Cabbage, tomatoes or potatoes are sometimes stuffed with the cold meat, onions and parsley.

> **"**His imagination is always on the boil, and the ideas bob up and down like potatoes and turnips in a pot-au-feu.**"**
>
> Paul Claudel
> *Endormie*, 1883

DEPENDING ON THE RECIPE

Precautions may have to be taken with some vegetables so as not to spoil the bouillon: potatoes must not be allowed to fall apart, and cabbage is best cooked separately.

THE MEAT

As Alexandre Dumas said, "The basis of a good pot-au-feu is the beef." It is essential to choose the right meat ■ *20*. Rib, chuck and shin are the best. The meat should be gelatinous, succulent and a little on the fatty side.

THE VEGETABLE BASKET

The meat should be accompanied by celeriac, carrots, turnips, onions and leeks.

MARROWBONE

Every pot-au-feu must contain marrowbone, and it should be shared out equally when the meat is served. The marrow is also delicious served at the start of the meal on hot toast with coarse salt.

WINE

Pot-au-feu is a simple and convivial dish from Lyons, and it therefore goes best with a good Beaujolais.(Brouilly, Morgon or Fleurie) served cool.

TWO WAYS OF COOKING POT-AU-FEU

Acording to the first method, the beef is placed in cold water, and its juices perfume the cooking liquid, which is then enriched by the savor of the vegetables. The second method has the meat placed in boiling water already flavored with a bouquet garni; in this way, the juices remain in the meat. The first concentrates on the quality of the bouillon, while with the second the ingredients retain all their flavor. Both ways are delicious.

The word "choucroute" comes from the Alsatian *sûrkrût*, which is in turn related to the German word *sauerkraut*, meaning "sour cabbage"; it refers to both fermented cabbage and the Alsatian dish made with it. There are many recipes for choucroute. For example, in the north the dish is cooked with goose fat, while in the south, chicken stock and even quartered apples are sometimes added. In his *France gastronomique*, Curnonsky suggests lining the bottom of the pan with the apples.

BAUMANN ◆ 383
Guy-Pierre Baumann is the king of choucroute. He runs several restaurants in Alsace and in Paris, and he has even created a fish choucroute. In his little restaurant in Place des Ternes, where it is as cosy and comfortable as any Alsatian brasserie, he cooks choucroute in the classical manner.

A HEALTHY DISH
Choucroute (fermented cabbage) is rich in vitamins, which are preserved by the fermentation, and in phosphorous and potassium. Choucroute is also very digestible, especially if it has been fermented with juniper berries (below). Even Captain Cook took it with him on his long sea voyages.

ALSATIAN WINES
These days, the white wines of Alsace are considered to be great wines. Sylvaner, light and pleasant, or Riesling, more complex and noble, go perfectly with choucroute. Those with a thirst are advised to have a light beer.

WHEN CABBAGE BECOMES CHOUCROUTE
Round white cabbage is finely sliced, salted and put in a barrel to ferment. The cabbage turns into choucroute after three weeks of explosive fermentation.

In Colmar, market gardeners used to bring their cabbage to market in carts or flat-bottomed boats.

THE MEAT
There should be plenty of choucroute on the plate, accompanied by potatoes and fresh and smoked pork chops, belly or shoulder) as well as sausages. There is an Austrian variety called *knacks*. Small *boudins blancs* or *boudins noirs* and tiny sausages called *colmarettes* can also be added.

PRACTICAL
INFORMATION

BY AIR

Paris is linked to all the world's major cities by the main international airlines. It is also linked to the principal French cities, by the French domestic airline Air Inter in particular. Various means of transport connect Orly and Roissy Charles-de-Gaulle, the two international airports, to the center of Paris.

INTO PARIS FROM ORLY

◆ AIR FRANCE COACH: A 30-minute journey from either Orly-Ouest or Orly-Sud terminals, with one stop at Montparnasse and its terminus at Invalides.

◆ ORLYBUS: The RATP buses leave every 15 minutes from both terminals and go right to Place Denfert-Rochereau. The journey time is about 50 minutes.

◆ EXPRESS BUS: This RATP bus links the

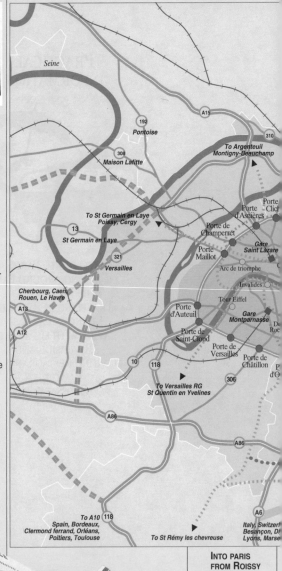

Seine

192 Pontoise

308 Maison Lafitte

To St Germain en Laye Poissy, Cergy

13 St Germain en Laye

321 Versailles

Cherbourg, Caen Rouen, Le Havre

A13

A12

10 118

To Versailles RG St Quentin en Yvelines

A86

A86

To A10 118 Spain, Bordeaux, Clermond ferrand, Orléans, Poitiers, Toulouse

To St Rémy les chevreuse

A15

310 To Argenteuil Montigny-Beauchamp

Porte d'Asnières Porte Clicl

Porte de Champerret

Gare Saint Lazare

Porte Maillot

Arc de triomphe

Invalides

Tour Eiffel

Porte d'Auteuil

Gare Montparnasse De Roc

Porte de Saint-Cloud

Porte de Versailles

Porte de Châtillon

306

A6 Italy, Switzerl Besançon, Di Lyons, Marse

airport with Villejuif-Louis-Aragon, a station on the Paris Métro ◆ 316.

◆ ORLYVAL: The automatic overhead métro takes passengers to the Antony RER station

(on line B)

◆ BY RER: The station on line C, Pont de Rungis Aéroport d'Orly, is accessible from both terminals via a free Paris Airports shuttle service. This line,

with many stops, crosses Paris from east to west. The main advantage of traveling by rail rather than road is that you avoid the frequent traffic jams on A6 motorway

INTO PARIS FROM ROISSY

◆ AIR FRANCE COACH: Journey time from the airport to the two stops in Paris, Porte Maillot and the Charles-de-Gaulle-Étoile terminus, is 40 minutes. Every hour another coach also serves Montparnasse station only.

◆ ROISSYBUS : The RATP bus links Roissy directly with

Map labels

Chantilly
(16)

A1 — Netherlands, Belgium
Calais, Dunkerque, Lille

Roissy
Charles de Gaulle

N2 — Senlis, Soissons

A1

N2

N3

Meaux, Châlons s/Marne

orte de chapelle — Porte de la Villette

Porte de Pantin

Gare de l'est

République

A3

Coulommiers

N34

Porte de Bagnolet

To Marne la vallée
Boissy-St Léger

stille

Nation

Germany
Metz, Nancy,
Reims, Strasburg

Gare de Lyon

Porte de Vincennes

N34

A4

Gare sterlitz

Porte de Bercy

A4

te lie

7

A86

Marne

A86

Seine

Rungis

7

ainebleau

Legend:
— Roads
═ Motorways
┼┼┼ SNCF
···· RER
···· Bus RATP
···· Bus Air France
···· Roissybus Orlybus
●●● Orlyval

CROSSING THE CHANNEL

Passenger trains for the Channel ports depart from London Victoria. Car and passenger ferries sail between Dover and Calais, Folkestone and Calais, Newhaven and Dieppe, and Southampton and Le Havre. Folkestone-Calais and Dover-Calais is also served by hovercraft. A TGV runs between Calais and Paris Gare du Nord. Ordinary train services link Paris with Dieppe and Le Havre. Journey times to Paris by car are about 2½ hours from Calais, about 1½ hours from Le Havre and Dieppe.

◆ LE SHUTTLE: The Channel Tunnel, linking Britain and France at Folkestone and Calais, is due to open in autumn 1994. There will be about four departures an hour at peak times. For those traveling by train, journey time from London Waterloo to Paris Gare du Nord is about 3 hours. The crossing itself takes about 35 minutes, but those traveling by car should allow a total of an hour, to take account of loading and customs formalities.

l'Opéra. This state-owned company also has a traditional regular bus service, which has frequent stops. The 350 goes to stations in the north and east of the city. The 351 goes to Place de la Nation. Journey time is about one hour, with departures every 15 to 20 minutes.

◆ BY RER: Line B, which crosses Paris from north to south, links Roissy with the Gare du Nord and with Châtelet: a free shuttle service links the air terminal with the station. Note that direct shuttles to Euro Disney leave regularly from both airports. Finally, you can also take a taxi to get into the city from either of the two air terminals. The journey costs between 150 and 250F.

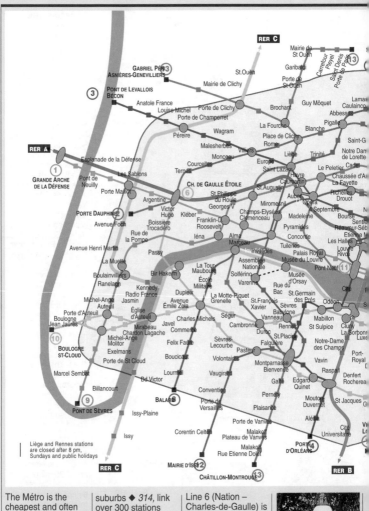

The Métro is the cheapest and often the quickest way to get around in Paris: 13 Métro lines (numbered from 1 to 13) and 4 RER lines (A, B, C and D), which serve the suburbs ◆ *314*, link over 300 stations throughout the capital. The Métro runs mainly underground, but some lines are overground.

Line 6 (Nation – Charles-de-Gaulle) is mainly elevated and offers some very fine views of Paris.

TIMETABLES
The Métro runs from 5.30 am until 1.00 am. You should allow 1½ minutes between stations and add 5 minutes if you need to change lines.

POINTS OF SALE

Métro stations, bus terminals, newsagents and Île-de-France railway stations (books of ten tickets only).

ATTENTION

Punch your ticket as you enter the station and retain it until you reach the exit: an inspector may ask to see it at any time.

VISITOR PACKAGES

◆ **PACKAGE 1**
A personalized one-day pass with a coupon allowing you to travel freely throughout Paris by Métro, bus, RER, funicular: 27F

◆ **ORANGE CARD**
One week's travel in Paris: 59F

◆ **PARIS VISITOR'S CARD**
The same principle as Package 1. However, this pass gives you discounts on: the Montparnasse Tower, the Arche de la Défense, La Cité des Sciences, the Canauxrama ◆ 326, the Vedettes du Pont-Neuf ◆ 326, the Musée Grévin, Roue Libre bicycle hire.
3 days: 90F
5 days 145F

◆ a "12 journey" weekly pass (2 journeys per day): 40F.

FARES

The fare is not related to the length of your journey: a single ticket allows you to travel freely on all lines. Remember that fares for suburban travel are higher.

◆ one single ticket : 6.50F
◆ a book of ten tickets (valid on the buses ◆ 318): 39F

◆ children under the age of four travel free of charge; four to ten, 50% off.

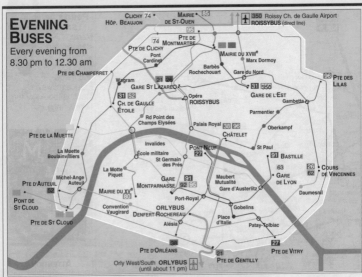

EVENING BUSES

Every evening from 8.30 pm to 12.30 am

CLICHY 74 •
HÔP. BEAUJON
MAIRIE DE ST-OUEN 85
350 Roissy Ch. de Gaulle Airport
ROISSYBUS (direct line)

PTE DE MONTMARTRE
74 PTE DE CLICHY
Pont Cardinet
95
MAIRIE DU XVIIIᵉ
Marx Dormoy

PTE DE CHAMPERRET
Wagram
Barbès Rochechouart
Gare du Nord
21 26
GARE ST LAZARE
31 52
CH. DE GAULLE ÉTOILE
Opéra
ROISSYBUS
31 350
GARE DE L'EST
96 PTE DES LILAS
Gambetta

Rd Point des Champs Elysées
Palais Royal
38 96
Parmentier
Oberkampf

PTE DE LA MUETTE
La Muette Boulainvilliers
Invalides
École militaire
St Germain des Prés
CHÂTELET
PONT NEUF
27
St Paul
91 BASTILLE
26 62 COURS DE VINCENNES

La Motte Piquet
GARE MONTPARNASSE
91 92 95
Maubert Mutualité
Gare d'Austerlitz
63
GARE DE LYON
Daumesnil

PTE D'AUTEUIL
Michel-Ange Auteuil
52
MAIRIE DU XV
80
Port-Royal
Gobelins

PONT DE ST CLOUD
PTE DE ST CLOUD
Convention Vaugirard
ORLYBUS
DENFERT-ROCHEREAU
Alésia
Place d'Italie
Patay-Tolbiac
27 PTE DE VITRY

38 PTE D'ORLÉANS
21
Orly West/South ORLYBUS (until about 11 pm)
PTE DE GENTILLY

BY BUS

◆ THE URBAN NETWORK

58 bus routes criss-cross Paris between the hours of 5.30 am and midnight. In the main the service stops as early as 8.30 pm, and at weekends. These times are displayed at every bus stop.

The routes are divided into zones; the fares are set depending on the number of zones: 1 ticket is valid for 2 zones. Once you have punched your ticket, keep it until you leave the bus, as an inspector could ask to see it. **Please note**: do not punch the orange card coupons or the visitor package.

◆ NOCTAMBUS

This system connects the *portes de Paris* (eg Porte d'Orléans, Porte de la Muette) with Châtelet between 1.00 am

(departure from the outskirts), or 1.30 am (departure from Châtelet), and 5.00 am. A bus leaves every 30 minutes. Passengers can get on and off where they like, as well as at fixed stops. Fare: 3 tickets. **Connections**: 1 extra ticket. There are 10 lines (see map). At bus stops, these buses are indicated by an owl logo.

◆ BALABUS

This bus operates only between April 15 and September 15 on Sundays and Bank Holidays between 12.30 pm and 9.30 pm. It is a tourist route, linking the Grande Arche with the Gare de Lyon. Cost: 3 tickets. Journey time about 45 minutes.

◆ ROISSYBUS

Leaves Rue Scribe, next to l'Opéra, every 15 minutes from 6 am until 11 pm. Cost: 30F. Journey time about 45 minutes.

◆ ORLYBUS

Leaves Place Denfert-Rochereau, following the same timetable as the Roissybus. It stops at the following stations: Dareau-Saint-Jacques, Glacière, Tolbiac and Porte de Gentilly. Cost 25F. Journey time to the airport about 30 minutes.

BY FUNICULAR This funicular climbs the slopes of Montmartre and takes you up to the Sacré Coeur, which commands some of the most spectacular views of Paris. Cost: 1 Métro ticket.

BY CAR

◆ CAR PARKS

Parking is restricted and those who ignore these regulations risk having their car towed away. It is far better to park in authorized zones, for which there is usually a charge. Parisian car parks are run by private companies and prices vary from 5 to 10F per hour for street parking (on a meter)

and from 8 to 15F per hour (decreasing rates) for underground parking.

◆ PETROL STATIONS

Many are located in underground car parks.

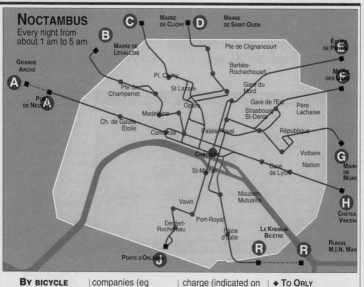

NOCTAMBUS
Every night from
about 1 am to 5 am

GRANDE
ARCHE

MAIRIE DE
LEVALLOIS

MAIRIE
DE CLICHY

MAIRIE
DE SAINT-OUEN

ÉGLISE
DE PA...

Pte de Clignancourt

Barbès-
Rochechouart

PORTE
DE NEUI...

Pte de
Champerret

Pl. Clichy

St Lazare

Gare du
Nord

MAIRI
DES LIL...

Ch. de Gaulle
Étoile

Madeleine

Opéra

Gare de l'Est
Strasbourg
St-Denis

Père
Lachaise

Concorde

Palais-Royal

République

CHÂTELET

Voltaire

G

St-Michel

Gare
de Lyon

Nation

MAIRI
DE
MONT...

Vavin

Maubert-
Mutualite

H

CHÂTEA
VINCENI

Denfert-
Rochereau

Port-Royal

Place
d'Italie

Le KREMLIN
BICÊTRE

RUNGIS
M.I.N. Mar

PORTE D'ORLÉANS

J

R

R

BY BICYCLE

Paris is not particularly well-suited for cyclists: cycle routes are rare and the roads dangerous. But outside Paris, there are woodlands that offer beautiful surroundings for leisurely cycle rides.

◆ **HIRING A BICYCLE**
RATP hires out bicycles at weekends in spring and summer. Rates are 20F to 45F per hour. There are also private rental companies (eg Bicloune and Paris by cycle).

BY TAXI

◆ **HOW TO USE THEM**
In the street: hail a taxi or go to a taxi rank (often located at a crossroads and indicated by a blue sign). Taxis for hire have their white light on. Passengers must sit in the back seats. A taxi may carry a maximum of 3 adults.

◆ **FARES**
The cost of a journey depends on two factors: the initial charge (indicated on the meter at the start of the journey), and the distance covered. Inside the *boulevard périphérique* (delineated by the *portes* – see map) two rates apply: rate A (daytime: 7 am to 7 pm) and rate B (nighttime: 7 pm to 7 am). Pick-up in the street: 12F. Pick-up following a phone call: depends on the distance and the time it takes the taxi to arrive. Allow roughly 22F for a 5-minute journey (rate A) and 27F (rate B); for a 10-minute journey allow 32F (A) and 43F (B). Rates per kilometer are 3.01F (A) and 4.68F (B).
At your destination, the meter will show these two figures added together. The driver adds the following supplements, which are not shown on the meter:
– 4th adult: 5F
– Pick-up at a station: 5F
– Luggage and bulky packages: 6F
– Animals: 3F
– Waiting/heavy traffic: 120F per hour.

◆ **TO ORLY
OR ROISSY** ◆ *314*
Rate C applies (suburbs). Allow about 220F (Orly) or 250F (Roissy)

◆ **"CONFORT PLUS"**
From June to September, the company G 7 Radio offers 150 top-of-the-range air-conditioned vehicles for comfort-conscious tourists. These vehicles can be hired for a basic fee of 500F per week. The cost of each journey undertaken is extra. For further information call 47 37 06 50.

BAT O BUS

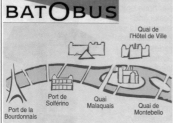

Quai de
l'Hôtel de Ville

Port de
Solférino

Quai
Malaquais

Quai de
Montebello

Port de la
Bourdonnais

BY BATOBUS

A boat ride with five ports of call, from the foot of the Eiffel Tower to the Hôtel de Ville. Stops: Port de la Bourdonnais, Port de la Solférino, Quai Malaquais, Quai de Montebello, Quai de l'Hôtel de Ville. Departures every 30 minutes from 10 am until 7.45 pm. Fare: 18F per port of call. Allow 6 to 12 minutes per port of call.

TAXIS

319

◆ LIVING IN PARIS

PARIS TOURIST OFFICE
27 Avenue des Champs-Elysées,
Paris 8th arrond. Tel. 49 52 53 41.

Staying in Paris, and of course living there, is expensive compared with life in provincial France. But generally, the cost of living in the capital is similar to that in other major European cities. Even so, to avoid being exploited, it is wise to be aware of Parisian customs and habits.

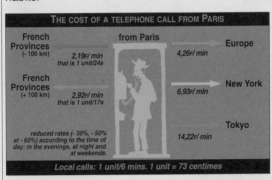

THE COST OF A TELEPHONE CALL FROM PARIS

	from Paris	
French Provinces (- 100 km)		**Europe**
2,19F/ min that is 1 unit/24s		*4,26F/ min*
French Provinces (+ 100 km)		**New York**
2,92F/ min that is 1 unit/17s		*6,93F/ min*
		Tokyo
reduced rates (- 30%, - 50% et - 60%) according to the time of day: in the evenings, at night and at weekends.		*14,22F/ min*

Local calls: 1 unit/6 mins. 1 unit = 73 centimes.

TO TELEPHONE
◆ Within Paris and its suburbs, numbers have 8 digits.
◆ From Paris to UK: dial 19 44 followed by the number, omitting the first 0.
◆ From Paris to USA: dial 191 and the number you require.
◆ From UK to Paris: dial 010 331, then an 8-digit number.
◆ From USA to Paris: 011 331 and then an 8-digit number.

POST OFFICE

Paris 1. Letters or postcards sent anywhere in the European Community need a 2.80F stamp. For other destinations, including the USA, this is 3.40F. Post offices are equipped with automatic franking machines. You can also consult Minitel (an electronic directory) free of charge.

Each area of Paris has several post offices, which are open until 7 pm (when the last post is collected). The only 24-hour post office is at 52 Rue du Louvre,

◆ New: the *Bi-bop*. This portable telephone allows you to make and receive calls, provided you are close to a transmitter. The network areas are indicated by a blue, white and green logo (sold by France Télécom).

PLACE DE L'UNIVERSITE

WHERE CAN YOU MAKE A CALL?
There are public card-operated telephones both in post offices and in the street. There are still a few coin-operated telephones (5F, 2F, 1F, 50c). Cafés often have telephones inside for the use of their customers, but these cost slightly more.

PHONE CARDS

Alexander Graham BELL
TELECARTE 50

These can be purchased in France Télécom shops, post offices and newsagents. Cost: 40F (50 units) or 96F (120 units).

ENTERTAINMENT GUIDES

The famous *Colonnes Morris* publicize current shows. Modern ones also incorporate a telephone box. Kiosks and newsagents sell comprehensive guides such as *L'Officiel des spectacles, Pariscope* and *Télérama*. Movie theaters change their programs on Wednesdays.
◆ Cut-price seats – tickets are available from: FNAC, Forum des Halles, Paris 1st arrond.; kiosks in the Les Halles RER station, Paris 1st arrond., and Place de la Madeleine, Paris 8th arrond.

MONEY AND BUREAUX DE CHANGE

Notes come in 20, 50, 100, 200 and 500F denominations. Coins come in 5, 10, 20, or 50 centime pieces and 1, 2, 5, 10 and 20F pieces. Banks and bureaux de change are generally open 9 am to noon and 2 pm to 5 pm. They are closed on Sundays and public holidays and sometimes on Saturdays.

BANK CARDS

◆ Visa cards can be used in cash dispensers in banks, savings banks and post offices and at *points argents* (cashpoints) in stations and airports. In the event of loss, theft or difficulty call 42 77 11 90.
◆ American Express: Roissy Terminal 1 (arrivals hall), Gare Montparnasse and Gare de Lyon (TGV arrivals), American Express offices: 11, Rue Scribe, Paris 9th arrond. Information: tel. 47 77 70 00.

HOW MUCH TO TIP

Tipping is always optional. Here are some situations where it is expected:
◆ Petrol stations: 5–10F for cleaning your windscreen or checking your tyre pressure and oil/water levels .
◆ Taxis: approximately 10 percent of the fare.
◆ Cafés: leave some small change in the waiters' saucer. You should be aware that your drink is charged differently at the bar (standing) from the seated areas (for sitting, expect to pay 3.50F more, sometimes even double the price at the bar). The price is even higher if you sit out on the terrace, or after 10 pm. As in restaurants, service is always included.
◆ Restaurants: 10–50F in cash depending on the type of establishment. About 10F to the cloakroom attendant, 10–20F to the doorman and car valet. A saucer in the toilets indicates that a few coins (1F or more) would be appreciated.

SOME PRICES

1 COFFEE: 5 TO 25F

1 SANDWICH: 10 TO 30F

GOING UP THE EIFFEL TOWER: 52F

1 HOUR'S BABYSITTING: 30 TO 40F

1 ENTRY TICKET FOR THE MUSÉE DU LOUVRE: 35F

1 THEATER TICKET: 100 TO 200F

1 MOVIE TICKET: 30 TO 50 F

1 DOUBLE ROOM: 300 TO 600F PLUS

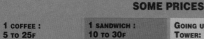

321

"We have now reached a very important part of gastronomy … that of wine, the intellectual part of the meal. Meat is but the material part" (Alexandre Dumas). Choosing a vintage ■ *38* is always difficult. In reputable restaurants, trust the judgment of the sommelier. Take advantage of the recession, which encourages restaurateurs to charge reasonably for what Pindar called the "milk of Venus".

HOW TO READ THE LABEL

Wherever they come from, all bottles of wine have a label. This gives legally required information and also, depending on the region of origin, certain specific and optional information. Here are two examples: a Burgundy and a

Bordeaux.
COMPULSORY INFORMATION (C):
◆ The name of the category (eg AOC: appellation d'origine contrôlée; VDQS: vin délimité de qualité supérieure, etc.)
◆ The name of the *appellation* (eg Volnay, Saint Emilion,

Bordeaux supérieur, Alsace)
◆ The name and address of the bottler
◆ The volume of the bottle
OPTIONAL INFORMATION (O):
◆ The brand name (eg Château Durand, Domaine des Gaulières)

◆ The vintage
◆ The classification (eg premier grand cru, cru classé)
◆ Where bottled
◆ Alcoholic content
◆ Any awards won

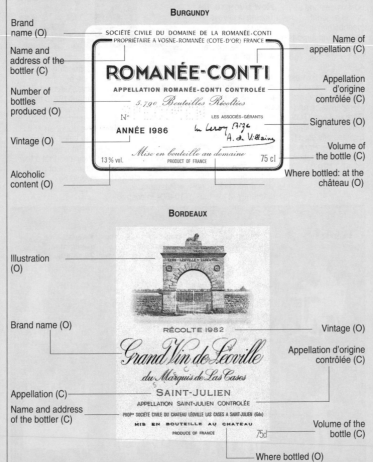

BURGUNDY

Brand name (O)

Name and address of the bottler (C)

Number of bottles produced (O)

Vintage (O)

Alcoholic content (O)

SOCIÉTÉ CIVILE DU DOMAINE DE LA ROMANÉE-CONTI
PROPRIÉTAIRE A VOSNE-ROMANÉE (COTE-D'OR) FRANCE

ROMANÉE-CONTI

APPELLATION ROMANÉE-CONTI CONTROLÉE

5.790 *Bouteilles Récoltées*

N°   LES ASSOCIÉS-GÉRANTS

ANNÉE 1986

Mise en bouteille au domaine

13 % vol.   PRODUCT OF FRANCE   75 cl

Name of appellation (C)

Appellation d'origine contrôlée (C)

Signatures (O)

Volume of the bottle (C)

Where bottled: at the château (O)

BORDEAUX

Illustration (O)

Brand name (O)

Appellation (C)

Name and address of the bottler (C)

RÉCOLTE 1982

Grand Vin de Léoville

du Marquis de Las Cases

SAINT-JULIEN

APPELLATION SAINT-JULIEN CONTROLÉE

PROP™ SOCIÉTÉ CIVILE DU CHATEAU LÉOVILLE LAS CASES A SAINT-JULIEN (Gde)

MIS EN BOUTEILLE AU CHATEAU

PRODUCE OF FRANCE   75cl

Vintage (O)

Appellation d'origine contrôlée (C)

Volume of the bottle (C)

Where bottled (O)

BOTTLES LARGE AND SMALL

Some examples of famous bottles: (from left to right) half bottle (37.5 cl), standard bottle (75 cl), magnum (1.5 l), double magnum (3 l) and jeroboam (4.5 l). There is also a Methuselah (6 l) and a Nebuchadnezzar (15 l)

EACH WINE HAS ITS OWN IDEAL DRINKING TEMPERATURE

The nature of each wine demands that it is drunk at a constant temperature. Only then will it be fully appreciated. It is all a question of molecules, of aroma and ideally of the temperature of the room in which it is being drunk!

Sweet wines: 6° C
Vinho Verde: 6° C
Riesling: 7° C
Sylvaner: 7° C
Champagnes: 7° C
Lambrusco: 8° C
Rosés: 9° C
Rosé or young wines: 10° C
Beaujolais: 11° C
Valpolicella: 11° C
Dry white wines: 11° C
"Yellow" wines: 11° C
Fruity red wines: 11° C
Sherry: 11° C
Vintage dry white wines: 13° C
Southern French red wines: 13° C
Sicilian red wines: 13° C
White Burgundies: 14° C
Côtes du Rhône: 14° C
Red Burgundies: 15° C

Chianti: 15° C
Red wines less than 5 years old: 15° C
Bordeaux wines: 16° C

WHICH WINES WITH WHICH FOODS

It is often recommended that certain wines be drunk with certain foods: the following list is a guideline.

◆ STARTERS AND HORS-D'OEUVRES
FOIE GRAS: Sauternes, Alsace (selection of fine grapes) or Quarts-de-Chaume
CHARCUTERIE: Côtes-du-Rhône Villages, Beaujolais, Saumur-champigny
SEAFOOD: White Graves, Alsace Sylvaner, Muscadet, white Hermitage
◆ FISH
SEA FISH: White Burgundies (Mersault, Puligny-Montrachet), white Graves, white Châteauneuf-du-Pape
FRESHWATER FISH: Alsace Sylvaner, white Mâcon, white Bellet, red Loire
◆ MEAT
RED MEAT: Red Bordeaux (Saint-Julien, Pauillac), red Burgundies (Rully, Mercurey)

WHITE MEAT: Red Côtes du Rhône, Cahors, Beaujolais, Saint Émilion
POULTRY: Burgundy, Saint Émilion, Graves
GAME: Gigondas, Châteauneuf-du-Pape, red Hermitage, Pommerol
◆ CHEESE
Red Graves, Saint-Estèphe, Nuits-Saint-Georges, Banyuls

(blue cheeses)

◆ DESSERTS
Banyuls (chocolate desserts), Champagne, Quarts-de-Chaume, Sauternes Beaumes de Venise (the sweet Muscat wine in France)

WHICH GLASS FOR WHICH WINE?

Many regions of France have their own particular type of glass. Here, from left to right, are the best known: the champagne flute (which purists maintain has never really been replaced by the tulip), Alsace glasses, Bordeaux glasses, Burgundy and white wine glasses.

◆ WINE WITH MEALS

THE RITUAL OF WINE

◆ **FILLING THE GLASS**
Generally, fill one-third full.

◆ **HOLDING THE GLASS**
To appreciate its color, hold by the foot and look at the wine from above.

◆ **SMELLING THE WINE**
Holding the glass in this way, put it on the table, swirl the wine around the glass five or six times and then smell it, with your nose deep in the glass.

◆ **DRINKING THE WINE**
Raise the glass to your mouth, still holding it in the same way. Start with just a small sip.

◆ **NOTES**
As distinct from handling a glass of spirits, always hold a glass of chilled wine by the base, to avoid warming it with your hands. Other wine glasses should also be held in this way so as not to dirty the glass and to release more aroma.

SERVING WINE

Decanting (pouring the wine from a bottle to a carafe) allows younger wines (less than ten years old) to "soften", if done one or two hours before drinking. The process re-oxygenates old wines thereby restoring their bouquet and leaving the sediment behind in the bottle. This is a delicate operation on two accounts. If it is done too soon, there is a risk of ending up with a stale, musty wine. Also, you must make sure that the sediment remains in the bottle; this may require the light of a candle held beneath the neck of the bottle (see opposite) while the wine is being decanted into a carafe.

WATER WITH MEALS

"It is an error to boast about drinking a great deal of mineral water," wrote the Latin poet Pliny the Elder. Despite this, the question is still asked, should one drink water with meals or not? There is no steadfast rule, even if gastronomes avoid water, making up for this between meals.

In top restaurants, water and wine are not mixed, and a separate glass is provided for each. But no one can really advise on which particular water to drink. For Pascal Martin, sommelier in the *Grand Hôtel* ▲ *256,* there is a simple rule: "Choose a water that is as neutral as possible." Spring waters and mineral waters such as Évian, Volvic or Vittel are popular. Some people find Contrexeville too salty. Save carbonated waters, especially the very gaseous ones like Perrier, until the end of a meal. If absolutely necessary, choose the lightest ones such as Badoit, or Ferrarelle (in Italian restaurants). Highly carbonated waters, such as Vichy (although some are milder than others), are better left for after meals, because they alter the flavor of foods too much. If you must drink water in a restaurant, request that it is not over-chilled. This often results in stomach upsets that can be wrongly blamed on the food! The ideal way to appreciate water would be to drink it at the temperature it left the spring. But perhaps that is just a little too much to ask!

<table>
<tr><td colspan="2">WINE VOCABULARY</td></tr>
</table>

WINE VOCABULARY

MATURITY: that has qualities unique to the variety of grape

ROUNDNESS: that is full-bodied

SHARPNESS: first impression; when this is absent the wine lacks character

FRESHNESS: combination of fruitiness and alcohol

ROBUSTNESS: due to tannins that assure longevity

BODY: a harmony of robustness and freshness

HARDNESS: a lack of maturity. This wine needs to age

LENGTH: the variable length of time aromas remain in the mouth

BITE: the presence of a fruity/tannic substance, which gives the impression of solidity

TANNIN: substance mainly from grape stalks which can play a role in the wine's composition

VANILLA: the character of young wines matured in new barrels, which give them their aroma

This price index for Bordeaux wines lists outstanding châteaux whose wines are quite often available at auction. Famous wines from other regions are not listed here because they are generally more difficult to find and more expensive (Romanée-Conti, for example, which can fetch up to 5000F a bottle). The index below gives average prices in 1993 sales.

	1929	1945	1953	1961	1966	1970	1975	1979	1982	1986
AUSONE (St-Émilion)	2 215	1 200	860	1 500	615	510	425	295	720	570
BEYCHEVELLE (St-Julien)	500	1 200	250	595	270	230	190	145	185	140
CALON SÉGUR (St-Estèphe)	480	660	340	550	270	210	215	120	190	130
CANON (St-Émilion)	950	750	320	460	300	200	200	125	260	170
COS D'ESTOURNEL (St-Estèphe)	1 025	900	440	725	230	295	210	210	260	180
GRUAUD-LAROSE (St-Julien)	930	820	620	720	315	255	220	220	250	150
HAUT-BRION (Graves)	1 760	2 500	1 155	1 860	700	540	475	470	575	340
LATOUR (Pauillac)	3 400	2 480	1 250	2 400	550	730	450	450	550	340
YQUEM (Sauternes)	3 600	4 525	2 550	1 750	1 350	1 385	1 360	1 040	860	980

© Cote Alain Bradfer, Alex de Clouet and Claude Maratier, 1993.

This index was compiled by wine expert Alex de Clouet, on the basis of blindfold tasting. It is only a selection. Variations in quality between different vintages can be seen, which is useful to know if you find a great wine at a reduced price on a menu!

	1900	1911	1928	1949	1955	1961	1970	1974	1978	1981	1982	1983	1984	1985	1986	1987	1988	1989	1990
BORDEAUX																			
SAINT-ÉMILION POMEROL	9	8	10	9	9	8	9	1	8	7	10	7	3	9	8	3	9	8	9
MÉDOC - GRAVES	9	8	10	9	9	10	9	1	8	7	10	7	4	8	10	3	8	9	9
SWEET WHITES	10	7	10	9	8	5	8	1	6	7	10	4	8	9	2	8	9	9	10
DRY WHITES	-	-	-	-	-	-	9	1	6	7	9	9	3	9	9	3	8	8	8
BURGUNDY AND CÔTES DU RHÔNE																			
RED BURGUNDY	-	10	6	9	8	8	4	6	10	7	4	9	3	9	4	3	8	9	9
WHITE BURGUNDY	-	-	-	-	8	7	7	6	9	7	7	9	5	9	6	7	7	10	9
CÔTES DU RHÔNE	-	-	-	-	-	9	9	4	10	7	7	9	3	10	4	4	9	9	8

The river Seine and its bridges, with the Eiffel Tower, Notre-Dame, Les Invalides, Place de la Concorde and many other attractions along its banks, are definitely the most famous vista in Paris. The river provides epicurean walkers wonderful opportunities to admire the most romantic city in the world. Many restaurants situated on the banks or on barges allow you to enjoy the capital from several different angles. What better than a walk along the river from Neuilly and Saint Cloud to the Île Saint-Louis?

1. Café de la Jatte

60 Bd Vital Bouhot, Ile de la Jatte, 92200 Neuilly sur Seine. Tel. 47 45 04 20 Surrounded by the Seine, but slightly set back. Set menus from 180F to 310F. Open every day, lunchtime and evenings. Private car park. ◆ 390

3. Quai Ouest

1200 Quai Marcel Dassault, 92210 Saint-Cloud Tel. 46 02 35 54. Located in a large boat-house on piles opposite the Bois de Boulogne. Open every day, lunchtime and evenings. Brunch on Sundays from midday to 5 pm. Set lunch menu: 100F. A la carte: 220F.
◆ 390

5. River Café

146 Quai de Stalingrad, 92130 Issy-les-Moulineaux. Tel. 40 93 50 20. Located on a moored barge, opposite the Ile Saint-Germain. Open every day, lunchtime and evenings. A la carte: 250F. ◆ 381

4. Le Cap Séguin

Opposite 36 Quai Le Gallo, 92100 Boulogne-Billancourt. Tel. 46 05 06 07. This restaurant situated on the quayside in front of the Parc de Saint-Cloud is decorated in nautical style: the plant-decked terrace and the dining rooms are laid out under a sail, and it is a pleasant place with a holiday atmosphere. A choice of fifteen dishes is available. Open every day, lunchtime and evenings. A la carte: 160F.

12. Pleasure Boats

Pont de l'Alma, Port de la Conférence, Paris 8. Tel. 42 25 96 10. Daily (except Mondays) dinner-cruise for 300F (350F on Sundays), and a dinner for 500F every day. Recommended for fine views.

THE GREAT RIVER SEINE

Whether actually on the Seine or further away, these restaurants afford a beautiful view of the river. They figure elsewhere in this guide and some of them are included in the section "Memorable Restaurants" ▲ 121.

7. Benkay
Hôtel Nikko, 61 Quai de Grenelle, Paris 15
◆ 365

9. Le Jules Verne
Eiffel Tower, Paris 7
▲ 169 ◆ 386

8. Les Monuments
Trocadéro, Paris 7
◆ 388

13. Le Musée d'Orsay Quai Anatole-France, Paris 7 ▲ 139 ◆ 370

15. Lapérouse
51 Quai des Grands-Augustins, Paris 6
▲ 135 ◆ 369

16. La Bûcherie
41 Rue de la Bûcherie, Paris 5
▲ 153 ◆ 375

17. Miraville
72 Quai de l'Hôtel-de-Ville, Paris 4
◆ 406

18. La Tour d'Argent 15-17 Quai de la Tournelle, Paris 5
▲ 147 ◆ 380

19. L'Institut du Monde arabe
1 Rue des Fossés-St-Bernard, Paris 5
▲ 148 ◆ 378

2. LES PIEDS DANS L'EAU
39 Bd du Parc, 92200 Neuilly-sur-Seine. Tel. 47 47 64 07. Specialties: Fish with oysters in winter. Set menu: 150F. A la carte: around 300F. Closed Saturday evenings and Sundays in winter; open seven days a week in summer.

14. VEDETTES DU PONT-NEUF
Ponton du Pont-Neuf, Square du Vert-Galant, Paris 1. Tel. 46 33 98 38. This company hires out its boats solely for private functions.

CANAUXRAMA
Bassin de la Villette, 13 quai de la Loire, Paris 19. Tel. 42 39 15 00. Theme cruises aboard pleasure boats on the Saint Martin canal, the Ourcq canal and the Seine, offering breakfast, snacks, refreshments, lunch, dinner or tea dances with champagne. This company also hires out its boats for seminars and private receptions.

10. ABOU DAOUD
Port Debilly, opposite 32 Av. de New York, Paris 16. Tel. 47 23 62 98; 47 23 62 96. Open every day,

lunchtime and evenings. Restaurant offering French-Lebanese cuisine on a wooden boat with an elephant figurehead. Inclusive dinner-dance (400F) with Oriental orchestra and belly dancer. Lunchtime set menu: 100F.

6. YACHTS DE PARIS
Port de Javel-haut, Paris 15. Tel. 44 37 10 20. Seasonal cuisine by chef Gérard Besson aboard the *Don Juan,* a 98-foot motor yacht, built in 1937 and restored in 1991. Eat in dock from 12.00-2.30 pm

Monday to Friday. Set price menus at 230F, 500F and 800F. Dinner cruise every night with set menus at 490F, 630F and 820F. Booking recommended. Private car park.

11. BATEAUX PARISIENS
Port de la Bourdonnais, Paris 7. Tel. 44 11 33 33. This company offers a lunch cruise at 300F and a dinner cruise at 550F. Open every day.

20. LE GRAND BLEU
10 Port de la Bastille, Paris 12. Situated on the quay, along the Saint-Martin canal, which links the Bastille with the Seine. Open lunchtime and evenings every day except Sunday evenings.

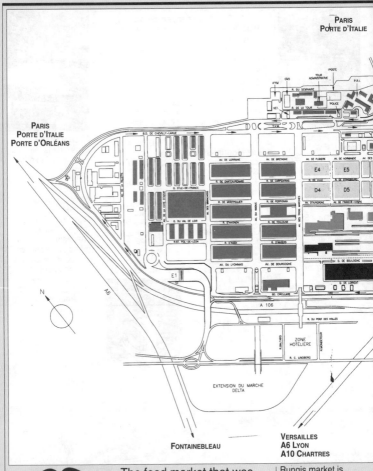

PARIS
PORTE D'ITALIE

PARIS
PORTE D'ITALIE
PORTE D'ORLÉANS

FONTAINEBLEAU

VERSAILLES
A6 LYON
A10 CHARTRES

EXTENSION DU MARCHE
DELTA

ZONE
HOTELIERE

The food market that was originally Les Halles ● *54*, in the city center, is now situated in Rungis ● *60*, to the south of Paris. Covering 625 acres, it is the largest market in France and its function is the wholesale distribution of perishable produce. Fruit and vegetables, meat, sea and freshwater fish, dairy produce, eggs and flowers from France and other countries are sold there. These five main sectors of the market support over five hundred related businesses, such as transport, banking, maintenance, syndicates and restaurants. The market is filled with people who are there to do business, but it is also open to anyone who just wants to look around.

Rungis market is really a town within a town and each sector has its own pavilion, warehouse, hall or open shed. The organization responsible for managing this enormous operation is Semmaris (Société d'économie mixte d'aménagement et de gestion du marché d'intérêt national), the major shareholder of which is the French State. Since its twentieth anniversary in 1989, Rungis market has become an international market serving Europe in particular.

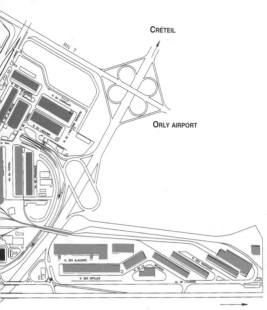

CRÉTEIL

RN 7

ORLY AIRPORT

ORLY AIRPORT

Legend:

- **Fruits and vegetables**
- **Dairy produce, caterers and equipment**
- **Sea and freshwater fish**
- **Meat**
- **Horticultural produce**
- **Services and administration**
- **Warehouses**

MARKET OPENING HOURS

OFFAL
5 am–11 am
Monday to Friday
CUT FLOWERS
6 am–11 am
Monday, Tuesday,
Thursday, Friday
and Saturday
FRUITS AND VEGETABLES
7 am–11 am
Monday to Friday
FISH
4 am–8.30 am
Tuesday to
Saturday
MEAT
5 am–9 am Monday
to Friday
DAIRY PRODUCE
7 am–12 noon
Monday to Friday
POULTRY AND GAME
5 am–10 am
Monday to Saturday

VISITING RUNGIS

At Rungis tourists may look but only those with business to do may buy. It is best to visit very early during the morning rush: all the buyers (including restaurateurs) are there. In the afternoon, the whole place is deserted and resembles a scene from the apocalypse. Recommended visits: seafood (followed by a pantagruelian sandwich in the eponymous restaurant) together with poultry and game. The offal hall is not recommended for those with weak stomachs.

TRAVELING TO RUNGIS

BY CAR
◆ From Paris and other routes via Porte d'Italie and Porte d'Orléans: take the A6 motorway, Rungis exit, after the Orly exit.
◆ From the south and the southwest: by the 186 main road towards Créteil, then Rungis exit.

From the east of Paris: by the A86 motorway: take the "Centre commercial régional" motorway link road and head for Rungis. There is a 37 F toll to pay at the entrance to Rungis.

BY PUBLIC TRANSPORT
Métro line N° 7, Villejuif-Louis-Aragon station: take RATP bus N° 185, which stops at several places inside the market. The line R Noctambus ◆ 318 serves Rungis every weekday night.

329

◆ GLOSSARY

* Term explained in the glossary

◆ YOUR PALATE ◆

Good food and pleasure in eating food, two bastions of a sort of "tastebud civilization," are both firmly rooted in the collective French consciousness. At least since the Middle Ages certain words have been used to evoke an attitude toward food that indicates perpetual abundance and that stands somewhere between an excess of pleasure and an excess of eating.

◆ BEC FIN :
A familiar expression to describe an epicure or gourmet*.

◆ FRIAND :
This word, dating from the Middle Ages, describes a pronounced taste for savory dishes (*frire* meaning "burning with desire"). It also signifies a refined palate capable of distinguishing good food from bad. However, during the 17th and 18th centuries, moral doubts were raised: were *friands* under the "effect of sensuality" and eating simply for pleasure (*Dictionnaire de l'Académie*, 1798) rather than to satisfy their hunger? Today, as much as ever, the French are devotees of *friandises*, "objects coveted by *friands*" (Jean-Louis Flandrin, *Chroniques de Platine* 1992).

◆ GASTROMANIA :
A perversion indicating an immoderate love of fine food (*bonne chère*).

◆ GASTRONOME:
A gastronome shows a keen interest in fine food, has a refined palate and is also blessed with a sound knowledge of culinary art and science. In short a gastronome is simultaneously a *gourmand*, *friand* and gourmet*, not to say enlightened! This 19th-century term is derived from the word "gastronomy"*. Today

it is commonly applied to a well-informed consumer who "tastes" and "knows".

◆ GASTRONOMY:
Joseph Berchoux used this word in 1801 in an alexandrine poem. It is, in fact, the French transcription of the title of a work by Archestrate, grandson of Pericles. In 1835 the Académie defined it as being "the art of creating good food". The Greek root of the word introduces an idea of legislation – "the legislation of the stomach" (*gaster*: stomach) – rather than of pleasure. And in 1825 Brillat Savarin stated: "Gastronomy is the reasoned knowledge of everything relating to man and his nourishment." The fact that the word caught on indicates a refinement in eating habits, evidence of democratization of taste. Since the 19th century the art of cooking has ceased to be the prerogative of aristocrats: it has descended into the street and everyone eats in restaurants now.

◆ GOURMAND :
A lover of *bonne chère** blessed with a hearty appetite. Today a *gourmand* is no longer simply a big eater, but also a *bec fin** who appreciates fine food. Until the end of the 18th century, this word described someone *goulu** and *avide** who ate to excess.

◆ GOURMANDISE :
Gluttony. One of the seven deadly sins: "the least virtuous of the sins" (Balzac).

◆ GOURMET :
In the 17th and 18th centuries a gourmet was a wine broker: in the 19th century he was "somebody who was knowledgeable about wines and knew how to taste wine" (*Dictionnaire de l'Académie* 1879). Recently the meaning of this word has widened and the *gourmand* is somebody of refined

taste who is knowledgeable about drink as well as food.

◆ A HEALTHY APPETITE ◆

Terms for over-eating are particularly numerous in the French language. Could this have anything to do with the fact that French is the language of Rabelais, whose characters moreover gave birth to new words that were synonyms for excess?

◆ AVIDE:
Hungry. From the Latin *avere* (to desire fervently). Note that the word "avare" has the same Latin origin. To eat hungrily is to eat selfishly, without leaving any for others. It is thus a solitary pleasure, which is strongly anti-gastronomic, since gastronomy is also the art of eating in company.

◆ BÂFRER:
To gobble, or eat gluttonously. This vulgar term may originate from the onomatopoeia *baf* or from the German radical *baf*: lips.

◆ CASSER LA CROÛTE:
To snack. Also a popular expression meaning "to eat". *Croûte* refers to a crust of bread, the staple food of the masses.

◆ EMPIFFRER (S') :
To stuff oneself. An expression in use since the 15th century.

◆ ENGOUFFRER:
This term appeared at the end of the 15th century. Its familiar use, meaning "to guzzle," is a contemporary one.

◆ FAIRE BONNE CHÈRE:
To put on a good spread, to welcome someone. The 11th-century word *chiere* came from the low Latin *cara* (face). By extension the laws of hospitality demand that you share your meal, so that *faire bonne chère* means "to produce a good meal." The implication is that eating well also involves eating

in the company of others.

◆ GARGANTUAN:
Originates from one of Rabelais's characters, Gargantua, father of Pantagruel. Balzac brought this word into use in the 19th century.

◆ GLUTTON:
In the 11th century the term was *gloton*, from the low Latin *gluttire* (to swallow) and *gluttus* (gullet).

◆ GOINFRE:
Greedy guts. The word first appeared around 1580 and has uncertain origins. It may come from the word *goujat* (boor or churl).

◆ GOULU:
Greedy. From the old French word *goule*, from which comes *gueule* (mouth).

◆ LIPPÉE:
Mouthful. From the word *lippe* (lip). Today a *franche lippé* is a blow-out. In La Fontaine's time it was a free meal.

◆ MORFAL:
Trencherman. Big eater. From *morfiler* or *morfier* (from the low Latin *morphia*: a mouthful) This very familiar term comes from military slang.

◆ PANTAGRUELIAN:
This term, dating from 1552 and resurrected in 1829, comes from Rabelais. It is the name of one of his characters, a giant called Pantagruel, a big eater.

◆ VORACE:
Ravenous. The word *vorage* dates from the beginning of the 16th century, and comes from the Latin *vorare*, meaning to tear with one's teeth.

◆ THE KITCHEN BRIGADE ◆

A team working in a kitchen is known as a *brigade*. This term obviously has military origins and indicates the discipline and organization that are necessary behind the scenes. Each person has a specific duty. Here are some terms of the trade.

◆ COMMUNARD:
Someone who prepares
food for the staff.

◆ COUP DE FEU:
A period of intense
bustle and activity when
the service is fully
stretched.

◆ ÉCHANSON:
Cut-bearer. Officer
responsible for serving
wine at the table of the
seigneur. He takes his
orders from the
*sommelier**. This word
goes back to the 12th
century. The *échanson*
is part of the
échansonnerie, serving
the drinks.

◆ GÂTE-SAUCE:
Inexperienced
*marmiton**.

◆ MAÎTRE D'HÔTEL:
In charge of service at
table.

◆ MARMITON:
Kitchen boy whose
menial duties include
looking after the
cooking pots.

◆ NIOLEUR:
Person specifically
responsible for the
pastries. From *nieules*,
cakes that were greatly
prized up until the last
century.

◆ OUBLIEUR:
The person who made
oublies, wafers cooked
between two irons.
Stands selling *oublies*
were found in the
streets.

◆ QUEUX:
Cook. From the Latin
coquus. An old term
already in use in the
seigneurial cooking of
the Middle Ages. Today
excellence in this
profession earns the
title *maîtrequeux*.

◆ RANG:
All the *commis* serving
in the dining-room.

◆ SOMMELIER:
Since the beginning of
the 19th century the
sommelier (from the
word *somme*,
responsible) has been
responsible for the
wine cellar and the
wines in the restaurant.
He was formerly
responsible for meals,
provisions and the
maintenance of an
establishment .

◆ TOQUE:
Chef's hat, the "emblem
of the culinary trades."
The word comes from

the Spanish *toca*, which
dates from the 15th
century.

◆ AT TABLE ◆

An enormous amount of
literature exists on the
subject of eating, and
the vocabulary that in
various degrees of
detail describes
everything relating to
this essential aspect of
everyday life is
particularly rich. Here
are some terms.

◆ À LA CARTE:
Meals offered dish by
dish, and not setting out
all the dishes as in
French-style service. À
la carte service was
introduced in
restaurants following
demand from the
'nouveau riches' of the
Revolution who did not
dare show their wealth
in public. Today
customers can choose
between à la carte,
where courses are
selected from the menu,
and set menus.

◆ COMMENSAL:
Someone who eats at
the same table. From
the Latin *cum* (with) and
mensa (table). Can
mean a familiar host.

◆ CONVIVE:
Guest invited to share
the meal.

◆ DESSERT:
Last part of a meal
before *desservir*
(clearing away).

◆ DÎNER:
This was the morning
meal in the 11th
century.

◆ ENTRÉE :
"The entrée precedes
the roast" and is
brought in, as its name
indicates, at the
beginning of the meal,
that is after the soup
and the hors d'oeuvre
and before the main
course. The term had
this meaning from the
17th century.

◆ ENTREMETS:
Dish served "between
two courses," after the
roast. This could be
savory or sweet. Today
an entremets is normally
a dessert.

◆ CHEESE:
Literally something that

is shaped in a mold. For
example *fromage de
tête* (pork brawn).

◆ HORS D'ŒUVRE:
Light dishes served at
the beginning of a meal
before the entrée. The
term appeared in
culinary language in the
17th century.

◆ MENU:
List of dishes in minute
(menu) detail.
Nowadays restaurant
menus include set
prices.

◆ RESTAURANT:
Originally broth from a
pot-au-feu - the
"restoring broth"
supposed to revive
those who drank it. The
word took on its current
meaning around 1765.

◆ SALAD:
Raw, savory edible
plants. From the
Provençal word *salada*,
a savory dish (from the
Latin *sal*: salt).

◆ FRENCH-STYLE SERVICE:
Until the 19th century all
the dishes were laid on
the table. Subsequently,
the guest served
himself from a dish held
by the waiter.

◆ ENGLISH-STYLE SERVICE:
The waiter presents the
dishes and serves each
guest.

◆ COOKING
VERBS ◆

Some recipes include
terms that describe very
precise processes. For
those who may wish to
use French cookbooks,
some of the most
common culinary tems
are explained here.

◆ ABAISSER:
To roll out dough with a
rolling pin.

◆ BARDER:
To cut lard (back fat)
into thin slices (bards)
and use to cover joints
of roast meat or the
underside of poultry.
Bards are held in place
by string.

◆ BLANCHIR:
To blanch. A first
cooking in boiling water
to remove the
bitterness.

◆ COLLER:
To thicken a sauce by
adding jelly or
gelatin.

◆ COMPOTER:
To stew, or cook for a
long time.

◆ CREVER:
To split. A term applied
to the cooking of rice or
barley: rice splits when
it is cooked but does
not lose its shape.

◆ DÉROBER:
To peel the skin (*robe*)
off potatoes boiled in
their skins (*en robe des
champs*).

◆ ÉCHAUDER:
To scald, or plunge into
boiling water.

◆ ÉMONDER:
To plunge almonds into
boiling water for a few
minutes so that they can
easily be peeled with
the fingers.

◆ ESCALOPER:
To cut into escalopes,
that is, thin slices.
Escalopes of meat were
formerly presented
stacked in the shape of
a ring with a well in the
center for the sauce.

◆ EXPRIMER:
To press a fruit or
vegetable in order to
extract its juice.

◆ FONCER :
To fill the base of a
receptacle with slices of
lard*, veal or pastry.

◆ LIER:
To thicken a sauce
using an egg yolk or
starch. "The aim of
thickening is to give
consistency to stocks
that are used as a base
for home made sauces"
(Marguerite de Saint-
Genès, *L'Art de la
cuisine*).

◆ LIMONER :
To remove the silt from a
fish that has been
plunged into hot water,
using a knife.

◆ LUTER:
To seal a terrine
hermetically using an
"edible cement" made
from flour and water, in
order to retain the flavor.

◆ MARINER:
To steep a piece of
meat in a marinade, a
simple preparation
made with such
ingredients as thyme,
parsley and vinegar that
slowly permeates the
meat.

◆ MONDER:
To grate the skin of
fruits.

◆ MIJOTER:
To simmer. "Generally

◆ GLOSSARY

cooking is done over a low heat. Dishes should be simmered not boiled fiercely..." (Marguerite de Saint-Genès, *L'Art de la cuisine*).

◆ MITONNER:
To soak and boil over a low heat for a long time.

◆ MORTIFIER:
To tenderize meat by hitting it hard or keeping it in a cool place for several days before cooking it.

◆ PARER:
To trim the skin, sinews and fat from meat to improve its appearance.

◆ REFAIRE:
To render. Turning poultry or game in the bottom of a pan over heat until the flesh swells.

◆ RISSOLER:
To brown, or expose to a high temperature to give a good color.

◆ TOURER:
A pastry-making term meaning to turn the dough once or more. To turn is to fold the dough into two or three after having rolled it out with a rollingpin.

◆ À LA CARTE ◆

Some dishes named after people or events.

STARTERS AND CHARCUTERIE

◆ BOUCHÉE À LA REINE:
Said to have been "invented" by Queen Marie Leszczynska, wife of Louis XV.

◆ GALANTINE:
From galatine (jelly). "There are galantines and terrines... and Spanish inns: you only find what you bring" (Robert Courtine, *Balzac à table*, 1976).

◆ VOL-AU-VENT:
Filled puff-pastry case. We owe the invention of this type of light *tourte* to the master chef Carême.

MEAT AND FISH

◆ COLBERT:
Preparation of certain types of fish. The name of Louis XIV's minister.

◆ GIBELOTTE:
Fricassée of rabbit (cut up and stewed) in white wine. From the old French *gibelet*, referring to a method of preparing poultry.

◆ MARENGO:
Chicken or veal sautéd in white wine with tomatoes. Legend has it that this dish was invented by Napoleon Bonaparte's cook on the eve of the battle whose name it took.

◆ NAVARIN:
Ragout of lamb accompanied by a selection of vegetables. The name comes from the Greek port Navarin on the Ionian Sea and the recipe from an inventive military cook.

VEGETABLES

◆ BRUNOISE:
Vegetables cut into very small pieces and cooked in butter.

◆ JULIENNE:
A way of cutting vegetables into fine matchsticks. The technique was perfected by a cook named Julienne.

◆ MATIGNON:
Finely cut young vegetables with ham. Almost certainly invented in the kitchens of the Hôtel de Matignon in the 18th century.

◆ MIREPOIX:
Vegetables cut *brunoise** style, enriched with lard* and ham. The Duke of Lévis-Mirepoix's cook perfected this dish in the 17th century.

◆ PONT-NEUF:
A method of preparing potatoes that takes its name from the oldest bridge in Paris: fried potatoes cut into regular slices were once sold by "friteurs" in shops on Pont-Neuf.

SALADS

◆ CHIFFONNADE:
A salad of leaves cut into fine strips.

◆ FRANCILLON:
Created from "from nothing" by Dumas junior for his play *Francillon*. A Parisian chef lit on the idea of copying the recipe

described and putting the dish on his restaurant menu.

DESSERTS

◆ BISCUITS À LA CUILLÈRE:
Sponge fingers. These cakes were introduced into France by Marie de Medicis' pâtissiers. They are so called because the mixture is tranferred to the baking sheet in spoonfuls (cuillerées).

◆ FRANGIPANE:
Named after someone called Frangipani. This may either be Count Frangipani, a friend of Queen Catherine de Medicis, to whom he dedicated a recipe invented by his cooks, based on wheatflour, or an Italian perfumer who invented almond flavoring.

◆ PETITS-FOURS:
Small pastries cooked in a moderate oven (petit four).

◆ BABA:
Cake invented and named by Stanislas Leszinsky, King of Poland, who, full of wonder at his recipe, christened it Ali-Baba.

◆ BELLE HÉLÈNE:
Poached pears coated in chocolate. Named after Offenbach's operetta, *La Belle Hélène* (1864), whose success inspired a pâtissier.

◆ MELBA (PÊCHE):
Sophisticated dessert of vanilla ice cream, poached pears and raspberries). Invented by August Escoffier for the opera singer Nellie Melba at the Carlton Hotel in London.

◆ RAMEQUIN:
Ramekin. From a Dutch word meaning "cream." A sweet or savory preparation cooked then served in small pots. The pot has taken the same name by extension.

◆ SAVARIN:
A type of Baba enriched with crème pâtissière and crystallized fruit. Named after Brillat-Savarin.

◆ SORBET:
From the Arabic

sherbet, a fruit syrup that was originally filtered through silk and kept in snow.

GARNISHES AND SAUCES

◆ AMÉRICAINE:
The term sauce "à l'armoricaine" is often applied to a preparation à l'américaine. But Armorica (Brittany) has nothing to do with this recipe. It was in fact perfected by Pierre Fraysse, a resident of Sètes who settled in Paris after returning from the United States.

◆ BÉARNAISE:
This ancient preparation has been known since the 16th century and was probably named after its inventor, a native of Béarn. Alternatively, it may take its name from the restaurant where it was served, the Pavillon Henri IV, which was previously called Le Béarnais.

◆ BÉCHAMEL:
A flour-based sauce invented during the reign of Louis XIV in the kitchens of the Marquis of Béchamel.

◆ CHASSEUR:
Preparation including mushrooms, shallots, tomatoes and stewed (compoté*) game.

◆ ESPAGNOLE:
A roux and a *fond** of tomatoes, mushrooms, a preparation of *mirepoix**: a classic dish for which French cooking is indebted to Spain. In fact when the Spanish Infanta married Louis XIV she brought with her her own cooks, who prepared a "burnt" sauce thickened with a roux.

◆ MAYONNAISE:
Numerous origins are given for this famous sauce, one of them being that the word for an egg yolk was *moyeu* in old French.

◆ ROUILLE:
Highly seasoned Provençal sauce named after its rusty color. Served with bouillabaisse and other fish dishes.

GUIDE TO THE RESTAURANTS OF PARIS

INFORMATION
Restaurant classified as listed building

SERVICE
● exceptional service
W particularly warm welcome

	INFORMATION	TERRACE (T) / GARDEN (G)	VIEW	PRIVATE DINING-ROOM	AIR CONDITIONING	SERVICE	WINE CELLAR	FOOD	PRICES
AIGUIÈRE (11e) - IT. 6				●	●			C	200-300
ALLARD (6e) - IT. 1	●			●	●			B	250-350
ALEXANDROS (17e) - IT. 3								F	80-108
ALSACE (8e) - IT. 4					●			R	200-300
AMAZIGH (16e) - IT. 3					●			F	230-330
AMBASSADE D'AUVERGNE (3e) - IT. 6	●			●	●			R	160-260
AMBASSADEURS (8e) - IT. 5	●			●	●	●	●	G	420-760
AMBROISIE (4e) - IT. 6	●			●	●	●	●	G	500-900
AMOGNES (11e) - IT. 6		T					●	C	160-280
AMPHYCLES (17e) - IT. 3		G			●		●	G	405-650
AMUSE BOUCHE (14e) - IT. 2						●	●	G	220-350
ANDROUET (8e) - IT. 7				●				Ch.	220-260
ANGELINA (11er) - IT. 5	●							C	170-200
ANTRE DU ROI PHILÈNE (16e) - IT. 3								F	200-300
APICIUS (17e) - IT. 3					●	●		G	400-700
ARMAND AU PALAIS-ROYAL (1er) - IT. 5	●							C	240
ARMES DE BRETAGNE (14e) - IT. 2					●			P	250-400
ARPÈGE (7e) - IT. 1				●	●	●	●	G	450-850
ASSIETTE (14e) - IT. 2							●	G	300-450
ASTIER (11e) - IT. 7					●			H	140-240
ATLAS (5e) - IT. 2			●		●			F	150-220
AUBERGADE (15e) - IT. 2		T				●		C	250-380
AUBERGE BASQUE (7e) - IT. 1					●			R	180-220
AUBERGE DE NICOLAS FLAMEL (3e) - IT. 6	●							C	150-250
AUBERGE DES DEUX SIGNES (5e) - IT. 2	●			●		W		C	310-410
AUBERGE LANDAISE (9e) - IT. 7				●		W		R	200-350
¡AY CARAMBA! (19e) - IT. 7								F	100-160
BALZAR (5e) - IT. 2	●							C	160-220
BARRAIL (15e) - IT. 1				●	●			C	180-280
BAUMANN-TERNES (16e) - IT. 3		T		●	●			R	160-220
BÉATILLES (17e) - IT. 3								C	220-320
BEAUVILLIERS (18e) - IT. 7	●	T		●	●	W	●	C	500-600
BELLECOUR (7e) - IT. 1				●	●			R	250-380
BENKAY (15e) - IT. 1		T	●		●			F	150-200
BENOÎT (4e) - IT. 6				●	●			C	300-420
BERRY'S (8e) - IT. 3								H	130-200
GÉRARD BESSON (1er) - IT. 6					●	●	●	G	280-680
BISTRO DE LA GARE (6e) - IT. 2	●	T			●			C	100-160
BISTROT D'À CÔTÉ (17e) - IT. 3	●				●			C	150-250
BISTROT DE L'ÉTOILE-LAURISTON (16e) - IT. 3								C	150-250
BISTROT DE PARIS (7e) - IT. 1				●				B	200-300
BISTROT DU PORT (5e) - IT. 2		T	●		●			C	180-300
BISTROT 121 (15e) - IT. 1								C	220-350
BLUE ELEPHANT (11e) - IT. 6				●	●			F	180-280
BŒUF SUR LE TOIT (8e) - IT. 4	●				●	●		C	160-230
BOFINGER (4e) - IT. 6					●	●		C	180-250
BOUCHUT (15e) - IT. 1		T				W		H	150-200
BOURDONNAIS (7e) - IT. 1		T		●	●	W		G	280-400
BRASSERIE DU LOUVRE (1er) - IT. 5								C	160-260
BRASSERIE FLO (10e) - IT. 7	●				●			C	140-240

CUISINE

- B bourgeois
- C classic
- F foreign
- Ch cheeses
- G gastronomic
- H home cooking
- R regional

IT. Refer to itineraries

PRICE À la carte prices as in the first quarter of 1993, including a starter, a main course and a dessert.

Restaurant	Information	Terrace (T) / Garden (G)	View	Private Dining-Room	Air Conditioning	Service	Wine Cellar	Food	Prices
BRASSERIE MUNICHOISE (1er) - IT. 5				●				F	170-250
BRASSERIE STELLA (16e) - IT. 3		T						B	180-280
BRISTOL (8e) - IT. 4		G		●	●	●		C	600-700
BÙCHERIE (5e) - IT. 2		T	●	●		●	●	C	300-400
BUTTE CHAILLOT (16e) - IT. 3		T						C	150-250
CABANON DES MAÎTRES NAGEURS (14e) - IT. 2		T						P	160-260
CAFÉ DE LA JATTE (NEUILLY) - IT. 3		T						C	200-300
CAFÉ DES THÉÂTRES (2e) - IT. 5				●				C	180-250
JACQUES CAGNA (7e) - IT. 1	●			●	●	●	●	G	450-600
CAGOUILLE (14e) - IT. 2		T						P	300-500
CALÈCHE (6e) - IT. 1							w	C	160-250
CAMÉLÉON (6e) - IT. 2	●						●	B	150-250
CAMPAGNE ET PROVENCE (5e) - IT. 2							●	R	180-280
CARPACCIO (8e) - IT. 3				●			●	F	320-500
CARRÉ DES FEUILLANTS (1er) - IT. 5	●			●	●	●	●	G	500-700
CARTES POSTALES (1er) - IT. 5								C	170-300
CASA BINI (6e) - IT. 1				●				F	160-220
CASA PEPE (5e) - IT. 2				●				F	200-250
CAVE PETRISSANS (17e) - IT. 3	●	T					w ●	H	180-250
CÉLADON (2e) - IT. 5	●							G	300-500
CÉLÉBRITÉS (15e) - IT. 1		T	●	●	●	●	●	G	350-550
CENTRE GEORGES-POMPIDOU (4e) - IT. 6		T	●	●				C	80-140
CERF-VOLANT (15e) - IT. 1							w	F	140-220
CHARDENOUX (11e) - IT. 6	●						●	B	150-250
CHARLIE DE BAB-EL-OUED (17e) - IT. 3				●				F	160-260
CHARLOT (9e) - IT. 7	●			●				P	250-450
CHARPENTIERS (6e) - IT. 1							w	H	150-220
CHARTIER (9e) - IT. 7	●							H	70-100
CHAT GRIPPÉ (6e) - IT. 2				●			●	G	250-350
CHATEAUBRIAND (10e) - IT. 7				●			w	F	220-380
CHIBERTA (8e) - IT. 3				●	●		●	G	395-700
CHIENG MAI (5e) - IT. 2		T		●				F	150-220
BERNARD CHIRENT (1er) - IT. 5				●	●		●	C	200-350
CIEL DE PARIS (15e) - IT. 2			●					C	220-340
CLAVEL (5e) - IT. 2				●				C	250-350
CLOS LONGCHAMP (17e) - IT. 3		G		●	●	●	●	G	408-650
CLOS DES MORILLONS (15e) - IT. 1				●				G	200-300
CLOSERIE DES LILAS (6e) - IT.2		T	●					C	150-380
CLOWN BAR (11e) - IT. 6								H	130-230
CLUB MANHATTAN (EURODISNEY) - IT. 6				●				F	140-250
COCHON D'OR (19e) - IT. 7	●			●				C	350-450
COCONNAS (4e) - IT. 6	●			●				C	220-350
COMPTOIR DU SAUMON (4e) - IT. 6				●				F	120-300
CONTI (16e) - IT. 3				●			●	G	290-400
COUGAR (17e) - IT. 3				●				P	345-450
COUPOLE (14e) - IT. 2	●			●				C	180-300
COURONNE (8e) - IT. 4				●	●	●	●	G	250-400
CROISSANT (2e) - IT.5	●							H	100-180
DATCHA LYDIE (15e) - IT. 1								F	150-250
DODIN-BOUFFANT (5e) - IT. 2	●	T		●				C	195

	Information	Terrace (T) / Garden (G)	View	Private Dining-Room	Air Conditioning	Service	Wine Cellar	Food	Prices
Dômarais (4e) - IT. 6	•	T						C	220-320
Dôme (14e) - IT. 2		T		•	•			P	300-500
Dominique (6e) - IT. 2				•	•			F	160-260
Drouant (2e) - IT. 5	•			•	•	•		C	300-500
Duquesnoy (7e) - IT. 1				•	•	•		G	380-580
Écaille du PCB (6e) - IT. 1					•			P	230-320
Écaille et plume (7e) - IT. 1				•	•			C	200-350
Échanson (14e) - IT. 2		T					•	C	150-200
Chez Edgard (8e) - IT. 4		T		•			•	C	200-300
Élysées du Vernet (8e) - IT. 3	•	G		•	•	•	•	R	300-400
Élysées-Lenôtre (8e) - IT. 4	•	T		•			•	G	400-700
Entre-Siecle (15e) - IT.				•	•		•	G	220-350
Entrecôte-Le Relais de Venise (17e) - IT. 3								C	100-150
Épopée (15e) - IT. 1		T					W	C	170-240
Erawan (15e) - IT. 1					•			F	180-250
Escargot-Montorgueil (1er) - IT. 6		T		•				C	200-350
Espace Champagne (1er) - IT. 5		T		•		•		C	200-250
Espace Hérault - Rabelais (5e) - IT. 2				•		•	W	R	150-250
Espadon (1er) - IT. 5	•	G		•	•	•	•	G	450-700
Etchegorry (13e) - IT. 2		T		•				R	150-230
Étoile marocaine (8e) - IT. 3					•			F	180-280
Fakhr el Dine (8e) - IT. 4					•			F	200-300
Famiglia Fuligna (17e) - IT. 3		T		•				F	170-250
Farigoule (15e) - IT. 1								R	150-220
Gérard Faucher (17e) - IT. 3		T				•	W	G	300-400
Henri Faugeron (16e) - IT. 3				•	•	•	W	G	550-700
Fell:ni (1er) - IT. 6				•	•			F	150-250
Ferme Saint-Hubert (8e) - IT. 5		T						CH.	120-180
Ferme Saint-Simon (7e) - IT. 1				•	•	•		C	220-320
Fermette Marbeuf (8e) - IT. 4	•	T				•	•	G	200-250
Chez Fernand (11e) - IT. 7								C	160-260
Jean-Claude Ferrero (16e) - IT. 3		G		•			W	G	315-540
Ferronnerie (7e) - IT. 1								B	180-250
Florence (7e) - IT. 1								F	200-300
Foc-Ly (7e) - IT. 1						•		F	180-250
Folies (11e) - IT. 7								F	140-240
Fond de cour (4e) - IT. 6		T		•				G	220-320
Fouquet's (8e) - IT. 4		T		•				B	240-440
Fouquet's Bastille (12e) - IT. 6		T				•		C	200-300
Fouquet's Europe (La Défense) - IT. 3				•		•	•	G	300-500
Fouta Toro (18e) - IT. 7								F	90-120
Chez Francis (8e) - IT. 4								C	200-300
French Line (8e) - IT. 4		T		•				C	180-220
Gallopin (2e) - IT. 5	•	T						H	220-300
Gazelle (17e) - IT. 3								F	120-150
Géorgiques (8e) - IT. 4				•	•	•		C	323-480
Goldenberg (17e) - IT. 3		T						F	150-200
Jo Goldenberg (4e) - IT. 6		T						F	150-250
Goumard-Prunier (1er) - IT. 5				•	•	•	•	P	350-700
Gourmandise (12e) - IT. 6								C	250-400

	INFORMATION	TERRACE (T) / GARDEN (G)	VIEW	PRIVATE DINING-ROOM	AIR CONDITIONING	SERVICE	WINE CELLAR	FOOD	PRICES
GRAND CAFÉ CAPUCINES (9e) - IT. 7				•	•			C	200-300
GRAND COLBERT (2e) - IT. 5	•			•	•			B	250-350
GRAND LOUVRE (1er) - IT. 5								F	80-108
GRAND VÉFOUR (1er) - IT. 5					•			R	200-300
GRAND VENISE (15e) - IT. 1					•			F	230-330
GRANDE CASCADE (16e) - IT. 3	•			•	•	•	•	R	160-260
GRANDGOUSIER (18e) - IT. 7	•			•	•	•	•	G	420-760
GRENADIN (8e) - IT. 3	•			•	•		•	G	500-900
GRILLE SAINT-HONORÉ (1er) - IT. 5		T					•	C	160-280
GRIZZLI (4e) - IT. 6		G		•	•	•	•	G	405-650
GUINGUETTE DE NEUILLY - IT. 3								G	220-350
GUY (6e) - IT. 1				•				CH.	220-260
JACQUES HÉBERT (15e) - IT. 2	•							C	170-200
IMPASSE (4e) - IT. 6						•		F	200-300
IMPRIMERIE (4e) - IT. 6					•			G	400-700
INCROYABLE (1er) - IT. 5	•					•		C	240
INSTITUT DU MONDE ARABE (5e) - IT. 2					•	•		P	250-400
JARDIN (8e) - IT. 3				•	•		•	G	450-850
JARDIN DU PRINTEMPS (8e) - IT. 4								G	300-450
JARDINS DE BAGATELLE (16e) - IT. 3					•			H	140-240
CHEZ JENNY (3e) - IT. 6			•	•	•			F	150-220
JOHNNY ROCK CAFÉ - IT. 4		T						C	250-380
JULES VERNE (7e) - IT. 3					•			R	180-220
JULIEN (10e) - IT. 7	•					W		C	150-250
CHEZ JULIEN (4e) - IT. 6	•			•		W		C	310-410
KAMBODGIA (16e) - IT. 3				•				R	200-350
KASAPHANI (11e) - IT. 7								F	100-160
KIM ANH (15e) - IT. 1	•							C	160-220
KINUGAWA (1er) - IT. 5				•	•			C	180-280
LAPÉROUSE (6e) - IT. 1		T		•	•			R	160-220
LASSERRE (8e) - IT. 4						W	•	C	220-320
LAURENT (8e) - IT. 4	•	T		•	•		•	C	500-600
LE DIVELLEC (7e) - IT. 1				•	•			R	250-380
LE DUC (14e) - IT. 2		T	•					F	150-200
LEDOYEN (8e) - IT. 4	•			•	•			C	300-420
LESCURE (1er) - IT. 5						•	•	H	130-200
LIPP (6e) - IT. 1					•			G	280-680
LOUBNANE (5e) - IT. 2	•	T						C	100-160
LOUIS XIV (10e) - IT. 7	•				•			C	150-250
LOUS LANDES (14e) - IT. 2								C	150-250
LUCAS CARTON (8e) - IT. 5				•				B	200-300
LUZ (7e) - IT. 1		T	•		•			C	180-220
LYONNAIS (17e) - IT. 3								C	220-350
MAIN À LA PÂTE (1er) - IT. 6				•	•	•		F	180-280
MAISON D'AMÉRIQUE LATINE (7e) - IT. 1	•				•	•		C	160-230
MAISON DU DANEMARK (8e) - IT. 3					•	W		C	180-250
MAISON DU VALAIS (8e) - IT. 5		T				W		H	150-200
MANOIR DE PARIS (17e) - IT. 3		T			•			G	280-400
MANSOURIA (11e) - IT. 6								C	160-260
MANUFACTURE (ISSY) - IT. 2	•				•			C	140-240

◆ CHOOSING A RESTAURANT

	INFORMATION	TERRACE (T) / GARDEN (G)	VIEW	PRIVATE DINING-ROOM	AIR CONDITIONING	SERVICE	WINE CELLAR	FOOD	PRICES
MARAÎCHER (4e) - IT. 6				•				F	170-250
MARÉE (8e) - IT. 3		T				•	•	B	180-280
MAXIM'S (8e) - IT. 5		G			•		•	C	600-700
MAXIM'S (ORLY) - IT. 2		T	•	•	•			C	300-400
MÉDITERRANÉE (6e) - IT. 2		T						C	150-250
MERCURE GALANT (1er) - IT. 5		T						P	160-260
DANIEL METERY (8e) - IT. 5		T						C	200-300
MEURICE (1er) - IT. 5				•		•	•	C	180-250
MINISTÈRES (7e) - IT. 1	•			•	•			G	450-600
MIRAVILE (4e) - IT. 6		T				W		P	300-500
MOI (16e) - IT. 3							•	C	160-250
MOISSONNIER (5e) - IT. 2	•						•	B	150-250
MOLLARD (8e) - IT. 7							•	R	180-280
MONDE DES CHIMÈRES (4e) - IT. 2				•		•	•	F	320-500
MONTPARNASSE 25 (14e) - IT. 2	•			•	•			G	500-700
MONUMENTS (16e) - IT. 3								C	170-300
MOROT-GAUDRY (15e) - IT. 1				•				F	160-220
AL MOUNIA (16e) - IT. 3				•		W	•	F	200-250
MUNICH (6e) - IT. 1	•	T						H	180-250
MUSÉE D'ORSAY (7e) - IT. 1	•					•	•	G	300-500
MUSES (9e) - IT. 7		T	•	•	•			G	450-650
NAPOLÉON (8e) - IT. 3		T	•	•	•	W		C	80-140
NAVARIN (11e) - IT. 6							•	F	140-220
NIOULAVILLE (11e) - IT. 7	•							B	150-250
ŒNOTHÈQUE (9e) - IT. 7					•			F	160-260
OLYMPE (15e) - IT. 1	•				•	W		P	250-450
ORANGERIE (4e) - IT. 2								H	150-220
OULETTE (12e) - IT. 6	•						•	H	70-100
OUM EL BANINE (16e) - IT. 3					•	W		G	250-350
PACTOLE (5e) - IT. 2					•	•	•	F	220-380
PARIS (6e) - IT. 1					•			G	395-700
PARIS-DAKAR (10e) - IT. 7		T			•		•	F	150-220
CHEZ PAULINE (1er) - IT. 5				•	•			C	200-350
PAVILLON DES PRINCES (16e) - IT. 3			•					C	220-340
PAVILLON MONTSOURIS (14e) - IT. 2					•	•	•	C	250-350
PAVILLON NOURA (8e) - IT. 4		G		•	•		•	G	408-650
PAVILLON PUEBLA (19e) - IT. 7					•			G	200-300
PERGOLÈSE (16e) - IT. 3		T		•				C	150-380
PERRAUDIN (5e) - IT. 2								H	130-230
PETIT BEDON (16e) - IT. 3					•			F	140-250
PETIT COLOMBIER (17e) - IT. 3	•				•			C	250-400
PETIT LAURENT (7e) - IT. 1	•							C	220-350
PETIT MARGUERY (13e) - IT. 2					•		•	F	120-300
PETIT MONTMORENCY (8e) - IT. 4					•			G	290-400
PETIT RÉTRO (16e) - IT. 3	P				•			P	345-450
PETIT RICHE (9e) - IT. 7	•			•	•	•	•	C	180-300
PETIT ZINC (6e) - IT. 1					•			G	250-400
PETITE BRETONNIÈRE (15e) - IT. 1	•							H	100-180
PETITE COUR (6e) - IT. 1								F	150-250
PETITE TOUR (16e) - IT. 3	•	T			•			C	250-350

	INFORMATION	TERRACE (T) / GARDEN (G)	VIEW	PRIVATE DINING-ROOM	AIR CONDITIONING	SERVICE	WINE CELLAR	FOOD	PRICES
PETITS CHANDELIERS (14e) - IT. 2	●	T						C	220-320
PHARAMOND (1er) - IT. 6		T		●	●			P	300-500
CHEZ PHILIPPE (11e) - IT. 7				●	●	●		F	160-260
PIED DE COCHON (1er) - IT. 6	●			●	●	●	●	C	300-500
PIERRE «FONTAINE GAILLON» (2e) - IT. 5				●				G	380-580
PIERRE AU PALAIS-ROYAL (1er) - IT. 5				●				P	230-320
PLANTATION (12e) - IT. 6				●			●	C	200-350
POÈTE IVRE (2e) - IT. 6		T					●	C	150-200
POLIDOR (6e) - IT. 2		T		●			●	C	200-300
POQUELIN (1er) - IT. 5	●	G		●			●	R	300-400
PORT-ALMA (16e) - IT. 4	●	T					●	G	400-700
POSTE (9e) - IT. 7				●	●			G	220-350
POULE AU POT (7e) - IT. 1							W	C	
PRÉ CATELAN (16e) - IT. 3		T						C	170-240
PRESSOIR (12e) - IT. 6				●				F	180-250
PRINCE DE GALLES (8e) - IT. 4		T		●		●		C	200-350
PRINCES (8e) - IT. 4		T		●	●	●	W	C	200-250
PRINTEMPS (9e) - IT. 7				●	●	●		R	150-250
PROCOPE (6e) - IT. 1	●	G		●				G	450-700
P'TITE TONKINOISE (10e) - IT. 7		T		●				R	150-230
QUACH (16e) - IT. 3				●				F	180-280
QUAI OUEST (SAINT-CLOUD) - IT. 3				●				F	200-300
YVES QUINTARD (15e) - IT. 2		T						F	170-250
RAAJMAHAL (15e) - IT. 1							W	R	150-220
RÉCAMIER (7e) - IT. 1		T			●	●	W	G	300-400
RÉGENCE-PLAZA (8e) - IT. 4				●	●			G	550-700
RELAIS D'AUTEUIL (16e) - IT. 3				●	●			F	150-250
RELAIS DE SÈVRES (15e) - IT. 1		T				●		Ch.	120-180
RELAIS LOUIS XIII (6e) - IT. 1				●	●	●	●	C	220-320
RELAIS-PLAZA (8e) - IT. 4	●	T		●				G	200-250
LE RESTAURANT (18e) - IT. 7							W	C	160-260
RESTAURANT A (5e) - IT. 2		G		●				G	315-540
RESTAURANT DU MARCHÉ (15e) - IT. 1								B	180-250
RESTAURANT OPÉRA (9e) - IT. 7								F	200-300
RISTORANTE (17e) - IT. 3				●				F	180-250
RIVER CAFÉ (ISSY) - IT. 2								F	140-240
JOËL ROBUCHON (16e) - IT. 3		T		●				G	220-320
ROI DU POT-AU-FEU (9e) - IT. 7		T		●				B	240-440
MICHEL ROSTANG (17e) - IT. 3		T			●	●	●	C	200-300
RÔTISSERIE D'ARMAILLÉ (17e) - IT. 3				●				G	300-500
RÔTISSERIE D'EN FACE (6e) - IT. 1								F	90-120
ROUDOULIÉ (11e) - IT. 6								C	200-300
SAMARITAINE - LE GRILL (1er) - IT. 6		T		●				C	180-220
SAN VALERO (NEUILLY-SUR-SEINE) - IT. 3	●	T						H	220-300
SAUDADE (1er) - IT. 6						●		F	120-150
GUY SAVOY (17e) - IT. 3				●	●			C	323-480
SÉBILLON-ÉLYSÉES (8e) - IT. 4		T						F	150-200
SENTEURS DE PROVENCE (15e) - IT. 1		T				●	●	F	150-250
CAROLL SINCLAIR (4e) - IT. 6				●	●			P	350-700
SIPARIO (12e) - IT. 6								C	250-400

339

	INFORMATION	TERRACE (T) / GARDEN (G)	VIEW	PRIVATE DINING-ROOM	AIR CONDITIONING	SERVICE	WINE CELLAR	FOOD	PRICES
SOFITEL (ROISSY) - IT. 7								C	220-350
SOLOGNE (12e) - IT. 6	●				●	●	●	C	200-250
SORMANI (17e) - IT. 3	●			●		●		R	240-350
SOUS L'OLIVIER (8e) - IT. 4	●			●	●		●	G	350-550
A SOUSCEYRAC (11e) - IT. 6						●	●	F	350-450
SQUARE TROUSSEAU (12e) - IT. 6	●	T G		●				C	450-600
TABLE D'ANVERS (9e) - IT. 7						W	●	C	180-280
TABLE DE PIERRE (17e) - IT. 3					●	W		G	300-400
TABLE RICHELIEU (11e) - IT. 6		T		●	●	W		H	200-350
TAGHIT (14e) - IT. 2	●	T						R	150-250
TAILLEVENT (8e) - IT. 3		T	●					C	160-230
TAKA (18e) - IT. 7				●	●	W	●	F	180-250
TAN DINH (7e) - IT. 1								G	280-380
TANTE LOUISE (8e) - IT. 5								H	180-280
TASHI DELEK (5e) - IT. 2				●	●			C	150-190
TÉLÉGRAPHE (7e) - IT. 1	●	T						H	120-220
TEMPS DE VIVRE (18e) - IT. 7		T	●			●	●	F	200-300
TERMINUS NORD (10e) - IT. 7	●	T G			●			G	320-480
TIMONERIE (5e) - IT. 2				●	●			F	150-250
TOIT DE PASSY (16e) - IT. 3		T G		●				C	300-500
TOTEM (16e) - IT. 3		T		●				R	220-270
TOUR D'ARGENT (5e) - IT. 2				●	●	●	●	F	120-250
TOUR DE MONTLHÉRY (1er) - IT. 6			●	●				G	420-600
CHEZ TOUTOUNE (5e) - IT. 2	●			●				C	170-270
TRAIN BLEU (12e) - IT. 6	●		●	●				B	220-300
TRAKTIR (15e) - IT. 1					●	●		F	180-260
TROU GASCON (12e) - IT. 6		T				W	●	F	140-170
TY-COZ (9e) - IT. 7								F	220-320
URI (15e) - IT. 1				●	●			F	250-400
VAGENENDE (6e) - IT. 1	●			●	●	●		G	320-520
VANCOUVER (8e) - IT. 3	●	T		●	●	●	●	G	450-800
VASSANTI (14e) - IT. 2	●	T		●				G	600-1000
VAUDEVILLE (2e) - IT. 5					●			P	450-750
VELLONI (1er) - IT. 6								P	360-700
VENANTIUS (9e) - IT. 7	●		●	●	●			G	500-700
VÉRO-DODAT (1er) - IT. 6		T			T			H	100-170
CHEZ LA VIEILLE (1er) - IT. 6	●	T		●				B	200-300
VIEUX MÉTIERS DE FRANCE (13e) - IT. 2		T		●				F	150-200
VIGNES DU PANTHÉON (5e) - IT. 2							●	C	230-330
VIN DES RUES (14e) - IT. 2		T			●	●	●	R	250-350
VIN SUR VIN (7e) - IT. 1	●			●	●	W		G	600-900
VISHNOU (14e) - IT. 2					●	W		P	230-330
VIVAROIS (16e) - IT. 3					●		●	R	220-320
VONG (8e) - IT. 4		G		●	●			F	200-320
WALLY LE SAHARIEN (4e) - IT. 2		T G		●				B	200-300
WEPLER (18e) - IT. 7		G		●				F	300-500
WILLI'S (1er) - IT. 5		T		●	●			F	200-220
YUGARAJ (6e) - IT. 1				●	●			G	280-600
YVAN (8e) - IT. 4								F	200-250
15, MONTAIGNE (8e) - IT. 4		T			●			C	180-280

* See addresses at the end of the guide
C Days closed not given
D dinner
L lunch
IT. refer to itineraries

	SATURDAY	SUNDAY	MONDAY	JULY	AUGUST	UNTIL 10PM	UNTIL 11PM	AFTER MIDNIGHT
AIGUIÈRE (11e) - IT. 6	D		•	•	•	•		
ALEXANDROS (17e) - IT. 1	•		•	•	*	•		
ALLARD (6e) - IT. 3	•		•	•		•		
ALSACE (8e) - IT. 4	•	•	•	•	•			24/24
AMAZIGH (16e) - IT. 3	D		•	•	•		•	
AMBASSADE D'AUVERGNE (3e) - IT. 6	•	•	•	*	*	•		
AMBASSADEURS (8e) - IT. 5	•	•	•	•	•	•		
AMBROISIE (4e) - IT. 6	•		•	•	*			
AMOGNES (11e) - IT. 6	•		•	•	•		•	
AMPHYCLES (17e) - IT. 3	D		•	•	•	•		
AMUSE BOUCHE (14e) - IT. 2	D		•	•	*	•		
ANDROUET (8e) - IT. 7	•		•	•	•		•	
ANGELINA (1er) - IT. 5	•	•	•	•	•	•		
ANTRE DU ROI PHILÈNE (16e) - IT. 3			•	•		•		
APICIUS (17e) - IT. 3			•	•		•		
ARMAND AU PALAIS-ROYAL (1er) - IT. 5	D		•	•	*		•	
ARMES DE BRETAGNE (14e) - IT. 2	•	•	•	•	•	•		
ARPEGE (7e) - IT. 1		D	•			•		
ASSIETTE (14e) - IT. 2	•	•		•		•		
ASTIER (11e) - IT. 7			•	C	C	•		
ATLAS (5e) - IT. 2	•	•	•	•	•		•	
AUBERGADE (15e) - IT. 2		L	•	•		•		
AUBERGE BASQUE (7e) - IT. 1	•		•	•		•		
AUBERGE DE NICOLAS FLAMEL (3e) - IT. 6	D	•	D	•	•	•		
AUBERGE DES DEUX SIGNES (5e) - IT. 2	D		•	•	•		•	
AUBERGE LANDAISE (9e) - IT. 7	•		•	•	*	•		
¡ AY CARAMBA ! (19e) - IT. 7	•	•	•	•	•		•	
BALZAR (5e) - IT. 2	•	•	•	•	•			1am
BARRAIL (15e) - IT. 1			•				•	
BAUMAN-TERNES (17e) - IT. 3	•	•	•	•	•			12am
BÉATILLES (17e) - IT. 3			•	•	*	•		
BEAUVILLIERS (18e) - IT. 7	•	D	•	•	•	•		
BELLECOUR (7e) - IT. 1	D		•	•		•		
BENKAY (15e) - IT. 1	•	•	•	•	•	•		
BENOIT (4e) - IT. 6			•	•		•		
BERRY'S (8e) - IT. 3	•		•	•	•			1am
GÉRARD BESSON (1er) - IT. 6			•	*	•	•		
BISTRO DE LA GARE (6e) - IT. 2	•	•	•	•	•			1am
BISTROT D'À CÔTÉ (17e) - IT. 3	D		•	•	*	•		
BISTROT DE L'ÉTOILE-LAURISTON (16e) - IT. 3	D		•	•	•			12am
BISTROT DE PARIS (7e) - IT. 1	D		•	•	•	•		
BISTROT DU PORT (5e) - IT. 2	•	•	•	•	•	•		
BISTROT 121 (15e) - IT. 1	•	•	•	•	•			12am
BLUE ELEPHANT (11e) - IT. 6	D	•	•	•	•	•		12am
BŒUF SUR LE TOIT (8e) - IT. 4	•	•	•	•	•			2am
BOFINGER (4e) - IT. 6	•	•	•	•	•			1am
BOUCHUT (15e) - IT. 1	D		•	•	•	•		
BOURDONNAIS (7e) - IT. 1	•	•	•				•	
BRASSERIE DU LOUVRE (1er) - IT. 5	•	•	•	•	•		•	
BRASSERIE FLO (10e) - IT. 7	•	•	•	•	•			1.30am

	SATURDAY	SUNDAY	MONDAY	JULY	AUGUST	UNTIL 10PM	UNTIL 11PM	AFTER MIDNIGHT
BRASSERIE MUNICHOISE (1er) - IT. 5	D		•	•				2am
BRASSERIE STELLA (16e) - IT. 3	•	•	•	•	•			1.30am
BRISTOL (8e) - IT. 4	•	•	•	•	•	•		
BÛCHERIE (5e) - IT. 2	•	•	•	•	•			12.30am
BUTTE CHAILLOT (16e) - IT. 3	•	•	•	•	•			12.30am
CABANON DES MAÎTRES NAGEURS (14e) - IT. 2	•	•	•	C	C		•	
CAFÉ DE LA JATTE (NEUILLY) - IT. 3	•	•	•	C	C			12am
CAFÉ DES THÉÂTRES (2e) - IT. 5	D		•	•	•			12am
JACQUES CAGNA (7e) - IT. 1	L		•	•	*	•		
CAGOUILLE (14e) - IT. 2	•	•	•	•	*	•		
CALÈCHE (6e) - IT. 1			•	•	*	•		
CAMÉLÉON (6e) - IT. 2	•			•				12.30am
CAMPAGNE ET PROVENCE (5e) - IT. 2	D		•	•	•		•	
CARPACCIO (8e) - IT. 3	•	•	•	•		•		
CARRÉ DES FEUILLANTS (1er) - IT. 5	D		•	•	•	•		
CARTES POSTALES (1er) - IT. 5	D		•	•	•			
CASA BINI (6e) - IT. 1	D		•	•	*			12am
CASA PEPE (5e) - IT. 2	D	D	D	•	•			2am
CAVE PETRISSANS (17e) - IT. 3			•	•	*	•		
CÉLADON (2e) - IT. 5			•	•	•			
CÉLÉBRITÉS (15e) - IT. 1	•	•	•	•	•			
CENTRE GEORGES POMPIDOU (4e) - IT. 6	•	•	•	•	•	•		
CERF-VOLANT (15e) - IT. 1	•		•	•	•	•		
CHARDENOUX (11e) - IT. 6			•	•	•			
CHARLIE DE BAB-EL-OUED (17e) - IT. 3	•	•	•	•	•	•		
CHARLOT (9e) - IT. 7	•	•	•	•	•			1am
CHARPENTIERS (6e) - IT. 1	•	•	•	•	•	•		
CHARTIER (9e) - IT. 7	•	•	•	•	•			
CHAT GRIPPÉ (6e) - IT. 2	D		•	•		•		
CHATEAUBRIAND (10e) - IT. 7	•			•		•		
CHIBERTA (8e) - IT. 3			•	•			•	
CHIENG MAI (5e) - IT. 2	•		•	•	*		•	
BERNARD CHIRENT (1er) - IT. 5	D		•	•	•			
CIEL DE PARIS (15e) - IT. 2	•	•	•	•	•		•	12am FS
CLAVEL (5e) - IT. 2	•	L		•	*			
CLOS LONGCHAMP (17e) - IT. 3			•	•	*	•		
CLOS DES MORILLONS (15e) - IT. 1	D		•	•	*	•		
CLOSERIE DES LILAS (6e) - IT. 2	•	•	•	•	•			2am
CLOWN BAR (11e) - IT. 6	D		•	•				1.30am
CLUB MANHATTAN (EURODISNEY) - IT. 6	•		•	•	•		•	
COCHON D'OR (19e) - IT. 7	•	•	•	*	*	•		
COCONNAS (4e) - IT. 6	•	•	•	•	•	•		
COMPTOIR DU SAUMON (4e) - IT. 6	•		•	•	•	•		
CONTI (16e) - IT. 3			•	•	•			
COUGAR (17e) - IT. 3	D		•	•	*	•		
COUPOLE (14e) - IT. 2	•	•	•	•	•			2am
COURONNE (8e) - IT. 4			•	•	•	•		
CROISSANT (2e) - IT. 5	•		•	•	•	•		
DATCHA LYDIE (15e) - IT. 1	•	•	•	•	•			
DODIN-BOUFFANT (5e) - IT. 2	•		•	•	*		•	

	SATURDAY	SUNDAY	MONDAY	JULY	AUGUST	UNTIL 10PM	UNTIL 11PM	AFTER MIDNIGHT
DÔMARAIS (4e) - IT. 6	D			●	●		●	
DÔME (14e) - IT. 2	●	●		●	●			12.45am
DOMINIQUE (6e) - IT. 2	●	●	●	★	★	●		
DROUANT (2e) - IT. 5	●	●	●	●	●	●		
DUQUESNOY (7e) - IT. 1	D		●	●	●	●		
ÉCAILLE DU PCB (6e) - IT. 1	D		●	●	●		●	
ÉCAILLE ET PLUME (7e) - IT. 1	D		●	★	★	●		
ÉCHANSON (14e) - IT. 2	●			●	●	●		
CHEZ EDGARD (8e) - IT. 4	●		●	●	★			12.30am
ÉLYSÉES DU VERNET (8e) - IT. 3			●	★	★		●	
ÉLYSÉES-LENÔTRE (8e) - IT. 4	D		●	●	●	●		
ENTRE-SIÈCLE (15e) ?	D		●	●	●			
ENTRECÔTE-LE RELAIS DE VENISE (17e) - IT. 3	●	●		●	●	●		
ÉPOPÉE (15e) - IT. 1	D		●	●	●	●		
ERAWAN (15e) - IT. 1	●		●	●	●	●		
ESCARGOT-MONTORGUEIL (1er) - IT. 6	●	●		●	●			1.30am
ESPACE CHAMPAGNE (1er) - IT. 5	●	●	●	●	●		●	
ESPACE HÉRAULT - RABELAIS (5e) - IT. 2			●	●		●		
ESPADON (1er) - IT. 5	●	●	●	●	●		●	
ETCHEGORRY (13e) - IT. 2	●		●		●	●		
ÉTOILE MAROCAINE (8e) - IT. 3	●	●	●	●	●	●		
FAMIGLIA FULIGNA (17e) - IT. 3	D	●	●	●	●		●	
FAKHR EL DINE (8e) - IT. 4	●	●	●	●	●			
FARIGOULE (15e) - IT. 1	●		L	●	★	●		
GÉRARD FAUCHER (17e) - IT. 3	D		●	●	★	●		
HENRI FAUGERON (16e) - IT. 3	★		●	●		●		
FELLINI (1er) - IT. 6	●		●	●	●		●	
FERME SAINT-HUBERT (8e) - IT. 5	●		L	●	●		●	
FERME SAINT-SIMON (7e) - IT. 1	D		●	●	★	●		
FERMETTE MARBEUF (8e) - IT. 4	●	●	●	●	●		●	
CHEZ FERNAND (11e) - IT. 7	●		●	●	★			
JEAN-CLAUDE FERRERO (16e) - IT. 3	★		●	●	★	●		
FERRONNERIE (7e) - IT. 1	●		D	●	★			
FLORENCE (7e) - IT. 1	●		●	●	●	●		
FOC-LY (7e) - IT. 1	●	●	●	●	Mon		●	
FOLIES (11e) - IT. 7	D		●	●	★	●		
FOND DE COUR (4e) - IT. 6	D		●	●	●		●	
FOUQUET'S (8e) - IT. 4	●	●	●	●	●			2am
FOUQUET'S BASTILLE (12e) - IT. 6	●		●	●	●			12am
FOUQUET'S EUROPE (DÉFENSE) - IT. 3			●	●	●	●		
FOUTA TORO (18e) - IT. 7	●	●	●	●	●			1am
CHEZ FRANCIS (8e) - IT. 4	●	●	●	●	●			1am
FRENCH LINE (8e) - IT. 4	●	●	●	●	●			2am
GALLOPIN (2e) - IT. 5			●	●	●		●	
GAZELLE (17e) - IT. 3	●		●	●	●		●	
GÉORGIQUES (8e) - IT. 4	D		●	●	●	●		
GOLDENBERG (17e) - IT. 3	●	●	●	●				12am
JO GOLDENBERG (4e) - IT. 6	●	●	●	●	●			1am
GOUMARD-PRUNIER (1er) - IT. 5	●			●	●	●		
GOURMANDISE (12e) - IT. 6	●			●	★	●		

◆ OPENING TIMES

	SATURDAY	SUNDAY	MONDAY	JULY	AUGUST	UNTIL 10PM	UNTIL 11PM	AFTER MIDNIGHT
GRAND CAFÉ CAPUCINES (9e) - IT. 7	●	●	●	●				★
GRAND COLBERT (2e) - IT. 5	●	●	●	●	●			1am
GRAND LOUVRE (1er) - IT. 5	●	●	●	●		●		
GRAND VÉFOUR (1er) - IT. 5			●	●	●	●		
GRAND VENISE (15e) - IT. 1	●			●		●		
GRANDE CASCADE (16e) - IT. 3				●	★			
GRANDGOUSIER (18e) - IT. 7	D		●	●	●	●		
GRENADIN (8e) - IT. 3			●	★	●		●	
GRILLE SAINT-HONORÉ (1er) - IT. 5	●		D	●	★	●		
GRIZZLI (4e) - IT. 6	●		D	●	★		●	
GUINGUETTE DE NEUILLY - IT. 3	●	●	●	●	●			
GUY (6e) - IT. 1	●		●	●	●			12.45am
JACQUES HÉBERT (15e) - IT. 2	●			●	★	●		
IMPASSE (4e) - IT. 6	D		●	●	★	●		
IMPRIMERIE (4e) - IT. 6	●	D	●	●	●			12am
INCROYABLE (1er) - IT. 5	●		L	●		●		
INSTITUT DU MONDE ARABE (5e) - IT. 2	●			●				12am
JARDIN (8e) - IT. 3	●	●	●	●	●	●		
JARDIN DU PRINTEMPS (8e) - IT. 4	●		●	●	●		●	
JARDINS DE BAGATELLE (16e) - IT. 3	●	●	●	●	●		●	
CHEZ JENNY (3e) - IT. 6	●	●	●	●	●			1am
JOHNNY ROCK CAFÉ (8e) - IT. 4	●	●	●	●	●			
JULES VERNE (7e) - IT. 3	●	●	●	●	●	●		
JULIEN (10e) - IT. 7	●	●	●	●	●			1.30am
CHEZ JULIEN (4e) - IT. 6	●	L		●	●	●		
KAMBODGIA (16e) - IT. 3	D		●	●			●	
KASAPHANI (11e) - IT. 7	●	●	●	●			●	
KIM ANH (15e) - IT. 1	●	●	●	●	●		●	
KINUGAWA (1er) - IT. 5	●		●	●	●	●		
LAPÉROUSE (6e) - IT. 1	●		D	●	●	●		
LASSERRE (8e) - IT. 4	●		D	●	●			
LAURENT (8e) - IT. 4	D			●	●		●	
LE DIVELLEC (7e) - IT. 1	●			●	●	●		
LE DUC (14e)	●			●	●	●		
LEDOYEN (8e) - IT. 4			●	●	★	●		
LESCURE (1er) - IT. 5	L		●	●	●	●		
LIPP (6e) - IT. 1	●	●	●	●	●			1am
LOUBNANE (5e) - IT. 2	●	●	D	●	●			12am
LOUIS XIV (10e) - IT. 7	●	●	●	●	●			1am
LOUS LANDES (14e) - IT. 2	D		●	●	●	●		
LUCAS CARTON (8e) - IT. 5	D		●	●	●	●		
LUZ (7e) - IT. 1	D		●	●	★	●		
LYONNAIS (17e) - IT. 3	D		●	●	●	●		
MAIN À LA PÂTE (1er) - IT. 6	●		●	●	●	●		
MAISON D'AMÉRIQUE LATINE (7e) - IT. 1			●	●	●	summer		
MAISON DU DANEMARK (8e) - IT. 3	●	★	●	●		★	★	
MAISON DU VALAIS (8e) - IT. 5	●		●	●	★		●	
MANOIR DE PARIS (17e) - IT. 3	D		●	●	●	●		
MANSOURIA (11e) - IT. 6	●		D	●	●	●		
MANUFACTURE (ISSY) - IT. 2	D		●	●	●	●		

	SATURDAY	SUNDAY	MONDAY	JULY	AUGUST	UNTIL 10PM	UNTIL 11PM	AFTER MIDNIGHT
MARAÎCHER (4ᵉ) - IT. 6	D		●	●	★		●	
MARÉE (8ᵉ) - IT. 3			●	●		●		
MAXIM'S (8ᵉ) - IT. 5	●	D	●	●		●		
MAXIM'S (ORLY) - IT. 2			●	●	●	●		
MÉDITERRANÉE (6ᵉ) - IT. 2	●	●	●	●		●		
MERCURE GALANT (1ᵉʳ) - IT. 5	D		●	●	●	●		
DANIEL METERY (8ᵉ) - IT. 5			●	●	●	●		
MEURICE (1ᵉʳ) - IT. 5	●	●	●	●	●	●		
MINISTÈRES (7ᵉ) - IT. 1	●		●	●	●			12am
MIRAVILE (4ᵉ) - IT. 6	D	●	●	●	●	●		
MOI (16ᵉ) - IT. 3	●		D	●	●		●	
MOISSONNIER (5ᵉ) - IT. 2	●	L		●	●	●		
MOLLARD (8ᵉ) - IT. 7	●	●	●	●	●			1am
MONDE DES CHIMÈRES (4ᵉ) - IT. 2	●			●	●	●		
MONTPARNASSE 25 (14ᵉ) - IT. 2	●		●	●	●	●		
MONUMENTS (16ᵉ) - IT. 3	●	D	●				●	
MOROT-GAUDRY (15ᵉ) - IT. 1			●	●		●		
AL MOUNIA (16ᵉ) - IT. 3		●		★	●		●	
MUNICH (6ᵉ) - IT. 1	●	●	●	●				1.30am
MUSÉE D'ORSAY (7ᵉ) - IT. 1	L	L		●	●	★		
MUSES (9ᵉ) - IT. 7			●	●	●	●		
NAPOLÉON (8ᵉ) - IT. 3			●	●		●		
NAVARIN (11ᵉ) - IT. 6	D	L	●	●	●	●		
NIOULAVILLE (11ᵉ) - IT. 7	●	●	●	●	★			1am
ŒNOTHÈQUE (9ᵉ) - IT. 7			●	●	●	●		
OLYMPE (15ᵉ) - IT. 1	D	D					●	
ORANGERIE (4ᵉ) - IT. 2	●		●	●	★			1am
OULETTE (12ᵉ) - IT. 6	D		●	●	C	●		
OUM EL BANINE (16ᵉ) - IT. 3	D		●	●	●		●	
PACTOLE (5ᵉ) - IT. 2	D		●	●	●	●		
PARIS (6ᵉ) - IT. 1			●	●	●	★		★
PARIS-DAKAR (10ᵉ) - IT. 7	●	●		●				12am
CHEZ PAULINE (1ᵉʳ) - IT. 5	L		●	●	●	●		
PAVILLON DES PRINCES (16ᵉ) - IT. 3	●	●	●	●	★	●		
PAVILLON MONTSOURIS (14ᵉ) - IT. 2	●	●	●	●	●	●		
PAVILLON NOURA (8ᵉ) - IT. 4	●	●	●	●	●			12am
PAVILLON PUEBLA (19ᵉ) - IT. 7	●			●	●	★	★	
PERGOLÈSE (16ᵉ) - IT. 3			●	●	●		●	
PERRAUDIN (5ᵉ) - IT. 2	D		D	●		●		
PETIT BEDON (16ᵉ) - IT. 3			●	●	★		●	
PETIT COLOMBIER (17ᵉ) - IT. 3		D	●	●		●		
PETIT LAURENT (7ᵉ) - IT. 1	D		●	●	★	●		
PETIT MARGUERY (13ᵉ) - IT. 2	●			●	★	●		
PETIT MONTMORENCY (8ᵉ) - IT. 4			●	●		●		
PETIT RÉTRO (16ᵉ) - IT. 3	●		D			●		
PETIT RICHE (9ᵉ) - IT. 7	●			●				12.45am
PETIT ZINC (6ᵉ) - IT. 1	●	●	●	●	●			2am
PETITE BRETONNIÈRE (15ᵉ) - IT. 1	D		●	●	●	●		
PETITE COUR (6ᵉ) - IT. 1	●	●	●	●			●	
PETITE TOUR (16ᵉ) - IT. 3	●		●	●	●	●		

◆ Opening Times

	SATURDAY	SUNDAY	MONDAY	JULY	AUGUST	UNTIL 10PM	UNTIL 11PM	AFTER MIDNIGHT
PETITS CHANDELIERS (14e) - IT. 2	•	•	•	•	•		•	
PHARAMOND (1er) - IT. 6	•		•	•	•			
CHEZ PHILIPPE (11e) - IT. 7			D	•	•			
PIED DE COCHON (1er) - IT. 6	•	•	•	•	•			★
PIERRE «FONTAINE GAILLON» (2e) - IT. 5	D		•	•	•			12.30am
PIERRE AU PALAIS-ROYAL (1er) - IT. 5			•	•			•	
PLANTATION (12e) - IT. 6	•		•	•	•		•	
POÈTE IVRE (2e) - IT. 6	•		•	•	•			
POLIDOR (6e) - IT. 2	•	•	•	•	•		Sun	12.30am
POQUELIN (1er) - IT. 5	D		•	•	•			
PORT-ALMA (16e) - IT. 4	•		•	•	★	•		
POSTE (9e) - IT. 7	D		•	•				2am
POULE AU POT (7e) - IT. 1	D		•	•	•		•	
PRÉ CATELAN (16e) - IT. 3	•	L	•	•	•			
PRESSOIR (12e) - IT. 6				•	•			
PRINCE DE GALLES (8e) - IT. 4	•	•	•	•	•			
PRINTEMPS LA TERRASSE (9e) - IT. 7	L		L	L	•			
PRINCES (8e) - IT. 4	•	•	•	•	L	•		
PROCOPE (6e) - IT. 1	•	•	•	•	•			1am
P'TITE TONKINOISE (10e) - IT. 7	•		•	•	•			
QUACH (16e) - IT. 3	D	•		•			•	
QUAI OUEST (SAINT-CLOUD) - IT. 3	•	★	•	•	•			12am
YVES QUINTARD (15e) - IT. 2	D		•	•	•			
RAAJMAHAL (15e) - IT. 1	•	•	•	•	★	•		
RÉCAMIER (7e) - IT. 1	•		•	•	•			
RÉGENCE-PLAZA (8e) - IT. 4	•	•	•	•	•			
RELAIS D'AUTEUIL (16e) - IT. 3	D		•	•	•			
RELAIS DE SÈVRES (15e) - IT. 1			•	•	•		•	
RELAIS LOUIS XIII (6e) - IT. 1	•		•	★				
RELAIS-PLAZA (8e) - IT. 4	•	•	D	•	★	•		1.30am
LE RESTAURANT (18e) - IT. 7	•		•	•	•		•	
RESTAURANT A (5e) - IT. 2	•	•	D	•	•		•	
RESTAURANT DU MARCHÉ (15e) - IT. 1	D			•	•	•		
RESTAURANT OPÉRA (9e) - IT. 7			•	•	•		•	
RISTORANTE (17e) - IT. 3	•		•	•		•		
RIVER CAFÉ (ISSY) - IT. 2	•	•	•	•	★		•	
JOËL ROBUCHON (16e) - IT. 3			•	★	•	•		
ROI DU POT-AU-FEU (9e) - IT. 7	•		•	★	•			
MICHEL ROSTANG (17e) - IT. 3	★		•	•	★	•		
RÔTISSERIE D'ARMAILLÉ (17e) - IT. 3	D		•	•	•		•	
RÔTISSERIE D'EN FACE (6e) - IT. 1	D		•	•	•		•	
ROUDOULIÉ (11e) - IT. 6	D		•	•	•			
SAMARITAINE - LE GRILL (1er) - IT. 6	L		L	L	•			
SAN VALERO (NEUILLY) - IT. 3	D		•		L	•		
SAUDADE (1er) - IT. 6	•		•	•	•	•	★	
GUY SAVOY (17e) - IT. 3			•	•	•			
SÉBILLON-ÉLYSÉES (8e) - IT. 4	•	•	•	•	•			12am
SENTEURS DE PROVENCE (15e) - IT. 1	D		•	•	•			
CAROLL SINCLAIR (4e) - IT. 6	D	★	•	•	★	•		
SIPARIO (12e) - IT. 6	•		•	•	•			12am

	SATURDAY	SUNDAY	MONDAY	JULY	AUGUST	UNTIL 10PM	UNTIL 11PM	AFTER MIDNIGHT
SOFITEL (ROISSY) - IT. 7	●	●	●	●	★			1am
SOLOGNE (12e) - IT. 6	D		●	●	●			
SORMANI (17e) - IT. 3			●	●	●	●		
SOUS L'OLIVIER (8e) - IT. 4			●	●	●	●		
A SOUSCEYRAC (11e) - IT. 6			●	●	●	●		
SQUARE TROUSSEAU (12e) - IT. 6	●		●	●	●	●		
TABLE D'ANVERS (9e) - IT. 7	D		●	●			●	
TABLE DE PIERRE - IT. 3	L		●	●	★		●	3.30pm
TABLE RICHELIEU (11e) - IT. 6	D	●	●	●	●			
TAGHIT (14e) - IT. 2	●	●	●	●	●	●		12am
TAILLEVENT (8e) - IT. 3			●	★	●			
TAKA (18e) - IT. 7	●		●	●	★	●		
TAN DINH (7e) - IT. 1	●		●	●	●			
TANTE LOUISE (8e) - IT. 5			●	●	●		●	
TASHI DELEK (5e) - IT. 2	●		●	●	●	●		
TÉLÉGRAPHE (7e) - IT. 1	●	●	D	●	●	●		12.30am
TEMPS DE VIVRE (18e) - IT. 7	●	●	●	●	●			
TERMINUS NORD (10e) - IT. 7	●	●	●	●	●		●	12.30am
TIMONERIE (5e) - IT. 2	●	●	●	●	●			
TOIT DE PASSY (16e) - IT. 3	D		●	●	★	●		
TOTEM (16e) - IT. 3	●	L	●	●	●	●		2am
TOUR D'ARGENT (5e) - IT. 2	●	●	●	●	●			
TOUR DE MONTLÉRY (1er) - IT. 6	●	●	●	●	●	●		★
CHEZ TOUTOUNE (5e) - IT. 2	●		●	●	●			
TRAIN BLEU (12e) - IT. 6	●	●	D	●		●		
TRAKTIR (15e) - IT. 1	●	●	●		●	●		12am
TROU GASCON (12e) - IT. 6			D	●	★			
TY-COZ (9e) - IT. 7	●		●	●	●			
URI (15e) - IT. 1	●		●	●	●			
VAGENENDE (6e) - IT. 1	●	●	●	●	●	●		1am
VANCOUVER (8e) - IT. 3			●	●	●			
VASSANTI (14e) - IT. 2	●		●	●	●	●		
VAUDEVILLE (2e) - IT. 5	●	●	D	●	●	●		2am
VELLONI (1er) - IT. 6	●		●	●	●			
VENANTIUS (9e) - IT. 7	D	D	●	●	★	●		
VÉRO-DODAT (1er) - IT. 6	●		●	●	●			
CHEZ LA VIEILLE (1er) - IT. 6			●	●	★	●		
VIEUX MÉTIERS DE FRANCE (13e) - IT. 2	●		L	●				
VIGNES DU PANTHÉON (5e) - IT. 2	D			●	●	●		
VIN DES RUES (14e) - IT. 2	L		●	●	●		●	
VIN SUR VIN (7e) - IT. 1	D			●	★			
VISHNOU (14e) - IT. 2	●	●	D	●	★	●		★
VIVAROIS (16e) - IT. 3			●	●	●		●	
VONG (8e) - IT. 4	●		●	●	●	●		
WALLY LE SAHARIEN (4e) - IT. 2	●		●	●	●			
WEPLER (18e) - IT. 7	●	●	D	●	●		●	1am
WILLI'S (1er) - IT. 5	●		●	●	●			
YUGARAJ (6e) - IT. 1	●	●	●	●	●		●	
YVAN (8e) - IT. 2	D		D	●	●		●	12am
15, MONTAIGNE (8e) - IT. 4	D		●	●	●			12am

This table shows the price range for each restaurant. The prices are classified in ascending order from the cheapest to the most expensive.

À la carte prices are those for first quarter of 1993, including a starter, a main course and a dessert. **IT**. refer to itineraries

FROM	TO	
70	100	CHARTIER (9ᵉ) - IT. 7
80	110	ALEXANDROS (17ᵉ) - IT. 3
80	120	TASHI DELEK (5ᵉ) - IT. 2
80	140	CENTRE GEORGES-POMPIDOU (4ᵉ) - IT. 6
90	120	FOUTA TORO (18ᵉ) - IT. 7
90	120	POLIDOR (6ᵉ) - IT. 2
100	150	ENTRECÔTE- RELAIS DE VENISE (17ᵉ) - IT. 3
100	150	PERRAUDIN (5ᵉ) - IT. 2
100	150	TEMPS DE VIVRE - IT. 7
100	160	¡ AY CARAMBA ! (19ᵉ) - IT. 7
100	160	BISTRO DE LA GARE (6ᵉ) - IT. 2
100	170	LESCURE (1ᵉʳ) - IT. 5
100	180	CROISSANT (2ᵉ) - IT. 5
100	180	VIN DES RUES (14ᵉ) - IT. 2
120	150	GAZELLE (17ᵉ) - IT. 3
120	180	FERME SAINT-HUBERT (8ᵉ) - IT. 5
120	180	MUSÉE D'ORSAY (7ᵉ) - IT. 1
120	180	PETIT RÉTRO (16ᵉ) - IT. 3
120	220	INCROYABLE (1ᵉʳ) - IT. 5
120	220	MINISTÈRES (7ᵉ) - IT. 1
120	300	COMPTOIR DU SAUMON (4ᵉ) - IT. 6
120	300	TRAKTIR (15ᵉ) - IT. 1
130	200	BERRY'S (8ᵉ) - IT. 3
130	200	NIOULAVILLE (11ᵉ) - IT. 7
130	230	CLOWN BAR (11ᵉ) - IT. 6
140	170	KASAPHANI (11ᵉ) - IT. 7
140	200	PARIS-DAKAR (10ᵉ) - IT. 7
140	220	CERF-VOLANT (15ᵉ) - IT. 1
140	240	ASTIER (11ᵉ) - IT. 7
140	240	BRASSERIE FLO (10ᵉ) - IT. 7
140	240	FOLIES (11ᵉ) - IT. 7
140	250	CLUB MANHATTAN (EURODISNEY) - IT. 6
140	260	MOI (16ᵉ) - IT. 3
150	160	ROI DU POT-AU-FEU (9ᵉ) - IT. 7
150	180	PETITS CHANDELIERS (14ᵉ) - IT. 2
150	190	IMPRIMERIE (4ᵉ) - IT. 6
150	200	BENKAY (15ᵉ) - IT. 1
150	200	BOUCHUT (15ᵉ) - IT. 1
150	200	ÉCHANSON (14ᵉ) - IT. 2
150	200	GOLDENBERG (17ᵉ) - IT. 3
150	200	LOUBNANE (5ᵉ) - IT. 2
150	200	POULE AU POT (7ᵉ) - IT. 1
150	200	PRINTEMPS (9ᵉ - IT. 7
150	200	P'TITE TONKINOISE (10ᵉ) - IT. 7
150	200	RESTAURANT A (5ᵉ) - IT. 2
150	200	SAMARITAINE - LE GRILL (1ᵉʳ) - IT. 6
150	200	TAKA (18ᵉ) - IT. 7
150	220	ATLAS (5ᵉ) - IT. 2
150	220	CHARPENTIERS (6ᵉ) - IT. 1
150	220	CHIENG MAI (5ᵉ) - IT. 2

FROM	TO	
150	220	FARIGOULE (15e) - IT. 1
150	230	ETCHEGORRY (13e) - IT. 2
150	250	AUBERGE DE NICOLAS FLAMEL (3e) - IT. 6
150	250	BISTROT D'À CÔTÉ (17e) - IT. 3
150	250	BISTROT DE L'ÉTOILE-LAURISTON (16e) - IT. 3
150	250	BUTTE CHAILLOT (16e) - IT. 3
150	250	CAMÉLÉON (6e) - IT. 2
150	250	CHARDENOUX (11e) - IT. 6
150	250	DATCHA LYDIE (15e) - IT. 1
150	250	ESPACE HÉRAULT - RABELAIS (5e) - IT. 2
150	250	FELLINI (1er) - IT. 6
150	250	JO GOLDENBERG (4e) - IT. 6
150	250	GRIZZLI (4e) - IT. 6
150	250	JARDIN DU PRINTEMPS (8e) - IT. 4
150	250	MARAICHER (4e) - IT. 6
150	250	RIVER CAFÉ (ISSY) - IT. 2
150	250	ROUDOULIÉ (11e) - IT. 6
150	250	TAGHIT (14e) - IT. 2
150	380	CLOSERIE DES LILAS (6e) - IT. 2
160	200	SIPARIO (12e) - IT. 6
160	220	BALZAR (5e) - IT. 2
160	220	BAUMANN-TERNES (16e) - IT. 3
160	220	CASA BINI (6e) - IT. 1
160	230	BŒUF SUR LE TOIT (8e) - IT. 4
160	230	GUINGUETTE DE NEUILLY (NEUILLY-SUR-SEINE) - IT. 3
160	250	CALÈCHE (6e) - IT. 1
160	250	MUNICHE (6e) - IT. 1
160	250	PETIT ZINC (6e) - IT. 1
160	250	RÔTISSERIE D'ARMAILLÉ (17e) - IT. 3
160	260	AMBASSADE D'AUVERGNE (3e) - IT. 6
160	260	BRASSERIE DU LOUVRE (1er) - IT. 5
160	260	CABANON DES MAÎTRES NAGEURS (14e) - IT. 2
160	260	CHARLIE DE BAB-EL-OUED (17e) - IT. 3
160	260	DOMINIQUE (6e) - IT. 2
160	260	CHEZ FERNAND (11e) - IT. 7
160	260	PROCOPE (6e) - IT. 1
160	260	QUACH (16e) - IT. 3
160	280	AMOGNES (11e) - IT. 6
170	200	ANGELINA (1er) - IT. 5
170	220	VÉRO-DODAT (1er) - IT. 6
170	240	ÉPOPÉE (15e) - IT. 1
170	250	BRASSERIE MUNICHOISE (1er) - IT. 5
170	250	FAMIGLIA FULIGNA (17e)3
170	270	JULIEN (10e) - IT. 7
170	270	URI (15e) - IT. 1
170	280	LE RESTAURANT (18e) - IT. 7
170	300	CARTES POSTALES (1er) - IT. 5
180	200	PLANTATION (12e) - IT. 6
180	220	AUBERGE BASQUE (7e) - IT. 1
180	220	BISTROT DU PORT (5e) - IT. 2

349

◆ Prices

FROM	TO	
180	220	FRENCH LINE (8ᵉ) - IT. 4
180	220	MONUMENTS (16ᵉ) - IT. 3
180	250	BOFINGER (4ᵉ) - IT. 6
180	250	CAFÉ DES THÉÂTRES (2ᵉ) - IT. 5
180	250	CAVE PETRISSANS (17ᵉ) - IT. 3
180	250	ERAWAN (15ᵉ) - IT. 1
180	250	FERRONNERIE (7ᵉ) - IT. 1
180	250	FOC-LY (7ᵉ) - IT. 1
180	250	GUY (6ᵉ) - IT. 1
180	250	PETIT RICHE (9ᵉ) - IT. 7
180	250	RÔTISSERIE D'EN FACE (6ᵉ) - IT. 1
180	250	SQUARE TROUSSEAU (12ᵉ) - IT. 6
180	250	VASSANTI (14ᵉ) - IT. 2
180	250	VELLONI (1ᵉʳ) - IT. 6
180	250	VIGNES DU PANTHÉON (5ᵉ) - IT. 2
180	260	KAMBODGIA (16ᵉ) - IT. 3
180	260	PETIT LAURENT (7ᵉ) - IT. 1
180	260	YVAN (8ᵉ) - IT. 4
180	280	BARRAIL (15ᵉ) - IT. 1
180	280	BLUE ELEPHANT (11ᵉ) - IT. 6
180	280	BRASSERIE STELLA (16ᵉ) - IT. 3
180	280	CAMPAGNE ET PROVENCE (5ᵉ) - IT. 2
180	280	ÉTOILE MAROCAINE (8ᵉ) - IT. 3
180	280	GRANDGOUSIER (18ᵉ) - IT. 7
180	280	IMPASSE (4ᵉ) - IT. 6
180	280	MANUFACTURE (ISSY) - IT. 2
180	280	ŒNOTHÈQUE (9ᵉ) - IT. 7
180	280	PIED DE COCHON (1ᵉʳ) - IT. 6
180	280	POÈTE IVRE (2ᵉ) - IT. 6
180	280	SAUDADE (1ᵉʳ) - IT. 6
180	280	TOUR DE MONTLÉRY (1ᵉʳ) - IT. 6
180	280	TY-COZ (9ᵉ) - IT. 7
180	280	WILLI'S (1ᵉʳ) - IT. 5
180	300	COUPOLE (14ᵉ) - IT. 2
180	300	PIERRE «FONTAINE GAILLON»(2ᵉ) - IT. 5
180	320	WEPLER (18ᵉ) - IT. 7
180	380	PACTOLE (5ᵉ) - IT. 2
190	300	PAVILLON MONTSOURIS (14ᵉ) - IT. 2
190	320	SÉBILLON-ÉLYSÉES (8ᵉ) - IT. 4
200	220	MAISON DU VALAIS (8ᵉ) - IT. 5
200	250	CASA PEPE (5ᵉ) - IT. 2
200	250	ESPACE CHAMPAGNE (1ᵉʳ) - IT. 5
200	250	FERMETTE MARBEUF (8ᵉ) - IT. 4
200	250	GRAND COLBERT (2ᵉ) - IT. 5
200	250	MANSOURIA (11ᵉ) - IT. 6
200	260	VAGENENDE (6ᵉ) - IT. 1
200	300	AIGUIÈRE (11ᵉ) - IT. 6
200	300	ALSACE (8ᵉ) - IT. 4
200	300	ANTRE DU ROI PHILÈNE (16ᵉ) - IT. 3
200	300	BISTROT DE PARIS (7ᵉ) - IT. 1

FROM	TO	
200	300	CAFÉ DE LA JATTE (NEUILLY) - IT. 3
200	300	CLOS DES MORILLONS (15e) - IT. 1
200	300	CHEZ EDGARD (8e) - IT. 4
200	300	FAKHR EL DINE (8e) - IT. 4
200	300	FLORENCE (7e) - IT. 1
200	300	FOUQUET'S BASTILLE (12e) - IT. 6
200	300	CHEZ FRANCIS (8e) - IT. 4
200	300	INSTITUT DU MONDE ARABE (5e) - IT. 2
200	300	LIPP (6e) - IT. 1
200	300	MAISON D'AMÉRIQUE LATINE (7e) - IT. 1
200	300	MONDE DES CHIMÈRES (4e) - IT. 2
200	300	NAVARIN (11e) - IT. 6
200	300	PETITE COUR (6e) - IT. 1
200	300	QUAI OUEST (SAINT-CLOUD) - IT. 3
200	300	RAAJMAHAL (15e) - IT. 1
200	300	RISTORANTE (17e) - IT. 3
200	300	SENTEURS DE PROVENCE (15e) - IT. 1
200	300	TERMINUS NORD (10e) - IT. 7
200	300	VAUDEVILLE (2e) - IT. 5
200	300	CHEZ LA VIEILLE (1er) - IT. 6
200	320	MAIN À LA PÂTE (1er) - IT. 6
200	350	AUBERGE LANDAISE (9e) - IT. 7
200	350	BERNARD CHIRENT (1er) - IT. 5
200	350	ÉCAILLE ET PLUME (7e) - IT. 1
200	350	ESCARGOT-MONTORGUEIL (1er) - IT. 6
200	350	GRILLE SAINT-HONORÉ (1er) - IT. 5
200	350	POSTE (9e)
200	350	RELAIS-PLAZA (8e) - IT. 4
200	350	TABLE RICHELIEU (11e) - IT. 6
200	350	VONG (8e) - IT. 4
200	400	PETIT BEDON (16e) - IT. 3
210	210	TABLE DE PIERRE (17e) - IT. 3
220	250	CAROLL SINCLAIR (4e) - IT. 6
220	260	ANDROUET (8e) - IT. 7
220	260	CHEZ JENNY (3e) - IT. 6
220	280	SAN VALERO (NEUILLY-SUR-SEINE) - IT. 3
220	300	GALLOPIN (2e) - IT. 5
220	300	CHEZ JULIEN (4e) - IT. 6
220	300	CHEZ TOUTOUNE (5e) - IT. 2
220	300	VIN SUR VIN (7e) - IT. 1
220	320	BÉATILLES (17e) - IT. 3
220	320	DOMARAIS (4e) - IT. 6
220	320	FERME SAINT-SIMON (7e) - IT. 1
220	320	FOND DE COUR (4e) - IT. 6
220	320	GRENADIN (8e) - IT. 3
220	320	KIM ANH (15e) - IT. 1
220	320	LYONNAIS (17e) - IT. 3
220	320	MOISSONNIER (5e) - IT. 2
220	320	OUM EL BANINE (16e) - IT. 3
220	330	MOLLARD (8e) - IT. 7

◆ Prices

FROM	TO	
220	340	CIEL DE PARIS (15e) - IT. 2
220	350	AMUSE BOUCHE (14e) - IT. 2
220	350	BISTROT 121 (15e) - IT. 1
220	350	COCONNAS (4e) - IT. 6
220	350	ENTRE-SIÈCLE (15e)
220	350	GRAND CAFÉ CAPUCINES (9e) - IT. 7
220	350	RESTAURANT DU MARCHÉ (15e) - IT. 1
220	350	TANTE LOUISE (8e) - IT. 5
220	380	CHATEAUBRIAND (10e) - IT. 7
230	320	ÉCAILLE DU PCB (6e) - IT. 1
230	330	AMAZIGH (16e) - IT. 3
230	330	LOUIS XIV (10e) - IT. 7
230	330	LUZ (7e) - IT. 1
230	330	AL MOUNIA (16e) - IT. 3
230	330	PETITE TOUR (16e) - IT. 3
230	330	CHEZ PHILIPPE (11e) - IT. 7
230	350	PIERRE AU PALAIS-ROYAL (1er) - IT. 5
240	240	ARMAND AU PALAIS-ROYAL (1er) - IT. 5
240	340	OLYMPE (15e) - IT. 1
240	340	GRAND LOUVRE (1er) - IT. 5
240	350	POQUELIN (1er) - IT. 5
240	360	TAN DINH (7e) - IT. 1
240	380	GRAND VENISE (15e) - IT. 1
240	440	FOUQUET'S (8e) - IT. 4
250	340	VIEUX MÉTIERS DE FRANCE (13e) - IT. 2
250	350	ALLARD (6e) - IT. 1
250	350	CHAT GRIPPÉ (6e) - IT. 2
250	350	CLAVEL (5e) - IT. 2
250	350	DODIN-BOUFFANT (5e) - IT. 2
250	350	LOUS LANDES (14e) - IT. 2
250	350	DANIEL METERY (8e) - IT. 5
250	350	ORANGERIE (4e) - IT. 2
250	350	CHEZ PAULINE (1er) - IT. 5
250	350	PAVILLON NOURA (8e) - IT. 4
250	350	PHARAMOND (1er) - IT. 6
250	350	YVES QUINTARD (15e) - IT. 2
250	350	SOUS L'OLIVIER (8e) - IT. 4
250	350	SOUSCEYRAC (11e) - IT. 6
250	350	TÉLÉGRAPHE (7e) - IT. 1
250	350	VANCOUVER (8e) - IT. 3
250	350	VISHNOU (14e) - IT. 2
250	350	WALLY LE SAHARIEN (4e) - IT. 2
250	350	YUGARAJ (6e) - IT. 1
250	350	AUBERGADE (15e) - IT. 2
250	350	BELLECOUR (7e) - IT. 1
250	350	PETIT MARGUERY (13e) - IT. 2
250	400	ARMES DE BRETAGNE (14e) - IT. 2
250	400	COCHON D'OR (19e) - IT. 7
250	400	COURONNE (8e) - IT. 4
250	400	GOURMANDISE (12e) - IT. 6

FROM	TO	
250	400	KINUGAWA (1er) - IT. 5
250	400	TIMONERIE (5e) - IT. 2
250	400	CHARLOT (9e) - IT. 7
250	450	TROU GASCON (12e) - IT. 6
250	500	MÉDITERRANÉE (6e) - IT. 2
260	320	OULETTE (12e) - IT. 6
260	360	SOLOGNE (12e) - IT. 6
260	380	PETITE BRETONNIÈRE (15e) - IT. 1
270	370	PETIT COLOMBIER (17e) - IT. 3
270	400	PORT-ALMA (16e) - IT. 4
270	400	RÉCAMIER (7e) - IT. 1
280	320	PAVILLON DES PRINCES (16e) - IT. 3
280	380	JACQUES HÉBERT (15e) - IT. 2
280	400	BOURDONNAIS (7e) - IT. 1
280	400	MUSES (9e) - IT. 7
280	600	MANOIR DE PARIS (17e) - IT. 3
280	680	GÉRARD BESSON (1er) - IT. 6
290	400	CONTI (16e) - IT. 3
290	450	NAPOLÉON (8e) - IT. 3
290	600	MEURICE (16e) - IT. 5
300	400	BÛCHERIE (5e) - IT. 2
300	400	ÉLYSÉES DU VERNET (8e) - IT. 3
300	400	GÉRARD FAUCHER (17e) - IT. 3
300	400	RELAIS D'AUTEUIL (16e) - IT. 3
300	400	TRAIN BLEU (12e) - IT. 6
300	420	BENOÎT (4e) - IT. 6
300	450	ASSIETTE (14e) - IT. 2
300	500	CAGOUILLE (14e) - IT. 2
300	500	CÉLADON (2e) - IT. 5
300	500	DÔME (14e) - IT. 2
300	500	DROUANT (2e) - IT. 5
300	500	FOUQUET'S EUROPE (LA DÉFENSE) - IT. 3
300	500	JARDINS DE BAGATELLE (16e) - IT. 3
300	500	MAISON DU DANEMARK (8e) - IT. 3
300	500	PAVILLON PUEBLA (19e) - IT. 7
310	410	AUBERGE DES DEUX SIGNES (5e) - IT. 2
310	450	MERCURE GALANT (1er) - IT. 5
320	480	JARDIN (8e) - IT. 3
320	480	GÉORGIQUES (8e) - IT. 4
320	500	CARPACCIO (8e) - IT. 3
320	500	SORMANI (17e) - IT. 3
320	520	LAPÉROUSE (6e) - IT. 1
320	520	MOROT-GAUDRY (15e) - IT. 1
320	540	JEAN-CLAUDE FERRERO (16e) - IT. 3
350	450	COUGAR (17e) - IT. 3
350	450	PERGOLÈSE (16e) - IT. 3
350	450	SOFITEL (ROISSY) - IT. 7
350	480	PARIS (6e) - IT. 1
350	500	MIRAVILE (4e) - IT. 6
350	500	MONTPARNASSE 25 (14e) - IT. 2

◆ Prices

FROM	TO	
350	500	Pressoir (12e) - IT. 6
350	500	Régence-Plaza (8e) - IT. 4
350	500	Relais de Sèvres (15e) - IT. 1
350	500	Restaurant Opéra (9e) - IT. 7
350	500	Toit de Passy (16e) - IT. 3
350	550	Grand Véfour (1er) - IT. 5
350	550	Table d'Anvers (9e) - IT. 7
350	600	Maxim's (8e) - IT. 5
350	600	Maxim's (Orly) - IT. 2
350	700	Goumard-Prunier (1er) - IT. 5
360	460	Venantius (9e) - IT. 7
360	700	Le Duc (14e) - IT. 2
360	700	Petit Montmorency (8e) - IT. 4
370	450	Relais Louis XIII (6e) - IT. 1
370	500	15, Montaigne (8e) - IT. 4
380	580	Duquesnoy (7e) - IT. 1
390	600	Vivarois (16e) - IT. 3
390	700	Chiberta (8e) - IT. 3
400	600	Marée (8e) - IT. 3
400	600	Prince de Galles (8e) - IT. 4
400	650	Amphycles (17e) - IT. 3
400	650	Clos Longchamp (17e) - IT. 3
400	700	Apicius (17e) - IT. 3
400	700	Élysées-Lenôtre (8e) - IT. 4
420	600	Jules Verne (7e) - IT. 3
420	760	Ambassadeurs (8e) - IT. 5
450	600	Jacques Cagna (7e) - IT. 1
450	600	Grande Cascade (16e) - IT. 3
450	600	Taillevent (8e) - IT. 3
450	650	Célébrités (15e) - IT. 1
450	700	Espadon (1er) - IT. 5
450	750	Le Divellec (7e) - IT. 1
450	800	Lasserre (8e) - IT. 4
450	850	Arpège (7e) - IT. 1
500	600	Beauvilliers (18e) - IT. 7
500	700	Carré des Feuillants (1er) - IT. 5
500	700	Ledoyen (8e) - IT. 4
500	700	Princes (8e) - IT. 4
500	900	Ambroisie (4e) - IT. 6
520	700	Michel Rostang (17e) - IT. 3
550	1000	Joël Robuchon (16e) - IT. 3
550	700	Henri Faugeron (16e) - IT. 3
550	800	Guy Savoy (17e) - IT. 3
600	700	Bristol (8e) - IT. 4
600	900	Lucas Carton (8e) - IT. 5
600	900	Pré catelan (16e) - IT. 3
600	1000	Laurent (8e) - IT. 4
650	1000	Tour d'Argent (5e) - IT. 2

◆ MICHELIN STARS NOW AND TWENTY YEARS AGO

(1) This is now Joël Robuchon's restaurant.
(2) Formerly called "Pierre au Palais Royal."
(3) "L'Espadron" restaurant in the hotel.

	1973	1993
GRAND VÉFOUR	★★★	★★
LASSERRE	★★★	★★
MAXIM'S	★★★	
TAILLEVENT	★★★	★★★
TOUR D'ARGENT	★★★	★★★
VIVAROIS	★★★	★★
ALLARD	★★	
DROUANT	★★	★
LA MARÉE	★★	★
LAPÉROUSE	★★	
LEDOYEN	★★★	★
LUCAS-CARTON	★	★★★
A SOUSCEYRAC	★	★
AUBERGE DU VERT GALANT	★	
BENOÎT	★	★
BISTROT 121	★	
COCONNAS	★	
ESCARGOT-MONTORGUEIL	★	
FOUQUET'S	★	
GRAND VENISE	★	
JAMIN	★	★★★ (1)
LAURENT	★	★★
LE DUC	★	
PRINCES	★	★
LOUIS XIV	★	
PETIT MONTMORENCY	★	
PHARAMOND	★	★
PIERRE	★	★ (2)
RÉGENCE-PLAZA	★	★
RELAIS LOUIS XIII		★
RITZ		★★ (3)
AMBROISIE (1985)		★★★
AMBASSADEURS (1985)		★★
AMPHYCLES (1989)		★★
APICIUS (1984)		★★
ARPÈGE (1987)		★★
GÉRARD BESSON (1978)		★★
JACQUES CAGNA (1975)		★★
CARRÉ DES FEUILLANTS (1987)		★★
CHIBERTA (nc)		★★
CLOS LONGCHAMP (1988)		★★
DUQUESNOY (1987)		★★
FAUGERON (1977)		★★
GOUMARD-PRUNIER		★★
LE DIVELLEC (1983)		★★
MICHEL ROSTANG (1977)		★★
PRÉ CATELAN (1976)		★★
GUY SAVOY (nc)		★★

A	Argentina			C	Cambodia					
As	Ashkenazi (Jewish East European cuisine)			CH	Switzerland					
				Cy	Cyprus					
B	Brazil			G	Germany					
				Gr	Greece					

	NORTH AFRICA	BLACK AFRICA	AMERICAS, WEST INDIES	CHINA	JAPAN	INDIA	REST OF ASIA	ITALY	SOUTHERN EUROPE	REST OF EUROPE	MIDDLE EAST
ALEXANDROS (17e) - IT. 3									Gr		
AMAZIGH (16e) - IT. 3	●										
ANTRE DU ROI PHILÈNE (16e) - IT. 3								●			
ATLAS (5e) - IT. 2	●										
¡ AY CARAMBA ! (19e) - IT. 7			M								
BENKAY (15e) - IT. 1					●						
BLUE ELEPHANT (11e) - IT. 6						Th					
BRASSERIE MUNICHOISE (1er) - IT. 5										Al	
CARPACCIO (8e) - IT. 3								●			
CASA BINI (6e) - IT. 1								●			
CASA PEPA (5e) - IT. 2									S		
CERF-VOLANT (15e) - IT. 1						V					
CHARLIE DE BAB-EL-OUED (17e) - IT. 3	●										
CHATEAUBRIAND (10e) - IT. 7								●			
CHIENG MAI (5e) - IT. 2						Th					
COMPTOIR DU SAUMON (4e) - IT. 6										●	
DATCHA LYDIE (15e) - IT. 1										Ru	
DOMINIQUE (6e) - IT. 2										Ru	
ERAWAN (15e) - IT. 1							Th				
ÉTOILE MAROCAINE (8e) - IT. 3	●										
FAKHR EL DINE (8e) - IT. 4											●
FAMIGLIA FULIGNA (17e) - IT. 3								●			
FELLINI (1er) - IT. 6								●			
FLORENCE (7e) - IT. 1								●			
FOC-LY (7e) - IT. 1				●			Th				
FOLIES (11e) - IT. 7							C				
FOUTA TORO (18e) - IT. 7		●									
GAZELLE (17e) - IT. 3		●									
GOLDENBERG (17e) - IT. 3										As	
JO GOLDENBERG (4e) - IT. 6										As	
GRAND VENISE (15e) - IT. 1								●			
GUY (6e) - IT. 1			B								
INSTITUT DU MONDE ARABE (5e) - IT. 2	●										
JARDIN DU PRINTEMPS (8e) - IT. 4				●		V					
JOHNNY ROCK CAFÉ (8e) - IT. 4			US								
KAMBODGIA (16e) - IT. 3							C				
KASAPHANI (11e) - IT. 7									Cy		
KIM ANH (15e) - IT. 1						V					

	NORTH AFRICA	BLACK AFRICA	AMERICAS, WEST INDIES	CHINA	JAPAN	INDIA	REST OF ASIA	ITALY	SOUTHERN EUROPE	REST OF EUROPE	MIDDLE EAST
KINUGAWA (1er) - IT. 5					•						
LOUBNANE (5e) - IT. 2											•
MAIN À LA PATE (1er) - IT. 6								•			
MAISON DU DANEMARK (8e) - IT. 3										•	
MAISON DU VALAIS (8e) - IT. 5										CH	
MANSOURIA (11e) - IT. 6	•										
MOI (16e) - IT. 3							V				
AL MOUNIA (16e) - IT. 3	•										
NIOULAVILLE (11e) - IT. 7					•		•				
OUM EL BANINE (16e) - IT. 3	•	R									
PARIS-DAKAR (10e) - IT. 7		•	WI								
PAVILLON NOURA (8e) - IT. 4											•
PETITS CHANDELIERS (14e) - IT. 2											
PLANTATION (12e) - IT. 6											
POETE IVRE (2e) - IT. 6							Th				
P'TITE TONKINOISE (10e) - IT. 7							V				
QUACH (16e) - IT. 3				•			V				
RAAJMAHAL (15e) - IT. 1						•					
RESTAURANT A (5e) - IT. 2				•							
RISTORANTE (17e) - IT. 3								•			
SAN VALERO (NEUILLY-SUR-SEINE) - IT. 3									S		
SAUDADE (1er) - IT. 6									P		
SIPARIO (12e) - IT. 6								•			
SORMANI (17e) - IT. 3								•			
TAGHIT (14e) - IT. 2	•										
TAKA (18e) - IT. 7		A			•						
TAN DINH (7e) - IT. 1				•			M				
TASHI DELEK (5e) - IT. 2							Ti				
TEMPS DE VIVRE (18e) - IT. 7											
TRAKTIR (15e) - IT. 1										Ru	
URI (15e) - IT. 1 - IT. 1							K				
VASSANTI (14e) - IT. 2						•					
VELLONI (1er) - IT. 6								•			
VISHNOU (14e) - IT. 2						•					
VONG (8e) - IT. 4											
WALLY LE SAHARIEN (4e) - IT. 2	•			•							
YUGARAJ (6e) - IT. 1						•					

357

◆ Ten Specialties and Where to Find Them

	Andouillette	Bouillabaisse	Boudin	Cassoulet	Choucroute	Confit	Cheeses Soufflés	Fish Seafood	Pot-au-feu	Grills Meats
Alsace (8e) - IT. 4					•					•
Ambassade d'Auvergne (3e) - IT. 6	•		•							
Androuet (8e) - IT. 7							•			
Armes de Bretagne (14e) - IT. 2								•		
Assiette (14e) - IT. 2		•	•							
Auberge basque (7e) - IT. 1				•		•				
Auberge landaise (9e) - IT. 7				•		•				
Balzar (5e) - IT. 2					•			•		
Barrail (15e) - IT. 1				•						
Baumann-Ternes (16e) - IT. 3					•			•		
Bellecour (7e) - IT. 1	•									
Benoit (4e) - IT. 6				•						
Berry's (8e) - IT. 3	•									
Bistrot d'à Côté (17e) - IT. 3	•									•
Bœuf sur le Toit (8e) - IT. 4								•		•
Bofinger (4e) - IT. 6					•			•		
Brasserie Flo (10e) - IT. 7					•			•		
Brasserie munichoise (1er) - IT. 5					•					
Brasserie Stella (16e) - IT. 3					•					
Butte Chaillot (16e) - IT. 3										•
Cabanon des maîtres nageurs (14e) - 2								•		
Cagouille (14e) - IT. 2								•		
Caméléon - IT. 2	•					•				
Charpentiers (6e) - IT. 1		•								
Chardenoux (11e) - IT. 6	•									
Charlot (9e) - IT. 7		•						•		
Closerie des Lilas (6e) - IT. 2	•							•		
Cochon d'Or (19e) - IT. 7	•		•							•
Cougar (17e) - IT. 3								•		
Coupole (14e) - IT. 2	•							•		
Dodin-Bouffant (5e) - IT. 2								•		
Dôme (14e) - IT. 2		•						•		
Duquesnoy (7e) - IT. 1						•				
Écaille du PCB (6e) - IT. 1								•		
Entrecôte - Relais de Venise (17e) - 3										•
Escargot-Montorgueil (1er) - IT. 6	•									
Espace Hérault - Rabelais (5e) - IT. 2				•		•				
Etchegorry (13e) - IT. 2				•		•				
Farigoule (15e) - IT. 1		•								
Ferme Saint-Hubert (8e) - IT. 5								•		
Chez Francis (8e) - IT. 4								•		
Fouquet's Bastille (11e) - IT. 6	•							•		
Gallopin (2e) - IT. 5	•									
Goumard-Prunier (1er) - IT. 5		•						•		
Grand Café Capucines (9e) - IT. 7								•		

358

	Andouillette	Bouillabaisse	Boudin	Cassoulet	Choucroute	Confit	Cheeses, Soufflés	Fish, Seafood	Pot-au-feu	Grills, Meats
Grand Colbert (2e) - IT. 5	•									
Grand Louvre (1er) - IT. 5				•		•				
Grizzli (4e) - IT. 6				•		•				
Chez Jenny (3e) - IT. 6					•					
Julien (10e) - IT. 7				•						•
Le Divellec (7e) - IT. 1									•	
Le Duc (14e) - IT. 2									•	
Louis XIV (10e) - IT. 7								•		
Lous Landes (14e) - IT. 2				•		•				
Luz (7e) - IT. 1									•	
Maison du Valais (8e) - IT. 5							•			
Marée (8e) - IT. 3								•		
Méditerranée (6e) - IT. 2								•		
Moissonnier (5e) - IT. 2	•		•							
Mollard (8e) - IT. 7								•		
Muniche (6e) - IT. 1	•				•					
Oulette (12e) - IT. 6						•				
Chez Pauline (1er) - IT. 5										•
Œnothèque (9e) - IT. 7	•									
Petit Riche (9e) - IT. 7	•									
Petit Zinc (6e) - IT. 1					•					
Pharamond (1er) - IT. 6	•									
Chez Philippe (11e) - IT. 7				•		•				
Pied de Cochon (1er) - IT. 6	•				•					
Port-Alma (16e) - IT. 4								•		
Poule au pot (7e) - IT. 1	•									
Procope (6e) - IT. 1								•		
Roi du pot-au-feu (9e) - IT. 7									•	
Rôtisserie d'Armaillé (17e) - IT. 3										•
Rôtisserie d'en face (6e) - IT. 1	•									•
Roudoulié (11e) - IT. 6						•			•	
Sebillon-Élysées (8e) - IT. 4								•		
Senteurs de Provence (15e) - IT. 1		•						•		
Sousceyrac (11e) - IT. 6	•			•						
Table d'Anvers (9e) - IT. 7		•								
Table de Pierre (17e) - IT. 3						•				
Table Richelieu (11e) - IT. 6								•		
Terminus Nord (10e) - IT. 7					•			•		•
Train bleu (12e) - IT. 6	•									•
Trou gascon (12e) - IT. 6				•						•
Vancouver (8e) - IT. 3		•						•		
Vaudeville (2e) - IT. 5					•			•		
Chez la Vieille (1er) - IT. 6										•
Vin des rues (14e) - IT. 2	•								•	
Wepler (18e) - IT. 7										•

* At weekends only

	DAYS	WEEKS	MONTHS
AMBASSADEURS		1-2	
AMBROISIE			1
AMPHYCLES	3-4		
APICIUS	4		
ARPÈGE		1	
GÉRARD BESSON	3-4		
BLUE ELEPHANT	3-4		
CARRÉ DES FEUILLANTS	8-10		
CARTES POSTALES		1	
ÉLYSÉES DU VERNET	4-5		
HENRI FAUGERON	4-5		
FERMETTE MARBEUF	4-5		
FLORENCE	2-4		
GRAND VÉFOUR	3		
JULES VERNE			1-2
LASSERRE		2	
LE DIVELLEC	3-4		
LUCAS CARTON		1	
MAIN À LA PÂTE	3-4		
MIRAVILE		1 *	
ORANGERIE	8		
PAVILLON MONTSOURIS	3 (summer)		
PRÉ CATELAN	3	2 (summer)	
JOËL ROBUCHON			2
GUY SAVOY		2	
TAILLEVENT			1
TOUR D'ARGENT			1
YVAN	4-5		
15, MONTAIGNE	5		

COMPULSORY BOOKING

Although restaurants have been particularly affected by the recession, you are still advised to book your table the day before, particularly at weekends. The bigger your party, the more essential it is to book. In some establishments that attract an international clientele or where the number of places is limited it is necessary to book a long time in advance. The periods referred to in the table give an indication: busy times are subject to seasonal variations; restaurants with a terrace or garden are particularly sought after in summer, as are restaurants such as the *Jules Verne* in the Eiffel Tower, which attracts many tourists. However, irrespective of the season, you can be lucky and find a quiet day. But you should not be under any illusions for restaurants such as *Joël Robuchon* or *Tour d'Argent*, which are sometimes full several months in advance. A word of advice if you are disappointed: try lunchtime, which is often less crowded. Also "business meals" or other offers are often a godsend.

350
RESTAURANTS

AU BON COIN

The following pages list more than 350 restaurants grouped under seven itineraries and in alphabetical order. Included are the hundred restaurants listed on pages 128-272, the twenty restaurants in the Foreign cuisine section (pages 273-304) and under French specialties (pages 305-312) and over two hundred other establishments. As many restaurants again are listed from page 333 onward.

For ease of reference, establishments are listed alphabetically, disregarding "le", "la", "les". Now it is just a matter of picking a restaurant from this wide range of Parisian eateries where you are going to treat yourself!

DIFFERENT CUISINES

Each entry is followed by a summary of the main theme of the restaurant.

BOURGEOIS
Traditional with distinctive atmosphere.
GASTRONOMIC
"Innovative" *haute cuisine*.
HOME COOKING
Traditional cooking.

CLASSIC
Literal interpretation.
FISH
Specializing in fish and seafood.
LYONNAIS,
VIETNAMESE, etc.
As the name indicates.

NOTES AND UPDATE

A few blank pages for you to record your personal impressions and add your own discoveries.

This section begins with updates certain restaurants have sent us since research was done ◆ 416.

ITINERARIES

The seven itineraries follow the same routes as those in the Gastronomic Itineraries section between pages 121 and 272, which describes the décor, history, food and general atmosphere of more than 100 memorable restaurants. The *arrondissements* are separated or grouped together as applicable. The descriptions of restaurants in the listings that follow reflect the honest opinions of our researchers at the time they visited the establishment, but a change of chef or of management could make all the difference, so do try them for yourself.

INDEX ◆ 433

This will help you to find the page and the itinerary relating to the restaurant you are looking for. The names of restaurants

included in the address book and in **Restaurants on and beside the Water** ◆ 326 are printed in bold type.

KEY TO SYMBOLS

	Credit cards		Garden
CB	Visa		Terrace
AE	American Express		Swimming pool
MC	Master Card		View
	Eurocard		Air conditioning
			Dining-room
			No animals
			Private car park
			Car valet

Miniature maps at the beginning of each itinerary show the relevant district(s). These maps are divided into frames indicating the different sections of the itinerary and the pages where more detailed maps corresponding to these divisions can be found.

SUBWAY
M: the closest subway station to the restaurant.

Each itinerary includes several maps on which the restaurants are indicated by a number. These numbers, which precede the name of the restaurant, are repeated in a white frame beneath each map.

ITINERARY 5 ◆

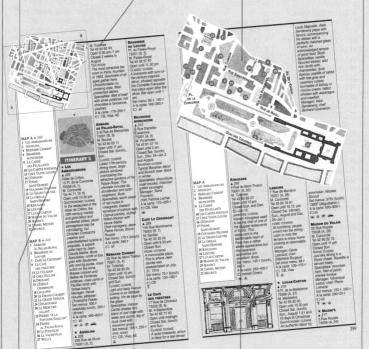

BRASSERIE DU LOUVRE
Pl. du Palais-Royal
75001 (B, 5)
M. Palais-Royal
Tel 44 58 37 87
Open until 11.30 pm
CLASSIC CUISINE
A brasserie with turn-of-the-century-inspired décor, situated opposite the Comédie Française that stays open after the show. Bar open until 1 am
Set menu: 95 f, 160 f
A la carte: 160–260 f
all

M. Tuileries
Tel 42 60 82 00
Open 9.30 am–7 pm
Closed 2 weeks in August
TEA ROOM
The most attractive tea room in Paris, founded in 1803. Gourmets of all ages gather here. Uncontestable no-smoking area. Well presented dishes. Specialties: filet of beef with straw potatoes, hot chocolate à l'ancienne, pastries.
A la carte: 170–200 f
CB, Visa, AE

MAP A ▲ 399
1 LES AMBASSADEURS
2 ANGELINA
4 BERNARD CHIRENT
5 BRASSERIE MUNICHOISE
9 LE CARRÉ DES FEUILLANTS
10 LES CARTES POSTALES
13 CHEZ TANTE LOUISE
15 L'ESPADON
17 FERME SAINT-HUBERT
21 GOUMARD-PRUNIER
22 LE GRAND LOUVRE
23 LA GRILLE SAINT-HONORÉ
26 KINUGAWA
28 LESCURE
27 LUCAS-CARTON
28 MAISON DU VALAIS
31 MAXIM'S
33 DANIEL MÉTERY
32 MEURICE

MAP B ▲ 400
3 ARMAND AU PALAIS-ROYAL
6 BRASSERIE DU LOUVRE
7 CAFÉ LE CROISSANT
8 CAFÉ DES THÉÂTRES
11 LE CELADON
12 CHEZ PAULINE
14 DROUANT
15 L'ESSENCE CHAMPAGNE
18 LE GALLIPOT
19 LE GRAND COLBERT
22 LE GRAND VÉFOUR
21 L'INCROYABLE
24 LA GRILLE
30 LE MERCURE GALANT
32 PIERRE "À LA FONTAINE GAILLON"
34 PIERRE AU PALAIS-ROYAL
35 LE POQUELIN
36 LE VAUDEVILLE
37 WILLI'S

ITINERARY 5

ARMAND AU PALAIS-ROYAL
▲ 222
2-6 Rue de Beaujolais
75001 (B, 4)
M. Bourse
Tel 42 60 05 11
Open until 11 pm
Closed Sat. (lunch), Sun.
CLASSIC CUISINE
Listed 17th-century dining-room, large windows overlooking the attractive gardens of the Palais-Royal. The clientele includes its stockbroker and actor neighbors. Book. Specialties: warm salad of red mullet in vinaigrette, braised escalope of salmon with Cyprus parsley, stuffed fatted chicken with sauce diable.
Manager: René Pouverin; chef: Fabrice Lechat
A la carte: 170–220 f
all

CAFÉ LE CROISSANT
▲ 209
146 Rue Montmartre
75002 (B, 7)
M. Sentier
Tel 42 33 35 04
Open until 8.30 pm
Closed Sun.
HOME COOKING
A memorable place. This is where Jean Jaurès was assassinated on July 31, 1914.
Set menu: 70 f (lunch)
A la carte: 100–180 f
all

BERNARD CHIRENT
▲ 209
28 Rue du Mont Thabor
75001 (A, 4)
M. Tuileries
Tel 42 60 60 05
Open until 10 pm
Closed Sat. (lunch) and Sun.
CLASSIC CUISINE
Light and tasty French cuisine in an intimate setting. Vin de pays Cantal cheese tart, blanc of cod roast with leeks and cumin, leg of duck civet with macaroni gratin.
Set menu: 185 f, 250 f (incl. wine)
CB, Visa, AE

LE CAFÉ DES THÉÂTRES
▲ 209
17 Rue de Choiseul
75002 (B, 8)
M. 4-Septembre
Tel 42 65 77 40
Open until midnight
Closed Sat. and Sun.
CLASSIC CUISINE
A quiet brasserie, which is ideal for a late dinner

▲ **ANGELINA**
▲ 228
226 Rue de Rivoli
75001 (A, 2)

396

Louis Majorelle. Alain Senderens plays with flavors, accompanying his dishes with a perfectly matched glass of wine. An acknowledged temple of good food. Book. Specialties: vanilla-flavored lobster, wild rice risotto with chanterelles, duck Apicius, pastilla of rabbit with foie gras and rosemary cutlets, tournedos of kidney in chorizo cream, fatted chicken with apple and endives.
Manager: Alain Senderens; chef: Bertrand Guéneron;

MAP A
1 LES AMBASSADEURS
2 ANGELINA
4 BERNARD CHIRENT
5 BRASSERIE MUNICHOISE
9 LE CARRÉ DES FEUILLANTS
10 LES CARTES POSTALES
13 CHEZ TANTE LOUISE
15 L'ESPADON
17 FERME SAINT-HUBERT
21 GOUMARD-PRUNIER
22 LE GRAND LOUVRE
23 LA GRILLE SAINT-HONORÉ
26 KINUGAWA
28 LESCURE
27 LUCAS-CARTON
28 MAISON DU VALAIS
31 MAXIM'S
33 MEURICE

KINUGAWA
▲ 282
9 Rue du Mont Thabor
75001 (A, 26)
M. Concorde
Tel 42 60 65 07
Open until 10 pm
Closed Sun. and Dec. 20–Jan.10
JAPANESE CUISINE
Kiyoshi Kinugawa used to be the chef of one of the biggest restaurants in Kyoto. This restaurant in the fashionable heart of Paris has a rather stylish appearance but the Japanese specialties are excellent. Book.
Set menu: 145 f (lunch), 250–450 f
A la carte: 250–400 f
except Diners

LESCURE
▲ 1 Rue de Mondovi
75001 (A, 26)
M. Concorde
Tel 42 60 18 91
Open until 10.15 pm
Closed Sun. (dinner), Sun. August and Dec. 25–Jan.1
HOME COOKING
At lunchtime, people crowd into the dining-room or onto the terrace to enjoy home cooking at reasonable prices.
Manager: Denis Lascaut; chef: Stéphane Burgaud
Set price menu: 98 f
A la carte: 150–170 f
all

★ **LUCAS-CARTON**
▲ 216
9 Place de la Madeleine
75008 (A, 27)
M. Madeleine
Tel 42 60 22 90
Open until 10.30 pm
Closed Sat. (lunch), Sun., August 1-21 and Christmas
GASTRONOMIC CUISINE
An authentic décor by

sommelier: Nicolas Bonnot
Set menu: 375f (lunch) 1300f (dégustation.)
A la carte: 600–900 f
all

MAISON DU VALAIS
20 Rue Royale
75008 (A, 28)
M. Concorde
Tel 42 60 22 72
Open until 11 pm
Closed Sun.
SWISS CUISINE
Just like dining in a Swiss chalet. Raclette is served freely. Specialties: mountain ham, filet of perch, cheese fondue.
Manager: Véronique Leduc; chef: Pierre Lemarle
Set menus: 150 f, 200 f
A la carte: 200–20 f
all

★ **MAXIM'S**
▲ 217
3 Rue Royale
75008 (A, 29)

399

★ **THE EDITOR'S FAVORITES**
A restaurant whose history, location, decoration and food are particularly appealing, interesting or attractive.

▲ **CROSS-REFERENCES**
Cross-referencing to a hundred memorable restaurants and those offering foreign cuisine or specialties indicates where they are described and where other information is given.

The letter and number that follow the address of each restaurant in the listing identifies the restaurant on the map.

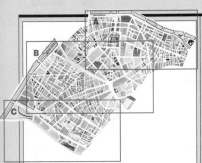

ITINERARY 1

ALLARD
▲ 144
41 Rue Saint-André-
des-Arts
75006 (A, 1)
M. St-Michel
Tel. 43 26 48 23
Open until 10 pm.
Closed Sun., Dec. 23–
Jan. 2 and August
BOURGEOIS CUISINE
*Turn-of-the-century
establishment with
original décor offering
bistro fare to a
cosmopolitan clientele.
Well-chosen "everyday"
wines. However, it is
expensive.*
Set menu: 150 F (lunch),
200 F
A la carte: 250–350 F
▭ all

★ **L'ARPÈGE**
▲ 137
84 Rue de Varenne
75007 (A, 2)
M. Varennes
Tel. 45 51 47 33
Open until 10.30 pm
Closed Sat. and Sun.
(lunch)
GASTRONOMIC CUISINE
*Minimalist and elegant
décor in keeping with
the meticulous
preparations of a
virtuoso chef, Alain
Passard. Service
impeccable. The set
lunch menu is
recommended. Open on
Sunday evenings, a
godsend! Book.
Specialties: Dublin Bay
prawns with caviar,
braised sea bass with
clams, lamb with truffle
fondue, "Louise
Passard" duck, tomate
confite aux douze
saveurs.
Manager: Alain Passard*
Set menus: 390 F
(lunch), 890 F (dinner)
A la carte: 450–850 F
▭ all

L'AUBERGADE
53 Av. de
La Motte-Picquet
75015 (B, 3)
M. La Motte-Picquet
Tel. 47 83 23 85
Open until 10.30 pm
Closed Sun. (dinner),
Mon., Dec. 27–Jan, 5
Easter and August
CLASSIC CUISINE
*Notable for holding its
prices and the quality of
its cuisine and
welcome.The menu has
two sources of
inspiration: Italy and
France. Interesting
lunch menu.
Specialties: salad of
skate with shellfish oil,
cassoulet of Dublin Bay
prawns and lobster
quenelles, sweet and
sour fillets of barbary
duckling in honey.
Managers: Pierre and
Rosanna Moisson; chef:
Jérôme Gaudin*
Set menu: 150 F (lunch)
A la carte: 250–380 F
▭ CB, Visa, AE
⌖

L'AUBERGE BASQUE
51 Rue de Verneuil
75007 (A, 4)
M. Solférino
Tel. 45 48 51 98
Open until 10.30 pm
Closed Sun. and
August
BASQUE CUISINE
*Authentic Basque
cuisine, a favorite with
connoisseurs for its
food and friendly
welcome. Local wines.
Specialties: piperade,
chipirons, duck dishes
such as magret and
confit, cassoulet.
Manager: Mrs Arraté;
chef: Michel Drouin*
Set menus: 105 F, 140 F
A la carte: 180–220 F
▭ CB, Visa
♨

★ **AUX
CHARPENTIERS**
▲ 131
10 Rue Mabillon
75006 (A, 5)
M. Mabillon
Tel. 43 26 30 05
Open until 11.30 pm
Closed Sun. and bank
holidays
HOME COOKING
*Established in 1874.
décor by master
craftsmen of the
Compagnons du Devoir.
Good setting, warm
welcome and interesting
wines.
Manager: Pierre
Bardèche; chef: Mr
Grondin*

A la carte: 150–220 F
▭ all

AUX SENTEURS DE PROVENCE
▲ 308
295 Rue Lecourbe
75015 (C, 6)
M. Balard
Tel. 45 57 11 98
Open until 10 pm
Closed Sat. (lunch),
Sun. and August 1–21
PROVENÇAL CUISINE
Modern, plush
surroundings. A daily
changing menu of
dishes that evoke the
smells of Provence
together with vins de
pays.
Specialties: aïoli,
bouillabaisse, bourride,
pieds paquets.
Manager: Leonardo
Dell'Omo
Chef: Frédéric Cabart

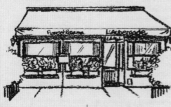

Set menu: 148 F (except
Fri. and Sat. dinner)
A la carte: 200–300 F
▭ all
⚓

LE BARRAIL
17 Rue Falguière
75015 (B, 7)
M. Pasteur
Tel. 43 22 42 61
Open until 10 pm
Closed Sat. and Sun.
CLASSIC CUISINE
The "Le Monde"
journalists' canteen.
Uninspiring décor but
the food is good, both
classic and innovative.
It is also reasonably
priced.
Set menus: 100 F, 150 F
▭ CB, Visa, AE, Euroc
▨ ☯ ⚘

LE BELLECOUR
22 Rue de Surcouf
75007 (A, 8)
M. Latour-Maubourg
Tel. 45 51 46 93
or 45 55 68 38
Open until 10.30 pm
Closed Sat. (lunch),
Sun. and August 1–30
LYONNAIS CUISINE
Charming old-fashioned
style bistro. Lyonnais

specialties recreated by
chef Denis Groset
and fine Burgundy
wines.
Specialties:
Lyonnais salads, roast
monkfish tail with three
types of cabbage,
boned and browned
saddle of rabbit with
turnips and mushrooms.
Manager: Gérald
Goutagny ;
Chef: Denis Croset
Set menus: 160 F, 250 F
(lunch weekdays.),
380 F
A la carte: 250–380 F
▭ all
▨ ☯

LE BENKAY
▲ 292
Hôtel Nikko
61 Quai de Grenelle
75015 (B, 9)
M. Bir-Hakeim

Tel. 40 58 21 26
Open until 10 pm
JAPANESE CUISINE
Modern Japanese
décor. Good views of
the Seine. Book.
Specialties: raw fish,
tempuras, grilled meats.
Manager: Mr Sato; chef:
Mr Chihara
Set menus: 130 F,
235 F, 300 F (lunch),
540 F, 590 F, 690 F
(dinner)
A la carte: 350–450 F
▭ all
▣ ⚲ ▨ ☯

LE BISTROT 121
121 Rue de la
Convention
75015 (B, 10)
M. Javel
Tel. 45 57 52 90
Open until midnight
CLASSIC CUISINE
1970's décor by Slavik,
generous servings and
pleasant wines at
reasonable prices.
Unfortunately, an air of
boredom prevails.
Specialties: escalope of
warm duck liver with
verjuice, whole grilled
calves' kidneys, leg of
rabbit with cider vinegar.

Managers: Pascal
and Stéphane Mousset;
chef: André Galbert
Set menus: 200 F, 285 F
(incl. wine and coffee)
A la carte: 220–350 F
▭ all
☯

LE BISTROT DE PARIS
▲ 143
33 Rue de Lille
75007 (A, 11)
M. Rue de Bac
Tel. 42 61 16 83
Open until 10.30 pm
Closed Sat. (lunch),
Sun, Dec 24- Jan. 2
BOURGEOIS CUISINE
Michel Oliver has
become famous for
demonstrating his
recipes on television.
His restaurant offers
classic cuisine and
excellent value for
money.
A la carte: 200–300 F
▭ CB, Visa, Euroc
▨

LE BOUCHUT
9 Rue Bouchut
75015
M. Sèvres-Lecourbe
Tel. 45 67 15 65
Open until 10.30 pm
Closed Sat. (lunch),
Sun. and August
HOME COOKING
A good local bistro for
enjoying good food in
peaceful surroundings.
Pleasant wines from the
Loire.
Set menu: 158 F
A la carte: 150–200 F
▭ CB, Visa
⚓

LE BOURDONNAIS
113 Av. de la
Bourdonnais
75007 (A, 13)
M. École Militaire
Tel. 47 05 47 96
Open until 11 pm
GASTRONOMIC CUISINE
Cozy décor, imaginative
and meticulous cooking
by Philippe Bardeau.
Delightful welcome from

Micheline Coat. Book.
Specialties: wild
mushroom vol-au-vent
with fumet of
chanterelles, grilled
John Dory with
barigoule of artichokes,
roast fillet of beef with
black pepper and subtle
garlic fritters.
Manager: Micheline
Coat
Set menus: 220 F
(lunch), 280 F (dinner),
380 F
A la carte: 280–400 F
▭ all
⚓ ▨ ☯

LA CALÈCHE
8 rue de Lille
75007 (A, 14)
M. Rue de Bac
Tel. 42 60 24 76
Open until 10.30 pm
Closed Sat., Sun., Dec
24-Jan. 2
and 3 weeks Aug.
CLASSIC CUISINE
This friendly
establishment in the
heart of the publishing
area is patronized by
writers and publishers.
Hearty food.
Manager: Michel
Pouget
Set menus: 130 F, 170 F
A la carte: 160–250 F
▭ all

CASA BINI
▲ 274
36 Rue Grégoire-
de-Tours
75006 (A, 15)
M. Odéon
Tel. 46 34 05 60
Open until 11 pm
Closed Sat. (lunch),
Sun., Christmas week
and Aug. 1–21
ITALIAN CUISINE
Attractive

Mediterranean décor, simple and very careful cuisine, using excellent ingredients. Two types of pasta, which change daily. Tuscan wines. Specialties: carpaccios, crostinis and pastas. Managers: Mrs Bini and Mrs Laurent; chef: Salvatore Esposito
Set menus: 130 F (lunch), 150 F (lunch)
A la carte: 160–220 F
▢ all
♨

★ LES CÉLÉBRITÉS
Hôtel Nikko
61 Quai de Grenelle
75015 (B, 16)
M. Bir-Hakeim
Tel. 40 58 21 28
Open until 10 pm
GASTRONOMIC CUISINE
Chic décor, good view of the Seine, smooth service and French gastronomy by Jacques Sénéchal, formerly of La Tour d'argent. Delicious desserts and excellent wines. Specialties: green asparagus and fresh morels in cream, warm salad of roast Dublin Bay prawns and chanterelles, bass in pepper, braised knuckle of veal with baby vegetables. Manager: Manuel Toncé
Set menus: 280 F, 680 F
A la carte: 350–550 F
▢ all
▣ ▦ ♨ ☀

LE CERF-VOLANT
▲ 296
1 Rue Nicolas-Charlet
75015 (B, 17)
M. Pasteur
Tel. 45 66 88 62
Open until 11 pm
Closed Sun. and August
VIETNAMESE CUISINE
Tasty fare at reasonable prices. An original cuisine without glutamate.
Set menus: 80 F, 105 F, 150 F (dinner), 220 F
A la carte: 140–220 F
▢ CB, Visa

LE CLOS DES MORILLONS
50 Rue des Morillons
75015 (C, 18)
M. Convention
Tel. 48 28 04 37
Open until 10.15 pm
Closed Sat. (lunch), Sun., Feb. 22-28 and August 8–24

GASTRONOMIC CUISINE
A quiet meeting-place in a tranquil backwater. Subtle cuisine by Philippe Delacourcelle. Good Loire wines. Specialties: baby potatoes stuffed with matelote of oysters, fillets of red mullet studded with orange rind and tapenade of dried tomatoes, saddle of rabbit with gratin of pumpkin in dill confit.
Set menus: 160 F (lunch), 230 F, 285 F
A la carte: 200–300 F
▢ CB, Visa, AE
♨

DATCHA LYDIE
▲ 280
7 Rue Dupleix
75015 (B, 19)
M. Dupleix
Tel. 45 66 67 77
Open until 10 pm
Closed Wed. and July 12–Sept 2.
RUSSIAN CUISINE
Friendly welcome and traditional fare prepared with care. Specialties: bortsch, smoked fish, fillet of beef Strogonoff.

Manager: Lydie Demme; chef: Daniel Demme
Set menu: 125 F
A la carte: 150–250 F
▢ CB, Visa

★ LE DIVELLEC
▲ 142
107 Rue de l'Université (corner of Rue Fabert)
75007 (A, 20)
M. Assemblée Nationale
Tel. 45 51 91 96
Open until 10 pm
Closed Sun., Dec 24-Jan. 4
FISH CUISINE
A fish restaurant frequented by fashionable Parisians. Impressive lobster press created by Christofle. Book. Specialties: seafood, sea bass roast in its

skin with confit of shallots, pan-fried red mullet with lettuce purée. Chef-manager: Jacques Le Divellec; sommelier: Pierre Laroche
Set menus: 270 F, 370 F (lunch)
A la carte: 450–750 F
▢ all
♨ ▣ ✗

DUQUESNOY
6 Av. Bosquet
75007 (A, 21)
M. École Militaire
Tel. 47 05 96 78
Open until 10.30 pm
Closed Sat. (lunch), Sun. and August 1-15
GASTRONOMIC CUISINE
Attractive light wood-paneled dining-room, perfect ingredients carefully prepared by

Jean-Paul Duquesnoy.
Faultless service, fine
Burgundies, good lunch
menu.
Specialties: creamy fish
soup with black truffle,
crispy scallops with
sesame, duck confit
and liver with truffle and
stuffed green cabbage.
Sommelier:
Mrs Duquesnoy
Set menus: 250 F
(weekday lunch), 420 F,
520 F
A la carte: 380–580 F
▢ CB, Visa, AE
☺

L'ÉCAILLE DU PCB
5 Rue Mabillon
75006 (A, 22)
M. Mabillon
Tel. 43 26 12 84
Open until 11 pm.
Closed Sat. (lunch) and
Sun.
FISH CUISINE
*The fish prepared by
the self-taught Pierre
Bardèche are redolent
of the Mediterranean.
Health-conscious
dishes.*
Good lunch menu.
Book.
Specialties: escabèche
of fresh sardines,
tureen of scallops
thickened with garlic
cream, Oriental-style
~onkfish osso-buco

Managers: Pierre and
Colette Bardèche
Set price menus: 125 F
(lunch), 210 F
A la carte: 230–320 F
▢ except Diners
☺

ÉCAILLE ET PLUME
25 Rue Duvivier
75007 (A, 23)
M. École Militaire
Tel. 45 55 06 72
Open until 10.30 pm
Closed Sat. (lunch),
Sun., 1 week in Feb.
and August 1-15
CLASSIC CUISINE
*Marie Naël presents
dishes from the days of
yore.
Seasonal cuisine based
on game and fish.*
Book.
Set menu: 175 F (lunch,
incl.wine)
A la carte: 230–320 F
▢ CB, Visa, MC
▦ ☺

L'ÉPOPÉE
89 Av. Émile-Zola
75015 (B, 24)
M. Charles Michel
Tel. 45 77 71 37
Open until 10.30 pm
Closed Sat. (lunch)
and Sun.
CLASSIC CUISINE
*Delightful welcome, in
this pretty flower-
decked dining-room.
Careful, light cuisine
based on good
ingredients, well
prepared, all for a
reasonable price.*
Manager: Yves
Millon;

chef:Patrick Léger
Set menu: 165 F
A la carte: 170–240 F
▢ CB, Visa, MC
☗

ERAWAN
▲ 296
76 Rue de la Fédération
75015 (B, 25)
M. La Motte-Picquet
Tel. 47 83 55 67
Open until 10.30 pm
Closed Sun. and August
THAI CUISINE
*Crowded and noisy, but
the décor is elegant, the
service efficient, and the
Thai dishes are
prepared with
sophistication.*
Set menus: 75 F (lunch),
132 F, 158 F, 175 F
A la carte: 180–250 F
▢ CB, Visa
☺ ⌧

LA FARIGOULE
▲ 308
104 Rue Balard
75015 (C, 26)
M. Javel
Tel. 45 54 35 41
Open until 10 pm
Closed Sun., Mon.
(dinner) and August
14–31
PROVENÇAL CUISINE
*Sun-drenched cuisine
and warm welcome in
an attractive dining-
room. Provençal wines.*
Specialties: aïoli,
bouillabaisse, pieds
paquets.
Manager: Anne-Marie
Gras; chef: Jean Gras
A la carte: 150–220 F
▢ CB, Visa

E-FRANCE

SAINT-GERMAIN

43

58 59
4 11   14

39

40

27

46

BD. SAINT-GERMAIN

BD. RASPAIL

47
42

37

64 36
55
33
57
1

62
51

28

32 22
53
5 49 15

45

RUE DE RENNES

367

LA FERME SAINT-SIMON

6 Rue de Saint-Simon
75007 (A, 27)
M. Rue du Bac
Tel. 45 48 35 74
Open until 10.15 pm
Closed Sat. (lunch),
Sun. and August 7–15
CLASSIC CUISINE
*Favored by a number of
politicians from the
neighboring National
Assembly as well as the
more glamorous
members of the fashion
and media crowd.
Fine ingredients are
selected by Francis
Mandenhende, while
the cooking is by
Thierry Meneux.
Perfect service, regional
wines. Good lunch
menu.
Specialties: velouté of
chicory and lobster
with chervil, blanc of
brill and oyster ravioli,
roast pigeon with
sorrel.*
Chef-manager: Francis
Mandenhende
Set menu: 160 F (lunch)
A la carte: 220–320 F
☐ CB, Visa, AE,
Diners
🔲 ☸ ✿

LA FERRONNERIE

18 Rue de la Chaise
75007 (A, 28)
M. Sèvres-Babylone
Tel. 45 49 22 43
Open until 11.30 pm
Closed Sun. and 3
weeks in August
HOME COOKING
*This rustic-style bistro
offering traditional
cuisine had a change
of owner at the
beginning of October
1993 but the emphasis
of the menu remains the
same as it has always
been.
Specialties: oven-roast
gigot of lamb, veal
kidneys, beef with
carrots.*
Manager: Mr Lejeune
chef: Jean-Pierre
Cloaguen
A la carte: 100–200 F
☐ CB, Visa

LE FLORENCE

▲ 274
22 Rue du Champ-
de-Mars
75007 (A, 29)
M. École Militaire
Tel. 45 51 52 69
Open until 10.30 pm
Closed Sun.
ITALIAN CUISINE
*An opulent dining-room
with antique wood-
paneling. Good menu in
a fairly traditional Italian
style. Book.
Specialties: feuilleté
pizza with aromatic
flavorings, piccata of
tuna with olive oil and
thyme, fillet of beef with
barolo.*
Manager:
Claude Étienne;
chef: Frédéric
Giraudeau
Set menus: 89 F (lunch),
180 F, 240 F
A la carte: 200–300 F
☐ all

FOC-LY

▲ 294, 296
71 Av. de Suffren
75007 (A, 30)
M. Sèvres-Lecourbe
Tel. 47 83 27 12
Open until 11 pm
Closed July and Mon.
in August
CHINESE-THAI
CUISINE
*Fine, carefully
prepared and subtly
spiced dishes,
incorporating the best
elements of Chinese
and Thai cuisine. It is
worth saving room for
one of their delicious
desserts. The service is
both efficient and
considerate. Book.*
Set menus: 108 F and
128 F (lunch), 135 F and
160 F (dinner, incl.
drinks)
A la carte: 180–250 F
☐ CB, Visa, AE
✿ ▣

The whole world comes to dine beneath the 16th-century beams of this splendid room where everything is peaceful and comfortable. Jacques Cagna is one of the great Parisian chefs. Incredible lunch menu, excellent wine list. Impeccable service. Book.
Specialties: salad of Dublin Bay prawn fritters with artichoke chips, fillet of sea bass stuffed with oysters, lobster roast in shellfish oil, noisettes of Pyrenean lamb roasted in tarragon juice, Brittany pigeon in honey and sauternes.
Manager: Anny Logereau ; chef: Jacques Cagna ; sommelier: Jacques Nicklès
Set menus: 260 F (weekday lunch), 480 F
A la carte: 450–600 F
▣ except Diners
▤ ☘

KAMAL
▲ 298
20 Rue Rousselet
75007 (A, 34)
M. Vanneau
Tel. 47 34 66 29
Open noon-2.30 pm; and 7.30–11.30 pm
Closed Sun.
INDIAN CUISINE
A restaurant of conspicuous finesse hidden away in a back street.
Specialties: chicken tika, fish tika, lamb tika and gratin of eggplants.
Manager: Mr Gopta
Booking preferred.
Set menus: 85 F; 129 F (dinner)
A la carte: 200–250 F
▣ AE, CB

KIM ANH
▲ 296
15 Rue de l'Église
75015 (B, 35)
M. Félix-Faure
Tel. 45 79 40 96
Open until 11.30 pm (dinner only)
VIETNAMESE CUISINE
Mr Kim Anh, the eponymous owner, gives a warm welcome in his small dining-room decorated with Vietnamese musical instruments. Caroline

Kim Anh creates exceptional, very fresh dishes. Unusual flavors, such as Chinese mint served with the nems. Well-chosen wines. Book.
Specialties: oven-baked stuffed crab, crawfish in caramel, selection of marinated kebabs.
Set menu: 200 F
A la carte: 220–320 F
▣ all

★ LAPÉROUSE
▲ 135
51 Quai des Grands-Augustins
75006 (A, 36)
M. St-Michel
Tel. 43 26 68 04
Open until 10.30 pm
Closed Sun., Mon.

(lunch), 2 weeks in August, Dec. 24
GASTRONOMIC CUISINE
Seductive Belle Époque decoration in the dining-rooms, plus cuisine with a strong flavor of southwestern France, by the Basque chef Gabriel Biscay, winner of the Meilleur Ouvrier de France award (Best Craftsman of France).
Specialties: lobster soup with chorizo and haricot beans, pigeon stuffed with chives and veal sweetbreads, veal kidneys with purple mustard.
Chef: Gabriel Biscay
Set menus: 250 F (lunch), 480 F
A la carte: 320–520 F
▣ CB, Visa, AE, Diners
▤ ☘

★ LE GRAND VENISE
▲ 274
171 Rue de la Convention
75015 (C, 31)
M. Convention
Tel. 45 32 49 71
Open until 10.30 pm
Closed Sun, Mon, Dec 24–Jan 2 and August
ITALIAN CUISINE
An opulent establishment serving classic Italian cooking, with a friendly welcome. Some interesting transalpine wines but unfortunately at American prices.
Specialties: minestrone, fried scampi, tortellini with ricotta, Venetian veal liver.
Manager: Anne Piprel
A la carte: 350–450 F
▣ CB, Visa, AE

GUY
▲ 288
6 Rue Mabillon
75006 (A, 32)
M. Mabillon
Tel. 43 54 87 61
Open until 12.45 am, Sat. lunch only
Closed Sun. and August 8–31
BRAZILIAN CUISINE
The food should be washed down with one of their excellent cocktails (batidas and

caipirinha).
Music on Monday evenings. Samba on Saturday afternoons with live band.
Specialties: feijoada, rabada (stewed oxtail), churrascos.
Manager: Erica Limouza; chef: Jacky Gaillarbois
Set menu: 99 F
A la carte: 180–250 F
▣ CB
▤ ☘

★ JACQUES CAGNA
▲ 143
14 Rue des Grands-Augustins
75006 (A, 33)
M. St-Michel
Tel. 43 26 49 39
Open until 10.30 pm
Closed Sat. (dinner), Sun., Dec. 24–Jan. 1 and 3 weeks in August
GASTRONOMIC CUISINE

★ **LIPP**
▲ *129*
151 Bd Saint-Germain
75006 (A, 37)
M. St-Germain-des-Prés
Tel. 45 48 53 91
Open until 2 am
BOURGEOIS CUISINE
*This early 20th-century
brasserie is popular just
because it is Lipp. The
food, in fact, has its ups
and downs. Go there to
rub shoulders with
fashionable Parisians.*
Manager: Claude de
Pronembourg
A la carte: 200–300 F
□ all
🍴 ♻

LE LUZ
4 Rue Pierre-Leroux
75007 (A, 38)
M. Vanneau
Tel. 43 06 99 39
Open until 10.15 pm
Closed Sat. (lunch)
and Sun.
FISH CUISINE
*Good fish dishes
served with a smile in a
small dining-room that
is packed at lunchtime.
Specialties: smoked eel
and galette of macaire
potatoes, escalope of
sea bream with vanilla,
escalope of veal
sweetbreads with
oysters.*
Chef -manager: Gilbert
Dugast
Set menus: 125 F, 155
F, 180 F (incl. wine)
A la carte: 230–330 F
□ all
♻ 🅿

**LA MAISON DE
L'AMÉRIQUE LATINE**
217 Bd Saint-Germain
75007 (A, 39)
M. Rue du Bac
Tel. 45 49 33 23
Open until 10.30 pm
(summer), lunch in
winter only
Closed Sat.,

Sun. and August
BOURGEOIS CUISINE
*Pleasant garden.
Patronized by
academics. The cooking
is variable, but the
"family hotel" ambiance
is truly delightful. Book.*
Set menus: 65 F (bar),
180 F (lunch)
A la carte: 200–300 F
□ none
♟ 🍴 ▤ ✗

LES MINISTÈRES
30 Rue du Bac
75007 (A, 40)
M. Rue du Bac
Tel. 42 61 22 37
Open until 12.30 am
Closed January 1
HOME COOKING
*A spacious brasserie in
the heart of the
publishing district.
Service often chaotic.*
Set menus: 72 F (lunch),
110 F
A la carte: 120–220 F
□ CB, Visa, AE,
Diners

★ **MOROT-GAUDRY**
8 Rue de la Cavalerie,
8th floor
75015 (A, 41)
M. La Motte-Picquet
Tel. 45 67 06 85
Open until 10.30 pm
Closed Sat. and Sun.
GASTRONOMIC CUISINE
*On the 8th floor of an
Art Deco building: from*

*the terrace good view
over the rooftops of
Paris and of the Eiffel
Tower on fine days.
Jean-Pierre Morot-
Gaudry offers a wide
and very personal wine
list and fine classic
cuisine. Good menu at
220 F. Book.
Specialties: ballottine of
guinea-fowl and pigeon,
side of hog-fish niçoise,
oven-baked wild duck
with Szechuan
spices and pepper.*
Set menus: 220 F
(incl.wine), 390 F,
550 F (incl. wine)
A la carte: 320–520 F
□ CB, Visa, AE
🍴 ▤ ♻

LE MUNICH
22 Rue Guillaume-
Apollinaire
75006 (A, 42)
M. St-Germain-des-Prés
Tel. 42 61 12 70
Open until 1.30 am
BOURGEOIS CUISINE
*In the Latin quarter, a
cramped dining-room
with Belle Époque
décor. The Layrac
brothers serve basic
dishes and the
ubiquitous choucroute
to post-theater diners.*
Manager: Gilbert Brunel
Set menu: 148 F
A la carte: 160–250 F
□ all
🍴 ♻ 🅿 ✗

★ **LE MUSÉE D'ORSAY**
▲ *139*
Musée d'Orsay
1 Rue Bellechasse
75007 (A, 43)
M. Solférino

Tel. 45 49 42 33
Open 11.30 am–2.30
pm (Thurs. until 9.30
pm)
Closed Mon.
CLASSIC CUISINE
*The ideal place for a
quiet lunch on the banks
of the Seine.
Unfortunately, the
quality of the food is
very inconsistent.*
Set menus: 72 F
(buffet), 95 F, 110 F,
135 F
□ CB, Visa, MC
🅿 ✗

OLYMPE
8 Rue Nicolas-Charlet
75015 (B, 44)
M. Pasteur
Tel. 47 34 86 08
Open until 11 pm
Closed Sat. (lunch),
Sun. (lunch), Mon.,
August 14–17
and Dec. 23–5
GASTRONOMIC CUISINE
*Olympe is no longer
there but the
exceptional food at
newly reduced prices
has convinced the loyal
clientele welcomed by
Albert Nahmias.
Interesting wines at
affordable prices.
Specialties: ravioli of
duck in gravy, crawfish
sautéed with garlic,
rabbit with pistou of
artichoke.*
Manager: Albert
Nahmias.

MAP (labels on map): RUE LECOURBE, RUE DE VAUGIRARD, RUE DE LA CONVENTION, RUE FALGUIÈRE, RUE BRANCION, BD. LEFEBVRE. Numbered markers: 65, 31, 52, 56, 18.

Set
menus:
149 F
(lunch), 189 F
(evening)
▭ all

LE PARIS
▲ 141
Hôtel Lutetia
23 Rue de Sèvres
75007 (A, 45)
(restaurant)
M. Sèvres-Babylone
Tel. 49 54 46 90
Open until 10 pm
Closed Sat., Sun.
and August
GASTRONOMIC AND
CLASSIC CUISINE
*Restaurant and
brasserie of a large
hotel with décor by
Slavik and Sonia Rykiel.
The young Philippe
Renard, winner of the
Meilleur Ouvrier de
France award (Best
Craftsman of France),
creates inspired and
innovative dishes.
Smooth service.
Specialties: warm
oysters with caviar on a
bed of watercress, roast
turbot steak with bacon,
truffled fondant of veal*

and risotto of foie gras.
*Manager: Jean-Marc de
Margerie ; chef: Philippe
Renard ; sommelier:
Mr Wielgosik*
Set menus: 250 F, 495 F
A la carte: 350–500 F

HÔTEL LUTETIA
45 Bd Raspail
(brasserie)
75006 (A, 45)
M. Sèvres-Babylone
Tel. 49 54 46 76
CLASSIC CUISINE
*Decorated to look like
the dining room of a
steamship.*
Set menus: 95 F (lunch
except Sun.), 150 F,
165 F (Sun. brunch),
185 F (Sun. lunch)
▭ all
☂ 🚗

LE PETIT LAURENT
38 Rue de Varenne
75007 (A, 46)
M. Varenne
Tel. 45 48 79 64
Open until 10.15 pm

Closed Sat. (lunch),
Sun. and August
CLASSIC CUISINE
*Politicians savor the
cuisine of Sylvain
Pommier in an elegant
Louis XVI décor. Perfect
ingredients, delicate
flavors, and intimacy, all
at very reasonable
prices.
Specialties: bisque of
Dublin Bay prawns with
croutons, sole meunière
in orange sauce, rabbit
confit with fennel.*
Set menus: 175 F, 240 F
A la carte: 250–350 F
▭ CB, Visa, AE,
Diners

LE PETIT ZINC
▲ 138
11 Rue Saint-Benoît
75006 (A, 47)
M. St-Germain-des-Prés
Tel. 42 61 20 60
Open until 2 am
CLASSIC CUISINE
*This is the former
Assiette au beurre
purchased by the
Layrac brothers. Has
the same menu, and is
as crowded as Le
Munich.*
Set menu: 158 F
A la carte: 160–250 F
▭ all

LA PETITE BRETONNIÈRE
2 Rue de Cadix
75015 (C, 48)
Garage 376, rue
de Vaugirard
M. Porte de Versailles
Tel. 48 28 34 39
Open until 10 pm
Closed Sat. (lunch),
Sun. and August
GASTRONOMIC CUISINE
Near the Porte de
Versailles. Alain La
Maison, a talented chef
inspired by the
traditions of south-
western France, shows
that this regional cuisine
need not be heavy.
First-class service, fine
wines. Specialties:
terrine of veal, warm
salad of pan-fried
scallops, mid section of
salmon stuffed with
oysters, magret of duck
roasted in truffle juices.
Set menu: 200 F (lunch)
A la carte: 350–400 F
☐ CB, Visa

LA PETITE COUR
▲ *134*
8 Rue Mabillon
75006 (A, 49)
M. Mabillon
Tel. 43 26 52 26
Open until 11 pm
CLASSIC CUISINE
In Saint-Germain-des-
Prés, Patrick Louvet
offers a lunch menu that
is excellent value for
money. Served under
the big tree on the small
terrace or in the
Napoleon III dining-
room. Book.
Specialties: millefeuille
of artichoke with foie
gras, supreme of
salmon with crawfish,
carré of roast lamb with
tarragon sauce.
Manager: Jean-
François Larpin; chef:
Patrick Guyadere
Set menus: 150 F
(lunch), 165 F (lunch),

185 F (dinner)
A la carte: 200–300 F
☐ CB, Visa
𝍖

LA POULE AU POT
121 Rue de l'Université
75007 (A, 50)
M. Invalides
Tel. 47 05 16 36
Open until 11 pm
Closed Sat. (lunch)
and Sun.
HOME COOKING
Décor and ambiance of
an old-fashioned bistro,
unpretentious cooking
at reasonable prices.
Specialties: poule au
pot, of course, but also
chitterlings in chablis.
Chef-manager: Jean-
Marie Plaf Debecker
A la carte: 150–200 F
☐ all
𝍖 ▦

LE PROCOPE
▲ *132*
13 Rue de l'Ancienne-
Comédie
75006 (A, 51)
M. Odéon
Tel. 43 26 99 20
Open until 1 am
CLASSIC CUISINE
One of the oldest sign-
boards in Paris: it was a
literary cafe in the 17th
century. It has now
been discovered by
tourists. Interesting
menu at 99 F.
Managers: Pierre and
Jacques Blanc;
chef: Mr Marty

Set menus: 99 F (lunch),
289 F (incl. wine)
A la carte: 160–260 F
☐ all
▦

RAAJMAHAL
▲ *298*
192 Rue de la
Convention
75015 (C, 52)
M. Convention
Tel. 45 33 29 39
or 45 33 15 57
Open until 10.45 pm
INDIAN CUISINE
Carved wood, hubbub,
oriental smells, hectic
service that is not
conducive to savoring
the specialties. This is
unfortunate, because
the food is good.
Manager: M. Kassam
Set menu: 59 F (lunch)
A la carte: 200–300 F
☐ all
𝍖 ⚘ 🄿

★ **LE RÉCAMIER**
▲ *140*
4 Rue Récamier
75007 (A, 53)
M. Sèvres-Babylone
Tel. 45 48 86 58
Open until midnight
Closed Sun.
BOURGEOIS CUISINE
At the end of a flower-
decked cul-de-sac, this
restaurant is a favorite
with politicians,
journalists and
publishers. The terrace
is a haven of tranquility.
Pleasant service,
extensive wine list.
Prices to match.
Specialties: cream of
lobster soup, scallops
steamed with seaweed,
Auvergne-style fillet of
veal.
Manager: Martin
Cantegrit; chef: Robert
Chassat
A la carte: 270–400 F
☐ all
𝍖 ▦ ⚘

LE RELAIS DE SÈVRES
Hôtel Sofitel
8-12 Rue Louis-Armand
75015 (C, 54)
M. Balard
Tel. 40 60 30 30
or 40 60 33 66
Open until 11 pm
Closed Sat., Sun.,
August and Dec
24–Jan 1
GASTRONOMIC CUISINE
The hotel restaurant.
Comfortable seating
and bold cuisine by
Martial Enguehard.

Delicious desserts, fine
wines and elegant
service.
Specialties: cream of
artichokes with lobster
quenelles, hot-pot of
sliced beef breast in
mushroom cocotte,
gratin of lentils with foie
gras.
Manager: Hervé de
Tergonde; chef: Martial
Enguehard; pâtissier:
Alain Gonnet
Set menus: 300 F
(lunch),
A la carte: 350–500 F
☐ all
▦ ⚘

LE RELAIS LOUIS XIII
8 Rue des Grands-
Augustins
75006 (A, 55)
M. St-Michel
Tel. 43 26 75 96
Open until 10.15 pm
Closed Mon. (lunch),
Sun.and July 24–August
24
CLASSIC CUISINE
Impressive décor of old
stone and Flemish
paintings. Cooking by
Christian Sochas
sometimes inconsistent.
Fine and expensive
wines.
Set menu: 240 F (lunch)
A la carte: 370–450 F
☐ all
▦ ⚘ 🥃 🄿

**LE RESTAURANT
DU MARCHÉ**
59 Rue de Dantzig
75015 (C, 56)
M. Convention
Tel. 48 28 31 55
or 45 32 26 88
Open until 10.30 pm
Closed Sat. (lunch),
Sun.
BOURGEOIS CUISINE
Genuine bistro
atmosphere and décor.
Good bourgeois house
specialties that come
round according to
season. Extensive wine
list.
Managers: Christiane
and Michel Massia;
chef: Christiane Massia
A la carte: 220–350 F
☐ CB

**LA RÔTISSERIE
D'EN FACE**
2 Rue Christine
75006 (A, 57)
M. St-Michel
Tel. 43 26 40 98
Open until 11 pm
Closed Sat. (lunch)
and Sun.

CLASSIC CUISINE
A branch of Jacques Cagna. It is the former Comptoir de l'Événement; commonly frequented by journalists. Pleasant dry Vouvray as an apéritif.
Set menu: 145 F (lunch), 185 F (dinner)
▭ CB, Visa, MC, Euroc
☻

TAN DINH
▲ 296
60 Rue de Verneuil
75007 (A, 58)
M. Solférino
Tel. 45 44 04 84
Open until 11 pm
Closed Sun. and August
VIETNAMESE CUISINE
The Vifian brothers' cuisine is exceptional: very meticulous, high-quality ingredients, amazing wine list. Price justified.
Specialties: Saigon salad with mango, sea-trout kebab with cardamom, Tan Dinh émincé of fillet of beef.
Set menu: 175 F (lunch)
A la carte: 240–360 F
▭ none
▦

LE TÉLÉGRAPHE
▲ 134
41 Rue de Lille
75007 (A, 59)
M. Rue du Bac
Tel. 40 15 06 65
Open until 12.30 am
CLASSIC CUISINE
Wood-paneling and green marble in Art Nouveau style, very pleasant garden-terrace. But in this enormous setting the service is icy. A new chef may improve the food.
Manager: Hubert de Ducla.
Set menu: 125 F (lunch), 175 F

A la carte: 250–350 F
▭ CB, Visa, AE
♣ ⑪

TRAKTIR
▲ 280
18 Rue Frémicourt and 51, rue Letellier
75015 (B, 60)
M. Commerce
Tel. 45 79 51 59
Open until midnight
Closed Mon. (lunch)
RUSSIAN CUISINE
Two dining-rooms. Atmosphere guaranteed in an establishment where tradition is respected. Live music in the evenings. Russian wines and vodkas.
Specialties: bortsch, stuffed blinis, Russian-style stuffed cabbage.
Manager: Nicolas Cherbakoff
Set menus: 90F (lunch), 120 F (lunch), 140 F (lunch), 150 F (lunch)
A la carte: 100–200 F
▭ CB, Visa
▦

URI
5 Rue Humblot
75015 (A, 61)
M. Dupleix
Tel. 45 77 37 11
Open until 10.30 pm
Closed Sun. and August
KOREAN CUISINE
A restaurant full of Koreans. Amazing meals served entirely as little bowlfuls of various dishes, some of them highly spiced. Book.
A la carte: 170–270 F
▭ CB, Visa
☻ ��

VAGENENDE
▲ 130
142 Bd Saint-Germain
75006 (A, 62)
M. St-Germain-des-Prés
Tel. 43 26 68 18
Open until 1 am
CLASSIC CUISINE
Originally a bouillon

restaurant, now with modern décor. Short wine list, nagging service. The food is almost boring.
Manager: Jacques Egurreguy; chef: Daniel Maciet
Set menu: 108 F
A la carte: 200–260 F
▭ CB, Visa, AE
⑂ ▦

VIN SUR VIN
20 Rue de Monttessuy
75007 (A, 63)
M. Alma-Marceau
Tel. 47 05 14 20
Open until 10 pm
Closed Sat. (lunch), Mon. (lunch), Sun., May 1–9, August 15–Sept. 1 and Dec. 23–Jan. 2
CLASSIC CUISINE
First class fresh ingredients and a cellar teeming with interesting finds. A winning combination at this lively establishment run by Patrice and Marc Vidal. Book.
Specialties: snails in pistou, brill and artichokes in meat gravy, fillet of beef in claret with bone marrow.
A la carte: 220–300 F
▭ CB, Visa, MC

YUGARAJ
▲ 298
14 Rue Dauphine
75006 (A, 64)
M. Odéon
Tel. 43 26 44 91
Open until 11 pm
Closed Mon. (lunch)

INDIAN CUISINE
Remarkable marriage of French wines and Bengali food. Probably the best Indian in Paris. Book.
Specialties: tandoori grilled eggplants, crab boulettes with cumin, lamb with cardamom and almonds.
Manager: Kulendran Meyapen; chef: Hukum Singh
Set menus: 130 F (weekday lunch), 180 F (dinner), 220 F
A la carte: 250–350 F
▭ CB, Visa, AE, Diners
▦ ♦

YVES QUINTARD
99 Rue Blomet
75015 (C, 65)
M. Volontaires
Tel. 42 50 22 27
Open until 10.30 pm
Closed Sat. (lunch), Sun. and August 1–23
GASTRONOMIC CUISINE
A gallery-restaurant. Original and well-prepared food by Yves Quintard. The 150 F menu is a bargain.
Specialties: gâteau of common crab caramelized in ginger, lemon sole in pastilla with fondue of courgette, pan-fried fillet of beef with cream of morels.
Set menu: 138 F (weekday lunch), 160 F
A la carte: 250–350 F
▭ CB, Visa
☻

MAP A ♦ 377

3 L'ATLAS
4 L'AUBERGE DES DEUX SIGNES
7 LE BALZAR
9 LE BISTROT DU PORT
10 LA BÛCHERIE
14 CAMPAGNE ET PROVENCE
16 CASA PEPE
18 CHEZ TOUTOUNE
19 CHIENG MAI
23 DODIN-BOUFFANT
28 L'ESPACE HÉRAULT – LE RABELAIS
30 INSTITUT DU MONDE ARABE
31 LOUBNANE
33 LA MÉDITERRANÉE
34 MOISSONNIER
35 LE MONDE DES CHIMÈRES
37 L'ORANGERIE
38 LE PACTOLE
40 PERRAUDIN
42 POLIDOR
43 RESTAURANT A
45 TASHI DELEK
46 LA TIMONERIE
47 LA TOUR D'ARGENT
50 LES VIGNES DU PANTHÉON
53 WALLY LE SAHARIEN

MAP B ♦ 378

1 L'AMUSE-BOUCHE
2 L'ASSIETTE
5 AUX ARMES DE BRETAGNE

6 AUX PETITS CHANDELIERS
8 LE BISTRO DE LA GARE
11 LE CABANON DES MAÎTRES NAGEURS
12 LA CAGOUILLE
13 LE CAMÉLÉON
15 LE CAROUBIER
20 LE CIEL DE PARIS
21 LA CLOSERIE DES LILAS
22 LA COUPOLE
24 LE DÔME
25 DOMINIQUE
26 LE DUC
27 L'ÉCHANSON
32 LOUS LANDÈS
36 MONTPARNASSE 25
44 LE TAGHIT
48 VASSANTI
51 LE VIN DES RUES
52 VISHNOU

MAP C ♦ 380

29 ETCHEGORRY
39 LE PAVILLON MONTSOURIS
41 LE PETIT MARGUERY
49 LES VIEUX MÉTIERS DE FRANCE

OFF MAP

17 LE CHAT GRIPPÉ

INNER SUBURBS

54 LA MANUFACTURE
55 MAXIM'S
56 RIVER CAFÉ

ITINERARY 2

L'AMUSE-BOUCHE
168 Rue du Château
75014 (B, 1)
M. Gaîté
Tel 43 35 31 61
Open until 10.30 pm
Closed Sat. (lunch),
Sun. and week of
August 15
CLASSIC CUISINE
*Delicious food by Gilles
Lambert, formerly at
Jacques Cagna. His
wife produces
marvelous desserts.
Specialties: saddle of
young rabbit in white
dandelion leaves and
warm foie gras salad,
fillet of sole meunière
with caramelized
chicory, pigeon roast in
honey and lemon.*
Set menu: 160 F (lunch
and dinner)
A la carte: 220–350 F
☐ CB, Visa

L'ASSIETTE
181 Rue du Château
75014 (B, 2)
M. Gaîté
Tel 43 22 64 86
Open until 10.30 pm
Closed Mon., Tue.,
August and 2 weeks in
Dec.
GASTRONOMIC CUISINE
*Extremely generous
helpings, relaxed
ambiance courtesy of
Lulu, the excellent cook,
queen of this former
charcuterie, which has a
painted ceiling. Book.
Specialties: rillettes of
mackerel, black-
pudding parmentier,
blanquette of scallops
with baby vegetables,
petit salé of duck,
chicken pot-au-feu with
truffles.*
A la carte: 300–450 F
☐ CB, Visa, AE

L'ATLAS
▲ 302
12 Bd Saint-Germain
75005 (A, 3)
M. Maubert Mutualité
Tel 44 07 23 66
Open until 11 pm

MOROCCAN CUISINE
*Moroccan restaurant
very close to the Institut
du Monde arabe.*
A la carte: 150–220 F
Y CB, Visa, AE, Diners
☼ ☺

L'AUBERGE DES DEUX SIGNES
▲ 148
45 Rue Galande
75005 (A, 4)
M. Maubert-Mutualité
Tel 43 25 46 56
and 43 25 00 46
Open until 10.30 pm
Closed Sat. (lunch),
Sun., May 1 and August
CLASSIC CUISINE
*Opposite Notre-Dame.
Georges Dhulster will
gladly give you a guided
tour of his superb
establishment with
medieval décor. Good
cooking by Olivier Cano,
regional wines,
reasonable prices.
Book.
Specialties: ravioli of
beef with potée of
cabbage and ginger,
escalope of pikeperch
à la nage, medallion of
capelin in a caul with
confit shallots, fillet of
beef with bone marrow.*
Set menus: 140 F
(lunch), 230 F
A la carte: 310–410 F
☐ none
☞

AUX ARMES DE BRETAGNE
108 Av. du Maine
75014 (B, 5)
M. Gaîté
Tel 43 20 29 50
or 43 20 01 67
Open until 11 pm
Closed August
FISH CUISINE
*This restaurant has an
old-fashioned air, with
an attentive car valet,
Napoleon III décor and
smooth service from a
side-table. Good sea
food and rich fish
cuisine, but expensive
and often dull.
Manager: Roland*

Boyer;
chef: William Dhenin
Set menu: 200 F
A la carte: 250–400 F
🍽 all
🌸 🚗

AUX PETITS CHANDELIERS
62 Rue Daguerre
75014 (B, 6)
M. Denfert-Rochereau
Tel 43 20 25 87
Open until 11 pm
REUNION CUISINE
The oldest Reunion restaurant in Paris. A series of several small dining-rooms which are quickly crowded. Go easy on the cocktails! Specialties: massalé, bichiques, cary de canard au chouchou.
Chef-Manager: Solange Lakermance
Set menus: 49 F, 80 F, 120 F
A la carte: 150–180 F
🍽 all

LE BALZAR
▲ 150
49 Rue des Écoles
75005 (A, 7)
M. Odéon
Tel 43 54 13 67
Open until 11 pm
Closed Dec. 24– Jan. 1 and August
CLASSIC CUISINE
Nothing has changed in this brasserie near the Sorbonne since 1931. It is still frequented by the Parisian intelligentsia. Buzzes at meal times. Avoid the tables near the entrance.
A la carte: 160–220 F
🍽 CB, Visa, AE

LE BISTRO DE LA GARE
▲ 154
59 Bd Montparnasse
75006 (B, 8)
M. Montparnasse
Tel 45 48 38 01
Open until 1 am
CLASSIC CUISINE
Good-sized long dining-room that has retained its Modern Style charm.

Mediocre cooking.
Manager: Édouard Chartier
Set menus: 59 F, 75 F, 90 F, 109 F
A la carte: 100–160 F
🍽 CB, Visa, MC
🍴 🌸

LE BISTROT DU PORT
13 Quai de Montebello
75005 (A, 9)
M. Maubert-Mutualité
Tel 40 51 73 19
Open until 10.30 pm
Closed Mon., Tue. (lunch)
CLASSIC CUISINE
Unrestricted view of Notre-Dame. Regional dishes and vins de pays. Specialties: Venetian-style cervelas of calamar, fricassée of veal with lemon-flavored vanilla.
Managers: Henri Garcia and Mona Guyot; chef: Henri Garcia
Set menu: 138 F
A la carte: 180–300 F
🍽 CB, Visa, MC
🔆 🍴 🌸

LA BÛCHERIE
▲ 153
41 Rue de la Bûcherie
75005 (A, 10)
M. Maubert-Mutualité
Tel 43 54 78 06
or 43 54 39 24
Open until 12.30 am
CLASSIC CUISINE
View of Notre-Dame from the terrace. Wood paneled dining-room, fireplace, contemporary art on the walls. The quality of the food and the fine clarets are good reasons for enjoying it. Book. Specialties: Dublin Bay prawns with cabbage, stuffed young turbot, fillet of beef with truffle juice, wild rabbit in muscadet.
Chef and sommelier: Bernard Bosque
Set menu: 230 F (incl. wine)

A la carte: 300–400 F
🍽 CB, Visa, AE, Diners
🍴 🔆 🚬 🌸

LE CABANON DES MAÎTRES NAGEURS
9 Rue Léopold-Robert
75014 (B, 11)
M. Vavin
Tel 43 20 64 14
Open until 11 pm
FISH CUISINE
Simple décor evocative of seaside holidays. Well prepared sea cuisine. Specialties: mussels in cider and in cream sauce, sea bream grilled with thyme, casserole of fresh cod.
Set menu: 100 F (lunch)
A la carte: 160–260 F
🍽 CB, Visa, MC
🍴

LA CAGOUILLE
10–12 Pl. Constantin-Brancusi (Rue de l'Ouest)
75014 (B, 12)
M. Gaîté
Tel 43 22 09 01
Open until 10.30 pm
Closed Dec. 24– Jan. 3
FISH CUISINE
Gérard Allemandou cooks fish in minimalist style. Pleasant terrace in summer, but the prices are on the steep side and the service leaves something to be desired. Superb selection of cognacs. Specialties: deep-fried fresh anchovies, cultivated mussels brûle-doigts, blanc of plaice in ginger sauce.
Special: 150 F
Set menu: 250 F
A la carte: 300–500 F
🍽 all
🍴

LE CAMÉLÉON
6 Rue de Chevreuse
75006 (B, 13)
M. Vavin
Tel 43 20 63 43
Open until 10.30 pm
Closed Sun., Mon. and August
BOURGEOIS CUISINE

A real old-fashioned bistro that has retained its original décor. Raymond Faucher, the proprietor, is a likeable character. Good food and pleasant wines. Specialties: pumpkin loaf with smoked bacon, provençal-style cod, sliced breast of duck with truffles.
Chef: Thierry Thibault
A la carte: 150–250 F
🍽 none

★ CAMPAGNE ET PROVENCE
▲ 308
25 Quai de la Tournelle
75005 (A, 14)
M. Maubert-Mutualité
Tel 43 54 05 17
Open until 11 pm
Closed Mon. (lunch), Sat. (lunch) and Sun.
PROVENÇAL CUISINE
Annex to Gilles Epié's Le Miravile. Alain Gérard prepares his sunshine dishes. Delightful wine list. Exceptional prices for the area. Book. Specialties: mussel soup with pistou, risotto with pumpkin and bacon, pollack with spicy coconut, tian of lamb with rosemary.
Set menu: 99 F (lunch)
A la carte: 180–280 F
🍽 CB, Visa

LE CAROUBIER
▲ 302
122 Av. du Maine
75014 (B, 15)
M. Gaîté
Tel 43 20 41 49
Open noon to 3 pm and 8 pm to midnight
Closed Sun. (lunch) and Mon. (lunch).
NORTH AFRICAN CUISINE
A pieds-noirs couple run this excellent establishment. Madame is in the kitchen. Monsieur runs the front of the house in a good-natured way. No obtrusive décor. Specialties: one of the best couscous in Paris. They serve a very good pastilla.
Manager: Pierre Michel
Set menu: 130 F (lunch and dinner), A la carte: 200 F
🍽 CB

CASA PEPE
▲ 276
5 Rue Mouffetard

75005 (A, 16)
M. Monge
Tel 43 54 97 33
Open until 11.30 pm
Closed lunchtime
SPANISH CUISINE
Toni, the proprietor, sings, greets, sits down at the table with everybody. Groups of guitarists and vocalists. Spanish (riojas) and French wines.
Specialties: tapas, zarzuela, paella.
Manager: Toni
Set menu: 250 F
A la carte: 200–250 F
CB all

LE CHAT GRIPPÉ
87 Rue d'Assas
75006 (off map, 17)
M. Rennes
Tel 43 54 70 00
Open until 10.30 pm
Closed Sat. (lunch), Mon. and August
GASTRONOMIC CUISINE
Near the Jardin du Luxembourg. Éric Thore, a protégé of Taillevent, has perfected a good classic cuisine. Exceptional clarets and noteworthy lunch menu. Book.
Specialties: salmon marinated in coulis of cucumber, duo of brandade and fresh cod, croquet of lamb with chive sauce.
Manager: Robert Bernacchia
Set menus: 160 F (weekday lunch), 235 F, 320 F
A la carte: 250–350 F
CB CB, Visa

CHEZ TOUTOUNE
5 Rue de Pontoise
75005 (A, 18)
M. Maubert-Mutualité
Tel 43 26 56 81
Open until 10.30 pm
Closed Sun., Mon. (lunch) and August
HOME COOKING
A welcome from Toutoune, famous for demonstrating her recipes on television. Quality cuisine. Book.
Set menu: 179 F
A la carte: 220–300 F
CB CB, Visa, AE

CHIENG MAI
▲ 296
12 Rue Frédéric-Sauton
75005 (A, 19)

M. Maubert-Mutualité
Tel 43 25 45 45
Open until 11.15 pm
Closed Sun., August 1-15 and Dec. 16–31
THAI CUISINE
One of the good Thai restaurants in Paris. Pleasant and attentive service. Book.
Specialties: Imperial Thai rouleau, steamed fish in banana leaves, émincé of gigot in young pepper and basil.
Set menus: 69 F, 90 F (lunch), 122 F, 136 F, 159 F, 173 F (dinner)
A la carte: 150–220 F
CB CB, Visa, AE, MC

LE CIEL DE PARIS
Tour Montparnasse
56th floor
75014 (B, 20)
M. Montparnasse
Tel 45 38 52 35
Open until 11.30 pm (midnight Fri. and Sat.)
CLASSIC CUISINE
Tourists come to enjoy good food on the 56th floor of the Tour Montparnasse while enjoying a fine aerial view of Paris.
Specialties: salad of skate with seven spices, tournedos of pikeperch with bone marrow, saddle of lamb and potatoes with smoked pork fillet.
Fixed menus: 205 F, 270 F
A la carte: 220–340 F
CB all

★ LA CLOSERIE DES LILAS
▲ 159
171 Bd Montparnasse
75006 (B, 21)

M. Port-Royal
Tel 43 26 70 50
Open until 2 am
CLASSIC CUISINE
Patronized by literary types. Avoid sitting beneath the coat hooks in the brasserie. Casual service, indifferent cooking. The tartare is famous, but better elsewhere. Book.
A la carte: 150–200 F (brasserie), 250–500 F (restaurant)
CB all

★ LA COUPOLE
▲ 156
102 Bd Montparnasse
75014 (B, 22)
M. Vavin
Tel 43 20 14 20
Open until 2 am
Closed Dec. 24 (dinner)
CLASSIC CUISINE
Jean-Paul Bucher has renovated this landmark of Parisian life. The restored Othon Friesz frescoes are even more stunning for it. The spirit of the place is intact, but the mediocre cooking somewhat "production line." Good seafood.
Set menus: 85 F (weekday lunch), 109 F (lunch and after 11 pm)
A la carte: 180–300 F
CB all

DODIN-BOUFFANT
25 Rue Frédéric-Sauton
75005 (A, 23)
M. Maubert-Mutualité
Tel 43 25 25 14
Open until 11 pm
Closed Sun., Sat. (lunch), 2 weeks in August and Dec.

23–Jan. 3
CLASSIC CUISINE
You come here to be seen or to see famous faces at close quarters. A place that lives on its reputation. Book.
Managers: Dany and Maurice Cartier; chef: Mark Singer
Set menu: 195 F (lunch and dinner)
CB all

LE DÔME
▲ 308
108 Bd Montparnasse
75014 (B, 24)
M. Vavin
Tel 43 35 25 81
Open until 12.45 am
Closed Mon.
FISH CUISINE
One of the best fish cuisines in Paris: fine ingredients, meticulous cooking by Franck Graux. Too noisy and crowded for a romantic tête-à-tête. Book.
Specialties: seafood, roast lobster with basil butter, cheeks of skate and coulis of tomato with vinegar, goujonnettes of John Dory with spices, bouillabaisse.
Manager: Claude Bras
A la carte: 300–500 F
CB all

DOMINIQUE
▲ 280
19 Rue Bréa
75006 (B, 25)
M. Vavin
Tel 43 27 08 80
Open until 10.30 pm
Closed July 15–August 15
RUSSIAN CUISINE
Combined bar, grocery store and restaurant.

One of the centers of Parisian Russia with a nostalgic Russia represented on the prints which decorate the walls. Wide range of vodkas.
Set menu: 153 F
A la carte: 160–260 F
☐ CB, Visa, AE, Diners
🚗 ♿

Le Duc
▲ 155
243 Bd Raspail
75014 (B, 26)
M. Raspail
Tel 43 20 96 30
Open until 10.30 pm
Closed Sun., Mon. and public holidays
FISH CUISINE
Good, fresh fish, meticulously cooked, and minimalist furnishings, which appeal to fashionable Parisians. A classic restaurant frequented by enthusiasts.

Specialties: raw sardines, lobster sautéed à l'orange, plain grilled bass, onglet of monkfish with two peppers.
Chef: Paul Minchelli
A la carte: 360–700 F
☐ none

L'Échanson
89 Rue Daguerre
75014 (B, 27)
M. Denfert-Rochereau
Tel 43 22 20 00
Open until 10.30 pm
Closed Sun., Mon., August 15–Sept. 6 and 1 week at Christmas
CLASSIC CUISINE
A wine restaurant with a few tables on the pavement in summer. Good light bistro dishes. Noteworthy wine list; some wines are available by the glass. Specialties: terrine of chicken livers with Vouvray, salmon roast in Guérande salt, ragout of lamb knuckle with Chinon.

Manager: Luc Desrousseaux
A la carte: 150–200 F
☐ CB, Visa, Euroc, MC
♿

L'Espace Hérault – Le Rabelais
8 Rue de la Harpe
75005 (A, 28)
M. St-Michel
Tel 46 33 00 56
Open until 10.30 pm
Closed Sat., Sun. and August
CUISINE FROM LANGUEDOC
A necessary haven of tradition in the Latin Quarter, which has been invaded by foreign "tourist-trap" restaurants. Here Patrick Pagès offers Languedoc fare washed down with regional wines. Prices as agreeable as the welcome. Book.
Specialties: stuffed squid à la sétoise, cassoulet lozérien, gigot of lamb with garrigue herbs.
Sommelier: Olivier Bompas
Set menus: 98 F (lunch), 140 F, 190 F, 250 F
A la carte: 150–250 F
☐ all ♿

GERMAIN

Bd. SAINT-MICHEL

RUE SAINT-JACQUES

RUE D'ULM

RUE MONGE

RUE JUSSIEU

ETCHEGORRY
▲ *306*
41 Rue Croulebarbe
75013 (C, 29)
M. Gobelins
Tel 44 08 83 51
Open until 10.30 pm
Closed Sun.
BASQUE CUISINE
For authentic southwestern French cooking with a penchant for the Pays Basque at very reasonable prices.
Specialties: foie gras, chipirons, cassoulet, confit.
Chef-manager: Henri Laborde
Set menus: 135 F, 150 F, 165 F, 200 F
A la carte: 150–230 F
all

INSTITUT DU MONDE ARABE
▲ *148, 300*
1 Rue des Fossés-Saint-Bernard
75005 (A, 30)
M. Jussieu
Tel 46 33 47 70
Open until 11 pm
Closed Sun. (dinner) and Mon.
LEBANESE CUISINE
Fine views of the Seine from the terrace. The mezzé are good, with an ample choice of uncooked meats. Grilled meats uninteresting.
Managers: Bou Antoun brothers
Set menus: 166 F (lunch), 195 F (dinner)
A la carte: 200–300 F
all

LOUBNANE
▲ *300*
29 Rue Galande
75005 (A, 31)
M. Maubert-Mutualité
Tel 43 26 70 60
Open until midnight
Closed Mon. (lunch)
LEBANESE CUISINE
Authentic Lebanese cuisine. Huge vaulted dining-room for receptions, with Oriental sitting room. Book.
Specialties: mezzé, mouloukhié, coley with flavored rice.
Set menus: 70 F (weekday lunch), 105 F (dinner, Sat., Sun. and public holidays)
A la carte: 150–200 F
toutes

LOUS LANDÈS
▲ *306*
157 Av. du Maine
75014 (B, 32)
M. Gaîté
Tel 45 43 08 04
Open until 10.30 pm
Closed Sat. (lunch), Sun. and August
SOUTHWEST CUISINE
Real southwestern French food served with excellent wines from that region. Unfortunately these rustic pleasures do not come cheaply.
Specialties: foie gras, matelote of eel, magret with Guérande salt, cassoulet.
Chef-manager: Hervé Rumen
Set menus: 190 F, 300F
A la carte: 250–350 F
CB, Visa, AE, MC

LA MÉDITERRANÉE
▲ *152, 308*
2 Pl. de l'Odéon
75006 (A, 33)
M. Odéon
Tel 43 26 46 75
Open until 11 pm
Closed May 1
FISH CUISINE
Opposite the Théâtre de l'Europe. The drawings on the menu are by Jean Cocteau.
Specialties: carpaccio of artichoke with green oysters, platter of roast sardines à la tapenade.
Manager: Laurence Bouquet; chef: Marc Richard
Set menu: 175 F
A la carte: 250–500 F
all

MAP B
1 L'AMUSE-BOUCHE
2 L'ASSIETTE
5 AUX ARMES DE BRETAGNE
6 AUX PETITS CHANDELIERS
8 LE BISTRO DE LA GARE
11 LE CABANON DES MAÎTRES NAGEURS
12 LA CAGOUILLE
13 LE CAMÉLÉON
15 LE CAROUBIER
20 LE CIEL DE PARIS
21 LA CLOSERIE DES LILAS
22 LA COUPOLE
24 LE DÔME
25 DOMINIQUE
26 LE DUC
27 L'ÉCHANSON
32 LOUS LANDÈS
36 MONTPARNASSE 25
44 LE TAGHIT
48 VASSANTI
51 LE VIN DES RUES
52 VISHNOU

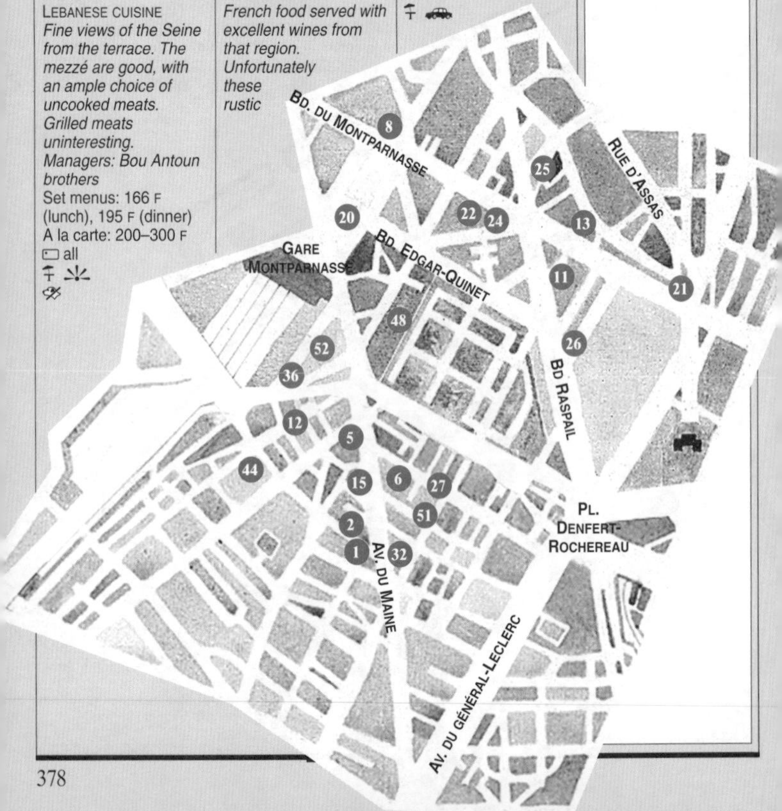

MOISSONNIER
28 Rue des Fossés-
Saint-Bernard
75005 (A, 34)
M. Jussieu
Tel 43 29 87 65
Open until 10 pm
Closed Sun. (dinner),
Mon. and August 1-
Sept. 7
LYONNAIS CUISINE
*An old-style bistro. In
the bar downstairs, the
décor hasn't changed
for three generations.
Monsieur Louis
manages the kitchen,
and Madame the front
of house. Wine served
in jugs.*
Chef-manager: Louis
Moissonnier
A la carte: 220–320 F
▭ CB, Visa

**LE MONDE
DES CHIMÈRES**
69 Rue Saint-Louis-
en-l'Île
75004 (A, 35)
M. Pont-Marie
Tel 43 54 45 27
Open until 10.30 pm
Closed Sun., Mon.
and public holidays.
BOURGEOIS CUISINE
*A 17th-century dining-
room with country
charm, dishes
concocted by Cécile
Ibane, who was a
television presenter.
You pay for the
reputation of the lady
and the décor.*
Set menu: 155 F
A la carte: 200–300 F
▭ CB, Visa, Euroc, MC

MONTPARNASSE 25
Hôtel Méridien
19 Rue du
Commandant-
Mouchotte
75014 (B, 36)
M. Montparnasse
Tel 44 36 44 25
or 43 20 61 03
Open until 10.30 pm
Closed Sat., Sun.,
public holidays, August

and 1 week at
Christmas
GASTRONOMIC CUISINE
*On level A in the
Méridien Hotel. Jean-
Yves Guého, who ran
the Méridien kitchens in
Hong Kong, concocts
delicious dishes.
Extensive lunch menu.
Impeccable service,
magnificent wine list,
superb cheese trolley.
Book.
Specialties: demi-deuil
of young cod and
scallops with truffles,
royal of squab with foie
gras, carré of suckling
calf roast and braised
with juniper berries.*
Managers: Jacques
Daumin and Gérard
Dubos; sommelier:
Gérard Margeon
Set menus: 230 F
(lunch), 290 F (dinner),
380 F (dinner)
A la carte: 350–500 F
▭ all
⊗ ✕ 🚗

L'ORANGERIE
28 Rue Saint-Louis-
en-l'Île
75004 (A, 37)
M. Pont-Marie
Tel 46 33 93 98
Open until 1 am, dinner
only
Closed Sun.
CLASSIC CUISINE
*The showbiz crowd and
tourists like this
attractive dining-room
with ancient beams and
large fireplace. But its
famous proprietor,
Jean-Claude Brialy, is
never seen there!
Over-rated.*
A la carte:
250–350 F
▭ CB,
Visa,
AE

LE PACTOLE
44 Bd Saint-Germain
75005 (A, 38)
M. Maubert-Mutualité
Tel 46 33 31 31
Open until 10.30 pm
Closed Sat. (lunch)
BOURGEOIS CUISINE
*The décor by Slavik, the
slightly humdrum but
light cuisine of Roland
Magne and a friendly
welcome from Noëlle,
his wife, have met with
deserved success.
Book.
Specialties: ravioli of
common crab, smoked
cod, fricassée of young
rabbit.*
Set menu: 149 F
(weekday lunch)
A la carte: 180–380 F
▭ CB, Visa, AE, MC,
Euroc
🍴 🍷

**★ LE PAVILLON
MONTSOURIS**
▲ 162
20 Rue Gazan
75014 (C, 39)
M. Cité Universitaire
Tel 45 88 38 52
Open until 10.30 pm
CLASSIC CUISINE
*This turn-of-the-century
villa in the Parc
Montsouris offers Belle
Époque charm to
passing gourmets.
Subtle combinations by
Stéphane Ruel.
Pleasant terrace on the
park. Interesting menu-
carte offer. Book.
Specialties: marbré of
pigeon with foie gras,
pan-fried tournedos of
tuna with braised
chicory, semi-wild
duckling served in two
helpings, soup of exotic
fruits in mint bergamot
jelly.*
Manager: Yvan
Courault;
pâtissier: Bernard Vatel
Set menus-A la carte:
189 F, 255 F
▭ all
🍴 🍷 ✕ 🚗

PERRAUDIN
▲ 152
157 Rue Saint-Jacques
75005 (A, 40)
M. Luxembourg
Tel 46 33 15 75
Open until 10.15 pm
Closed Sat. (lunch),
Sun., Mon. (lunch) and
August 14–31
HOME COOKING
*Students from the
nearby Sorbonne are
enthusiasts of this
bistro. As in the old
days regulars' napkins
are kept in pigeon
holes. Attractive prices.*
Set menu: 59 F (lunch)
A la carte: 100–150 F
▭ none
🍴 ✕

**★ LE PETIT
MARGUERY**
9 Bd du Port-Royal
75013 (C, 41)
M. Gobelins
Tel 43 31 58 59
Open until 10.30 pm
Closed Sun. Mon.,
August and Dec.
24–Jan. 2
BOURGEOIS CUISINE
*One of the most
authentic bourgeois
bistros in the capital,
run by the charming
Cousin brothers.
Generous helpings and
regional wines. Book.*
Set menus: 160 F
(lunch), 200 F (dinner),
320 F, 450 F
A la carte: 250–380 F
▭ all
🍴 🍷

POLIDOR
▲ 151
41 Rue Monsieur-
le-Prince
75006 (A, 42)
M. Odéon
Tel 43 26 95 34
Open until 12.30 am
(Sun. 11 pm)
HOME COOKING
*Budding writers
frequent the Polidor, sit
where 19th-century
writers sat, and eat
heartily. They find the
napkin pigeon holes for
regulars as appealing
as the waitresses'*

MAP C

29 ETCHEGORRY
39 LE PAVILLON
   MONTSOURIS
41 LE PETIT MARGUERY
49 LES VIEUX MÉTIERS
   DE FRANCE

BD DE PORT-ROYAL

BD ARAGO

BD AUGUSTE-BLANQUI

RUE DE LA SANTÉ

RUE DE TOLBIAC

PL. D'ITALIE

---

uniforms, and their
smiles. A seat of
nascent literature. All
for dream prices.
Set menus: 55 F
(weekday lunch), 100 F
(lunch Sun.)
A la carte: 90–120 F
☐ none

RESTAURANT A
▲ *294*
5 Rue de Poissy
75005 (A, 43)
M. Cardinal Lemoine
Tel 46 33 85 54
Open until 11 pm
Closed Mon.
CHINESE CUISINE
18th-century cuisine. No
glutamate and the
sauces in the
"casseroles" have
simmered for 48 hours.
Sculpted ice creams
and vegetables, shaped
rice pastry with
demonstration during
meals. Specialties:
maritime roll, gambas
with nougatine,
casserole of crab in

beer.
Chef-manager: Kien
Huynh
Set menu: 108 F
A la carte: 150–200 F
☐ CB, Visa, AE
♨

LE TAGHIT
▲ *302*
63 Rue de l'Ouest
75014 (B, 44)
M. Gaîté
Tel 43 20 25 57
Open until midnight
ALGERIAN CUISINE
The Taghit, a
"Restaurant of the
desert," offers unique
couscous and tajines
in Paris, accompanied
by three semolinas:
flavored with barley,
orange flower and
desert herbs.
A la carte: 150–250 F
☐ CB, Visa

TASHI DELEK
4 Rue des Fossés-
Saint-Jacques
75005 (A, 45)

M. Jussieu
Tel 43 26 55 55
Open until 10.30 pm
Closed Sun. and Mon.
(lunch)
TIBETAN CUISINE
Enter this colorful
establishment and be
initiated into the strange
flavors of Tibet.
A long journey for a
small price.
Specialties: steamed
ravioli with vegetables
and cheese, homemade
noodles, curry of gigot
with rice and yellow
lentils.
A la carte: 80–180 F
☐ CB, Visa
♨

LA TIMONERIE
35 Quai de la Tournelle
75005 (A, 46)
M. Maubert-Mutualité
Tel 43 25 44 42
Open until 10.30 pm
Closed Mon. (lunch) and
Sun.
GASTRONOMIC CUISINE

Original dishes created
by Philippe de
Givenchy. Slightly
stilted ambiance, good
lunch menu.
Specialties: ravioli of
duck with ginger, grilled
tuna and piperade of
uncooked ham, pig's
cheek with vegetables
in gravy and crispy rind.
Set price menu: 195 F
(lunch)
A la carte: 250–400 F
☐ CB, Visa, AE, Diners
♨ **P**

★ **LA TOUR D'ARGENT**
▲ *147*
15–17 Quai de la
Tournelle
75005 (A, 47)
M. Maubert-Mutualité
Tel 43 54 23 31
Open until 10.30 pm.
Closed. Mon.
GASTRONOMIC CUISINE
A landmark! Foreigners
rave about this very
famous restaurant. The
formal welcome, luxury
décor, tables covered
with sumptuous
glassware and
magnificent silver, the
view of the Île de la
Cité, the grand service,
David Rigway's
prodigious wine cellar
make it one of the
jewels in French luxury.
Manuel Martinez
presents top-quality
cooking in the great
French tradition. Book.
Specialties: brouillade
of eggs with truffles,
roast turbot with
woodland mushrooms,
tournedos of wild
salmon Taria, duckling
Tour d'Argent, fillet of
beef Tour d'Argent,
cushion of veal
sweetbreads with
lobster, pear Jean
Charpini, chocolatine

with morello cherries.
Manager: Claude Terrail
Set menu: 375 F (lunch)
A la carte: 650–1 000 F
🍽 All
⛷ 🚗 🐎 🚙

VASSANTI
3 Rue Larochelle
75014 (B, 48)
M. Gaîté
Tel 43 21 97 43
Open until 10.30 pm
Closed Mon. (lunch)
and Tue. (lunch)
INDIAN CUISINE
Fine Indian cuisine in
carved wood
surroundings; pleasant
service by waiters in
traditional costume.
Book.
Set menus: 99 F, 130 F
(lunch)
A la carte: 180–250 F
🍽 except AE

**LES VIEUX MÉTIERS
DE FRANCE**
▲ 164
13 Bd Auguste-Blanqui
75013 (C, 49)
M. Corvisart
Tel 45 88 90 03
and 45 81 07 07
Open until 10.30 pm
Closed Sun. and Mon.
GASTRONOMIC CUISINE
The Compagnons du
Tour de France built the
half-timbered façade
and made the Louis XIII
furniture.
Technically faultless
cuisine. The unusual
surroundings, pleasant
food and rich wine list
are the stuff of dreams.
Book.
Specialties: papillote of
foie gras with salted
crunchy cabbage,
lobster roast in herb
butter, cheek of beef
simmered in brouilly,
Bresse chicken with
morel mushrooms.
Chef-manager: Michel
Moisan; sommelier:
Franck Favier
Set menus: 165 F, 300F
A la carte: 250–340 F
🍽 CB, Visa, AE, Diners
🚗 🐌

**LES VIGNES
DU PANTHÉON**
4 Rue des Fossés-
Saint-Jacques
75005 (A, 50)
M. Jussieu
Tel 43 54 80 81
Open until 11 pm
Closed Sat. (lunch),
Sun.
HOME COOKING

Maison fondée en 1582

Updated bistro cuisine
in this wine restaurant,
which offers a fine
selection of
southwestern vintages.
Specialties: eggs en
meurette, quercynoise
pan-fried queen
scallops, Troyes
chitterlings in sancerre.
Set menu: 89 F (lunch)
A la carte: 180–250 F
🍽 CB, Visa

LE VIN DES RUES
▲ 310
21 Rue Boulard
75014 (B, 51)
M. Denfert-Rochereau
Tel 43 22 19 78
Open from 10 am to 8
pm (lunch: 1 pm-3 pm)
Late opening Wed. and
Fri. 9 pm to midnight
Closed Sun., Mon.,
Feb. 14–21 and August
HOME COOKING
This bistro evokes the
romantic Paris of
Jacques Prévert and
Robert Doisneau.
Lyonnais-inspired
cuisine. The best place
to celebrate the arrival
of Beaujolais nouveau.
Book.
Chef-manager: Jean
Chanrion
A la carte: 100–200 F
🍽 none

VISHNOU
▲ 298
13 Rue du
Commandant-
Mouchotte
75014 (B, 52)
M. Montparnasse
Tel 45 38 92 93
Open until 11.30 pm
(Fri. until 2 am)
INDIAN CUISINE
Welcome in traditional
costume, superb saris
displayed on the walls.
Good Indian cuisine
with a menu that allows
you to sample a range
of tandooris, particularly
the tasty cubes of
salmon. The salted
lassis (yogurt-based
drinks) are
exceptional.
Set menus: 95 F,
150 F (lunch), 220
F, 230 F
A la carte: 250–350
F

🍽 all

WALLY LE SAHARIEN
▲ 302
16 Rue Le Regrattier
75004 (A, 53)
M. Pont-Marie
Tel 43 25 01 39
Open until 11.30 pm
Closed Sun. and Mon.
(lunch)
SAHARAN CUISINE
Wally's couscous is as
delicious as it is
unusual: it is presented
Saharan style with no
accompanying stock or
vegetables. If you come
from that part of the
world, home-sickness is
guaranteed. Book.
Specialties: pastilla with
pigeon, hand-rolled
couscous with lamb
méchoui and merguez.
Chef-manager: Wally
Shouaki
Set menu: 300 F (incl.
wine)
A la carte: 250–350 F
🍽 CB, Visa, AE
🚗 🐌 🍽

**INNER
SUBURBS**

★ **LA MANUFACTURE**
20 Esplanade
Manufacture
(opposite 30 Rue
Ernest-Renand)
Issy-les-Moulineaux
Tel 40 93 08 98
Open until 10.30 pm
Closed Sat. (lunch),
Sun.
CLASSIC CUISINE
A tobacco factory
converted into a very
trendy

plant-decked bistro. "To
order: great bourgeois
dishes" a notice
proclaims.
Specialties: confit of
pig's ears in salad,
lightly roast sea bream
and celery juice, magret
of duck with black
radish and juniper.
Chef-manager: David
Van Laer
Set menu: 180 F
Set price dégustation
menu: 250 F (dinner)
🍽 CB, Visa, AE

★ **MAXIM'S**
Orly Airport
Orly-Ouest Terminal
Tel 46 86 87 84 or 46 87
16 16
Open until 10 pm
Closed Sat., Sun.,
public holidays and
August
CLASSIC CUISINE
The younger brother of
Maxim's Paris.
View of the airport from
the terrace.
Manager: Jean-Marie
Janisson; chef: Gilles
Jouanin; sommelier:
Denis Brayer
Set menu: 290 F
A la carte: 350–600 F
🍽 all

★ **RIVER CAFÉ**
◆ 326
46 Quai Stalingrad
Issy-les-Moulineaux
Tel 40 93 50 20
Open until 11.30 pm
CLASSIC CUISINE
The ideal spot to eat on
the banks of the Seine
close to Paris. Unusual
surroundings and good
cuisine appreciated by
neighboring advertising
executives or
employees of French
national television.
Managers: Thierry
Monassier and Manuel
Heurtier;
chef: Thierry Papin
A la carte: 150–250 F
🍽 all

MAP A ◆ *384*
4 Amphyclès
6 Apicius
8 Baumann-Ternes
9 Les Béatilles
10 Le Berry's
11 Le Bistrot d'à côté
16 Cave Petrissans
27 La Gazelle
28 Gérard Faucher
29 Goldenberg
31 Le Grenadin
33 Il Ristorante
42 Le Manoir de Paris
43 La Marée
44 Michel Rostang
59 La Table de Pierre

MAP B ◆ *387*
2 Alexandros
3 Amazigh
5 L'Antre du roi Philène
7 Au Petit Colombier
12 Le Bistrot de l'Étoile-Lauriston
15 Le Carpaccio
17 Charlie de Bab-el-Oued
18 Chiberta
19 Clos Longchamp
20 Conti
21 Le Cougar
22 Élysées du Vernet
23 Entrecôte-Le Relais de Venise
24 L'Étoile marocaine
25 Famiglia Fuligna
32 Guy Savoy
34 Le Jardin
39 Kambodgia
40 Le Lyonnais
41 La Maison du Danemark (Copenhague and Flora Danica)
47 Napoléon
50 Le Pergolèse
51 Le Petit Bedon
57 La Rôtisserie d'Armaillé
58 Sormani
60 Taillevent
63 Le Vancouver

MAP C ◆ *389*
1 Al Mounia
13 Brasserie Stella
14 La Butte Chaillot
26 Faugeron
36 Jean-Claude Ferrero
37 Joël Robuchon
38 Le Jules Verne
45 Le Moï
46 Les Monuments
48 Oum El Banine
52 Le Petit Rétro
53 La Petite Tour
55 Quach
56 Le Relais d'Auteuil «Patrick Pignol»
61 Le Toit de Passy
62 Le Totem
64 Le Vivarois

OFF MAP
30 La Grande Cascade
35 Les Jardins de Bagatelle
49 Le Pavillon des princes
54 Le Pré catelan

INNER SUBURBS
65 Le Café de la Jatte
66 Fouquet's Europe
67 La guinguette de Neuilly
68 Quai Ouest
69 San Valero

◆

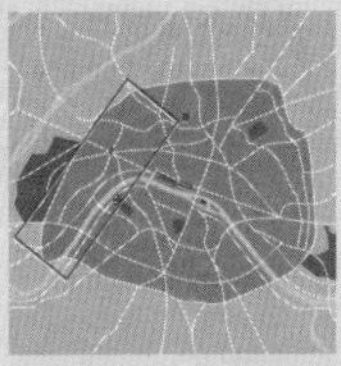

ITINERARY 3

Al Mounia
▲ *302*
16 Rue de Magdebourg
75016 (C, 1)
M. Trocadéro
Tel 47 27 57 28
Open until 10.30 pm
Closed Sun. and July 15–Sept. 1
Moroccan Cuisine
Copper trays, silk cushions, waiters in traditional costume. Good couscous and tajines. Book.
A la carte : 230–330 F
CB, Visa, AE

Alexandros
18 Rue Saint-Ferdinand
75017 (B, 2)
M. Argentine
Tel 45 74 75 11
Open until 10 pm
Closed Sun. and August 15–23
Greek Cuisine
Everything from the starters to the desserts is homemade by Dolly Alexandros. Incredible value for money. Specialties: souvlaki, pikilia, calmars à la crétoise, suckling pig. Chef-manager: Dolly Alexandros
A la carte : 85–108 F
none

Amazigh
▲ *302*
2 Rue La Pérouse
75016 (B, 3)
M. Kléber
Tel 47 20 90 38
Open until 11 pm
Closed Sat. (lunch) and Sun.
Moroccan Cuisine
This chic restaurant offers a wide range of tajines and couscous. Book.
A la carte : 235–330 F
CB, Visa

Amphyclès
78 Av. des Ternes
75017 (A, 4)
M. Porte Maillot
Tel 40 68 01 01
Open until 10.30 pm
Closed Sat. (lunch) and Sun.
Gastronomic cuisine
Fashionable Paris dines chez Philippe Groult, Joël Robuchon's former number 2. Intimate atmosphere, small decorative garden. Subtle and creative cooking, fine wines, noteworthy lunch menu. Book. Specialties: mesclun of red mullet with a light pepper vinaigrette, cream of baby leeks with crawfish, lobster carapace with spices, Lozère roast lamb in lavender perfumed persillade. Sommelier: Hubert Notais
Set menus: 260 F (lunch), 580 F, 780 F
A la carte: 405–550 F
except AE

L'Antre du roi Philène
▲ *274*
16 Rue Lauriston
75016 (B, 5)
M. Charles de Gaulle-Étoile
Tel 45 00 25 03
Open until 10.15 pm
Closed Sat., Sun., August and Dec. 15–27
Franco-Italian Cuisine
A Breton chef, Italian hostess, eclectic cooking, disparate wine list. Altogether very attractive. Book. Chef-managers: Frank Businelli and Silvia Tomaschu
Set menus: 139 F, 175 F, 320 F (dégustation)
A la carte : 205–300 F
CB, AE, Visa

★ **Apicius**
▲ *175*
122 Av. de Villiers
75017 (A, 6)
M. Périere
Tel 43 80 19 66
Open until 10 pm
Closed Sat., Sun. and August.
Gastronomic cuisine
Elegant modern décor. Jean-Pierre Vigato offers apparently classic dishes with a creative twist. One of the best Parisian eateries. Book. Specialties: lobster consommé with bone

marrow, shellfish and frogs' legs flan with sauce poulette, skate with rock salt, veal sweetbreads on a spit, duck tourte.
Sommelier: Hervé Milet
Set menu : 480 F (dinner)
A la carte : 405–700 F
▭ CB, Visa, AE
🐾 🚗

AU PETIT COLOMBIER
45–42 Rue des Acacias
75017 (B, 7)
M. Argentine
Tel 43 80 28 54
Open until 10.30 pm
Closed Sat., Sun. (lunch) and August 1–17
CLASSIC CUISINE
Warm welcome in the reception with fireplace. Comfortable, flower-decked dining-rooms. Regional dishes realized by the excellent technician, Bernard Fournier. The lunch menu is a bargain. Book.
Specialties: spit-roast eggs with fresh truffles, sweet and sour noix of scallops, fatted chicken with truffle juice, veal sweetbreads à l'anglaise.
Set menus: 200 F (lunch), 350 F (dinner)
A la carte: 265–370 F
▭ CB, Visa, AE
🔆 🐾 🎭 P

BAUMANN-TERNES
▲ 312
64 Av. des Ternes
75017 (A, 8)
M. Porte Maillot
Tel 45 74 16 66
Open until midnight
ALSATIAN CUISINE
Nostalgic photos and posters of Alsace on the walls. One of the capital's fashionable brasseries, which is not always justified.
Specialties: seafood, fish, choucroute.
Manager: Agnès Kehres
Set menu: 160 F
A la carte: 165–220 F
▭ all
🍴 🔆 🐾

LES BÉATILLES
127 Rue Cardinet
75017 (A, 9)
M. Malesherbes
Tel 42 27 95 64
Open until 10.30 pm
Closed Sat., Sun., Feb. holidays and 3 weeks in

August
CLASSIC CUISINE
Friendly welcome in this unpretentious and flower-decked establishment. Good dishes at truly interesting prices. Set menus perfect.
Specialties: lasagna of red mullet, matelote of oysters and galette of pig's trotters, béatilles of lamb.
Chef: Christian Bochaton
Set menus : 130 F (lunch), 180 F, 290 F (dinner)
A la carte : 225–320 F
▭ all

★ LE BERRY'S
46 Rue de Naples
75008 (A, 10)
M. Europe
Tel 40 75 01 56
Open until 1 am
Closed Sat. (lunch). Sun.
HOME COOKING
Annex of the adjacent restaurant, Le Grenadin, where Patrik Cirotte officiates.
The kitchens are shared. Very tasty bistro cooking.
A la carte: 135–200 F
▭ CB, Visa

LE BISTROT D'À CÔTÉ
Corner of 10 Rue Gustave-Flaubert and 20 Rue Rennequin
75017 (A, 11)
P. Garage Banville
Tel 42 67 05 81
Open until 10.30 pm
Closed Sat. (lunch), Sun. and August 1–15
CLASSIC CUISINE
Charming former grocery store with marble pay-desk and mirrors. Michel Rostang has developed the menu.
Specialty: game. Wines served by the glass.
Other premises: 16 Avenue de Villiers (47 63 25 61). Book.
Sommelier: Alain Ronzatti
Set menu: 198 F
A la carte: 145–250 F
▭ CB, Visa, AE
🐾

LE BISTROT DE L'ÉTOILE-LAURISTON
19 Rue de Lauriston
75016 (B, 12)

M. Charles de Gaulle-Étoile
Tel 40 67 11 16
Open until midnight
Closed Sat. (lunch) and Sun.
CLASSIC CUISINE
Chic and spacious surroundings in this bistro set up by Guy Savoy. Same qualities as the other branches. Book.
Chef: William Ledeuil
A la carte: 155–250 F
▭ all

BRASSERIE STELLA
133 Av. Victor-Hugo
75016 (C, 13)
M. Victor-Hugo
Tel 47 27 60 54
Open until 1.30 am
BOURGEOIS CUISINE
Regional cooking and seafood.
A la carte : 185–280 F
▭ CB, Visa, AE
🍴

LA BUTTE CHAILLOT
112 Av. Kléber
75016 (C, 14)
M. Trocadéro
Tel 47 27 88 88
Open until midnight
CLASSIC CUISINE
Another Guy Savoy bistro with a decidedly modern décor. The clientele gathers around the fireplace in winter and the fountain in summer. Book.
Chef: Franck Paquier
Set menus: 110 F (weekday lunch), 150 F (after 10 pm)
A la carte: 155–250 F
▭ CB, Visa, AE, MC
🍴

★ LE CARPACCIO
▲ 274
Hôtel Royal-Monceau,
37 Av. Hoche
75008 (B, 15)
M. Charles de Gaulle-Étoile
Tel 45 62 76 87
Open until 10.30 pm
Closed August
ITALIAN CUISINE
In the Royal-Monceau hotel.

Some of the best transalpine cooking in Paris served with a smile. The evening menu offers a wide range of dishes and the wine list some unusual discoveries. Book.
Specialties: mini pasta gnocchis with ragout of beef, saffron risotto and beef bone marrow, Venetian-style calves' liver.
Manager: Jean-Pierre Allais; chef : Angelo Paracucchi; sommelier : Bruno Malara
Set menus: 250 F (lunch), 300 F (dinner)
A la carte: 325–500 F
▭ all
🚗 🐾 🎭

CAVE PETRISSANS
30bis Av. de Niel
75017 (A, 16)
M. Ternes
Tel 42 27 52 03
Open until 10.30 pm
Closed Sat., Sun. and August 5–22
HOME COOKING
M. Petrissans opened his wine cellar in 1880. Today it is one of the best in Paris and a restaurant has been added. Marie-Christine Allemoz continues her grandfather's work. Good cooking, splendid wine list, wine by the glass.
Chef: Jacques Bertrel
Set price menu: 155 F
A la carte: 185–250 F
▭ CB, Visa, AE
🍴

CHARLIE DE BAB-EL-OUED
▲ 302
95 Bd Gouvion-Saint-Cyr
75017 (B, 17)
M. Porte Maillot
Tel 45 74 34 62
Open until 11 pm
ALGERIAN CUISINE
Marvelous décor and mosaics, fountains, moucharabiehs and palm trees. Couscous and tajines. Book.

383

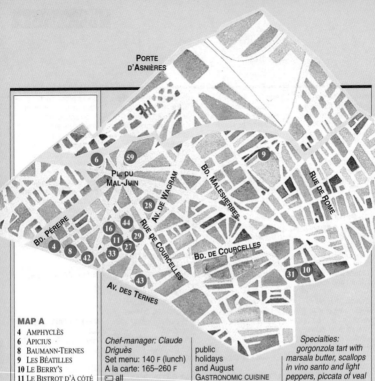

PORTE
D'ASNIÈRES

PL. DU
MAL-JUIN

BD. MALESHERBES

AV. DE WAGRAM

RUE DE ROME

BD. PEREIRE

RUE DE COURCELLES

BD. DE COURCELLES

AV. DES TERNES

Chef-manager: Claude Driguès
Set menu: 140 F (lunch)
A la carte: 165–260 F
☐ all
♨ ✍

CHIBERTA
3 Rue Arsène-Houssaye
75008 (B, 18)
M. Charles de Gaulle-Étoile
Tel 45 63 77 90
Open until 10.30 pm
Closed Sat., Sun., public holidays, August and Dec. 24 -Jan. 3
GASTRONOMIC CUISINE
One of the temples of Parisian society. Faultless cooking : Philippe Da Silva skilfully recreates classic dishes. Book.
Specialties : salad of smoked eel and creamed caviar, panfried salmon with bacon potatoes, confit of roast duckling in caraway, pan-fried calves' liver in vinegar and buttercup persillade.
Manager: Louis-Noël Richard
Set menu: 290 F
A la carte: 395–700 F
☐ all
♨ 🚗

CLOS LONGCHAMP
Hôtel Méridien
81 Bd Gouvion-Saint-Cyr
75017 (B, 19)
M. Porte Maillot
Tel 40 68 30 40 or 40 68 00 70
Open until 10.30 pm
Closed Sat., Sun.,

public holidays and August
GASTRONOMIC CUISINE
Jean-Marie Meulien skilfully creates very personal preparations in the Hôtel Méridien at Porte-Maillot, complemented by wines chosen by notable sommelier Didier Bureau. Impeccable service. Book.
Specialties: chestnut soup with cagouilles, sea bream with bone marrow and young peppers, truffade of duck in wine, entrecôte in sauce mareyeur.
Manager: Francis Coulon
Set menus: 250 F (weekday lunch), 450 F (dinner except public holidays)
A la carte: 408–650 F
☐ all
♨♨ ▦ ♨ 🅿

CONTI
72 Rue de Lauriston
75016 (B, 20)
M. Boissière
Tel 47 27 74 67
Open until 10.30 pm
Closed Sat., Sun. and August
GASTRONOMIC CUISINE
Michel Ranvier reinterprets transalpine cuisine, adding a little creative genius that transforms it into a personalized cuisine. Good choice of Italian wines and interesting menu. Book.

Specialties: gorgonzola tart with marsala butter, scallops in vino santo and light peppers, piccata of veal and baby artichokes in poivrade.
Manager: M. Abyaghi; sommelier: Philippe Cabalé
Set menu: 265 F (weekday lunch, incl. wine and coffee)
A la carte : 295–400 F
☐ all
♨

LE COUGAR / TAIRA
10 Rue des Acacias
75017 (B, 21)
M. Argentine
Tel 47 66 74 14
Open until 10.30 pm
Closed Sat. (lunch), Sun. and week of August 15
FISH CUISINE
Preparations by a protégé of Joël Robuchon and Jacques Cagna are served in an understated décor. Taira Kurihara cooks meticulously with sophisticated imagination. Fine menus.
Specialties: queen scallops stuffed with tarragon, pan-fried John Dory with caramel of Dublin Bay prawns, fillet of gray sea bream in a rock salt crust.
Set menus: 150 F (lunch), 170 F, 320 F (dinner)
A la carte: 345–450 F
☐ CB, Visa, AE, Diners
♨

ÉLYSÉES DU VERNET
25 Rue Vernet
75008 (B, 22)
M. George-V
Tel 47 23 43 10
Open until 10 pm
Closed Sat., Sun. and
July 23–August 24
PROVENÇAL CUISINE
*Hotel restaurant. Under
the Belle Époque glass
canopy, try the
generous southern
dishes. Bustling service
and impressive wine
cellar. Book.
Specialties: effeuillée of
cod with sea urchins,
shelled spider crab with
gnocchi of potimarron,
duck in orange sauce.
Manager: Alain Moser;
chef: Bruno Cirino;
sommelier: Angel Plata*
Set menus: 270 F, 420 F
(dinner)
A la carte: 305–400 F
▭ all
🏛 🍴 🍷 🚗

**ENTRECÔTE-LE
RELAIS DE VENISE**
271 Bd Péreire
75017 (B, 23)
M. Porte Maillot
Tel 45 74 27 97
Open until 10.30 pm
Closed Good Friday
and July
CLASSIC CUISINE
*It is fashionable to
queue in front of this
local restaurant at busy
times. Cramped tables
and top-quality meats
for a hurried and
sophisticated clientele.
Single dish: entrecôte
with French fries and
walnut salad. Choice of
desserts.*
A la carte : 105–150 F
▭ CB, Visa, MC.
Checks none
🍴

L'ÉTOILE MAROCAINE
▲ 302
56 Rue de Galilée
75008 (B, 24)
M. George-V
Tel 47 20 44 43
Open until 10.30 pm
MOROCCAN CUISINE
*Tasty Moroccan
experience in this
annex of the Timgad
(17th arr.). Book.*
A la carte: 185–280 F
Y CB, Visa
▭ CB, Visa
🍷

FAMIGLIA FULIGNA
▲ 274
2 Rue Waldeck-

Rousseau
75017 (B, 25)
M. Porte Maillot
Tel 45 74 20 28
Open until 11 pm
ITALIAN CUISINE
*Family restaurant
specializing in pasta.
Music in the evenings.
Manager: Michela
Fuligna; chef: Gianni
Fuligna*
A la carte: 175–250 F
▭ all
🍴 🅿

FAUGERON
▲ 167
52 Rue de Longchamp
75016 (C, 26)
M. Iéna
Tel 47 04 24 53
Open until 10 pm
Closed Sat. (May-
Sept.), Sat. dinner (Oct.-
April), Sun., Dec 23–
Jan. 2, August
GASTRONOMIC CUISINE
*First the exceptional
welcome from the chef's
wife. Then the faultless
service and Jean-
Claude Jambon, the
"Best Sommelier in the
world." Lastly the
perfect classic
food by Henri Faugeron.
A great Parisian eatery.
Book.
Specialties: millefeuille
of artichoke with
smoked salmon, lobster
roast in sate, tournedos
of grouper with truffle
extracts, curry of jarret
of veal in sauternes,
parmentier of young
rabbit with dill.*
Set menus: 290 F
(lunch), 550 F (incl.
wine)
A la carte : 555–700 F
▭ CB, Visa
🍴 🍷 🚗

LA GAZELLE
▲ 304
9 Rue Rennequin
75017 (A, 27)
M. Ternes
Tel 42 67 64 18
Open until 11.30 pm
Closed Sun.
AFRICAN CUISINE
*Cameroon specialties,
with a few other recipes
from Black Africa. A
musician plays the
khora in the evenings;
singer Fridays and
Saturdays.
Chef-manager: Marie
Koffi Nketsia*
Set menus: 95 F, 130 F
A la carte: 125–150 F
▭ CB, Visa, AE

GÉRARD FAUCHER
123 Av. de Wagram
75017 (A, 28)
M. Périere
Tel 42 27 61 50
Open until 10 pm
Closed Sat. (lunch),
Sun. and August 15
GASTRONOMIC CUISINE
*Delightful welcome from
Nicole Faucher in an
elegant dining-room.
Gérard Faucher
transforms simple
ingredients into tasty
combinations. Superb
lunch menu. Book.
Specialties: millefeuille
of spinach and raw
beef, potato galette with
different types of cod,
lamb with eggplants
and anchovy sauce.
Sommelier: Martial
Tréguier*
Set menus: 200 F
(lunch), 420 F
(dégustation)
A la carte: 305–400 F
▭ all
🍴 🍷

GOLDENBERG
▲ 284
69 Av. de Wagram
75017 (A, 29)
M. Ternes
Tel 42 27 34 79
Open until midnight
CENTRAL EUROPEAN
CUISINE
*You can taste the
specialties from this
shop in the adjacent
small room.
Specialties: zakouski,
smoked herrings and
salmon, special breads
Chef: Patrick
Goldenberg.*
Set menu: 98 F
A la carte: 155–200 F
▭ CB
🍴

★ **LA GRANDE
CASCADE**
▲ 171
Bois de Boulogne,
Allée de Longchamp

(opposite the
racecourse)
75016 (off map, 30)
M. Av. Henri-Martin
Tel 45 27 33 51
Open until 10.30 pm
Closed Dec. 20–Jan. 20
and Nov.1-March 31
(dinner)
CLASSIC CUISINE
*In a hunting lodge built
by Haussmann between
the Bagatelle rose
garden and the
Longchamp racecourse.
Turn-of-the-century
dining-room with a
superb glass canopy,
impeccable service and
impressive wine list.
Book in summer.
Specialties: brouillade
of eggs with truffles,
salmon with smoked
bacon and cabbage,
fillet of beef with
mushrooms, sweet and
sour duckling with fried
ginger.
Manager: André Menut;
chef: Jean Sabine*
Set menu: 285 F (lunch)
A la carte: 455–600 F
▭ CB, Visa, AE, Diners
🏛 🍴 🖼 🚗

LE GRENADIN
44 Rue de Naples
75008 (A, 31)
M. Europe
Tel 45 63 28 92
Open until 10 pm
Closed Sat., Sun., week
of July14 and week of
August 15, Christmas
holidays
GASTRONOMIC CUISINE
*Patrick Cirotte creates
very individual dishes.
Warm welcome from his
wife in two small dining-
rooms. Well-chosen
wine list.
Specialties: oxtail salad
with chicons and poppy
seeds, fillet of sea
bream à la bière de
mars, nage of pork filet
mignon with spices.*
Set menus: 188 F,
238 F, 298 F, 320 F
A la carte: 305–400 F
▭ CB, Visa, AE
🍷

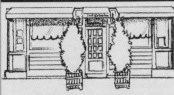

★ **GUY SAVOY**
▲ 177
18 Rue Troyon
75017 (B, 32)
M. Charles de Gaulle-
Étoile
Tel 43 80 40 61
and 43 80 36 22
Open until 10.30 pm
Closed Sat. (lunch) and
Sun.
GASTRONOMIC CUISINE
Superb contemporary
paintings, impeccable
service, chic Parisian
and international
clientele, together with
a few stars. But the real
star is in the kitchen :
Guy Savoy creates
dishes as unusual as
they are exquisite, well
supported by a brilliant
sommelier, Éric Mancio.
Book.
Specialties: pan-fried
mussels and field
mushrooms in "turf and
surf" sauce, crispy veal
trotters with herb salad
and parsley dressing,
oven-baked herb-
studded John Dory,
saddle of lamb roast
with a ragout of broad
beans, poached and
grilled pigeon
and its giblets in risotto.
Set menu: 750 F
A la carte: 450–800 F
▭ except Diners

IL RISTORANTE
▲ 274
22 Rue de Fourcroy
75017 (A, 33)
M. Ternes
Tel 47 63 34 00
Open until 10.30 pm
Closed Sun. and August
10–24
ITALIAN CUISINE
Here you can taste
fresh pasta skilfully
prepared by the Sicilian
owner, Rocco Anfuso.
Book.
Set menu: 165 F (lunch)
A la carte: 205–300 F
▭ CB, Visa, AE

LE JARDIN
▲ 176
Hôtel Royal-Monceau

37 Av. Hoche
75008 (B, 34)
M. Charles de Gaulle-
Étoile
Tel 45 61 98 00
Open until 10.30 pm
GASTRONOMIC CUISINE
Luxury hotel restaurant.
Circular dining-room
surmounted by a glass
canopy, picture windows
overlooking a garden-
terrace. Sublime
desserts are the
finishing touch to
Bernard Guilhaudin's
cooking. Fantastic wine
list. Book.
Specialties: crispy
Dublin Bay prawns with
basil and mango and
papaya sauce, steamed
sea bass with fennel
and aromatic
seasonings, side of
pigeon with olives and
pithiviers of its giblets,
veal sweetbreads roast
with lemon and celeriac
confit.
Manager: Jean-Pierre
Allais; sommelier:
Stéphane Lochon
Set menu: 280 F
A la carte: 320–480 F
▭ toutes

**LES JARDINS
DE BAGATELLE**
▲ 172
Bois de Boulogne,
Parc de Bagatelle.
Route de Sèvres à
Neuilly
75016 (off map, 35)
Tel 40 67 98 29
Open until 11.30 pm
Closed Jan.
CLASSIC CUISINE
The terrace is idyllic in
summer and the stables
décor picturesque. Very
classic cuisine. Book.
Manager: Michel
Bouquet; chef: Philippe
Gouriot
Set menu: 230 F
A la carte: 305–500 F
▭ all

★ **JEAN-CLAUDE
FERRERO**
▲ 166
38 Rue Vital

75016 (C, 36)
M. Passy
Tel 45 04 42 42
Open until 10.30 pm
Closed Sat. (summer),
Sun., May 1–18 and
August 10– Sept. 5
GASTRONOMIC CUISINE
Warm welcome from
Andrée Ferrero in this
Second Empire private
townhouse. Jean-
Claude Ferrero
concocts skilfully
adapted traditional
dishes. Local gourmets,
people from
showbusiness, politics
and finance come here
to taste the best all-
truffle menu in France
(800 F). Book.
Specialties: bavarois of
peppers in virgin oil,
roast gambas in garlic
petals, chicken en
vessie with vegetables,
truffle and goose liver,
blanquette of veal à
l'ancienne.
Set menus: 200 F
(lunch), 280 F and 350 F
A la carte: 315–540 F
▭ except Diners

★ **JOËL ROBUCHON**
▲ 168
59, Av. Raymond-
Poincaré
75016 (C, 37)
M. Victor-Hugo
Tel 47 27 12 27
Open until 10.15 pm
Closed Sat., Sun.
and July 5– August 1
GASTRONOMIC CUISINE
The whole world beats
a path to Joël
Robuchon, leader of
French gastronomy.
Comfortable dining-
room, privacy, fine
service and sommelier
extraordinaire, Antoine
Hernandez. But above
all, Joël Robuchon
himself in the kitchens
concocts divine,
unrivaled dishes
attracting the crowds.
Book.
Specialties: caviar jelly
with creamed
cauliflower, tarte friande
of truffles with onions
and smoked bacon,
creamed beans with
coconut truffée, pan-
fried fresh cod with
aromatic seasonings,
free range guinea-fowl
and foie gras roast with
confit potatoes in sauce,
simmered pig's head
Île-de-France.

Set menus: 890 F,
1200 F
A la carte: 555–1 000 F
▭ CB, Visa, AE, Diners

★ **LE JULES VERNE**
▲ 169
Champ-de-Mars,
2nd level of the Eiffel
Tower (south pillar lift)
75007 (C, 38)
M. Champ-de-Mars
Tel 45 55 61 44
Open until 10.30 pm
GASTRONOMIC CUISINE
The most gastronomic
postcard of Paris.
Unrivaled view of the
capital by day or night
from the second level of
the tower. Attractive
black décor by Slavik,
smooth welcome and
chic clientele. The
creative and
sophisticated cooking of
Alain Reix contributes to
the success of the
place. Book.
Specialties: matelote of
grouper with mushroom
and artichoke ravioli,
crépinette of pigeon
wing and pithiviers of its
legs, fillet of Sisteron
lamb with raw pan-fried
artichokes.
Manager: Pierre Ody;
sommelier: Amar
Chebrek
Set menu: 290 F
(weekday lunch)
A la carte: 420–600 F
▭ all

KAMBODGIA
▲ 296
15 Rue Bassano
75016 (B, 39)
M. Iéna
Tel 47 23 31 80
Open until 11 pm
Closed Sat. (lunch)
and Sun.
INDO-CHINESE CUISINE
Oriental wood paneling
and embroideries,
private corners and
small cushions. Subtle
cuisine, friendly service.
Book.
Manager: Yves Vatelot;
chef: Bui Thichi
Set menu: 170 F (lunch)
A la carte: 185–260 F
▭ CB, Visa, AM

LE LYONNAIS
26 Rue d'Armaillé
75017 (B, 40)
M. Argentine
Tel 45 72 00 82
Open until 10.30 pm

Closed Sat. (lunch) and Sun.
LYONNAIS CUISINE
A pleasant Lyonnais bistro just outside Neuilly. Relaxed welcome and reasonable prices.
Chef-manager: Yves Bourrier
Set menus: 118 F (lunch), 168 F, 225 F
À la carte: 225–320 F
☐ CB, Visa, MC
[symbol]

MAISON DU DANEMARK (COPENHAGUE AND FLORA DANICA)
▲ *282*
142, Av. des Champs-Élysées
75008 (B, 41)
M. George-V
Tel 43 59 20 41
Open until 10.30 pm
Closed (Copenhague only) Sun., public holidays, Jan. 1–7 and August
DANISH CUISINE
Two restaurants in the same building. Downstairs, the Flora Danica with its pleasant patio. Upstairs, the Copenhague, which is comfortable and chic.
Specialties: smoked or marinated fish, all kinds of salmon, mignons of reindeer, pre-salted duck.
Manager: Mr Engström; chef: Denis Schneider
Set menus: 250 F, 510 F (for 2)
À la carte: 305–500 F
☐ CB, Visa, AE, Diners
[symbols]

LE MANOIR DE PARIS
6 Rue Pierre Demours
75017 (A, 42)
M. Wagram
Tel 45 72 25 25
Open until 10 pm
Closed Sat. (lunch) and Sun.
GASTRONOMIC CUISINE
At the helm, Francis Vandenhende, who has put Gilles Méry in charge of the kitchens, although he still creates the desserts himself. Mediterranean specialties. Book.
Specialties: pastilla of young rabbit with rosemary and wild dandelion leaves, green oysters, shellfish and seafood à l'étouffée, carré of suckling pig roast with sage and stuffed cabbage and braised haunch.
Sommelier: Rémy Aspect
Set menus: 240 F, 295 F (lunch), 260 F, 390 F (dinner)
À la carte: 285–600 F
☐ all
[symbols]

LA MARÉE
▲ *308*
1 Rue Daru
75008 (A, 43)
M. Courcelles
Tel 43 80 20 00
Open until 10.30 pm
Closed Sat., Sun. and August
FISH CUISINE
Virtuoso service and fine choice of fish dishes

concocted by Bernard Pinaud : fine ingredients skilfully prepared and sumptuous wine cellar. Décor of Flemish paintings
Specialties: Belon oysters in champagne, lobster in cassolette, common crab in mildly spiced sauce, grilled sea bass with fennel.
Manager: Éric Trompier
À la carte: 405–600 F
☐ all
[symbols]

MICHEL ROSTANG
▲ *176*
20 Rue Rennequin
75017 (A, 44)
M. Ternes
Tel 47 63 40 77
Open until 10.30 pm
Closed Sat. (lunch) and Sat. (in summer), Sun.
GASTRONOMIC CUISINE
One of the leading lights of Parisian gastronomy. Two dining-rooms, one of which overlooks the kitchens via a picture window. Attractive décor, impeccable service, excellent wine list and cooking by the master, Michel Rostang. Book.
Specialties: galette of spleen with caviar and herb salad, pavé of pikeperch roast in its skin, veal sweetbreads pan-fried simply with lobster, carrots and shellfish juice in sauternes, hot bitter chocolate tart.

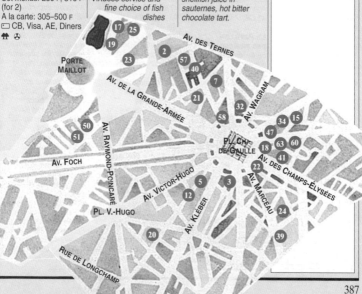

Set menus: 285 F (lunch), 495 F, 680 F (except public holidays)
A la carte: 525–700 F
▭ except Diners
🍸 ⚘ 🚗

LE MOÏ
▲ 296
7 Rue Gustave-Courbet
75016 (C, 45)
M. Victor-Hugo
Tel 47 55 81 26
Open until 11 pm
Closed Sun. and Mon. (lunch)
VIETNAMESE CUISINE
This was once a chic rendezvous. Now reopened after a lengthy closure, it offers delicate dishes worthy of its earlier days. Book.
Manager: Huguette Oggeri; chef: Agnès Fabre
A la carte: 145–260 F
▭ CB, Visa, AE
⚘

LES MONUMENTS
1 Pl. du Trocadéro
75016 (C, 46)
M. Trocadéro
Tel 44 05 90 00
Open until 10.30 pm
Closed Tue.
CLASSIC CUISINE
In the Musée des Monuments Français. Terrace affords a good view of the Eiffel Tower and the Seine. Reasonable prices. Specialties: feuilleté of asparagus, scallops with hazelnuts, duck with mango.
Set menu: 150 F (Sat. and Sun. lunch)
A la carte: 185–220 F
▭ except AE and Diners
🍸 🌿 ⚘

NAPOLÉON
38 Av. de Friedland
75008 (B, 47)

M. Charles de Gaulle-Étoile
Tel 42 27 99 50
Open until 10.30 pm
Closed Sat. and Sun.
GASTRONOMIC CUISINE
A stone's throw from the Arc de Triomphe. Sophisticated décor, perfect service and subtle dishes by a promising young chef, Karl Vandelverbe. Specialties: aumônière of common crab with orchid and fresh herb butter, John Dory with cream of sea urchins, Challans duckling roast with polenta and confit gizzards.
Manager: Guy-Pierre Baumann
Set menus: 170 F, 240 F and 280 F
A la carte: 295–450 F
▭ all
⚘ 🐦

OUM EL BANINE
▲ 302
16 bis Rue Dufrénoy
75016 (C, 48)
M. Rue de la Pompe
Tel 45 04 91 22
Open until 11 pm
Closed Sat. (lunch) and Sun.
MOROCCAN CUISINE
This Moroccan restaurant offers subtle and authentic traditional cuisine.
Chef-manager: Maria Seguin
Set menu: 150 F (lunch, incl. wine or tea)
A la carte: 225–320 F
▭ CB, Visa, AE

LE PAVILLON DES PRINCES
69 Av. de la Porte-d'Auteuil
75016 (off map, 49)
M. Porte-d'Auteuil
Tel 47 43 15 15
or 46 51 82 20

Open until 10.30 pm
GASTRONOMIC CUISINE
This charming fin de siècle villa on the edge of the Bois de Boulogne at the entrance to Roland-Garros square offers covered or summer terraces overlooking the garden. Reasonable prices. Specialties: red tuna with tian of vegetables, sauté of lamb with sage, duck cooked in two different ways.
Manager: Pascal Bonnichon; chef: Patrick Lenotre; sommelier: Loïc Boulmert
Set menus: 180 F, 270 F
A la carte: 285–320 F
▭ all
🍸 ⚘ 🅿

LE PERGOLÈSE
40 Rue Pergolèse
75016 (B, 50)
M. Argentine
Tel 45 00 21 40
Open until 11 pm
Closed Sat., Sun. and August
CLASSIC CUISINE
Two dining-rooms where you can eat well cooked but unoriginal dishes.
Chef-manager: Albert Corre
Set menus: 230 F, 300 F
A la carte: 355–450 F
▭ except Diners
🍸 ⚘

LE PETIT BEDON
38 Rue Pergolèse
75016 (B, 51)
M. Argentine
Tel 45 00 23 66
Open until 11 pm
Closed Sun.
CLASSIC CUISINE
In this establishment the décor is as bourgeois as the cuisine. Warm welcome. Book.
Chef: Pierre Marchesseau; sommelier: Jean-Marc Lamour
Set menu: 150 F, 175 F, 260 F (incl. wine)
A la carte: 205–400 F
▭ CB, Visa, AE, Diners
⚘

LE PETIT RÉTRO
5 Rue Mesnil
75016 (C, 52)
M. Victor-Hugo
Tel 44 05 06 05
Open until 10.30 pm
Closed Sun. and Mon. (lunch)
HOME COOKING

An attractively decorated old style bistro. Friendly service, well cooked tasty and unpretentious dishes. Specialties: cream of cucumber glazed with goat's cheese, salmon tartare with dill, lamb roasted with thyme flowers.
Manager: Chantal de Corbiac; chef: Frédéric Renoux
A la carte: 125–180 F
▭ CB, Visa
🍸

LA PETITE TOUR
11 Rue de la Tour
75016 (C, 53)
M. Passy
Tel 45 20 09 97
Open until 10.30 pm
Closed Sun.
CLASSIC CUISINE
A flower-decked dining-room in Passy in keeping with the area. Cocoon-like atmosphere. Book.
Chef-manager: Freddy Israël
A la carte: 225–330 F
▭ all

★ **LE PRÉ CATELAN**
▲ 173
Bois de Boulogne, Route de Suresnes
75016 (off map, 54)
M. Av. Henri-Martin
Tel 45 24 55 58
Open until 10 pm
Closed Sun. (dinner), Mon., Feb. 15–30
GASTRONOMIC CUISINE
A stone's throw from l'Étoile and La Défense, this restaurant on the edge of the Bois de Boulogne is a haven of tranquility for stressed businessmen. Very professional service, extensive wine list. Book.
Specialties: black risotto of Dublin Bay prawns with citronnella and Thai basil, mignonnettes of sea bass in maraîchère with fennel, pig's trotters caramelized in truffle juice, roast duck in tamarind sauce.
Chef-manager: Roland Durand; sommelier: Marlène Vandramelli
Set menus: 320 F (lunch), 400 F, 690 F
A la carte: 605–900 F
▭ all
🌳 🍸 🚗

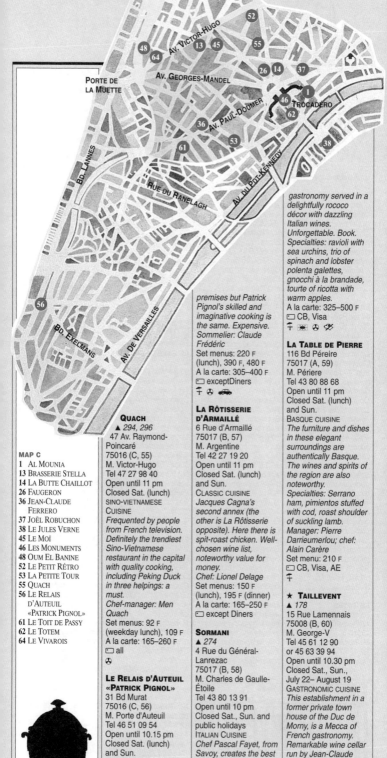

PORTE DE
LA MUETTE

AV. VICTOR-HUGO

AV. GEORGES-MANDEL

AV. PAUL-DOUMER

TROCADERO

BD. LANNES

RUE DU RANELAGH

AV. DU PDT-KENNEDY

BD. EXELMANS

AV. DE VERSAILLES

MAP C
1 AL MOUNIA
13 BRASSERIE STELLA
14 LA BUTTE CHAILLOT
26 FAUGERON
36 JEAN-CLAUDE
    FERRERO
37 JOËL ROBUCHON
38 LE JULES VERNE
45 LE MOÏ
46 LES MONUMENTS
48 OUM EL BANINE
52 LE PETIT RÉTRO
53 LA PETITE TOUR
55 QUACH
56 LE RELAIS
    D'AUTEUIL
    «PATRICK PIGNOL»
61 LE TOIT DE PASSY
62 LE TOTEM
64 LE VIVAROIS

QUACH
▲ 294, 296
47 Av. Raymond-
Poincaré
75016 (C, 55)
M. Victor-Hugo
Tel 47 27 98 40
Open until 11 pm
Closed Sat. (lunch)
and Sun.
SINO-VIETNAMESE
CUISINE
*Frequented by people
from French television.
Definitely the trendiest
Sino-Vietnamese
restaurant in the capital
with quality cooking,
including Peking Duck
in three helpings: a
must.
Chef-manager: Men
Quach*
Set menus: 92 F
(weekday lunch), 109 F
A la carte: 165–260 F
□ all
⊕

**LE RELAIS D'AUTEUIL
«PATRICK PIGNOL»**
31 Bd Murat
75016 (C, 56)
M. Porte d'Auteuil
Tel 46 51 09 54
Open until 10.15 pm
Closed Sat. (lunch)
and Sun.
GASTRONOMIC CUISINE
Newly renovated

*premises but Patrick
Pignol's skilled and
imaginative cooking is
the same. Expensive.
Sommelier: Claude
Frédéric*
Set menus: 220 F
(lunch), 390 F, 480 F
A la carte: 305–400 F
□ exceptDiners
⊕ ⊕ ⊕

**LA RÔTISSERIE
D'ARMAILLÉ**
6 Rue d'Armaillé
75017 (B, 57)
M. Argentine
Tel 42 27 19 20
Open until 11 pm
Closed Sat. (lunch)
and Sun.
CLASSIC CUISINE
*Jacques Cagna's
second annex (the
other is La Rôtisserie
opposite). Here there is
spit-roast chicken. Well-
chosen wine list,
noteworthy value for
money.
Chef: Lionel Delage*
Set menus: 150 F
(lunch), 195 F (dinner)
A la carte: 165–250 F
□ except Diners

SORMANI
▲ 274
4 Rue du Général-
Lanrezac
75017 (B, 58)
M. Charles de Gaulle-
Étoile
Tel 43 80 13 91
Open until 10 pm
Closed Sat., Sun. and
public holidays
ITALIAN CUISINE
*Chef Pascal Fayet, from
Savoy, creates the best
Italian dishes in Paris.
This is top quality*

*gastronomy served in a
delightfully rococo
décor with dazzling
Italian wines.
Unforgettable. Book.
Specialties: ravioli with
sea urchins, trio of
spinach and lobster
polenta galettes,
gnocchi à la brandade,
tourte of ricotta with
warm apples.*
A la carte: 325–500 F
□ CB, Visa
⊕ ⊕ ⊕ ⊕

LA TABLE DE PIERRE
116 Bd Péreire
75017 (A, 59)
M. Périere
Tel 43 80 88 68
Open until 11 pm
Closed Sat. (lunch)
and Sun.
BASQUE CUISINE
*The furniture and dishes
in these elegant
surroundings are
authentically Basque.
The wines and spirits of
the region are also
noteworthy.
Specialties: Serrano
ham, pimientos stuffed
with cod, roast shoulder
of suckling lamb.
Manager: Pierre
Darrieumerlou; chef:
Alain Carère*
Set menu: 210 F
□ CB, Visa, AE
⊕

★ TAILLEVENT
▲ 178
15 Rue Lamennais
75008 (B, 60)
M. George-V
Tel 45 61 12 90
or 45 63 39 94
Open until 10.30 pm
Closed Sat., Sun.,
July 22– August 19
GASTRONOMIC CUISINE
*This establishment in a
former private town
house of the Duc de
Morny, is a Mecca of
French gastronomy.
Remarkable wine cellar
run by Jean-Claude
Vrinat, outstanding
service, subtle cooking*

389

by Philippe Legendre.
Book.
Specialties: chausson of lobster in sauce ravigote, stuffed red mullet en crépine with black olives, duck liver with pain d'épice and ginger, strudel of rabbit with shallots.
A la carte: 455–600 F
CB, Visa, MC

LE TOIT DE PASSY
94 Av. Paul-Doumer
75016 (C, 61)
M. La Muette
Tel 45 24 55 37
Open until 10.30 pm
Closed Sat. (lunch), Sun. and some public holidays.
GASTRONOMIC CUISINE
On the 6th floor, opposite the Eiffel Tower. The roof terrace is open on fine days. Many fine wines to accompany Yannick Jacquot's excellent dishes. Book.
Specialties: foie gras of duck poached in Graves, pan-fried turbot in ginger sauce, roast Pauillac lamb and broad beans, hare cooked in three ways.
Set menus: 275 F, 295 F (lunch), 380 F, 495 F (dinner)
A la carte: 355–500 F
CB, Visa, AE

LE TOTEM
Palais de Chaillot
17 Pl. du Trocadéro
75016 (C, 62)
M. Trocadéro
Tel 47 27 74 11
Open until 2 am

Closed Sun. (dinner)
CLASSIC CUISINE
The restaurant in the Palais de Chaillot. For good views over the Place du Trocadéro and for its terrace.
Set menus: 55 F, 98 F, 125 F, 155 F, 195 F
A la carte: 105–200 F
CB, Visa

LE VANCOUVER
▲ 308
4 Rue Arsène-Houssaye
75008 (B, 63)
M. Charles de Gaulle-Étoile
Tel 42 56 77 77
or 42 56 50 52
Open until 10 pm
Closed Sat., Sun. and Dec 24– Jan 2
FISH CUISINE
A stone's throw from l'Étoile. Top-quality fish subtly cooked by Jean-Louis Decout.
Specialties : pan-fried scallops au naturel, sea bream in cider, lasagna of Dublin Bay prawns, bouillabaisse parisienne.
Managers: Jean-Louis and Chantal Decout
Set menu: 190 F
A la carte: 255–350 F
CB, Visa, AE

★ LE VIVAROIS
▲ 170
192 Av. Victor-Hugo
75016 (C, 64)
M. Av. Henri-Martin
Tel 45 04 04 31
Open until 10 pm
Closed Sat., Sun. and August
GASTRONOMIC CUISINE
Sumptuous, slightly passé backdrop for Claude Peyrot, inspired creator and mentor of numerous young chefs. The "à la carte" menu is constantly changing according to season and the master's inspiration. Perfect sommelier (Jean-Claude Vinadier),

quality service. One of the capital's leading restaurants.
Specialties: warm oysters in curry sauce, ravioli Rastellini, pourpre of turbot Sylvestre, cock in Pommard, whole cooked calves' kidneys.
Set menu: 345 F (lunch)
A la carte: 395–600 F
CB, Visa, AE, Diners

INNER SUBURBS

LE CAFÉ DE LA JATTE
▲ 326
60 Bd Vital-Bouhot
Neuilly-sur-Seine
Tel 47 45 04 20
Open until midnight
CLASSIC CUISINE
A vast space on the charming Île de la Jatte. Unusual interior décor and pleasant terrace on fine days. A fashionable place. The food is good but the service sometimes less than friendly.
A la carte: 205–300 F
all

FOUQUET'S EUROPE
CNIT
Paris-La Défense
Tel 46 92 28 04
Open until 10.30 pm
Closed Sat. and Sun.
GASTRONOMIC CUISINE
Alexandre Faix, a protégé of Joël Robuchon, prepares wonderful food in the futuristic décor of the CNIT. Faultless service.
A la carte: 305–500 F
all

LA GUINGUETTE DE NEUILLY
12 Bd Georges-Seurat
Île de la Jatte
Neuilly-sur-Seine
Tel 46 24 25 04
Open until 10.30 pm
CLASSIC CUISINE

A balcony overlooking the Seine, terraces, well executed classic cuisine and a friendly unpretentious welcome.
Book.
Specialties: leeks with ocean prawns, goujonnettes of sole with whisky, calves' kidneys in port.
A la carte: 165–230 F
except AE

QUAI OUEST
▲ 326
1200 Quai Marcel-Dassault
Saint-Cloud
Tel 46 02 35 54
Open until midnight (Sun. brunch noon to 5 pm)
CLASSIC CUISINE
Take care as you cross the road to reach this boathouse on the banks of the Seine. Pleasant décor with a fireplace. Attractions for children and jazz evenings. Original bistro dishes.
Managers: René Pourcharesse and Éric Watler; chef: Jean-Yves Guichard
Set menu: 100 F (lunch)
A la carte: 205–300 F
all

SAN VALERO
▲ 276
209 ter, Av. Charles-de-Gaulle
Neuilly-sur-Seine
Tel 46 24 07 87
Open until 10.30 pm
Closed Sat. (lunch), Sun., public holidays and Dec. 24– Jan 2
SPANISH CUISINE
A family business that has banned hackneyed Spanish food. Comfortable surroundings, well-spaced tables and tasty little dishes accompanied by good Iberian wines.
Specialties: paellas, pimientos al piquillo, suckling lamb with herbs.
Manager: Faustino Valero; chef: Javier Valero
Set menu: 150 F (except Sat.), 190 F
A la carte: 225–280 F
CB, Visa, AE, Diners

ITINERARY 4

L'ALSACE
▲ *312*
39 Av. des Champs-
Élysées
75008 (A, 1)
M. Champs-Élysées-
Clémenceau
Tel 43 59 44 24
Open 24 hours a day
ALSATIAN CUISINE
*A typical Parisian
brasserie offering the
inevitable seafood and
choucroute.*
A la carte: 200–300 F
▭ all
♫

AU JARDIN
DU PRINTEMPS
▲ *294, 296*
32 Rue de Penthièvre
75008 (B, 2)
M. Miromesnil
Fax 43 59 32 91
Tel 43 59 44 48
Open until 11 pm
Closed Sun. and August
SINO-VIETNAMESE
CUISINE
*This restaurant is
frequented by
fashionable Parisians,
members of the
Academie Française
and ministerial staff.
The service is attentive
and dishes dainty.
Manager: Tan Le Bieng;
chefs: the Tan brothers*
Set menu: 200 F (lunch)
A la carte: 150–250 F
▭ CB, Visa, AE
▦ ♫ ✕ **P**

AU PETIT
MONTMORENCY
26 Rue Jean Mermoz
75008 (B, 3)
M. Franklin-D-Roosevelt
Tel 42 25 11 19
or 45 61 01 26
Open until 10.30 pm
Closed Sat., Sun. (from
Easter to Oct.) and
August
GASTRONOMIC CUISINE
*Here an international
clientele mingles with
fashionable Parisians.
Daniel Bouché serves
an extremely personal
cuisine, stamping his
trademark on an
intelligent and
multifaceted menu.
Specialties: custard
mold with sea urchins,*

*grilled salmon and
pimento potatoes, hare
royale and ribbon
noodles with wild
mushrooms coulis.
Sommelier: Nicole
Bouché*
A la carte: 360–700 F
▭ CB, Visa
▦ ♫ ✕

★ LE BŒUF
SUR LE TOIT
▲ *201*
34 Rue du Colisée
75008 (B, 4)
M. St-Philippe-du-Roule
Tel 43 59 83 80
Open until 2 am
CLASSIC CUISINE
*A magnificent Flo Group
brasserie with 1930's
décor. The kitchen
cacophony does not
mar the always
courteous service.
Manager: Jean-Paul
Bucher; chef: Philippe
Souaidé*
Set menus: 109 F (lunch
and from 11 pm)
A la carte: 160–230 F
▭ CB, Visa, AE,
Diners
♫

LE BRISTOL
▲ *199*
Hôtel Bristol
112 Rue du Faubourg-
Saint-Honoré
75008 (B, 5)
M. Champs-Élysées-
Clémenceau
Tel 42 66 91 45
Open until 10.30 pm
CLASSIC CUISINE
*The restaurant of the
Hotel Bristol, the luxury
hotel next door to the
Elysée. Superb wood-
paneled dining-room,
pleasant patio in
summer. Stunning wine
cellar. The cuisine,
mainly rather old-
fashioned, is expensive.
Manager: Raymond
Marcelin; chef: Emile
Tabourdiau*
Set menus: 360 F,
450 F, 620 F
A la carte: 600–700 F

▭ all
♨ ⌂ ⚘ ♫ ✕ 🚗

CHEZ EDGARD
▲ *186*
4 Rue Marbeuf
75008 (A, 6)
M. Franklin-D-Roosevelt
Tel 47 20 51 15
Open until 12.30 am
Closed Sun. and
August 1–23
CLASSIC CUISINE
*Key politicians and
journalists are at home
here. The showbiz
world draws inspiration
from the wine cellar to
help forget the
somewhat soporific
cuisine.
Manager: Paul
Benmussa; chef: Jean-
Pierre Cassagne*
A la carte: 200–300 F
▭ all
⌂ ▦

CHEZ FRANCIS
▲ *200*
7 Place de l'Alma
75008 (A, 7)
M. Alma-Marceau
Tel 47 20 86 83
or 47 23 39 53
Open until 1 am
CLASSIC CUISINE
*Opposite the Pont de
l'Alma. This brasserie,
with décor by Slavik, is
where the fashion
crowd meet.*
Set menus: 120 F, 180 F
(incl. wine)
A la carte: 200–300 F
▭ all

CHEZ VONG
▲ *294, 296*
27 Rue du Colisée
75008 (A, 8)
M. St-Philippe-du-Roule
Tel 43 59 77 12
Open until midnight
Closed Sun.
SINO-VIETNAMESE
CUISINE
*Pleasantly disorienting
turn-of-the-century
décor. Subtle cuisine
and highly attentive
service.
Specialties: Swallow's*

391

nest soup, shark's fin with cinnamon flowers, glazed young pigeon.
A la carte: 200–350 F
☐ all
▩ ⚙

LA COURONNE
Hôtel Warwick
5 Rue de Berri
75008 (A, 9)
M. George-V
Tel 45 63 14 11
Open until 10.30 pm
Closed Sat., Sun. and August
GASTRONOMIC CUISINE
*The restaurant of the Warwick Hotel. Paul Van Gassel gives his absolutely first-class ingredients a touch of the south of France. Service and wine cellar equally fine. Book.
Specialties: consommé of rosevals and goat's cheese ravioli, noisettes of pikeperch in beetroot sauce, fillet of roast lamb with purple artichokes.
Manager: Charles Pelletier; sommelier: Christophe Fromentin*
Set menus: 220 F (weekday lunch), 270 F (dinner)
A la carte: 250–400 F
☐ all
⚙ ✄ 🚗

L'ÉLYSÉE-LENÔTRE
▲ 191
Carré Marigny
10 Av. des Champs-Élysées
75008 (B, 10)

M. Concorde
Tel 42 65 85 10
Open until 10.30 pm
Closed Sat. (lunch)
GASTRONOMIC CUISINE
*Behind the trees of the Carré Marigny is a charming Belle Époque villa. Lunch under the glass canopy or on the terrace. Faultless dishes prepared by Paul Huyart. Superb wine list chosen by Olivier Poussier. Book.
Specialties: glazed sea bream with grilled shallots, roast side of pork in Noilly, roast young pigeon with spring vegetables.
Manager: Richard Meric*
Set menu: 300 F (lunch, incl. wine.), 340 F, 580 F (dinner)
A la carte: 400–700 F
☐ CB, Visa, AE, Diners
🍴 ▩ 🚗

FAKHR EL DINE
▲ 300
3 Rue Quentin-Bauchart
75008 (A, 11)

M. Franklin-D-Roosevelt
Tel 47 23 74 24
Open until 12.30 am
LEBANESE CUISINE
*Run by the Bou Antoun brothers, who also manage the restaurant in the Insitute du Monde arabe.
Specialties: mezze, roast bass in sesame oil, spit-roasted marinated lamb émincé.
Chef: Fouad Sfeir*
Set menu: 75 F (lunch), 160 F
A la carte: 200–300 F
☐ all
⚙

★ LA FERMETTE MARBEUF
▲ 193
5 Rue Marbeuf
75008 (A, 12)
M. Franklin-D-Roosevelt
Tel 47 20 63 53 and 47 23 31 31

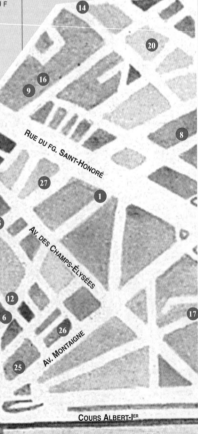

Open until 11.30 pm
Closed May 1 and
Dec. 24
GASTRONOMIC
CUISINE
A turn-of-the-
century restaurant
with listed décor.
Fashionable Paris
adores the unfailingly
classic cuisine of Gilbert
Isaac. This
establishment was the
first to offer menus
consisting of AOC
ingredients. Pleasant
terrace, extensive wine
cellar, extremely
disciplined service.
Specialties: galette of
crab with courgettes,
fricassé of sweet and
sour sole, magret of
duck with green pepper.
Manager: Jean Laurent
Set menu: 160 F
A la carte: 200–250 F
▭ all
☗ ▦ ◂

FOUQUET'S
▲ 180
99 Av. des Champs-
Élysées
75008 (A, 13)
M. George-V
Tel 47 23 70 60
Open until 2 am
BOURGEOIS CUISINE
José Artur records his
radio program here
every evening. There
are so many celebrities
that the less famous
have difficulty finding a
table, particularly as
entry is carefully vetted.
Expensive cuisine in the
spirit of the times.
Manager: Maurice
Casanova; chefs: Pierre
Ducroux and Guy
Krenzer
Set menu: 250 F
A la carte: 240–440 F
▭ all
☗ ▦ ◂

FRENCH LINE
▲ 192
235 Rue du Faubourg-
Saint-Honoré
75008 (A, 14)
M. St-Philippe-du-Roule
Tel 44 09 06 00
Open until 2 am
CLASSIC CUISINE
A luxury brasserie
opened in March 1993.
Tea room with pianist,
piano bar from
10.30 pm. Seafood.
Set menu: 175 F
A la carte: 180–220 F
▭ all
☗ ▦

LES GÉORGIQUES
36 Av. George-V
75008 (A, 15)
M. George-V
Tel 40 70 10 49
Open until 10 pm
Closed Sat. (lunch)
and Sun.
CLASSIC CUISINE
A peaceful dining-room
frequented by a well-
dressed business
clientele.
Warm welcome and
impeccable service.
Very precise and
accurate cuisine
prepared by a
young Japanese
chef, Katsumaro
Ishimaru.
Book.
Specialties: consommé
with lobster ravioli,
selection of fish with
fines-herbes sauce, fillet
of beef Rossini.
Set menus: 180 F
(lunch), 360 F
A la carte: 320–480 F
▭ CB, Visa, AE
▦ ◔ ✗

JOHNNY ROCK CAFÉ
▲ 290
13 Rue de Berry
75008 (A, 16)
M. George-V
Tel 47 23 07 72
Open from noon to 2 am
(restaurant).
TEX-MEX CUISINE
This, the former City
Rock Cafe, is still a vast
bistro where noise is an
essential ingredient of
success.
Specialties: fajitas
(beef and poultry with
corn pancakes,
guacamole and various
sauces), gigantic
hamburgers and fries
with salads.
Manager: Michel Axel
Set menu: 65 F (lunch)
A la carte : 120–250 F
▭ AE, Visa

★ LASSERRE
▲ 188
17 Av. Franklin-
Roosevelt
75008 (A, 17)
M. Franklin-D-Roosevelt
Tel 43 59 53 43
and 43 59 67 45
Open until 10.30 pm
Closed Mon. (lunch),
Sun. and August
GASTRONOMIC CUISINE
The temple of tradition.
In summer, the roof is
open to the sun and the
stars. Commissionaires,
bell-hops and maîtres
d'hôtel whirl around
giving top-quality
service. Eminently
classic cuisine by
Bernard Joinville. Book.
Specialties: hot belon
oysters with Chablis
and morels, parmentier
of cod with scallops,
soufflé of sole, duck in
orange.
Manager: René
Lasserre; sommelier:
Jean-Pierre Le Goff
A la carte: 450–800 F
▭ CB, Visa, AE, Gold,
Diners
☗ ▦ ◔ ✗ ◂

★ LAURENT
▲ 196
41 Av. Gabriel
75008 (B, 18)
M. Champs-Élysées-
Clémenceau
Tel 42 25 00 39
Open until 11 pm
Closed Sat. (lunch),
Sun. and public holidays
GASTRONOMIC CUISINE
One of the nicest
terraces in Paris.
Directoire décor in the
dining-room. Philippe
Braun, one of Joël
Robuchon's protégés,
prepares good dishes
and Philippe
Bourguignon is a
perfect sommelier.
Book.

Specialties: cold tomato
soup with quail's eggs
and blanched liver, side
of roast sea bream with
onions and asparagus,
loin of suckling veal
bourgeois.
Manager: Edmond
Ehrlich
Set menu: 380 F
A la carte: 600–1 000 F
▭ all
☗ ▦ ◔ ✗ ◂

LEDOYEN
▲ 197
Carré des Champs-
Élysées, 1 Av. Dutuit
75008 (B, 19)
M. Champs-Élysées-
Clémenceau
Tel 47 42 35 98
Open until 10.30 pm
Closed Sat., Sun.
and August
GASTRONOMIC CUISINE
The Napoleonic dining-
room upstairs serves
Ghislaine Arabian's
remarkable cuisine. Of
Flemish origin, she has
kept the taste of hops
and her specialty is
gingerbread rolls
shaped like little people.
A rich and inventive
cuisine, which is
becoming increasingly
successful. Book.
Specialties: quick-
smoked mussel soup,
roast turbot in Gard
beer, leg of rabbit in a
cream casserole, oven-
baked lobster, cream
with speculos and
chocolate.
Manager: Jean-Paul
Arabian
Set menu: 290 F (lunch),
480 F
A la carte: 500–700 F
▭ CB, Visa, AE,
Diners
◔ ▦ ✗ ◂

OLSEN
▲ 282
8 Rue du Commandant
Rivière
75008 (A, 20)
M-St-Philippe-du-Roule
Tel 45 61 22 64
Open until 11 pm
Closed Sun.
NORDIC CUISINE

MAP B

Young, relaxed restaurant.
Specialties: Danish smoked salmon, seafood from the Baltic (around the island of Bornholm).
Set menu-buffet: 175 F (evenings)
A la carte: 150–200 F
☐ AE, CB

PAVILLON NOURA
▲ 300
21, av. Marceau
75008 (A, 21)
M. Alma-Marceau
Tel 47 20 33 33
Open until midnight
LEBANESE CUISINE
The former Ramponneau restaurant has

become an elegant dining-room serving mezze (an assortment of small hot and cold dishes).
Manager: the Bou Antoun brothers; chef: Elie Azar
Set menus: 156 F, 190 F (lunch), 220 (dinner), 280 F, 320 F
A la carte : 250–350 F
☐ CB, Visa, AE, Diners
☗ ⛟

LE PORT-ALMA
▲
10 Av. de New-York
75016 (A, 22)
M. Passy
Tel 47 23 75 11
Open until 10.30 pm
Closed Sun. and August
FISH CUISINE
Pleasant welcome and comfortable dining-room.
Paul Canal's dishes are meticulously cooked and subtly flavored.
Book.
Specialties: shellfish minestrone, grilled lobster with tarragon, small John Dory braised in star anise.
Managers: Paul and Sonia Canal
Set menu: 200 F (lunch)
A la carte: 270–400 F
☐ all
☗ ▦ ⚘

LE PRINCE DE GALLES (MARIOTT)
▲ 185
Hôtel Prince de Galles.
33, Av. George-V
75008 (A, 23)
M. George-V
Tel 47 23 55 11
Open until 10.30 pm
GASTRONOMIC CUISINE
In the Prince de Galles hotel. Trompe l'oeil décor, delightful patio. Subtle concoctions by Dominique Cécillon, combining tradition and innovation.
Musical brunch on Sundays.
Specialties: lobster marinière in Sauternes and ginger, fillet of duckling in mango sauce, saddle of wild rabbit with red cabbage.
Manager: Willy Libert; sommelier: Franck Hardy
Set menus: 225 F (incl. wine, except Sun.), 250 F (brunch)
A la carte: 400–600 F
☐ CB, Visa, AE, Diners, MC
▦ ⚘ ⛟ ⛟

LES PRINCES
▲ 183
Hôtel George-V
31 Av. George-V
75008 (A, 24)
M. George-V
Tel 47 23 54 00
Open until 10.30 pm
CLASSIC CUISINE
A luxury hotel restaurant. The 1930's-style interior décor and leafy patio are

popular with the great and the good. The cuisine is far from unforgettable.
Specialties: satiné of veal fillet and sweetbreads with morel

mushrooms, quail
cutlets with almond
persillade, turbot soufflé
with Dublin Bay prawns.
Manager: Mr Biteau;
chef: Jacky Joyeux
Set menus: 350 F, 450 F
A la carte: 500–700 F
□ all
♀ ♃ ▦ ⊛ 🚗

**15, MONTAIGNE –
LA MAISON BLANCHE**
▲ 190
15 Av. Montaigne
75008 (A, 25)
M. Franklin-D-Roosevelt
Tel 47 23 55 99
Open until 11 pm
Closed Sat. (lunch) and
Sun.
GASTRONOMIC CUISINE
Paris is seen in all its
splendor through the
picture windows of this
chic restaurant with fine
modern décor, situated
above the Champs-
Elysées theater. Very
pleasant terrace and
excellent cooking by
José Martinez, plus fine
wines from an extensive
list. Book.
Specialties: confit of
warm vegetables,
oyster fritters, tian of
vegetables and pan-
fried Dublin Bay prawns,
caramelized saddle of
lamb with mango, roast
pigeon with chard.
Manager: René Durand,
Pascal Vignes;
sommelier: Jean-
Jacques Michel
A la carte: 370–500 F
□ CB, Visa, AE, MC
♃ ▦ ⚒ ⊛ 🚗

**LE RÉGENCE-PLAZA
AND LE RELAIS-PLAZA**
▲ 186
Hôtel Plaza-Athénée
25 and 21 Av.
Montaigne
75008 (A, 26)
M. Franklin-D-Roosevelt
Tel 47 23 78 33
and 47 23 46 36
Open until 10.30 pm
(Le Régence) ; 1.30 am
(Le Relais)
GASTRONOMIC AND
CLASSIC CUISINE
In the Grand Hôtel
Plaza. The Régence
has a sumptuous Louis
XVI dining-room.
Celebrities from the
worlds of politics,
fashion and the media
come to enjoy Gérard
Sallé's delicate cuisine.
Meals are served on the
patio in summer.
The Relais is a
luxurious brasserie
with 1930's-style
décor where good,
simple cooking is
admirably served. Well-
dressed clientele.
Specialties (at the
Régence): artichoke
hearts in émietté of
common crab, Dublin
Bay prawns royale with
saffron fumet, calves'
liver with grapes,
supreme of fatted
chicken in fleurette
sauce with truffle juice.
Managers: Patrice
Jeanne (Régence),
Werner Kuchler
(Relais); sommelier:
Didier Thomas
Set menus: 330 F (lunch

Sun., Le Régence),
285 F (Le Relais)
A la carte: 350–500 F
and 200–350 F
□ all
♀♀ ▦ ⊛ ✄

LE SÉBILLON-ÉLYSÉES
66 Rue Pierre-Charron
75008 (A, 27)
M. Franklin-D-Roosevelt
Tel 43 59 28 15
Open until midnight
CLASSIC CUISINE
A brasserie in the
former Ascot piano bar.
Comfortable English
pub atmosphere, with
wood paneling, stained
glass windows and
leather-covered
benches.
Manager: Gérard Joulie;
chef: Dominique Allory
A la carte: 190–320 F
□ CB, Visa, AE,
Diners
⊛

SOUS L'OLIVIER
15 Rue Goethe
75016 (A, 28)
M. Alma-Marceau
Tel 47 20 84 81
Open until 10.30 pm
Closed Sat., Sun.
and public holidays
CLASSIC CUISINE
Members of the nearby
CNPF adore William
Warnault's traditional
cuisine. The terrace is
irresistible in fine
weather.
Set menu: 175 F
(evening)
A la carte: 250–350 F
□ CB, Visa, AE
♃

YVAN
1 bis Rue Jean-Mermoz
75008 (B, 29)
M. Franklin-D-Roosevelt
Tel 43 59 18 40
or 42 89 16 69
Open until midnight
Closed Sat. (lunch)
and Sun.
GASTRONOMIC CUISINE
The highly media-
conscious Yvan
Zaplatilek offers an
original style of cuisine,
which is strongly
influenced by his
Flemish origins. The
menu is very good and
he also has an
interesting wine cellar.
Book.
Specialties: salad of
lamb's tongues and
endive with pears, fillet
of sea bream with two
kinds of celery, leg of
rabbit with lemon confit,
veal sweetbreads
seared with leeks,
capers and truffles.
Set menus: 168 F, 188 F
(lunch), 238 F, 278 F,
298 F
A la carte: 180–260 F
□ all
⊛ ✄

ITINERARY 5

★ LES AMBASSADEURS
▲ 222

Hôtel de Crillon
10 Pl. de la Concorde
75008 (A, 1)
M. Concorde
Tel 44 71 16 16
Open until 10.30 pm
GASTRONOMIC CUISINE
In the restaurant of the Hôtel de Crillon, the 18th-century marble and gold décor and somewhat stilted, plush atmosphere may be intimidating, but Christian Constant's creative and unembellished cuisine is exquisite. A superb cellar kept by Jean-Claude Maître. Book. Specialties: confit of foie gras with Sauternes jelly and fig purée, roast turbot on the bone, Bresse chicken and Belles de Fontenay potatoes, roast carré of Pauillac lamb with Tarbes beans. Manager: Hervé Houdre; pâtissier: Christophe Felder
Set menus: 330 F (weekday lunch), 590 F (dinner)
A la carte: 450–800 F
□ all
▦ ☻ ✄ 🚗

★ ANGELINA
▲ 228

226 Rue de Rivoli
75001 (A, 2)
M. Tuileries
Tel 42 60 82 00
Open 9.30 am–7 pm
Closed 2 weeks in August
TEA ROOM
The most attractive tea room in Paris, founded in 1903. Gourmets of all ages gather here. Uncomfortable no-smoking area. Well-presented dishes. Specialties: fillet of beef with straw potatoes, hot chocolate à l'ancienne, pastries.
A la carte: 170–200 F
□ CB, Visa, AE

ARMAND AU PALAIS-ROYAL

2–6 Rue de Beaujolais
75001 (B, 3)
M. Bourse
Tel 42 60 05 11
Open until 11 pm
Closed Sat. (lunch), Sun.
CLASSIC CUISINE
Listed 17th-century dining-room, large picture windows overlooking the attractive gardens of the Palais-Royal. The clientele includes its stockbroker and actor neighbors. Book. Specialties: warm salad of red mullet in vinaigrette, braised escalope of salmon with Cyprus parsley, stuffed fatted chicken with sauce diable. Chef-managers: Jean-Pierre Ferron, Bruno Roupie
Set menu: 170 F (lunch)
A la carte: 240 F
□ all

BERNARD CHIRENT

28 Rue du Mont Thabor
75001 (A, 4)
M. Tuileries
Tel 42 86 80 05
Open until 10 pm
Closed Sat. (lunch) and Sun.
CLASSIC CUISINE
Light and tasty French cuisine in an intimate setting. Vin de pays by the glass. Specialties: mature Cantal cheese tart, blanc of cod roast with leeks and cumin, leg of duck civet with macaroni gratin.
Set menus: 185 F, 250 F (incl. wine)
□ CB, Visa, AE
☻

BRASSERIE DU LOUVRE

Pl. du Palais-Royal
75001 (B, 5)
M. Palais-Royal
Tel 44 58 37 87
Open until 11.30 pm
CLASSIC CUISINE
A brasserie with turn-of-the-century-inspired décor, situated opposite the Comédie Française that stays open after the show. Bar open until 1 am.
Set menu: 95 F, 160 F
A la carte: 160–260 F
□ all

BRASSERIE MUNICHOISE
▲ 312

5 Rue Danielle-Casanova
75001 (A, 6)
M. Pyramides
Tel 42 61 47 16
Open until 2 am
Closed Sat. (lunch), Sun., Dec. 24–Jan 2 and August
BAVARIAN CUISINE
Typical Bavarian décor and Munich beer. Book in winter. Specialties: choucroute, roast knucke, charcoal-grilled sausages. Manager: René Pouverin; chef: Fabrice Lechat
A la carte: 170–220 F
□ CB, Visa

CAFÉ LE CROISSANT
▲ 209

146 Rue Montmartre
75002 (B, 7)
M. Sentier
Tel 42 33 35 04
Open until 8.30 pm
Closed Sun.
HOME COOKING
A memorable place. This is where Jean Jaurès was assassinated on July 31, 1914.
Set menu: 70 F (lunch)
A la carte: 100–180 F
□ CB
🍴

LE CAFÉ DES THÉÂTRES

17 Rue de Choiseul
75002 (B, 8)
M. 4-Septembre
Tel 42 65 77 40
Open until midnight
Closed Sat. (lunch) and Sun.
CLASSIC CUISINE
A quiet brasserie, which is ideal for a late dinner

in a district that teems with cinemas and theaters, including the neighboring Opéra-Bouffe.
Chef: Jacques Roulland; manager: Alain Blaise
Set menus: 78 F, 115 F, 173 F (aperitif and wine incl.)
A la carte: 180–250 F
☐ all

★ **LE CARRÉ DES FEUILLANTS**
▲ 226
14 Rue de Castiglione
75001 (A, 9)
M. Tuileries
Tel 42 86 82 82
Open until 10.30 pm
Closed Sat. (lunch),
Sun. and August
GASTRONOMIC CUISINE
A former convent, with décor by Slavik. Traditional cooking, mainly from the southwest of France, on which the famous Alain Dutournier works his magic. Unforgettable and truly great wine cellar. Book.
Specialties: Brittany lobster in white gaspacho, barigoule of poivrades and snails, cod with fresh coconuts, grilled half duckling in anchoïade, knuckle of veal in cocotte with eggplants.
Set menus: 260 F (lunch), 560 F
A la carte: 500–780 F
☐ CB, Visa, AE, Diners, JCB
⊞ ♨ ✁

LES CARTES POSTALES
7 Rue Gomboust
75001 (A, 10)
M. Pyramides
Tel 42 61 02 93
Open until 10.30 pm
Closed Sat. (lunch),
Sun. and public holidays
CLASSIC CUISINE
French food interpreted by a Japanese chef and served in a tiny dining-room. Book.
Specialties: galette of crab in a grapefruit vinaigrette, half-cooked

half-raw side of brill, braised oxtail in Médoc wine.
Manager: Lionel Guillois; chef: Yoshimasa Watanabe
Set menus: 135 F (weekday lunch), 285 F
A la carte: 170–300 F
☐ except AE
✁

LE CÉLADON
15 Rue Daunou
75002 (B, 11)
M. Opéra
Tel 47 03 40 42
Open until 10 pm
Closed Sat., Sun.,
public holidays and August
GASTRONOMIC CUISINE
The restaurant of the Hôtel Westminster. Comfortable, cozy, very professional but rather starchy service. Imaginative preparations by Joël Boilleaut, but can be very expensive.
Specialties: veal sweetbread with truffle oil, fresh salmon with Oriental flavors, fillet of lamb with caraway seeds.
Manager: Volker Zach.
Set menus: 220 F, 400 F
A la carte: 300–500 F
☐ all
⊞ ♨ 🅿

★ **CHEZ PAULINE**
5 Rue Villedo
75001 (B, 12)
M. Pyramides
Tel 42 96 20 70
or 42 61 79 01
Open until 10.30 pm
Closed Sat. (lunch),
Sun.
BOURGEOIS CUISINE
A top-of-the-range bistro. Molded ceilings, imitation red leather, wall mirrors. Pleasant service. Burgundy-inspired cuisine.
Specialties: mussel salad au pistou, calf's head salad with gribiche sauce, roast sea bass in salt crust, stuffed cabbage "Chez

Pauline."
Chef-manager: André Génin
Set menu: 220 F
A la carte: 250–350 F
☐ CB, Visa, AE, Euroc
⊞ ♨

CHEZ TANTE LOUISE
41 Rue Boissy-d'Anglas
75008 (A, 13)
M. Concorde
Tel 42 65 06 85
Open until 10.30 pm
Closed Sat., Sun.
and August
CLASSIC CUISINE
1930's bistro décor. Regulars enjoy the friendly welcome, comfort and careful service. Dishes meticulously prepared from excellent ingredients. You can look around the wine cellar.
Manager: Éliane and Bernard Lhiabastres; chef: Michel Lerouet
Set menus: 168 F, 235 F.
A la carte: 215–350 F
☐ all
⊞ ♨

★ **DROUANT**
▲ 204
16–18 Pl. Gaillon
75002 (B, 14)
M. 4-Septembre
Tel 42 65 15 16
Open until 10.30 pm
Closed Dec. 25 (dinner) and Jan.1 (dinner)
CLASSIC CUISINE
This is where the Prix Goncourt is awarded. The smooth service and Louis Grondard's excellent dishes attract fashionable society and

those who like to stay up late. Good clarets. Book. Specialties: charlotte of Dublin Bay prawns with eggplant confit, heart of fillet in a beef jelly with Chinon, roast young pigeon in potato case.
Manager: Louis

Grondard
Set menu: 290 F (weekday lunch)
A la carte: 300–500 F
☐ all
⊞ ♨ 🚗

L'ESPACE CHAMPAGNE
110 Galerie de Valois
75001 (B, 15)
M. Palais-Royal
Tel 42 96 04 09
Open until midnight
CLASSIC CUISINE
Main attractions are the terrace overlooking the Palais-Royal gardens and the ubiquitous champagne, either to drink or in the cooking. Jazz piano on Thursdays, Fridays and Saturdays.
Manager: Gérard Bonnemort; chef: Norredine Embarkia
Set menus: 125 F, 165 F, 290 F
A la carte: 200–250 F
☐ CB, Visa, AE
⊻ ⊤ ⊞ ♨

★ **L'ESPADON**
▲ 224
Hôtel Ritz
15 Pl. Vendôme
75001 (A, 16)
M. Opéra
Tel 42 60 38 30
Open until 11 pm
Closed August
GASTRONOMIC CUISINE
The restaurant of the Ritz Hotel. In the kitchen Guy Legay prepares fine, modern dishes, and is particularly good at updating the classics. Both the wine cellar and the service are impeccable. Book.
Specialties: millefeuille

of sea bass and salmon with spinach shoots and cuttlefish with dill, aiguillettes of duck with blueberries and clafoutis of olives, grenadine of veal in sauce bergère.
Sommelier: Jean-Michel Deluc

Set menus: 350 F
(lunch), 550 F (dinner)
A la carte: 450–700 F
▭ all
♟ 🍸 🐌 ⌘ 🚗

**FERME
SAINT-HUBERT**
21 Rue Vignon
75008 (A, 17)
M. Madeleine
Tel 47 42 79 20
Open until 10.30 pm,
11.30 pm Fri. and Sat.
Closed Sun.
CHEESE CUISINE
*This cheesemonger has
added a restaurant to
his store, where his
most popular specialties
– feuilleté of roquefort,
fondue and raclette –
can be sampled.*
A la carte: 120–180 F
▭ except Diners
♟

GALLOPIN
▲ 207
40 Rue Notre-Dame-
des-Victoires
75002 (B, 18)
M. Bourse
Tel 42 36 45 38
Open until 11.30 pm
Closed Sat. and Sun.
HOME COOKING
*Stockbrokers working in
the area lunch in this
marvelous 19th-century
bistro, which has
retained its original
décor.*
Chef-manager: Gérard
Wagrez
Set menu: 150 F
(dinner, incl. wine)
A la carte: 220–300 F
▭ all
♟

**★ GOUMARD-
PRUNIER**
▲ 222
9 Rue Duphot
75001 (A, 19)
M. Madeleine
Tel 42 60 36 07
Open until 10.30 pm
Closed Mon. and 15
August
FISH CUISINE
*The chef cooks
exceptionally fresh fish
to perfection. The
service is meticulous
and the wine cellar is
particularly attractive.
Book.
Specialties: warm
shellfish salad au
naturel, lobster with
cayenne sauce, whole
pan-fried small red
mullet, grilled sea bass
with olives and sautéed
eggplant.*
Manager: Jean-Claude
Goumard;
chef: M. Landriot;
sommelier: Thierry
Moinnereau;
pâtissier: Charlie
Poitevin
A la carte: 350–700 F
▭ all
🖼 ♟

**★ LE GRAND
COLBERT**
▲ 211
2 Rue Vivienne
75002 (B, 20)
M. Bourse
Tel 42 86 87 88
Open until 1 am
Closed July
25–August 25
HOME COOKING
*In the Vivienne gallery,
taken over by Joël
Fleury, this superb
brasserie is well on the
way to becoming one of
the most notable in
Paris.
Specialties: fish soup,
whiting Colbert, beef
gros sel, chitterlings.*
Chef: Jean-Luc Rozec
Set menu: 155 F
A la carte: 200–250 F
▭ except Diners
♟

LE GRAND LOUVRE
Musée du Louvre,
under the Pyramid
75001 (A, 21)
M. Louvre
des Antiquaires
Tel 40 20 53 41
Open until 10 pm
Closed Tue.
CUISINE FROM THE
SOUTHWEST
*The best museum
restaurant in Paris.
Authentic southwestern
French cuisine
supervised by André
Daguin, the great chef
from Auch, who is also
responsible for
choosing the wines.
Reasonable prices.
Specialties: foie gras,
garbure with duck confit.*
Set menu: 170 F
A la carte: 240–350 F
▭ CB, Visa, AE, Diners
🖼 ♟ 🐌

★ LE GRAND VÉFOUR
▲ 213
17 Rue de Beaujolais
75001 (B, 22)

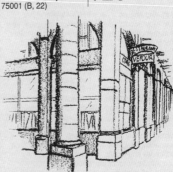

M. Bourse
Tel 42 96 56 27
Open until 10.15 pm
Closed Sat., Sun.
and August
GASTRONOMIC CUISINE
*A restaurant with
superb late 18th-century
décor, where it is easy
to imagine dining in the
company of the ghosts
of Camille Desmoulins
and Colette. After
surviving more than his
fair share of financial
problems, Guy Martin's
restaurant is now doing
very well. Book.
Specialties: terrine of
eggplant with
anchovies, supreme of
plaice with tomato and
basil fondue, roast
Bresse pigeon,
steamed calves' liver.*
Chef-manager:

Guy Martin; sommelier:
Patrick Tanusier
Set menu: 305 F (lunch)
A la carte: 350–550 F
▭ all
🖼 ♟ 🐌 🚗 🍸

**LA GRILLE
SAINT-HONORÉ**
15 Pl. du Marché-
Saint-Honoré
75001 (A, 23)
M. Pyramides
Tel 42 61 00 93
Open until 10.30 pm
Closed Sun., Mon.
(lunch), August 7–23
and Dec. 24–Jan. 2
HOME COOKING
*Generous, but slightly
predictable, even
boring, cuisine in the
comfortable
surroundings of a
former bistro. Book.*
Chef-manager: Jean
Speyer
Set menu: 180 F, 230 F
A la carte: 200–350 F
▭ all
🍸 🖼 ♟

L'INCROYABLE
▲ 212
26 Rue de Richelieu
75001 (B, 24)
M. Palais-Royal
Tel 42 96 24 64
Open until 9 pm
Closed Sun. and Mon.
(dinner)
HOME COOKING
*A canteen offering
pleasant food and, more
remarkably, good value
for money in the heart
of an otherwise
expensive district.*
Chef-manager:
Claudette Breyer
Set menus: 60 F
(weekday lunch), 70 F
(dinner), 100 F
A la carte: 120–220 F
▭ CB, Visa, AE
🍸

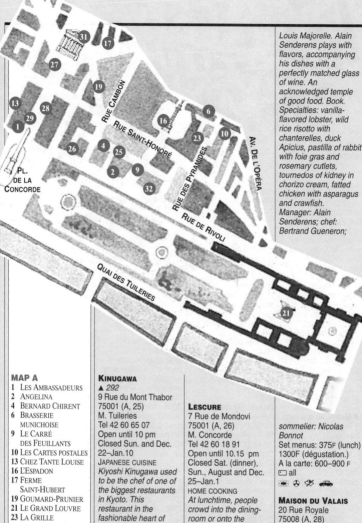

Louis Majorelle. Alain Senderens plays with flavors, accompanying his dishes with a perfectly matched glass of wine. An acknowledged temple of good food. Book. Specialties: vanilla-flavored lobster, wild rice risotto with chanterelles, duck Apicius, pastilla of rabbit with foie gras and rosemary cutlets, tournedos of kidney in chorizo cream, fatted chicken with asparagus and crawfish.
Manager: Alain Senderens; chef: Bertrand Gueneron;

MAP A

KINUGAWA
▲ 292
9 Rue du Mont Thabor
75001 (A, 25)
M. Tuileries
Tel 42 60 65 07
Open until 10 pm
Closed Sun. and Dec. 22–Jan.10
JAPANESE CUISINE
Kiyoshi Kinugawa used to be the chef of one of the biggest restaurants in Kyoto. This restaurant in the fashionable heart of Paris has a rather sterile appearance but the Japanese specialties are excellent. Book.
Set menu: 145 F (lunch), 545 F
A la carte: 250–400 F
🔲 except Diners
🍽 🕭

LESCURE
7 Rue de Mondovi
75001 (A, 26)
M. Concorde
Tel 42 60 18 91
Open until 10.15 pm
Closed Sat. (dinner), Sun., August and Dec. 25–Jan.1
HOME COOKING
At lunchtime, people crowd into the dining-room or onto the terrace to enjoy home cooking at reasonable prices.
Manager: Denis Lascaud; chef: Stéphane Burgaud
Set price menu: 98 F
A la carte: 100–170 F
🔲 CB, Visa
🍽 🕭

★ LUCAS-CARTON
▲ 216
9 Pl. de la Madeleine
75008 (A, 27)
M. Madeleine
Tel 42 65 22 90
Open until 10.30 pm
Closed Sat. (lunch), Sun., August 1-21 and 10 days at Christmas
GASTRONOMIC CUISINE
An authentic décor by

sommelier: Nicolas Bonnot
Set menus: 375F (lunch) 1300F (dégustation.)
A la carte: 600–900 F
🔲 all
🍽 🕭 🕭 🚗

MAISON DU VALAIS
20 Rue Royale
75008 (A, 28)
M. Concorde
Tel 42 60 22 72
Open until 11 pm
Closed Sun.
SWISS CUISINE
Just like dining in a Swiss chalet. Raclette is served freely.
Specialties: mountain ham, fillet of perch, cheese fondue.
Manager: Véronique Leduc; chef: Pierre Lemerle
Set menus: 150 F, 200 F
A la carte: 200–20 F
🔲 all
🍽 🕭 🕭

★ MAXIM'S
▲ 217
3 Rue Royale
75008 (A, 29)

399

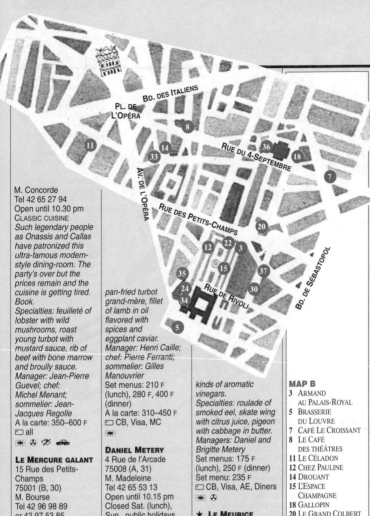

MAP labels: BD. DES ITALIENS · PL. DE L'OPÉRA · RUE DU 4-SEPTEMBRE · AV. DE L'OPÉRA · RUE DES PETITS-CHAMPS · RUE DE RIVOLI · BD. DE SÉBASTOPOL

M. Concorde
Tel 42 65 27 94
Open until 10.30 pm
CLASSIC CUISINE
Such legendary people as Onassis and Callas have patronized this ultra-famous modern-style dining-room. The party's over but the prices remain and the cuisine is getting tired. Book.
Specialties: feuilleté of lobster with wild mushrooms, roast young turbot with mustard sauce, rib of beef with bone marrow and broully sauce.
Manager: Jean-Pierre Guevel; chef: Michel Menant; sommelier: Jean-Jacques Regolle
A la carte: 350–600 F
all

LE MERCURE GALANT
15 Rue des Petits-Champs
75001 (B, 30)
M. Bourse
Tel 42 96 98 89
or 42 97 53 85
Open until 10.30 pm
Closed Sat. (lunch),

Sun. and public holidays
CLASSIC CUISINE
Peace and comfort in a 19th-century dining-room. Predictable classic cuisine.
Specialties: lobster salad with citrus fruits,

pan-fried turbot grand-mère, fillet of lamb in oil flavored with spices and eggplant caviar.
Manager: Henri Caille; chef: Pierre Ferranti; sommelier: Gilles Manouvrier
Set menus: 210 F (lunch), 280 F, 400 F (dinner)
A la carte: 310–450 F
CB, Visa, MC

DANIEL METERY
4 Rue de l'Arcade
75008 (A, 31)
M. Madeleine
Tel 42 65 53 13
Open until 10.15 pm
Closed Sat. (lunch), Sun., public holidays and 1 week in August.
GASTRONOMIC CUISINE
Daniel Metery was taught by some of the greatest masters and has not forgotten it. Here there is an amazing menu, including dishes incorporating various

kinds of aromatic vinegars.
Specialties: roulade of smoked eel with citrus juice, pigeon with cabbage in butter.
Managers: Daniel and Brigitte Metery
Set menus: 175 F (lunch), 250 F (dinner)
Set menu: 235 F
CB, Visa, AE, Diners

★ **LE MEURICE**
▲ 227
Hôtel Meurice
228 Rue de Rivoli
75001 (A, 32)
M. Tuileries
Tel 44 58 10 50
Open until 11 PM
GASTRONOMIC CUISINE
A luxury hotel restaurant with a regal décor overlooking the Tuileries gardens. Very inventive cuisine, exceptional service and a fine wine cellar. Prices are reasonably stable. Book.
Specialties: cream of cauliflower with smoked eel clams, fine potato tart with gizzard cepes and duck liver, steamed fillet of John Dory with cinnamon, roast Bresse goose with black stuffing.
Manager: Philippe Roch; chef: Marc

MAP B
3 ARMAND AU PALAIS-ROYAL
5 BRASSERIE DU LOUVRE
7 CAFÉ LE CROISSANT
8 LE CAFÉ DES THÉÂTRES
11 LE CÉLADON
12 CHEZ PAULINE
14 DROUANT
15 L'ESPACE CHAMPAGNE
18 GALLOPIN
20 LE GRAND COLBERT
22 LE GRAND VÉFOUR
24 L'INCROYABLE
30 LE MERCURE GALANT
33 PIERRE "À LA FONTAINE GAILLON"
34 PIERRE AU PALAIS-ROYAL
35 LE POQUELIN
36 LE VAUDEVILLE
37 WILLI'S

Marchand; sommelier:
Antoine Zochetto
Set menus: 300 F
(lunch), 380 F (dinner)
A la carte: 285–600 F
▭ all
🍽 ⌀ ✗ 🚗

PIERRE "À LA FONTAINE GAILLON"
▲ 206
1 Pl. Gaillon
75002 (B, 33)
M. 4-Septembre
Tel 42 65 87 04
or 47 42 63 22
Open until 12.30 am
Closed Sat. (lunch),
Sun. and August
CLASSIC CUISINE
*A listed 17th-century
private mansion.
Wonderful façade
overlooking the square
where parasols are put
out on the terrace in
summer, near the Autin
fountain. There is a
paneled dining-room
with a lot of character,
but unfortunately the
food isn't up to the
same standard as the
décor. Book in summer.*
Manager: Roland
Boyer; chef: Patrick
Broença
Set menu: 165 F
(dinner)

A la carte: 180–300 F
▭ all
🍴 🍽 ⌀

PIERRE AU PALAIS-ROYAL
10 Rue Richelieu
75001 (B, 34)
M. Palais-Royal
Tel 42 96 09 17
or 42 96 27 17
Open until 10 pm
Closed Sat., Sun.,
public holidays and
August
CLASSIC CUISINE
*In the shadow of the
Palais-Royal. A
restaurant with
peaceful, opulent
dining-rooms, and a
traditional cuisine drawn
from the French
regional repertoire.
Specialties:* snails and
frogs' legs with morels,
skate wing with a knob
of butter, shredded beef
à la ménagère.
Manager: Daniel and
Nicole Dez; chef: Roger
Leplu
Set menu: 230 F (lunch)
A la carte: 230–350 F
▭ except AE

LE POQUELIN
17 Rue Molière
75001 (B, 35)

M. Pyramides
Tel 42 96 22 19
Open until 10.30 pm
Closed Sat. (lunch),
Sun. and August 1–20
CLASSIC CUISINE
*Next door to the
Comédie-Française.
Regional dishes at
sensible prices
considering the fact that
the district can be very
expensive.
Specialities:* pan-fried
foie gras with dried fig
purée, roast pikeperch
with wild mushrooms,
roast saddle of lamb
with thyme.
Manager: Maggy
Guillaumin;
chef: Michel Guillaumin
Set menus: 154 F, 185 F
A la carte : 240–350 F
▭ all
🍽 ⌀

LE VAUDEVILLE
▲ 208
29 Rue Vivienne
75002 (B, 36)
M. Bourse
Tel 40 20 04 62
Open until 2 am
CLASSIC CUISINE
*A Flo Group brasserie
in the purest Art Deco
style, with a lively late
night scene.*

Manager: Jean-Paul
Bucher;
chef: Jean-François
Thorel
Set menu: 109 F (lunch),
185 F, 109 F (after 11
pm)
A la carte: 200–300 F
▭ all
🍴

WILLI'S
13 Rue des Petits-
Champs
75001 (B, 37)
M. Bourse
Tel 42 61 05 09
Open until 11 pm
Closed Sun.
CLASSIC CUISINE
*Opposite the National
Library. The style is out
of date, the tables
tightly packed and the
menu skeletal.*
Manager: Mark
Williamson;
chef: François Yon
Set menu: 155 F
A la carte: 180–280 F
▭ CB, Visa

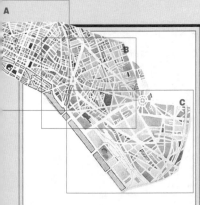

ITINERARY 6

À L'IMPASSE

4 Impasse Guémenée
75004 (B, 1)
M. Bastille
Tel 42 72 08 45
Open until 10 pm
Closed Sat. (lunch),
Sun., Mon. (lunch)
and August
HOME COOKING
*Family cooking in a
local bistro that has
welcomed some famous
patrons in the past,
including the actor
Gérard Depardieu.
Manager: Maryse
Collard; chef: Hugues
Vulcain*
A la carte: 180–280 F
▭ CB, Visa, MC
🍴 🅿

Set menu: 175 F
A la carte: 250–350 F
▭ CB, Visa, AE

L'AIGUIÈRE

37 bis Rue de Montreuil
75011 (B, 3)
M. Faidherbe-Chaligny
Tel 43 72 42 32
Open until 10.30 pm
Closed Sat. (lunch) and
Sun.
CLASSIC CUISINE
*An establishment that,
from the flowers on the
table to the pictures on
the walls, pays attention
to detail. Friendly
welcome, dishes
prepared with
intelligence and
imagination. Pleasant
piano accompaniments.
Good menus with fair
prices.
Manager: Patrick
Masbatin; chef : Pascal
Viallet*
Set menus: 115 F
(weekday lunch), 175 F,
248 F
A la carte: 200–300 F
▭ all
♿

À SOUSCEYRAC

▲ *306*
35 Rue Faidherbe
75011 (B, 2)
M. Faidherbe-Chaligny
Tel 43 71 65 30
Open until 10 pm
Closed Sat. (lunch),
Sun. and August
CUISINE FROM QUERCY
*Provincial ambiance
and décor, a number of
interesting traditional
dishes from the Lot
region, and a good
choice of excellent
regional wines.
Specialties: terrine of
lobster and foie gras in
jelly, hare royale,
cassoulet.
Chefs: Patrick
and Gabriel Asfaux*

L'AMBASSADE
D'AUVERGNE

▲ *240*
22 Rue du Grenier-
Saint-Lazare
75003 (A, 4)
M. Etienne-Marcel
Tel 42 72 31 22
Open until 10.30 pm
Closed 2 weeks in
summer
CUISINE FROM
AUVERGNE
*Near the Georges
Pompidou Center.
Medieval façade, oak
beams. Regional
dishes, well-stocked
wine cellar. A
fashionable place.
Book.
Specialties: cabbage
and roquefort soup,
chestnut black pudding,*

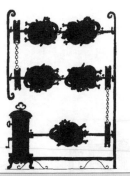

leg of lamb brayaude.
Managers: the Petrucci family;
chef: Patrick Hun
A la carte: 160–260 F
except Diners

L'AMBROISIE
▲ *239*
9 Pl. des Vosges
75004 (B, 5)
M. Chemin-Vert
Tel 42 78 51 45
Open until 10.15 pm
Closed Sun., Mon., Feb. holidays and 3 weeks in August
GASTRONOMIC CUISINE
A great restaurant in a plum location on the Place des Vosges, in the former Hôtel de Luynes. Discreet entrance into a simple dining-room, pleasant welcome from Danièle, the chef's wife, gourmet and sparkling clientele. Bernard Pacaud is an artist in the kitchen, although somewhat austere. Impeccable service, magnificent wine list, for an exceptional meal. Book.
Specialties: spiced terrine of Landes duck foie gras with confit fennel, pastilla of tuna with dried apricots, marinière of braised sea bass and fennel with green olives, crispy calves' ears stuffed with rillons of caramelized veal sweetbreads.
Chef-manager: Bernard Pacaud
A la carte: 500–1 000 F
Visa

LES AMOGNES
243 Rue du Faubourg-Saint-Antoine
M. Faidherbe-Chaligny
75011 (B, 6)
Tel 43 72 73 05
Open until 11 pm
Closed Sun. and Mon.
CLASSIC CUISINE
A flower-decked country inn a stone's throw from the Opéra, where the regulars rub shoulders with the trendy. Thierry Coué cooks meticulously and with character. Wines of all price ranges. Book.
Specialties: soup of mussels with Le Puy lentils, side of cod on pavé of eggplant, cabbage stuffed with rabbit and rosemary.
Chef-manager: Thierry Coué
Set menu: 160 F
CB, Visa, EC, MC

L'AUBERGE DE NICOLAS FLAMEL
51 Rue de Montmorency
75003 (A, 7)
M. Arts-et-Métiers
Tel 42 71 77 78
Open until 11.30 pm
Closed Sat. (lunch) and Sun.
CLASSIC CUISINE
The oldest listed building in Paris, dating from 1407. Fine dining-rooms with old stone and beams but doubtful décor. Good dishes by Laurent Delcros.
Specialties: Roman ravioli in cream of mushrooms, pavé of cod with spices, saddle of lamb in oil of thyme.
Manager: Nathan Hercberg
Set menus (lunch): 48 F, 72 F, 98 F
A la carte: 150–250 F
CB, Visa

AU PIED DE COCHON
▲ *236*
6 Rue Coquillière
75001 (A, 8)
M. Les Halles
Tel 42 36 11 75
Open 24 hours
CLASSIC CUISINE
Night owls are already familiar with this turn-of-the-century brasserie, which is open night and day. The ideal place for seafood, pigs' trotters and onion soup.
Managers: Pierre and Jacques Blanc; chef: Jean-Claude Tretot
A la carte: 180–280 F
all

AU PRESSOIR
257 Av. Daumesnil
75012 (C, 9)
M. Michel Bizet
Tel 43 44 38 21
Open until 10.30 pm
Closed Sat., Sun., 1st week in Feb. and 4 weeks in August
GASTRONOMIC CUISINE
Comfortable, opulent dining-room, warm welcome and creative cuisine by Henri Séguin. Service and wine cellar to match.
Specialties: potato cakes with foie gras, brandade of cod with asparagus, rabbit with coriander.
Set menu: 380 F
A la carte: 350–600 F
all

AU TROU GASCON
▲ *306*
40 Rue Taine
75012 (C, 10)
M. Daumesnil
Tel 43 44 34 26
Open until 10 pm
Closed Sat., Sun., Dec. 25–Jan. 3. and August
CUISINE FROM THE SOUTHWEST
One of the best restaurants in the district. Jacques Faussat cooks southwestern French dishes to perfection. Fine wines are served, also from that region.
Specialities: chestnut bouillon with breast of hen pheasant, sole with market garden produce, cassoulet with Tarbes beans, persillé of young rabbit à la bohémienne.
Managers: Alain and Nicole Dutournier
Set menus: 200 F, 450 F
A la carte: 250–450 F
all

★ **BENOÎT**
▲ *235*
20 Rue Saint-Martin
75004 (A, 11)
M. Châtelet
Tel 42 72 25 76
Open until 10 pm
Closed Sat., Sun. and August
BOURGEOIS CUISINE
A popular rendezvous for businessmen and politicians. Dishes prepared by a cook who is as reliable as a metronome. Book.
Specialties: ox tongue in liver parfait, skate in mustard butter, compotier of beef à la parisienne, cassoulet.
Manager: Michel Petit; chef: Patrick Crochet
A la carte: 300–420 F
none

BLUE ELEPHANT
▲ *296*
43 Rue de la Roquette
75011 (B, 12)
M. Bastille
Tel 47 00 42 00
Open until midnight
Closed Sat. (lunch)
THAI CUISINE
Exotic plants, a small bridge, a waterfall and waiters dressed in traditional costume all combine to evoke the

atmosphere of dining well in Thailand. The menu tells you which dishes are hot and spicy. Good food. Book.
Manager: Manuel Da Motta-Veiga; chef: Oth Sombath
Set menus: 150 F (weekday lunch), 265 F, 295 F
A la carte: 180–280 F
all

★ **BOFINGER**
▲ *240*
5–7 Rue de la Bastille
M. Bastille
75004 (B, 13)
Tel 42 72 87 82
Open until 1 am
CLASSIC CUISINE
A superb Belle Époque brasserie just a stone's throw from the futuristic Opéra, in a lively

district. Exorbitantly
priced seafood.
Booking preferred.
Manager: Mr Alexandre;
chef: Patrice Macrez
Set menu: 166 F
A la carte: 180–250 F
▢ all
♨

CAROLL SINCLAIR
36 Bd Henri-IV
75004 (B, 14)
M. Bastille
Tel 42 72 17 09
Open until midnight
Closed Sun. (dinner),
Mon. (lunch)
CLASSIC CUISINE
A former interior
decorator whose
delicate and
sophisticated cuisine
brings all Paris
gourmets flocking to the
door.
Specialties: small
couscous of Dublin Bay

prawns, fondant of beef
in its juices with chenas,
calves' kidneys à la
goutte de sang cooked
in two different ways.
Chef-manager:
Caroll Sinclair
Set menus: 120 F, 177
F, 277 F
A la carte: 220–250 F
▢ all

CENTRE GEORGES-POMPIDOU
19 Rue de Beaubourg
6th floor
75004 (A, 15)
M. Les Halles
Tel 48 04 99 89
Open until 9 pm (11 pm
Fri. and Sat.)
Closed Tue. and
evenings in winter
CLASSIC CUISINE
On the top floor of the
Georges Pompidou
Center, a cafeteria, self-
service and traditional
restaurant. Beautiful
view over the rooftops
of Paris.
Set menus: 85 F, 105 F,
130 F
A la carte: 55–140 F
▢ except AE
🍴 ⌖ 📷 ♨

CHARDENOUX
▲ 252
1 Rue Jules-Vallès
75011 (B, 16)
M. Charonne
Tel 43 71 49 52
Open until 10.30 pm
Closed Sat., Sun.
and 1 month in summer
BOURGEOIS CUISINE
A friendly welcome
awaits in this listed
bistro with marble
counter and engraved
glass panels.
Vins de pays. Book.
Specialties: leeks
vigneronne, cod
Florentine, pan-fried

onglet with mushrooms.
Chef: Bernard
Passavant
A la carte: 150–250 F
▢ CB, Visa, AE

★ CHEZ JULIEN
1 Rue du Pont-Louis-
Philippe
75004 (A, 17)
M. Pont-Marie
Tel 42 78 31 64
Open until 11 pm
Closed Sat (lunch),
Sun., Mon. (lunch)
and 3 weeks in summer
BOURGEOIS CUISINE
A former bakery and
patisserie with superb
original frontage,
adjacent to the church
of Saint-Gervais, in the
heart of old Paris, with a
good view of the Île de
la Cité.
Set menu: 140 F (lunch)
A la carte: 220–300 F
▢ CB, Visa, MC
🍴 📷

★ CHEZ LA VIEILLE
▲ 232
1 Rue Bailleul
75001 (A, 18)
M. Louvre
Tel 42 60 15 78
Closed evenings, Sat.,
Sun., public holidays
and August
BOURGEOIS CUISINE
A number of politicians

and performers choose this as their favorite bistro.
Chef-manager: Adrienne Biasin
A la carte: 200–300 F
☐ CB
🞔

LE CLOWN BAR
11 Rue Amelot
75011 (A, 19)
M. Bréguet-Sabin
Tel 43 55 87 35
Open until 11 pm
Closed Sun., public holidays and August
HOME COOKING
Some very good little dishes served in a listed décor with frescoes of clowns recalling the neighboring Hiver circus. Warm ambiance but the smoky atmosphere in the evening is repugnant. Book.
Manager: Joël Vitte; chef: Emmanuel Lannel
A la carte: 130–230 F
☐ none

COCONNAS
2 bis Pl. des Vosges
75004 (B, 20)
M. Chemin-Vert
Tel 42 78 58 16
Open until 10.15 pm
Closed Mon., Tue. (winter)
and Jan 15–Feb.15
CLASSIC CUISINE
The terrace beneath the arcades of the Place des Vosges attracts tourists. The food is not of a very high standard. Book.
Manager: Claude Terrail; chef: Hervé Poulleau
Set menu: 160 F
A la carte: 220–350 F
☐ all
🞗

COMPTOIR DU SAUMON
▲ 282
60 Rue François-Miron
75004 (A, 21)
M. St-Paul

Tel 42 77 23 08
Open until 10 pm
Closed Sun.
SCANDINAVIAN CUISINE
Primarily a food shop with a small room where you can sample specialties such as smoked fish washed down with vodka.
Manager: Mr Pringault; chef: Nicolas Vassor
Set menus: 100 F, 145 F
A la carte: 120–300 F
☐ CB, Visa, AM
🞒

DÔMARAIS
▲ 238
53 bis Rue des Francs-Bourgeois
75004 (A, 22)
M. St-Paul
Tel 42 74 54 17
Open until 11.30 pm
Closed Sat. (lunch), Sun. and Mon.
CLASSIC CUISINE
Interesting restaurant in an old auction room with rococo décor. Honest, straightforward cooking. There is live music on Friday evenings. Book. Specialties: carpaccio of sea bream with ginger, magret of duck with cider vinegar, roulade of chicken with Noilly.
Manager: Dominique Ratni; chef: Claude Lauzet
Set menus: 175 F (lunch), 285 F (Wed., Thur.), 285 F, 385F; (Fri., Sat.)
A la carte: 220–320 F
☐ CB, Visa, AE
🞗

L'ESCARGOT-MONTORGUEIL
▲ 233
38 Rue de Montorgueil
75001 (A, 23)
M. Les Halles
Tel 42 36 83 51
Open until 11 pm
Closed Jan.1, May 1 and August

CLASSIC CUISINE
A Second Empire-style bistro with basic but genuine dishes.
Manager: Kouikette Terrail; chef: Christian Delplanque
Set menus: 130 F (lunch), 190 F, 250 F, 320 F (dinner)
A la carte: 200–350 F
☐ all
🞗

FELLINI
▲ 274
47 Rue de l'Arbre-Sec
75001 (A, 24)
M. Pont-Neuf
Tel 42 60 90 66
Open until 11 pm
Closed Sat. (lunch) and Sun.
ITALIAN CUISINE
Good transalpine cooking served in a beautiful dining-room with stone walls or in a vaulted cellar. There is another establishment at 58 Rue de la Croix-Nivert, in the 15th arrondissement.
Manager: Flavio Mascia
Set menu: 110 F (lunch)
A la carte: 150–250 F
☐ CB, Visa
🞒 🞔

LE FOND DE COUR
3 Rue Sainte-Croix-de-la-Bretonnerie
75004 (A, 25)
M. St-Paul
Tel 42 74 71 52
Open until 11 pm
Closed Sat. (lunch) and Sun.
GASTRONOMIC CUISINE
A pleasant welcome can be expected in this 17th-century private townhouse. In summer you can sit on the terrace and enjoy the sun. A fashionable restaurant. Piano bar in the basement. Specialties: rillettes of smoked salmon, fresh pasta with shredded crab, fillet of swordfish aumônière.
Manager: Philippe Gwizz; chef: Olivier Lecam

Set menus: 188 F (lunch), 258 F
A la carte: 220–320 F
☐ except Diners
🞔 🞗

FOUQUET'S BASTILLE
▲ 242
130 Rue de Lyon
75012 (B, 26)
M. Bastille
Tel 43 42 18 18
Open until midnight
Closed Sun.
CLASSIC CUISINE
This deluxe brasserie near the Opéra welcomes the night owls of the Bastille district with its decisively modern décor. The cuisine is unimpressive.
Manager: Charles Casanova; chef: Patrick Michaux
Set menu: 100 F
A la carte: 200–300 F
☐ all
🞗 🞒

GÉRARD BESSON
5 Rue du Coq-Héron
75001 (A, 27)
M. Les Halles
Tel 42 33 14 74
Open until 11.30 pm
Closed Sat. evening, Sun. and Dec. 25–Jan.1.
GASTRONOMIC CUISINE
Close to Les Halles. Gérard Besson cooks like one of the greats. He is both a traditionalist and an innovator. This mecca of French gastronomy is not always madly cheerful but has a fine wine cellar and attentive service. Book. Specialties: marbré of aiguillettes of braised beef and foie gras in port wine jelly, salad of green beans, civet of eels and sole in Bordeaux wine, roast duck served in two helpings.
Chef-manager: Gérard Besson; sommelier: Véronique Perrin
Set menus: 260 F (lunch), 650 F, 750 F, 900 F
A la carte: 280–680 F
☐ all
🞒

LA GOURMANDISE

271 Av. Daumesnil
75012 (C, 28)
M. Porte Dorée
Tel 43 43 94 41
Open until 10.30 pm
Closed Sun., Mon.
(dinner), and August
8–28
CLASSIC CUISINE
On the edge of the Bois
de Vincennes. Good
cooking by Alain
Denoual, classic but not
heavy. Book.
Specialties: oyster and
seaweed soup, brill with
Dublin Bay prawns,
roast lamb with fresh
figs.
Set menus: 92 F
(children), 135 F, 165 F,
220 F and 320 F
A la carte: 250–400 F
▭ CB, Visa, AE

LE GRIZZLI

7 Rue Saint-Martin
75004 (A, 29)
M. Châtelet
Tel 48 87 77 56
Open until 11 pm
Closed Sun.
and Dec. 24–Jan. 3
CUISINE
FROM THE SOUTHWEST
Bear leaders used to
come here at the
beginning of the 20th
century. The spiral
staircase and manual
service lift remain.
Cheerful welcome and
generous dishes from
southwestern France.
Terrace overlooking the
pedestrian street.
Manager: Bernard
Areny; chef: Patrick
André
Set menus: 110 F
(lunch), 145 F
A la carte: 150–250 F
▭ except Diners
⌘

L'IMPRIMERIE

101 Rue Vieille-
du-Temple
75004 (A, 30)
M. Hôtel de Ville
Tel 42 77 93 80
Open until midnight
CLASSIC CUISINE
Worth a visit for the
view over the gardens
of the Picasso museum,
menus that are good
value for money, the
gourmand's platters
(60 F) and the savory
tarts. Wines are served
by the glass or the
bottle.
Specialties: nage of
cauliflower with

coriander, gigotin of
monkfish, rump steak
with bone marrow and
wild mushrooms.
Manager: Bernard
Buchollzer
Set menus: 151 F, 178 F
A la carte: 150–250 F
▭ CB, Visa, AE
⌖ ⊞

★ JO GOLDENBERG

▲ 237, 284
7 Rue des Rosiers
75004 (A, 31)
M. St-Paul
Tel 48 87 20 16

Open until midnight
ASHKENAZE CUISINE
The temple of
Ashkenaze cuisine in
the heart of the Marais
district. Don't let the
noise, the crowd or the
elbow-to-elbow seating
bother you.
Specialties: borsch,
chopped liver with
onions, stuffed carp,
boiled chicken.
Manager: Jo
Goldenberg
A la carte: 150–250 F
▭ all
⌖

LA MAIN À LA PÂTE

▲ 274
35 Rue Saint-Honoré
75001 (A, 32)
M. Louvre
Tel 42 36 64 73
or 45 08 85 73
Open until 12.30 am
Closed Sun.
ITALIAN CUISINE
An assiduous clientèle
seems to appreciate the
plastic plants in the
winter garden, the fine
transalpine wine list and
the sometimes
unreliable Italian
cooking of Annita
Bassano. Book.
Manager: Livio Bassano
Set menus: 114 F
(weekday lunch), 176 F
A la carte: 200–320 F
▭ CB, Visa, AE,
Diners
♛ ✿

MANSOURIA

▲ 302
11 Rue Faidherbe
75011 (B, 33)
M. Faidherbe-Chaligny
Tel 43 71 00 16
Open until 11.30 pm
Closed Sun. and Mon.
(lunch)
MOROCCAN CUISINE
Not far from the Opéra-
Bastille where the "in"
crowd meets. The
cuisine is original. Book.
Chef-manager: Fatima
Hal
Set menus: 99 F (lunch),
164 F (dinner)
A la carte: 200–250 F
▭ CB, Visa

LE MARAÎCHER

5 Rue Beautreillis
75004 (B, 34)
M. Sully-Morland
Tel 42 71 42 49
Open until 11 pm
Closed Mon., Sun.,
public holidays and
August
CLASSIC CUISINE
Stone walls and
fireplace, attentive
waiters, careful cuisine
and a smart young
clientele.
Specialties: cassolette
of mussels with saffron
and steamed
vegetables, fresh
golden cod with
courgette tagliatelle,
oven-roast pigeon.
Set menu: 120 F (lunch)
A la carte: 250–350 F
▭ CB, Visa, MC, EC
⌖

LE MIRAVILE

72 Quai de l'Hôtel-
de-Ville
75004 (A, 35)
M. Pont-Marie
Tel 42 74 72 22
Open until 10.30 pm
Closed Sat. (lunch) and
Sun.
GASTRONOMIC CUISINE
The fashionable
restaurant. Here, Gilles
Épié accomplishes feats
of genius, according to
some, or flirts with
disaster, according to
others. In any case, he
gets himself talked
about and the customers
crowd in. The welcome
is really very pleasant in
the frescoed, marble-
floored dining-room.
Booking is strongly
recommended.
Specialties:
caramelized foie gras
fritters with port wine,

carpaccio of tuna with
mature Parmesan, roast
gigot of suckling lamb,
strong pure malt coffee
tart.
Chef: Gilles Épié.
Set menu: 200 F
▭ CB, Visa
⌖ ✿ ▱

LE NAVARIN

3 Av. Philippe-Auguste
75011 (C, 36)
M. Nation
Tel 43 67 17 49
Open until 10 pm (Fri
and Sat. 10.30 pm)
Closed Sat. (lunch),
Sun. (dinner), a few
days in August and Dec.
23–6
CLASSIC CUISINE
Close to Place de la
Nation. Chefs François
Moyet and Jean-Pierre
Reynaud offer lamb-
based specialties such
as shoulder in salt crust,
navarin, baeckeoffe au
Riesling.
Chef-managers:
François Moyet
and Jean-Pierre
Reynaud
Set menus: 98 F,
(lunch), 168 F and 245 F
A la carte: 200–300 F
▭ CB, Visa

L'OULETTE

▲ 306
Pl. Lachambeaudie
75012 (C, 37)
M. Dugommier
Tel 40 02 02 12
Open until 10.15 pm
Closed Sat. (lunch)
and Sun.
CUISINE FROM THE
SOUTHWEST
Specialties from
southwestern France,
adjusted and adapted
by an imaginative chef,
Marcel Baudis. The
wine is wonderful but
expensive.
Specialties: Aunt
Antonia's "all pork"
salad, escabèche of
squid, Béarn-style
garbure, dish of
Pyrenean suckling
lamb.
Managers: Marcel
Baudis and Alain
Fontaine
Set menus: 150 F, 280 F
(incl. wine)
A la carte: 260–320 F
▭ CB, Visa, AE
⌖ ✿ ▣

★ PHARAMOND

▲ 234
24 Rue de la Grande-

MAP B

Truanderie
75001 (A, 38)
M. Les Halles
Tel 42 33 06 72
Open until 10.30 pm
Closed Sun. and Mon.
(lunch)
CUISINE FROM
NORMANDY
There are ceramics, a spiral staircase and big mirrors in this establishment, which dates from 1832. Good Normandy cuisine. Book.
Specialties: maraîchère of chicken oyster-piece with hazelnuts, tripe à la mode de Caen, "Petite Normande" fillet mignon of veal.
Manager: Jocelyne Faget-Roguez; chef: Claude Gerber
A la carte: 250–350 F
CB, Visa, AE, Diners

LA PLANTATION
▲ 286
5 Rue Jules-César
75012 (B, 39)
M. Bastille
Tel 43 07 64 15
Open until 11 pm
Closed Sun.
WEST-INDIAN CUISINE
For authentic Creole cooking in an exotic setting, and where service with a smile is the norm.
Specialties: feuilleté of clams, colombo de vivano.
Set menus: 98 F, 120 F (lunch), 240 F (dinner)
A la carte: 180–200 F
CB, Visa, AE

LE POÈTE IVRE
▲ 296
8 Rue Léopold-Bellan
75002 (A, 40)
M. Sentier
Tel 40 26 26 46
Open until 10.30 pm
Closed Sun. and public holidays
THAI CUISINE
Guaranteed romance in an unusual curiosity shop. Authentic service and exquisite Thai cuisine. Book.
Specialties: papaya salad with prawns, sautéed pork with ginger, magret of duck in pimento sauce with coconut milk and pineapple.
Set menus: 125 F, 180 F
A la carte: 180–280 F
CB, Visa, AE

LE ROUDOULIÉ
▲ 306
16 Rue La Vacquerie
75011 (B, 41)
M. Voltaire
Tel 43 79 27 46
Open until 10.30 pm
Closed Sat. (lunch)

and Sun.
CUISINE FROM THE
SOUTHWEST
A former bistro with unusual décor. Friendly atmosphere.
Specialties: roast rabbit stuffed with young vegetables, veal sweetbreads à l'ancienne, Auge Valley pavé of veal.
Managers: Miguel and Christine Vilar; chef: Miguel Vilar
Set menus: 72 F (weekday lunch), 92 F (dinner), 175 F
A la carte: 150–250 F
CB, Visa, AE

**LA SAMARITAINE -
LE GRILL**
Magasin 2 Rue
de la Monnaie, 6th floor
75001 (A, 42)
M. Pont-Neuf
Tel 42 33 96 70
Open until 3 pm (tea room 3–6 pm)
Closed Sun.
CLASSIC CUISINE
From the terrace on the 10th floor (cold buffet from June to September 15: 110 F), a commanding view of the Pont-Neuf.
A la carte : 150–200 F
all

SAUDADE
▲ 278
34 Rue des
Bourdonnais
75001 (A, 43)
M. Châtelet
Tel 42 36 03 65
Open until 10.30 pm
(11 pm Fri. and Sat.)
Closed Sun.
PORTUGUESE CUISINE
Cod in various guises
features in all of the star
dishes, but it is worth
trying some of the less
well-known Portuguese
specialties as well.
Noteworthy wine list
including some
exceptional ports.
Manager:
Antonio Simoes;
chef: Joaquim
Serralheiro
A la carte: 180– 280 F
▭ CB, Visa, AE,
Diners
⌖ ✥

SIPARIO
▲ 274
69 Rue de Charenton
75012 (B, 44)
M. Ledru-Rollin
Tel 43 45 70 26
Open until midnight
Closed Sun., August

7–23 and 1 week at
Christmas
ITALIAN CUISINE
The décor consists of
frescoes of giant
vegetables, the tables
are well spaced and the
welcome is friendly. In
winter, northern Italian
cuisine, in summer a trip
to the Mezzogiorno.
Fine transalpine wines.
Book.
Specialties: vitello
tonato, filetto
scioglimbocca,
spaghetti with lemon
and green pepper.
Manager: Roberto
Ferrari;
chef: Salsi Mauro
Set menu: 100 F (lunch)
A la carte: 160–200 F
▭ all

LA SOLOGNE
164 Av. Daumesnil
75012 (C, 45)
M. Gare de Lyon
Tel 43 07 68 97
Open until 10.30 pm
Closed Sat. (lunch),
Sun. and public holidays
GASTRONOMIC CUISINE
A fine restaurant run by
a young couple, with
Didier Maillet in the
kitchens. Meticulous
cooking and classic

preparation. Game in
season.
Specialties: calves' foot
terrine with pleurotes
and aigrelette sauce,
roast cod with saffron
cabbage confit, navarin
of lamb.
Chef-manager: Didier
Maillet
Set menu-carte: 150 F
▭ all

**LE SQUARE
TROUSSEAU**
1 Rue Antoine-Vollon
75012 (B, 46)
M. Ledru-Rollin
Tel 43 43 06 00
Open until 11.30 pm
HOME COOKING
Turn-of-the-century
moldings, frescoes and
benches. Pleasant
atmosphere and good
bistro cooking. There is
a terrace for use in fine
weather. Book.
Manager: Philippe
Damas;
chef: Laurent Rivallain
Set menu: 120 F (lunch)
A la carte: 180–250 F
▭ CB, Visa
⌖

LA TABLE RICHELIEU
276 Bd Voltaire
75011 (C, 47)
M. Nation
Tel 43 72 31 23
Open until 11 pm

Closed Sat. (lunch)
CLASSIC CUISINE
Daniel Rousseau has transformed this brasserie into a comfortable dining-room with pictures on display and for sale. Good cooking with many dishes featuring seafood.
Managers: Daniel and Évelyne Rousseau
Set menus: 145 F (weekday lunch), 260 F
A la carte: 200–350 F
☐ CB, Visa, AE
♿

LA TOUR DE MONTLÉRY (CHEZ DENISE)
5 Rue des Prouvaires
75001 (A, 48)
M. Les Halles
Tel 42 36 21 82
Open 24 hours
Closed Sat., Sun. and July 14– August 15
CLASSIC CUISINE
Bistro décor and ambiance. Chic,

sometimes famous clientèle. Generous helpings served on plates decorated by Moretti.
Manager: Denise Benariac;
chefs: Bernard Noèl and Michel Anfray
A la carte: 180–280 F
☐ CB, Visa

★ LE TRAIN BLEU
▲ 243
Gare de Lyon
20 Bd Diderot
75012 (B, 49)
M. Gare de Lyon
Tel 43 43 09 06
Open until 10 pm
BOURGEOIS CUISINE
This station buffet is the only one of its kind in the world and is a listed building. Unusual décor, with frescoes depicting the destinations of trains departing from the Gare de Lyon. Good, traditional food is assiduously served. Book.
Specialties: hot Lyons

sausage with parsley potatoes, soufflé of brill with mushrooms, roast gigot of lamb forézienne.
Manager : Philippe Chazal; chef : Michel Comby
Set menus: 195 F (lunch), 280 F (dinner)
A la carte: 300–400 F
☐ all

VELLONI
▲ 274
22 Rue des Halles
75001 (A, 50)
M. Les Halles
Tel 42 21 12 50
Open until 11 pm
Closed Sun. and August 15–30
ITALIAN CUISINE
Delicious Tuscan cuisine, pleasant welcome and good wines.
Specialties: duck and pleurote salad with balsamic vinegar, baconcini of veal à la romaine, spinach and ricotta ravioli.

Manager: Stefano Cuccini; chef: Jean-Michel Calvert
Set menu: 130 F
A la carte: 180–250 F
☐ all

VÉRO-DODAT
▲ 230
19 Galerie Véro-Dodat
75001 (A, 51)
M. Louvre
Tel 45 08 92 06
Open until 10 pm
Closed Sun., public holidays and 10 days in August
CLASSIC CUISINE
Very atmospheric former dairy-restaurant in the superb Véro-Dodat gallery. Pleasant terrace.
Specialties: rémoulade of black radishes with smoked fillet of goose, sautéed prawns with pleurotes in champagne sauce, civet of chicken braised in beer.
Set menu: 129 F
☐ CB, Visa, AE
⚓

ITINERARY 7

ANDROUET
41 Rue d'Amsterdam
75008 (A, 1)
M. St-Lazare
Tel 48 74 26 90
Open until 10 pm
Closed Sun. and public
holidays
CHEESE CUISINE
At street level this
famous
cheesemonger's store
attracts passers-by. The
restaurant is upstairs.
Specialties: Camembert
croquettes, lobster with
roquefort, fondue
savoyarde.
Chef: Marc Labourel
Set menus: 125 F, 175 F
(lunch), 195 F, 230 F
(dinner)
A la carte: 220–260 F
⊡ all
▣

★ **ASTIER**
44 Rue Jean-Pierre-
Timbaud
75011 (B, 2)
M. Parmentier
Tel 43 57 16 35 and
43 38 25 56 (except
1–6 pm)
Open until 11 pm
Closed Sat., Sun.,
2 weeks at Christmas
and spring and 5 weeks
in summer
HOME COOKING
Good bistro dishes and
choice of wines at
moderate prices.
Managers: Bertrand
Vergnaud and Jean-Luc
Clerc
Set menu: 130 F
⊡ CB, Visa
⌘

**AU CHATEAUBRIAND,
LA GALLERIA**
▲ 274

23 Rue de Chabrol
75010 (B, 3)
M. Gare de l'Est
Tel 48 24 58 94
Open until 10.15 pm
Closed Sun., Mon.,
August and 1 week in
winter
ITALIAN CUISINE
Charming welcome,
assiduous service and
good cuisine but prices
are high.
Chef-manager: Guy
Bürkly
Set menu: 150 F
(weekday lunch)
A la carte: 220–380 F
⊡ CB, Visa, AE
⌘ ⌀

★ **AU COCHON D'OR**
192 Av. Jean-Jaurès
75019 (C, 4)
M. Porte de Pantin
Tel 42 45 46 46
Open until 10.30 pm
BOURGEOIS CUISINE
Close to the Cité des

Sciences but this
Cochon d'Or evokes
Les Halles in the old
days. A fine institution,
well run in, well oiled
and very well
maintained. Superb
bouquets of flowers and
very high-quality meat.
Manager: René Ayral;
chef: Candid Muck
Set menu: 240 F
A la carte: 350–450 F
⊡ all

AU PETIT RICHE
▲ 261
25 Rue Le Peletier
75009 (A, 5)
M. Richelieu-Drouot
Tel 47 70 68 68
Open until 12.15 am
Closed Sun.
BOURGEOIS CUISINE
The décor dates from
1860 but there's nothing
old-fashioned about the
customers: journalists,
artists, financiers and
auctioneers fortify
themselves here with
simple home cooking in
a relaxed atmosphere.

Manager: Gérard
Lejeune; chef: Marc
Bertin
Set menu: 160 F
A la carte: 180–250F
⊡ all
▣

L'AUBERGE LANDAISE
▲ 306
23 Rue Clauzel
75009 (A, 6)
M. St-Georges
Tel 48 78 74 40
Open until 10.30 pm
Closed Sun. and August
3–25
CUISINE FROM THE
SOUTH-WEST
A rustic dining-room,
top-quality ingredients,
careful cuisine, pleasant
service, but if it lacks
pizzazz, then the
collection of armagnacs
will sweeten the bill.
Specialties: Landes
piperade, cassoulet,
duck confit.

Chef-manager:
Dominique Morin
Set price menu: 180 F
A la carte: 200–350 F
⊡ all
▣

¡ AY CARAMBA !
▲ 290
59 Rue de Mouzaïa
75019 (C, 7)
M. Danube
Tel 42 41 23 80
Open every evening
until 11 pm and Fri., Sat.
and Sun. lunch
TEX-MEX CUISINE
Musical ambiance
provided by the
Mariachi Mezcal band.
Elbow-to-elbow
evenings, not for lovers
seeking privacy.
Mexican cocktails and
wines.
A la carte: 100–160 F
⊡ all

BEAUVILLIERS
▲ 272
52 Rue Lamarck
75018 (A, 8)
M. Anvers

Tel 42 54 54 42
Open until 10.45 pm
Closed Mon. (lunch)
and Sun.
CLASSIC CUISINE
*A charming former
bakery on the
Montmartre hill: leafy
terraces, Second
Empire reception
rooms, dining-room
decorated with wedding
bouquets.
Good cooking by Gilles
Renault, tempting wine
cellar, unforgettable
welcome from Edouard
Carlier.
Specialties: sauté of
lobster in ragout, boned
young rabbit in chopped
parsley jelly cooked in
Bourgogne aligoté,
supreme of guinea fowl
cooked slowly,
aiguillettes of Challans
duck with peaches.*
Manager: Édouard
Carlier; chef: Jean-
François Renard;
sommelier: Marc Moine
Set menus: 185 F, 300 F
(weekday lunch), 320 F
(dinner)
A la carte: 500–600 F
▭ CB, Visa, AE, JCB
🛠 🖼 ♿ ✍

**CHARLOT "ROI
DES COQUILLAGES"**
▲ 270
12 Pl. de Clichy
75009 (A, 9)
M. Place Clichy
Tel 48 74 49 64
Open until 1 am
FISH CUISINE
*Enjoy the fish in the
frescoes as those on
the plates are a
disappointment.*
Manager: Pierre and
Jacques Blanc; chef:
Didier Lizard
Set menu: changed
every month.
A la carte: 250–450 F
▭ all
♿

★ **CHARTIER**
▲ 262
7 Rue du Faubourg-
Montmartre
75009 (A, 10)
M. Rue Montmartre
Tel 47 70 86 29
Open until 9.30 pm
HOME COOKING
*Superb Belle Époque
canteen serving cheap
dishes in a chaos that
has delighted
generations of students.*
Manager: René
Lemaire;
chef: Yves Lepeut
Set menu: 82 F (incl.
wine)
A la carte: 70–100 F
▭ CB, Visa
✍

**CHEZ FERNAND
ET LES FERNANDISES**
17 and 19 Rue de
la Fontaine-au-Roi
75011 (B, 11)
M. Goncourt
Tel 43 57 46 25
and 48 06 16 96
Open until 10.30 pm
Closed Sun., Mon.
3 weeks in August
CLASSIC CUISINE
*Everything is made on
the premises in these
two neighboring bistros.
The service is
sometimes sketchy but
the Normandy cuisine is
fortifying.*
Chef: Fernand Affelille
Set menu: 130 F
A la carte: 160–260 F
▭ CB, Visa, AE

CHEZ JENNY
▲ 268, 312
39 Bd. du Temple
75003 (B, 12)
M. Filles du Calvaire
Tel 42 74 75 75
Open until 1 am
ALSATIAN CUISINE
*Listed Spindler
marquetry and
waitresses in traditional
costume in this shrine to
choucroute.*
Manager: Adolphe
Bernard; chef: Michel
Dionnet
Set menu: 98,50 F (incl.
wine)
A la carte: 220–270 F
▭ except CB and Visa
🛠 🖼

**LES FOLIES
("CHEZ ROSINE")**
▲ 296
101 Rue Saint-Maur
75011 (B, 13)
M. St-Maur
Tel 43 38 13 61
Open until 11 pm
Closed Sat. (lunch),
Sun. and August 15–30
CAMBODIAN CUISINE
*Modern décor
complemented by
stunning Cambodian
objets d'art. Rosine Ek
prepares sophisticated
and tasty dishes. Book.
Specialties: green
papaya salad with
prawns, marinated
grilled meat and fish.*
Chef-manager: Rosine
Ek
Set menus: 48 F, 98 F

(weekday lunch), 108 F,
128 F, 148 F, 198 F
A la carte: 140–240 F
CB, Visa, AE

★ **FLO**
▲ *259*
7 Cour des
Petites-Écuries
75010 (B, 14)
M. Château-d'Eau
Tel 47 70 13 59
Open until 1.30 am
CLASSIC CUISINE
*This brasserie, dating
from 1886, is on a par
with others in the group
that bears its name.
Manager: Jean-Paul
Bucher; chef: Philippe
Dubreuil*
Set price menus: 109 F
(weekday lunch), 109 F
(from 11 pm), 185F
A la carte: 140–240 F
all

FOUTA TORO
▲ *304*
3 Rue du Nord
75018 (A, 15)
M. Marcadet-
Poissonniers
Tel 42 55 42 73

Open until 1 am
Closed lunch and Tue.
AFRICAN CUISINE
*A small Senegalese-run
dining-room. A musician
plays every evening
under the fans.
Specialties: pastel (fish
fritter), mafé of chicken,
African couscous.
Manager: Moctar
Gueye; chef:
Aïssata Gueye*
A la carte: 90–120 F
none

**LE GRAND CAFÉ
CAPUCINES**
▲ *254*
4 Bd. des Capucines
75009 (A, 16)
M. Opéra
Tel 47 42 19 00
Open 24 hours
CLASSIC CUISINE
*This brasserie, which
almost never closes,
has reconstituted its
Belle Époque décor.
Intense activity at
mealtimes, diligent
waiters, chic*

*clientele.
Manager: Pierre and
Jacques Blanc; chef:
Christian Linay*
Set menu: 185 F in
summer, 119 F after
11 pm.
A la carte: 220–350 F
all

★ **JULIEN**
▲ *264*
16 Rue du Faubourg-
Saint-Denis
75010 (B, 17)
M. Strasbourg-St-Denis
Tel 47 70 12 06
Open until 1.30 am
Closed Dec. 24
CLASSIC CUISINE
*A restaurant dating from
the late 19th century:
magnificent Art Nouveau
mahogany counter.
Fashionable clientele
and actors come and eat
after the show.
Manager: Jean-Paul
Bucher; chef:
Emmanuel Rault*
Set menus: 109 F (lunch
and from 11 pm), 185 F
A la carte: 170–270 F
all

KASAPHANI
122 Av. Parmentier
75011 (B, 18)
M. Goncourt

Tel 48 07 20 19
Open until 11.30 pm
Closed Mon. and Sat.
(lunch)
CYPRIOT CUISINE
*Warm welcome in this
establishment offering
tasty food at low prices.
The wines are Greek
and the Cypriot dishes
should be tried.
Specialties: grilled
olives, gambas
gratinéed with feta
cheese, pork marinated
in wine and coriander,
flat Cyprus sausages.
Chef-managers: Pavlos
and Georges Melodias*
Set menus: 50 F, 85 F
(lunch)
A la carte: 140–170 F
CB, Visa

LE LOUIS XIV
▲ *266*
8 Bd. Saint-Denis
75010 (B, 19)
M. Strasbourg-St-Denis
Tel 42 08 56 56
Open until 1 am
Closed May 1 and
August 31
CLASSIC CUISINE
*This kitsch-as-can-be
restaurant on one of the
famous theater*

boulevards is
frequented by actors.
Specialties: seafood,
spit-roast chicken, gigot
of lamb with dwarf
kidney beans.
Manager: Gérard
Flottès-Descombes;
chef: Patrick Noblet
Set menus: 138 F, 158 F
A la carte: 220–330 F
⊟ all

MOLLARD
▲ 258
113 Rue Saint-Lazare
75008 (A, 20)
M. St-Lazare
Tel 43 87 50 22
Open until 1 am
CLASSIC CUISINE
A superb modern-style
brasserie that is listed
as a historic monument.
This magnificent
establishment deserves
better food and service
than it has at present.
Manager: Bernard
Gauthé;
chef: Gérard Kerlidou
Set menu: 183 F (incl.
wine)
A la carte: 220–330 F
⊟ except CB and Visa

LES MUSES
Hôtel Scribe
1 Rue Scribe
75009 (A, 21)
M. Opéra
Tel 44 71 24 26
Open until 10.30 pm
Closed Sat., Sun.,
public holidays and
August
GASTRONOMIC CUISINE
The hotel restaurant.
Pierre Miecaze skilfully
prepares top-quality
ingredients in a wood-
paneled and old stone
décor a stone's throw
from the Opéra.
Specialties : ravioli of
Vire chitterlings and
mustard-flavored tripe
stock, Dublin Bay
prawns tempura,
Sisterons lamb with
coriander.
Manager: Gérard
Toupet;
chef: Pierre Miecaze
Set menus: 190 F, 250 F
A la carte: 280–400 F
⊟ all
▦ ✿ 🚗

NÏOULAVILLE
▲ 296
32–34 Rue de l'Orillon
75011 (B, 22)
M. Belleville
Tel 43 38 30 44
or 43 38 95 23

Open until 1 am
CHINESE CUISINE
The welcoming dining-
room seats up to 500
diners. You hail
waitresses pushing
covered trolleys of food
and select what you
want to eat. The turmoil,
exotic preparations and
smells in this Chinese
canteen transport you to
another world.
Manager: Pangam Lam
Set menu: 46 F (buffet
lunch)
A la carte: 130–200 F
⊟ all

L'ŒNOTHÈQUE
20 Rue Saint-Lazare
75009 (A, 23)
M. Notre-Dame-de-
Lorette
Tel 48 78 08 76
or 40 16 10 27
Open until 10.30 pm
Closed Sat., Sun.,
Feb. holidays., May 1–8
and August 7–28
CLASSIC CUISINE
Daniel Hallée, wine
expert and prince of
brandies, accompanies
his wines with a very
personalized cuisine.
Specialties: confit of
quail on lettuce,
poached pibales
(elvers) with herbs,
bœuf bourguignon.
A la carte: 300–350 F
⊟ CB, Visa
✿

PARIS-DAKAR
▲ 304
95 Rue du Faubourg-
Saint-Martin
75010 (B, 24)
M. Gare de l'Est
Tel 42 08 16 64
Open until 11.30 pm
Closed Mon.
SENEGALESE CUISINE
This establishment
describes itself as "the
most African African
restaurant." Beautiful
Senegalese décor. The
food is served on
wooden plates and a

musician plays the
African guitar.
Specialties: red bean
fritters, chicken yassa,
mafé of beef.
A la carte: 140–200 F
⊟ except Diners

LE PAVILLON PUEBLA
Parc des Buttes-
Chaumont
Entrance corner Av.
Simon-Bolivar and Rue
Botzaris
75019 (C, 25)
M. Buttes-Chaumont
Tel 42 08 92 62
Open until 10 pm.
Closed Sun., Mon., 1
week Feb. and 2 weeks
August
GASTRONOMIC CUISINE
A flower-decked
Second Empire villa in
the Buttes-Chaumont
park. Tasty and very
personal cuisine by
Christian Vergès. Warm
welcome, pleasant
service and fine wines.

Meals served in the
garden in summer.
Managers: Christian
and Jacqueline Vergès;
chef: Christian Vergès
Set menus: 180 F, 230 F
A la carte: 300–500 F
⊟ all
▦▦ 🚗

**CHEZ PHILIPPE
("AUBERGE
PYRÉNÉES-
CÉVENNES")**
106 Rue de la
Folie-Méricourt
75011 (B, 26)

M. Goncourt
Tel 43 57 33 78
Open until 10.30 pm
Closed Sat., Sun.,
public holidays and
August
GASTRONOMIC CUISINE
A real inn with
sausages and hams
hanging from the
beams. Friendly,
unpretentious
atmosphere. Good,
copious regional dishes,
fine wines.
Manager: Philippe
Serbource ;
chef: Jean-Paul Rol
A la carte: 230–330 F
⊟ CB, Visa, AE
✿

LA P'TITE TONKINOISE
▲ 296
56 Rue du Faubourg-
Poissonnière
75010 (B, 27)
M. Bonne-Nouvelle
Tel 42 46 85 98
Open until 10 pm
Closed Sun., Mon., Dec.
22.– Jan. 5 and August
1 – Sept. 15
VIETNAMESE CUISINE
Authentic Vietnamese
cuisine. You pay a fair
price for a good meal
and the welcome is
friendly.
Managers: Odette
and Henry Costa;
chef: Michel Costa
A la carte: 150–200 F
⊟ CB, Visa

**LA POSTE/
CASABLANCA**
22 Rue de Douai
75009 (A, 28)
M. Blanche
Tel 42 80 66 16
La Poste has been
renamed and its
address has changed
(you enter from the
other side) but its
telephone number is the
same. Under Moroccan
influence the cuisine
has changed for the
better. This 19th-
century private

AV. JEAN-JAURÈS

BASSIN DE LA VILLETTE

RUE DE CRIMÉE

RUE MANIN

AV. SECRÉTAN

PARC DES
BUTTES-
CHAUMONT

BD. SÉRURIER

BD. DE LA VILLETTE

AV. S. BOLIVAR

RUE DE BELLEVILLE

MAP C
4 AU COCHON D'OR
7 ¡ AY CARAMBA !
25 LE PAVILLON PUEBLA

townhouse
was formerly the
home of Georges Bizet.
Chef: Nicolas Hahn
Set menu: 200 F
🍴 ☯

**LE PRINTEMPS –
LA TERRASSE**
64 Bd. Haussman
9th floor
75009 (A, 29)
M. Opéra
Tel 42 82 62 76
Open until 7 pm
Closes with store
CLASSIC CUISINE
*Fine views of
Haussmann's
boulevards, the
Madeleine and the
Opéra Garnier. Parasols
and solarium. Self-
service.*
A la carte : 70–100 F
🖭 except Diners
🔆 🍴

LE RESTAURANT
32 Rue Véron
75018 (A, 30)
M. Blanche
Tel 42 23 06 22
Open until 11 pm
Closed Sat.(lunch), Sun.
and Mon. (lunch)
CLASSIC CUISINE
*In a modern setting, the
young chef, Yves
Péladeau, produces a
range of fine dishes.
Well-chosen wines at
honest prices.
Specialties: velouté of
pumpkin with steamed
queen scallops, fillet of*

hog-fish cooked in its
skin, guinea fowl in
coarse salt and
cabbage with white
wine.
*Manager: Yves
Péladeau*
Set menu: 170 F
(weekday lunch)
Set menu-carte: 120 F
(dinner)
🖭 all

RESTAURANT OPÉRA
▲ 255
5 Pl. de l'Opéra
75009 (A, 31)
M. Opéra
Tel 40 07 32 32
Open until 11 pm
Closed Sat., Sun.,
August and one week in
February
BOURGEOIS CUISINE
*Next door to the Opéra.
Spectacular Napoleon
III décor but expensive,
rather uninteresting
cuisine and exorbitantly
priced wines. It is a
case of paying over the
odds for a good
location.
Manager: Bernt Schutz*
A la carte: 350–500 F
🖭 except CB, Visa and
MC
☯

LE ROI DU POT-AU-FEU
▲ 310
34 Rue Vignon
75009 (A, 32)
M. Madeleine
Tel 47 42 37 10
Open until 10.30 pm
Closed Sun. and July

15–August 15
HOME COOKING
*A proper pot-au-feu,
with bowl of soup,
marrowbone and
vegetables.
Manager: Daniel Anée;
chefs: Pascal Poilly and
Daniel Anée.*
A la carte: 145–160 F
🖭 CB, Visa

**★ LA TABLE
D'ANVERS**
2 Pl. d'Anvers
75009 (A, 33)
M. Anvers
Tel 48 78 35 21
Open until 11.30 pm
Closed Sat. (lunch),
Sun. and August 1–15
GASTRONOMIC CUISINE
*The Conticinis
(Christian the chef and
Philippe the pâtissier)
have teamed up to
produce stunning
dishes, forming a
dynamic duo in which
each rivals the other in
his own sphere:
vegetables, spices and
desserts. Fine Italian
wines and perfect
service.
Specialties: galette of
red mullet in pistou of
chickpeas, black
pudding hachis
parmentier, grilled
pigeon and salsify with
coriander, Riviera
chocolate with lavender
and lemon.
Sommelier: Jean-
Christophe Moulin.*
Set menus: 160 F, 340 F

(lunch), 190 F, 420 F, 480 F (dinner)
A la carte: 350–550 F
all

TAKA
1 Rue Véron
75018 (A, 34)
M. Blanche
Tel 42 23 74 16
Open until 10.30 pm
Closed Sun., public holidays and one month in summer
JAPANESE CUISINE
Japanese specialties are excellent and offer good value for money. The dining-room is cramped and people willingly wait for tables to become available.
Specialties: raw fish, grilled meats, fondues.
Manager: Okamoto Taka; chef: Hiroshi Taka
Set menu: 110 F (lunch)
A la carte: 150–200 F
CB, Visa

LE TEMPS DE VIVRE
13 Rue André del Sarte
75018 (A, 35)
M. Château-Rouge
Tel 42 58 47 26
Open until 23 h
Closed Sun. (lunch) and Mon.
ARGENTINIAN CUISINE
The pictures on the walls are by the owners. Loud tangos in the background.
Argentinian wines.
Specialties: locro, beef in chimichurri sauce.
Chef-managers: Mr and Mrs Perez
A la carte: 100–150 F
except AE

TERMINUS NORD
23 Rue de Dunkerque
75010 (B, 36)
M. Gare du Nord
Tel 42 85 05 15
Open until 12.30 am
Closed Dec. 24 (dinner)
CLASSIC CUISINE
Situated near the Gare du Nord, with attractive décor dating from 1925. Efficient service, seafood, choucroute and many great classics of brasserie cuisine.
Manager: Jean-Paul Bucher;
chef: Jean-Luc Blanlot.
Set menus: 185 F (lunch incl.wine and coffee), 109 F (after 11 pm)
A la carte: 200–300 F
all

TY-COZ
▲ *260*
35 Rue Saint-Georges
75009 (A, 37)
M. St-Georges
Tel 48 78 42 95
Open until 10.30 pm
Closed Sun. and Mon.(dinner)
BRETON CUISINE
Traditional Breton food and décor in a pretty dining-room with exposed beams.
Specialties: stuffed mussels, grilled lobster, monkfish in cider, pancakes.
Chef-manager: Marie-Françoise Lachaud
Set menu: 170 F (dinner)
A la carte : 180–280 F
CB, Visa, AE, Diners

VENANTIUS
Hôtel Ambassador
16 Bd. Haussmann
75009 (A, 38)
M. Richelieu-Drouot
Tel 42 46 92 63
or 48 00 06 38
Open until 10.30 pm
Closed Sat., Sun. and August
GASTRONOMIC CUISINE
Gérard Fouché officiates under the Corinthian capitals of this luxury hotel restaurant. Inspired by the dishes of south-western France, fine ingredients, meticulous cooking and good wines. The service is rather forced.
Specialties: civet of oysters and flat truffled duck sausages, stuffed sole in pain d'épice and soured sauce, pan-fried fillet of beef poêlé in rioja sauce.
Manager : Béatrice Ruggieri;
chef: Gérard Fouché;
sommelier: Tony Decarpentrie
Set menu: 250 F
A la carte: 360–460 F
all

LE WEPLER
14 Pl. de Clichy
75018 (A, 39)
M. Place Clichy
Tel 45 22 53 24
Open until 1 am
CLASSIC CUISINE
This is the ideal place to observe the comings and goings in the Place Clichy. Inside, the waiters' ballet is worth watching.
Specialties: pork brawn, steamed hog-fish in artichoke barigoule, cheek of beef pot-au-feu.
Manager: Michel Bessière
Set menu: 150 F
A la carte: 180–320 F
CB, Visa, AE, Diners

◆ UPDATE

Months of work go into the preparation of a guide like this and during this period restaurants are constantly changing, particularly during a recession.

Good news for consumers: prices have sometimes returned to their former levels and regional dishes are making a comeback. Bad news: restaurants are disappearing or changing hands faster than we can record in the foregoing pages. However, a few changes and new additions are noted below.

ADDITIONS OR CHANGES

AU PETIT BŒUF
188 Av. Jean Jaurès
75019
M. Porte de Pantin
Tel 42 39 44 44
Next to the restaurant, Au Petit Bœuf (shared kitchens), for a quick snack when visiting the Grande Halle de la Villette.
Dish of the day at 55 F

BISTROT DU DÔME
2 Rue de la Bastille,
75004
M. Bastille
Tel 48 04 88 44
For an evening at the Opera House this new annex to the famous Dôme ▲ 308, offers excellent seafood at relatively reasonable prices. Set price for desserts (35 F) and wines (98 F)
A la carte: 220–50 F

CARRÉ KLÉBER
11 bis Rue de Magdebourg
75016
M. Trocadéro
Tel 47 55 82 08
This will prove whether the Troisgros are good mentors: the young Christophe Delaunay, who was their protégé, is promising but has yet to prove himself.
Set menu: 160 F

CASA OLYMPE
48 Rue Saint-Georges
75009
M. St-Georges
Tel 42 85 26 01
Dominique Versini is the champion of gastronomes and the darling of the media. After having officiated at Chez Olympe, then on the top floor of the Virgin Megastore, she now has her own restaurant offering regional dishes in the former Casa Miguel, that she remembers as one of the least expensive restaurants in Paris.
Set menu: 170 F

DALLOYAU-LE PLEYEL
252 Rue du Faubourg Saint-Honoré
75008
M. Ternes
Tel 45 62 89 71
You need no longer go to concerts at the Pleyel on an empty stomach. Another outlet for the famous caterer. The cakes and sorbets are worth a second opinion.
First menu: 130 F

EXPLORER'S TRADING POST
47 Rue Vavin,
75006
M. Vavin
43 26 66 61
Australia has come to Paris. For fans of Mel Gibson and grilled ostrich.
A la carte: 120–200 F

AUX ÎLES MARQUISES
15 Rue de la Gaieté
75014
M. Edgar-Quinet
Tel 43 20 93 58
A fish restaurant. It is not new – Carcot, Piaf and many other artists of the late Bobino frequented it – but the prices have to some extent returned to their former level: a reason to return there.
Set menus: 130 F, 150 F

INDRA
10 Rue du Commandant Rivière
75008
M. St-Philippe-du-Roule
Tel 43 59 46 40
Harmonious marriage of the culinary traditions of northern India with western tastes. Sophisticated cooking exuding inimitable tastes and subtle flavors.
Set menus: 220 F (lunch) and 300 F
A la carte: 250–300 F

LE RELAIS DU PÉRIGORD
15 Rue de Tolbiac
75013
M. Porte d'Ivry
Tel 45 83 07 48
This restored establishment not far from the Pont de Tolbiac, so dear to Léo Malet, offers robust dishes from the South-West.
Set menu: 135 F

LE SELF DU PALAIS DE LA FEMME
94 Rue de Charonne
75011
M. Charonne
Tel 46 59 30 00
A sign of the times: a private company has taken over this self-service restaurant in the Salvation Army hostel. A surprising and vast building of note from the turn-of-the-century (seats over 500). Curiosity value.
Meals: 40–60 F

CHEZ PIERROT
18 Rue Étienne Marcel
75002
M. Etienne Marcel
Tel 45 08 00 48
A stone's throw from Les Halles and Beaubourg where the best and the worst come and go, a good solid bistro.
Set menu: 139 F

FRANCO ET GIACOMO
115 Av. Jean-Jaurès
75019
M. Laumière
Tel 42 00 04 77
A good Italian restaurant. An evening daily not renowned for its jokes (Le Monde, naturally) had no hesitation in declaring it "Little Italy on the Buttes-Chaumont."
A la carte: 100–50 F

RE-OPENING SHORTLY

TAILLEVENT-PRUNIER TRATKIR
Jean-Claude Vrinat, owner of the famous Taillevent, is preparing to re-open the amazing bar-fishmongers-restaurant Prunier in the Avenue Victor-Hugo ▲ 222 at the end of 1994. Let's hope that the Art Deco and the spirit of the place remain.

LE PRINCE DE GALLES
▲ 394
The restaurant in the Prince de Galles hotel will re-open sometime in 1994 following renovation.

CHANGE OF NAME

LE COUGAR ◆ 384
Is now called Le Taira.

LA POSTE ◆ 413
This establishment offering Moroccan-inspired cuisine has been re-christened Le Casablanca.

CLOSED OR CHANGED

These establishments appear in this guide, which went to press before they could be deleted:

CLAVEL ◆ 335
Closed.

L'ENTRE-SIÈCLE ◆ 336
Closed.

GRANDGOUSIER ◆ 337
Closed.

LE TOTEM ◆ 390
At the time of going to press, Le Totem (Palais de Chaillot) was closed indefinitely for renovation.

◆ NOTES

> **"I HAVE MORE MEMORIES THAN IF I HAD LIVED A THOUSAND YEARS."**
>
> CHARLES BAUDELAIRE

APPENDICES

ESSENTIAL
◆ READING ◆

◆ BRILLAT-SAVARIN:
*Physiologie du goût,
ou méditation de
gastronomie
transcendante* (1826),
with a foreword by
Roland Barthes,
Hermann, Paris, 1975.
◆ COURTINE (R.):
*Larousse
gastronomique*,
Larousse.
◆ GUY (C.): *Histoire
de la gastronomie
en France*, Nathan,
Paris, 1985.

◆ HISTORY ◆

◆ ANDRÉ (J.):
*L'Alimentation
et la Cuisine à Rome*,
Les Belles Lettres,
Paris, 1981.
◆ ARON (J.-P.):
*Le Mangeur du XIXe
siècle*, Payot, 1989.
◆ BERNARD (A.) with
PATOU-MATHIS (M.):
*La Cuisine
préhistorique*,
Pierre Faniac.
◆ BLOND (G. and G.):
*Histoire pittoresque de
notre alimentation*,
Fayard, Paris, 1960.
◆ CASTELOT (A.):
L'Histoire à table,
Plon-Perrin, 1972.
◆ DES OMBIAUX (M.):
*L'Art de manger et son
histoire*, Payot, Paris,
1928.
◆ DION (R.): *Histoire
de la vigne et du vin
en France, des
origines au XIXe siècle*,
Flammarion, 1959.
◆ FRANKLIN (A.): *La Vie
privée d'autrefois: la
cuisine* (1888),
Slatkine, 1980.
◆ GILLET (P.): *Par mets
et par vins: voyages et
gastronomie en
Europe aux XVIe et XVIIe
siècles*, Payot, 1985.
◆ GRIMOD DE LA
REYNIÈRE (A.B.L.):
*Manuel des
amphitryons*, Métailié,
1993.
◆ GRIMOD DE LA
REYNIÈRE (A.B.L.):
*L'Almanach gourmand
1803-1810*, F. P.
Lobies, 1973.
◆ HEMARDINQUER
(J.-J.): *Pour une
histoire de
l'alimentation*, Armand
Colin, Paris, 1961.
◆ HIEATT (C. B.),
BUTLER (S.): *Pain, vin
et venaison: un livre
de cuisine médiévale*,
France-Amérique,
1977.
◆ LEHOUCQ (R.):
Le Ménagier de Paris,
Connaissance du
Moyen Age, Lille.
◆ LÉO (J.): *Le Baron
Brisse: un gastronome
du second Empire*,
Grenier des
Collectionneurs, 1992.
◆ LÉVI-STRAUSS (C.):
*Mythologiques:
l'origine des manières
de la table*, Plon, 1968.
◆ MENELL (S.):
*Français et Anglais à
table, du Moyen Age à
nos jours*, Flammarion,
1987.
◆ NEIRINCK (E.)
and POULAIN (J.-P.):
*Histoire de la cuisine
et des cuisiniers*,
Jacques Lanore,
Malakoff, 1988.
◆ NERCESSIAN (A.):
*La Cuisine romaine
antique*, Glénat.
◆ POURTEAU (F.):
*Les fins mets de
l'histoire*, Éditions de
l'Humanité - Messidor,
1988.
◆ REDON (O.), SABBAN
(F.) and SERVENTI (S.):
*La Gastronomie au
Moyen Âge*, Stock,
1992.
◆ RIVAL (N.): *Grimod
de La Reynière, le
gourmand
gentilhomme*,
Le Pré-aux-Clercs,
1983.
◆ RODIL (L.): *Antonin
Carême de Paris*,
Jeanne Laffitte, 1992.
◆ SCOTTO (les sœurs)
and HUBERT-BARE (A.):
*L'Héritage de la
cuisine française*,
Hachette pratique
(coll. L'Héritage de la
cuisine).
◆ TOUSSAINT-SAMAT
(M.): *Histoire naturelle
et morale de la
nourriture*, Bordas,
1990.
◆ VERDOT (C.):
*Historiographie de la
table*, Paris, 1833.
◆ WHEATON (B.K.):
*L'Office et la Bouche.
Histoire des mœurs
de la table en France:
1300-1789*, Calmann-
Lévy, Paris, 1984.

◆ DICTIONARIES ◆

◆ CHATELAIN-COURTOIS
(M.): *Les Mots du vin
et de l'ivresse*, Belin
(coll. Le Français
retrouvé), Paris,
1984.
◆ COURTINE (R. J.):
*Dictionnaire des
fromages*, Larousse
(coll. Les Dictionnaires
de l'homme du
XXe siècle), Paris, 1972.
◆ CRAPLET (C. and J.):
*Dictionnaire des
aliments et de la
nutrition*, Le Hameau,
Paris, 1979.
◆ DUMAS (A.):
*Le Grand Dictionnaire
de cuisine* (1873),
Veyrier, 1978.
◆ GUILLEMARD (C.):
*Les Mots d'origine
gourmande*, Belin (coll.
Le Français retrouvé,
n° 14), Paris, 1986.
◆ GUILLEMARD (C.):
*Les Mots de la cuisine
et de la table*, Belin,
Paris, 1990.
◆ VICAIRE (G.):
*Bibliographie
gastronomique depuis
le commencement de
l'imprimerie à 1890*,
London, 1954.

ART AND
◆ DECORATION ◆

◆ AUZET (R.): *Pains
décorés et pièces
artistiques*, Jérôme
Villette, 1992.
◆ COLLECTION:
*Restaurants parisiens
et décoration
1800–1914*, in *Les
Décors des boutiques
parisiennes*,
Délégation artistique
de la Ville-de-Paris,
1987.
◆ DIÉGO-DORTIGNAC
(G.): *La cuisine de
Toulouse-Lautrec*,
Editions Scala, Paris
1993
◆ FISHER (M.K.F):
*L'Art de présenter
les plats*, Jacques
Lanore-Henri
Laurens.
◆ GROSS (G. M.):
*Le Nouvel Art de
plier les serviettes*,
Solar (Arts de la
maison).
◆ JOYES (C.): *Les
Carnets de cuisine
de Monet*, Editions du
Chêne, 1991.
◆ LIS (M.): *Le Jardin
sur la table*, Actes Sud,
1991.
◆ MENEAU (M.) AND
CAEN (A.): *Musée
gourmand, le peintre
et le cuisinier*, Editions
du Chêne, 1992.

◆ DISHES ◆

◆ ANDROUET (P.):
*Un fromage pour
chaque jour*, éd. de
Verfèvre, Paris, 1981.
◆ BERGIER (J.-F.):
Une histoire du sel,
Office du Livre,
Lausanne, 1984.
◆ BIANQUIS (L.): *Foie
gras*, Hachette/CIL,
1992.
◆ BOISARD (P.):
*Le Camembert,
mythe national*,
Calmann-Lévy.
◆ BOISARD (P.):
*Les Meilleurs
Desserts*, Reader's
Digest selection.
◆ BOISARD (P.):
*Pâtisserie
contemporaine et
traditionnelle en
Europe*, Kramer,
diff. Vilo.
◆ BROCHARD (G.):
L'Agenda du thé,
Editions du Chêne,
1992.
◆ BUTEL (P.): *Histoire
du thé*, Desjonquères,
1990.
◆ CALVEL (R.): *Le Goût
du pain*, Jérôme
Villette, 1990.
◆ CHARLON (R.):
*Coquillages
et crustacés*,
Ouest-France
(Monographies), 1993.
◆ COURCELET (P. and
B.):
La Route des épices,
Bordas, Paris, 1991.
◆ DARD (P.) and TURLAY
(J.-C.): *Fromages
d'aujourd'hui*,
Robert Laffont.
◆ FRUCHTEL (I.):
Légumes, Hachette-
CIL (Petits albums
cuisine).
◆ FRUCHTEL (I.):
*Le Grand Livre de
la pomme de terre*,
Images.
◆ GARNIER (A.): *Pains
et viennoiseries*.
◆ GODECKEN (H.):
Le Caviar, Jeanne
Laffitte, 1992.
◆ HARWICH (N.):
Histoire du chocolat,
Desjonquères, 1992.
◆ ILLY (F. and R.):
Du café à l'express,
Abbeville Press
France,
diff. Flammarion.
◆ JACOB (H. E.):
L'épopée du café,
Le Seuil, Paris, 1953.
◆ JACOB (H. E.):
*Histoire du pain depuis
6 000 ans*,

Le Seuil, Paris, 1958.
◆ LALLEMAND (R.):
Le Pot-au-feu,
Jeanne Laffitte, 1992.
◆ LE GOFF (J.):
Le Sel dans l'histoire,
Annales, 1961,
pp. 956-961.
◆ LEONI (G.) and
FERRERI (B.): *Les
Meilleurs
Champignons
comestibles*,
De Vecchi.
◆ MAURO (F.):
Histoire du café,
Desjonquères, 1991.
◆ MEYER (J.): *Histoire
du sucre*,
Desjonquères, 1991.
◆ NORMAN (J.): *Les
épices*, Hatier, 1991.
◆ PASTOUREAU (M.),
RAVENEAU (A.) and
BUREN (R.): *Le Bœuf,
histoire, symbolique et
cuisine*, Sang de la
terre (Beaux livres).
◆ RAYNAL (J.): *Épices
et produits coloniaux*,
Bibliothèques,
diff.Distique, 1992
(L'écrivain voyageur).
◆ RIERA (C.):
*La Pomme dans tous
ses états*, Jeanne
Laffitte, 1991.
◆ ROCCHIA (J. M.):
*De la truffe en général
et de la rabasse en
particulier*, Barthélemy,
(Du goût et
de l'usage).
◆ ROGERS (F.):
Pommes, Michel
Aveline, diff. Distique
(Cuisines).
◆ ROGERS (F.): *Citrons
et agrumes*, Michel
Aveline, 1991.
◆ SEMONIN (J.-P.)
and DUPONT (J.-C.):
*La Cuisine des
poissons d'eau douce*,
Jérôme Villette, 1991.
◆ VANNIER (P.) and
MEILLER (D.):
*Le Grand Livre des
fruits et des légumes*,
La Manufacture, 1991.
◆ VERGNE (E.):
Poissons et crustacés,
Hachette.
◆ VERGNE (E.):
Les Viandes, Hachette,
1992.
◆ VERGNE (E.):
Volailles, Hachette.
◆ VIARD (H.):
Fromages de France,
Dargaud 1980
(Rustica sens
pratique).
◆ VIARD (M.) and
GAILLARD (P.): *Les
Jardins des épices*,
Du May (Empreintes).

◆ ZIEHR (W.): *Paysan,
meunier, boulanger.
Le pain à travers les
âges*, Éditions Hermé,
Paris, 1959.

◆ WINES ◆

◆ BRADFER (A.),
DE CLOUET (A.) and
MARATIER (C.): *La Cote
des meilleurs vins
de France*, Solar.
◆ CHABOT (Y.):
*Cuisinons aux vins
de France*, Société
des Éditions de
France.
◆ CHARPENTIER (L.):
Le Mystère du vin,
Robert Laffont, Paris,
1981 (coll. Énigmes de
l'Univers).
◆ CHEVET (H.):
A chaque plat son vin,
De Vecchi (De Vecchi
poche).
◆ CHOKO (A.): *La cote
des vins*, l'Amateur.
◆ CLARKE (O.):
*Nouvelle encyclopédie
illustrée des vins de
France*, Solar, 1992.
◆ COLLECTION:
Le Grand Atlas du vin,
Atlas, 1992.
◆ DOUTRELANT (P.-M.):
*Les Bons Vins et les
Autres*, Le Seuil, 1976
(coll. Points actuels).
◆ DUSSERT-GERBER (P.):
*Guide Dussert-Gerber
des Vins de France*,
Albin Michel, 1987.
◆ HUET (M.) and
LAUZERAL (V.):
*Dictionnaire
des vins et alcools*,
Hervas, 1991.
◆ JOHNSON (H.):
*Le Nouvel Atlas
mondial du vin*,
Robert Laffont, 1986.
◆ KAUFFMANN (J.-P.):
Un repas, quels vins?,
S.A.E.P., 1991.
◆ LEGAY (G.) and LEPRÉ
(G.): *Magie d'un
palace et de ses vins*,
Olivier Orban.
◆ MASTROJANNI (M.):
*Le Grand Livre des
vins de Loire*, Solar,
1991.
◆ MOTHE (F.): *Toutes
hontes bues*, Albin
Michel, 1991.
◆ OLNEY (R.): *Yquem*,
Flammarion.
◆ PAUMARD (B.) and
LENOIR (J.): *Le Nez des
vins*, Jean Lenoir.
◆ PEYNAUD (E.): *Le
Goût du vin: le grand
livre de la dégustation*,
Dunod, 1983.
◆ PICHONNAT (B.) and

GLATRE (E.): *Cognac: la
part des anges*,
Hervas, 1990.
◆ RABAUDY (N. DE)
and POUTEAU (J.-L.):
Les Vins de rêve,
Solar, 1991.
◆ SEWARD (D.):
*Histoires des vins
monastiques. Les
moines et le vin*,
Pygmalion-Gérard
Watelet, Paris,
1982.
◆ WOUTAZ (F.),
DE MONZA (J.-P.) and
CELLIER (J.):
*Atlas des vins de
France*, Jean-Pierre
de Monza, 1992.

◆ PARIS
AND FRANCE ◆

◆ ARON (J.-P.): *Essai
sur la sensibilité
alimentaire à Paris au
XIXe siècle*, Cahier
des annales, Armand
Colin, Paris, 1967.
◆ COURTINE (R. J.): *Les
Cent Merveilles de la
cuisine française*,
Le Seuil, Paris,
1971.
◆ COURTINE (R.): *La Vie
parisienne: cafés et
restaurants de
boulevards 1814–
1914; le ventre de
Paris; la rive gauche*,
Perrin, Paris, 1985.
◆ CURNONSKY and
GIRARD (S.):
*Cuisine et vins de
France*, Larousse,
1992.
◆ ESCAIG (G.): *La
Petite Bible des hôtels
et restaurants
parisiens*, Roland
Escaig, 1992.
◆ GAIN (R.): *Les Plus
Beaux Restaurants de
Paris*, Gallimard, Paris,
1989.
◆ GIRARD (S.) and
MEURVILLE (E. DE):
*L'Atlas de la France
gourmande*, Jean-
Pierre de Monza,
1991.
◆ HÉRON DE VILLEFOSSE
(R.): *Histoire et
géographie
gourmandes de Paris*,
Éditions de Paris,
Paris, 1956.
◆ HILLAIRET (J.):
*Connaissance du
vieux Paris*, Éditions
de Minuit, Paris,
1954.
◆ LARGE (P.-F.):
*Des Halles au Forum:
métamorphoses au
cœur de Paris*,

L'Harmattan, 1992.
◆ LEBEY (C.): *Les
100 Recettes des
bistrots parisiens*,
Robert Laffont, 1988.
◆ MONCAN (P. de)
and MAHOUT (C.): *Le
Guide des passages
de Paris*, SEESAM-
RCI, Paris, 1991.
◆ PITTE (J.-R.):
*Gastronomie
française*, Fayard,
Paris, 1991.
◆ PITTE (J.-R.):
*Gastronomie
française: histoire
et géographie d'une
passion*, Fayard,
1992.

◆ REGIONAL
CUISINE ◆

◆ AUGER-HOLDERBACH
(P.): *La Cuisine
paysanne en
Rouergue*, Editions du
Rouergue (Traditions).
◆ BIANQUIS (L.):
Cuisine créole,
Hachette/CIL.
◆ BLANC (G.) and
VENCE (C.): *Le Grand
Livre de la volaille*,
Robert Laffont, 1991.
◆ BOUCHARD (J.-P.): *La
Grande Cuisine du
Bordelais*, Solar, 1992.
◆ CHANOT-BULIER (C.):
*Vieilles recettes de
cuisine provençale*,
Tacussel, 1990.
◆ CHARIAL-THUILIER
(J.-A.): *Bouquet de
provence*, Solar, 1991.
◆ CHARLON (R.):
Savoureuse Bretagne,
Éditions Ouest-France
(Beaux livres).
◆ CHAUVIREY (M.-F.):
*Les Bonnes Recettes
des landes*, Lavielle,
1991.
◆ CLÉMENT (M.-C. and
D.): *Sologne
gourmande, ou le
Cahier secret de
Silvine*, Albin Michel.
◆ COMPAS (R.): *Grand
livre de la cuisine
normande*, Charles
Corlet.
◆ COURTINE (R.): *Le
Guide de la cuisine
des terroirs*,
La Manufacture, 1992.
◆ CUNY (J.-M.) and
CARPENTIER (B.): *La
cuisine lorraine*,
Gérard Klopp.
◆ DAGUZAN (J.-F.): *La
Cuisine gasconne*,
Publisud, 1990.
La Riviera à table,
Albin Michel.
◆ FALCOU (F.), CARPLET

(C.) and Carplet-
Meunier (J.): *Le
Cassoulet de
Castelnaudary*, Lyon
Josette,1991.
◆ Falcou (F.), Carplet
(C.) and Carplet-
Meunier (J.): *Le Guide
critique des aliments
allégés*, Lyon Josette,
1991.
◆ Ferniot (J.): *Carnet
de croûte. Le tour de
France d'un
gastronome*,
Robert Laffont, 1980.
◆ Fisher (M.K.F.):
*La Cuisine des
provinces de France*,
S.I. Time, Time-Life,
1969 (La cuisine à
travers le monde*)*.
◆ Gérard (A.): *Cuisine
provençale*, Hachette /
CIL.
◆ Grison (P.) and
Godet (M.): *Merveilles
de la cuisine
lyonnaise*, Édisud.
◆ Hell-Girod (G.):
*Le Livre de la cuisine
alsacienne*,
Gérard Klopp, 1991.
◆ Humbert (M. T.)
and Sweeney (J. T.):
*Les Confréries en
Bourgogne*,
La Manufacture, 1992.
◆ Lacave (M.) and Gas
(A.): *Paysages
gourmets: Languedoc
oriental*, Éditions de
Borée, 1991.
◆ Lacave (M.) and Gas
(A.): *Paysages
gourmets: le Lot-et-
Garonne*, Éditions de
Borée,1991.
◆ Lagréoulle (C.): *Les
Bonnes Recettes du
Béarn*, Lavielle, 1991.
◆ Lebey (C.) (under
the supervision of):
*La Franche-Comté.
Produits du terroir et
recettes
traditionnelles*,
Albin Michel / CNAC
(L'Inventaire du
patrimoine culinaire de
la France).
◆ Lebey (C.) (under
the supervision of):
*L'Île- de-France.
Produits du terroir et
recettes
traditionnelles*, Albin
Michel / CNAC
(L'Inventaire du
patrimoine culinaire de
la France).
◆ Lebey (C.) (under
the supervision of):
*Nord-Pas-de-Calais.
Produits du terroir et
recettes
traditionnelles*, Albin

Michel / CNAC
(l'Inventaire du
patrimoine culinaire de
la France).
◆ Lizambard (D. and
M.): *La Grande
Cuisine de Savoie*,
Solar, 1991.
◆ Lizambard (D. and
M.): *La Grande
Cuisine d'Alsace*,
Solar, 1992.
◆ Maria (J.) and de la
Peppa (G.): *Et vive la
cuisine niçoise*,
Z'Éditions, 1990.
◆ Matignon (B.):
*Cuisine et gastronomie
bretonne aux algues*,
Coop Breizh, Spézed.
◆ More (J.):
*Bourgogne
gourmande*,
Flammarion.
◆ Nazet (M.): *Cuisine
et fêtes en Provence*,
Édisud.
◆ Pourteau (R.):
*Gastronomie en
Poitou-Charente*,
Comité Art de Vivre,
1992.
◆ Reboul (R.): *La
Cuisinière provençale*,
Tacussel, réédition
1992.
◆ Robaglia (S.):
*Margaridou. Journal et
recettes d'une
cuisinière au pays
d'Auvergne*.
◆ Rouanet (M.): *La
Cuisine amoureuse,
courtoise et occitane*,
Loubatières, 1991.
◆ Saint-Lebe (N.):
*Cuisines pyrénéennes.
La saveur des recettes
traditionnelles*, Milan,
Beaux Livres
Pyrénéens.
◆ Saulnier (J.): *La
Cuisine créole*, Jean-
Pierre Taillandier.
◆ Sloimovici (A.):
*Ethnocuisine de la
Bourgogne*,
Jeanne Laffitte, 1992.

Foreign
◆ cuisine ◆

◆ Auger-Alvarez (I.):
Cuisine espagnole,
Hachette/CIL.
◆ Aris (P.): *La Cuisine
espagnole*,
Albin Michel, 1991.
◆ Armengaud (C.):
*La Suède à dos de
cuillère*, Actes Sud.
◆ Bahloul (J.):
*Le Culte de la table
dressée: rites et
traditions de la table
juive algérienne*,
Métailié, 1983.

◆ Belhadj (A. M.):
*La Cuisine
méditerranéenne*,
Publisud, 1990.
◆ Botkine (F.):
Cuisine russe,
Hachette/CIL.
◆ Chiche-Yana (M.):
*La Table juive, recettes
et traditions de fête*,
Édisud, 1991.
◆ Bouayed (Z.):
Cuisine algérienne,
Hachette/CIL.
◆ Choinska (F.):
*Cent recettes de
cuisine juive*, Robert
Laffont, Paris, 1968.
◆ Collection: *Traité
de cuisine chinoise.
Les Techniques de
base* (t. I) ; *200
recettes de base* (t. II);
*Spécialités de
poissons et crustacés*
(t. III) ; *Recettes pour
la santé* (t. IV), Saint-
Honoré, diff.
Multimédia.
◆ Comelade (E.): *La
Cuisine catalane*
Robert Laffont (2 vol.).
◆ Cousin (F.) and
Monzon (S.) (under the
supervision of):
*Cuisines du monde.
Gestes et recettes*,
Éditions du CNRS.
◆ Dekura (H.): *Cuisine
japonaise*, Solar.
◆ Del Passo (S. and
F.): *Douceur et passion
de la cuisine
mexicaine*, Éditions de
l'Aube, 1991.
◆ Domingo (X.),
Husserot (P.) and
Revel (J.-F.): *Le Goût
de l'Espagne*,
Flammarion, 1992.
◆ Esquerre Anciaux
(M.): *Dictionnaire de la
cuisine des Ardennes*,
Christine Bonneton,
1992.
◆ Hadjiat (S.): *La
Cuisine d'Algérie*,
Publisud, 1990.
◆ Hom (K.): *Saveurs
de Chine*, Flammarion,
1991.
◆ Huynh (K.): *200
Recettes de cuisine
chinoise traditionnelle*,
Jacques Grancher,
1991.
◆ Jacobs (S.): *La
Cuisine des îles
grecques*.
◆ Jaguar: *Les
Merveilles de la
cuisine africaine*,
Jaguar, 1991.
◆ Jaguar: *Les
Merveilles de la
cuisine asiatique*,
Jaguar, 1991.

◆ Johnson-Bekaert
(S.): *États-Unis, la
cuisine des origines*,
Éditions de l'Aube,
1991.
◆ Losco (I.): *La
Cuisine italienne*,
Jacques Grancher,
1992.
◆ De Medici (L.):
*L'Héritage de la
cuisine italienne*,
Hachette, 1991.
◆ De Medici (L.):
Saveurs d'Italie, Robert
Laffont, 1992.
◆ Mordelet (J.):
*Saveurs des palais
d'Orient. 130 recettes
du Bosphore au
Caucase*, Éditions
de l'Aube (Cuisines
migrantes).
◆ Peter (M.), Maine
(M.) and Pejean (J.):
*Recettes du monde
entier*, L.G.F., 1991
(Livre de poche).
◆ Ribère (R.): *La
Bonne Cuisine
des Antilles*, Solar
(Cuisine).
◆ Stouff (L.):
*L'Histoire de la table
provençale* (livre de
recettes méridionales),
Alain Barthélemy,
1992.

◆ Literature ◆

◆ Aragon (L.): *Les
Beaux Quartiers*,
Denoël, 1936.
◆ Aymé (M.): *Le Vin de
Paris*, Gallimard, Paris,
1947.
◆ Barthes (R.):
Mythologies, Le Seuil,
Paris, 1957.
◆ Borrel (R.),
Senderens (A.) and
Naudin (J. B.): *Proust:
la cuisine retrouvée*,
Editions du Chêne,
1992.
◆ Chatelet (N.):
Histoires de bouches,
Gallimard, 1988.
◆ Chatelet (N.):
A contresens, Mercure
de France, 1989.
◆ Chatelet (N.):
*Le Corps à Corps
culinaire*, Le Seuil,
1977
◆ Clément (M.-C. and
D.): *Colette
gourmande*, Albin
Michel, 1990.
◆ Courtine (R.) and
Desmur (J.):
*Anthologie de la
littérature
gastronomique*,
Trévise, Paris, 1970.
◆ Courtine (R.)

and Desmur (J.): *Anthologie de la poésie gourmande*, Trévise, Paris, 1970.

◆ Courtine (R.): *Balzac à table*, Robert-Laffont, 1976.

◆ Courtine (R.): *Simenon et Maigret passent à table*, Robert Laffont, 1992.

◆ Courtine (R.): *Le Cahier de recettes de Mme Maigret*, Robert Laffont, Paris.

◆ Delteil (J.): *La Cuisine paléolithique*, Robert Morel éditeur, 1972.

◆ Hemingway (E.): *Paris est une fête*, Gallimard, 1964.

◆ Nignon (E.) and Paine (A.): *éloges de la cuisine française*, François Bourin, 1992.

◆ Revel (J.-F.): *Un festin en paroles: histoire littéraire de la sensibilité gastronomique de l'Antiquité à nos jours*, Pauvert, Paris, 1979.

◆ Sand (C.): *À la table de Georges Sand*, Flammarion.

CHEFS' ◆ OWN WORDS ◆

◆ Amiard (H.): *Portraits de chefs*, Contrejour, 1992.

◆ Bazet (M.) and Ordonez (M.): *La Cuisine des mousquetaires*, Éditions de la Presqu'île.

◆ Bocuse (P.): *Cuisine de France*, Flammarion, 1991.

◆ Bras (M.): *Le Livre de Michel Bras*, Éditions du Rouergue.

◆ Cedus: *Desserts de chefs*, B.P.I.

◆ Escoffier (A.): *Souvenirs inédits*, Jeanne Laffitte, 1985.

◆ Gagnaire (P.) (master chef at the *Pierre-Gagnaire*, Saint-Étienne, Loire): *La cuisine immédiate*, Robert Laffont, 1988.

◆ Guegan (B.): *La Fleur de la cuisine française où l'on trouve les meilleures recettes des meilleurs cuisiniers, pâtissiers et limonadiers de France du XIIIᵉ au XIXᵉ siècle* (with notes and a glossary by B. Guegan), Paris, 1920.

◆ Guerard (M.) (master chef at the *Prés d'Eugénie*, Eugénie-les-Bains, Landes): *La Cuisine gourmande*, Robert Laffont, 1978.

◆ Lamazère (R.): *Le Magicien de la cuisine*, Michel Lafon.

◆ Le Divellec (J.): *Les Poissons*, Jean-Pierre Taillandier.

◆ Lenôtre: *Lenôtre, desserts traditionnels de France*, Flammarion, 1991.

◆ Loiseau (B.): *L'Envolée des saveurs*, Hachette, 1992.

◆ Oliver (R.): *Grand inventaire de la cuisine française*, Albin Michel.

◆ Peyrot (C.) and Vence (C.): *La Cuisine de l'émotion*, Robert Laffont, 1992.

◆ Peyrot (C.): *Le Vivarois*, Robert Laffont, 1992.

◆ Poilâne (L.): *Guide de l'amateur de pain*, Robert Laffont, 1991.

◆ Robuchon (J.): *Ma cuisine pour vous*, Robert Laffont, 1991.

◆ Robuchon (J.) and Wells (P.): *Le Meilleur et le Plus Simple*, Robert Laffont, 1992.

◆ Rouff (M.): *La Vie et la Passion de Dodin-Bouffant, gourmet* (1924), Stock, 1984 (out of print).

◆ Senderens (A.): *Figues sans barbarie*, Robert Laffont, 1992.

◆ Senderens (A.) (master chef at the *Lucas-Carton*, Paris) and Senderens (E.): *La Cuisine réussie: les 200 meilleures recettes de l'Archestrate*, Jean-Claude Lattès, 1981.

◆ Senderens (A.) and Trehin (Dr): *Manger c'est la santé*, Jean-Claude Lattès, 1992.

◆ Troisgros (J. and P.): *Cuisiniers à Roanne*, Robert Laffont, Paris, 1977.(coll. Les recettes originales).

◆ Verge (R.): *Les Légumes de mon moulin*, Flammarion.

ACKNOWLEDGMENTS

Grateful acknowledgment is made to the following for permission to reprint previously published material:

◆ Charles Scribner's Sons: Excerpts from *A Moveable Feast* by Ernest Hemingway, copyright © 1964 by Mary Hemingway, copyright renewed 1992 by John H. Hemingway, Patrick Hemingway, and Gregory Hemingway. Reprinted by permission of Charles Scribner's Sons, an imprint of Macmillan Publishing Company.

◆ Random House, Inc.: Excerpt from *Within a Budding Grove* from *Remembrance of Things Past, Vol. I*, by Marcel Proust, translated by C. K. Scott Moncrieff and Terence Kilmartin, copyright © 1981 by Random House, Inc. and Chatto & Windus. Reprinted by permission of Random House, Inc.

◆ Editions Gallimard: Excerpt from *Le Piéton de Paris* by Léon-Paul Fargue. Copyright © 1932 by Editions Gallimard. Reprinted in the UK, US and Canada by permission of Editions Gallimard, Paris.

Excerpt from *La Lettre dans un Taxi* by Louise de Vilmorin. Copyright © 1973 by Editions Gallimard. Reprinted in the UK, US and Canada by permission of Editions Gallimard, Paris.

Excerpt from *Le Fichier Parisien* by Henri de Montherlant. Copyright © 1974 by Editions Gallimard. Reprinted in the UK, US and Canada by permission of Editions Gallimard, Paris.

Excerpt from *Paris Vecu* by Léon Daudet. Copyright © 1929 by Editions Gallimard. Reprinted in the UK, US and Canada by permission of Editions Gallimard, Paris.

Excerpt from *Histoires* by Jacques Prévert. Copyright © 1963 by Editions Gallimard. Reprinted in the UK, US and Canada by permission of Editions Gallimard, Paris.

Excerpt from *Le Vin de Paris* by Marcel Aymé. Copyright © 1947 by Editions Gallimard. Reprinted in the UK, US and Canada by permission of Editions Gallimard, Paris.

Excerpt from *Nadja* by André Breton. Copyright © 1963 by Editions Gallimard. Reprinted in the UK, by permission of Editions Gallimard, Paris.

Excerpt from *Le Parti-Pris des Choses* by Francis Ponge. Copyright © 1942 by Editions Gallimard. Reprinted in the UK, by permission of Editions Gallimard, Paris.

◆ LIST OF ILLUSTRATIONS

◆ LIST OF ILLUSTRATIONS

ILLUSTRATORS

COVER :
Philippe Biard.

NATURE :
Pascal Robin,

François Desbordes, Jean Chevallier, Catherine Lachaux, Gismonde Curiace, Anne Bodin, Patrick Mérienne.

ART OF LIVING :
Polly Raynes, James Robins, Jean-Philippe Chabot

DECORATION AND FURNITURE :
Sandra Doyle, Kevin Hart

ITINERARIES :
Jean-Marc Lanusse (*Le Procope*), Philippe Biard (*Le Train Bleu*).

PRACTICAL INFORMATION AND ADDRESS BOOK :
Maurice Pommier, Régis Haghebaert, Anne Bodin, Vincent Brunot.

CARTOGRAPHY :
John Kent, Anne Bodin, Emmanuel Calamy (computer retouching).

INFOGRAPHY :
Paul Coulbois, Danièle Guitton (practical information tables), Kristof Chemineau, Cyrille Mallié, Nathalie Pujebet.

Our thanks to the musée de Nogent-sur-Marne and to Jean-Christophe Gourvenec.

INDEX

Restaurants found in the address book are indexed in bold type
BENOIT : one of the editors' choices, **Grand Venise :** other restaurants

Restaurants found in the address book are indexed in bold type
BENOIT : one of the editors' choices, **Grand Venise :** other restaurants

Restaurants found in the address book are indexed in bold type
BENOIT : one of the editors' choices, **Grand Venise :** other restaurants

INDEX ◆

In bold, the restaurants found in the address book
BENOIT : one of the 100 editors' choices, **Grand Venise** : other restaurants